CASPIAN SEA

Baku

R. Aras

Julfa

Tabriz
Ardebil • Astara

WEST AZERBAIJAN
EAST

Enzeli
Mahabad
Rasht
Shahsavar
Piranshahr

GILAN MAZANDARAN

Qazvin
Sari

KURDISTAN
Marivan
Penjwin Paveh Sanandaj
TEHRAN Damavand

Qasr-e
Shirin
Kermanshah Hamadan
KERMANSHAHAN Assadabad
Gilan-e Gharb Nahavand
Naft-e Shah Arak

Mandali
Mehran

Al Kut Dehloran
Musian Andimeshk
Dezful

Amarah Bostan Masjid-e Suleiman
Susangard
Ahvaz

KHUZISTAN Ramhormuz

Qurna
Khorramshahr Behbahan
Basra
Umm Qasr Abadan Bandar Khomeini

Fao
Kuwait

Kharg Is.
Bushahr

AL HASA

THE

Taheri
Asaluyeh

GULF

Ras Tanura
Lavan Is.

Bandar Lengeh

Little Tunb Is.
Sirri Is.
Abu Musa Is.
Sharjah

Dubai

Abu Dhabi

Gonbad-e Kavus
R. Atrak

Gorgan
Kabkan

Damghan
Mashhad

KHURASAN

Reyshahr
Semnan

Manzariyeh

Qom

Tabas

Birjand
Tayabad
Herat

R. Hari-Rud

Yazd

Rafsanjan

Shiraz

FARS

Zahedan

BALUCHISTAN
Iranshahr

SISTAN

Bandar Abbas
Qeshm Is. Larak Is.
Henqin Is.
Greater Tunb Is.
Strait of Hormuz

Jask

Gwadar

Gulf of Oman

R. Helmud

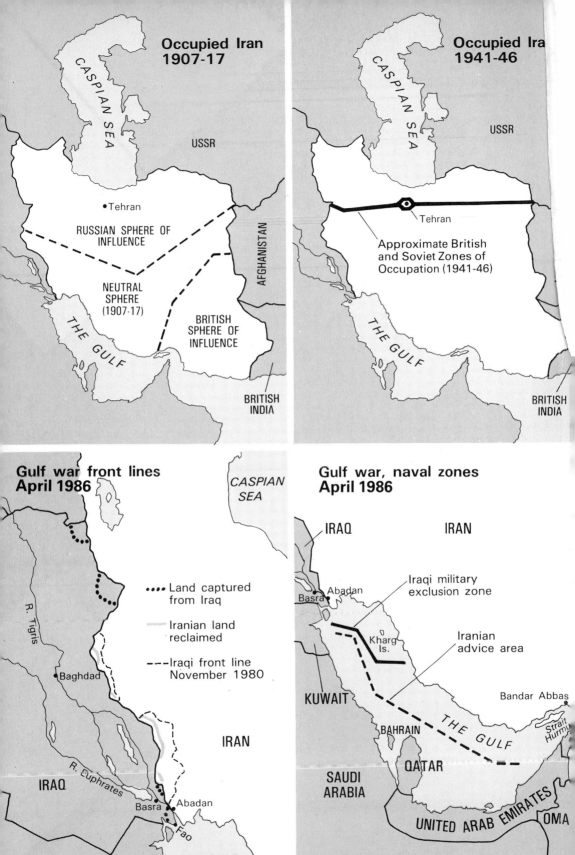

Occupied Iran 1907-17

CASPIAN SEA

USSR

•Tehran

RUSSIAN SPHERE OF INFLUENCE

AFGHANISTAN

NEUTRAL SPHERE (1907-17)

BRITISH SPHERE OF INFLUENCE

THE GULF

BRITISH INDIA

Occupied Ira 1941-46

CASPIAN SEA

USSR

Tehran

Approximate British and Soviet Zones of Occupation (1941-46)

THE GULF

BRITISH INDIA

Gulf war front lines April 1986

CASPIAN SEA

•••• Land captured from Iraq

Iranian land reclaimed

– – – Iraqi front line November 1980

R. Tigris

Baghdad

R. Euphrates

IRAQ

Basra

Abadan

Fao

IRAN

THE GULF

Gulf war, naval zones April 1986

IRAQ

IRAN

Basra

Abadan

Iraqi military exclusion zone

Kharg Is.

Iranian advice area

Bandar Abbas

KUWAIT

BAHRAIN

THE GULF

Strait Hurmu

QATAR

SAUDI ARABIA

UNITED ARAB EMIRATES

OMA

IRAN UNDER THE AYATOLLAHS

The Author
Dilip Hiro was born in Pakistan, and educated in India, Britain and America. He now lives in London and is a full-time writer and freelance journalist, contributing articles to such publications as the *Sunday Times*, *Washington Post*, *Wall Street Journal*, *Boston Globe*, *Guardian* and *International Herald Tribune*. His other books include *Inside India Today* (1976), *Black British, White British* (1971) and *Inside the Middle East* (1982).

BY THE SAME AUTHOR

Inside the Middle East
Inside India Today
The Untouchables of India
Black British, White British

FICTION

Interior, Exchange, Exterior (Poems)
Apply, Apply, No Reply and *A Clean Break* (Two plays)
To Anchor a Cloud (A play)
A Triangular View (A novel)

DILIP HIRO

IRAN UNDER THE AYATOLLAHS

ROUTLEDGE & KEGAN PAUL
London and New York

First published in 1985
Paperback edition, with corrections and
new Postscript, published in 1987 by
Routledge & Kegan Paul Ltd
11 New Fetter Lane, London EC4P 4EE, England

Published in the USA by
Routledge & Kegan Paul Inc.
in association with Methuen Inc.
29 West 35th Street, New York, NY 10001

Set in Times
by Columns of Reading
and printed in Great Britain
by T.J. Press (Padstow) Ltd, Cornwall

British Library Cataloguing in Publication Data

Hiro, Dilip
Iran under the Ayatollahs.

1. Iran—Politics and government—1979-
I. Title
955'.54   DS318.8

ISBN 0-7102-1123-6

CONTENTS

ABBREVIATIONS

AH	After Hijra (Migration of Prophet Muhammad)
AIOC	Anglo-Iranian Oil Company
APOC	Anglo-Persian Oil Company
Awacs	Airborne Warning and Control Systems
BBC	British Broadcasting Corporation
b/d	barrels/day
Cento	Central Treaty Organisation
CIA	Central Intelligence Agency
CRC	Cultural Revolution Committee
EEC	European Economic Community
FBI	Federal Bureau of Investigation
GCC	Gulf Cooperation Council
GDP	Gross Domestic Product
GNP	Gross National Product
HIID	Headquarters for the Implementation of the Imam's Decree
ICJ	International Court of Justice
ICO	Islamic Conference Organisation
IRC	Islamic Revolutionary Council
IRG	Islamic Revolutionary Guards
IRP	Islamic Republican Party
KDP	Kurdish Democratic Party
KGB	Komitet Gosudarstvenoy Bezopasnosti (Committee for State Security)
MAAG	Military Assistance Advisory Groups
MERIP	Middle East Research and Information Project

MIR	Mujahedin of the Islamic Revolution
MI6	Military Intelligence 6
MMM	Movement of Militant Muslims
MPRP	Muslim People's Republican Party
NAM	Non-Aligned Movement
Nato	North Atlantic Treaty Organisation
NDF	National Democratic Front
NIOC	National Iranian Oil Company
NRC	National Resistance Council
NSP	National Salvation Party
NVOI	National Voice of Iran
OAPEC	Organisation of Arab Petroleum Exporting Countries
OMC	Organisation of Militant Clergy
OPEC	Organisation of Petroleum Exporting Countries
PDP	People's Democratic Party
PLO	Palestine Liberation Organisation
RCC	Revolutionary Command Council
RDF	Rapid Deployment Force
SAIRI	Supreme Assembly of Islamic Revolution in Iraq
SAM	Surface to Air Missile
Savak	Sazman-e Amniyat Va Ittilaat-e Keshvar (Organisation of National Security and Intelligence)
UAE	United Arab Emirates
UAR	United Arab Republic
UN/UNO	United Nations Organisation
US/USA	United States of America
USSR	Union of Soviet Socialist Republics

GLOSSARY OF ARABIC AND PERSIAN WORDS

abi/abu: father
adha: sacrifice
akhtar: star
al/el/ol/ul: the
Alawi: follower or descendant of Imam Ali
alim (pl., ulema): religious-legal scholar
amal: hope
amniyat: security
ansar: helper
aram: comfort
ashura: (lit.) tenth; (fig.) tenth of Muharram
asr: period or age
asrar: secrets
ayandegan: the future
ayatollah: sign or token of Allah
azadegan: the free
azadi: freedom
azm: grand or chief
baath: renaissance
bab: door
bait: place or house
bakhtar: west
balagheh: eloquence
bamdad: morning
basij: mobilisation
bayan: declaration
bedouin: nomads
bemukh: brainless
bin: son
chador: (lit.) sheet; (fig.) veil
cherikha: guerrillas
dar: house or realm
dawla: state or government

din: faith
duniya: world
-e: of
eid: festival
Eid al Adha: the Festival of Sacrifice
Eid al Fitr: the Festival of 'Breaking the Fast'
emruz: today
fajr: dawn
faqih: religious jurist
fatah/fath: victory
fatwa: religious decree
fedai (pl., fedaiyan or fedaiyin): self-sacrificer
fermandeh: commander
fitr: breaking the fast
furqan: distinction
habl: rope
hadith: action or speech of Prophet Muhammad or an Imam
hajj: pilgrimage (to Mecca)
haram: religiously forbidden
hazrat: title for a prophet or imam
hejab: veil
Hezbollah: Party of Allah
Hezbollahi: member of the Party of Allah
hidaya: guidance
hijra: migration
hojatalislam: proof of Islam
homafar: an airman, named after homa, a mythical Iranian bird
hukumat: government
ibn: son
ijtihad: interpretative reasoning
imam: (lit.) one who leads prayers in a mosque; (fig.) religious leader
inqilab: revolution
islam: state or act of submission (to the will of Allah)
istiqlal: independence
ittihad: unity
ittilaat: information
jihad: (lit.) struggle in the name of Allah; (fig.) holy crusade or war
jumhouri: republic
kar: labour
kargar: worker
kashf: revelation
kayhan: world
keshvar: nation
khabranameh: newsletter

khabrigan (sing., khabra): experts
khalq: people
khariji: outsider
khat: line or side
khums: one-fifth (of profits)
maasuma: innocent
mahdi: one who is guided by Allah
majlis: assembly
maktabi: one who follows Islam comprehensively
mardom: people
marja: source
markazi: central
masail: unclear points of Sharia
matin: firm
matla: rising
mawali: client
medina: city
melli: national
melliyun: nationalist
misbah: lamp
mizan: scales
mobin: clear
Mousavi: a descendant of Imam Mousa al Kazem
mubarak: blessed
muhammad: praiseworthy or blessed
mujahed (pl., mujahedin): (lit.) one who volunteers for jihad; (fig.)
   combatant
mujtahid: one who practises ijtihad
munafiqin (sing., munafiq): hypocrites
muntazar: expected
muqaddas: holy
muslim: one who accepts Islam
mustazafin (sing., mustazaf): the needy or the oppressed
nahaj: path
nahzat: movement
nauruz: new day
niqab: mask
parcham: flag
pasdar (pl., pasdaran): guard
payam: message
paykar: combat
peik: courier
quds: holy
quran/koran: recitation

rah: path or road
reza: contentment
rida: contentment
safir: blast of a trumpet
saltane: kingdom
sayyed: a male descendant of Prophet Muhammad
sazman: organisation
sepahadar: commander
shah: king
shahbanu: queen
shahed: witness
shah-en-shah: emperor
shaikh: (lit.) old man; (fig.) a title of respect accorded to a wise man
sharh: description
Sharia: Islamic law
shatt: river
shia: partisan
suf: wool
sultan: ruler
sunna: tradition
sunni: one who follows sunna
tabaqah: class or category
taghut: personification of evil
taqlid: emulation
tariq: road
tasis: foundation
tauhid: divine unity
tauzih: clarification
tudeh: masses
ulema: body of religious-legal scholars
umma: nation or community
urf: customary law
va: and
vahid: unit
vali: lord
vilaya: ruler
vilayat: rule
wa: and or by
waqf: religious endowment
-ye: of
zakat: alms
zaman: present time

ISLAMIC CALENDARS: LUNAR AND SOLAR

The traditional Islamic calendar is lunar, and dates from 15 July 622 AD, the day of the hijra (migration) of Prophet Muhammad from Mecca to Medina. On average a lunar year contains 354 days. The Islamic lunar months, with their duration, are: Muharram (30 days), Safar (29), Rabia Awal (30), Rabia Thani (29), Jumada Awal (30), Jumada Thani (29), Rajab (30), Shaaban (29), Ramadan (29), Shawal (30), Dhul Qaada (29), and Dhul Hijja (30).

In 1925 AD the Iranian parliament adopted the solar calendar beginning with the hijra. The solar year begins on the spring Equinox, 21 or 22 March, and is divided into six consecutive months of thirty-one days each, and the rest of thirty days, except the last. The solar months are: Farvardin (31 days), Urdibehesht (31), Khurdad (31), Tir (31), Murdad (31), Shahrivar (31), Mihr (30), Aban (30), Azar (30), Dey (30), Bahman (30), and Isfand (29 days, normally; 30 days in a leap year).

Since a lunar year is shorter than a solar year by eleven days, it takes thirty-four lunar years to equal roughly thirty-three solar years. That is, there is an approximate difference of three years between a lunar century and a solar one. A person who is 100 years old by a solar calendar is 103 years old by a lunar calendar.

To change an Islamic solar date to a Christian solar date, add 621 or 622, depending on the month of the year. To convert an Islamic lunar date to a Christian solar date, divide it first by 1.031, and then add 621 or 622.

PREFACE

My purpose in writing this book is to offer a political and economic history of Iran which, while dealing primarily with the events before and after the 1978-9 revolution, takes into account the Islamic heritage of Iranian society. That is why I begin with a brief history of Islam and the rise of an Islamic state which came to include Iran. I then shift the focus on Iran, and the Safavid and Qajar dynasties which ruled it from 1501 onwards. Chapter 2 deals with the Pahlavi dynasty which started in 1926: Reza Pahlavi until 1941, followed by his son Muhammad Reza Pahlavi. It highlights the uneasy relations that existed between the state and the mosque. The conflict between them – personified by the Shah, the ruler, and Ayatollah Ruhollah Khomeini – reached a climax in June 1963. Khomeini lost, and was deported. The second clash between them came fifteen years later, and forms the core of Chapter 3. This time the Shah went, for good.

I devote the second, and the longest part of the book to the Islamic entity that arose out of the ashes of the Pahlavi kingdom. As before, I have divided each chapter into sections. In Chapter 4 I concentrate on the immediate problems that the Islamic regime had to face, and the governmental style and the constitution it offered the nation. The crisis caused by the seizure of the American embassy and diplomats in November 1979 is the main subject of the next chapter. Against this background I examine the differences between Khomeini and his chief theological rival, Ayatollah Muhammad Kazem Shariatmadri, and narrate the history of the Mujahedin-e Khalq (People's Combatants).

Chapter 6 deals primarily with the Iraq-Iran war and its integration into the domestic politics of Iran, and secondarily with the ousting of President Abol Hassan Bani-Sadr. In the next chapter I describe the effect on the government of the armed struggle waged against it by the Mujahedin-e Khalq, and discuss the impact of the war on the economy. The final chapter of this section weighs the pros and cons of the Gulf War. It also provides a survey of the various revolutionary organisations which have been established, and the extent to which society has been Islamised. These provide important pointers to the future of Iran.

Part III deals with Iran's relations with the outside world. In Chapter 9 I set the current Iranian-Soviet relations in a historical context. I do the same in the subsequent chapter regarding Iran's ties with Western powers – concentrating first on Britain and then on America. Lastly I focus on Tehran's links with Arab Gulf states and other neighbours – and Syria, Lebanon and the Palestinians. I end this part of the book with a brief description of how Iranian leaders evaluate themselves and their revolution within the Islamic world.

In my conclusion I analyse the nature of the Iranian revolution by examining the social forces at work in its favour and against it. I speculate on the effect that Khomeini's departure will have on the government and the opposition. I also consider different ends to the Gulf War, and the impact each outcome will have on the future of the Islamic revolution.

My three visits to Iran after the revolution, lasting nearly four months, were useful in gaining first hand knowledge and understanding of the changes that Iran has undergone. Besides Tehran and its outlying towns and villages, I visited Qom, Khomein (the birth place of Khomeini), and various cities in Azerbaijan and Khuzistan.

A word about place names, and the spellings of Arabic and Persian words. I have used the term 'the Gulf' for the gulf that divides Iran from the Arabian Peninsula. But I have listed the two other names in vogue – the Arabian Gulf and the Persian Gulf – in the index. There is no standard way of spelling Arabic and Persian names. I have used one of the most widely used spellings in the English-speaking world, and stuck to it – except when the spelling of an author is different from mine. There I have simply reproduced the published spelling. A particular difficulty arises when different spellings of a proper name, or an object, begin with a different letter. Common examples are Koran and Quran, and Ghom and Qom. I have solved this problem by using one spelling in the text but including both in the index.

In general I have tried to be simple and consistent. Instead of writing 'a' ', I have chosen 'aa'; and instead of following the example of authors who write Shiite and Alawite (but never Sunnite), I have stuck to Shia, Alawi and Sunni. I have used the terms Mujahedin-e Khalq and Mujahedin interchangeably; and so also Fedai Khalq and Fedai. Since most of the Arabic words which appear in the text are part of the Persian vocabulary, I have prepared a combined glossary of Arabic and Persian words.

Rial is the Iranian unit of currency. Rials 75 to 85 are worth one American dollar.

In Iran, whereas a religious title always precedes a person's name, a secular title often follows it. For instance, Ayatollah Khomeini, but Muhammad Reza Pahlavi Shah. The following Arabic and Persian words signify religious or secular titles: ayatollah, dawla, hazrat, hojatalislam, imam, mahdi, saltane, sayyed, sepahdar-e azm, shah, shahbanu, shah-en-shah, shaikh and sultan.

Dilip Hiro
June 1984

INTRODUCTION

Iran has produced more surprises in six years than most countries do in sixty. A revolutionary movement sprang up in Iran at a time of economic prosperity, military strength and political stability. It was led by a seventy-five-year-old cleric, Ayatollah Ruhollah Mousavi Khomeini, operating from abroad. He relied heavily on Islam, and Islamic customs and festivals, to energise the movement and destroy the Pahlavi dynasty. In the process the movement neutralised the region's strongest military machine. The clergy, who provided most of the revolutionary leadership, possessed neither an organised political party of their own nor a blueprint of the social order to be created in the post-Pahlavi Iran.

In 1977 Iran was in its fifteenth year of economic growth. During that period per capita income increased fivefold in real terms. Between 1973 and 1977 the statutory minimum wage rose from Rials 80 to Rials 210. Iran was the most powerful country in the region. Its military was unflinchingly loyal to the ruler, Muhammad Reza Pahlavi Shah. Its intelligence services and political police were formidable. On the eve of the New Year Day 1978, the visiting American president, Jimmy Carter, called Iran 'an island of stability in one of the most troubled areas of the world'.

When the revolutionary movement gathered steam during the summer of 1978, the Shah did not trust the reports he was getting. One day he flew over the capital in a helicopter to survey the demonstrations against him. The experience shattered him. He could not believe that these were the same subjects who only a few months earlier had lined the streets of the eastern city of Mashhad in their tens of thousands to greet him. With his domestic base gone, his support abroad also fell rapidly. Even the US government, the staunchest of his backers, became equivocal. When Carter was asked at a press conference in December whether the Shah would survive, he replied: 'I don't know. . . . That's something in the hands of the Iranian people.'

Within a year the region's most stable island had become the most turbulent.

The emergence of Khomeini as the undisputed leader of the revolutionary movement was another major surprise. He had been in exile for thirteen years when political agitation began in Iran. He had in the past briefly led protests against the Shah. But he was by training, and inclination, a theological teacher, not a politician. He was certainly not a revolutionary, nor even a serious student of revolution. (Very few in the West had heard of him. He had published many books, but even the American Central Intelligence Agency had not acquired a single title.) Despite his lack of knowledge of the dynamics of a revolution, he soon recognised the revolutionary potential of the protest which began in early 1977. He made astute use of Islamic history and Iranian nationalism to create and encourage anti-monarchical militancy. His spartan style of life won him popular standing among people who were sick of the corrupt and luxury-living politicians. The fact that he was a man of God gave him the spiritual authority that secular leaders lacked. He kept his message simple. And like revolutionary leaders before him, he united the disparate opposition to the established order under the highest demand: an end to the monarchy.

Revolutionaries everywhere face their toughest test when challenging the military. Iran was no exception. How to overcome a force of over 400,000 armed men totally loyal to the Shah – that was the most crucial problem which the revolutionary leaders faced. To this Khomeini offered a unique solution. He urged the strategy of 'fighting' soldiers through martyrdom. Let the army kill as many as it wanted, until the soldiers were shaken to their hearts with the massacres they had committed, he said. Then the army would collapse, he predicted. And it did. On the morrow of the revolution, there was not a single soldier left in the capital.

That the revolution would succeed was as much of a surprise to revolutionaries as it was to the Shah and his foreign backers. Asked as to when exactly he expected the revolution to win, Khomeini's elder brother, Ayatollah Murtaza Pasandida, replied that he did not expect the revolution to succeed at all. It seemed to be more a divine miracle than a human endeavour.

The coalition of diverse religious and secular forces, which overthrew the Shah, broke up almost immediately after the event. The Islamic regime, which followed the Shah, was plagued with acute political, economic and security problems. Such conditions were conducive to the success of the counter-revolutionary forces at home and abroad, intent on destroying the revolutionary state. There were times when Iran seemed on the verge of civil war. But, leaving aside the Kurdish region in the north-west, civil strife did not erupt. That was another major surprise.

Abroad, Iran challenged the United States of America, seizing its diplomats. A second rate regional power thus confronted a super-power. America came close to punishing Iran militarily, but stepped back at the last moment on the ground that the military chaos created in Iran by such an action would help the Soviets to increase their influence in the Islamic Republic. In the end Iran got away with holding American hostages for fourteen months without being punished for it in a dramatic fashion.

The Iranian regime experienced economic difficulties due to the Western boycott imposed in the spring of 1980. But these did not amount to widespread shortages of consumer goods. The main reason why Tehran was able to withstand Western pressure was that it was able to operate its oil industry efficiently. That was a surprise. Few foreign observers had thought Iran capable of running its oil industry unaided by outside experts. By having caused a crisis in the world oil markets due to the revolution, which led to the doubling of oil prices, Iran was able to earn as much as before by keeping its exports at half the pre-revolution level.

Where American and British embargoes hurt Iran most was in the field of military hardware and spare parts. Iran was equipped almost exclusively with American and British weapons. And it was forced to fight a war, when it was invaded by Iraq in September 1980. The Iraqi action was not unexpected. But the Iranian response was. Most foreign observers had by then concluded that the Khomeini regime had lost its popularity, and that an Iraqi invasion would trigger off uprisings among ethnic minorities, the military and the urban middle classes. What actually happened was the exact opposite. The nation rallied round the Islamic leaders and stopped the Iraqi advance – and offered the world another major surprise. Future historians are likely to single out the Iraq-Iran war as the event which enabled the Islamic leaders to consolidate their regime in Iran.

Once the immediate danger to the Republic's integrity had passed, sharp differences between orthodox Islamic forces, represented by the Islamic Republican Party, and liberal Muslims, now represented by President Abol Hassan Bani-Sadr, came to the surface. Khomeini could no longer maintain his distance from the internecine conflict tearing the Republic apart. He sided with the IRP. This caused the most damaging rift yet within the portals of power in Tehran. All the disaffected sections of society backed Bani-Sadr. It was a formidable, but poorly organised coalition of forces.

Yet it was not enough to defeat Khomeini. He remained popular with poor and lower middle class Iranians, who formed the bulk of the population, and who had become politically active in the process of the revolution. As such, the defeat of Bani-Sadr was expected. What was not expected was the size and virulence of the violence that the opposition forces, led by the Mujahedin-e Khalq, unleashed against the Khomeinist regime. The deaths by a bomb explosion of seventy-two leaders of the Republic was the most severe blow that the state had received so far. Two months later, in August 1981, came the assassinations of the Republic's president and prime minister by an incendiary device. A force, which had succeeded in penetrating so deeply into the inner sanctum of power in Tehran, had to be considered a serious threat to the regime: so thought many domestic and foreign analysts. Hopes arose of an imminent demise of the Islamic regime, or at least a fully fledged civil war. But once again such predictions proved false. The government reacted with unprecedented violence, resorting to wholesale arrests, searches and summary executions. There was a chance that such behaviour would prove counter-productive, that it would alienate even more people and pave the way for the overthrow of the regime. But it did not. That the Islamic leaders managed to crush the Mujahedin challenge and ward off a civil war was a major surprise.

Having survived numerous threats to the Republic, internal and external, Khomeini loosened the state's grip over the citizen. The government felt secure enough at home to pursue the war with greater vigour than before. In the spring of 1982 it expelled the Iraqis from its soil. In July it invaded Iraq. Having been a victim of aggression, Iran was widely expected to be wary of invading Iraq. But once again the Islamic regime baffled foreign observers.

Over the next two years Iran launched a series of offensives, each time making some gains. Its offensives in early 1984 secured it the Majnoon islands, in the marshy land near the border in the south, with huge oil reserves. In the process Iran had alienated both superpowers: a unique achievement. For, in all the major conflicts in the Third World since the Second World War, the superpowers have always taken opposite sides.

One consequence of this was that Iran was forced to fall back on its own resources, and only those. By the spring of 1984 Iraq had borrowed nearly $40,000 million to prosecute the war. But the Islamic Republic had borrowed nothing abroad. In fact it had paid back virtually all of the international debts it had inherited from the previous regime.

In short, the Islamic Republic has proved more durable and resilient than most foreign observers had expected. It has maintained Iran's territorial integrity, kept the economy ticking over, and prosecuted the war with vigour. It has been able to achieve this by mobilising the bulk of the Iranian people on the basis of something they all believe in: Islam.

Most commentators describe Iran as an example of the Islamic revival that has been sweeping the Muslim world over the past decade or so. Such a statement overlooks the variation in religiosity that exists between different sections of Muslim society. The major divide is between working and lower middle class Muslims on one side, and upper middle and upper classes on the other. In Iran the former were as religious during the Shah's rule as they are now. They provided the overwhelming majority of 3.2 million pilgrims to the shrine of Imam Ali Reza in Mashhad in 1974.[1] They can hardly be said to have undergone an Islamic revival: they have been deeply religious all along. The term 'Islamic revival' applies to upper middle and upper class Muslims. During the Pahlavi era in Iran they – the ruling elite – were secular and Westernised. They were alienated from the popular religio-cultural environment of their country. That is now changed. As a result of the revolution, they have lost all political power.

Since the clergy are the new rulers of Iran, there is no longer the religio-cultural chasm that existed betwen the ruler and the ruled during the Pahlavi period. Most working and lower middle class Muslims now identify with the Islamic Republic, and feel they have a stake in the system. That explains why they have rallied round the Islamic leaders to safeguard the revolution. But they remain an enigma to Western observers, who have all along underestimated their potential. That is the main source of error in assessing the events in Iran before and after the revolution – and a string of wrong predictions. It is in this context that Iran can be seen to have offered the world a series of surprises since 1977.

PART I

BEFORE THE ISLAMIC REVOLUTION

THE ISLAMIC HERITAGE

The events of 1978-9 in Iran have proved to be unique in more ways than one. Together they constituted a revolution, and not a coup backed later by popular support. It was a phenomenon in which millions of people participated, and where the participants avoided violent confrontation with the armed forces. The revolutionary movement was led primarily by clerics, who followed the guidelines issued by Ayatollah Ruhollah Mousavi Khomeini, then living abroad. Khomeini used religious festivals and customs to give an ever increasing impetus to the revolutionary process and carry it to its final victory.

If nothing else, the success of the revolution has underlined the importance of Iran as an Islamic state. This is a recreation of the past, in so far as Iran was for long an important actor in the history of Islam. 'Over the centuries Iran stood as the second pole in the political developments and the great dynastic struggles of Islam,' notes Eqbal Ahmed, a Pakistani scholar. 'It played the polar role . . . in the first great dynastic shift from the Ummayads to the Abbasids, and in the rise and sustenance of subsequent dynasties such as Safavids and, culturally, of the Moguls.'[1]

In a sense Iran represented the eastern branch of Islam, which originated in western Arabia in the seventh century. It was through Iran that Islam spread to the Indian subcontinent, where today there are more Muslims than anywhere else in the world.

Islam, in Arabic, means state of submission; and the one who has submitted to the will of Allah – the one and only God – is called Muslim. In Arabia, the faithful were united in their belief in Allah and his precepts, as conveyed through Muhammad (praiseworthy), his messenger.

Muhammad was born in 571 to Abdullah of the Hashem clan of the merchant tribe of Quraish in Mecca, a trading post, and a place of pilgrimage for the worshippers of idols at the sanctuary of Kaaba, in western Arabia. When he was about forty, he began preaching revelations in Arabic that purportedly came to him from the archangel Gabriel. (These utterances, delivered in rhythmic prose, were noted down, and compiled into 114 chapters of varying lengths to form a book – the Quran – which took its definitive form a few years after Muhammad's death.)

The early revelations concerned mainly the omniscience and omnipotence of Allah, the compassionate; the evils of idol worship; and the concept of divine judgement. Since Muhammad's monotheistic teachings were antithetical to the idol worship practised at Kaaba, these angered the Meccan merchants, who profited by the arrival of the pilgrims.

In July 622 local hostility drove Muhammad and a dozen of his followers out of Mecca to Medina, an oasis town about 300 miles to the north-east. Here the feuding tribes of Aus and Khazraj welcomed him as an arbiter. The subsequent acceptance of Islam – the faith then being preached by Muhammad – helped the Medinese to end their feuding and live in peace as Muslims. Muhammad became the military and civil governor of Medina. This is reflected in the later (Medinese) part of the Quran, which deals mainly with daily problems of administration.

By the time of Muhammad's death in 632, Dar al Islam – the Domain of Islam – contained most of western Arabia, including Mecca. During Prophet Muhammad's short, fatal illness, intense rivalry broke out between his close aides for the succession. The contenders were Abu Baqir, father of Aisha, the Prophet's youngest wife; and Ali ibn Abi Talib, the Prophet's cousin and son-in-law. Whereas Abu Baqir led the public prayers during Muhammad's illness, the Prophet chose Ali to wash his body, a singular honour.

While Ali and other Muslims were mourning the Prophet and burying him, Abu Baqir and Ummar ibn Khattab, father of Hafsa, the Prophet's other wife, called a meeting of the community elders. After much debate, the assembly elected Abu Baqir as the caliph – successor – to the Prophet.

Abu Baqir died two years later, in 634. During that time he nominated Ummar ibn Khattab as his successor. However, before taking up the position, Ummar secured the community leaders' approval. He ruled for ten years. The disappointed Ali largely withdrew from active public life. But Fatima, his wife, often denounced Ummar for delivering wrong judgements. One such verdict so infuriated the defendant – named Firuz, an Iranian slave of an Arab – that he assassinated Ummar. The victory of Arab Muslims over the Iranian army of the Sassanians in 637 at Qadisiya had marked the arrival of Islam in Iran.

By the time of Ummar's death Dar al Islam contained not only

Arabia but also Syria, Iraq, Egypt and part of Iran. Ummar left behind an electoral council of six. It included Ali ibn Abi Talib and Uthman ibn Affan, a member of the Ummayad clan, which enjoyed higher status than the Hashemi clan within the Quraish tribe, and which was led by Abu Sufian. The council chose Uthman as the caliph.

Uthman favoured fellow-Ummayads brazenly. His policies created a class of wealthy landowners in Mecca, Medina and Taif. They took to a luxurious way of life. This enraged the faithful among nomadic tribes. In 656 tribal malcontents attacked Uthman's house in Medina and assassinated him. Following this Ali, regarded as 'the best among the Muslims', was chosen as caliph.

Ali was opposed by Muawiya Abi Sufian, governor of Syria and brother-in-law of the Prophet, and Aisha, the Prophet's surviving wife. They both demanded that Uthman's death be avenged. Having been elected by Uthman's assassins and their defenders, Ali could not concede the demand. A battle ensued between the forces of Ali and Aisha. Ali won. Following this, most of the military governors of Dar al Islam swore allegiance to Ali. He moved the capital from Medina to Kufa in Iraq, and prepared to confront Muawiya.

This happened at Siffin, on the banks of the Euphrates, in 659. When the battle was going against them, the forces of Muawiya stuck pages of the Quran to their lances. This brought the fighting to a standstill. Ali was pressured to accept arbitration. The arbiters ruled in favour of Muawiya. Ali refused to step down. Some of the erstwhile supporters of Ali, called Kharijis (Outsiders), were so enraged by Ali's having agreed to arbitration in the first place that they decided to kill both Ali and Muawiya, and make a clean start.

They succeeded in assassinating Ali in 661 – but not Muawiya, who managed to escape. He was later proclaimed the caliph in Jerusalem. Hassan, Ali's oldest son, was declared the caliph in Kufa. But soon Hassan was persuaded by Muawiya's emissaries to retire to Medina on the understanding that after Muawiya's death, the caliphate would return to the Hashemi clan, specifically to the House of the Prophet. Hassan died of poisoning in 669. And Muawiya nominated his son, Yazid, as the caliph during his lifetime, thus setting up dynastic rule – something that had not happened thus far in Dar al Islam.

By the time Muawiya died in 680, those who had supported Ali as the caliph all along came to be called Shiat Ali – Partisans of Ali – or simply Shia. They argued that because Ali had been divinely appointed successor to Prophet Muhammad, and because Allah's message had been most clearly received by Ali and his family, only the descendants of this first truly Muslim family were fit to rule Dar al Islam.

From this arose the concept of Imamat: that is, only Imams, the descendants of Ali and Fatima, can rule Muslims on behalf of Allah;

and the Imams, being divinely inspired, are infallible.[2] This view was not shared by Sunnis (those who follow the tradition), who regarded the caliphs to be fallible interpreters of the Quran, the Word of Allah. Whereas Sunnis believe in three basic precepts – monotheism, prophethood, and resurrection – Shias believe in two more: Imamat and justice.

When Yazid proclaimed himself the caliph, Hussein, Ali's oldest surviving son, refused to accept this. Yazid despatched his soldiers against Hussein. They attacked Hussein and his seventy-two followers at Karbala, twenty-five miles from Kufa, the base of Hussein, killing all the males, except Zain al Abidin, the ailing twenty-two-year-old son of Hussein, and Muhammad al Baqir, his four-year-old son.

Zainab, Hussein's sister, upheld the Shia cause until Zain al Abidin (the fourth Imam, after Ali, Hassan and Hussein) had fully recovered. From then on, Shiaism attracted dissident and revolutionary elements in Dar al Islam. Under the Ummayads, society had become stratified: Ummayad aristocrats at the top, and the conquered non-Arab peoples, called mawalis (clients) at the bottom – with ansars (helpers) and nomadic Arab tribes inbetween. This provided recruits to the Shia side.

Alienated from the system, the mawalis joined a series of rebellions that were led by members of the Hashem clan, the traditional rivals to the Ummayads. With each successive failure, the rebel leaders retreated further into the easternmost province of Dar al Islam, which now included all of Iran.

It was in Khurasan, the easternmost part of Iran, that an anti-Ummayad revolt, led by the descendants of Abbas al Hashemi, finally gathered momentum. The Abbasids drew their inspiration from Shia ideas; and their agents made it appear that they were fighting on behalf of the legitimate members of the House of the Prophet.

When, after their victory over the Ummayads in 750, the Abbasids revealed that they were the descendants of Abbas al Hashemi, an uncle of the Prophet, Shias were disappointed. The Abbasid origins lay with a man two generations older than the House of the Prophet. Yet Jaafar al Sadiq, the sixth Shia Imam, acquiesced to the Abbasid power. In return, the Abbasid caliph honoured Jaafar al Sadiq while keeping him under discreet surveillance. This was the beginning of peaceful co-existence between the Shia Imam's followers and the Sunni state.

During the Abbasid rule (751-1258), conducted from Baghdad, three branches of Shiaism crystallised: Zaidis or Fivers; Ismailis or Seveners; and Imamis, Jaafaris or Twelvers. Zaidis share the first four Imams of Twelvers, and follow a different line beginning with Zaid, son of Muhammad ibn al Hanafiya, a half brother of Imam Hussein ibn Ali.[3] Since they did not claim infallibility for their Imams they were in least conflict with Sunni caliphs. Zaidi principalities existed in north Iran in the ninth century.

Ismailis share the first six Imams with Twelvers, and follow a different line beginning with Ismail, the older, militant son of Jaafar al Sadiq. An Ismaili group set up the Fatimid caliphate in north Africa, which after conquering Egypt in 969, rivalled the Abbasids.

Those who followed Mousa al Kazem, the younger, moderate son of Jaafar al Sadiq, came to be known as Jaafaris – and later as Twelvers. After Mousa al Kazem came Ali al Rida (or Reza, in Persian), Muhammad al Taqi Javad, Ali al Naqi, Hassan al Askari, and Muhammad al Muntazar. The Twelvers believe that Muhammad al Muntazar, the infant son of the eleventh Imam, went into occultation in 873, leaving behind four special assistants. When this line became extinct in 939, there was no longer an infallible interpreter of the will of the twelfth Imam. The Twelvers believe that the situation will change only when the Mahdi (Rightly Guided One) appears to institute a just society.

Once the Imam had disappeared, the Sunni caliph felt secure enough to accept Shias as a separate religious-legal group. Following the death of Harun al Rashid in 809, the caliph's effective power began declining, with Dar al Islam's eastern part being increasingly usurped by semi-independent Iranian dynasties. Indeed, in 932 Baghdad fell into the hands of Ahmed Muizz al Dawla, a Buyid king, who was a Twelver. But neither he nor his descendants attempted to institute Shiaism at the caliph's court or abolish the Abbasid caliphate. Instead, the Buyids maintained a puppet caliphate until their overthrow in 1055. During their rule, four collections of Shia hadith – sayings and doings of Shia Imams – were codified. In legal terms, this put Shias on a par with four Sunni codes of Sharia, canon law: Hanafi (founded by Abu Hanifa, died 767), Maliki (by Malik ibn Aus, died 795), Shafei (by Idris al Shafei, died 820), and Hanbali (by Ahmed ibn Hanbal, died 855).

In 936 Muizz al Dawla introduced public commemoration of Imam Hussein's death. This continued until the overthrow of the Buyids by Tughril Seljuk, a Sunni. The Oghuz Turks and the Mongols, who followed the Seljuks as rulers of the eastern sector of Dar al Islam, including Iran, were Sunni. So too were the members of the Ilkhan dynasty, founded by Halagu in the 1250s, which lasted until 1335.

Towards the close of the fourteenth century, Iran was absorbed into the empire of Timur Lang (died 1405) which extended from the Oxus river to the eastern shores of the Mediterranean. With the death of Shah Rukh, a Sunni, in 1447, the empire disintegrated.

While debates between Sunnis and Shias were going on, another form of religious expression and concern – one directed more towards the inner self rather than the outer world – developed within Islam under the name of Sufism. The term was derivative of *suf*, wool, linked to the woollen garments that the early followers wore as a sign of asceticism. Almost all of the classical Sufi masters were Sunni. Prominent among them was Abu Hamid al Ghazali who lived in the Abbasid Baghdad of the eleventh century. During the following century Sufism became popular throughout the Islamic world.

From the time of the Mongol invasions of Iran during the fourteenth century, a certain rapprochement developed between Iranian Sufism and Shiaism. This was exemplified by a Sufi order called Safavid, which was centred around Ardebil. The order was Sunni in its origin but later moved towards Twelver Shiaism.

The power vacuum created by the death of Shah Rukh in mid-fifteenth century aroused the temporal ambitions of the Safavids. Aided by militant tribesmen, who combined their Sufi beliefs with veneration for Imam Ali, Shah Ismail, the Safavid chief, captured Tabriz in 1501. Within seven years Shah Ismail extended his domain from Herat, Afghanistan, to Baghdad.

Once in power, the Safavids adopted orthodox Twelver Shiaism to appeal to the heterodox sentiments of the populace, particularly tribesmen, and to differentiate themselves from the competing Sunni Ottoman Turks eager to incorporate Iran into their empire. The Safavids imported orthodox ulema (religious-legal scholars) from southern Iraq, Syria and Lebanon, and by declaring Twelver Shiaism as the state religion, conferred power, status and wealth upon them.

In return, the ulema allowed the temporal ruler to extend his authority so as to ensure 'order and tranquillity'. They declared the Safavids to be the descendants of the seventh Imam, Mousa al Kazem. Shah Ismail and his successor Shah Tahmasp tried to present themselves as the 'Allah's shadow on the Earth'. In his enthusiasm to spread Shiaism, Shah Ismail enjoined all preachers to publicly curse the first three caliphs: Abu Baqir, Ummar ibn Khattab, and Uthman ibn Affan. Shia ranks grew. By the early eighteenth century, most Iranians were Shia.

But in the late 1710s, when Shah Sultan Hussein tried by force to convert the Sunni tribes in Afghanistan to Shiaism, they rebelled. They invaded and captured Isfahan, the Safavid capital, in 1722. But they ruled only for eight years. During that period they tried, unsuccessfully, to reimpose Sunnism in Iran. Their successors, the Afshars, attempted to modify Shiaism in such a way as to make it acceptable to Sunni opinion. But they too were unsuccessful. The next dynasty, the Zands, supported Shiaism.

The Qajar period

With the Safavids' fall, most of the Shia ulema left Isfahan for Shia holy cities of Najaf and Karbala in Ottoman Iraq. Here the ulema became increasingly literalist, interested more in transmitting religious knowledge than in encouraging interpretative reasoning, ijtihad. It was not until the early 1780s that the literalist tradition began to wane under the forceful opposition of the prestigious Aqa Baqir Muhammad Behbahani (died 1803). He argued that a mujtahid, a practitioner of interpretative reasoning, was needed to interpret the basic foundations of the faith, and that every believer must choose a mujtahid as a source of emulation, marja-e taqlid. 'The need to follow the rulings of a living mujtahid, who was less fallible than any temporal ruler, gave a basis for power in the hands of the mujtahids that was far greater than that of the Sunni ulema,' notes Nikki R. Keddie, an American specialist on Iran.[4] Thus mujtahids acquired a basis for making political decisions, impinging on Islamic principles, independently of temporal rulers. From this arose the independence exercised by the Shia ulema during Iran's subsequent history.

Iran was now ruled by the Qajars who were Shia. Having defeated the Zand ruler in 1779, Aqa Muhammad Khan Qajar had conquered most of Iran by 1790. He was succeeded seven years later by his nephew, Fath Ali Shah, who frequently patronised the ulema.

Under Fath Ali Shah's benign rule, the ulema consolidated their position. They administered vast religious endowments, waqfs. They also collected religious taxes: khums, one fifth of profits, and zakat (alms), 2.5 per cent of income. They used these funds to run educational, social and charitable institutions as well as theological colleges. The ulema conducted Sharia courts which dealt with personal and family matters. In the process of enforcing court verdicts, they took to leading private armies composed of religious students and the fugitives they had sheltered. They enjoyed higher esteem among the faithful than the local Friday prayer leaders and judges – dealing with crimes according to the urf, customary law – appointed by the Qajar king. Moreover, they felt uniquely independent since their superiors, living in Najaf and Karbala, were outside the jurisdiction of the Qajars.

Steady erosion of the Qajar authority caused by the pressures applied by European nations, particularly Britain and Czarist Russia, after the Napoleonic wars of 1803-15, led to an increase in clerical power. As rivals, Britain and Russia were keen to see that Iran did not become a protectorate of the other. Thus, rivalry between these imperialist powers ensured the continued existence of an independent Qajar dynasty, however weak.

A nationalist urge to recover some of the territory ceded to Russia, as a result of the 1804-13 war, led to the ulema to pressure Fath Ali Shah to declare jihad (holy war or crusade) against Russia in 1826. Iran lost the war and signed the Turkomanchai Treaty in 1828.[5] The next year, angered by the aggressive behaviour of the Russian troops in Tehran, a crowd attacked the Russian mission in the capital, and killed almost all its members.

As a result, Britain's relations with Iran improved. This lasted until Abbas Mirza, the crown prince, prepared to attack Herat in 1833. His premature death in that year opened up the contest for the throne. Britain and Russia both backed Fath Ali Shah's son, Muhammad Mirza. The ulema opposed him mainly because of his Sufi leanings. Despite this, Muhammad Mirza became the shah (king) in 1834. He gave trade concessions first to Britain and then to Russia.[6] These hurt the interests of Iranian merchants who were close to the ulema.

During the long reign of Nasser al-Din Shah (1848-96), the gulf between the monarch and the ulema widened. Two major factors contributed to this: growing autocracy and corruption of the Qajar court, and the drive by Qajar ministers to implement social and economic reform. The introduction of a secular school system by the government in 1851 was bitterly opposed by the ulema, since it broke their monopoly over education.

The Shah's extravagance made him increasingly dependent on Britain and Russia; and this alienated the ulema from the court. In 1859 work began on a telegraphic system in Iran by the British. In the course of completing this thirteen-year-long project, British officials penetrated Iran as no other foreigners had ever done. The rising importance of the British at the Qajar court became dramatically clear when, in 1872, the Shah gave Baron Paul Julius de Reuter, a Briton, exclusive rights for seventy years for railways, tramways, roads, telegraph lines, irrigation works, all minerals (except gold and silver), a state bank, and customs collection for an advance of £40,000, and 60 per cent of the profits from the customs concession.[7] The deal was, quite simply, outrageous. The ulema protested vehemently, as did many others at home and abroad. The opposition to it became so intense that the Shah cancelled it in 1873.

Five years later, the Shah visited Russia. On his return, he formed the Iranian Cossack Brigade, officered by Russians. Its strength rose gradually to 2,000. Since the Shah used it as the palace guard, and since it was the only properly disciplined and trained unit of the army, its importance grew.

In 1889, in lieu of the cancellation of the 1872 concessions, the Shah granted banking and mineral privileges to Baron de Reuter. According to these, Reuter's Imperial Bank of Persia had the exclusive right to issue bank notes. These notes competed with the traditional notes and bills of exchange of Iranian merchants, and caused much resentment among traders and artisans: the two classes that had already been badly hit by European imports.

Traditionally close to the mosque, these classes backed the idea of offering united opposition to foreign, particularly British, domination of Iran – an idea then being propounded by Jama al-Din Afghani/ Assadabadi,[8] an Iranian-born Islamic thinker and writer.

But this had little impact on the Shah. Deeply indebted, on 8 March 1890 he offered a fifty-year monopoly of purchase, sale and manufacture of the entire tobacco crop of Iran to Major G.F. Talbot of the British-owned Imperial Tobacco Company for a personal gift of £25,000 to him, and an annual fee of £15,000 plus 25 per cent of profits to the state.[9] The yearly consumption of 10,000 tons of tobacco in Iran indicated the magnitude of the deal. The concession was kept secret until *Akhtar* (Star), an Istanbul-based Persian paper, divulged it many months later.

In January 1891, leaflets attacking corruption at the court were distributed clandestinely in Tehran. The Shah suspected Afghani to be the instigator, and exiled him to Iraq. There he contacted Mirza Hassan Shirazi, the leading Shia authority of the day, and won his support. This in turn encouraged the Iranian clergy to mount a campaign in Tehran, Isfahan, Mashhad and Tabriz against the tobacco concession. In early December, Shirazi declared tobacco to be haram (religiously forbidden), and instructed the faithful to stop smoking until the Shah had cancelled the concession to Talbot. The result was a near-total boycott. The government's effort to crush the protest by firing at the demonstrators in Tehran failed. The movement enjoyed wide public support, because it affected landholders, shopkeepers and exporters. For the first time the Shah's concession to foreigners affected ordinary citizens. On 25 January 1892, following a mob attack on his palace, the Shah rescinded the concession.

By giving a successful lead to popular protest, the ulema showed that they were an important and vital political force. This episode was to prove to be the forerunner of something bigger: the Constitutional Revolution. Interestingly, telegraphic facilities aided the protest leaders to coordinate their activities throughout Iran as well as stay in constant touch with Shirazi and other senior ulema in Iraq. About nine decades later cassette tapes were to become the main instrument in inspiring and sustaining a popular campaign against the monarch.[10]

However, a politically weakened Nasser al-Din Shah became even more dependent on the British. To pay the compensation of £500,000 to the aggrieved Imperial Tobacco Company, he raised a loan from Reuter's Imperial Bank of Persia. In return he authorised the bank's agents to collect customs duties in south Iran and the Persian Gulf. This incensed Afghani. Now exiled in London, he conducted an anti-Shah campaign through a monthly journal published there and smuggled into Iran. Afghani tried to build up a movement under clerical leadership for the overthrow of the Shah. But before the anti-royalist campaign could gather momentum, the Shah was killed. On 1 May 1896, he was shot dead at Shah Abdul Azim mosque near Tehran by Mirza Muhammd Reza Kermani, a merchant who had once been Afghani's student.

Muzzafar al-Din's accession to the throne caused no change in the strained state-ulema relations. Weak and spendthrift, the new Shah raised a series of loans from the British and the Russians by awarding an oil concession in 1901 to a British subject, William Knox D'Arcy, and further lowering tariffs on Russian goods in 1903. Because these tariffs included wines and spirits, prohibited by Islam, the ulema declared them to be haram, religiously forbidden.

The ulema's move emboldened the opposition which took to distributing anti-government leaflets. The opposition was encouraged by the anti-royalist papers published in Cairo and Calcutta and smuggled into Iran, and by the events in Russia. The defeat of Russia in the Russo-Japanese war of 1904 led to constitutional reform there. In late October 1905, Czar Nicholas agreed to convene a parliament with legislative powers. The news uplifted the Iranians agitating for a constitution.

In December Tehran's governor ordered a public beating of two old, respected sugar wholesalers for overcharging. The incident led to an instant closure of the bazaar. Later some 2,000 merchants and theological students, led by Sayyed[11] Muhammad Tabatabai, took sanctuary inside Abdul Azim mosque, and made four demands of the court, including the enforcement of the Sharia, and the establishment of a House of Justice. The Shah held out for a month while Tehran was crippled by a general strike. Finally he conceded the demands.

But the Shah failed to keep his promise. Matters came to a head in mid-July 1906, during the holy month of Muharram. In a sermon Sayyed Jamal al-Din Isfahani, a militant cleric, attacked the government for its autocracy, injustice and lack of a constitution. When he was arrested, theology students marched on the police station holding him. One of them was killed when police opened fire. The next day soldiers from the Cossack Brigade fired on the funeral procession of the theology student, killing twenty-two. In protest Tehran's eminent clerics led their families and some 2,000 theology students to the holy city of Qom, thus bringing all of the capital's religious institutions to a standstill. In the capital, now under military control, 14,000 merchants and mullahs sought refuge in the spacious garden of the British embassy. The protestors now raised their major demand from a House of Justice to a Majlis-e Melli, National Assembly.

Negotiations ensued between the court, the religious leaders in Qom and the merchant elders in Tehran. Faced with a continued general strike in the capital, the Shah capitulated. On 5 August he issued a decree that an 'Assembly of Delegates' be elected by 'princes, the doctors of divinity [ulema], the Qajar family, the nobles and notables, the landowners, merchants, and the guilds'.[12]

The constitutional movement was backed by propertied classes as well as religious and intellectual leaders. The former, consisting of landowners, administrators, merchants and artisans wanted Iran to be free of European domination so that they could develop their own potential, unfettered by the Shah's practice of giving economic concessions to Europeans. Religious leaders felt, rightly, that reduction in the monarch's authority would increase their power in manipulating tribal chiefs, feudal aristocrats and clerics.

With many of the guilds electing clerics as their representatives, the ulema occuped a majority of the 106 seats of the Majlis.[13] It met in early October. During the next two months they passed a set of Fundamental Laws. Later, in the following year, they produced a set of Supplementary Fundamental Laws. Each of these was signed by a different Shah. The ulema were divided broadly into purists and pragmatists. The purists argued that in the absence of the Twelfth Imam – popularly known as Imam al Zaman (The Imam of the Present Time) or Hazrat Vali-e Asr (Ruler of the Age) – the present government of the Cruel should be replaced by a constitutionalist government of the Wise Mujtahids. The pragmatists, commanding a large majority in the Majlis, agreed with the purists' sentiment, but found it impossible to implement it.

The pragmatists were subdivided among moderates and radicals. The moderates, led by Sayyed Muhammad Tabatabai and Sayyed Abdullah Behbahani, wanted to check the monarch's arbitrariness along the lines laid out in such European constitutions as that of Belgium. The radicals, led by Shaikh Fazlollah Nouri, wanted to limit the ruler's power within an Islamic framework.

On sovereignty, the radicals argued that since sovereignty had been delegated by Allah to the Imam, and then on to the mujtahids, it did not rest with the people. Their view was opposed by the moderate clerics as well as secular constitutionalists. The latter won. 'Sovereignty is a trust confided [as a Divine gift] by the People to the person of the King,' stated Article Thirty-five.[14]

The final document, modelled along the Belgian constitution, was a compromise between moderate and radical views, with radical clergy winning a few points. It was framed within an Islamic context. Article

One declared Jaafari or Twelver Shiaism to be the state religion. Only a Jaafari Shia could become the king, a minister or a judge. Article Thirty-nine enjoined upon the monarch to 'promote the Jafari doctrine' and 'to seek help of the holy spirits of the Saints of Islam to render service to the advancement of Iran'. Article Eight differentiated between Muslims and non-Muslims. Article Eighteen specified free education, provided it did not contravene the Sharia. However, the control of education lay with the government. 'The foundation of schools with the funds of the government and the nation, and compulsory instruction, must be regulated by the Ministry of Science and Arts, and all schools and colleges must be under the supreme control and supervision of that Ministry', stated Article Nineteen. The next Article declared the press to be free within the framework of the Sharia. Article Twenty-two required the right of free association to be dependent on the organisation's stand towards Islam. Article Twenty-seven confirmed the right of Sharia courts to exist.[15]

The Majlis deputies passed the Fundamental Laws unanimously, and rushed them to the Shah, who was mortally ill. He ratified them on 30 December 1906, and died five days later. When his son, Muhammad Ali, ascended the throne, he tried to emulate his dictatorial grandfather, Nasser al-Din Shah. Some months later the Majlis produced the longer Supplementary Fundamental Laws, which outlined the bill of rights for citizens, and a parliamentary form of government, with power concentrated in the legislature at the expense of the executive. Significantly, Article Two of this set of laws specified that no bill passed by the Majlis was valid until a committee of five mujtahids – elected by the Majlis from a list of twenty submitted by the ulema – had judged it to be in conformity with Islam. That is, the committee of the mujtahids could only exercise veto power, and not act as a creative body in its own right, as radical clergy had wanted. In practice, however, this article was never implemented. The Qajar rulers ignored it, as did the Pahlavis.

Muhammad Ali Shah refused to ratify the Supplementary Fundamental Laws. This led to demonstrations and the assassination of Prime Minister Amin al-Sultan. The Shah was shaken: he signed the document on 7 October 1907. Taken together, the Fundamental Laws and the Supplementary Fundamental Laws formed the Iranian constitution.

This augured a new epoch in Iranian history: the era of constitutional monarchy. The success of the Constitutional Revolution went down badly with Czarist Russia as well as Imperial Britain, which feared its spread to British India. This consideration, coupled with the rising threat of Germany, led Britain to settle its century-old dispute with Russia in Tibet, Afghanistan and Iran. The result was the Anglo-

Russian Entente signed secretly on 31 August 1907. According to this, the northern region of Iran, and part of the central zone, including Tehran and Isfahan, were placed under Russian 'sphere of influence'; the south-eastern region, adjoining British India and Afghanistan, under British 'sphere of influence'; and the rest, designated 'neutral zone', was left open to both powers. When this became public knowledge in early 1908, it demoralised the Iranian constitutionalists.

Like the Russian Czar, the Iranian Shah wanted to destroy the parliament and the constitutionalist movement. And like the Czar, the Shah became a target of assassination by his militant opponents. An attempt to kill him in mid-June failed. In reply he mounted a coup against the elected government. On 23 June he ordered the Cossack Brigade to bomb the Majlis building, then being defended by 7,000 lightly armed constitutionalists. In the fighting that ensued over 250 people were killed. The Shah dissolved the Majlis, declared martial law under the Cossack Brigade, and waged a reign of terror against the constitutionalists.

A civil war ensued. The Shah's efforts to suppress the constitution-alist movement in the provinces were thwarted when the royalist troops encountered armed resistance in Tabriz. In the south-west, Bakhtiari tribes sided with the constitutionalists to liberate Isfahan from the Shah's troops. They then marched to Tehran where, on 13 July 1909, they met up with the victorious constitutionalists from Tabriz. Thus overwhelmed, the Shah sought refuge in the Russian embassy. His abdication in favour of his twelve-year-old son, Ahmed, signalled the collapse of the royalist counter-revolution. But this was not the end of the conflict.

On 5 August the cabinet decreed the convening of the Second Majlis – Shaura-ye Melli (National Consultative Assembly). Elections followed and the new Majlis met in November. It approved the appointment of William Morgan Shuster, an American economist, as the treasurer-general, to shore up the state's dwindling revenue. The Russian and British governments protested. Shuster organised a special tax collecting force, and used it everywhere, including the Russian zone of influence. This angered the Czar. Russian forces occupied Enzeli and Rasht in November 1911, while the Czar issued an ultimatum that if Shuster were not dismissed within two days Russian forces would occupy Tehran. Shuster was sacked as the Russians began a march on Tehran. To placate the Czar, Nasser al Mulk, the Iranian regent, dismissed the Majlis for having voted to defy the Russian ultimatum. Although the Regent did not abrogate the constitution, his dismissal of the Second Majlis marked the end of the Constitutional Revolution.

Throughout this period, extending from December 1905 to

November 1911, the ulema were actively involved in political life, something they were not to repeat as a body until the late 1970s. They were moved as much by an urge to expand their socio-political domain at the expense of the secular authority as by economic gain. Many of the senior clerics were related to wealthy merchants who found their ambition to establish large scale commercial or industrial enterprises frustrated by the Shah's preference for Europeans in the economic development of Iran.

For the next decade the ulema were far less politically active, partly because normal life was disrupted by the First World War. Iran's declared neutrality meant very little: Britain and Czarist Russia were allies against the Central Powers, at least until the Bolshevik Revolution of November 1917. With the subsequent renunciations of Czarist imperialist policies by the Bolsheviks, nationalist Iranians turned increasingly against the British. Popular pressure brought down the government of the pro-British Hassam Khan Vossuq al Dawla in June 1920. But that still left the British in charge of the Cossack Brigade (purged of Russian officers after the Bolshevik Revolution) as well as the important ministries of war and finance. At the same time, lacking control of the Majlis, the British failed to secure ratification of the 1919 Anglo-Persian agreement, which amounted to Iran becoming a virtual protectorate of Britain.[16]

In early 1921 Bolshevik Russia and Iran decided to delineate their borders according to the 1881 Akhal-Khurasan Treaty and normalise relations. This prompted Britain's policy-makers to decide on stabilising Iran as a buffer state against the rising tide of Bolshevism in order to safeguard the British empire in India. As for containing nationalist and socialist tendencies in Iran itself, Britain opted for an enlightened strategy of working for the implementation of long overdue socio-economic reform through a strong, centralised state.

Aware of the ineffective administration that the Qajar elite, allied to feudal aristocracy, had provided to Iran, the British decided to supplant Qajar power with a new and strong force. In Colonel Reza Khan – a man of modest origins from a village in Mazandaran, now commanding the powerful Cossack Brigade – the British found their protégé.

On the night of 21 February 1921, forty-five-year-old Reza Khan led a force of 3,000 from Qazvin (the British military headquarters in the north) to Tehran, and overthrew the government of Sepahdar-e Azm Fathollah Gilani without any resistance. All this was accomplished in great secrecy, and very few then suspected Reza Khan to be in league with the British. Having assured the Shah that the coup was meant to safeguard the court from revolution, Reza Khan proposed Zia al-Din Tabatabai, a pro-British journalist, as prime minister. The Shah complied.

As the army commander, Reza Khan joined the cabinet led by Zia al-Din Tabatabai. The two leaders promised to end internal disintegration and foreign occupation, and carry out socio-economic reform. To dramatise their independence from the British they signed a treaty with Bolshevik Russia and submitted it to the Majlis for ratification.[17]

In May Reza Khan eased out Zia al-Din Tabatabai as premier. The next cabinet was headed by Ahmed Qavam al-Saltane, a rich plantation owner in Gilan, with Reza Khan as war minister. In August 1922 this government appointed an American economist, Arthur C. Millspaugh, as the treasurer-general, to increase its revenue to maintain an enlarged army. By merging 7,000 Cossacks and 12,000 members of the gendarmerie into the army, Reza Khan had created a unified fighting force of 40,000.

With this army under his command, Reza Khan conducted a series of successful campaigns against tribal and other revolts in the provinces during 1922-3. In October he returned triumphantly to Tehran only to discover a plot against his life. He decided to lead the government while retaining his control of the war ministry.

Premiership further fuelled Reza Khan's ambition. But he knew that he could not confront the Shah until and unless he had the backing of Shia leadership in Qom and Najaf. Therefore he cultivated clerical figures. He allowed Sayyed Abol Hassan Isfahani and Shaikh Muhammad Hussein Naini – the eminent Shia ulema freshly expelled from Najaf by the British, the new masters of Iraq – to tour Iran and propagate their views. Since Isfahani and Naini were then based in Qom, Reza Khan's decision won him much approval in the Iranian Shia circles.

In order to avoid a direct confrontation with the Shah, Reza Khan toyed with the idea of turning Iran into a republic: something Mustapha Kemal Ataturk had done in Turkey in October 1923. But the religious leaders regarded Kemalism as secularist, and therefore unIslamic. Knowing this, the court gave currency to Reza Khan's republican inclinations, hoping thus to alienate him from influential clerics. Reza Khan could not afford to let this happen.

His chance came when the British, having overcome the political crisis in Iraq, decided to let Isfahani and Naini return. On the eve of their departure in April 1924, Reza Khan visited them in Qom, and took the opportunity to disown republicanism. 'Since my only personal aim and method from the beginning has been, and is, to preserve and guard the majesty of Islam and the independence of Iran . . . I and all other people in the army have from the very beginning regarded the preservation and protection of the dignity of Islam to be one of the greatest duties,' he said. 'And we [the mujtahids and I] ultimately saw it necessary to advise the public to halt the use of the term, republic.'[18]

In October, the prestigious Calcutta-based *Al Habl al Matin* (The Firm Rope) published a manifesto attributed to Isfahani and Naini in which they said: 'It is obligatory for us to inform the people not to deviate from this Muslim circle [the government of Reza Khan] which gives currency to Islam. Those who oppose this command will be considered infidels.'[19]

Thus fortified, Reza Khan marched with 22,000 troops to the oil-rich Khuzistan, where the semi-independent Shaikh Muhammad Kazal had refused to pay taxes. Shaikh Kazal surrendered unconditionally. This confirmed the supremacy of Reza Khan and his army.

In January 1925, while Ahmed Shah Qajar was on a European tour, Reza Khan made a pilgrimage to Najaf and Karbala. In Najaf he called on Isfahani and Naini. He strengthened his ties with them by letting them believe that if he were made the ruler of Iran, he would implement the Islamic articles of the constitution, particularly the one about the mujtahids vetting all legislation. But he failed to co-opt them into a plan to block the Shah's return from Europe.

The next month Reza Khan sought and secured emergency powers from the Majlis, including the title of the commander-in-chief of the armed forces. He encouraged an anti-Qajar campaign. It reached a peak in October when Ahmed Shah Qajar was abroad, in Paris. On 25 October the Majlis voted by eighty votes to five, with thirty abstentions, to depose Ahmed Shah Qajar and appoint Reza Khan Pahlavi as regent. (Following the law passed in the spring, which required all citizens to acquire a birth certificate and a surname, Reza Khan had chosen for his family the name of an ancient Iranian language, Pahlavi.) Reza Khan Pahlavi immediately banned gambling and sale of alcohol, slashed bread prices and promised to enforce moral conduct and 'the true laws of sacred Islam'.[20]

As regent, he ordered the convening of a constituent assembly of 260 members. Using his unchallenged power, he secured the election of his backers to the assembly. On 25 December, leaving aside three abstainers, the assembly unanimously proclaimed him the monarch of Iran. Four months later, dressed in military uniform and royal jewels, Reza Khan Pahlavi crowned himself the Shah-en-Shah – King of Kings – of Iran. Thus began the Pahlavi dynasty.

THE PAHLAVIS

Soon after ascending the throne, Reza Pahlavi Shah created a national civil service and a police force. He centralised and modernised the state. His policies accelerated the pace of economic development, engendering a rising class of commercial and industrial bourgeoisie, and enlarging the size of the modern middle classes: secular teachers, lawyers, doctors, engineers, technicians, civil servants and journalists. He considered the ulema to be ill-equipped to deal with the problems of modern times, and steadily curtailed their power in their traditional fields of law, education, and religious endowments, waqfs.

This contrasted with his behaviour before he became monarch. Then he had courted the ulema and taken their views seriously. For instance, when he was overseeing the drafting of a bill for military conscription in the early spring of 1925, he listened to the clerical leaders, many of whom argued that a two-year stint in a secular institution, such as the military, would erode the beliefs of the faithful. He agreed to exempt clergy and theological students from conscription. In addition, he promised to 'preserve the greatness of Islam and the ulema leadership' so that 'in carrying out their convictions and intentions . . . they would not meet obstacles'.[1]

The Law of Military Conscription passed in May 1925 incorporated the promised exemption, but created an examination body of lay religious experts to check the claim of a theological student applying for exemption. This was a subtle, but important, intrusion by the state into ecclesiastical matters. However, taking education as a whole, the principle of state supremacy, enshrined in Article Nineteen of the constitution, had already been implemented in the Education Law of 1911. This law specified a council for organising the affairs of theological schools.

Although Reza Pahlavi Shah did not need the ulema's approval as much as he did before his elevation to kingship, he still had to work with the Sixth Majlis (1926-8), where 40 per cent of the deputies were ulema.[2] Therefore he had to tread carefully when it came to reforming the administration of waqfs and the legal system – composed of urf (customary) courts dealing with the state and its administration, and Sharia courts involved with matters of family, property and commerce.

The Shah devised the strategy of combining universally popular measures with socio-economic reform which ran contrary to clerical interests. In 1927 he dismissed Millspaugh and unilaterally cancelled the economic privileges – called Capitulations – accorded to European powers over the past century. He then increased tariffs on imports. These moves were enthusiastically received by merchants, artisans and clerics. Merchants had already been pleased by the Commercial Code of 1925 which, by legalising joint companies, had opened the way for their rapid economic advancement.

Intent on providing Iran with a comprehensive legal framework, the government introduced a civil code to the Majlis. The code combined the highly acclaimed abrogation of the Capitulations with controversial provisions for subordinating Sharia courts to the state and increasing the powers of the government's waqf department. When the ulema protested, the justice minister temporised by adding 'provisional' to the code. The Provisional Civil Code was passed in May 1928, and laid the foundation for future tussles between clerics and the state.

The Shah wanted to create a national Iranian identity out of many ethnic ones, often dramatised by the dress. Out of this arose the Uniformity of Dress Law of 1928. It required all males to wear Western-style dress and a round peaked cap, later to be called a Pahlavi cap. Only genuine clerics and theological students were exempted. And, just as in the case of military conscription, the onus was on the applicant to prove his bona fides. In retrospect, this law was to prove to be the turning-point in the Shah-ulema relationship, with power shifting decidedly in favour of the Shah.

A government decree of January 1929 restricted the definition of a theological student or teacher. This led to protest. The police took to harassing theological students in Qom. This behaviour caused the moderate Ayatollah Abdul Karim Hairi-Yazdi to join the outcry against the state decree. But the Shah ignored the protest. Instead, his government tightened its control of religious schools by appointing examining boards for them. It was one of the many steps taken to reduce the number of religious students and teachers. These were effective. During the next decade the number and size of theological schools in Tehran, Isfahan, Tabriz and Mashhad declined considerably.

In a series of moves the government reduced the power of Sharia courts run by the ulema. The Law of Sharia Courts of 1930 restricted them to marriage, divorce, guardianship, and deciding only the innocence or guilt of the accused. The attorney general and state courts were given the authority to decide which cases were to be handled by Sharia courts, and what sentences to pass on those who had been found guilty by them. The Law Concerning the Registration of Documents and Property of 1932 ended the right of the Sharia court to act as registrar of documents: something that had been a major source of income to the ulema. Finally, a law passed in December 1936 barred clerics from acting as judges in state courts.

While Reza Pahlavi Shah lost ground among the clergy, he gained popularity among civil servants, merchants and the commercial bourgeoisie, because of his aggressively nationalist economic policies. In 1930 he transferred the Imperial Bank of Persia's exclusive right to issue notes to the recently established Bank Melli (National Bank). To insulate Iran from the ill-effects of the 1929 economic depression, he nationalised import-export trade under the Monopoly of Foreign Trade Law of 1931. Dissatisfied with low oil royalties, he unilaterally cancelled the concession to the British-owned Anglo-Persian Oil Company in November 1932 – a step that was welcomed with rejoicing in the streets. After the company had taken the case to the League of Nations the Shah signed a new agreement with it in April 1933 under the League's aegis. It offered better terms to Iran, including the reduction of the concession area of 500,000 square miles to 100,000 square miles in two stages.[3] During that year a Scandinavian consortium began work to finish the railway from the north to the south, first begun in 1927.

Having thus enhanced his popular standing, the Shah tackled the ulema on their most secure base: the waqfs, religious endowments, the prime source of income and social prestige for the clergy. The state's involvement in the administration of waqfs went back to the Safavid period. Between the overthrow of the Safavids by the Afghan rebels in the early 1720s and the rise of the Qajars sixty years later, the number and size of waqfs fell considerably. But once significance of the mujtahid in the life of the believers had been re-established in the early nineteenth century – during the rule of the pro-ulema Fath Ali Shah – the situation changed. With the mujtahid's increasing involvement in the daily life of the faithful, the importance of waqfs as a financial source for the mujtahid's social welfare agencies grew. Following the Constitutional Revolution, the system was rationalised.

During Reza Pahlavi Shah's rule, the Civil Code of 1928 included various clauses on religious endowments. These provided the foundation on which the 1934 Law of Waqfs was built. This law and the subsequent administrative statute of May 1935 boosted the powers of the waqfs department of the ministry of education. It was authorised to take over all the religious endowments with no or unknown administrators, and to supervise others by approving or disapproving their budgets. It was also empowered to transform a waqf into private property or prohibit such a development.

In the course of implementing this law the state took over many religious schools. This, and the establishment of the Faculty of Theology at Tehran University in 1935, gave the government direct control over a majority of the religious schools' managements, teachers and students, and strengthened the hands of the Shah in his ongoing conflict with the ulema.

Inspired by his visit to the secularist Turkey in 1934, Reza Shah tried to improve women's social status. He ordered all public places and educational institutions to open their doors to women. In 1935 he outlawed the veil – particularly chador, an all-embracing shroud, commonly used by Iranian women. The ulema opposed this, since the veil is sanctified by the Quran.[4]

The Shah also decreed that all men must replace their Pahlavi caps with European felt hats. This interfered with the Islamic way of praying, which requires the believer to touch the ground with his forehead in the course of the prayer. Many Muslims defied the order. The matter came to a head at the shrine of Imam Ali Reza, the eighth Imam, in Mashhad on 10 July 1935: the twenty-fourth anniversary of the Russian bombing of the shrine. Despite threats by the police, the faithful refused to don brimmed hats. For two days there was a stand-off between the pilgrims and the security forces. On the third day the troops summoned from Azerbaijan entered the shrine and fired, killing over 100 people, including women and children, and wounding nearly 250.[5] The event shocked the nation. Realising the gravity of the army's action, the Shah ordered an inquiry. When the investigators put the blame on the shrine's administrator, the Shah had him executed.

But this had little impact on the general direction of the Shah's policies in religious matters that he had been following over the past decade. He sought to prohibit the popular mourning of the death (in Najaf) of Shaikh Naini, revered as Iranian Shias' marja-e taqlid. Having banned in 1939 self-flagellation in public on the anniversary of Imam Hussein's death on the tenth of Muharram, the Shah tried to stop the public performance of Shia passion plays preceding the mourning, and prohibit the pilgrimage to Mecca.

Since the Shah needed a pliant Majlis to implement his policies without question, he resorted to manipulating elections. With the help of the police chief he would draw up a list of desirable candidates for the benefit of the interior minister, who conducted the polling. The minister would then send these names to provincial governors-general, who would pass them on to the local electoral councils, meant to supervise the balloting. As these councils consisted mainly of men who were close to the interior ministry, they complied readily. Not surprisingly, the number of ulema in the Majlis declined rapidly. The Eleventh Majlis (1936-8) did not have a single well-known cleric.[6]

With 30 to 40 per cent of government expenditure going to development projects during the 1930s,[7] there was much economic growth. The regime made a special effort to foster industry, particularly textiles and food processing. The building of 14,000 miles of new roads, and the completion of the Trans-Iranian Railway by August 1938, gave impetus to industrialisation. During the 1930s, 230 new factories were established.[8] As the state was part-owner of 200 of these, and the sole owner of the rest, the Shah and his courtiers enriched themselves by making legal and illegal deals.

After the rise of Adolf Hitler in Germany in 1933, the Shah tried to use Berlin as a counterpoint to the commercial and political dominance of London and Moscow. Hitler's autocracy and ultra-nationalism had special appeal for Reza Shah. Political and economic ties between Tehran and Berlin grew stronger. By the time the Second World War broke out in September 1939, Germany accounted for nearly half of Iran's foreign trade.[9] German experts were then engaged in the construction of Iranian roads, railways and docks – as well as the organising of the Youth Corps.

Reza Shah declared Iran to be neutral in the conflict. In the winter of 1940-1, as the war went in favour of the Axis Powers, the British protested against the presence of German agents in Iran. In mid-1941 there were an estimated 2,000 Germans in the country.[10]

The German invasion of the Soviet Union on 22 June 1941 alarmed the British. They saw it as part of a pincer movement, its other arm being the German thrust into north Africa, to crush the British resistance. Soon after the USSR joined the Allies, it sent a note of protest to the Shah about the German agents in Iran, drawing his attention to Articles 5 and 6 of the 1921 Iranian-Soviet Treaty.[11] The Allies deliberately played up the issue of German spies. Their real fear was the possibility of the Shah upgrading his strong sympathies with Germany into a military alliance. This had to be aborted at all costs, they decided, and Iran secured to provide an Allied supply route to the USSR.

On 25 August 1941 Soviet and British troops marched into Iran at five different places. Iranian resistance collapsed after two days, and a ceasefire was signed on 28 August. The Soviet forces occupied the northern part of Iran, and the British the southern part. On 16 September, fearing that Soviet troops were marching down from Qazvin to Tehran with the intention of deposing him, Reza Pahlavi Shah abdicated in favour of his twenty-three-year-old son Muhammad Reza. He left immediately for the island of Mauritius, then a British colony.[12]

'Reza Shah's work for rapid modernisation from above, along with his militantly secularist cultural and education programme, helped to create the situation of "two cultures" in Iran,' comments Nikki R. Keddie. 'The upper and new middle classes became increasingly Westernised and scarcely understood the traditional or religious culture of most of their compatriots. On the other hand, peasants and urban bazaar classes continued to follow the ulema, however politically cowed the ulema were. . . . These classes associated "the way things should be" more with Islam than with the west.'[13] This was to have an important bearing on the rise of a revolutionary movement in the late 1970s.

Muhammad Reza Pahlavi Shah

The end of Reza Shah's fifteen-year-long dictatorship brought relief and joy to many in Iran, including the ulema. His successor was too young and inexperienced to rule autocratically, even if he wanted to. In any case, with his kingdom occupied by foreign powers, and his army reduced to the role of safeguarding internal security, he could only reign, not rule. His regime was beset with acute problems stemming from the war: dislocation of transport, declining production, shortages of food and other necessities, hoarding and profiteering and soaring inflation. Prices rose sevenfold in three years.

People suffered. So did the theological schools dependent on leasing out waqf properties. Yet it was important for the long-term health of the waqfs that they should remain adequately endowed. To this end, the new Shah reversed the rule which allowed the waqf properties to be sold commercially. He also amended the 1911 Education Law to help improve the management of religious schools. He wanted to show the ulema that he cared for religious institutions.

Yielding to clerical pressures he annulled his father's bans on Shia passion plays and pilgrimage to Mecca. He even instructed government offices to observe the Islamic prohibitions during the fasting month of Ramadan: a small but highly visible step. The changed circumstances emboldened many urban women to appear veiled in the streets. The police tended to ignore their defiant act. Aware of the absence of active support for him among any segment of society, the young Shah wanted to win the sympathies of the ulema, the one group in daily touch with the masses.

When the Second World War finally ended in August 1945 it did not lead to an immediate withdrawal of foreign troops from Iran. As such, the Shah still could not exercise proper authority. It was only after Soviet forces had withdrawn in May 1946, and the Shah's forces had quelled rebellions in Azerbaijan and Kurdistan in December that the Shah acquired enough confidence to assert his power.[14] A year later he dismissed Premier Ahmed Qavam al Saltane, the very politician who had been instrumental in the re-imposition of the Shah's authority in Azerbaijan. However, Ibrahim Hakimi, the Shah's choice for premier, faced stiff competition from Muhammad Mussadiq, a strong personality. Hakimi managed to win, but only by one vote.

Not surprisingly, when in early January 1948 a group of ulema issued a religious decree, fatwa, that women must wear a veil while shopping, Premier Hakimi reacted tepidly. All he did was to appeal to Ayatollah Muhammad Mousavi Behbahani, the capital's clerical leader, to help stop attacks on unveiled women by zealot men.

Like Ayatollah Muhammad Hussein Borujerdi, Behbahani was a moderate. That is, both these leaders stressed that clergy must stay away from day-to-day politics. Their view was opposed by Ayatollah Abol Qassem Kashani, a militant cleric, who had been imprisoned twice: in 1942 by the British occupiers for his anti-British activities, and then briefly in 1947 by Qavam al Saltane. While Kashani was popular with second rank clerics and itinerant mullahs, Borujerdi and Behbahani, being part of the clerical elite, were the favourites of senior clergy.

Soon after the Second World War, Kashani had founded a political party, Mujahedin-e Islam (Combatants of Islam). It drew its strength from small traders, theological students and older leaders of the bazaar merchant families. It demanded cancellation of all the secular laws passed by Reza Shah, the application of Sharia (as stated in the constitution), re-introduction of the veil for women and, interestingly, protection for Iranian industries.

Kashani's third arrest, followed by banishment to Lebanon, came in the wake of an unsuccessful assassination attempt on the Shah by a press photographer on 4 February 1949 at Tehran University. The attacker was killed on the spot. But because his identity papers showed him to be working for the *Parcham-e Islam* (Flag of Islam), a religious publication, and belonging to the journalists' union, then affiliated to a pro-Communist labour federation, the Shah hit out at the Islamic and Communist forces. He imposed martial law and banned the communist Tudeh (Masses) Party.

At the Shah's behest the Majlis passed a law which restricted political activity. The moderate ulema leaders rallied round the ruler. A conference of 2,000 clergy called by Borujerdi in Qom on 20-21 February decided against political activism by clergy, and threatened to derecognise any cleric who defied the directive.

But this did not deter many senior clerics from issuing religious decrees in favour of the nationalisation of the Anglo-Iranian Oil Company, a subject that dominated elections to the Sixteenth Majlis, held from July 1949 to February 1950. Kashani stood for nationalisation. In this, he argued, he was following the example of Mirza Hassan Shirazi of Tobacco Protest fame. In December he called on all 'sincere Muslims and patriotic citizens' to fight the enemies of Islam and Iran by 'joining the nationalisation struggle'.[15] Supporting Kashani, the prestigious Ayatollah Muhammad Taqi Khonsari quoted the Prophet's hadith: 'He who upon waking does not concern himself with the affairs of Muslims is not himself a Muslim'.[16] Such statements had a profound impact on young Islamic militants. On 7 March 1951, while the nation was in the grip of a heated debate on oil nationalisation, Khalil Tahmasibi, a member of the clandestine Fedaiyan-e Islam (Self-sanctificers of Islam), assassinated the pro-British Premier General Ali Razmara inside a Tehran mosque.

Reflecting the national mood, the Sixteenth Majlis first passed a motion on 15 March for the principle of oil nationalisation, and then on 28 April spelled out the steps for the takeover of the AIOC. By seventy-nine votes to twelve, it also recommended that Muhammad Mussadiq, leader of the National Front, be appointed premier. The Senate[17] too supported the nationalisation legislation. On 1 May the Shah gave his assent to the oil nationalisation bill, and appointed Mussadiq premier.

Kashani was actively involved in bringing about this outcome. His followers, drawn mainly from the Tehran bazaar, were prominent in the pro-Mussadiq demonstrations before and after Mussadiq's elevation to premiership. Kashani was moved as much by anti-imperialist feelings as by an Islamic vision of fusion of politics and religion. 'Islamic doctrines apply to social life, patriotism, administration of justice and opposition to tyranny and despotism,' he said. 'Islam warns its adherents not to submit to foreign yoke. This is the reason why the imperialists are trying to confuse the minds of the people by drawing a distinction between religion and government and politics'.[18] Similar sentiments were to be expressed many years later by another ayatollah – Ruhollah Khomeini – and fuel the forces of revolution.

Having failed to thwart Iran's oil nationalisation plans, the British government, aided by Western petroleum companies, spearheaded a successful boycott of Iranian oil. The Iranian oil industry declined sharply. Faced with a deteriorating economy, Mussadiq sought emergency economic powers from the Seventeenth Majlis on 13 July. Three days later, using his constitutional prerogative, he appointed a minister of war. The Shah refused to accept Mussadiq's nominee, and thus relinquish his active command of the military. Mussadiq resigned in protest. The Shah nominated Qavam al Saltane as premier. This led to five days of strikes, rioting and demonstrations. Kashani attacked Qavam al Saltane as 'the enemy of religion, freedom and national independence'.[19] On 21 July the Shah relented, and recalled Mussadiq.

Qavam al Saltane resigned. On 3 August the Majlis gave Mussadiq emergency powers for six months, and elected Kashani speaker for a year. The Mussadiq-Kashani combine represented an alliance of the modern and traditional middle classes, both of whom wanted to rid Iran of foreign domination, whether political or economic.

During the next few months, as the Western boycott of Iranian oil began to hurt Iran further, this alliance became strained. When, for instance, the economic minister prepared to open new bakeries in an attempt to lower food prices, the traditional guilds of the bazaar, instigated by Kashani, protested at the government's interference with a free market system.[20]

The erosion of support among the traditional middle classes made the Mussadiq government increasingly dependent on the following that the Tudeh Party could muster in the street, the oil industry and the civil service. This further alienated the clerical leaders from the government. In January 1953 there was a clash in Qom between the followers of Ayatollah Borujerdi and those of the leftist-inclined Ayatollah Ali Akbar Burqui. Mussadiq found himself in an invidious position. He could not criticise Burqui, who had been a staunch backer of oil nationalisation. At the same time he could not afford to alienate the powerful Borujerdi. In fact, earlier, yielding to pressures by Borujerdi and Behbahani, Mussadiq had dropped his plans for enfranchising women. He had also banned the sale of alcohol. The Shah too had been equally solicitious of the religious leaders. In his inaugural address to the Seventeenth Majlis in early June he had committed himself to strengthening the foundations of Islam and propagating its principles.[21]

In mid-January 1953 Mussadiq approached the Majlis for an extension by a year of his emergency powers. This was opposed among others by Kashani. In the end, Mussadiq secured the extension, but the break between him and Kashani was now complete. That is, the alliance between the modern and the traditional middle classes, forged earlier, broke down long before the major conflict – between the Shah and the government – came to a head. Something similar was to happen more than a quarter century later *after* the overthrow of the Shah.

The Shah: flight and return

The Shah was alarmed at the way Mussadiq used his emergency powers. He ordered Reza Shah's illegally acquired lands returned to the state, cut the court budget, and forbade communication between the Shah and foreign diplomats. Mussadiq appointed himself acting minister of war. To dramatise his disapproval, the Shah threatened on 27 February to leave Iran soon. Through this tactic he meant to galvanise all his forces and confront Mussadiq. Unwilling to engage in such an exercise just then, Mussadiq persuaded the Shah to change his mind.

To reconcile the monarch with the prime minister, the Majlis appointed an eight-member committee. A fortnight later it recommended that since the constitution put the military under the government's jurisdiction, the Shah should give up his active command of the military to the minister of war, Mussadiq. The Shah refused. Mussadiq offered to forego his emergency powers if the Shah would relinquish his control over the armed forces, but to no avail. An impasse ensued. Ayatollahs Borujerdi and Behbahani offered to mediate, but nothing came of it. On 24 May, fifty-four of the fifty-seven Majlis deputies present voted for the bill to implement the committee's recommendation. (The current strength of the 136-member Majlis was seventy-nine, since elections to the remaining seats had been postponed.) With this, the Shah's powers were reduced to what they were at the time of his accession to the throne.

In July, Kashani failed to be re-elected speaker of the Majlis. This gave Mussadiq much area for manoeuvre. To break the political deadlock, he asked his Majlis supporters to resign so that he could order fresh elections without the Shah's concurrence. Fifty-six deputies did so, thus causing de facto dissolution due to lack of quorum. On 27 July he ordered a referendum on the dissolution of the Majlis. This was held from 3 to 10 August. Since the opposition boycotted it, Mussadiq won practically all the votes.[22]

By now two powerful, but clandestine, forces were busily planning the overthrow of the Mussadiq government: royalist military and gendarmerie officers, and the American Central Intelligence Agency. The officers had been organised by Senator General Fazlollah Zahedi under the aegis of the clandestine Committee to Save the Fatherland. The fifty-six-year-old Zahedi was totally loyal to the Pahlavis, having served under Colonel Reza Khan in the Cossack Brigade. Most of his early recruits came from the 200 officers retired or dismissed by the Mussadiq government during 1952. They joined the innocuous sounding Retired Officers Club. Zahedi and others got in touch with the British Secret Service, MI6 (Military Intelligence 6). The government was not unaware of this, for on 13 October 1952 it arrested a general and three businessmen for plotting against it with a 'foreign embassy'.[23] Nine days later Mussadiq cut off diplomatic ties with Britain. The British MI6 left behind a working group under Assadollah Rashidian, a rich businessman, with extensive contacts among the strongmen of the Tehran bazaar. However, recognising the immense difficulties of operating in a country where Britain no longer had its embassy, the MI6 approached the American CIA and got it interested in the idea of overthrowing the Mussadiq government, which was said to be slipping dangerously into the Soviet orbit.

By the spring of 1953 the CIA had become the prime mover of the project, codenamed Operation Ajax. It was placed under Kermit Roosevelt, the CIA's area chief for the Middle East. Helped by the CIA, Zahedi's Committee to Save the Fatherland won over important military and intelligence officers. They set out to destabilise the government by arming dissident tribes, and building up contacts with anti-Mussadiq clerical figures, and such leaders of the strongmen of Tehran's bazaar as Shaaban Jaafari, commonly known as Bemukh (Brainless).[24] Kermit Roosevelt arrived in Iran on 19 July by road from Iraq.

On the night of 1-2 August Roosevelt met the Shah clandestinely at the royal palace. Together they worked out a four-point plan: an alliance with the ulema; organising publications, crowds, and monitoring of the opposition through paid agents; consolidating the support of royalist military officers; and an overall coordination of the operations with General Zahedi and his 'friends'.[25] They had a series of meetings, the last one being on 8-9 August.

The next day marked the end of the week-long referendum on the dissolution of the Majlis. On 12 August Mussadiq declared that he would dissolve the Majlis and order fresh elections. That day the Shah and his wife flew to their holiday villa on the Caspian Sea. From there, on 13 August, the Shah sent two orders: one dismissed Mussadiq, and the other appointed General Zahedi (who had gone underground in July to avoid arrest[26]) as prime minister.

Colonel Nematollah Nasseri, the commander of the Imperial Guards, tried to serve the Shah's decree on Mussadiq at the prime minister's residence on the night of 15-16 August. But he found his forces surrounded by the royalist troops commanded by General Taqi Riahi, the chief of staff, who had been tipped off earlier by a 'royalist' officer. Nasseri was arrested, and his forces disarmed. This signalled the failure of the royalist-CIA coup. But this was not the end of the drama.

On the morning of 16 August the Shah and his wife, Soraya Isfandiari, fled in their private plane first to Baghdad and then to Rome. Jubiliant Mussadiq partisans took to the streets in Tehran and elsewhere. One section of Mussadiq's National Front demanded proclamation of a republic while the other proposed a referendum to redesignate the monarch as the constitutional head of state. The Tudeh Party called for an immediate break with the United States.

Three days of rioting and demonstrations, coupled with increasingly radical demands by the demonstrators, unnerved Mussadiq. They also caused an open rift between the National Front's moderate wing and the Tudeh Party.

On the afternoon of 18 August the US ambassador, Loy Henderson, met Mussadiq to complain of the harassment being meted out to the Americans, and to promise American aid if law and order were restored. Mussadiq decided to bring the situation under control. He ordered police and army into the streets next day to break up the demonstrations. This was his undoing.

It provided a cover to the royalist officers and Zahedi's Committee to Save the Fatherland to mount a coup against the Mussadiq government. It also gave an opportunity to the American and British agents, financed generously by CIA cash, to collect pro-Shah crowds from south Tehran to provide a veneer of populism to what was essentially a military operation by the anti-Mussadiq forces.

The pro-Shah demonstrators in south Tehran, where the vast bazaar is situated, materialised with the assistance of clerical leaders as well as pro-Western merchants and their allies: they feared a seizure of power by the Tudeh Party if Mussadiq continued in office. Led among others by Shaaban Jaafari Bemukh, the demonstrators marched to central Tehran where they met up with pro-Shah troops who had arrived from the Hamadan garrison 200 miles away.

They had two major targets in mind: the Tehran Radio building and the prime minister's residence. Tehran Radio station proved comparatively easy to seize. As soon as it fell to the royalists, they announced that the Shah's order appointing Zahedi as premier had been implemented. This was untrue. Just then Zahedi was engaged in a battle to capture the prime minister and his residence, being defended by loyalist troops. It took Zahedi thirty-five Sherman tanks and nine hours to overpower the pro-Mussadiq forces.[27] All told, 164 soldiers and demonstrators died on 19 August.[28] Three days later the Shah and his wife returned to Tehran to much public acclaim.

The 19 August 1953 coup laid the foundation for royal dictatorship which lasted a quarter of a century. It destroyed any chance that Iran had of evolving as a Western-style democracy. The Shah set out systematically to wreak vengeance on his opponents. He set up military tribunals to punish all those who had participated in anti-royalist activities. These were to become a permanent feature of the Pahlavi regime. The persecution of the Shah's adversaries went on for two years, and claimed 5,000 lives.[29] In addition, it drove about 50,000 men into self-exile.[30]

In a sense the events of March 1951 to August 1953 were a re-run of the history of the Constitutional Revolution. Then the Anglo-Russian Entente of 1907 had prepared the ground for the subsequent end of the revolution through Russian pressure and British complicity. Now America – a power which most secular nationalists had initially considered to be benevolently neutral to them in their dispute with the British – had clandestinely combined with Britain to overthrow a government which represented popular nationalist interests.

At the same time recent events were different from those of 1905-11. Whereas the traditional middle classes, led by the ulema, played a leading role in the constitutional movement, they were only junior partners in the oil nationalisation movement, which was led by the representatives of the modern middle classes, whether in the National Front or the Tudeh Party. This had happened because of the suppression suffered by the ulema during Reza Shah's rule, and because of the large expansion in the size of the modern middle classes during that period. A quarter of a century later, for different reasons, the roles were to reverse once again.

The second coming

The Shah was generous with praise and patronage to all those who had opposed Mussadiq and worked for his comeback. At the same time he was not indiscriminate. For instance, while he was warmly approving of Ayatollah Behbahani, he kept Ayatollah Kashani at bay, considering him unreliable and essentially rebellious. The state-directed press gave wide coverage to the activities of Behbahani. On the eve of Behbahani's pilgrimage to Mashhad in October, the Shah solicited the Ayatollah to pray for him at Imam Ali Reza's shrine so that he could meet 'the needs of the poor'.[31] Shia leaders responded in kind. In the course of his Iranian travels, Ayatollah Mahdi ibn Abol Qassem Shahrastani, an Iraqi marja-e taqlid, regretted the events of 1951-3, and said that in his talks with the local ulema he had heard things that were 'entirely in praise of the Shah'.[32] The Shah's regime, still trying to find its feet after the traumatic experience of the Mussadiq period, welcomed such statements with gratitude.

Senior religious leaders offered public approval of the repression that the Shah unleashed on the Tudeh Party in 1954-5. In contrast, they acquiesced discreetly when the Shah meted out similar treatment to the Fedaiyan-e Islam, a militant, underground organisation, in late 1955. Formed in 1945 by a young theological student, Sayyed Navab Safavi (alias Sayyed Mujtaba Mirlohi), it went beyond the customary call for the application of the Sharia as provided by the constitution, and demanded a ban on tobacco, alcohol, cinema, opium, gambling, and even the wearing of foreign dress. It advocated the re-introduction of the veil for women, and such Sharia prescriptions of punishment as cutting off a hand for stealing. It advocated comprehensive land reform, nationalisation of industry and various social welfare measures. Since it drew its following from the lower sections of bazaari society – porters, shop assistants, hawkers, peddlers[33] – it was complimentary to Kashani's Mujahedin-e Islam. Not surprisingly, Fedaiyan leaders were close to Kashani.

The Fedaiyan used assassination as a political weapon. Their first target was Ahmed Kasravi, a leading secularist lawyer and historian. He was assassinated in early 1948. Their second victim was Abdul Hussein Hazhir, Court minister, considered by them to be an agent of British imperialism and a sympathiser of Bahais, a heretical sect. He was murdered on 4 November 1948. Then came the assassination of the pro-British Premier General Razmara in March 1951 which, as stated earlier,[34] triggered off public jubilation, and led the Majlis to approve oil nationalisation.

When Mussadiq became premier, Fedaiyan leaders expected a cabinet seat or two in his government. Their hopes were disappointed. They turned against Mussadiq. Fedaiyan activists attempted to kill Hussein Fatimi, a special aide to the prime minister. Mussadiq ordered the arrest of Navab Safavi. The situation changed briefly, after Mussadiq's second term of office in late July 1952. At Kashani's intercession, Mussadiq released twenty-eight Fedaiyan members, including Tahmasibi, the assassin of Razmara.[35] But as Kashani moved away from Mussadiq, so did the Fedaiyan. They accused Mussadiq of falling under Western and leftist influences.

After the August 1953 coup the Fedaiyan did not moderate their policies or actions. They condemned the inequitable oil agreement which the Shah signed with the Western consortium in August 1954 and which the Majlis ratified two months later. On 18 November 1955, a Fedaiyan member, Muzzafar Ali (alias Dhul Qadr) tried unsuccessfully to kill Premier Hussein Ala. The Shah ordered an all-out campaign against the organisation. Its members and sympathisers were arrested by the score, and trials were initiated against all those accused of assassinations. Kashani was imprisoned briefly, and released only after he had publicly dissociated himself from the organisation, and privately promised not to protest against the expected executions of the leading Fedaiyan. On 16 January four Fedaiyan leaders, including Navab Safavi, Khalil Tahmasibi and Muzzafar Ali, were executed. But the organisation continued to exist.

Since his comeback the Shah had gone out of his way to project himself as a saviour of Islam. Along with his wife, Soraya, he took to visiting the holy shrines in Qom, Mashhad and Karbala. They made a pilgrimage to Mecca. He offered easy access to the Court for Ayatollah Behbahani, and took care to keep the favour of Ayatollah

Borujerdi. In return, they refrained from commenting on the Shah's secular decisions. For instance, they said nothing about the unfair agreement that the Shah entered into with the Western oil consortium in the summer of 1954, which led to strikes by bazaar merchants.

But religious matters were something else. Feeling confident of their elevated status at the Court, Borujerdi and Behbahani pressed the Shah to outlaw the Bahai sect. Bahaism stemmed from Babism, whose origin went back to 20 May 1844: the day when Sayyed Ali Muhammad Shirazi, a merchant from Shiraz, declared that he was the bab (door) to the Hidden (Twelfth) Imam. He was opposed by the ulema, particularly when in his book *Bayan* (Declaration) he compared himself to Prophet Muhammad. He was executed on 9 July 1850 in Tabriz. During the next two years the Babi movement in Iran was destroyed.

In the exiled Babi community of Baghdad, Mirza Hussein Ali, a Mazandaran-born aristocrat, rose to prominence. He declared himself Bahaollah, Glory of Allah, in 1863. As all Babis followed him, they now came to be called Bahais. Among other things Bahaollah said that religion was evolving. Since this ran counter to the traditional view of Islam as the last, most perfect, revealed Word of Allah, the ulema declared Bahaism heretical. By the time Bahaollah died in Acre, Palestine, in 1892, Bahaism had evolved as a universalist, pacifist faith without formal clergy.

Shia clergy were vehemently against Bahaism, and called on the state to stamp it out. In June 1903 there was anti-Bahai rioting in Yazd, an important Bahai centre. By denying vote to the apostates of Islam, Article Five of the 1906-7 constitution disenfranchised Bahais. The charges of spying for the British during the First World War, levelled against Abbas Afindi, son of the sect's founder, reflected a popular feeling that the Bahais were linked to Britain. Responding to a campaign against them in the early 1930s, Reza Shah closed down Bahai schools.

Now Ayatollah Borujerdi advocated anti-Bahai policies. During the month of Ramadan in 1955 (April-May), his lieutenant, Shaikh Abol Qassem Muhammad-Taqi Falsafi, attacked Bahaism and Bahais in his sermons on the state radio. He argued that by opposing Islam, Bahaism was weakening the state and monarchy. The anti-Bahai campaign by the ulema suited the Shah: it diverted public attention away from the problems of the ailing economy. And by identifying with the widely prevalent prejudice against Bahais, the Shah's regime improved its popularity. On 7 May General Teimur Bakhtiar, Tehran's military governor, led a contingent of troops and police to seize the Bahai Spiritual Centre in the capital. Borujerdi and Behbahani praised the government action.[36]

Reiterating that he would continue to propagate Jaafri Shiaism, as specified in the constitution, the Shah promised to close down the occupied Bahai Spiritual Centres in Tehran and Shiraz. However, he resisted the clerical pressures to outlaw Bahaism and purge the government of all Bahais. Sustained anti-Bahai propaganda led to attacks on the life and property of Bahais, whose numbers were variously estimated at 10,000 to 1,000,000.[37] When the Bahai International Headquarters in Haifa, Israel, complained to the United Nations on human rights grounds, the chief Iranian delegate to the UN said that there were no Bahais in Iran at all.

By early August the nation's attention was turned to the forthcoming celebrations of the second anniversary of the Shah's return, and the ceremonials of the first ten days of Muharram ending in the public mourning of Imam Hussein's murder on Ashura (tenth). With anti-Bahai passions cooled, the Shah quietly handed back the Bahai centres to the local communities. Simultaneously, steps were taken to excise all references to Bahais and Bahaism from history books, and increase religious instruction at school.

Having improved his public standing, the Shah felt confident enough in October to join the pro-West Baghdad Pact (later to be called the Central Treaty Organisation, Cento), a military alliance of Turkey, monarchist Iraq, Pakistan and Britain. The Shah's decision was backed by Jaafar Behbahani, a nephew of Ayatollah Behbahani, who was the ulema leadership's spokesman in the Majlis. He described the Baghdad Pact as being defensive and well within the UN Charter's collective security clauses. Referring to the 1946 Azerbaijan crisis caused by Moscow's refusal to withdraw its troops from northern Iran after the Second World War, he praised the UN, American and the Iranian military for countering Soviet expansionism.[38] Behbahani's pro-American views were very much in vogue in Tehran.

American influence in Iran rose dramatically in the aftermath of Mussadiq's overthrow. Between August 1953 and December 1956 America provided Iran with military and economic aid of $414 million.[39] With US aid came thousands of Americans, a development much deplored by nationalist Iranians, secular and religious. Iran's oil revenue jumped from $34 million in 1954-5 to $181 million two years later. With the state treasury receiving and spending such vast sums, corruption increased. This troubled the ulema, guardians of the nation's moral health.

The Shah was aware of the damage that the rising corruption was causing his regime. When he appointed Hussein Ala, a former Court minister, prime minister in April 1955, he instructed him to root out corruption. His earlier dismissal of the influential General Zahedi as premier showed his increasing confidence and determination to arrogate all power to himself. The Shah had set the trend on his comeback when he ordered the martial law administrators to report to him directly.

In 1955 he set up a political police force under military officers to gather intelligence and repress opposition: a prelude to Savak, Sazman-e Amniyat Va Ittilaat-e Keshvar (Organisation of National Security and Intelligence). The law of 20 March 1957 formalised the situation. The functions of Savak, described in Article Two, included 'the gathering of information necessary to protect national security; to prevent the activity of groups whose ideology is contrary to the constitution; to prevent plots against national security'.[40] Since Savak was a political police force run by army officers, all Savak agents were by law military personnel: their actions could only be judged by the permanent military tribunals. Savak was attached to the prime minister's office, and its head had the status of deputy prime minister.

By the time Savak was formally established, the Shah had smashed not only the Tudeh Party but also all the constituents of the National Front, formed by Mussadiq in 1949. Abroad, he had strengthened his links with the US by subscribing to the Eisenhower Doctrine of January 1957, which promised support to any Middle East government against 'overt armed aggression from any nation controlled by international communism'.[41]

However, there was nothing in this doctrine to enable the Shah, or any other ruler in the region, to forestall an internal coup by military leaders. The overthrow in July 1958 of the Iraqi king, Faisal II, by nationalist, republican officers underlined this only too well. The Iraqi coup alarmed the Shah. He intensified repression of the opposition at home. He approached President Dwight Eisenhower to sign a mutual defence pact. Eisenhower declined. Instead, in March, the US president signed an executive agreement with the Shah within the definition of the Eisenhower Doctrine. In return the Shah promised to spend US aid on economic development rather than on financing imports of consumer goods. He also agreed to liberalise the political system. This came in the form of introducing controlled party politics in 1959: Premier Manuchehr Eqbal heading the ruling Melliyun (Nationalist) Party, and Assadollah Alam, a boyhood friend of the Shah, leading the opposition Mardom (People's) Party.

Thus, by the late 1950s the Shah had laid the necessary political-economic infrastructure for rapid economic development under state-dominated capitalism: a process set to expand the size of the modern middle and upper classes – white collar professionals, and commercial and industrial bourgeoisie – and diminish the size of the traditional upper and middle classes: feudal lords, tribal chiefs, clerics, bazaar merchants and craftsmen. To facilitate rapid growth of capitalism, the

Shah needed to break the shackles of feudalism, the strong feudal element being the landed gentry. Half of the cultivated land of 4.5 million hectares belonged to absentee landlords.[42] Among them were the religious endowments managed by clerics. On the other hand 40 per cent of all rural households were landless, and only 5 per cent of the peasants were owner-occupiers, the rest being tenant farmers.[43] Redistribution of land was overdue, and the Shah decided to act.

This caused unease among not only landed aristocracy but also senior clerics, determined to hold on to the vast waqf lands. The ulema leaders had other grievances against the Shah as well. He had failed to counter the tide of corruption; he had been concentrating increasing power into his hands; and he had attempted to enfranchise women. Although a collision between the Shah and the mosque was avoided on land reform due to the concessions made by the Pahlavi ruler, the roots of the conflict were not removed.

The White Revolution

In December 1959 the Manuchehr Eqbal government submitted a draft bill on land reform to the Nineteenth Majlis (1956-60). In a letter to Jaafar Behbahani in mid-February, Ayatollah Borujerdi expressed his opposition to the bill, describing it as being contrary to the Sharia and the constitution. He blamed the Shah's advisers for it. He was worried specifically about the the takeover, or break-up, of the religious endowments – the source of revenue which paid for the upkeep and running of mosques and religious schools, and the financing of the Shia ceremonials during Muharram. Borujerdi's protest was effective. The agrarian reform legislation, passed in May 1960, included many exemptions, including one to waqfs. This satisfied Borujerdi.

The emasculated law fell into disuse almost immediately. The term of the Nineteenth Majlis ended in June; and elections to the next Majlis were rigged so blatantly that they set off protest in the streets. The Shah asked the deputies to resign. They did. The government of Eqbal fell.

Fresh elections to the Majlis were held under the premiership of Jaafar Sharif-Emami. The twentieth Majlis met in February 1961, with the ruling Melliyun Party commanding sixty-nine seats and the opposition Mardom sixty-four (out of a total of 200). Sharif-Emami gave way to Ali Amini as the head of the government. A wealthy aristocrat, Amini had been finance minister in Mussadiq's cabinet from May 1950 to mid-July 1952. He again served as finance minister in Zahedi's government after the August 1953 coup. He was appointed Iranian ambassador to the US in 1955. There he became a friend of

Senator John F. Kennedy. With Kennedy becoming president in January 1961, pressure grew on the Shah to implement wide-ranging reform and appoint Amini as prime minister. The Shah complied in early May 1961. Since Amini wanted a free hand to carry out reform he advised the Shah to dissolve the Majlis. The Shah did so, on the ground of electoral irregularities, and took to ruling by decree.

This happened at a time when the ulema were feeling leaderless in the wake of Borujerdi's death in March 1961 after sixteen years of being the marja-e taqlid. His religious position now went to Ayatollah Muhsin Hakim in Najaf. As an Arab by birth living in Iraq, Hakim lacked an intimate knowledge of Iranian affairs. This suited the Shah, but not the Iranian ulema.

Leaving aside the small pro-Shah minority among them, the ulema fell roughly into three categories: conservative, centrist and radical. The conservatives supported Borujerdi's line of staying out of politics. With Borujerdi gone, their leadership passed on to the triumvirate of Ayatollahs Muhammad Reza Golpaygani, Shehab al-Din Marashi-Najafi and Muhammad Kazem Shariatmadari: the seniormost clerics of Qom. They opposed the idea of state takeover of land above a certain ceiling, an important part of the agrarian reform law. They saw it as an attack on private property, a right sanctified by the Sharia, and therefore inviolable.

The centrists disagreed with Borujerdi's directive of keeping away from politics, but did little in practice to defy it. They tended to concentrate on the educational and social aspects of the Shia institutions. Their best known spokesmen were Ayatollahs Murtaza Motahhari and Muhammad Husseini Beheshti, both of them based in Tehran. They were in touch with Ayatollah Mahmoud Taleqani, a leader of the radicals, who also lived in the capital. On land reform, he argued that of the private, state, waqf and waste lands, the last category should be given to the landless for reclamation to help them end their destitution. As a group, the radicals stood for popular participation in the parliamentary process and limiting of the Shah's powers.

In Qom the radical viewpoint was now being articulated by Hojatalislam Ruhollah Mousavi Khomeini, a comparatively junior cleric, who came into prominence after Borujderdi's death. He openly criticised the Shah for violating the constitution by failing to call new elections within a month of the dissolution of the Majlis. On the agrarian reform he directed his fire against the provision for agricultural cooperatives, to be financed by US aid, to handle both production and marketing. This, he argued, would damage the interests of the traditional bazaar. Unlike some conservative clerics, he did not seem to have attacked the land redistribution aspect of the agrarian reform.[44]

Disregarding the criticism of Khomeini and others, the Shah took two major steps on 11 November 1961. He arrogated to himself the authority to initiate legislation, and instructed Premier Amini to implement the 1960 land reform law. A few days later he issued an edict which authorised the cabinet to rule by decree until the Majlis had reassembled. He directed Amini to pass laws on village, town and provincial councils with a view to building democracy from bottom upwards (and thus prepare the ground for fresh Majlis elections) and to reform tax and educational systems.

On 9 January 1962 the cabinet approved a new agrarian reform law which extended and strengthened the previous one. Hassan Arsanjani, agriculture minister, began implementing it immediately. Landlords had to sell the land above one village to the government and receive compensation on the basis of previous tax assessments; and the excess land was then to be sold to the sharecroppers cultivating it.[45]

About a fortnight later Tehran University students clashed with troops. The government arrested nine public figures, including Jaafar Behbahani, the leading spokesman of the ulema in the Majlis. This further soured relations between the state and the mosque. By now the Amini administration had alienated not only the clergy but also large landlords (due to the agrarian reform), politicians (by refusing to call Majlis elections), and top civilian and military officers (by its anti-corruption drive).

This made it easier for the Shah to ease out Amini whose independent-mindedness had always grated upon him. In the course of preparing the budget for the next Iranian year, beginning 21 March (the vernal equinox), Amini proposed cuts in military expenditure to reduce a huge deficit. The Shah, as the commander-in-chief, rejected these. In the conflict that developed, Amini attempted to secure the backing of the US administration. He failed. In mid-July the Shah forced him to resign, and appointed Assadollah Alam, the Court minister, as premier.

Although Alam retained Arsanjani as agriculture minister, the pace of reform slowed down. Alam concentrated on implementing the idea of multi-layered democracy. He published an electoral decree on local councils. Unlike the Majlis electoral law, this one did not specify that the candidates had to be male and Muslim. This, and the absence of the customary reference to the Quran in such a document, led the ulema to oppose the decree with a series of protests in November. Khomeini was prominent in this, and published his attack in the form of a pamphlet entitled *Local Government Administration in the Islamic Manner*.

Angered, the Shah launched a frontal attack on the ulema,

describing them as reactionary and opposed to Islamic concepts of equality. He threatened on 11 December to amend the 1962 Land Reform Act to include waqf lands. On 6 January 1963 he launched a six-point White Revolution. Besides the agrarian reform, it included forest nationalisation, sale of public sector factories to pay compensation to landlords, votes for women, profit-sharing in industry, and eradication of illiteracy.

The state-run media lumped together the secular National Front (which while favouring reforms opposed the unconstitutionality of their implementation) and religious opposition, and labelled them as 'reactionary'. They launched a campaign for the support of the White Revolution. The followers of the National Front and militant clerics resorted to street protest and called for a boycott of the referendum.[46] On 25 January, the referendum day, as the National Front central committee members and leading opposition clerics were being taken to jail, the Shah was distributing lands to peasants in the county of Qom. 'No one can claim that he is closer to God or the Imams than I am', he declared to the assembly of peasants.[47]

According to the government 5.6 million voters, amounting to 91 per cent of those eligible, participated in the referendum. Of these 99.9 per cent said 'Yes' to the White Revolution.[48] The next month women were enfranchised. None of this discouraged the Pahlavi regime's opponents.

As the opposition, led chiefly by radical ulema, prepared to show its strength on 21 March, the New Year Day, Nauruz, the government launched an offensive of its own. In early March the pro-regime *Ittilaat* published a series of editorials arguing that the minority of clerics, who were opposing reforms, had allowed their personal prejudice to colour their interpretation of the Sharia, and that the state's reforms were in conformity with the Sharia. Describing Islam, and other monotheistic religions, as 'eternal', it added: 'By the same token, religion is a matter apart from politics. Politics is an everyday term, religion an eternal one'.[49]

Such statements were anathema to radical clergy, particularly Khomeini, and inflamed the situation. Despite dire warnings by the authorities, anti-Shah demonstrations were held on Nauruz in Qom, Tehran, Shiraz, Mashhad and Tabriz. In Qom these were led by theological students who had been agitating against the scheduled opening of liquor shops in the holy city containing the shrine of Fatima, Hazrat-e Maasuma (the Revered Innocent), sister of Imam Ali Reza. Paratroopers and Savak agents attacked theological schools in Qom and Tabriz. Unofficial estimates of those killed by the security forces were put at 'hundreds'.[50] Khomeini was arrested the next day, but released shortly after.

Speaking in honour of the dead, Khomeini attacked the 'tyrannical regime' of the Shah which by its 'inhuman acts' was trying to deflect the Muslim people of Iran from 'the great aim of Islam: to prevent oppression, arbitrary rule, and the violation of the law . . . and to establish social justice'.[51] Throughout April sporadic demonstrations continued in Qom. To punish the theological students, the government suspended their exemption from conscription. This only raised tempers. More and more residents of Qom began siding with the religious students and Khomeini.

Tension rose sharply in late May as the holy month of Muharram approached. More and more pictures of Khomeini began appearing in the bazaars of Qom, Tehran and many other cities of Iran, an index of his rising popularity. On 3 June, the tenth of Muharram, in his address to the faithful, Khomeini launched a personal attack on the Shah. 'You miserable wretch, isn't it time for you to think and reflect a little, to ponder where all this is leading you?' he asked rhetorically. 'The religious scholars and Islam are some form of Black Reaction! And you have carried out White Revolution in the midst of all this Black Reaction!' He then referred to a number of preachers in Tehran being taken to Savak offices and ordered 'not to say anything bad about the Shah, not to attack Israel, and not to say that Islam is endangered'. But, he went on, 'all our differences with the government comprise exactly these three [points]. Does the Savak mean that the Shah is Israeli? . . . Mr Shah, do you want me to say that you don't believe in Islam, and kick you out of Iran? Do you know that when one day something changes, none of these people who surround you will be your friends?'[52] The speech electrified the audience. It turned the Ashura procession into a vast anti-Shah demonstration.

The next day copies of Khomeini's speech appeared on the walls of Fatima's shrine and the adjoining Faiziya theological college. Thousands gathered to read and discuss it.[53] It established Khomeini as a fearless leader with strong convictions ready to attack the dreaded Shah's policies and personality in public. Overnight it turned him into a national hero among the religious masses who despised the royal autocracy but dared not express their feelings or views.

Equally it made him a prime target for persecution by the Shah: a trial for subversion, even treason, ending in capital punishment. But the Shah decided not to make a martyr of Khomeini. Confident that he had crushed the movement against him once and for all, the Shah decided to do no more than order Khomeini's arrest. In retrospect this proved to a blunder on the Shah's part: it cost him the Peacock Throne some fifteen years later.

Khomeini was arrested in the early hours of 5 June, 15 Khurdad. The news spread instantly, and led to anti-government demonstrations, first in Qom, and then in Tehran, Mashhad, Tabriz, Varamin and Kashan. The anti-Shah feelings, that had been accumulating over the past decade, erupted violently. The rioting that accompanied the demonstrations was severe: together they acquired the proportions of an insurrection, later to be called the 15 Khurdad Uprising. The scale and severity of the popular anger against his regime unnerved the Shah. He himself took control of the government and the riot control operations. He declared martial law in the riot-torn cities, and pressed tanks and troops into action with orders to 'shoot to kill'. Among the thousands of Iranians arrested were twenty-eight ayatollahs.[54] All the National Front leaders had been jailed on the eve of the referendum on the White Revolution.

It took troops two days of 'shoot to kill' to crush the uprising. According to the government, eighty-six people were killed and 150 wounded.[55] But one American academic, who witnessed the army firing outside the Tehran bazaar, put the number of dead and injured at 'many thousands'.[56] Writing in the *Payam-e Emruz* (Today's Message) of Tehran, Dr A.R. Azimi estimated the number of dead at 10,000.[57] 'Thousands were massacred by the army, an event symbolised in popular memory with the image of thousands of black-shirted marchers en route from Qom to Tehran being strafed by air force planes', writes Michael M.J. Fischer, an American social anthropologist specialising in Iran.[58]

By unleashing the firepower of modern military on unarmed civilians, the Shah cowed the populace. This became apparent when the ulema's call for a national strike on 11 June drew poor response. By acting brutally, the Shah quickly crushed a major, desperate attempt by popular opposition to thwart his ambition to consolidate the royalist autocracy.

Since the end of the Nineteenth Majlis in June 1960, rule by decree had become the norm rather than exception. The following year had seen the dissolution of two parliaments on the ground of electoral irregularities. After that the Majlis had ceased to exist. The absence of parliament fuelled Muhammad Reza Shah's dream of becoming an absolute ruler of Iran. Having smashed the secular opposition – first the Tudeh and then the National Front – he now turned his guns against his clerical opponents. In the confrontation that developed dramatically on 5 June 1963, he established his superiority. The conflict was not yet over, but the direction in which it was to be finally resolved was by now settled.

The recent land reform had brought about some fundamental changes which favoured the Shah and Iranian capitalism. The agrarian reform legislation helped increase the Shah's power in the countryside where the majority of Iranians lived. It did so partly by reducing the traditional power of the big landlords, and partly by increasing the presence and authority of the state bureaucracy in villages. By encouraging landlords to invest their compensation funds in urban development and industry, the Shah gave them an increasing stake in the capitalist development of Iran. The rise of capitalism was also aided by the sale of public sector factories to private entrepreneurs, one of the points of the White Revolution, a 'revolution' which had earned the scorn of Khomeini among others.

The Shah versus Khomeini

Having beaten the opposition, the Shah decided to relax his iron grip a little, and to apply a veneer of parliamentarism to his absolutist rule. On 3 August he released Khomeini from jail, and placed him under house arrest in Qaitariye, a suburb of the capital. He did so partly in response to the protest lodged by thirty-five ayatollahs, who said that since Khomeini was a marja-e taqlid, they were bound to obey him. By being kept in jail, Khomeini was being prevented from performing his Islamic duties, something contrary to the constitution which held Twelver Shiaism to be the state religion.[59]

Majlis elections were scheduled for 17 September, with women entitled to vote for the first time. Khomeini called on the faithful to stay away. This put an end to his limited freedom. He was once again taken to prison: a fate that fell to all those leaders, religious or secular, who advocated electoral boycott. Among the groups to contest the elections was the Progressive Centre, an elitist club of civil servants, which had been engaged by the Shah as his personal research bureau after the 5 June 1963 uprising. Led by Hassan Mansur, son of a former premier, Ali Mansur, the Progressive Centre won forty of the 217 Majlis seats. But once the Twenty-second Majlis had assembled in early October 1963, more than 100 deputies joined it. In December Mansur renamed it the New Iran Party, and limited its membership to 500.[60] Three months later Mansur replaced Assadollah Alam as prime minister.

In early April 1964, following a Savak statement that Khomeini had agreed that he would not act 'contrary to the interest, and law and order, of the state', he was released. So were 250 other public figures, religious and secular, arrested earlier for promoting election boycott. But this had no effect on those opposition figures who had been arrested on different charges. For instance, Ayatollah Mahmoud Taleqani and Mahdi Bazargan, leaders of the Liberation Movement of Iran (Nahzat-e Azadi-e Iran) sentenced to ten years' imprisonment in January 1964, remained incarcerated. Once free, Khomeini denied that he had given any promise to the government. His subsequent behaviour made this abundantly clear.

Two months later the issue of granting diplomatic immunity to the American citizens, military or civilian, engaged in military projects in Iran caught the popular imagination. Public opinion was so strongly against this that the otherwise docile Majlis deputies were unwilling to pass the appropriate bill. This was the case even after the government had told them that the bill was part of the deal for getting $200 million in credits from Washington to buy American weapons. It was with great difficulty that the government managed to get it through, by a narrow majority, in late October. A few days later the bill to accept US credits was passed.

These bills stirred up old memories, of the days of the Capitulations to European powers. A staunch supporter of Iranian independence, Khomeini was fiercely against Iran becoming a dependency of America, or any other foreign power. On 27 October, addressing a meeting outside his house in Qom, he said: 'American cooks, mechanics, technical and administrative officials, together with their families, are to enjoy legal immunity, but the ulema of Islam, the preachers and servants of Islam, are to live banished or imprisoned'.[61] He then put his views in writing, which were circulated clandestinely as a pamphlet. 'Today, when colonial territories are bravely freeing the bonds that have chained them, the so-called progressive Majlis . . . votes for the most shameful and offending decrees of the ill-reputed government', it said.[62]

On 4 November Khomeini was arrested for 'instigating against the country's interests, security, independence and territorial integrity'. He was taken to Tehran's Mehrabad airport and put on a plane bound for Turkey. He lived in Bursa near Istanbul for about a year. In October 1965 he moved to Najaf, the Shia holy place with the shrine of Imam Ali, where many decades ago, his grandfather, Sayyed Ahmed Mousavi al Hindi,[63] had met Yusuf Khan Kamaraei, a notable from Khomein, an Iranian town.

Ahmed Mousavi al Hindi married Kamaraei's daughter, and went to live in Khomein, a town 220 miles south-west of Tehran. Mustapha, their only son, grew up there, but went to Najaf for his Islamic studies. He became one of the leading clerics of the time. He married and raised a family of six – three sons, three daughters – in Khomein, where he was the town's chief clergyman. In that capacity he ordered the execution of a man who defied the Islamic injunction of fasting between sunrise and sunset during Ramadan by eating in public. In February 1903 he was murdered by the friends of the executed man.

Ruhollah, born on 24 September 1902 (20 Jumada Thani 1320 AH), was then five months old. Mustapha Mousavi left behind little for the sustenance of his family. Ruhollah was educated under the supervision of his aunt. At six he was instructed in the Quran. He finished his Persian education at fifteen. For the next four years he did his Islamic studies and jurisprudence under the supervision of his elder brother, Murtaza Pasandida. He then joined the religious school in Arak, forty miles from Khomein, run by Ayatollah Abdul Karim Hairi-Yazdi, who had been a student of Mirza Hassan Shirazi, the leader of the Tobacco Protest.

When Hairi-Yazdi moved to Qom in 1922 to reorganise religious education there, Khomeini went with him. In 1925 Khomeini completed his studies in the Sharia, ethics and spiritual philosophy. Two years later, at twenty-five, he married Khadija, daughter of Mirza Mohammed al Saqafi, an older member of the circle of Hairi-Yazdi's disciples. Of the eight children they had, five survived: two sons (Mustapha and Ahmed) and three daughters (Farida, Sadiqa and Fatima).

In 1929 Khomeini wrote a thesis on ethics and spiritual philosophy in Arabic, entitled *Misbah al Hidaya* (The Lamp of Guidance), which impressed his teachers. Over the years he established himself as a learned teacher of ethics and philosophy as well as an extraordinarily disciplined and orderly person. He was particularly noted for interrelating ethical and spiritual problems with contemporary social issues, and urging his students to regard it as part of their religious duty to work for the solution of current social problems. Living and teaching in Qom, the spiritual centre of Iran, helped Khomeini to witness major events of the country from a vantage point.

After Hairi-Yazdi's death in 1936, Khomeini joined those ulema who wanted the departed leader's position as the supreme religious authority to go to Ayatollah Borujerdi. This happened. But the hope of Khomeini and some others that in that capacity Borujerdi would take steps to counter Reza Shah's moves towards secularisation and totalitarianism were disappointed.

However, encouraged by Borujerdi, Khomeini published a book, entitled *Kashf al Asrar* (The Secrets Revealed) in late 1941. Written as a rebuttal to a work which advocated secularism, Khomeini's book was basically political. His targets were secularism and Reza Shah's dictatorial rule. He argued that since the laws enforced during Reza Shah's rule had not been vetted by a committee of mujtahids, as the constitution specified, they must be repealed. 'We say that the government must be run in accordance with God's law, for the welfare of the country; and the people demand it', he wrote. 'That is not feasible except with the supervision of the religious leaders. In fact this principle has been approved and ratified in the constitution, and in no way conflicts with public order, the stability of the government, or the interests of the country'.[64]

In 1945 Khomeini graduated to the rank of hojatalislam, one below that of ayatollah.[65] This meant that he could now collect his own circle of disciples, who would accept his interpretations of the Sharia and hadith (the sayings and actions of Prophet Muhammad). A way was now prepared for his elevation to the next level: an ayatollah. Following Borujerdi's death in 1961, Khomeini's disciples and admirers pressed him to publish his interpretations, hoping thus to secure him the position left vacant by Borujerdi. The result was a book entitled *Tauzih al Masail* (Clarification of Points of the Sharia). It immediately secured the author the rank of an ayatollah. His work was later to be described by an American specialist on Iran, Marvin Zonis, as 'a rigorous, minute, specific codification of the way to behave in every conceivable circumstance, from defecation to urination to sexual intercourse to eating to cleaning the teeth'.[66]

In the late 1940s Khomeini's hostility to Muhammad Reza Shah became widely known. Following the warmth that developed between the Shah and Borujerdi, after an unsuccesssful attempt on the monarch's life in early 1949, the ministry of education successfully pressured Borujerdi to stop Khomeini teaching at the prestigious Faiziya seminary (established in the Safavid period). Khomeini then took to giving lectures first at Salmasi mosque near his house and later at Mahmoudi mosque in the main street of Qom.[67]

During the initial stage of the oil nationalisation movement, Khomeini stood on the sidelines. In its latter phase he was critical of Mussadiq for falling under the influence of the Tudeh Party, which he detested. He was equally opposed to the American influence which rose sharply in the aftermath of the August 1953 coup. He decried the deal that the Shah made with the Western oil consortium a year later, and deplored the government's over-dependence on Western investments. Later he openly condemned 'the plundering of the nation's wealth' by 'traitors' in the government allied to 'imperialism'.[68]

Ayatollah Kashani's death in 1962 created a vacuum in the leadership of the radical clergy. Given the prestige and status that Khomeini, now sixty years old, had by then acquired, it seemed almost natural that he should become the doyen of militant ulema. That is what brought him into direct conflict with the Shah whose secularist and dictatorial policies he had always abhorred. In a series of sermons at the Faiziya seminary in early 1963 he attacked the White Revolution as phoney. This established him as a national figure. As described earlier, he went on to challenge the Shah, and lost.

For a year he suffered exile in the unfamiliar territory of Turkey. It was only after he had moved to Najaf, the place where his father and grandfather had spent many years, that he felt somewhat at home. He was also physically and spiritually near to his native country. It was here, in Najaf, that he was to formulate a blueprint for a contemporary Islamic state that he was to found in Iran in 1979.

The economic march

With the last credible source of public opposition removed, the Shah tightened his grip over the state and society of Iran. He further strengthened Iran's economic, military and cultural ties with the West. Oil was to be the source of Iran's rapid economic progress, signalled by the launching of the Third Plan (1964-7) with the target of 6 per cent annual growth rate.[69] To induce the Western oil companies to raise output, Premier Mansur gave their consortium further concessions in mid-January 1965.

These were blatantly unfair to Iran, and incensed many nationalists, secular and religious. In fact, such was the anger of a group of militant theological students, including some members of a successor organisation of the Fedaiyan-e Islam, that they fatally wounded Mansur on 21 January. They took this action partly to avenge the expulsion of Khomeini from Iran. Expectedly, there were large scale arrests of suspected assassins and their sympathisers.

The Shah himself became a target for assassination on 10 April. The attempt failed, and the attacker – a conscript in the Imperial Guards – was killed instantly by royal bodyguards. Hundreds of arrests followed. Most of the suspects were tortured by Savak, which was by now using torture almost routinely.

On Mansur's death, the Shah had promoted the finance minister, Amir Abbas Hoveida, to premiership. A brother-in-law of Mansur, Hoveida was then deputy leader of the New Iran Party. He came from an eminent family of civil servants, and began his career in the diplomatic service. He then joined the National Iranian Oil Company. He left it to found the New Iran Party. As finance minister he proved popular with businessmen. His close ties with the business community continued throughout his twelve-and-a-half-year-long term as prime minister. These years witnessed an impressive growth in the economy, particularly after the dramatic oil price rise in late 1973.

The decade of 1963-72 saw the completion of two ambitious five-year plans. They developed the economy in both rural and urban areas. As a result of agrarian reform, the proportion of land owned by 45,320 absentee landlords fell from 50 per cent of the total to 20 per cent. The number of peasant proprietors rose from 1,162,000 to 2,800,000, with a third of them owning more than five hectares.[70] A 1967 law encouraged those with smallholdings to sell these to state-run farm cooperatives for shares in the cooperatives. All told, feudal relations in agriculture were severely weakened. $1.2 billion was invested in irrigation facilities, land reclamation, and the subsidised use of agricultural machinery, chemical fertilisers and pesticides. About a quarter of a million hectares were brought under irrigation. The use of fertilisers rose twenty times, to one million tons, and that of tractors seventeen times, to 50,000.

Yet the annual increase in agricultural output was only about 2.5 per cent, and lagged behind the 3 per cent population growth. The fault lay with the government's policy of giving incentives to big landlords and large agricultural corporations, and neglecting small and middle-sized peasant owners whose productivity was much higher than that of others.

By contrast the increase in industrial production was truly impressive. Between 1963 and 1977 the number of factories rose from 1,902 to 7,989. Among these were new steel mills, oil refineries, aluminium smelters, machine tool factories and assembly plants for tractors, lorries and cars. The annual rate of industrial growth quadrupled, from 5 per cent to 20 per cent.[71]

The seeds of this development had been sown in the Second Plan (1955-62), when it was decided to develop mining and heavy and intermediate industries, and manufacture consumer articles for the domestic market. In 1960 came the first agreement to assemble passenger cars. Two years later the Geological Institute was established to conduct the first comprehensive mineral survey of Iran.

Investment in industry, which amounted to $2.5 billion during the period 1955-64, rose sharply in the subsequent decade, and was coupled with an investment of $3.9 billion in electric power plants, roads, railways, ports and communications. During the latter period, output of cement and coal rose threefold to 4.3 million tons and 900,000 tons respectively; steel and aluminium sheets ninefold, to 275,000 tons; iron ore forty-fivefold, to 900,000 tons; and motor vehicles fifteenfold, to 109,000.[72]

Between 1959 and 1972, the share of industry in the Gross Domestic Product rose from 13.6 per cent to nearly 20 per cent, whereas that of agriculture fell from 30 per cent to 16 per cent.[73] The 7.6 per cent difference between these changes was taken up by the increase in the share of services in the GDP.

Public education and health services improved dramatically. During the decade of 1963-72 the number of hospital beds doubled, and that of doctors nearly trebled, to 12,750. Between 1963 and 1977 the educational system underwent a threefold expansion. The doubling of enrollment to secondary schools was modest, but the rise in the student body of technical, vocational and teacher training colleges was staggering: from 14,240 to 227,500. The expansion in the university population too was equally dramatic: from 24,885 to 154,215. There was also an impressive increase in the number of Iranian students at foreign, mainly Western, universities: from 18,000 to 80,000.[74]

The money to finance these ambitious plans came from the fast rising oil output, and US aid, which ceased only in 1972.[75] Oil income shot up from $450 million in 1963 to $4,400 million ten years later.[76] This enabled the Shah not only to expand the military, particularly the air force, and modernise it, but also Savak. During the decade of 1963-72, the annual military budget rose from $170 million to $1,915 million.[77]

As the commander-in-chief, the Shah kept a close eye on the military leadership, personally vetting all promotions above the rank of major. He ensured the loyalty of senior officers by keeping them under the constant surveillance of military intelligence, J2 Department (set up by Reza Shah in 1933 on the lines of the French Deuxième Bureau), and rewarding them with generous salaries and fringe benefits during service, and important jobs in public sector undertakings after retirement.

Though nominally attached to the prime minister's office, Savak operated under military protection, and thus came within the direct jurisdiction of the Shah. All Savak officials held army ranks. By 1972 it had grown so large that its annual budget of $225 million was one-eighth of the military's.[78]

The increase in Savak activities stemmed from its obsession with countering subversion, the promulgation of a series of repressive measures by the government, and the expansion of the university population, a potential source of opposition. Savak had by now perfected its methods of intimidation: harassment; interference with mail and telephone; denial of job, promotion, passport or exit visa; pressures on the suspect's family and friends; arrest without charge; lengthy detention without trial; exile to outlandish places in the country; and finally the threat of murder. 'In the name of protecting the interests of state, Savak could interrogate, imprison, and eliminate individuals without challenge or scrutiny,' wrote Robert Graham, a British journalist posted in Tehran.[79]

Book censorship was introduced in 1966. Since half of the books then published were religious, Savak resorted to regular raids on mosque libraries to confiscate banned works.[80] From there it was only a small step to interference with the day-to-day decisions of the ministry of information and culture. Savak's need to tap telephones and telexes led it to vet the decisions of the post and communications ministry.

Likewise, Savak became an integral part of the daily life of universities. It combined the vetting of all university appointments with the monitoring of classroom lectures through informers recruited among students. But there was one institution of Iranian university students which Savak could not control or even reliably monitor: the Confederation of Iranian Students operating among Iranian students in Europe and America since 1960. The situation changed somewhat in the US when Richard Nixon, soon after becoming president in January 1969, allowed Savak to operate inside the US, an unprecedented step.[81]

Following the June 1967 Arab-Israeli war, which underlined the explosive instability of the Middle East, American interest in Iran, already high, increased further. American military and civilian presence in Iran rose perceptibly: a phenomenon resented by most urban Iranians. They found their way of expressing dissent – mildly – whenever an opportunity presented itself. For instance, in the 1968 local election 90 per cent of Tehran's voters abstained, a record.

Abroad, Khomeini was active. He kept up a steady stream of anti-Shah pamphlets and tape recordings, which were smuggled into Iran. In April 1967 he addressed an open letter to Premier Hoveida, castigating him for allocating Rials 4,000 million (about $500 million) – 'half of it taken from the national treasury and the other half extorted directly from the bazaar merchants and others by force and intimidation'[82] – for the Shah's coronation on 26 October, his fortieth birthday.[83]

In that year the ulema raised their voice against the Family Protection Law. It gave women the right to apply for divorce without the husband's permission, required a married man to secure the present wife's consent before taking a second one, and transferred family affairs from Sharia courts to secular courts. The ulema contended that these provisions clashed with the Sharia.

The simmering discontent in Iran found an outlet in March 1970 when bus fares in Tehran were raised. University students demonstrated against the rise. Five of them were killed in a police firing that followed, and about a thousand were arrested. In May religious and secular dissidents condemned an American industrial exposition and an allied business seminar in the capital as further manifestations of the inequitable sale of Iran's natural resources to the US. Two of the speakers at an anti-government rally – Ayatollah Muhammad Reza Saidi and Ahmed Nikadaudi, a polytechnic student – were arrested and tortured to death.[84]

In June, following the death of Ayatollah Muhsin Hakim, the marja-e taqlid resident in Najaf, forty-eight ulema of Qom sent condolences to Khomeini. For this the government banished them to faraway places in the country. Yet mild protest persisted. In December university students in Tehran and elsewhere demonstrated against the government. This led to a partially successful strike in Qom. 'Long live Khomeini' was one of the most frequent slogans raised by the strikers.

Khomeini utilised the annual pilgrimage to Mecca (in January-February 1971) to address open letters to the Muslims of Iran and elsewhere through his Najaf-based emissaries. Referring to the Shah's scheduled celebrations in October of 2,500 years of unbroken monarchy in Iran, Khomeini warned: 'Anyone who organises or participates in these festivals is a traitor to Islam and the Iranian nation'.[85]

Two other events in February were to prove momentous in retrospect. In that month Western oil companies signed an agreement on oil prices and royalties with Iran, Iraq and Saudi Arabia as representatives of all the Gulf states, thus recognising for the first time the principle of collective bargaining.[86] This laid the foundation for the dramatic oil price rise in late 1973 through the Organisation of Petroleum Exporting Countries.

On 8 February thirteen armed members of the Sazman-e Cherikha-ye Fedai Khalq-e Iran (The Organisation of the Iranian People's Self-Sacrificing Guerrillas of Iran) – a Marxist-Leninist organisation, commonly known as Fedai Khalq – attacked a gendarmerie post in Siakal on the littoral fringes of the Caspian forest. Their attack was repulsed. But the event marked the beginning of a guerrilla campaign against the state which continued until the Shah's downfall. Six months later the Sazman-e Mujahedin-e Kalq-e Iran (Organisation of the People's Combatants of Iran) – a leftist Islamic organisation popularly called the Mujahedin-e Khalq – launched a series of guerrilla actions to disrupt the preparations for the celebration of 2,500 years of monarchy at Persepolis, once the capital of the Achemenian dynasty.

By then other anti-Shah forces too were focussing their attention on the Persepolis festivities. Following the paratroopers' success in foiling the Qom theological students' attempt to commemorate the anniversary of the death of Ayatollah Saidi in May, the Qom students published leaflets and wall posters contrasting the Shah's planned extravagance in Persepolis with the fate of the people in the famine-stricken provinces of Fars and Baluchistan-Sistan. As in the case of the Shah's coronation festivities, the government had resorted to exacting contributions from merchants and others. 'Even within entrepreneurial classes there was much grumbling at what amounted to forced levies, large monetary contributions to the [Persepolis] celebrations,' noted Richard W. Cottam, an American academic.[87] Faced with mounting opposition, the Shah arrested 600 to 1,000 dissidents, and banned access to Persepolis and its environs.

On 15 October while the Shah regally entertained sixty-eight kings, queens, princes, princesses and heads of state at Persepolis, hundreds of thousands of dissident students and bazaar merchants in Tehran and elsewhere undertook a token fast in protest. The government put the expenses for the celebrations at $40 million. But according to unofficial estimates, which included the cost of building special roads and other facilities in the area, and the posting of the army, the figure was $120 million.[88]

Khomeini found the occasion appropriate to attack the institution of monarchy openly and unambiguously. 'Tradition relates that the Prophet said that the title of King of Kings, which is [today] borne by the monarchs of Iran, is the most hated of all titles in the sight of God,' Khomeini declared from Najaf. 'Islam is fundamentally opposed to the whole notion of monarchy. . . . Monarchy is one of the most shameful and disgraceful reactionary manifestations.'[89]

Monarchy was one of the subjects that Khomeini had tackled systematically in a series of lectures which he gave to his students in 1970, and which were published the following year under the title: *Hukumat-e Islam: Vilayat-e Faqih* (Islamic Government: Rule of the Faqih). Khomeini argued that the ulema should go beyond the traditional prescribing of do's and don'ts for the believers, and wait passively for the return of the Hidden Imam. They must commit themselves to ousting corrupt officials and repressive regimes, and to replacing them with the ones led by Islamic jurists. He called on the theological students of Najaf, Qom and Mashhad to 'instigate and stimulate the masses'.[90]

Faced with such a challenge to his legitimacy, the Shah set out to undermine the influence of the traditional clergy by supplanting them with a new breed processed by the institutions of his regime. Going by Article Thirty-nine of the constitution (which required the monarch to promote Jaafari Shiaism), the Waqf Organisation established the Department of Religious Corps and Religious Affairs. After initiating a programme of training groups of Religious Propagandists for posting in rural areas, this department undertook the formation of the Religious Corps in August 1971 with a batch of thirty-nine graduates of theology faculties of the Universities of Tehran and Mashhad. Along with the already functioning Literacy Corps, the Religious Propagandists and Religious Corps were hailed by the regime as 'the mullahs of modernisation'.[91]

This development caused concern among the ulema. They saw that what the Shah had initiated was far more damaging to them in the long run than anything else he had done so far to undermine their authority and status. The monarch was creating an alternative body of clergy, loyal to him and his ideas. They feared that state-sponsored clergy would create their own constituency among the villagers benefiting from the land reform measures – and among urban youth growing up in an environment of economic prosperity and rising cultural influence of the West. In May 1972 Ayatollah Hassan Tabatabai, an eminent cleric exiled to Iraq, attacked the Religious Corps and Religious Propagandists for trying to turn the faithful away from the traditional ulema. This only steeled the regime to keep up the pressure on the ulema.

About two months later the Waqf Organisation's Methods and Policy Committee sent a secret memorandum to Premier Hoveida outlining a strategy for dividing the ulema and discrediting Khomeini.[92] Ever since the leftist Arab Baath Socialist Party seized power in Iraq in July 1968, relations between Iran and Iraq had been tense. With Iraq signing a friendship and cooperation treaty with the Soviet Union in April 1972, the tension between the two neighbours rose sharply. Given this, said the Committee, the Iranian government and media should present Khomeini as a partisan of the Iraqi regime. But Khomeini had been unhappy at the way the secularist Baathist government had been treating Shia clerics in the shrine cities of south Iraq, and had expressed his wish to leave for Lebanon, only to have it rejected by the authorities. All this was common knowledge among Iranian ulema, who had conveyed this to the faithful. As such, the Waqf Organisation's tactic to discredit Khomeini as an unpatriotic, pro-Iraqi exile failed.

But the policy of dividing the clergy by using bribes to co-opt the fence-sitters and punishing those who refused to cooperate was adopted, and implemented with success, as years rolled on. The exiling in late 1973 of forty eminent clerics to obscure parts of Iran for their sympathies with Khomeini was a case in point. However, none of this had any impact on the traditional religiosity of the Iranian masses. If anything, the Shah's increasing authoritarianism and repression of the ulema, and the rush of modernism, made ordinary Iranians more, not less, religious. The dramatic rise in the number of pilgrims to Imam Ali Reza's shrine in Mashhad was indicative of this. In 1964 Mashhad received 220,000 pilgrims; ten years later the figure was 3,200,000.[93] In a country of some thirty million people, or about six million families, this meant every other family sending a pilgrim to Mashhad once a year.

On his part the Shah too seemed to be undergoing a change. Having usurped all temporal power in Iran, he began to see himself as an agent of God. 'I believe in God, and that I have been chosen by God to perform a task', he said in his interview with Oriana Fallaci, an Italian journalist, in late August 1973. 'My visions are miracles that saved the country. My reign saved the country, and it had done so because God is on my side.'[94]

The Shah's megalomania was to rise even further as Iran's income from oil rocketed later that year. He dreamt of, and often talked about, making Iran the fifth most powerful nation in the world – after the US, the Soviet Union, Japan and West Germany.

The oil boom

After the coup against Mussadiq the Shah, following the advice of the US government, did not abolish the National Iranian Oil Company formed by the 1951 oil nationalisation law. Starting in 1957, the NIOC began signing deals for exploration and production of oil (outside the concession area of the Western oil consortium) with small, independent oil companies. The first such agreement was with Italy's Ente Nazionale Idrocaburi. The deal gave the NIOC 75 per cent of the profits: a vast improvement on the 50 per cent being paid by the Consortium, consisting of eight major American, British, French and Dutch oil companies.

Iran was one of five founder members of the Organisation of Petroleum Exporting Countries formed in 1960 in Baghdad.[95] OPEC strove to enter into collective bargaining with oil majors, then operating as a virtual cartel, with a view to negotiating output and prices, but failed. Among OPEC's leading aims outlined in June 1962, and reiterated six years later, was the direct development of a member state's hydro-carbon resources by its government. As stated earlier, it was not until February 1971 that the oil majors finally consented to collective bargaining with Iran, Iraq and Saudi Arabia on behalf of all the Gulf states. This agreement required the oil majors to pay 55 per cent of their profits as tax. OPEC members then pressed for a share in the running of the local oil industry. They reached an agreement with major oil corporations in October 1972 whereby the oil companies of Abu Dhabi, Kuwait, Qatar and Saudi Arabia immediately acquired 25 per cent of the shares of the foreign concessionaries.[96]

This was the background against which the Shah announced, on the tenth anniversary of the White Revolution, in January 1973, that the NIOC would take over all the operations and ownership of the Western oil consortium operating in Iran. This happened on 20 March, the last day of the Iranian year 1352. The consortium formed the Oil Services Company of Iran to provide expertise to the NIOC in the running and developing of oilfields in Khuzistan. In return it received part of Iranian oil for marketing abroad. So twenty-two years after the Majlis, moved by popular pressure, had passed the oil nationalisation bill, its implementation was carried out by the monarch who was now more closely linked with the West than ever before.

During the October 1973 Arab-Israeli war the Organisation of Arab Petroleum Exporting Countries[97] imposed oil blockades on the countries aiding Israel, and thus set the stage for a dramatic price rise. Since Iran was not a member of OAPEC, it did not join the oil embargo. Nonetheless, it benefited by the jump in oil price during the last three months of 1983: from $2.55 to $11.65 a barrel. Iran's oil revenue shot up from $4.4 billion in 1973 to $11.65 billion in the following year, with the production unchanged at around 2.2 billion barrels.[98]

With this the Shah drastically upgraded the current Fifth Plan (1973-7), and overheated both the civilian and military economies. Annual growth, which had fluctuated between 4.5 per cent and 15.3 per cent during the period 1963-73, jumped to 34 per cent in 1974 and 42 per cent in the following year.[99] Inflation rose too, and reached an annual rate of 30 to 35 per cent. But so far, the advantages of the booming economy outweighed the disadvantages.

The Shah noticed that the ruling New Iran Party was taking all the credit for the economic achievement, and giving no quarter to the opposition Mardom Party. Fearing that the minority party might become the base for genuine and open opposition to his regime, he decided to include it in the government as well. This meant setting up a single political entity. Accordingly, on 8 March 1975, the Rastakhiz (Resurgence) Party was inaugurated with Hoveida as its leader.

It contested elections to the Twenty-fourth Majlis in June, and secured five million votes out of seven million cast. Since the monarch had visualised the Rastakhiz as the link between him and the nation, he called on every Iranian who 'believes in the constitution, the monarchy, and the 6th Bahman [White] Revolution' to join it.[100]

Oddly, the Shah founded a single party at a time when the accelerated pace of capitalist development had stratified the politically important urban population into six distinct classes: the royals and the upper class at the top; the working class, industrial and non-industrial, at the bottom; and the middle classes, traditional and modern, in between.

The royalty consisted of the monarch and his brothers, sisters and cousins: a total of sixty-odd families. Then followed about a thousand families, graded according to the length of their aristocratic roots. At the top were those aristocratic entrepreneurs who had begun investing in urban projects before the agrarian reform; then came those who had done so after the reform. Next followed about 200 elderly politicians, and former civil and military officers, who thrived on the government contracts awarded to the companies they directed. With the defence budget rising sharply from $225 million in 1966 to $9,500 million ten years later,[101] the size and frequency of military contracts alone grew dramatically. Finally came the non-aristocratic entrepreneurs, most of them dating back to the days of the Second World War.

About a million families belonged to the traditional middle class, with half of them originating in the bazaar. However, the propertied bazaaris were divided into two broad layers: the upper, consisting of wholesalers, commission agents, brokers, middlemen, money-changers and workshop owners; and the lower, made up of shopkeepers, artisans and craftsmen. A typical bazaar was controlled by the government-regulated guild system, which had been virtually untouched by the political radicalisation of the period 1941-53. As a national institution the bazaar dealt with three-quarters of wholesale trade and two-thirds of retail.[102]

Then there were traders and entrepreneurs who functioned apart from the bazaar. They owned not only the 420,000 village workshops, often weaving carpets, and 440,000 medium-sized commercial farms, but also the shops outside the bazaar.

Both these groups were related to the ulema. Within religious circles, properly qualified clerics from recognised theological colleges stood above itinerant preachers, Friday prayer leaders and procession organisers. All these, along with 15,000 theological students and teachers, totalled 100,000.

At 650,000, the modern middle class had doubled over the past generation, with a 462,000 strong student body in vocational and technical colleges and Iranian and foreign universities, waiting to enlarge it even further. It consisted of 304,000 civil servants, 208,000 teachers, and 61,000 white collar professionals and managers.[103] Together they amounted to 6.5 per cent of the total labour force of 10 million.[104]

Over 2.5 million families belonged to the urban working class, industrial and non-industrial. Since 1963 this class had expanded fivefold. Two-thirds of the 900,000 industrial workers were employed in factories engaging less than ten persons. The non-industrial working class consisted of 400,000 persons engaged in distribution and other services, and 1.2 million construction workers, peddlers, hawkers and menials.[105] The latter were to be called by the revolutionary regime the mustazafin, the needy or the oppressed.

Most of the mustazafin were recent arrivals from villages where, as landless peasants or former nomads, they had worked as agrarian labourers, construction workers, shepherds or rural workshop employees. Their kinsmen in rural areas, still performing these tasks, amounted to 1.1 million families. So the mustazafin in the town and the country together amounted to 23 per cent of the national workforce, and the urban and rural wage-earners as a whole to 36 per cent, the largest single class.

It was against this socio-economic background that the Pahlavi ruler tried to solve the problems created by an overheated economy, and simultaneously to confront the traditional middle classes in his continuing craving for power and glory. In the process he alienated all sections of society except the upper class, and paved the way for his downfall.

Inflation was a pressing problem. To tackle it the Hoveida government passed an anti-profiteering law. Soon hundreds of young Rastakhiz recruits were out in the bazaars checking prices. Within two weeks of the law, 7,750 traders were arrested, another 10,000 fined, and 600 shops closed down.[106] The anti-profiteering campaign continued, with 10,000 Rastakhiz students acting as vigilantes, and special guild courts, formed by Savak, dealing with the accused. By the end of 1975, besides collecting a quarter of a million fines from traders, the guild courts had handed out further punishments to 180,000 other offenders, exiled 23,000 shopkeepers from their bazaars, and imprisoned 8,000 traders.[107] That is, a majority of the half a million bazaaris had been punished one way or the other by the authorities. To further weaken bazaari wholesalers and retailers, the government established state purchasing corporations for such essentials as wheat, meat and sugar.

The Rastakhiz leaders set up party offices in the bazaars, and resorted to exacting levies from traders. Assisted by a freshly passed law, they dissolved the old guilds, and replaced the loosely formed Higher Councils of Guilds with the state-sponsored Chambers of Guilds.

As if this were not enough the government-controlled press mounted a well-orchestrated campaign to raze the bazaars in city centres and build highways, and to replace neighbourhood shops with super-markets. The existing supermarkets were enjoying cheap bank credit at a 12 per cent interest rate while the bazaari merchants had to pay 25 to 100 per cent interest on their borrowings. Feeling pressured, the merchants turned to their age-old allies: the ulema.

But the ulema were themselves under attack. The endowments in their charge were being audited by the agents of the Rastakhiz Party. Their publishing activities were banned when the authorities restricted religious publishing only to the Waqf Organisation. All this went hand in hand with the Rastakhiz government's attempts to project the Shah not only as the Political Leader but also the Spiritual Leader. To make the point dramatically it introduced the royalist calendar, dating back to the pre-Islamic Achemenian dynasty, on the completion of half a century of the Pahlavi rule on 24 April 1976. While the justice minister called for stricter enforcement of the 1967 Family Protection Law, strengthened in 1975, by secular courts, the Waqf Organisation further expanded the Religious Corps. Finally, following the July 1971 memorandum of the Waqf Organisation, the government had begun paying sinecures to pro-regime ulema, and recruiting clerics as Savak agents.[108]

Yet some of the government's actions inadvertently helped the ulema. For instance, in its drive to lower inflation, the authorities controlled food prices. This in turn reduced farm incomes and drove tens of thousands of marginal farmers to cities, thus accelerating the exodus from villages. As devout Muslims, the rural poor looked to the ulema for guidance and succour. They continued the tradition when they migrated to urban centres, thus enlarging the congregations of the urban-based clerics and clerical power base. The census figures of 1966 and 1976 showed the size and rapidity of the emigration from villages: the proportion of those living in the towns with 100,000-plus inhabitants to the national population rose from 21 to 29 per cent.[109]

Such influx into urban centres overstretched the existing facilities: housing, electricity, water supply. Expansion of these facilities was inhibited by shortages of men and materials. At one time, for instance, there was no cement available for civilian projects because of the frantic pace of military construction. Such shortages, coupled with the arrival of tens of thousands of foreign managers and technicians ready to pay exorbitant rents, caused rent explosion. In five years rents rose by 300 per cent, often eating up nearly half of the earnings of many middle class families.

Discontent was rife in the modern middle class. But it lacked any outlet for expression. There was only one political party, the Rastakhiz, and all the newspapers and journalists were affiliated to it. With Rastakhiz nominees controlling radio and television and the ministries of information and the arts and culture, censorship was now stricter than ever before. The number of books published fell from 4,200 in 1974 to 1,300 two years later.[110] The Writers Association, formed in 1976, was denied an official licence because its members refused to join the Rastakhiz Party. Already twenty-two leading novelists, poets and film-makers were in jail for being critical of the government.

During that year a study by the Geneva-based International Commission of Jurists concluded that Iran's government was systematically violating basic human rights and using torture against its citizens.[111] Savak and other security forces were particularly brutal in their handling of the guerrilla organisations' members. By mid-1975 they had killed fifty Mujahedin-e Khalq guerrillas. They had also meted out similar treatment to the Fedai Khalq members. As a result the leaders of both these organisations were compelled to review their tactics.

Now, only the anti-Pahlavi ulema were in a position to offer a semblance of public opposition through periodic statements and demonstrations. Khomeini's exile helped them. Beyond the reach of the Iranian regime, Khomeini was in a country whose government was at best uncooperative with the Shah, and at worst bitterly hostile. In March 1975 Khomeini lost no time in condemning the Rastakhiz. This party, he said, was set on attacking Islam, violating constitutional freedoms, destroying agriculture, and squandering large sums on foreign arms.[112]

On the eve of the Rastakhiz's formation, the Faiziya seminary students in Qom went on srike. Over 250 of them were arrested, and the seminary closed down indefinitely. Savak then arrested all the leading pro-Khomeini ulema in the country. The list included Ayatollahs Muhammad Beheshti and Hussein Ali Montazeri, and Hojatalislams Muhammad Reza Mahdavi-Kani and Ali Hussein Khamanei: some of the ulema who were later to become the leading figures of the revolutionary regime. Undeterred by this, Ayatollah Hassan Ghaffari, an old Tehran cleric, preached against the government. He was put in jail where he was tortured to death. But there was no end to overt opposition to the Pahlavi king. Echoing Khomeini's views, Ayatollah Sadiq Rouhani issued a religious decree in April against the Rastakhiz Party, forbidding his followers to join it.[113]

Clerical hostility came to the surface when the Shah introduced the royalist calendar in April 1976. Since the calendar broke away from the Islamic heritage, Hojatalislam Abol Hassan Shamsabadi of Isfahan attacked it. A few days later he was found murdered. The local bazaar went on strike in protest. On 5 June theology students in Qom organised a demonstration to commemorate the 15 Khurdad Uprising. It was the largest such gathering in the city since the fateful events of thirteen years ago. It gave a lie to the Shah's claim made a year earlier that opposition to his rule was confined to 'a handful of nihilists, anarchists and Communists'.[114]

Ironically, one of the clauses of the treaty that the Shah signed with Iraq in March 1975, mainly to settle border disputes, began to work against him, and for Khomeini. It required both countries to ease border crossings. In the subsequent talks the Baghdad government agreed to allow 130,000 Iranian pilgrims to the Shia holy places in Iraq.[115] It was the first time since 1969 – when relations between Iran and Iraq reached breaking point – that Iranians were allowed in such large numbers to visit Karbala and Najaf, Khomeini's base. With this it became comparatively easy for Khomeini to maintain regular contact with his acolytes in Iran, and guide them in their struggle against the Pahlavi regime through smuggled tape recordings.

This development came at about the same time as Jimmy Carter became the president of America. In his election campaign in the autumn of 1976 Carter had named Iran as one of the countries where the US should do more to protect civil and human liberties. Once in office in January 1977, Carter stressed human rights as an integral part of his foreign policy, hinting that the states violating human rights might be denied American weapons or aid, or both. This applied as much to Iran as it did to many authoritarian states in Latin America. Inadvertently, it set the scene for a revolutionary change in Iran.

THE END OF MONARCHY

In late 1976 the Shah felt secure, confident of the popularity of his policies at home. He was therefore open to suggestions for some relaxation of his authoritarian rule, particularly if they came from Washington, the chief source of the arms supplies for the military build-up he had begun in 1972.[1] The impetus to listen to the Carter administration's views on human rights was all the more, since turning a deaf ear to them could have jeopardised further flow of US weapons. In any case the Shah needed to offer a quid pro quo to the US government for something else he wanted from it: reliable information about the aid then being given by the Palestine Liberation Organisation and other radical Arab institutions to the Iranian guerrilla organisations. These were the factors that led the Shah to loosen his iron grip over the state apparatus.

Liberalisation, which began in February 1977 with the release of 357 political prisoners, gathered momentum in the summer. Each concession by the Shah brought further demands from the opposition. Both the modern and traditional middle classes became active, but in different ways. Writers, academics, politicians, lawyers and even judges resorted to addressing open letters to the Pahlavi ruler, whereas bazaar merchants and theological students adopted militant methods: processions, demonstrations and clashes with the police.

Being close to the city poor, both politically and geographically, the traditional middle class provided leadership to the urban underclass which eventually adopted the revolutionary slogan 'Death to the Shah', and stuck to it. To be sure, popular demands were raised in stages, and were orchestrated by Khomeini from abroad.

The revolutionary process went through seven steadily rising stages before reaching its goal of the Shah's overthrow. These lasted over the following periods: February to October 1977; November to December 1977; January to June 1978; July to 8 September (Black Friday) 1978; 9 September to 5 November 1978; 6 November 1978 to 16 January 1979; and 16 January to 11 February 1979.

The first stage: February to October 1977

The release of political prisoners in February encouraged intellectuals to express themselves. In March Ali Asghar Hajj Sayyed Javadi addressed an open, critical letter to the Shah, and circulated it. A former editor of the *Kayhan* (World) newspaper, Javadi had had a chequered career. He had started as a Tudeh member in his youth and had then become a social democrat. Over the next fifteen years he had emerged as an essayist on Islam and socialism, and had become popular with a large body of religious laymen. Now he was active with the Writers Association.

Javadi's action came at a time when the Shah was busy refurbishing his international image. He permitted the International Commission of the Red Cross to visit twenty prisons. He gave personal audiences to the representatives of the International Commission of Jurists and Amnesty International, a London-based human rights organisation, both of which had been critical of the Iranian regime. He opened up a subversion trial to the public, and promised to restrict the powers of the military tribunals which had been established in the wake of the August 1953 coup. And he made no move against Javadi.

Encouraged, Javadi published a 200-page essay, critical of the state of contemporary Iran, in May. Again the Shah took no action against him. This emboldened fifty-three laywers to send a letter to the Shah alleging government interferences in the judicial system, and announcing the formation of the Committee to Safeguard Independence of Courts. The next month a group of forty writers addressed a letter to Premier Hoveida asking him to lift censorship. More importantly, on 12 June three National Front leaders published an open letter to the Pahlavi king, and distributed 20,000 copies of it. Describing the government as 'based on a system of despotism dressed up as lawful monarchy', they called on the Shah 'to desist from authoritarian rule, to submit absolutely to the principle of constitutionality, revive the people's rights, respect the constitution and the Universal Declaration of Human Rights, abandon the single party system, permit freedom of the press and freedom of association, free all political prisoners, allow exiles to return, and establish a government based on a majority which has been popularly elected and which considers itself answerable to the constitution'.[2]

A week later came the news of the death of forty-four-year-old Ali Shariati – an Islamic intellectual, actively opposed to the Shah – in Southampton, England, during his travels in Europe. It was widely believed that he had been killed by Savak. This shocked and angered the middle classes. Dissident authors and publishers formed the Group for Free Books and Free Thought. Sixty-four lawyers called for the abolition of military tribunals. These developments occurred at a time when, in the sweltering heat of summer in Tehran and other cities, public tempers were running short due to frequent power failures. Tempers among the capital's underclass rose sharply when the authorities demolished the illegally built shacks in central Tehran occupied by the rural immigrants working in the booming construction industry. Those made homeless protested, only to receive police bullets, which left some of them dead.

The Shah felt a need to make a dramatic gesture to appease the rising tide of discontent. He moved Premier Hoveida to the Imperial Court, and gave his job to Jamshed Amouzgar, a fifty-one-year-old technocrat. The leader of the 'progressive liberal' wing of the Rastakhiz Party, Amouzgar favoured cooling the overheated economy to reduce inflation and relieve shortages, and further loosen the state's hold over society. Soon after assuming office on 6 August, Premier Amouzgar liberalised judicial rules: he opened all trials to the public, and required the security authorities to produce a detainee before a magistrate within twenty-four hours.

But as the regime unscrewed the lid gradually, more and more of the accumulated grievances of the past came to the surface. In September fifty-four judges wrote to the supreme court stating that the government had violated the constitution, particularly the independence of the judiciary. Thirty opposition politicians, headed by Mahdi Bazargan, formed the Iranian Committee for the Defence of Freedom and Human Rights. In October 120 lawyers set up the Association of Iranian Jurists, which in turn appointed a working group to publicise Savak torture and monitor prison conditions. Dissident academics formed the National Organisation of University Teachers and demanded academic freedom.

By now the National Front had been revived, and so had the Liberation Movement of Iran and the Tudeh. The National Front, led by Karim Sanjabi and Shahpour Bakhtiar, was renamed the Union of National Front Forces. The Liberation Movement, dating back to 1961, was still headed by Mahdi Bazargan. All of these parties had begun publishing semi-clandestine publications.

The second stage: November to December 1977

Although Khomeini was not to engage popular attention until early November, he was active during the summer. In his taped messages in August to September he called on the ulema to form Komitehs (derivative of Comité, Committee) in mosques to guide the faithful struggling against the oppressor king. The bazaaris in Tehran formed the Society of Merchants, Traders and Craftsmen with the objective of curtailing the activities of the Rastakhiz Party. In early October the Islamic students at Tehran University demonstrated against co-education. During that month there were ten days of poetry readings at the Iranian-German Cultural Centre devoted to poetry of protest which had been suppressed for so long.

In late October sudden death visited the family of Ayatollah Khomeini in Najaf. His forty-five-year-old son, Mustapha, in perfect health, was found dead in bed. Since Islam does not allow autopsy, the actual cause of the death could not be established. It is likely that he was poisoned. Many saw the hand of Savak in this.[3] It seems probable that Savak tried to get even with Khomeini for the assassination attempt on Princess Ashraf in southern France on 13 September. She had escaped unhurt, but one of her companions was killed and another wounded.

The twin of Muhammad Reza Pahlavi, Ashraf was entitled to regency if the Shah died while his son, Reza Cyrus (born in 1960), was still a minor. She was close to her brother, and had easy access to him. She was the overlord of the ministries of culture and information, and thus of radio and television. To most Iranians she was the epitome of moral and material corruption that permeated the Court. Her three marriages, her frequent jaunts abroad, her dazzling social life among the international elite, and her alleged sexual appetite: all these were grist to the gossip mills of the bazaar and surrounding districts.[4] In fact her mores were also the subject of much adverse comment among the upper class as well. 'The opposition, be it bourgeois, the left, or the clergy, have made Princess Ashraf and her lifestyle the main target of their criticism,' Fereydoun Hoveida, the Iranian ambassador at the UN, told Parviz Radji, the Iranian ambassador to Britain. 'Many people's susceptibilities have been genuinely offended by her alternate visits to Mecca and Monte Carlo [casinos].'[5] So the attack on Ashraf's life did not arouse much genuine sympathy among Iranians, whatever their social standing.

This was not the case with the mysterious death of Mustapha Khomeini. It created a groundswell of sympathy with his family, particularly his father. Given the Shia custom of offering condolences to the bereaved on the fourth, seventh and fortieth days of the death, the Iranian public had ample opportunity to express its grief. And it did. On 4 November, a Friday, a mourning procession for Mustapha Khomeini gathered in south Tehran. It clashed with the police outside the bazaar.

On 15 November while Iranian students in the US were demonstrating against the Shah's visit to the White House in Washington, D.C., their colleagues in Tehran took to the streets in sympathy. Clashes with the police followed in both cities. More students clashed with police after attending poetry reading sessions organised by the Writers Association at Aryamehr University in the capital on 15, 16 and 19 November. Those arrested sought lawyers from the Association of Iranian Jurists. Tried by civilian courts (and not military tribunals, as had been the case so far), they were either released or given light sentences. This was a major step forward for the opposition. It weakened the long-held fear among the Iranians that opposing the Pahlavi ruler meant Savak torture and stiff prison sentences by military courts meeting in secret.

The Shah realised this, and tried to revert to his old ways. Savak pressured the Writers Association to drop its demands of freedom of expression and an end to censorship. A government circular black-listed the lawyers who had signed various open letters. Savak set up the clandestine Committee of Revenge. Its members assaulted opposition leaders and planted bombs in their offices. Warning that the government's patience was running out, Rastakhiz officials set up the Resistance Corps, consisting of policemen in civilian clothes. The Corps specialised in breaking up protest meetings. The authorities drastically reduced traffic between Iran and Iraq, and resorted to confiscating all personal belongings of the travellers at the border. One consequence of this was an abrupt rise in the price of the smuggled tape-cassettes of Khomeini's speeches – to $25 a piece or more.

But the Shah was not content with merely taking repressive actions. He wanted to regain the initiative that had been seized by his opponents. One way to achieve this was to go on the offensive against the ulema in general and Khomeini in particular. He seemed to remember the well-orchestrated campaign that he had mounted against the ulema in March 1963 on the issue of land reform. Since that tactic worked then, might it not do so now? The only difference was that this time he was best advised to focus on a single cleric: Khomeini.

The third stage: January to June 1978

On 7 January, the Women's Day, the *Ittilaat* published an unsigned article entitled 'Iran, and the Black and Red Reactionaries'. (Its author was later revealed to be none less than the information minister, Dariush Humayun.) It opened with a few general statements on the White Revolution and the 'Black Reaction' of the clergy. It then referred to a religious leader chosen to direct the 'Black Reaction' as 'an adventurer, without faith, and tied to the centres of colonialism . . . a man with a questionable past, linked to the more superficial and reactionary colonialists'. He was Ruhollah Khomeini, better known as 'the Indian Sayyed'. While his links with India had never been exposed, it was obvious that he had contacts with the British. In his youth he wrote romantic poetry signed 'Al Hindi' (The Indian). Now he opposed the Shah's reforms. He received a lot of money from the English, through an Arab, to carry on fighting the Shah.[6]

The article enraged Qom in the same way as had Khomeini's arrest in June 1963. The bazaar and theological colleges closed down in protest. On 9 January, 4,000 religious students demanded restoration of freedom to the faithful in the mosques. When they were confronted by armed police pointing loaded guns at them, many of the protestors offered themselves fearlessly to the security forces. They set a pattern which was to be followed by tens of thousands of protestors during the next turbulent year. This time, ten to seventy-two of them lost their lives.[7]

Khomeini responded by immediately calling for more demonstrations. Ayatollah Shariatmadari described the police behaviour as 'unIslamic', and said that if demanding a return to the constitution was 'black reaction' then he was a black reactionary. He joined eighty-seven religious and secular leaders in their call to the public to stay away from work on the fortieth day of the mourning for those killed in Qom by the security forces.

But this had no effect on the government's plans to demonstrate its popular standing. On 26 January 100,000 to 300,000 people rallied in Tehran to celebrate the fifteenth anniversary of the White Revolution. This, however, was to prove to be the last show of strength by the Shah's partisans.

Three days before the fortieth-day memorial to the Qom martyrs, due on 18 February, the grand ayatollahs of Iran urged the faithful to join the mourning processions. They did. There were peaceful demonstrations in eleven cities where main bazaars and universities closed down. But rioting broke out in Tabriz when police shot down a young demonstrator. The rioters, consisting mainly of poor, alienated young immigrants from the surrounding countryside, attacked seventy-three targets: police stations, the Rastakhiz Party offices, liquor shops, the movie houses showing sexy films, and the large banks owned by the rich elite (where only records were destroyed). For the first time they raised the cry 'Death to the Shah!'. Some policeman changed to civilian clothes in order to avoid shooting the rioters while others joined Savak agents and shot them from cruising cars. The local army garrison refused to fire on the protestors. This introduced a new factor in the anti-Shah movement, one which was to grow in importance over the next year.

The Tabriz uprising continued for two days. The Shah declared martial law, sacked the provincial governor-general as well as six police chiefs, and despatched to the city a general armed with tanks, helicopter gunships and armoured personnel carriers. By the time order was restored, more than 100 people had been killed and over 600 injured.[8] The troops stayed on until 3 March.

Khomeini was quick to comment. In a speech at Shaikh Ansari mosque in Najaf on 19 February, he referred to the shutdowns in Tehran, Tabriz, Mashhad and Qom. 'These closings represent a form of active protest against the person of the Shah,' he said. 'The people have identified the true criminal. It was obvious before . . . but some people didn't recognise him as such or didn't dare to speak out. Thanks be to God, this barrier of fear has [now] collapsed.'[9] A week later, after he had received a full report on the Tabriz uprising, Khomeini addressed a congratulatory message to 'the upright men and honourable youths of Tabriz and all those who have risen up . . . with the cries of "Death to the Shah!" '.[10]

This gave an impetus to the move to celebrate nationally the fortieth day mourning of those killed in Tabriz. The commemoration fell on 29 March. Demonstrations occurred in fifty-five urban centres. All except five were peaceful. As in Tabriz, the rioters attacked banks, police stations, royal statues, select cinemas, liquor shops, and the Rastakhiz Party offices. In Yazd, the scene of the most violent confrontation between mourners and police, five to 100 people died. Once again the Shah had to take personal charge of directing the riot control operations to end the three-day-long cycle of rioting and police firing.

Far more violence occurred on the next fortieth day mourning of those killed in the 19 to 31 March disturbances. The demonstrators and the police clashed in twenty-four cities and towns. The Shah himself commanded the armoured troops used in Tehran to quell the rioters. In Qom the protestors dispersed only after the authorities had cut off the electricity and sent in troops to fire at the crowds. It was not until 12 May that order was restored. Three days later a 25 per cent rise in petrol prices triggered off another bout of rioting. All told, the cycle of violence had by now caused the deaths of twenty-two to 250 people and injuries to 200 to 600.[11]

Given this, both the Shah and the moderate clergy, guided by Shariatmadari, wanted to avoid violence on the next fortieth day mourning processions due on 19 June. The Shah offered an olive branch to the ulema and the bazaar. He paid a widely publicised visit to the Imam Ali Reza shrine in Mashhad. He promised to re-open Qom's Faiziya seminary, closed since 1975, and increase the quota of pilgrims to Mecca. He banned pornographic movies. He called off the anti-inflation campaign which had badly hit the bazaar: he disbanded the price inspectorate teams and released the merchants serving prison sentences for overcharging. He cancelled the plan for a state-run marketing system. On 6 June he removed the much hated General Nematollah Nasseri, head of Savak since 1965, and posted him as ambassador to Pakistan. He instructed his royal relatives to sever all business connections.

Shariatmadari called on his followers to stay away from the demonstrations scheduled for 19 June. In an interview to the press he said that all he wanted was the return of the constitutional government, and that he did not care whether the Shah left or stayed.[12] This was at variance with Khomeini's stand. Khomeini urged his followers to keep up the protest until the 'evil regime' had been overthrown.[13] In the end, the 19 June protest passed off peacefully.

But by now the Amouzgar government's recessionary measures of the past ten months had created favourable conditions for the rise of protest on economic grounds. This drew industrial and non-industrial working classes into the anti-Shah agitation, and transformed it into a revolutionary movement.

The fourth stage: July to 8 September 1978

In order to reduce excessive inflation and deficit financing, Amouzgar tightened up credit facilities and pared down the over-ambitious Fifth Plan, curtailing or axing many industrial plans and construction projects. He limited wage rises and cancelled the customary annual bonus to office employees and workers. As a result, inflation fell from 30 to 35 per cent in 1977 to 7 per cent the following year. But so did economic growth: from 14 per cent in 1977 to 2 per cent in the first half of 1978.[14] This was the end of fifteen years of continued prosperity. During the period 1963-77 real per capita income had increased fivefold, from $200 a year to $1,000.[15]

Between 1973 and 1977 alone, the daily minimum wage rose from Rials 80 to Rials 210. During those years the economy was short of labour. But by mid-1978 there were 400,000 unemployed in the country. With the urban construction growth slumping from 32 per cent in 1977 to 7 per cent the following year, the take-home wage of a construction worker fell by nearly a third.[16]

For factory workers and office staff, the cancellation of the annual bonus came at a time when the hold of Savak over their unions was slackening.[17] In any case there was now less fear of Savak and courts than before. Working class protest began mildly in June, and caught on in September. It expressed itself in strikes as well as participation in demonstrations, swelling them many times their previous sizes. On 22 July tens of thousands of workers joined a funeral procession for a Mashhad cleric killed in a car accident. In the clashes with the police that followed, and the inevitable firing, at least forty people were killed. This sent a new shock wave throughout the country. Most urban centres staged the seventh day mourning processions for the Mashhad dead. Rioting erupted in major cities.

This provided a prelude to the fasting month of Ramadan which started on 5 August, the Constitution Day of Iran. On its eve the Shah pledged to hold '100 per cent free' elections to the Majlis due in June 1979. Few Iranians took his promise seriously. For the next twenty-nine days as the faithful prayed daily at a mosque and listened to the preacher's sermon – sometimes accompanied by Khomeini's taped speeches – before breaking the fast after sunset, anti-Shah sentiment rose sharply.

'Ramadan sermons provided a perfect and powerful vehicle for spreading a basically political message, urging men to rise and act against tyranny,' wrote the editors of *The Dawn Of The Islamic Revolution, Volume I.* 'Preachers drew on the Shiite themes of struggle and martyrdom. The Pahlavis did not have to be directly mentioned. It was not difficult to draw a parallel between the hated figures of Yazid and Muawiya and the Shah, or between the Ummayad dynasty, with its bent for luxury and pomp, and the Pahlavi dynasty.'[18]

As a result there were a series of riots and demonstrations from 7 to 16 August in Mashhad, Shahsaver, Tabriz, Ahvaz, Behbahan and Shiraz (where the annual arts festival, declared 'lewd' by the local ulema, was cancelled). On 17 August demonstrators took control of Isfahan. It was only after the Shah had declared martial law in the city, and sent in troops, that the government regained full control after two days. Over 100 people died in army firings.[19] But something far worse was yet to come.

On 19 August a fire inside the Rex Cinema in Abadan killed 410 men, women and children. The government blamed religious fanatics; the public accused Savak. It was hard to see why anti-Shah elements would attack a cinema in a working class neighbourhood showing a contemporary Iranian-made film, entitled *The Deer*, which had passed the censors with considerable difficulty. The deliberate closing of the cinema doors, and the tepid response of the local fire station, strengthened popular suspicion of Savak involvement. The next day angered mourners shouted 'Burn the Shah' and 'Death to the Shah'.

After the mysterious death of Khomeini's son in October 1977, and the virulent anti-Khomeini article in the *Ittilaat* in January 1978, the Abadan cinema fire was the single most important event to inflame public feelings against the Pahlavi ruler. 'All indications are that the heart-rending incident in Abadan has the same origin as the massacres that have taken place in other cities,' said Khomeini on 21 August. 'The regime may commit similar savage acts in other cities of Iran. . . . All our speakers and preachers should make clear to the people the dangers that threaten the continuation of the liberating Islamic Revolution.'[20]

The Islamic speakers followed Khomeini's directive. There was no let up in popular protest. Abadan was in turmoil. The nightly rioting by the mourners reached a peak on the seventh day mourning of the Rex Cinema victims. In a fiery speech Ayatollah Kazem Dehdashti, the local religious leader, demanded the Shah's removal.

Realising the depth of anti-regime feeling among his subjects, the Shah tried to defuse the situation. On 27 August he removed Amouzgar as premier, and appointed Jaafar Sharif-Emami, chairman of the Senate, to form a government of 'national reconciliation'. As deputy-custodian of the super-affluent Pahlavi Foundation, Sharif-Emami was close to the monarch, the Foundation's custodian. A grandson of an ayatollah, he knew most of the moderate religious leaders. He was thus well-equipped to conciliate them. But he had to move fast.

On 31 August, the fortieth day memorial of the Mashhad massacre, Ayatollah Abol Hassan Shirazi of Mashhad issued a fourteen-point manifesto which summed up the ulema's demands. These included abrogation of all anti-Islamic laws, freedom of expression for the ulema, banning of casinos and cinemas, release of all Islamic prisoners, invitation to Khomeini and other exiles to return, punishing of those responsible for the deaths of the demonstrators, dismissal of Bahais from all official posts, restricting cabinet appointments to Jaafari Shias, and clerical and secular supervision of the Majlis elections.[21] Fourteen cities witnessed violent disturbances on 31 August, and deaths of fifty to 100 people.

Sharif-Emami acted swiftly. He set up a ministry of religious affairs, released many leading clerics in jail since 1975, and abolished the royalist calendar. He shut down the casinos belonging to the Pahlavi Foundation, ended subsidies to the Rastakhiz Party, and lifted censorship. He declared that seventy police and army officers would be dismissed for their part in the suppression of the recent riots.[22]

On the other side Ayatollah Shariatmadari agreed to give the new government three months to return to the constitution, adding that if it failed he would renew civil disobedience. Sharif-Emami won the cooperation of the opposition leaders in arranging a peaceful celebration of Eid al Fitr (Festival of 'Breaking the Fast'), due on 4 September, in Tehran by promising to keep the army out of public view.

The festival passed off quietly in all major urban centres. In the capital two marches – one from the affluent north and the other from the lowly south – met in the city centre, and then headed for the Shahyad Square to the west. About a third of the marchers were women, a new development which was to acquire great significance as the conflict between the people and the regime sharpened. The confluence of the marchers from the economically disparate halves of the city symbolised a coalition of all classes (except the very affluent) in their struggle against the Pahlavi dynasty: students in jeans, workers in overalls, clerics in ecclesiastical robes, women in chador, and merchants and professionals in suits. The size of the procession, estimated at half a million, indicated what the extensive networks of the the ulema and the secular opposition leaders could achieve. Given that it was a day of festivities after the rigour of month-long fasting (between sunrise and sunset), and that the soldiers had been confined mainly to side streets, the marchers greeted them with flowers, and shouted such slogans as 'The army is part of the nation'.

Khomeini sensed danger in the conciliatory steps taken by Premier Sharif-Emami and the peaceful celebration of Eid al Fitr. 'Pay no attention to the deceptive words of the Shah, his government, and its supporters, for their only aim is to gain another reprieve for their satanic selves,' he warned in a statement on 6 September. 'The Shah and his government are in a state of armed rebellion against the justice-seeking people of Iran, against the constitution, and against the liberating decrees of Islam. They are therefore traitors, and to obey them is to obey the taghut [personification of evil]. Do not give them the slightest respite, and inform the whole world of their barbarous deeds with your strikes and protest demonstrations.' He then addressed the military in a clear move to drive a wedge between them and the Shah: a tactic which was to prove crucial in the last stages of the revolutionary movement. He thanked the army for not firing on the huge Eid al Fitr marches in the country (in which a total of four million people participated). Extending his hand to 'all those in the army, air force and navy who are faithful to Islam and the homeland', Khomeini called on them to 'renew your bonds with the beloved people and refuse to go on slaughtering your children and brothers for the sake of the whims of this [Pahlavi] family of bandits!'. He concluded by urging 'speakers and writers' to 'do their utmost to explain the thoughts that are agitating our brothers in the army, and [that] the Iranian peoople must respect them, for they are our brothers'.[23]

The next day, 7 September, half a million people marched from north Tehran to the Majlis building in central Tehran, shouting 'Death to the Shah', 'Khomeini is our leader', and 'We want an Islamic government'. This was a record gathering, with many thousands of marchers wearing the white shrouds of martyrs, showing their willingness to die. The tide of militancy was rising. Neither the opposition leaders' appeals for restraint nor the government's ban on demonstrations on 6 September succeeded in halting the daily processions that the protestors in the capital had been mounting since Eid al Fitr.

Khomeini referred to the marches of Eid al Fitr and 7 September as 'a referendum' that 'the Shah's regime has no place in Iran'. Addressing 'the great ulema of Islam and great politicians who have no fear of the Shah', he urged them to 'ever more strengthen the excellent resistance, morale and spirits of society, and close your ranks to confront the enemy of the Iranian nation'.[24]

Muhammad Reza Pahlavi Shah realised that unless he took drastic action immediately the situation would get out of control. He therefore pressured the cabinet overnight to impose six-month-long martial law in a dozen cities, including Tehran. He gave the job of the military governor of the capital to General Gholam Ali Oveissi, nicknamed the 'Butcher of Tehran' for his actions during the June 1963 upheaval.

Martial law and daylight curfew went into force at 6 am the next day, a Friday, the weekly holiday and the day of communal prayers. Many of the protestors gathering in the streets of south Tehran were unaware of the curfew. So were the 15,000 people who had crowded into the Jaleh Square in eastern Tehran, a residential area of bazaari merchants and employees. At 8 am troops and tanks surrounded the square. Without warning the soldiers fired to kill. Pandemonium broke out. Assisted by helicopter gunships, the soldiers drove the protestors into the narrow lanes radiating out of the square. By the time they had cleared the area by noon, some 1,600 people lay dead. In south Tehran the residents confronted the soldiers with barricades and Molotov cocktails, and received bullets in return. Repeating his tactics of June 1963, General Oveissi used helicopter gunships to clear out the rioters from south Tehran slums. At the end of the day the government announced eighty-seven dead and 205 injured. This was a lie. For, during the next few days the Bchesht-e Zahra cemetery, on the edge of south Tehran, issued 4,290 burial certificates.[25] Due to the bloodbath that occurred on 8 September, 17 Shahrivar (in the Iranian calendar), the day was called the Black Friday.

The Shah's atrocity showed to the Iranians that the Pahlavi had not changed at all, and that he was quite capable of massacring thousands in order to maintain his absolutist power. They saw, as Khomeini had warned, that the Shah's earlier concessions were a ruse to gain time to muster his forces and crush his opponents. The people were angered and disgusted by the outrage committed on the Black Friday. But, as the Shah was to discover soon, they were not cowed. If anything, the events of the Black Friday steeled the resolve of the anti-Shah forces. Any compromise with the Shah was out. With this Iran entered a period of stark choices: a revolution by the masses or a counter-revolution by military officers led by the Pahlavi ruler.

The fifth stage: 9 September to 5 November 1978

The Shah pressed on with his repressive measures. He reintroduced censorship, arrested opposition leaders and extended martial law to more cities. He persuaded the Iraqi government to place Khomeini under house arrest in Najaf.[26] At the same time he tried to refurbish the image of the Imperial Court. He ordered all the royals to give up their government positions. Yielding to Premier Sharif-Emami's pressure to rid the Court and the government of Bahais, he forced Hoveida to resign as Court minister, and dismissed his own Bahai physician, Dr Abdul Karim Ayadi, as well as four Bahai generals, including the managing director of Iran Air.

But the Shah's concessions were too few and too late. And there was no way he could wipe out the bloody events of the Black Friday. It soon became obvious that though the Shah had the power to order periodic massacres of his subjects he could no longer make them comply with his repressive decrees. For instance, when on 12 September General Oveissi sent censors to two Tehran newspaper offices, all the 4,000 employees walked out. Unable to enforce censorship, Premier Sharif-Emami lifted it on 15 September.

Three days later the regime's credibility received a bodyblow from an unexpected quarter. That day the employees of the Central Bank (Bank Markazi) of Iran released a statement which showed that 177 affluent Iranians had recently sent abroad a total of $2,000 million. Sharif-Emami had transferred $31 million, and General Oveissi $14 million. The list included the royals as well as top politicians, civil servants and military officers. The members, relatives and retainers of the royal family had collected vast sums by peddling influence at the Court and receiving generous grants from the Pahlavi Foundation. Senior politicians and civil servants had accumulated large fortunes from kickbacks on government contracts and bonuses from the Pahlavi Foundation. Top military officers had enriched themselves from bribes and commissions on proliferating military contracts with the tacit approval of the Shah, who thus wanted to strengthen their loyalty to the regime. Now by rushing to transfer their cash assets abroad, the Iranian elite was showing its lack of confidence in the Pahlavi dynasty's durability. This boosted the morale of the opposition.

Information released by the Central Bank staff revealed that thirteen top military officers had recently exported $253 million abroad. This had a debilitating effect on the morale of conscripts, who formed 50 per cent of the infantry, and who received a stipend of $1 a day. Being drawn from all sections of society, young conscripts were more receptive to Khomeini's ideas than professional soldiers or officers. In the coming weeks and months this was to prove to be the fatal weakness of the Shah's army.

By the time of the Central Bank revelations, disaffection had spread to the crucial, state-owned National Iranian Oil Company. Oil refinery workers in Tehran, Tabriz, Isfahan and Shiraz downed tools, and demanded the lifting of martial law. On 22 September the NIOC staff in Ahvaz went on strike. Their example was followed on 1 October by 10,000 workers in Khuzistan. They demanded higher wages. While workers were demonstrating their opposition to the regime increasingly through strikes on economic and political grounds, the rich were showing their loss of confidence in the Peacock Throne by massive transfers of their funds abroad. In late September the capital flight from Iran reached the level of $50 million a day.[27]

In early October fifty major manufacturing and service establishments were shut down by strikes. They ranged from the petro-chemical complex in Bandar Shahpour (now Bandar Khomeini) to the National Bank (Bank Melli) in Tehran to the copper mines near Kerman. Postal workers, bank employees, hospital staff, journalists, miners and customs officers combined their demands for wage rises of 50 to 100 per cent with calls for the dissolution of Savak, the ending of martial law, and the return of Khomeini.

But the Shah had different ideas. At his behest, Khomeini was expelled from Iraq. After an unsuccessful attempt to cross into Kuwait by road, Khomeini flew to France on 6 October. Khomeini's expulsion sparked off three days of strikes and demonstrations in Iran. Those participating included not only bazaaris and students but also most of the employees in the public sector: postal service, airline, railways, hospitals, oil industry and so on.

Faced with such a massive challenge, and intent on defusing the situation before the fortieth day memorial of the Black Friday's martyrs due on 17 October, the Shah tried desperately to prove his reformist credentials. He dissolved the Rastakhiz Party in late September. On 2 October he initiated a series of amnesties which were to continue until his birthday on 26 October. Addressing the Majlis on 6 October, he promised that liberalisation would continue, as would the arrests of corrupt officials.

On being installed in a Paris suburb, Khomeini found that he had much greater freedom of action there than in Najaf. And he used it.

He gave four to five interviews a day to the international media. On 11 October in a message to the Iranian people he declared the fortieth day after the Black Friday as a day of public mourning. 'Your blood is being shed for the same cause as the blood of the Prophets and the Imams and the righteous,' he said. 'You will join them [in heaven]; and you have no cause to grieve, therefore, but every reason for joy.' He repeated his call to the army to refrain from shooting their brothers and sisters, and stressed the Islamic nature of the current struggle being launched with the objective of 'the overthrow of the corrupt Pahlavi regime and the liberation of the destiny and resources of our country from foreign control'.[28]

The bloody demonstrations of 17 and 18 October produced their share of martyrs. For the first time *all* workers went on a two-day strike. And the trend continued. By the third week of October strikes had spread to 'almost all the bazaars, universities, high schools, oil installations, banks, government ministries, post offices, railways, newspapers, customs and port facilities, internal air flights, radio and television stations, state-run hospitals, paper and tobacco plants, and other large factories'.[29] The cumulative effect was a general strike, the like of which Iran had not experienced before. The Shah was rattled. He floated the idea of constitutional monarchy through Sharif-Emami who was in touch with the leaders of the National Front and the Liberation Movement. To test Khomeini's response to the Shah's proposal, Mahdi Bazargan, the Liberation Movement chief, flew to Paris on 23 October. Karim Sanjabi of the National Front followed him. Their trips to Paris signified that the initiative to solve the political crisis was now firmly in the hands of Khomeini. And he knew it.

Khomeini pushed his advantage by hitting the regime where it hurt most: petroleum. He called on the oil employees to stop working. Responding instantly, they went on an indefinite strike on 31 October. This was a severe blow to the state treasury: a loss of some $74 million a day, most of it in foreign currencies. Premier Sharif-Emami called it 'treason' and sent troops to the oilfields.

The next day Khomeini was once again the focus of public attention. In Tehran hundreds of thousands of people marched to commemorate the fourteenth anniversary (by the Iranian calendar) of his expulsion from Iran. Ayatollah Shariatmadari, the most respected cleric inside Iran, endorsed Khomeini's stand. 'Our demands are the same,' he declared.[30] On 4 November, speaking in Paris, Karim Sanjabi ruled out any possibility of compromise with the Shah. He did so after meeting Khomeini. These two statements formally sealed an alliance between secular and religious opposition leaders on the basis of the common objective of ending the Pahlavi dynasty and the acceptance of

Khomeini as the supreme leader of the anti-Shah coalition.

On 4 November at Tehran University, protesting students tried to demolish the Shah's statue at the main gate. In the mêlée a conscript handed over his rifle to the protestors. This angered his sergeant. He fired his sub-machine gun, and killed thirty to sixty students. The event was significant. It showed that the troops' loyalty to the monarch was slipping, and that the 413,000 strong armed forces were no longer the rock solid foundation of the Pahlavi regime as had been assumed so far.

The news of the students' deaths spread fast. They inflamed popular feelings, and led to an upheaval in Tehran of the same scale as had occurred earlier in Tabriz and Isfahan. The following day, 5 November, the bazaar closed in protest, and stayed shut for a week. Student demonstrators from north Tehran and working class protestors from south Tehran met along Reza Shah Avenue (now Inqilab Avenue) to form a shouting mass of 200,000 people. Then a section of the procession went on a rampage, attacking liquor stores, banks, cinemas, luxury hotels, American and British airline offices, and the ministries of information and culture. They destroyed the Shah's portraits by the hundred. Despite the comparative restraint by the military government in ending the rioting, sixty-five people were killed by the security forces.

There were unconfirmed reports of mutiny in the garrisons situated in Isfahan, Hamadan and Babol, and near the capital. The occurrence of large scale rioting in Tehran, despite the martial law, worried the Shah. He concluded that he would have to use a still blunter weapon to reimpose his will on the people, whose disaffection had reached unprecedented proportions. The next step was to discard the facade of a civilian administration and install a military government. That is what he did. It was a measure of his growing desperation shared by his most powerful foreign backer: the US government.

The sixth stage: 6 November 1978 to 16 January 1979

The Shah replaced Sharif-Emami with General Gholam Reza Azhari, commander of the Imperial Guards, on 6 November and asked the new prime minister to form a military government to end 'violence and unrest'. This was a reference to the rioting that had rocked Tehran the day before. Actually, the Shah had decided two days earlier to form a military administration, once he had received assurances from Washington that it would support such a move.[31] The eruption of rioting in the capital provided the ruler with a handy excuse to do what he was going to do anyway. President Carter had been in close touch with the Shah throughout the latter part of the crisis. On 31 October Carter had received the Shah's son, Reza Cyrus, on the latter's birthday at the White House, and greeted him with the statement: 'Our friendship with Iran is one of the most important bases on which our entire foreign policy depends'.[32] Earlier, in the midst of intense negotiations to bring about peace between Egypt and Israel at the presidential retreat of Camp David, Carter had phoned the Shah to reassure him of US backing in the aftermath of the events of the Black Friday.[33]

While placing Iran under military government, the Shah made it appear as if he were backing down. 'I once again repeat my oath before the Iranian nation and undertake not to tolerate the past mistakes, unlawful acts, oppression and corruption, but to make up for them,' he said in a nation-wide television address on 6 November. 'I have read the revolutionary message of you, the people, the Iranian nation. I guarantee that in the future the Iranian government will be divorced from tyranny and oppression, and will be run on the basis of the constitution and social justice.'[34]

To prove his sincerity, the very next day the Shah ordered the arrest of thirteen prominent figures of his regime, including General Nasseri (for illegal arrest and torture during his tenure as the head of Savak), former premier Hoveida, and Dariush Humayun, the author of the anti-Khomeini article in the *Ittilaat*. He appointed a commission to investigate the Pahlavi Foundation. He conceded many of the economic demands of the civil servants and public sector employees, and found the money by cancelling $4,000 million worth of advanced weapons, including seven Airborne Warning and Control Systems (Awacs), 160 F-16 and seventy F-4 combat aircraft.

But the Shah's other face was in evidence as well. Six of the ten-member cabinet of Azhari were generals. General Oveissi, the capital's military governor, was appointed labour minister and given the task of ending the oil workers' strike. He imposed martial law in the oil-rich province of Khuzistan, arrested the strike committee, and ordered soldiers to shoot at gatherings of two people or more.

In Paris Khomeini remained steadfast. If the Shah had really heard 'the revolutionary message' of the people, the Ayatollah retorted, he would abdicate and offer himself for an Islamic trial. Warning that anybody cooperating with the government would be considered a traitor to Islam, Khomeini urged the faithful to continue strikes and demonstrations until the hated monarchy was overthrown.[35]

His views were shared by Bazargan and Sanjabi after talks with him in Paris in early November. Bazargan said that the Iranian people wanted to replace monarchy with 'an Islamic system of government'. Sanjabi called for a referendum to establish a national government

'based on the principles of Islam, democracy and national sovereignty'.[36] But before he could repeat his demand for a referendum in
Tehran on 11 November, he was arrested.

This set off a general strike in Tehran, followed by three days of
rioting in the oil cities of Khuzistan. Then, yielding to the military
pressures, 60 per cent of the oil workers resumed work on 16
November on the condition that they would produce just enough to
meet home demand and pay for essential foreign imports, nothing
more. This meant an output of 1.1 million barrels/day instead of the
5.3 million barrels/day produced before the strike.

The Shah's absence at the Army Day ceremonies on 17 November
confirmed persistent rumours of his lapse into deep depression and his
estrangement from his wife, Farah Diba. Any lingering hopes in his
mind of direct US intervention to save his throne were soon dashed.
On 18 November Soviet President Leonid Brezhnev warned the US
against interference in Iran's domestic affairs.[37] This was no symbolic
gesture. It was based on two articles in the 1921 Iranian-Russian
Treaty: these authorised Moscow to move its troops into Iran if a third
party carried out an armed intervention in Iran.[38] These articles were
the basis for the Soviet march into Iran in August 1941. Cyrus Vance,
US secretary of state, replied publicly that America had no intention
of getting involved in Iran's internal affairs. This statement was a
morale booster for the anti-Shah forces.

On 21 November troops in Mashhad shocked the nation by chasing
demonstrators into the shrine of Imam Ali Reza and shooting them.
This was a re-run of the events of 10 July 1935 which, even in those
comparatively halcyon days, had traumatised the faithful throughout
the country and led to the execution of the shrine's administrator.[39]
Now the outraged Iranians awaited the word from Khomeini.

It came on 23 November. Condemning the military government as
'contrary to the law of the land and Sharia', Khomeini called on the
people to oppose it, and deny it taxes and assistance. 'It is the duty of
all oil company officials and workers to prevent the export of oil, this
vital resource,' he said. He instructed the seminary students and ulema
leaving for villages and provincial towns 'to enlighten their inhabitants'
that 'an Islamic state is not [to be] the protector of capitalists and big
landlords. Let them be assured that Islam stands on the side of the
weak, the peasants and the needy'. Alluding to the forthcoming month
of mourning, Muharram, he called on the faithful to 'organise your
gatherings without referring to the authorities, and if you are
prevented from holding them, gather in public squares, in thorough-
fares and streets, and proclaim the sufferings endured by Islam and
Muslims, and the treacherous acts of the Shah's regime'.[40]

Khomeini's instructions set off demonstrations, peaceful as well as violent, over the next week in fifty urban centres. On 26 November Mashhad witnessed a march by 1,500,000 people, and Qom by 200,000. Daunted by the sight, the military commanders ordered their soldiers to withdraw to the barracks. This was the first time since 21 July 1952, during the oil nationalisation movement, that anything like this had happened. Not surprisingly, the government banned all meetings except those held inside a mosque.

Tension rose sharply as Muharram approached. Anticipating trouble, Premier Azhari declared that night curfew would be strictly enforced, and that no permits for (religious) demonstrations would be issued. Ayatollah Shariatmadari scoffed at the idea of the faithful having to secure government permission to commemorate Imam Hussein's martyrdom. Ayatollah Taleqani, the recently released clerical leader of Tehran, advised the people to express their opposition to the Shah by shouting 'Allah is great' from roof-tops at certain times. Khomeini declared that it was the duty of the faithful to die, if necessary, to defeat the oppressive regime, that Muslim soldiers should desert if ordered to shoot their Muslim brothers or sisters, and that oil workers should blow up oil wells in case of military intervention.[41]

The National Front leaders called for a general strike on the first and the tenth days of Muharram, which began on 2 December. On the first three nights of Muharram, thousands of men wearing white shrouds, signifying their readiness to die, defied night curfew. Soldiers fired at them. About 700 of them lost their lives in various cities. This led the oil workers to go on an indefinite strike on 5 December.

That day Premier Azhari agreed to allow marches on Ashura, the tenth day of Muharram, if the opposition leaders promised to lead them personally along prescribed routes and refrained from direct attacks on the Shah. He released Karim Sanjabi and 471 other political prisoners the next day.

On Tasua, 9 Muharram, a Sunday, a march of 300,000 to 1,000,000 people in Tehran, headed by Ayatollah Taleqani and Karim Sanjabi, took six hours to pass the city centre on its way to the Shahyad Square. It ended peacefully, as did most such marches in other cities. Khomeini's instruction to theological students and teachers to spread the word in rural areas about the revolutionary movement had worked. For the first time these urban marches drew large number of supporters from surrounding villages.

Ashura, 10 Muharram (11 December), saw nearly two million people in the capital, led once again by Taleqani and Sanjabi, pass through the city centre for eight hours to reach the Shahyad Square. There, the marchers ratified a seventeen-point charter by acclamation. It demanded an end to monarchy, acceptance of Khomeini as the leader, establishment of an Islamic government, rejuvenation of agriculture, social justice for the deprived masses, protection of religious minorities, and the return of all exiles. This event conferred legitimacy on the opposition – an alliance of religious and secular forces – as the genuinely representative government of the Iranian people.

The Shah and his military government viewed the event with nervous alarm. Over the next three days the army went on a rampage in fifty-five urban centres. In Isfahan and Najafabad alone troops killed at least forty people. But attempts by military officers, as well as such civilians as Ardeshir Zahedi, a son-in-law of the Shah, to stage pro-Shah demonstrations were dismal failures. Khomeini warned that the 'mentally deranged' Shah would commit further atrocities. He appealed to the soldiers not to fire on the demonstrators. His call for a general strike was taken up by the National Front leaders: they decided on 18 December as the strike day.

Premier Azhari tried frantically to end strikes in the oil industry and government ministries. By ordering the arrests and dismissals of militant NIOC employees he was able to intimidate a section of the oil workers to resume production. Elsewhere he failed. The general strike on 18 December was a success. That strengthened the civil servants' resolve to continue their stoppage.

What is more, the army began to show signs of serious cracks. On the day of the general strike, dissident soldiers in Tabriz went beyond their refusal to shoot the demonstrators: 500 of them, equipped inter alia with a dozen tanks, went over to the opposition. In the holy cities of Qom and Mashhad hundreds of desertions had sapped the morale of the army garrisons there. Those remaining had threatened to obey the ulema rather than their officers.[42] Such a state of affairs was widespread, and was confirmed by an army general after the Shah's departure. He confessed that, unable to rely on their ranks, the officers had often to do the firing themselves.[43] Even more disturbing to the Shah were the intelligence reports that in such provincial cities as Kermanshah and Hamadan, the soldiers had begun clandestinely passing on arms to the local Revolutionary Komitehs.[44] So now a section of the army was actually aiding the revolutionaries.

Not surprisingly, the Shah concluded that his military administration had reached a dead end, and that the only way out was to co-opt a leader of secular opposition to form the next government. He decided on the National Front. On 21 December he asked one of its leaders, Gholam Hussein Sadiqi, to form a government. Sadiqi agreed, subject to Khomeini's approval. Khomeini refused it.

On 23 December the assassination of two NIOC officials, one American and the other Iranian, triggered off a spate of resignations by oil workers. Output fell dramatically. Three days later, realising that it had only one week's supply of heating oil for Tehran, in the middle of winter, the government stopped all oil exports. It introduced fuel rationing. By now the strikes in factories, bazaars, government ministries and banks had seized up the economy. Most of the ministries and other offices were occupied by strike committees.

With the civil servants on strike, and the administrative institutions paralysed, the task of governing the country fell increasingly on the military, which was ill-equipped for the job. It became more brutal than before. There were many examples of wanton violence by the army. In one instance, on 27 December, troops in Tehran fired on a mourning crowd of middle class men and women for four hours. The next day in Qazvin soldiers shot 600 people in a mourning procession.[45]

With oil production running at two-fifths of the domestic demand, shortage of heating oil and kerosene grew acute. In the capital, public transport and garbage collection were suspended. The Shah was eager to find a civilian premier before 30 December, which had been declared by Khomeini as the Day of Mourning for the past year's Qom martyrs (according to the Islamic calendar). On 29 December Shahpour Bakhtiar, sixty-two-year-old leader of the National Front, agreed to form a government on the (unwritten) conditions that the Shah would immediately go abroad on holiday, and that he would act as a constitutional monarch in the future. This won Bakhtiar an instant expulsion from his party.

On 30 December, the Day of Mourning, there were massive demonstrations in most of the major cities and towns. A dozen of them turned violent. Mashhad and Isfahan fell into the hands of the demonstrators. Two days later the Shah said that he would like to take a vacation 'if the situation permitted'.[46] On 3 January Bakhtiar received a 'vote of intent' in the Majlis as well as the Senate. 140 of the 165 Majlis deputies (in a house of 268) voted for him. That day, without consulting Bakhtiar, the Shah appointed General Abbas Karim Gharabaghi as the new chief of staff of the armed forces to replace General Azhari.

None of this made any difference to Khomeini. He declared that any government appointed by the Shah was illegal, and that strikes and demonstrations must continue. From now on Khomeini concentrated on isolating the Bakhtiar administration while at the same time pressing on with his ultimate objective of overthrowing the Shah.

Aware of the hardship being caused by paucity of heating oil to millions of Iranians, Khomeini instructed the oil workers to produce enough to meet the domestic needs. This meant an output of 700,000 barrels/day instead of 5,300,000 barrels/day before the current turmoil.

On his return to Iran after his second visit to Paris, Bazargan carried Khomeini's message to the oil workers in Khuzistan. This produced the desired result on 5 January.

That day there were huge demonstrations in all major cities against Bakhtiar, who had by now secured the backing of Shariatmadari. On 6 January Premier Bakhtiar presented his full cabinet to the Shah. Bakhtiar took a series of steps to show that his government marked a dramatic break with the past. He seized the assets of the Pahlavi Foundation. He combined the release of the remaining political prisoners with a promise to disband Savak. He pledged to withdraw Iran from Cento, and ordered the cancellation of weapons purchase contracts worth $7 billion, and oil sales agreements with South Africa and Israel.[47]

To prove his radical bona fides, Bakhtiar supported *two* Days of Mourning for the Qom martyrs (according to the Iranian calendar): one called by Shariatmadari on 7 January, and the other by Khomeini a day later. In the event, the demonstrations on 8 January turned out to be much larger than those staged a day earlier. Half a million people marched in Mashhad. They were all peaceful.

On 7 January newspapers reappeared after an interval of two months. But elsewhere there was no sign of an end to the strikes which affected bazaars, educational institutions, factories, and state-run services and industries. The strikers were waiting for the Shah to leave the country as promised. But, as was to be revealed later, the Shah stayed on to finalise plans for a military coup to overthrow the Bakhtiar government and recall him from abroad. On 9 January he appointed General Abdul Ali Badrai, commander of the Imperial Guards, as the commander of the army,[48] with a view to ensuring the success of the coup to be led by Badrai.

Bakhtiar sensed the growing impatience of the public about the Shah's promised departure. On 11 January he announced that the monarch would leave for the US the following week. To facilitate his departure, the next day the government announced the formation of a nine-member Regency Council on 12 January. Headed by Sayyed Jalal al-Din Tehrani, the Council included Bakhtiar and General Gharabaghi.[49] That day demonstrators marched in thirty cities and towns to demand the Shah's abdication, Bakhtiar's dismissal, and Khomeini's return.

Meanwhile Khomeini had been laying the foundation for a system to replace monarchy. 'In accordance with the rights conferred by the laws of Islam and on the basis of the vote of confidence given to me by the overwhelming majority of the Iranian people', he announced the establishment of the Council of the Islamic Revolution on 13 January. Its task was to examine and study conditions for the formation of a provisional government to be charged with convening a constituent assembly to produce a constitution for the Islamic Republic, holding elections, and transferring power to the elected representatives.[50]

Congratulating the officials who had refused to cooperate with the Bakhtiar government, Khomeini called on the people to continue the struggle 'until the establishment of an Islamic Republic that guarantees freedom of the people, independence of the country, and attainment of social justice'. He made a distinction between 'a few slavish and bloodthirsty individuals in the army' wishing to mount a coup, and 'the honourable officers and commanders of the army' who deserve the Iranian people's respect. 'The army belongs to the people, and the people belong to the army', he said.[51]

Behind Khomeini's distinction between good and bad military officers lay the fact that he had charged the Tehran-based members of the Islamic Revolutionary Council (whose names were withheld to safeguard their lives)[52] to negotiate an agreement with the military leadership, and thus avoid bloodshed. The next fortnight saw the most intense round of talks yet between various parties in Tehran and Paris: Khomeini and his aides, the Islamic Revolutionary Council members in Tehran, the Iranian military leaders, US president's special envoy General Robert Huyser, Premier Bakhtiar and the Shah.

On 16 January, Tuesday, the Shah finally left for Aswan, Egypt, for a 'vacation'. He decided against going to the US. Expecting to be recalled after a military coup, he wanted to stay on in the region. He had delayed his departure for about a week partly to finalise plans for a coup and partly to take with him three royal crowns, the largest one studded with 3,380 jewels.[53] On six consecutive days the Pahlavi king despatched a contingent of Imperial Guards from his Niavaran Palace in northern Tehran to the strike-bound head office of the Central Bank in the city centre to collect the crowns stored, along with the famous Peacock Throne, in an underground vault. But the trips proved futile. The bank officials who knew how to operate the combination locks to enter the vault were on strike and could not be found.[54]

As soon as the Shah left, euphoria gripped the Iranian people. Hundreds of thousands of them took to the streets in the capital and elsewhere to celebrate the occasion. They carried the ulema on their shoulders. Other cruised around in cars blowing horns in joy. Everywhere lights were turned on. Crowds set out systematically to pull down the statues of Muhammad Reza Pahlavi and his father. The deliberateness with which they conducted the exercise was in sharp contrast to their frantic efforts after the Shah's earlier escape on 16 August 1953.

Also, this time, the chief of staff, General Gharabaghi, declared that the military would support the legal government, and that there would be no coup. The statement was made in response to what Khomeini had said on 13 January. On that day he had combined his warning against a military coup with an assurance that the army would suffer no harm as a result of the Shah's departure. Khomeini's tactic of splitting the officer corps and wooing the ranks was proving effective. For following his 13 January statement, civilians began putting flowers in the soldiers' guns, and troops took to displaying Khomeini's portraits on their vehicles.

The supremacy of Khomeini was recognised, indirectly, even by Bakhtiar. On the day the Shah left he despatched Jalal al-Din Tehrani, the Regency Council head, to Paris to win Khomeini's endorsement for his government. But Khomeini was not taken in by the gesture. He refused to see Tehrani.[55]

Khomeini knew that he was on a winning streak, but he also knew that victory was still not his. The Shah was far too cunning and power-thirsty to give up the Peacock Throne for ever. 'The Shah's departure without abdication does not change anything,' he said.[56]

There were still a few major battles to be fought and won before the revolutionary struggle could claim lasting success. Bakhtiar's government had to be toppled, and the powerful royalist elements in the Iranian military isolated and overpowered. The only way to ensure final victory was to wield the two weapons which had brought the anti-Shah movement thus far: strikes and marches.

The final stage: 16 January to 11 February 1979

Khomeini called for mass demonstrations on the fortieth day memorial of Imam Hussein's martyrdom, due on 19 January. National Front leaders and their followers stayed away from this commemoration. Despite this, the march in Tehran attracted a million people, in Mashhad half a million, and in Qom about a quarter of a million.

The need for a continued show of popular backing for the revolutionary movement was now as urgent as before. For, General Gharabaghi's pledge of loyalty to the Bakhtiar government was proving hollow. Eight of the seventeen generals and admirals posted in Tehran were in touch with the Shah either directly or through General Abdul Ali Badrai, commander of the army. These included Generals Hashemi Nehzad, Parvez Amin Afshar and Ali Rashabi of the Imperial Guards; General Manuchehr Khosrowdad, commander of the paratroopers; General Amir Hussein Rabii, commander of the air force; and General Mahdi Rahimi, commander of the military police and the military governor of the capital.[57]

To discourage a precipitate action by the royalist generals, Ayatollah

Taleqani warned on 22 January that the Iranian people would launch a jihad (holy crusade) against the army if it attempted a coup. The next day the Imperial Guards put on a show of strength at the parade ground of their Lavizan base for the benefit of foreign journalists. Their commander said that *all* military units were loyal to the Shah. The intention was to deter Khomeini from returning to Tehran to offer prayers on the next Friday, 26 January, and commemorate the anniversary of the Prophet Muhammad's death on the following day. Khomeini showed no sign of altering his plans. Therefore the next day, 24 January, tanks and armoured vehicles occupied Tehran's civilian airport at Mehrabad to forestall Khomeini's return. Later the military closed all Iranian airports for the next three days. These moves had the full backing of Bakhtiar. On 26 January some 100,000 people marched to the Mehrabad airport. They clashed with the military, and twenty-eight of them died. But the following day, the anniversary of the Prophet's death, when half a million people took to the streets, the army commanders withdrew their troops.

Behind the scenes frantic talks were in progress to break the impasse. A compromise formula was hammered out. Bakhtiar would hand over his resignation to Khomeini, who would then instruct him to form a transitional government with a mandate to hold elections to produce a representative government. In the end Khomeini rejected this plan. On 29 January he declared: 'The former Shah was illegal; the two assemblies [i.e., the Majlis and the Senate] and Bakhtiar are illegal; and I won't receive an illegal official'.[58]

By 29 January all civilian airports of Iran were re-opened except the one in the capital. The next day air force technicians (called homafars[59]) seized Tehran's airport, and compelled Bakhtiar to order its re-opening. They thus set the scene for Khomeini's return. That day, amid rumours of an impending military coup, the Imperial Guards staged an impressive parade in the capital as an advance warning to Khomeini's local supporters, now swelled by an influx of a million people from outside Tehran.

Khomeini, his aides, and journalists boarded a specially chartered aeroplane in Paris on the evening of 31 January, and arrived in Tehran the next morning. 'It was an occasion of unbridled rejoicing, for which there has probably been no parallel in modern world,' wrote Mohamed Heikal. 'If the Hidden Imam had in truth reappeared after eleven hundred years, the fervour could hardly have been greater. People were shouting "The soul of Hussein is coming back!", "The doors of paradise have been opened again!", "Now is the hour of martyrdom!", and similar cries of ecstasy.'[60] Three million people had lined up the streets to greet Khomeini. 'I'll appoint a government with the support of the nation,' he declared on arrival. 'I'll slap the Bakhtiar government in the mouth.' Since the official authorities had disowned responsibility for Khomeini's security, the Revolutionary Komitehs had taken over the task, and marshalled their guards for the purpose. Seeing that the airport and the roads had become jammed with people, the Revolutionary Komitehs decided to take Khomeini by helicopter to Alaviya high school in east Tehran, which was to become his headquarters for a month.

Bakhtiar found himself in an invidious position. On one hand he wanted to restrain military leaders from mounting a coup; and on the other he needed their help to dissuade Khomeini from appointing an alternative government.

On 2 February, Friday, after paying homage to the dead at the Behesht-e Zahra cemetery near Tehran, Khomeini ordered the formation of the Central Komiteh. He instructed it to examine the dozens of Revolutionary Komitehs which had sprung up in the capital (and which had been steadily taking over administrative powers as the Bakhtiar government had weakened daily), dissolve the unreliable ones, and coordinate the genuine ones. He began receiving a steady stream of leaders of many organisations offering him their support and loyalty. On 3 February he announced that the Islamic Revolutionary Council had drafted a republican constitution which would be offered to the people for their vote.[61] That day air force homafars (technicians) staged pro-Khomeini demonstrations at Tehran's civilian and military airports, a foretaste of the events to come.

Intermediaries intervened to forestall a head-on collision between Khomeini and Bakhtiar. A compromise was reached. Bakhtiar promised not to arrest the provisional government appointed by Khomeini, and merely call it 'a shadowy administration'. Khomeini agreed to refrain from immediately presenting the draft republican constitution for a referendum. This meant that the 1906 constitution continued to exist nominally, for the period of transition.

On 5 February, Monday, Khomeini appointed Mahdi Bazargan prime minister of the provisional Islamic government. With this, Iran entered a period of two competing governments – with the one associated with the ancien régime trying desperately to win popular support through a series of radical reforms. Bakhtiar presented the Majlis with bills abolishing Savak and withdrawing Iran from Cento. He lifted the ban on demonstrations and eased the curfew. But he was fighting a losing battle.

Plagued by mounting desertions the military – the mainstay of the Pahlavis and now Bakhtiar – was rapidly disintegrating. On Wednesday, 7 February, representatives of the air force personnel clandestinely met Khomeini and swore allegiance to him. Their lead was soon followed by representatives of the army and navy ranks.[62]

The next day, 8 February, airmen in uniform joined pro-Khomeini demonstrations in support of Premier Bazargan. They called on Khomeini's headquarters and chanted: 'Khomeini, we're only a small part of your army'. This event brought to a breaking point the tension that had been simmering between pro-Khomeini and pro-Shah elements in the armed forces for some time.

The following day, 9 February, at Doshan Tapeh air base in eastern Tehran (near the revolutionary stronghold of Jaleh Square), homafars and uniformed civilian workers refused to arm combat aircraft with bombs on the ground that the high command planned to bomb and strafe Iranian cities. The Bakhtiar government used army police to arrest the protestors' leaders, and despatched an Imperial Guards detachment to the air base. Three miles to the west of the base, at the Tehran University campus, Bazargan urged the huge congregation of the faithful, gathered for the Friday afternoon prayer, to continue their strikes until Bakhtiar had resigned.

Clips of the Friday prayer congregation and Khomeini's activities of the day were shown on television that evening. Watching Khomeini on television, hundreds of air cadets and homafars (whose leaders had by now established contacts with the leftist and Islamic guerrillas in the city) burst into anti-Bakhtiar slogans. In the fighting that erupted between them and the Imperial Guards unit, twenty-three American military advisers attached to the air base were trapped inside a bunker.[63] With the capital now rife with stories of the events at Doshan Tapeh air base, and mounting fears of a military coup, the leftist guerrilla organisations as well as the ulema-led Revolutionary Komitehs went on the alert. They immediately threw a cordon around Khomeini's headquarters.

William Sullivan, US ambassador to Iran, was anxious to secure the immediate release of the American advisers trapped at the Doshan Tapeh base. The Imperial Guards unit there felt beleaguered. Responding to the pleas from these sources, Bakhtiar despatched Imperial Guards reinforcements to the air base. But when they tried to approach their destination they found the Damavand Road leading to it occupied by civilian guerrillas and the base itself taken over by mutinous airmen. Their tanks and armoured vehicles became the targets of the hand grenades and machine gun fire of the guerrillas. By the time the battle ended in the rout of the Imperial Guards, some 200 people were dead on both sides.

Having captured the armoury at Doshan Tapeh airbase, the guerrillas, and airmen and army deserters rushed arms and ammunition to the Tehran University campus, where youthful volunteers snapped them up. Most of the city's 200,000 reservists, experienced in the use of arms, were eager to fight for the revolution. Now their moment had come. Alarmed by the prospect of a popular, armed uprising, the Bakhtiar government instructed the state radio at 2 pm to announce curfew for 4 pm. Khomeini countered this immediately. 'Nobody should go home,' Khomeini said. 'Everybody should stay in the streets.'[64] His word spread like wildfire.

During the next twenty-four hours (10-11 February) armed revolutionaries, and army and air force deserters, went about systematically destroying what remained of the Shah's once formidable war machine. First they captured an arms factory and nine police armouries. With this they increased their fire power and their armed ranks. All told they distributed some 300,000 weapons, including 75,000 sub-machine guns.[65] Thus armed, the revolutionaries fought the only element of the Shah's military ready and willing to do so: the 30,000 strong Imperial Guards, consisting of two armoured divisions. But they were equipped with tanks and armoured vehicles which were unsuitable for the street battles that ensued. Yet only one of the two Imperial Guards divisions was defeated, with the other remaining intact. Later it was to make an unsuccessful attempt to stage a coup.

The revolutionary forces captured the capital's prisons, television station, Majlis building and military academy. And one by one they overran the military bases at Ishratabad, Shahpur, Bagh-e Shah – and even Lavizan, the Imperial Guards headquarters. The military apparatus in Tehran was destroyed – with commanders dispersed, arrested or killed, and ranks abandoning their weapons and uniforms and melting into the populace.

On the morning of 11 February, Sunday, the twenty-six generals and admirals of the Military Supreme Council met in Tehran under the chairmanship of General Gharabaghi to review the situation. At 2 pm the Council issued a statement. 'The Iranian military has the duty to defend the independence and integrity of the country and has . . . tried to defend the legal government and carry out this duty in the best possible manner,' it read. 'With due consideration for the circumstances the Military Supreme Council . . . [decided] to announce the military's neutrality in the present political crisis and ordered the troops to return to their garrisons.'[66] In the words of Gharabaghi, the Military Supreme Council reached this decision in order 'to prevent further bloodshed, to preserve the unity and integrity of the armed forces threatening to split into royalist and Islamic camps, and prevent civil war'.[67] Four hours later music on the National Radio of Iran was interrupted by an announcer who said that the station had been secured by 'the forces of the revolution'. He read out General Gharabaghi's statement.

This marked the official end to the fighting in Tehran which had so far claimed 654 dead and 2,804 injured.[68] The following day as Premier

Bazargan announced the names of three deputy premiers, the revolutionary forces captured the Shah's Niavaran Palace and other places of resistance, and Bakhtiar went underground. The twelfth of February became the official birthday of the post-Pahlavi regime. The next day Bazargan presented his full cabinet of ten ministers to Khomeini.

On 14 February pro-Shah troops launched an attack on radio and television stations. Immediately calls went out on these stations for popular support to repulse the assault. Thousands of armed revolutionaries appeared, and defeated the royalists after forty-five minutes of fighting. That day leftist guerrillas attacked and briefly occupied the US embassy in Tehran on the ground that Savak agents had taken refuge there and were hiding secret documents.[69] Among the provincial cities which experienced fighting between pro-Shah and pro-Khomeini forces were Abadan, Babol, Mahabad, Kermanshah, Hamadan, Yazd, Mashhad and Tabriz. In fact, whereas by 14 February Tehran fell under the full control of the revolutionaries, Tabriz was then in the throes of fighting between the rival sides. It was only on 16 February that the royalists finally conceded defeat there.

With this, an era came to an end in Iran and the region.

The downfall of the Shah: an analysis

In the conflict between royalists and revolutionaries both sides suffered heavily. Between the police firings on the Qom theological students in January 1978 and the Shah's downfall in February 1979, the anti-royalists lost 10,000 to 40,000 lives.[70] During that period the Iranian army's strength fell from nearly 300,000 to a little over 100,000, mainly due to desertions. Months of civil unrest and strikes severely crippled the economy. Yet the Shah gave up only in extremis. If the revolutionaries had not been led by someone as astute and steadfast as Ayatollah Khomeini, they would most likely have failed to overthrow the Pahlavi dynasty. It is still hard to believe that the region's most powerful monarch, backed by a loyal military force of over 400,000 was dethroned by a movement of ordinary, unarmed citizens.[71]

Personal reasons partly explained why the Shah did not end his liberalisation policies in the face of rising protest. In early 1978 he learnt from his French doctors that he had cancer and that it was well-advanced. As Reza Cyrus was then a minor, it was decided to groom Shahbanu Farah Diba as the future ruler.[72] Since she could not be expected to be as autocratic as her husband, it was best to continue the liberalisation process begun earlier. Out of this overall strategy came the decision to appoint Sharif-Emami as the premier in late August, to conciliate the Shah's most powerful adversaries: the ulema.

America backed this move. The Carter administration believed that political and economic reform was overdue in Iran, and felt that though it would be accompanied by some turmoil, the net effect would be to secure the future of the Peacock Throne.

Such thinking overlooked two major problems. By late August the anti-Shah movement had progressed to a point where its demands were well ahead of what the monarch could be expected to concede. Secondly, the adverse effects of the Shah's overambitious military and economic plans, initiated in the early 1970s, had reached a stage where these could not be eliminated except by throwing out the very regime which had launched them.

Between 1972 and 1978, the military budget jumped from $1,375 million to $9,940 million, and amounted to a quarter of the national budget.[73] During that period Iran placed $20,000 worth of arms contracts with American companies. Kickbacks were an accepted and established practice on such deals. The size of the kickbacks can be gauged by the fact that a modest contract for British Chieftain tanks in 1971 had netted a commission of £1 million ($2 million at the current rate of exchange) to an eminent Iranian.[74] In addition there were military contracts being awarded at home. These yielded handsome fortunes to the top military brass. Foreign and domestic contracts were the chief sources of the funds sent abroad by the military leaders mentioned earlier.[75]

With the economic development projects running at $12.6 billion in 1977-8,[76] there were immense opportunities for kickbacks for influential royals and politicians, and senior civil servants. Then there were state-run agencies importing wheat, sugar and tea. Finally there was the state-owned National Iranian Oil Company doing an annual business of $18 billion to $21 billion.

The Shah was at the apex of a hierarchy of parasites fattening themselves off the Iranian economy. He was followed by lesser Pahlavis and their relatives, a total of some sixty-five families. Of the $2,000 million exported annually during the period 1973-8 half of it belonged to the Pahlavis.[77] The Pahlavi Foundation, set up by the Shah in 1958 as a charity organisation out of the sale of crown lands to the tenants, came in handy to the Pahlavis as a means of funnelling their funds out of Iran.

Initially the Foundation had concentrated on running hospitals, orphanages and youth centres, and financing the education of Iranian students abroad. Later, however, it controlled the country's fifth largest bank – Omran Bank – and through it, lucrative real estate, hotels, casinos and holiday resorts. In 1978 its assets amounted to $3,200 million. Over the years it became a powerful economic weapon

in the hands of the Shah, its chief custodian. Through it he could buy
off those who spoke out against him and reward those who had done
his bidding without getting the state machinery involved. And it
provided him with a vehicle to portray himself as a generous,
charitable ruler. But as the protest movement gathered momentum,
this veneer wore off, and the Pahlavi Foundation became more a
political liability to the monarch than an asset.

Ultimately, therefore, the Shah had to depend on the state's
repressive agencies – Savak, police and military – to maintain himself
in power. With some 60,000 people working for Savak, full time and
part time,[78] Savak was effective. Its ruthlessness was well documented
by the International Commission of Jurists inquiry in 1977. The ICJ's
interviews with 3,087 prisoners showed that 90 per cent of them had
been beaten, 80 per cent whipped with rods or cables, more than half
burned with cigarettes, and up to 40 per cent seared with hot rods.[79]
But once the Pahlavi ruler had allowed such an inquiry to be
conducted, and had combined it with an end to secret trials for
political dissidents by military courts, the fear of Savak waned.

Later, as the protest movement escalated, religious speakers at the
fortieth day memorials for the dead delivered fiery anti-Shah speeches
before congregations which included Savak agents. These officials
dared not arrest the offenders while the ceremonies lasted. And, once
the congregation dispersed, the offending speakers melted into the
protective crowd. Repeated failure of Savak officials to arrest and
prosecute the anti-Shah speakers discredited the once-feared political
police. A final blow came in September 1978, when the newly
appointed premier, Sharif-Emami, purged Savak of thirty-four top
officials. This severely demoralised Savak personnel.

As the crisis deepened, the Shah was left with only the military to
crush the challenge to his authority. However, the task of quelling
street rioting could only be assigned to the infantry, a section of the
army which derived half of its strength from conscripts. Unlike
professionals, conscripts had no loyalty to their units. Also, being
young, they were more susceptible to Khomeini's appeals not to shoot
the demonstrators, the majority of whom were often young. The
conscripts' faith in their commanders plummeted when it was revealed
in mid-September 1978 that they had been transferring vast sums
abroad.

Among the sections of the army made up wholly of professionals,
the Imperial Guards and the paratroopers were pre-eminent. In case of
the ultimate challenge to the Shah, they were expected to fight for the
Peacock Throne, and overpower other sections of the army, if need
be. This was also expected of the air force personnel. The air force,
which had expanded rapidly, was about 100,000 strong in 1977. It split

into two factions: non-commissioned homafars and young air cadets on one side and senior ranks on the other. This happened partly because the revolutionary movement had gone on for so long and so intensely that it had permeated all but the senior ranks of the force, and partly because of the ubiquitous presence of American advisers in the force, which caused much resentment among young Iranians.

What is more, the methods and systems used by the Shah to maintain a tight control over the military worked against his interests once he had left the country in mid-January. To obviate any chance of a military coup against him, the Shah had banned a meeting of two or more generals, and instituted a command structure which excluded any coordinated action by the generals. Aware of the elaborate system of informers working under the direction of the special J2 Department, the generals had strictly obeyed the rule about meetings with their colleagues. Now, with the Shah gone, they were unable to work together partly because they had never done so before, and partly because they lacked a command structure to do so. Despite the frantic efforts of General Huyser of the US military, the Iranian generals failed to produce and implement a unified strategy to forestall Khomeini.

As for the Shah's own tactics of dealing with his adversaries, he acted erratically – hitting them with an iron fist one day and offering them an olive branch the next. His vacillation contrasted with the decisiveness he had displayed during the past crises in October 1946 (the Azerbaijan crisis), July 1952 (the oil nationalisation movement), August 1953 (the Mussadiq government), July 1962 (the Ali Amini government), and June 1963 (the confrontation with Khomeini). But the Shah had been decisive only when he had had the unequivocal backing of the military at home and the US government abroad. This time military leaders were unhesitatingly behind him. But the Carter administration in Washington was divided. One faction led by the national security adviser, Zbigniew Brzezinski, urged tough action against the opposition while the other, led by secretary of state, Cyrus Vance, advised compromise.

Some totally unexpected events worked against the Shah. A prime example was the mysterious fire in an Abadan cinema house. It took him by surprise; and there was nothing in his vast armoury he could use to counter its adverse effect on his regime. He also showed poor judgement. He thought that by getting Khomeini away from Iraq he would lessen his impact on the Iranian people. He gave a tacit nod of approval to the French president, Valéry Giscard d'Estaing, before the latter admitted Khomeini to France. Judging by the international publicity that Khomeini received in Paris, the Shah realised that he had blundered. But by then it was too late.

In any case the Shah faced a situation which strongly disfavoured him. Both objective and subjective factors favoured the opposition. By the time the banner of protest was raised in early 1977, the Shah's policies had alienated all but the top elite. The longstanding alienation of bazaaris and the ulema from the Pahlavi regime had been made worse by the monarch's onslaughts on their economic and social standing. The professionals and intellectuals resented their exclusion from the decision-making apparatus of the regime. This was particularly true of those Iranians who had been educated in European and American universities during the radical years of the late 1960s and early 1970s.

Since their timid trade unions were controlled by Savak, and strikes banned, industrial workers blamed the Court for their accumulating grievances. To this rising discontent was added the rootlessness and impatience of the vastly enlarged sub-proletariat. They had all heard of the billions of dollars that Iran was earning by exporting oil, and they knew of the luxurious life-style of the elite that this wealth supported; but they had seen very little of it themselves. The anger and impatience was all the more among the young. With nearly two-thirds of Iranians being under thirty in the mid-1970s, the young were in a clear majority. They had no memory of the August 1953 coup, and only a vague notion of the Shah's brutality in suppressing the June 1963 uprising. As such they were not inhibited from challenging the Pahlavis.

Initially, these disparate classes lacked both a common objective and a charismatic leader around whom they could all unite. But as the protest movement, initiated by intellectuals and professionals, gathered pace, Ayatollah Khomeini emerged as the undisputed leader of the anti-Shah forces. Khomeini had vocally and consistently opposed the Shah since the deaths of Ayatollahs Borujerdi and Kashani in the early 1960s. His exile was a living proof of this. Two of Khomeini's personal characteristics endeared him to the Iranian people: his spartan style of life and his refusal to compromise. He had no worldly possessions. He led an austere existence, eating simply, sleeping on the floor, and saying his prayers without fail. 'Khomeini . . . acted like a "man of God" who sought not worldly power but spiritual authority', states Ervand Abrahamian, an American specialist on Iran. 'Similarly, in a decade notorious for cynical, bland, corrupt, defeatist, and inconsistent politicians, Khomeini appeared to be thoroughly sincere, defiant, dynamic, consistent and most important of all, incorruptible.'[80]

Khomeini made astute use of Shia history and Iranian nationalism to engender and encourage anti-royalist militancy not only among the bazaaris and the ulema but also the urban underclass. The February

1978 upheaval in Tabriz, caused chiefly by the sub-proletariat, coming soon after the turmoil in Qom, showed that his tactic was working. In this way Khomeini also outmanoeuvred such moderate clerical leaders as Shariatmadari who wanted only a return to constitutional monarchy.

The Islamic leftists, such as the Mujahedin-e Khalq, were already committed to a revolutionary overthrow of the Pahlavis. So too were the Marxist-Leninist Fedai Khalq. Later, even the cautious Tudeh leaders adopted this programme.

As for such non-Marxist laymen as Mahdi Bazargan and Karim Sanjabi, it was left to Khomeini to draw them into the revolutionary column. During his meeting with Khomeini in Paris in late October 1978, Bazargan told the Ayatollah that he did not want revolution. 'The people are not ready to cope with freedom,' Bazargan argued. 'They must be accustomed to it by teaching them to develop politically, by seizing power in small steps – first education, then the press, then the magistracy, then the economy, and then the army.' Khomeini disagreed. 'No gradualism, no waiting. We must not lose a day, not a minute. The people demand an immediate revolution.'[81] Like many great revolutionary leaders before him, Khomeini had his finger on the pulse of the masses. He also had a shrewd sense of timing.

Ayatollah Khomeini had the sagacity and charisma to unite all the disparate forces along the most radical demand: dethronement of the Shah. He kept the alliance together through a turbulent period by championing the causes of each of the groups in the anti-Shah coalition, and by maintaining a studied silence on such controversial issues as democracy, agrarian reform, the ulema's role in the future Islamic republic, and the status of women. He aroused hopes of deliverance and improvement in different strata of society. The traditional middle classes saw in Khomeini an upholder of private property, a partisan of the bazaar, and a believer in Islamic values. The modern middle classes regarded Khomeini as a radical nationalist wedded to the programme adopted earlier by Mussadiq: ending royal dictatorship and foreign influence in Iran. The urban working class backed Khomeini because of his repeated commitment to social justice which, it felt, could only be achieved by transferring power and wealth from the affluent to the needy. Finally, the rural poor saw the Ayatollah as their saviour: the one to provide them with arable land, irrigation facilities, roads, schools and electricity.

Actually Khomeini did more than merely hold the anti-Shah movement together. He helped to create ever-increasing popular upsurge to push it forward in greater and higher tides. He did so by making consistent use of the fortieth day mourning of the martyrs, by using the month of Ramadan to charge the nation with revolutionary fervour, and finally by transforming the traditional Ashura processions into demonstrations for the revolution. With the aid of the re-enactment of the passion plays of the early days of Islam, he helped to create a revolutionary play of modern times. This was a unique phenomenon.

The Ayatollah's other outstanding contribution to the history of revolutions lay in devising and implementing an original set of strategy and tactics to neutralise the Pahlavi's powerful military. Khomeini was aware of the strategy favoured by the Mujahedin-e Khalq and the Fedai Khalq: guerrilla attacks on selected targets to lead to increased repression which would arouse the masses to participate in an armed struggle against the regime. Khomeini disagreed with this, arguing that if people were to wage an armed struggle against the military, this would create 'a chain of revenge'. Bloodshed would make the army close ranks, and stand by the Pahlavis. He therefore chose the strategy of 'moral attack' on the army. 'We must fight the army from within,' he said. 'We must fight from within the soldiers' hearts. Face the soldier with a flower. Fight through martyrdom, because the martyr is the essence of history. Let the army kill as many as it wants, until the soldiers are shaken to their hearts by the massacres they have committed. Then the army will collapse, and thus you will have disarmed the army.'[82] Such an advice appealed to the martyr complex that lies deeply embedded in the psyche of Shia Iran. At the same time he warned the soldiers that if they fired at their brothers and sisters 'it is just as though you are firing at the Quran'.[83] Since these words came from a grand ayatollah, a marja-e taqlid, and since most of the troops were Shia, they were effective. In short, Khomeini devised revolutionary tactics which stemmed from the specific religio-cultural environment of Shia Iran.

The mosque played a crucial part in the revolution, both as an institution and as a place of prayer and congregation. Since it was impractical for the state to regularly suppress the mosque, it offered opportunities to the revolutionaries that no other place did. Khomeini knew this, and used it. He urged the ulema to base local Revolutionary Komitehs in mosques. He thus created an institution which proved invaluable during the last, crucial months of the revolutionary movement. Of all the spontaneous or directed revolutionary bodies that sprouted during the final stage of the revolution, the Revolutionary Komitehs proved to be the most broad-based and most effective. They were prominent in organising distribution of essential goods, including heating oil, during the last general strike. And they were the ones to take over administrative and police powers, once the Shah had departed. Not surprisingly, they continued to exist long after the Shah's downfall and the founding of the Islamic Republic.

PART II

THE REVOLUTION

THE FOUNDING OF THE ISLAMIC REPUBLIC

Once the revolutionary forces had expelled the Shah and neutralised the military, their unity began to crack. This was inevitable. After all, the various groups within the movement had different visions of what should follow the Shah's overthrow. Militant ulema loyal to Ayatollah Khomeini and their lay allies wanted an Islamic regime of an orthodox mould, led by clerics. Lay Islamic radicals, headed by Mahdi Bazargan in the Liberation Movement, favoured a less rigid model than Khomeini loyalists. Liberal, secular forces, represented by the National Front of Karim Sanjabi, aspired to create social democracy in Iran. The leftist Islamic strand of the movement, dominated by the Mujahedin-e Khalq, wanted to create an egalitarian Islamic society through fusion of Islam and Marxism. Such Marxist-Leninist groups as the Fedai Khalq and the Tudeh visualised the current revolution as a step towards a socialist revolution to follow.

In addition there were regional organisations: the Kurdish Democratic Party in Kurdish areas; the Cultural and Political Society of the Turkoman People in the Turkoman region; the Islamic Unity Party in Baluchistan and Sistan; and the Cultural, Political, and Tribal Organisation of the Arab People in Khuzistan. Since these parties controlled local Revolutionary Komitehs they wielded considerable power. While holding different political views, they were all united on the issue of developing their distinct ethnic, cultural or sectarian identity, and exercising political autonomy at provincial level.

A salient feature of the immediate post-Pahlavi period was the explosion of freedom that occurred. Having broken the shackles of a long-established authoritarian tyranny, Iranian people were for the first time able to exercise the rights of free speech, assembly and association that they had only dreamt of before. They had had to mount a revolution to attain these rights; and now that they had overthrown the Shah, they wanted to enjoy the fruits of their bloody struggle. The new regime, which had come into existence espousing the cause of freedom, was in sympathy with the prevalent mood. In any case, even if it wanted to curtail basic freedoms, it lacked the necessary machinery to do so.

The regime faced the daunting problems of coping with an ailing economy and producing an effective system of governance. While the final authority was exercised by Khomeini, state power was divided between the government led by Mahdi Bazargan and the Islamic Revolutionary Council headed by Ayatollah Motahhari. In theory, day-to-day administration was to be conducted by the Bazargan government, and formulation of overall policies by the IRC. However, in practice, the division was not so clear-cut. Top civil servants were not always loyal to their ministers, and the cabinet and the IRC shared certain members, including seventy-two-year-old Bazargan.

Mahdi Bazargan had a long and chequered political career. A French-trained engineer, he began teaching at Tehran University in 1941. He was a pioneer in promoting Islamic consciousness among professionals. Later he became a leading member of the Iran Party, a secular nationalist body. When the Iran Party was banded together with two other organisations by Muhammad Mussadiq into the National Front in 1948, Bazargan emerged as a prominent member of the Front. He became the first managing director of the National Iranian Oil Company. With Mussadiq's downfall, Bazargan's star waned. Arrested on charges of 'treason and anti-state activity' in mid-May 1955, Bazargan spent his years in jail until the thaw of 1960-1. After his release he teamed up with Ayatollah Taleqani to form the Liberation Movement of Iran. They saw the organisation as a link between Shiaism and modern political ideas and movements. It was open to both lay and clerical Iranians. Bazargan urged the ulema to participate in politics. This was the main theme of his address to the Second Congress of Islamic Societies in September 1962.[1] He called for a boycott of the referendum on the White Revolution in January 1963, and received a ten-year prison sentence. After his release he stayed out of politics. But as soon as there were faint signs of protest he became active.

The imprisonment of Bazargan in 1963 (and later of Taleqani) did not impair the activities of the Liberation Movement and its sponsored Islamic Student Society in North America and Europe. In North America these bodies were led by Ibrahim Yazdi and Mustapha Chamran, and in France by Sadiq Qutbzadeh and Abol Hassan Bani-Sadr. These leaders were in constant touch with Khomeini during his exile in Najaf. Later, when Khomeini took up residence in a Paris suburb in the autumn of 1978, they became part of his entourage. Yazdi, Qutbzadeh and Bani-Sadr were among the lay members of the Islamic Revolutionary Council appointed by Khomeini in mid-January 1979, and so was Bazargan.

Khomeini's choice of Bazargan as prime minister of the provisional Islamic government was shrewd. Bazargan's anti-authoritarian credentials were impeccable. While he was a learned Islamic scholar and an ally of militant ulema, he was himself a layman. All the three deputy premiers that he chose on 12 February – Yazdi, Abbas Amir, Entezam and Muhammad Hashem Sabbaaghian of the National Front – were laymen too. He appointed the moderate Karim Sanjabi as foreign minister, and promised the US embassy that he would ensure the safety of American citizens. All this went down well with modern middle classes at home and Western capitals abroad. At this juncture it was necessary for the fledgling regime to reassure these elements.

But Bazargan lacked charisma and popular appeal. He was also a reluctant revolutionary whose government failed to provide the right combination of firmness and innovation that was needed to tackle the pressing problems. The government needed to recover the 300,000 weapons distributed to young revolutionaries in the capital between 9 and 11 February, establish a new security organisation which excluded former Savak employees and which elicited popular cooperation, overhaul the judicial system to suit the new conditions, punish those found guilty of perpetrating massacres during the pre-revolutionary turmoil, and purge royalist elements from the military, civil service, oil industry and the media.

Appeals by Bazargan and Khomeini to armed citizens to surrender their weapons, acquired by them during the monarchy's last days, yielded poor results. For tactical and ideological reasons, the secular and Islamic leftist guerrilla organisations refused to give up their arms. The Fedai Khalq openly rejected the call saying that it was their 'duty to safeguard the revolution'. Khomeini called them 'a group of bandits and unlawful elements'.[2] On 22 February the Fedai announced plans for a peaceful march to Khomeini's headquarters the next day to present him with a set of demands during a private meeting. Khomeini described them as 'non-Muslims at war with Islam' and their march as being 'against the Sharia'. He added, 'I'll not permit these opportunists to come to my house'.[3]

In the event the Fedai held a rally at the Tehran University campus. It drew a predominantly middle class audience of 70,000. While describing him as a great anti-imperialist fighter, the Fedai speakers called on Khomeini to reveal the names of the Islamic Revolutionary Council members, and to replace secret trials by the revolutionary courts (set up by Khomeini) with open trials by the people's courts in order to inform and educate the masses. The resolution passed at the rally demanded that all the classes and sections of Iranian society who had participated in the revolution must now have a voice in the running of the state. 'Such participation is not possible without the setting up of workers' cells in factories, barracks and offices,' it said.[4]

Of course Khomeini had no intention of leading Iran towards a Marxist socialist state. Nor did he sympathise with those who wanted a democratic Iran along Western lines. 'Democracy is another word for usurpation of God's authority to rule,' he declared on his return to Qom on 1 March.

Four days later half a million people assembled to commemorate the anniversary of the death of Muhammad Mussadiq in his home town of Ahmedabad, sixty miles south-west of Tehran. The rally, addressed among others by National Front leaders, resolved to form the National Democratic Front open to 'all groups and people believing in a democratic and anti-imperialist struggle', and appointed a commission of eight under the chairmanship of Hedayatollah Matine-Daftari, a grandson of Mussadiq, to accomplish the task.[5]

Later ten groups, including the National Front (now functioning as the Union of National Front Forces), joined the National Democratic Front. Since none of them believed in an armed struggle, their members had no weapons to surrender to the authorities. Those who decided to give up their arms did so to local mosques, which worked in conjunction with about a thousand Revolutionary Komitehs in the country, being assisted by a medley of poorly organised militias. Some of the Komitehs in Tehran and elsewhere held prominent military and civilian members of the ancien régime. In an atmosphere charged with daily tales of Savak torture and brutality by the thousands of recently released prisoners, there were popular demands for the execution of the eminent figures of the past.

Khomeini had acted swiftly to set up a secret Islamic revolutionary court in Tehran. On 15 February it handed out death sentences to Generals Nematollah Nasseri, Mahdi Rahimi, Manuchehr Khosrowdad and Reza Naji. Five days later it ordered the execution of four more generals, including Parvez Amin Afshar of the Imperial Guards. Soon after came the execution of Captain Munir Taheri held responsible for the deaths caused by fire at Abadan's Rex Cinema. Capital punishment was awarded according to the Sharia for the Islamic crimes of 'causing corruption on earth' and 'fighting Allah'. Protests were voiced about summary executions at home and abroad. Replying to these, Hojatalislam Muhammad Reza Mahdavi-Kani, the IRC member in charge of the Revolutionary Komitehs, said: 'We must purify society in order to renew it'.[6]

Revolutionary courts functioned outside the jurisdiction of the justice ministry, which had itself been directed by Khomeini to expedite its decisions and abolish the appeals system. Despite private protests by Bazargan and Taleqani, Khomeini allowed summary executions to continue until the middle of March, when their number had reached sixty-eight. He did this partly to satisfy the popular demand for revenge against the past tyrants, partly to make a dramatic break with the slow, graft-ridden process of justice of the monarchical period, and partly to abort a genuine threat of a coup by former military and Savak officers.

On 16 March Khomeini halted summary trials until procedures for revolutionary justice had been promulgated, and said that future trials would be held under the direct supervision of the IRC and the provisional government. Three weeks later he issued a decree which outlined the basic rules of revolutionary justice. These precluded the use of lawyers by defendants. In mid-May Khomeini ruled that the death sentence was to be given only to those who had murdered or given orders to kill.[7]

Within a few days of his return to Qom, Khomeini ordered the formation of the Mustazafin Foundation to consolidate the properties of the Pahlavis and the assets accumulated by others through improper means, and to use the income from these for the welfare of the mustazafin (deprived). Khomeini himself directed the purging of the uppermost ranks of the military and the civil service. During his exile in Paris he had been briefed by General Faridun Jam[8] about the loyalties of individual generals and their immediate subordinates. This helped Khomeini to quickly fill in the vacancies left by the removal of most of the top layer of military hierarchy with pro-Islamic officers. He did the same with senior civil servants.

The Ayatollah left the task of purging the intermediate and lower levels of military and civilian bureaucracies to the IRC and the government. However the IRC was better placed to act than cabinet ministers. Since IRC members had an exclusive access to Savak files they held an immense power over middle rank civil servants. This gave an advantage to the IRC over the government.

Also, the IRC commanded exclusive loyalties of two powerful revolutionary organisations: Komitehs and courts. In March 1979 the IRC was said to have thirteen members, seven of them clerics: Ayatollahs Taleqani, Beheshti, Motahhari and Abdul Karim Mousavi-Ardebili; and Hojatalislams Hashemi-Rafsanjani, Mahdavi-Kani and Muhammad Javed Bahonar. Its six lay members were: Bazargan, Bani-Sadr, Qutbzadeh, Yazdi, Yadollah Sahabi and Ali Akbar Moinfar. The IRC was led by Motahhari.

It soon became obvious that Khomeini favoured the IRC. On 7 March he publicly described the provisional government as 'weak'. As such, the IRC came to exercise legislative, executive and judicial powers. Either independently, or in coordination with the cabinet, it introduced legislation. It supervised the judicial system. Furthermore, directed by Khomeini to produce a draft constitution, the IRC appointed a committee of experts to do so. The Committee was headed by Beheshti.

Since Khomeini had in his edict of 5 February instructed the Bazargan government to hold a referendum on the issue of 'changing the political system of the country to an Islamic Republic', public debate centred around the wording of the question to be placed before voters, and the exact title of the republic. Khomeini summarily dismissed the suggestion of 'People's Democratic Republic' made by the Fedai Khalq. He also rejected the title 'Democratic Islamic Republic' favoured by the National Democratic Front and most of the regional parties. 'Do not use this word "democratic",' he said, addressing the theological students of Qom. 'That is a Western idea. We respect Western civilisation, but will not follow it.'[9]

The question on the ballot paper read, 'Should Iran be an Islamic Republic?'. Therefore the National Democratic Front, the Fedai, and most of the regional parties boycotted the referendum. But the impact of their decision was nullified by two moves made by the regime: lowering of the voting age from eighteen to sixteen, thus enfranchising hundreds of thousands of youthful demonstrators of the past year; and extending the voting period from one day to two days. Official figures put the voter turnout on 30 and 31 March at 89 per cent. Polling was particularly heavy in urban working class districts. Given the religious eminence of Khomeini, there was widespread feeling among the faithful that failure to vote for the Islamic Republic would mean being branded infidel.[10] Since the identity card of a person using his vote was stamped, a non-participant was easy to spot. According to the government, 98.2 per cent of the 20,251,000 voters said 'Yes' to the Islamic Republic. The Ayatollah declared 1 April as 'the first day of the Government of God'.

When Khomeini saw the results of the referendum, he considered offering the draft constitution to voters on a simple 'Yes/No' basis, thus skipping the intermediate step of an elected constituent assembly debating the document and approving it: something he had promised in his 13 January 1979 statement. Ayatollah Shariatmadari disagreed with this, arguing that such a complex document as the constitution needed to be thoroughly examined by an elected body of experts.

Following many postponements the draft constitution was leaked to the press by the Islamic Revolutionary Council on 28 April. (The constitution will be discussed later.) It led to a free and spirited debate. Such a reaction led Khomeini to reconsider the idea of a large elected constituent assembly. He now favoured a smaller consultative assembly to be nominated by him. Other clerical leaders argued for the original proposal of a representative constituent assembly. Yadollah Sahabi, minister for constitutional transition, intervened. With his aid, consensus grew around the concept of a smaller constituent assembly to be called the Assembly of Experts (Khabrigan). Its seventy-three members (each representing half a million people) were to study the draft constitution, as well as all the amendments that had been submitted, and produce the final version for vote in a referendum. The elections to the Assembly of Experts were scheduled for early August.

By the time this vote was held, Khomeinists were able to field candidates of their own political party – the Islamic Republican Party – and canvass support for them in their own newspaper, the *Jumhouri-ye Islami* (Islamic Republic). In fact the party had been established within a month of the revolution, and the paper some weeks later.

The party was founded by Ayatollahs Beheshti, Mousavi-Ardebili and Bahonar, and Hojatalislams Hashemi-Rafsanjani and Ali Hussein Khamanei. Its manifesto stated that the main problem was to guard the revolution and foil counter-revolutionary attempts to reinstitute the Pahlavi dynasty. Open to all those who believed in the Islamic revolution, the party aimed to infuse Islamic principles into political, economic, cultural and military spheres of society. This could be achieved by purging society of the symptoms of the royal dictatorship and colonialism of the past; establishing basic human freedoms of speech, publication and association; transforming corrupt bureaucracy into an honest civil service; ending economic dependence on foreigners and their plunder of Iran's natural resources; and changing the educational system. The party wanted the army to defend the country and not be used as an instrument for suppressing the nation. The basic unit of the party organisation was to be a cell, consisting of fifteen active cadres. A congress of the party delegates would meet biennially to elect all of the thirty members of the central committee, the party's highest executive arm.[11]

Aside from recruiting individual members, the founders encouraged the Islamic Associations – that had been formed in factories, offices, educational institutions and military bases – to affiliate to the Islamic Republic Party. Also they tried to get the IRP members at Qom and Mashhad theological colleges posted as Friday prayer leaders in villages and small towns, thus helping the party to extend itself throughout Iran.

While some of the IRC's clerical members were busy setting up a political party on a national scale, two of its lay members – Yazdi and Qutbzadeh – concentrated on encouraging three small Islamic militias to amalgamate into a single unit, to be called the Mujahedin of the Islamic Revolution. Thus they helped to create a single force of 6,000 armed men.[12] Khomeini backed the idea of a centralised, anti-leftist militia. On 6 May he issued an order to establish the Islamic Revolutionary Guards (Pasdaran-e Inqilab-e Islami), a special force responsible to the Central Revolutionary Komiteh, 'to protect the Islamic revolution'. He appointed Ayatollah Hassan Lahouti as the head of the new organisation. The Islamic Revolutionary Guards Corps was officially formed on 16 June. Armed with sub-machine guns, the IRG guarded key offices and leaders, monitored the activities of the leftists and liberals, and broke up demonstrations and strikes. They also kept watch on army barracks and police stations, and strove to prevent sabotage, particularly in border areas.

Initially the various Islamic militias had some Mujahedin-e Khalq adherents in their ranks. But they were steadily eased out. The hard core of these militias – and later of the IRG – was composed mainly of a few hundred Islamic militants who had received military training in the Palestine Liberation Organisation camps in the Shia-dominated south Lebanon. Fresh recruits came chiefly from those youths who had been active in the anti-Shah demonstrations. The example of sixteen-year-old Hamid from east Tehran was typical. A few days after his school closed in late October 1977, he and some friends went to the Tehran University campus. They found it locked, but managed to break in. That day soldiers shot and killed fifty-four Tehran University students. After that Hamid went to many demonstrations. When the crisis grew more serious, he found himself taken to an air force base. 'They gave me a gun and told me to shoot at the tanks' driving mirrors,' he said. 'Someone showed me how to do it. . . . There were a lot of us shooting at the same time. After the fighting was over, I became a revolutionary guard in my area.'[13]

A typical revolutionary guard came from a lower middle class or poor urban family, and was totally dedicated to Khomeini and the Islamic revolution. 'The Islamic Revolutionary Guards are a people's militia,' said Sadiq Tabatabai, a deputy premier. 'They are not completely under the control of the [Bazargan] government, but they remain the guardians of the opinion of the majority. . . . They are necessary. The people don't as yet trust the army fully.'[14]

Indeed most observers saw revolutionary guards as a counter-force to army troops often led by officers whose loyalty to the Islamic republic was suspect. At the same time the revolutionary regime found itself beleagured by the actions of dissidents agitating for the acceptance of their ethnic, political or economic demands. The only effective way Islamic leaders could successfully confront their adversaries was by expanding and strengthing the IRG. And they did.

All in all, within the first six months of its existence, the Islamic regime set up new institutions in the administrative, political, judicial, economic and security fields of the polity: the Revolutionary Komitehs, the Islamic Republican Party, revolutionary courts, the Mustazafin Foundation, and the Islamic Revolutionary Guards. It also conducted a referendum on the country's political system and held elections to the Assembly of Experts to produce a constitution.

Ethnic rebellions and other problems

Regional nationalists were the first to challenge the new regime's authority. They were the strongest in Kurdish areas in north-west Iran. The three million Kurds there were more numerous than the other national minorities taken together: 1.5 million Baluchis in the south-east, over half a million Arabs in the south-west, and nearly 300,000 Turkomans in the north-east. About a third of the Kurds lived in Kurdistan province, with the rest concentrated in West Azerbaijan, Kermanshahan and East Azerbaijan.

As descendants of the Indo-European tribes that settled in south-eastern Turkey, north-western Iran, and north-eastern Iraq, Kurds trace their distinct history as mountain people to the seventh century BC. It was not until fourteen centuries later that they embraced Islam. Like Persians they retained their language, but unlike them they remained Sunni in their beliefs. During the Second World War, the Kurdish region was occupied by Soviet troops. In early 1945 Kurdish nationalists formed the Democratic Party of Kurdistan, commonly known as the Kurdish Democratic Party. It formed the Kurdish People's Republic of Mahabad in December. The republic lasted a year before being overthrown by the forces sent by Tehran. The KDP was outlawed, but never fully destroyed. On the whole the left-leaning Kurds were against the Shah. They participated actively in the revolutionary movement. During that period local power was seized by the Revolutionary Komitehs, composed of the members of the KDP and the followers of Shaikh Izz al-Din Husseini, a popular Sunni religious leader, based in Mahabad. A similar situation arose in most of the Kurdish districts of the adjoining three provinces, especially West Azerbaijan, where Kurds lived in uneasy rivalry with the Azeri-speaking Turks.

After the revolution, when the central government tried to establish control in Kurdish areas, it encountered resistance. On 21 February Shaikh Husseini sent a list of demands to Premier Bazargan. It included the formation of a regional Kurdish government, with control over all internal matters, declaration of Kurdish as an official language along with Persian, and use of local Kurdish fighters (known as Peshmargas) as the internal security force. He received no reply from Tehran.

On 18 March fighting broke out between Kurdish nationalists and central forces in Sanandaj, the capital of Kurdistan. Abdul Rahman Qassemlou, the KDP leader – who had during the last days of his exile in France conferred with Khomeini in Paris – rushed to Qom to see the Ayatollah. Following this meeting, Khomeini despatched Ayatollah Taleqani to Sanandaj to bring about a ceasefire and confer with Kurdish leaders. A ceasefire came into effect on 23 March. Two days later Ibrahim Yunisi, a Kurd, was appointed the province's governor-general. Taleqani reportedly conceded the idea of regional autonomy to Kurdish leaders, but on his return to Qom he failed to gain Khomeini's concurrence.

Taleqani was soon sent on a similar mission to the Turkoman area. On 27 March fighting erupted between Turkoman partisans and central troops in Gonbad-e Kavus. Like their Kurdish counterparts, Turkoman nationalists demanded regional autonomy. Despite Taleqani's intervention and Bazargan's assurance that the constitution-makers would pay special attention to ethnic minorities, a ceasefire did not come into effect until 2 April.

Later that month a KDP meeting in Naqadeh, West Azerbaijan, was attacked by gunmen. This led to clashes between the Kurds and the Azeri-speaking Turks. These lasted three days. There were over 1,000 casualties, and some 12,000 Kurds were made homeless. The central forces sent to the town to restore order sided with the Turks against the Kurds.[15] This created widespread ill-will against the Tehran government among Kurds.

Having failed to persuade Khomeini to concede regional autonomy to national minorities, Taleqani advocated the establishment of elected councils at local, county and provincial levels with powers to deal with social, economic, cultural, educational and health issues. On 10 May he submitted this plan to the committee receiving amendments to the constitution. This divided the Kurds. One faction led by Shaikh Ahmed Muftizadeh, the Friday prayer leader of Sanandaj, accepted Taleqani's proposal as satisfactory while the other faction, led by Shaikh Husseini, rejected it as inadequate. The radicals went on to hold a conference on self-determination in late June in Sanandaj and repeat their autonomist demands. On 13 July Kurdish guerrillas clashed with the Islamic Revolutionary Guards in Marivan, and killed thirteen guards. This was a prelude to widespread fighting which broke out in August and continued for three months.

Other minorities were active too. The Islamic Unity Party in Baluchistan-Sistan demanded regional autonomy, appointment of Baluchs to important provincial posts, and teaching of Baluchi in schools. More importantly, the Arab minority in Khuzistan became restive. In mid-March Arab representatives demanded greater share of oil revenue, priority for Arabs in local jobs, and teaching of Arabic as the first language.[16] Arab aspirations were forcefully articulated by their religious leader, Ayatollah Muhammad Taher Khaqani. He came under pressure from pro-Khomeini elements. On 23 April he threatened to leave the country unless the powers of local Revolutionary Komitehs in Khuzistan were controlled. Three days later 100,000 Arabs in Khorramshahr demonstrated in favour of Khaqani and regional autonomy.

Soon militant Arabs resorted to hit and run attacks on the central forces and oil installations. This caused apprehension and anger in Tehran. On 30 May Arab nationalists staged a demonstration in Khorramshahr. Ahmed Madani, the province's governor-general, ordered troops to fire on the demonstrators. They killed twenty-one to 100 people. Yet demonstrations went on for two more days.[17] Madani's action embarrassed the regime's leading figures. By using troops' firepower to disperse unarmed protestors, Madani had done something which the Shah used to do, and which the leaders of the Islamic regime had specifically ruled out. Troops were to be employed only for external defence, they had promised.

The Khorramshahr incident accelerated the creation of the Islamic Revolutionary Guards: it happened a fortnight later. As a result, when 2,500 Arabs demonstrated in Abadan in July, they were dispersed by thirty armed revolutionary guards, assisted by some 200 men carrying metal bars and sticks.[18]

Those assisting the IRG were Hezbollahis, members of the Hezbollah (Party of Allah). Later, this shadowy organisation was found to have surreptitious links with the Islamic Republican Party. It was to play an important role in the street at crucial moments in the history of the revolution. In addition, another militant Islamic body had become active: the Fedaiyan-e Islam. Following the release of the Fedaiyan-e Islam members during the Shah's last days, the organisation was revived by Hojatalislam Sadiq Khalkhali, a prominent cleric of Qom. Addressing a public rally soon after the revolution, Khalkhali promised death to every member of the Shah's family. Such a task was apparently to be performed by the members of the Fedaiyan-e Islam. On 7 December they probably assassinated Mustapha Shafiq, a nephew of the Shah, in Paris.

Assassination squads were busy on the other side as well. On 23 April General Muhammad Vali Qarani, the Islamic regime's first chief of staff, was killed by three armed men.[19] They were later arrested, and found to be members of the Furqan (Distinction). It was a religious organisation which did not regard the Imams to be infallible, merely inspired leaders, and had a poor opinion of the ulema. It considered Khomeini and other clerical leaders as unworthy of leading an Islamic revolution. In short, it claimed to oppose the present regime from an intensely purist viewpoint.

It claimed a second victim on 1 May: fifty-six-year-old Ayatollah

Motahhari. A widely respected scholar, he was the author of many books. As chairman of the Islamic Revolutionary Council, he was the second most powerful man in the country. His murder shocked Khomeini and the IRC. In an interview with *Le Monde* (The World) of Paris, Khomeini blamed these assassinations on American agents. In so far as the Furqan was formed at the time of the June 1963 uprising by Savak, itself trained by the American CIA,[20] Khomeini's statement was not off the mark.

On 12 May the *Ayandegan* (Future), a liberal newspaper, published Khomeini's interview with *Le Monde*, and a long feature article setting out the Furqan's background and ideology. The article claimed that the organisation was following the line of the late Ali Shariati, an eminent Shia thinker and scholar, to whom public homage was often paid by the regime. Khomeini called the paper 'depraved' and 'unIslamic'. His statement that he would no longer read the *Ayandegan*, and that he expected the faithful to follow suit, was read out on radio and television, and repeated in mosques.

This episode encouraged the IRC and the government to flesh out Article Nineteen of the 1906-7 constitution which guaranteed free press within the framework of the Sharia, and to rationalise the chaotic publishing scene which had emerged in the aftermath of the revolution. Disregarding the licensing law, publishers had taken to bringing out publications without an official permit. As a result, the number of publications had jumped from twenty-five during the Shah's rule to an estimated 225.[21]

The government published a press law in early June, which among other things prescribed three years' imprisonment for insulting a prominent clerical or governmental personality. But it had to postpone the implementation. It encountered opposition from many quarters, including Shariatmadari; it lacked an effective enforcement agency; and it found itself facing a much bigger problem when it released the second draft of the constitution in mid-June.

In the background lay an ailing economy, a result of many months of political upheaval. With the flight of 130,000 local and foreign industrial managers and technicians,[22] hundreds of factories and workshops had closed down or suffered steep falls in production. Shortages of raw materials had bedevilled inexperienced managements. Sometimes, unemployed workers, led by leftists, resorted to demonstrations and sit-ins. Often leftist-dominated workers' councils either took over management functions or bargained forcefully with existing managements on wages and working conditions, resorting sometimes to strikes.

The authorities reacted in a number of ways. They broke up demonstrations and strikes with the aid first of the Mujahedin of

Islamic Revolution and then of the Islamic Revolutionary Guards, dissolved the leftist workers' councils and encouraged the formation of the Islamic Associations, and nationalised the businesses left behind by the departed owners or directors.

However, the government take-over was not to be limited to the abandoned establishments. Premier Bazargan announced on 8 June that the government had acquired twenty-two privately-owned banks.[23] Two more nationalisation decrees issued during the next four weeks applied to fifteen insurance companies, including eight foreign-owned companies, and the factories assembling aircraft and shipping vessel parts, and motor vehicles. All this gave the government a tighter control over the economy, and was in tune with the regime's egalitarian tendencies.

But repairing the economy was still a formidable task. And so far the regime had little to show by way of success in tackling the ethnic discontent in outlying provinces. The most it could do was to hope that the recently established revolutionary organisations would take root and help it to solve urgent problems in the near future by widening and consolidating its popular base. However, the most pressing, and fundamental, need of the hour was drafting and passing an Islamic constitution. Going by the official leaks, it promised to be an original document of its kind.

The constitution

The draft constitution presented to the nation in late April 1979 did not contain the doctrine of Vilayat-e Faqih (Rule of the Faqih), first expounded as a political theory by Khomeini in a series of lectures in 1970, and later published as *Hukumat-e Islami: Vilayat-e Faqih*. Even then, the draft aroused much controversy. Some leading clerics opposed the idea of direct intervention by the ulema in the day-to-day running of the government as specified in the draft. There was also protest by the leaders of ethnic minorities who wanted greater powers for non-Persian speaking regions. The degree of controversy disappointed Khomeini, who had anticipated smooth sailing. The second draft published in mid-June failed to satisfy the critics. Given this, and the unstable conditions existing in the country, IRP leaders decided to keep the doctrine of Vilayat-e Faqih out of the discussion on the constitution. But that did not mean that they had abandoned the idea. They decided that only after they had secured reasonable stability in the country, would they introduce and adopt this crucially important doctrine of Khomeini. Therefore the draft constitution that the constituent assembly, elected in August, met to discuss lacked the concept of Vilayat-e Faqih. It was in the course of the deliberations by the assembly – which was dominated by the IRP – that it was introduced, discussed and adopted.

In his book on the subject Khomeini urges the subordination of political power to Islamic precepts, criteria and objectives, calls on the ulema to bring about an Islamic state and participate in its legislative, executive and judicial organs, and offers a programme of action to establish an Islamic state.

Khomeini describes the movement to reduce Islam to a mere system of ritual and worship as a deviation from the true faith: a development much encouraged by the imperialist West to weaken Muslims and their countries. Since Islam is above all a divine law, Khomeini argues, it needs to be applied as a form of state. Only a government can properly collect the Islamic taxes of khums and zakat and spend them honestly on the needy – as well as enforce Islamic injunctions about the duties of the believer and punishment of the transgressor. 'It is a logical necessity that there must be a government which undertakes to put the [Islamic] rules into practice and to apply all [Islamic] measures absolutely,' he writes.[24]

An Islamic government requires an Islamic ruler. All Muslims agree that an Islamic ruler must be a Just Faqih, religious jurist. He must know the Sharia thoroughly, and must be absolutely just in its application. According to Shias, their Imams possessed these qualifications. In fact, being infallible and superior human beings, they were more than Just Faqihs.

In the absence of an Imam – who has been missing for the past eleven centuries – Muslims must find an alternative to an Imam in order to avoid living in anarchy or under an alien, atheistic government. Although lacking the infallibility and personal superiority of an Imam, a Just Faqih is qualified to head an Islamic state. The Just Faqih is to be assisted by jurisprudents at various levels of legislative, executive and judicial bodies. The function of a popularly elected parliament is to resolve the conflicts that are likely to arise in the implementation of Islamic doctrines. The actual administration is to be carried out by civil servants who are familiar with the laws pertinent to their specific jobs. However, judicial functions are to be performed only by the jurisprudents who are steeped in the knowledge of the Sharia. Such jurisprudents are also to oversee the actions of the legislative and executive branches. The overall supervision and guidance of parliament and the judiciary is to rest with the Just Faqih, who must also ensure that the executive does not exceed its powers. Finally, since the overriding purpose of the Islamic government is to meet the needs of its citizens, jurisprudents must ensure that wealth does not become concentrated in the coffers of a few through their exploitation of human beings or natural resources.

At its simplest, the Vilayat-e Faqih is the rule of the divine law as interpreted and applied by the Just Faqih. Since he does not rule according to his own will, the system is not dictatorial. And, as the position of the Just Faqih is not hereditary, the system is certainly not monarchical.

Since Khomeini visualises people as a political force, the system can be described as republican, but within an Islamic context. 'The great reformist movements in history did not possess power at their inception,' he writes. 'The cadres of the [reformist] movement would draw the attention of the people to oppression and awaken them to the dangers of submitting to the rule of the tyrants, then the people became the active force which sweeps all the obstacles in its way.'[25]

What makes Khomeini's thesis attractive to many Muslims is that it is simple, direct and free of non-Islamic influences. It is derived from the first principles of Islam, and avoids convoluted, hairsplitting religious arguments which leave most religious laymen baffled. Moreover, as Sami Zubaida, a British specialist on Islamic sociology, points out, 'It is conducted exclusively in traditional Islamic discussions with hardly any reference to Western or Western-inspired politico-ideological notions.'[26] There is no reference here to nationalism, democracy or socialism.

During the revolutionary upheaval, Khomeini's aides made a special effort to downgrade the importance of *Hukumat-e Islami*. They thought that to publicise a definite outline of what Khomeini had in mind for the post-Pahlavi Iran would destroy the unity of the disparate anti-Shah forces.

After the revolution, prominent among those who opposed Khomeini's views on an Islamic political system was Ayatollah Shariatmadari. On 24 May Shariatmadari said, 'In Islam there is no provision that the ulema must absolutely intervene in matters of state'. There were only two exceptions to this: if parliament is about to enact a law which contravenes the Sharia, and when there is no leader available to establish order in society. Khomeini declared that those who did not believe in the political leadership of the ulema were enemies of the revolution. 'It is not for the ulema to involve themselves in politics, that is for the government,' replied Shariatmadari. 'We must simply advise the government when what they do is contrary to Islam. . . . It is the duty of the government to govern. There should be no direct interference from spiritual leaders.'[27]

A contemporary of Khomeini, Muhammad Kazem Shariatmadari was born in Tabriz of an Azeri-speaking family. He came to Qom in 1924 a few years after Khomeini had done so. Shariatmadari found himself in tune with the cautious, conservative Ayatollah Borujerdi, and rose steadily in clerical ranks. After Borujerdi's death, Shariatmadari became a grand ayatollah, a development which pleased the Azeri-speaking people, who form about a fifth of the national population. When the ulema came into increasing conflict with the Shah during the latter's implementation of the White Revolution, Shariatmadari joined the anti-Shah protest. At the peak of the strife in June 1963, he was arrested. But this experience did not radicalise him. When the Shah sent him condolences on the death of Ayatollah Hakim in June 1970, Shariatmadari was effusive in declaring his loyalty to the monarch. Later that year, when Qom theological students called a one-day protest strike, he did not join. It was only after the security forces had broken into his theological college in January 1978 and killed two of his students, that he publicly turned against the Shah. But even then he limited his basic demand to a return to the 1906-7 constitution. He tried to calm the situation by advising his followers to keep away from the street demonstrations of 19 June. It was not until after a military government had been installed in early November that Shariatmadari joined the two other grand ayatollahs in Qom to attack 'the tyrannical state apparatus' and call for 'the dismantling of the despotic imperialist system'.[28]

Once the Shah had been overthrown, differences between moderate Shariatmadari and radical Khomeini surfaced almost immediately. When in early February Khomeini described opposition to the provisional Islamic government as apostasy, Shariatmadari said that in his view peaceful criticism or opposition should not be punished.[29] On his return to Qom in March Khomeini paid Shariatmadari a courtesy call. But they continued to disagree. Shariatmadari objected to the wording of the question on Iran's political system, and suggested: 'What kind of political system would you prefer?'.[30] However, he did not carry his objection to the point of boycotting the referendum. He participated, and voted for the Islamic Republic.

Later, during the deliberations of the constituent assembly, Shariatmadari opposed the incorporation of the doctrine of Vilayat-e Faqih into the constitution. He argued that the concept was contentious, with some ulema interpreting it narrowly as guardianship of minors and widows, while others (such as Khomeini) doing so in broad political terms.[31]

But the criticisms of Shariatmadari as well as those of regional autonomists went unheeded before and after the convening of the constituent assembly. The second draft of the constitution, published in mid-June, showed this clearly. In addition, Khomeini seemed intent on dropping the plan for a directly elected constituent assembly. The end result was a deep division within the Islamic camp. This was the first serious crisis of the Islamic Republic. Troubled by this, Ayatollah Golpaygani, the oldest of the four grand ayatollahs resident in Qom, invited the other three – Khomeini, Shariatmadari and Marashi-Najafi – to his residence. After an hour-long meeting on 19 June, they gave a call for national unity and declared that they were united in their resolve to preserve the Islamic Republic. However, on the following Friday, 22 June, a rally held by those who favoured a representative constituent assembly was broken up by Khomeini loyalists.

The next week witnessed intense talks between various parties to find a compromise, with Yadollah Shabi playing a mediatory role. As stated earlier,[32] the crisis ended with an agreement to convene a popularly elected Assembly of Experts to discuss and finalise the constitution. On 30 June the polling date for the elections to the Assembly of Experts was announced. The next day the cabinet met in Qom, with Khomeini presiding. This was done to reassure the people that the regime was united behind the Ayatollah. To bring about better coordination between the government and the Islamic Revolutionary Council, it was decided on 19 July to appoint four IRC members to Bazargan's government: Mahdavi-Kani and Hashemi-Rafsanjani as deputy ministers of interior, Bahonar as deputy minister of education, and Bani-Sadr as deputy minister of economy and finance.

But the situation remained unchanged for those who stood outside the portals of power. Such secular opposition groups as the National Democratic Front, the Fedai Khalq and the Kurdish Democratic Party complained of clerical bias in the screening of candidates for the Experts' Assembly, the shortness of the campaign period, and violent harassment by Khomeinists. Therefore they boycotted the poll.

On the eve of the election, the boycotters were joined by the Muslim People's Republican Party which, associated with Shariatmadari, enjoyed much support among the Azerbaijanis, whether living in East and West Azerbaijan provinces or outside. But the MPRP's decision was taken so near the polling day, 3 August, that its leader, Rahmatollah Moqadem-Maraghehi, found himself elected a member from East Azerbaijan. So too did Qassemlou of the KDP, from West Azerbaijan. About eleven million people voted to elect seventy-three representatives to the Assembly, including a member each from the Christian, Zoroastrian and Jewish communities.

The Assembly met on 19 August, and immediately declared Qassemlou's election as null and void. Of the seventy-two experts, forty-five were clerics. Thirty-six of them were either members of the Islamic Republican Party or were in sympathy with it. Of the twenty-seven lay experts, eleven belonged to the IRP or were sympathetic to it. Thus two-thirds of the experts were with the IRP, actively or passively. The Assembly elected Ayatollah Montazeri, a one time student of Khomeini, as its president, and Ayatollah Beheshti, the IRP's general secretary, as its deputy president. It finished its job on 15 November. When the constitution was put to a referendum on 2 and 3 December, it won 99.5 per cent of the 15,785,956 votes cast.

Divided into twelve chapters, the constitution contains 175 principles. The constitution-makers left intact the doctrine of the Vilayat-e Faqih. But they conceded the demand of the predominantly Sunni Kurds, Baluchs and Arabs that non-Shia sects be officially put on par with Twelver Shiaism. They allowed the use of regional languages in the media and their teaching in schools. They also made a token compromise on the question of decentralisation of political power as demanded by many regional autonomists.

'The official religion of Iran is Islam and the Twelver Jaafari school of thought; and this principle shall remain eternally immutable,' states Principle Twelve. 'Other Islamic schools of thought including the Hanafi, Shafei, Maliki, Hanbali and Zaidi schools, are to be accorded full respect, and their followers are free to act in accordance with their own jurisprudence in performing their religious devotions. These schools enjoy official status for the purposes of religious education and matters of personal status. . . . In areas where Muslims following one of these schools of thought constitute the majority, local regulations within the bounds of the jurisdiction of local councils, are to be in accordance with the respective schools.'[33]

Principle Two describes the Islamic Republic as 'a system based on the belief in . . . religious leadership and continuous guidance, and its fundamental role in the permanency of Islam's Revolution'. Principle Five states that in the absence of Hazrat Vali Asr (Lord of the Age, the missing Twelfth Imam). 'the governance and leadership of the nation devolve upon the just and pious faqih who is acquainted with the circumstances of his age; courageous, resourceful, and possessed of administrative ability; and recognised and accepted as leader by the majority of the people'. The duties and powers of the Leader are listed in Principle 110. As the commander-in-chief of all armed forces, and the head of the Supreme Defence Council, he has the authority to appoint or dismiss the chief of the general staff and the commanders of the military's three branches as well as the Islamic Revolutionary Guards Corps, and declare war or peace. He has the authority to approve presidential candidates, and appoint the president on his election, or dismiss him after the supreme court has found him politically incompetent and in violation of his duties towards the Majlis, the National Consultative Assembly.[34] He has the right to appoint 'the highest judicial authorities' and the Islamic jurists on the Council of Guardians, which vets all legislation passed by the Majlis.

In short, the Leader is a cross between the head of state and the chief justice.

The procedure to find a successor, or successors, to Khomeini – who is specifically named in Principle One as 'Grand Ayatollah Imam Khomeini' – is outlined in Principle 107. 'Experts elected by the people will review and consult among themselves concerning all persons qualified to act as marja-e taqlid and leader,' it states. 'If they discern outstanding capacity for leadership in a certain marja-e taqlid, they will present him to the people as their leader; if not, they will appoint three or five marja-e taqlids possessing the necessary qualifications for leadership and present them as members of the Leadership Council.'

On the question of sovereignty – a subject of much controversy in 1906[35] – the Islamic constitution provides a compromise. 'Absolute sovereignty over the world and man belongs to God, and it is He who has placed man in charge of his social destiny,' reads Principle Fifty-six. 'No one can deprive man of this God-given right, nor subordinate it to the interests of a given individual or group. The people exercise this God-given right by the paths specified in the principles below.' After stating that powers of government in the Islamic Republic consist of 'the legislative, the judiciary, and the executive powers', Principle Fifty-seven adds, 'These powers are independent of each other, and communication between them will be ensured by the president of the republic'. That the system must be representative is underlined by Principle Six. It states that 'the affairs of the country must be administered on the basis of public opinion expressed by means of elections, including the election of the president, the representatives of the National Consultative Assembly, and the members of councils, or by means of referendums in [certain] matters'.

Next to the marja-e taqlid and leader, the president (who must be Shia) is the most powerful figure. 'He is responsible for implementing the constitution and organising relationship between the three powers,' states Principle 113. 'He is also the head of the executive power, except for the affairs pertaining directly to the Leader.' Elected directly for a four-year term by an absolute majority of the votes cast, the president is the chief executive who signs and executes the laws passed by the Majlis. He nominates a Majlis deputy as the prime minister; and once his nominee has won the endorsement of the Majlis, he administers the oath of office. He approves cabinet ministers proposed by the premier before they are presented to the Majlis for a vote of confidence.

To ensure that Majlis decisions do not contradict the ordinances of Islam and the constitution, Principle Ninety-one specifies the establishment of a twelve-member Council of the Guardians. Six 'just faqihs, conscious of current needs and the issues of the day' are to be appointed by the Leader or the Leadership Council; and six jurists, specialising in different branches of law, are to be elected by the Majlis from a list of qualified candidates submitted by the Supreme Judicial Council. The tenure of the Guardians Council is six years: but after the (very) first three years, two members of each group will be changed by lottery. (In contrast, the life of the Majlis is four years.) The Majlis must send all its regulations and laws to the Guardians Council. All the guardians vote on a law's compatibility with the constitution, but only the six faqihs do so on its compatibility with Islamic precepts.

The constitution attempts to meet the demand for regional autonomy by offering a multi-tiered system of government. 'In accordance with the command of the Quran contained in the verses "Their affairs are by consultation among them" and "Consult them on affairs", councils and consultative bodies – such as the National Consultative Assembly, the Provincial Councils, and the City, Neighbourhood, Division, and Village Councils – belong to the decision-making and administrative organs of the country', reads Principle Seven. Chapter Seven, consisting of Principles 100 to 106 pertains to the councils below the national level. One of these specifies that elections to the councils are to be held 'according to the principles of national unity, territorial integrity, rule of the Islamic Republic and sovereignty of the central government'. Principle 101 refers to the formation of the Supreme Council of Provinces, composed of representatives from each province, in order to 'prevent discrimination and gain cooperation in planning development and welfare programmes for the provinces'. However, since the constitution did not provide for directly elected provincial assemblies, it failed to meet the main demand of ethnic minorities.

In judiciary, the Supreme Judicial Council is the highest authority. It is on the basis of the standards and criteria laid down by the Supreme Judicial Council that the supreme court is to be established. The head of the supreme court and the prosecutor general must be mujtahids (just, Islamic jurists) well-versed in judicial matters; and they are to be appointed by the Leader in consultation with the supreme court judges. The minister of justice, to be chosen by the prime minister from a list submitted by the Supreme Judicial Council, has the responsibility for 'all the problems concerning relations between the judiciary, the executive and the legislature'. One of the important functions of the judiciary – described as 'an independent power' – listed in Principle 156 is 'restoring public rights and expanding justice and legal freedoms'.

Chapter Three, consisting of twenty-three principles, concerns 'Rights of the People'. Principle Twenty-one guarantees the rights of women 'in all areas according to Islamic standards'. Then follow principles guaranteeing rights to private property, religious freedom, and press freedom. 'Publications and the press are free to present all matters except those that are detrimental to fundamental principles of Islam or the rights of the public', states Principle Twenty-four. 'The formation of political and professional parties, associations and societies, as well as religious societies, whether they be Islamic or pertain to one of the recognised religious minorities, is freely permitted on the condition that they do not violate the principles of independence, freedom, national unity, the criteria of Islam, or the foundation of the Islamic Republic,' reads Principle Twenty-six. 'No one may be prevented from joining these groups or forced to participate in them.'

The right to property is qualified. 'The government has the responsibility of confiscating all wealth resulting from usury, usurpation, bribery, embezzlement, theft, gambling, misuse of endowments, misuse of government contracts and transactions, the sale of uncultivated lands and other categories of land inherently subject to public ownership, the running of houses of ill-repute, and other illicit sources,' states Principle Forty-nine. 'When appropriate, such wealth must be restored to its legitimate owner, and if no such owner can be identified, it must be placed in the public treasury. The application of this principle must be accompanied by due investigation and verification in accordance with the law of Islam and carried out by the government.'

A citizen is guaranteed 'freedom of access' to courts of law. 'Both parties in a dispute have the right in all courts of law to select a lawyer,' reads Principle Thirty-five. 'If they are unable to do so, arrangements must be made to provide them with legal counsel'. Principle Thirty-eight forbids torture, and adds that punishment of those violating the ban 'will be determined by law'. Principle Thirty-five prohibits 'inspection of letters and failure to deliver them, the recording and disclosure of telephone conversations, the disclosure of telegraphic and telex communications or wilful failure to transmit them, wire-tapping, and all forms of covert investigation' except as provided by law.

Taken together, the bill of rights included in the Islamic constitution seemed fairly comprehensive. It was included mainly at the insistence of Ayatollah Taleqani, Yadollah Sahabi (of the Liberation Movement), and Bani-Sadr. Significantly, none of them was a member of the Islamic Republican Party, which dominated the Assembly of Experts. In theory, IRP leaders were not averse to incorporating such rights in the constitution. After all, their own manifesto had committed the party to eradicating all the symptoms of the royal dictatorship and guaranteeing basic human freedoms.[36]

However, making statements of intent was one thing and resolving real crises quite another. While the country prepared for elections to the Assembly of Experts, and while the members of the Assembly were engaged in debating the constitution for three months, events moved fast and in unexpected directions. The task of creating a new order out of the shambles of the old was proving too formidable for those in power. By and large the new leaders lacked experience, either administrative or political. This meant that Khomeini had to become more involved in the running of the government than expected. Before the revolution he had seen his role as an arbiter, intervening only to resolve major crises. He therefore felt no need to stay on in the capital, and left after four weeks there. But such was the magnitude of the problems erupting in quick succession that he had to revise his plans. Soon he became the centre of governmental decision-making. With this, he gave the Islamic regime a style that reflected his personality: militant, firm, persistent and intolerant of opposition.

Khomeini's style of government

Aware of the repression that the people had suffered during the Pahlavi period, Khomeini allowed freedom of expression but only to those who were firmly within the Islamic camp. In fact, on major issues he would let Islamic leaders divide into hardline and moderate camps, and develop their arguments. He would then come down in favour of the hardliners. This pattern can be seen in the way Khomeini tackled the major problems afflicting the Islamic regime: the future of the newly formed revolutionary bodies within and outside the state machinery; the purging of monarchical and unIslamic elements from all state organisations; and relationship with opposition, whether ethnic or ideological, or both. While dealing with immediate problems, Khomeini did not lose sight of the long-term objective of the Islamic revolution: cleansing society of all unIslamic influences of the past.

Soon after Khomeini had formalised the existence of revolutionary courts in early April, the Revolutionary Komitehs came under fire. On 13 April a militia controlled by a Komiteh in Tehran arrested Ayatollah Taleqani's two (leftist) sons and a daughter-in-law. This caused widespread outcry. Taleqani protested, and left Tehran for an undisclosed destination. Foreign minister Karim Sanjabi resigned in protest against the Komitehs' arbitrary behaviour. The arrested persons were released. On 17 April Taleqani announced from his village that he had retired from politics so as 'not to give a chance to dictatorship and despotism to return'.[37] Taleqani's followers held a large rally near the Tehran University campus. The next day the capital witnessed two marches, one in support of Taleqani and the other against him. The Islamic Revolutionary Council issued a statement praising Taleqani, and explaining that Islamic militias were not completely under its control. In Qom Taleqani called on Khomeini. The following day Taleqani said that he accepted Khomeini's leadership and approved of his actions. Khomeini in turn declared that the Revolutionary Komitehs would continue to exist until 'the authority of the [provisional Islamic] government has been established'.[38] In short, in the debate on the Revolutionary Komitehs' future, sparked by the arrests of Taleqani's sons, Khomeini came down firmly in favour of continuing the Komitehs.

As for his relationship with Taleqani, Khomeini repaired it fast, and went on to strengthen it. After Ayatollah Motahhari's murder on 1 May, he (secretly) appointed Taleqani chairman of the IRC. On the eve of Ramadan (in late July), Khomeini named Taleqani the Friday prayer leader of Tehran. Taleqani richly deserved the honours.

Born in 1910 in Taleqan, a village in Mazandaran, Sayyed Mahmoud Taleqani went to Qom's Faiziya seminary in the 1930s. After graduation in 1938, he taught at Sepah Salar theological school in Tehran. The following year he was jailed for six months for delivering anti-Shah lectures – the first of many imprisonments which kept him behind bars for a total of fifteen years. During the oil nationalisation movement he backed Mussadiq. After the 1953 coup he was arrested for having once given shelter to Navab Safavi, the Fedaiyan-e Islam leader. One of the founders of the Liberation Movement of Iran, Taleqani was close to Bazargan. Of his many books, *Kar va Malikiyat dar Islam* (Labour and Property in Islam) was the best known. In it he argued that since God had created the world for human kind, with no intention of dividing up society into exploiting and exploited segments, a classless society is enjoined by Islam. As such, Taleqani was popular with both Islamic and secular leftists. He was known to be close to the Mujahedin-e Khalq, and was arrested in June 1977 on charges of his links with this party. He was tortured. Mounting public pressure during the revolutionary turmoil compelled the Shah to release him in early November 1978. He was one of the original members of the Islamic Revolutionary Council. Soon after the revolution, he became Khomeini's chief trouble-shooter. In terms of popular support, which spanned a wide political spectrum, he was second only to Khomeini. To quote *The Iranian*, a Tehran-based weekly, Taleqani provided 'balance to the political line-up: a factor as important to Khomeini, who could rely on Taleqani to moderate his own harsh statements, as it was to Bazargan'.[39]

Among the issues on which the Islamic Revolutionary Council, now guided by Taleqani, focussed was revolutionary justice. In late June the IRC sent a bill to the Bazargan government setting out the jurisdiction of revolutionary courts. They were to deal with cases of counter-revolutionary activity, espionage, murder, torture, armed robbery, and cultivation of poppies used for producing opium. Early next month the IRC recommended the release of all former military and Savak officials except those specifically accused of murder or torture. Khomeini confirmed this.[40] But this was not to be a prelude to the dismantling of the whole system. For the attempt by the justice minister in late October to persuade Khomeini to abolish revolutionary courts failed. In the Ayatollah's view, these courts had a crucial role to play in the march of Islamic revolution; and that march had hardly begun.

Revolutionary courts now operated under the overall direction of Ayatollah Mahdi Hadavi, the chief justice, and Ayatollah Muhammadi Gilani Reyshahri, the prosecutor general. Their offices were in the Qasr prison complex on the eastern outskirts of the capital. Here the prison mosque was the venue of the most serious trials.

One day in August 1979, Hussein Mabor, a former agent of Savak, was in the dock, accused of murder and torture. Male witnesses sat on one side of the hall, and women, clad in chador, on the other. The prosecutor, a tall cleric in black robes, read out the indictment detailing the accused's participation in the torture and murder of many innocent people. 'He went to war against Allah and His prophet Muhammad,' concluded the prosecutor.

'I joined Savak to serve the King and my country,' said Mabor in his defence. 'My family is very religious. . . . My superiors criticised me for not being hard enough and did not even allot me a flat to live in.'[41] Then came a stream of witnesses. One of them described how a woman demonstrator arrested in a demonstration had died under torture by him. Addressing him directly, another said: 'Remember how you gave me electric shocks, hung me from the ceiling by my wrists, threw salt water over my burns caused by your cigarettes.' Mabor was overcome by remorse. Covering his face, he began to sob.[42] Since the Quran enjoins that 'A life be taken for a life', and since revolutionary courts functioned within the framework of Quranic injunctions, Mabor was destined for the firing squad.

Raising arms against the Islamic government was another capital offence. This was the one being committed by thousands of Kurdish guerrillas. The armed actions of the Kurds had created a dilemma for the regime: to use or not to use the military to quell their rebellion. When the fighting first erupted in Kurdistan in mid-March, General Qarani, the chief of staff, despatched former Imperial Guards units and helicopter gunships to the region. Qarani's action was so embarrassingly reminiscent of the Shah's behaviour that Ahmed Madani, then defence minister, dismissed Qarani. (But two months later Madani, now the governor-general of Khuzistan, used troops to break up a demonstration by unarmed Arabs.)

Once a ceasefire was established in Kurdistan, the government decided formally not to use troops to put down ethnic rebellions. With the formation of the Islamic Revolutionary Guards in mid-June, the role of maintaining internal security was taken up by its ranks. In late June Kurdish nationalists, angered by the absence of regional autonomy in the revised draft constitution, clashed with the IRG in three cities of Kurdistan. Twelve people died. This led General Azizollah Seif Amir Rahimi, commander of military police, to demand on 9 July the reversal of the policy of non-interference by the military in ethnic rebellions. He also alleged that military commanders were conspiring to 'discredit the Islamic Republic'.[43] Taqi Riyahi, defence minister, dismissed General Rahimi. But the latter replied that he would leave only if Khomeini ordered him to. The next day the Ayatollah's office announced that Khomeini wanted Rahimi to stay. Riyahi resigned a week later, and Khomeini had a meeting with Rahimi and Bazargan in Qom. On 21 July General Nasser Farbod, the chief of staff, was dismissed and replaced by General Hussein Shakari. From then on the ban on engaging troops to fight Kurdish rebels was off. This was one more example of Khomeini siding with hardliners in a conflict between them and moderates.

The changes in the military leadership coincided with the induction of four IRC members into the Bazargan government and the appointment of Taleqani as the Friday prayer leader of Tehran. Khomeini orchestrated these moves as a prelude to using the holy month of Ramadan, beginning on 25 July, to rally his supporters to confront and overpower the opposition, and press ahead with his programme of Islamising society.

Ramadan began with a ban on music on radio and television. Khomeini argued that music had an opium-like effect on the listeners and made them indolent. (As such, the ban did not apply to martial music.) During the next week or so the faithful were urged to participate in the elections to the Assembly of Experts. As stated earlier, the NDF and the Fedai Kahlq boycotted this poll. These were Tehran-based parties, and their action made them prime targets for the regime's wrath. But this did not bother the Fedai leaders.

After all, the Fedai Khalq had a history of combat and confrontation since its formation in 1971 out of the merger of two groups which traced their origins to 1963. The Fedai attack on the Siakal gendarmerie post in early 1971 won the party hundreds of young recruits. Most of them were from middle class, professional families. They were organised in half a dozen northern cities. Believing in the 'Propaganda by the Deed' doctrine of Ernesto Che Guevara, the Latin

American revolutionary, the party hoped that the consequent repression by the Shah would lead to increased resistance by the masses, and trigger off a people's revolution. It forged links with the Popular Front for the Liberation of Palestine, led by George Habash; and its leading members received training in the Palestinian camps of Lebanon.[44] The party cadres attacked police stations and banks, bombed American and British embassies, and assassinated police and Savak informers. This went on for five years. The party suffered heavily. Some 10,000 of its members, actual or suspected, were jailed; and about 180 party activists were killed by the security forces in armed clashes, executions and torture.[45] The people's revolution failed to materialise. The party split into two factions, with the moderate wing concentrating on political work among industrial workers.

When Savak became overstretched in the autumn of 1977, the Fedai revived its guerrilla activity with the assassination of the Mashhad police chief in October. Between then and early February 1979, the party claimed to have staged fifteen guerrilla actions, including attacks on police stations, army barracks and the gendarmerie headquarters in Tehran.[46] At the same time party members and sympathisers were active in the anti-Shah demonstrations. During the February 1979 fighting, the Fedai captured many police stations and the Savak headquarters. Later the party turned the former Savak premises into its own head office.

Once the Fedai's demand for a share in state power had been rejected by Khomeini, the party, led by Mustapha Madani, went into opposition. In March it adopted the Kurdish slogan 'Autonomy for Kurds, Democracy for Iran', and combined it with a boycott of the referendum on Iran's political system. The party had an active membership of 5,000 in Greater Tehran; and its rally in late June on the Tehran University campus drew a largely middle class crowd of 50,000. As government pressure on the organisation mounted, hundreds of Fedai activists left for Kurdistan to join the Kurdish guerrilla movement there. Those who remained were determined to resist the efforts of Khomeini loyalists to monopolise political and other power.

Confrontation came when the government, having completed the Experts' Assembly election, decided to enforce the two month old press law. On 7 August the Islamic Revolutionary Guards occupied the offices of the *Ayandegan* and confiscated the day's issue.[47] Those who opposed the government action demonstrated the next day, and were dispersed by revolutionary guards. For the next few days the opposition forces worked feverishly to show their collective strength in the street. The result was an impressive protest march on 12 August – called by the National Democratic Front and backed by the Fedai and the Mujahedin. It was attacked by Khomeinists. In the fighting that ensued hundreds of people were injured, and many booths selling opposition papers were destroyed.

But this was not the end. The next day contingents of the IRG besieged the head offices of the Fedai and the Mujahedin, the latter situated in the former headquarters of the Pahlavi Foundation. The armed Fedai and Mujahedin guards offered resistance. A stalemate ensued. Appeals were made to Ayatollah Taleqani to intervene. He did. Due to his moderating efforts further bloodshed was avoided. But the Fedai and the Mujahedin had to give up their premises respectively to the government and the Mustazafin Foundation. The same fate befell the Tudeh: it was expelled from its modest building near the Tehran University campus. The end result was a triumph for the government and the IRG.

This was the most difficult task that the two-month-old Islamic Revolutionary Guards had undertaken in the capital so far; it was also the most public. By accomplishing it successfully, it established itself as an effective internal security force. In its anti-leftist campaign the IRG had the full backing of Khomeini. 'Let no one expect that the corrupt and American or non-American left will be able to reappear in this country,' he said on 16 August. 'We gave them time and treated them mildly in the hope that they would stop their devilish acts. . . . We can, when we want, in a few hours throw them in the dustbin of death.'[48]

Having established its authority, the government pressed its advantage. It banned forty-one opposition papers on 20 August, including the publications of the NDF, Tudeh, Fedai and Mujahedin. On 8 September it declared that since the companies owning the Ittilaat and the Kayhan publishing complexes were 'illegally acquired assets', they were to be taken over by the Mustazafin Foundation. These publishing companies were then purged of all unIslamic journalists and employees, and the hands of the recently formed Islamic Associations in these establishments were strengthened. This meant that both the popular afternoon dailies of Tehran, the *Ittilaat* and the *Kayhan*, each with a circulation of about 100,000, were now to be run by the semi-official Mustazafin Foundation. Of the three morning dailies, the *Jumhouri-ye Islami* (circulation 40,000) belonged to the IRP, and the *Inqilab-e Islami* (Islamic Revolution), with a circulation of 30,000, to Bani-Sadr; and the *Bamdad* (Morning), with a circulation of 100,000, was, in the words of a resident Pakistani journalist, 'three per cent independent'.[49] As for radio and television, it remained firmly under government control, as in the pre-revolution days.

With religious fervour rising during Ramadan, Khomeini was in no mood to tolerate armed challenge to the Islamic government's authority. When Kurdish guerrillas resisted the arrival of revolutionary guards in Paveh by capturing the town on 16 August, Khomeini reacted angrily. He branded the KDP leaders as 'corrupt', and called for their arrest. He personally ordered the military and the IRG to re-take the town. This meant an all-out fight between Kurdish rebels and government forces. Over the next few weeks the troops and revolutionary guards captured all the important Kurdish urban centres, including Mahabad, the stronghold of Kurdish nationalists. But the central government achieved this only by deploying a large majority of its 110,000 army troops in Kurdistan.

Even then, rural areas remained under the control of the coalition of Kurdish autonomists, now composed of the KDP, the Fedai, and the Komala (a Kurdish acronym, meaning the Revolutionary Organisa-tion of the Kurdish Toilers) led by Jaafar Shafei. These groups had sided with peasants in their struggle against big landlords during the Shah's rule and the revolutionary movement. 'Silenced under the Shah, the Kurdish villagers had their sweet revenge when they occupied farmlands during the revolution,' reported a correspondent of *The Iranian*. 'Armed with weapons seized from army barracks and guard posts, these villagers have sown their crops and are now awaiting to take the harvest. To them, autonomy means achieving real land reform.'[50]

Given this, Kurdish fighters were soon able to consolidate their support in the rural and mountainous areas of Kurdistan, and launch a series of successful offensives against the central forces in urban centres. They crowned their victories with the recapture of Mahabad on 31 October. This forced the Tehran government to negotiate with them. A more suitable climate for talks was created by the occupation of the US embassy in Tehran by Islamic militants in early November: an action enthusiastically endorsed by Kurdish fighters. In mid-November both sides reached a formal ceasefire agreement.

The Kurdish conflict saw the IRG fighting alongside the army in a difficult terrain. However, the bulk of the new revolutionary force was deployed in Iranian cities. It was at the disposal of the revolutionary authorities to assist them inter alia in cleansing the civil service, military and oil industry of all unIslamic elements. The radical members of the IRC found Premier Bazargan lackadaisical in implementing a thoroughgoing purge. For instance Bazargan had openly said that purging in the army would not be extended below the brigadier-general level.[51] That this was a point of continued friction between the prime minister and IRC radicals was confirmed by Abbas Zamani (alias Abu Sharif), the commander of the IRG, in an interview with the Beirut-based *Al Safir* (The Trumpet Blast), published on 1

December. 'The Bazargan government wanted . . . to prevent the revolutionary guards from arresting the civil servants and military officers accused of collaborating with the Shah's regime,' said Zamani. 'Bazargan did not want to allocate funds to the Islamic Revolutionary Guards or supply it with arms and ammunition. . . . They tried to prevent the expansion of the IRG.'

The Khomeini regime was keen to consolidate its hold over the oil industry, its sole earner of foreign exchange and its single most important source of revenue. Soon after taking office, Bazargan appointed Hassan Nazih, a human rights lawyer, as chairman of the National Iranian Oil Company. Nazih made no effort to mask his secularist views. Addressing the National Lawyers' Congress in late May, he disputed Khomeini's statement that those who did not accept the leadership of the ulema were against the revolution. He stated that Islam was incapable of solving the complex problems of modern society. Ayatollah Beheshti condemned Nazih's statements and demanded his prosecution. Seven members of the NIOC board of directors threatened to resign if action were taken against Nazih. Beheshti did nothing.

But the conflict was not resolved. For it was decided in the inner sanctum of the revolutionary power to depute Hojatalislam Shahab al-Din Eshraqi, a son-in-law of Khomeini, to mount a sustained campaign against the NIOC chairman. An unknowing Nazih kept up his independent stance. In July, objecting to the procedures adopted for the elections to the Experts' Assembly, he refused to enter the contest. On the other side, working in league with the Union of Islamic Associations and Syndicates of Oil Industry, Eshraqi charged that Nazih had failed to purge the industry of corrupt officials and reduce the inordinately high pay differentials between workers and top managers, and had disbursed company funds to such organisations as the Iranian Committee for the Defence of Freedom and Human Rights. Nazih responded by attacking the ulema for meddling in the policy-making decisions of the NIOC. He did so in an address to an economic seminar in mid-September. That sealed his fate. Khomeini dismissed him on 28 September, and ordered the prosecutor general to investigate the charges against him. This was one more example of Khomeini ending an ongoing controversy by siding with hardliners.

The same day Premier Bazargan abolished Nazih's post, created a new ministry of oil, and appointed Ali Akbar Moinfar, an IRC member and a religious layman, as oil minister. Bazargan acted thus in order to deflect pressures on him to appoint a cleric as the NIOC's new chairman.

By now an institution set up by Khomeini after the revolution had taken root, and emerged as the country's largest economic conglomerate. This was the Mustazafin Foundation. With the immediate acquisition of the Pahlavi Foundation, which owned 20 per cent of the assets of all privately-owned companies,[52] the new Foundation was well on its way to becoming an economic giant. Over the months it acquired the assets of tens of thousands of affluent Iranians who fled the country before and after the revolution, and of all those who were executed. In the immediate aftermath of the revolution, poor families from south Tehran were accommodated by the Revolutionary Komitehs in the confiscated mansions of the wealthy in north Tehran, with the luxury items auctioned off, and routine household goods given away to the needy. By early October the Mustazafin Foundation owned more than 100 companies engaged in such diverse activities as hotels, construction, real estate, agriculture, household goods manufacture, tyres, paper manufacture, publishing and food processing. The Foundation was divided into thirteen departments, and had branches in all important provincial towns. The creation of the Mustazafin Foundation, combined with the nationalisation measure of June-July, gave the regime powerful leverage in economic matters.

In all the decisions that Khomeini took in conducting the multifarious affairs of society, he rarely modified his stance. One of the few examples was the issue of women's dress. On the eve of the International Women's Day on 8 March, Khomeini suspended the Family Protection Law of 1967/75 and banned co-education. He also ruled that women employees in government ministries must dress 'according to Islamic standards', that is, wear a veil. This set off protest demonstrations by women. Day after day thousands of women protestors marched through the capital's streets. A demonstration on 11 March was met by revolutionary guards firing over the heads of protesting women. The next day the demonstrators were stoned, and attacked by knife-wielding men. On 13 March, responding to public protest and private pleas, the Ayatollah's office announced that Khomeini had said that a chador was a desirable, not compulsory, form of dress for women.[53] Behind the scenes Ayatollah Taleqani played a crucial role in persuading Khomeini to soften his ruling.

Taleqani provided a much-needed balance in this formative period of the republic. He sat easily between Premier Bazargan and Khomeini as politician-administrators. He also sat easily between Ayatollah Shariatmadari and Khomeini when it came to interpreting the Sharia. In addition, he was a valuable bridge between the regime and the leftist forces represented by the Mujahedin and the Fedai. However, his success in aborting a bloody confrontation between the IRG and the armed Mujahedin and Fedai militants proved to be his last. He died of a heart attack in his sleep on 9 September. He was mourned deeply and widely, with Tehran witnessing the largest mourning procession ever.

Having humbled the opposition during Ramadan, and having established the supremacy of the Islamic government, Khomeini relaxed somewhat. When, for instance, on the re-opening of the Tehran University in early October, the Mujahedin, the Fedai and other leftist groups established their offices on the campus, the authorities turned a blind eye. About then the government lifted its ban on the *Mardom* (People), the organ of the Tudeh, and other opposition papers, and overlooked the appearance of semi-clandestine publications of other groups. However, the rumour that the *Ayandegan* would reappear under the overall supervision of the Mustazafin Foundation proved unfounded.

Mild relaxation at home seemed to tie in well with the provisional government's effort to mend fences with the US, the single most important backer of the Shah. With the recall in early April of William Sullivan, the American ambassador during the revolutionary upheaval, and the Bazargan government's acceptance of Bruce Laingen as the new chargé d'affaires two months later the stage seemed set for reconciliation between Tehran and Washington.[54]

But neither of the two administrations had realised the full implications of the parallel system of conducting foreign relations that had evolved in Iran. Whereas Khomeini's office in Qom concerned itself primarily with promoting Islam and Islamic interests abroad, the foreign ministry in Tehran focussed on promoting national interests, of which Islam was one aspect. Khomeini pursued his objective by quietly sending off personal emissaries to foreign countries with specific assignments, and by secretly posting acolytes as personal ambassadors to important Islamic states, and by instructing certain foreign ministry officials to report to him directly.[55] In a way Khomeini was following the tradition of the grand ayatollahs in Qom and elsewhere. It was customary for them to send personal envoys abroad and post their own representatives in important Islamic places. But the scale of Khomeini's operations, backed by the power of the Iranian state, was unprecedented.

What further complicated Tehran-Washington relations was the fact that the running of the Iranian embassy in the American capital was supervised by the Islamic Association of the embassy staff.[56] To avoid the scrutiny of the Islamic Association, the acting Iranian chargé d'affaires in Washington, Shahriar Rouhani, a son-in-law of the foreign minister, Ibrahim Yazdi, resorted to having secret meetings with US state department officials. Yazdi himself repeated the pattern when he attended the United Nations General Assembly session in New York in late September. He had secret meetings with US officials at the UN on 4 and 6 October.[57] Meanwhile, the US defence department announced that America had resumed delivery of aircraft parts to Iran.

Behind these talks lurked the possibility of President Carter allowing the Shah into America from Mexico for medical treatment. (Iran was then pressing Mexico to extradite the Shah to face a series of charges in Iran.) The US administration was divided on the issue. Henry Precht, the state department's Iran director, proposed withholding the decision until after Iran had elected its president and Majlis, and after the US embassy in Tehran had improved its guard. Others argued for letting in the Shah immediately. He was reported to be grievously ill, and the specialised medical treatment he needed was unavailable outside the US.

The division within the American government was exposed dramatically and damagingly. On 20 October Henry Precht arrived in Tehran offering further help in equipping Iranian military. Two days later Carter allowed the Shah to fly to New York secretly for a gall bladder operation. Khomeini took this to be one more example of American duplicity. Now that the Shah was in New York, demands went up from the Iranian government and people that he should be extradited immediately to stand trial for his political and economic crimes. The news on 26 October, his birthday, that he had advanced lymph node cancer did nothing to soothe Iranian tempers.

The arrival of the Shah in America confirmed Khomeini's worst fears. He had felt all along that the US would never accept the Shah's deposition with equanimity, and that it would try to repeat history by reinstalling Muhammad Reza Pahlavi on the Peacock Throne. In his message on 2 November (Friday) to Iranian students – preparing to commemorate the deaths of Tehran University students on 4 November 1978 – Khomeini urged them to 'expand your attacks against America and Israel with full force, and to compel the US into extraditing this criminal, deposed Shah'.[58]

This set the scene for a dramatic event the next day: the seizure of the American embassy and diplomats. It was to mark the formal end of the first phase of the revolution and the beginning of the next.

During the opening phase Khomeini laid out the line along which the Islamic revolution was to progress. His starting point was the March 1979 referendum with a 98.2 per cent vote for an Islamic republic: a fact mentioned in Principle One of the constitution. By virtue of this vote, and other actions taken earlier by the Iranian people, Khomeini regarded himself to be the final authority to decide the future course of the revolution.

He argued that since both society and the regime were Islamic there was no place in it for those who were opposed to Islam or questioned the overriding importance of Islam in life. Such political parties as the Fedai Khalq, which believed and propagated Marxism, a materialist, atheistic ideology, were patently unIslamic. Then there were those who used Islam as a cover to hide their Marxist convictions and ideology. Such people were hypocrites, and ought to be exposed. Finally came the deviants, those who accepted and acted on wrong interpretations of the Sharia. Khomeini considered himself to be the ultimate arbiter in deciding who or what was Islamic, and who or what was not. All the non-Islamic forces had to eliminated from the government administration, military, judiciary, public and private enterprises and educational institutions. This was to be achieved by a combination of government decisions and popular actions.

But identifying and neutralising non-Islamic elements was only one function of the Islamic regime and its leaders. Their other major function was to purify society, which had been corrupted by alien influences over the past few centuries, and Islamise it. Corrupt behaviour and customs had to be ended. Alcohol and gambling were banned, and so were night clubs, pornographic films and mixed bathing. Society needed to be Islamised in a positive sense. Therefore Friday noon prayer and sermons were made the focal point of the week. The sermons were used to inform and educate the faithful. All Friday prayer leaders were appointed by Khomeini, and they were required to report to him.

Those who resisted the Islamic government were to be punished along the lines set out in the Sharia. Such Islamic crimes as raising arms against the Islamic state or spreading corruption in society were to be awarded capital punishment.

This was the ideological framework which Khomeini laid out, and within which he operated during this phase of the revolution, and after.

THE AMERICAN HOSTAGE CRISIS

The seizure of the American embassy on 4 November by militant students was a well-planned affair, a culmination of a process which began in the immediate aftermath of the Shah's downfall in February. Among the generals to be interrogated and executed on 15 February was Nematollah Nasseri. The boss of Savak from April 1965 to June 1978, he had been arrested by Premier Azhari under martial law regulations for illegal arrests and torture. In his confessions to his Islamic interrogators he told them that Savak had an undercover agent, codenamed Hafiz, inside the US embassy in Tehran. The Central Revolutionary Komiteh contacted Hafiz and offered him immunity if he would continue the past activity. Since Hafiz was neither Iranian nor American he felt vulnerable. He cooperated with the revolutionary regime. Before he was allowed to leave the country in early September, he passed on two sets of documents to Hojatalislam Hashemi-Rafsanjani, then deputy minister of the interior. These documents contained secret cables exchanged between Cyrus Vance and William Sullivan, and later Bruce Laingen. These showed that, contrary to its public statements, the Carter administration was actively considering admitting the Shah into the US. Also the US embassy in Tehran was courting dissident officers in the military, and Kurdish and Azerbaijani leaders.[1]

Alarmed by this, the top Islamic leadership resolved to act. A secret decision was made at the highest level to plan a take-over of the American embassy with a view to seizing all the documents there. Hojatalislam Ahmed Khomeini, the thirty-five-year-old son of the Ayatollah, was put in overall charge of the project. His chief lieutenant was Hojatalislam Muhammad Mousavi Khoiniha, the thirty-eight-year-old head of the Tehran University Revolutionary Komiteh. Khoiniha worked with the activists of the Islamic Associations at Tehran's major universities, Habibollah Payman, the head of the Movement of Militant Muslims, and the leaders of the Mujahedin of the Islamic Revolution. Payman had a long history of active opposition to the Pahlavi king. During his first imprisonment, which began in 1957, he shared a cell with Ali Shariati, a promising Islamic thinker and philosopher. After the failure of the June 1963 uprising, Payman established the Movement for Iranian National Liberation, which believed in armed struggle. When the 1977-8 revolutionary agitation started, Payman was in jail. He was released in November 1978. Immediately he founded the Movement of Militant Muslims, an organisation which attracted young, radical laymen. In mid-September, after he and the MIR and the universities' Islamic Associations leaders had been given the detailed layout and plans of the American embassy complex in central Tehran, they engaged forty to fifty of their hardcore supporters on the project.

This happened at a time when relations between Tehran and Washington were improving. Laingen, the American chargé d'affaires, visited Washington in late September. In a briefing to American correspondents there he suggested that they should be less critical of Khomeini.[2] During his meeting with Yazdi in New York in October, Vance told the Iranian foreign minister that the Carter administration considered the Shah to be finished, and accepted the Islamic revolution, and their common enmity to the Soviet Union made Iran and the US natural allies. Yazdi reported this to a sceptical Khomeini on his return to Tehran. On 20 October came Henry Precht's statement of American willingness to supply fresh weapons to Iran. However, the effect of these American gestures was nullified by the admission of the Shah into the US. The public mood in Iran turned rapidly anti-American.

Bazargan and Yazdi left Tehran on 1 November for Algiers to attend the twenty-fifth anniversary of the launching of the Algerian war of national liberation. The next day, while Khomeini was urging students to intensify their attacks on the US to secure the Shah's return, Bazargan and Yazdi had a meeting with Zbigniew Brzezinski, who had been a most vociferous supporter of the Shah and had opted for a military coup against the revolution. Iranian television showed Bazargan and Yazdi cordially shaking hands with Brzezinski – a gesture which sealed their fate.

On 4 November, the Mujahedin of the Islamic Revolution and the Movement of Militant Muslims were two of the many organisations scheduled to participate (officially) in the Students' Day demonstrations and rally. But the 450 activists of the universities' Islamic Associations, the MMM and MIR, who had gathered at a point a quarter of a mile from the US embassy, never arrived at the Tehran University campus to join the rally. Instead, they attacked the embassy, and took complete charge of it within three hours. The embassy staff tried to destroy as many secret papers as they could by using shredders and incinerators. But the forty to fifty assailants who entered the main embassy building moved with speed and precision, and captured most of the documents intact. They also preserved the shreds: these were later to be painstakingly reconstructed. During the following months these documents proved to be a treasure trove to the Islamic leadership. It used them to discredit and eliminate most of its opponents and even some of its lukewarm supporters.

Bazargan's cabinet met the next day. Among other things it decided to abrogate the March 1959 mutual military cooperation agreement with the US. On 6 November, protesting against 'the irresponsible intervention in governmental affairs' by militant students, Bazargan resigned. Khomeini accepted his resignation, and ordered the Islamic Revolutionary Council to take over the administration. The IRC requested all ministers to stay on. They did, except Yazdi. He resigned two days later. His job went to Bani-Sadr who was already in charge of finance and economic affairs. Meanwhile, the militant students – calling themselves Khat-e Imam, Followers of the Imam's Line – had declared that American diplomats would be released after the US had returned the Shah to Iran. Such an exchange was out of the question, said the Carter administration. The result was a crisis which lasted more than fourteen months.

Iran's confrontation with the US quickened the pace of the revolution, and gave meaning to the slogan raised on the day the Shah left Iran: 'After the Shah, the Yankee imperialism'. By concentrating Iranian attention on the past and present misdeeds of the US in Iran the American hostage crisis united the nation, and strengthened the radicals within the regime at the expense of the moderates. It proved to young Iranians that Khomeini and his followers were as staunchly anti-imperialist as the Fedai or the Mujahedin. To that extent it seriously damaged the growth prospects of these leftist organisations. The crisis provided the regime with a palpable issue to educate the masses politically, and rally popular support for the Islamic constitution and participation in presidential and parliamentary elections.

By the time the referendum on the Islamic constitution was held in early December, Iran and America were poised firmly against each other. Khomeini rejected the offer of talks with a delegation being sent by the US president. Carter stopped the shipments of $300 million worth of military spare parts that had been paid for during the Shah's days. He then instructed the US attorney general to start deportation proceedings against those Iranian students residing illegally in America. On 11 November, while Iranian papers published documents, released by the students occupying the US embassy, revealing US-British plots in Iran, Khomeini described Carter as 'an enemy of humanity'.[3] The next day Carter banned the import of Iranian oil. On

14 November he froze the Iranian assets deposited in US banks, estimated to be between $8,000 and $10,000 million. As American and British warships began joint naval exercises in the Arabian Sea, off the Hormuz Strait, Iran closed its territorial waters and airspace to US ships and aircraft.

On the eve of Muharram, beginning on 20 November, Khomeini said that whereas last Muharram the Iranian people had faced the Shah, a child of the Mother of Corruption, America, today they faced the Mother herself.[4] The following day as millions of Iranians marched against US imperialism, the Militant Students occupying the American embassy said that all hostages would be 'destroyed' if the US was to use military force against Iran. With the release of five female and eight black American hostages (on Khomeini's orders), the total now stood at fifty-three: fifty inside the embassy and three, including Laingen, at the foreign ministry.

Khomeini used the hostage crisis to rally voters for the referendum on the constitution, scheduled immediately after Ashura, 1 December. 'We are facing a satanic power today, and it wants to destroy our country,' he said on 28 November. 'Don't let the foundation of the Islamic Republic be weakened or the enemies of Islam fulfil their dreams.'[5] Yet the turnout was halfway between the figures for the Islamic Republic referendum (twenty million) and the Experts' Assembly (eleven million). Of the 15,785,956 who voted, 99.5 per cent approved the constitution.[6]

Part of the reason for the lack of overwhelming voter participation lay with Shariatmadari. He refused to endorse the constitution, and abstained from voting. And so did many of the three million voters in East and West Azerbaijan provinces. With this, the conflict that had existed between Shariatmadari and Khomeini since the revolution became sharper. Over the next several weeks there were repeated clashes between their respective supporters.

Shariatmadari versus Khomeini

Ayatollah Shariatmadari believed in the ultimate sovereignty of Iranian people. He therefore objected to Principle 110 of the Islamic constitution. This gave the Leader the right to vet the popularly elected president, thus subordinating the principle of national sovereignty to the doctrine of the Vilayat-e Faqih, Rule of the Jurist. 'We seem to be moving from one monarchy to another,' he said.[7]

On the eve of the referendum Shariatmadari issued a two paragraph statement. The first said that the constitution was acceptable in Islamic terms. The second said that there was a contradiction between

Principles Fifty-six and 110. Principle Fifty-six stated that no one could deprive man of 'his God-given right' of determining 'his social destiny'. But Principle 110 conferred this right on the Leader by authorising him to vet the popularly elected president. The state-run television showed the first paragraph of Shariamadari's statement, but not the second.

The suppression of the critical paragraph by television angered Shariatmadari's followers. On 5 December they clashed with Khomeini's supporters in Qom. In the mêlée a guard outside Shariatmadari's house was killed. The next morning there was a protest demonstration outside Khomeini's house in Qom. The outbreak of violence within the Islamic camp was an extremely serious matter, and worried Khomeini. Later that day, accompanied by Ahmed, his son, Khomeini called on Shariatmadari. This was a public gesture of goodwill and compromise by Khomeini, an unprecedented step. It highlighted the gravity of the situation. But it came too late to stop thousands of pro-Shariatmadari demonstrators in Tabriz marching that day to the local radio and television building and seizing it. They also took over the governor-general's residence and other public buildings.

When local revolutionary guards tried to regain control of the government buildings they were resisted by the armed militants of the Muslim People's Republican Party. On 8 December Shariatmadari alleged that promises made to him by 'revolutionary leaders' had been broken. The next day, as a team of Islamic Revolutionary Council members, led by Bani-Sadr, left for Tabriz, Khomeini described the events in that city as 'rebellion against the rule of Islam'.[8] In Qom the Faiziya seminary and other Islamic centres called for the dissolution of the MPRP. Shariatmadari replied that the demand was unnecessary, and publicly confirmed that he had abstained from voting in the referendum on the constitution. This had an immediate impact on the people in Tabriz, where Bani-Sadr was engaged in negotiations with Azerbaijani leaders. There were further clashes between Shariatmadari partisans and security forces; and this strengthened the hands of local leaders in their talks with Bani-Sadr. Most Azerbaijanis felt hurt that their venerable ayatollah, Shariatmadari, who was for long a most respected leader of Iranian Shias, had been elbowed out of the limelight by recent events and the machinations of the aides around Khomeini, the shining star. Matters had reached a point where Shariatmadari was not being consulted even on Azerbaijani affairs, they complained.[9] Bani-Sadr promised redress of many Azerbaijani grievances.

As a result the reconciliation rally held in Tabriz on 13 December was attended by half a million people. It adopted a ten-point charter, the first point being that all administrative and religious posts in the two Azerbaijani provinces must be approved by Shariatmadari.[10] The next day Khomeini and Shariatmadari sent their personal envoys to Tabriz to finalise the agreement between the IRC team and the Azerbaijani leaders. Both sides compromised. The MPRP leaders declared that they were 'suspending' their party. This was reported to be in exchange for an unpublicised promise by Khomeini and the IRC to discuss amending the constitution in consultation with Shariatmadari. It was agreed to form a joint committee of the nominees of Khomeini and Shariatmadari for the purpose.

But the compromise proved stillborn. Shariatmadari chose Hassan Nazih and Rahmatollah Moqadem-Maraghehi as his representatives on the constitutional committee. Both of them were wanted by the prosecutor general. Angered by Shariatmadari's decision, Khomeini refused to name his nominees. There were now repeated demands by Khomeinists to ban the MPRP. Khomeini charged that the events in the Azerbaijani region were being instigated by the US. In this he was relying on the claims made by the Militant Students that they had discovered papers in the US embassy which showed that the MPRP leader Moqadem-Maraghehi had been spying on behalf of America: a charge that had led the prosecutor general to order his arrest. Shariatmadari retorted that blaming the US for everything would not solve any problem. 'Under the Shah I was not free to speak, and they came to my house and killed my students,' he said in a Friday sermon on 28 December. 'Under this government I am still not free to speak, and they came to my house and killed a guard.'[11]

Fighting broke out that day in Tabriz between revolutionary guards and MPRP militants, with the latter taking nine guards as hostage. This incensed Khomeini. Shariatmadari advised the immediate release of the guards, but insisted that the constitutional powers of the Leader must be reduced. Khomeini rejected this. In a statement on 3 January he said that 'belief in Principle 110 is a must' for all candidates for presidency.[12]

The following day the partisans of the two leaders clashed in Tabriz and Qom after the Friday prayer meetings. One hundred people were injured. While revolutionary guards occupied the MPRP headquarters in Tabriz, MPRP militants took over the radio and television building. On 5 January revolutionary guards besieged Shariatmadari's house in Qom. That day pro-Khomeini supporters took to the streets throughout the country to protest against the 'deviants'. There was little doubt in the Khomeini camp as to who these deviants were and who was leading them. 'The plotters are the very same people who never for a moment opposed the Shah's regime, who until yesterday supported the monarchical constitution, who are linked with the CIA, who do not recognise the Islamic Republic's constitution and who have not voted for it affirmatively,' said Hojatalislam Khoiniha – the leader of the Militant Students and Khomeini's representative on radio and television, and interior and national guidance ministries – at a Tehran rally. 'These plotters covered themselves with religious cloak.'[13]

Clashes between the two sides continued for the next few days in Tabriz and Qom. The situation in Qom became so serious that on 7 January the control of the city was handed over to the Islamic Revolutionary Guard. Two days later Tabriz witnessed large scale rioting. It left ten people dead, over 100 injured, and more than fifty banks destroyed. To defuse the situation two clerical leaders in Qom, Ayatollahs Marashi-Najafi and Sadiq Rouhani, called on Shariatmadari and advised reconciliation with Khomeini. Their effort failed.

Shariatmadari was reluctant to give in. He knew that he had to act before the presidential poll on 25 January legitimised the constitution, with its Principle 110 intact. He was aware of the immense support he had gathered behind himself. Those who backed him included moderate ulema throughout the country, a majority of the Azeri-speaking Iranians, the disaffected modern middle classes and monarchists. Taken together, this was a formidable coalition, with the MPRP alone claiming a membership of three million, far larger than the IRP's claim. In case the presidential election went ahead as planned, Shariamadari wanted to field a strong candidate from his side. For he reckoned that no candidate would secure the requisite 51 per cent of the vote in the first round, and that there would be a second round between the two leading contenders.

On his part Khomeini was determined to stop Shariatmadari now, before the presidential poll, rather than later. And he used the method employed before to great effect: unleash his followers into the street on a religiously significant day. The occasion was the fortieth day commemoration of Imam Hussein's death, on 9 January. Throughout Iran millions of Shias marched in support of Khomeini, and demanded punishment for the deviants in Qom and Tabriz. Primed by the widely publicised revelations of the Militant Students about contacts between the US and Moqadem-Maraghehi, the marchers backed Khomeini's claim that the developments in Azerbaijan were the handiwork of America.

These marches paralysed Shariatmadari and MPRP leaders. On the night of 11/12 January revolutionary guards attacked the new headquarters of the MPRP in Tabriz, and killed four people. Later that day the revolutionary court in Tabriz ordered the execution of eleven Azerbaijani leaders on charges of fighting God, armed rebellion against the Islamic Republic and terrorism. A week later came the news of the arrest of twenty-five air force officers in Tabriz for plotting a coup.[14]

This was the end of Shariatmadari's attempt to institutionalise his power base in the form of a political party. He proved to be a poor tactician. He failed to realise the difference between his confrontation with Khomeini in June and now. Earlier he was on surer ground: he was trying to make Khomeini stick to what he himself had promised five months back – namely, a representative constituent assembly. In this Shariatmadari had widespread support within the religious establishment. But now he demanded amendment to the constitution which had already been adopted by an elected assembly. He had much less clerical backing on this than was the case in June. What is more, when Khomeini compromised by calling on him and agreeing later to appoint a joint commission to study amendments to the constitution, Shariatmadari did not respond in kind. He nominated two persons who were being sought by the prosecutor general. He should have known that Khomeini would never accept them. If Shariatmadari meant to escalate his conflict with Khomeini, he should have strengthened the disparate coalition of forces that had lined up behind him before so doing. But he did not. He should have known that Khomeini was a past master in the game of confrontation: he had fought the Shah and won against all the odds. Shariatmadari should have known too that he himself had neither the aptitude nor stamina for confrontational politics. So by pitting himself against a veteran of many fights, Shariatmadari virtually ensured his own defeat. In the process he inadvertently enhanced Khomeini's popularity.

Outside the Azerbaijani region, popular attention was now fixed on the forthcoming presidential election, a unique event in Iranian history. Soon after the polling date was announced in mid-December, Khomeini let it be known that he did not want the ulema to monopolise all power. That ruled out Ayatollah Beheshti, the general secretary of the Islamic Republican Party, as a presidential candidate. By the time the election commission had winnowed down 106 hopefuls to twenty-six on 13 January, serious contenders were down to about six.

Jalal al-Din Farsi, the IRP candidate, had the backing of a majority of his party's central committee, and of important Islamic centres in Qom. But when his nationality came under shadow by a revelation that his father had been an Afghan national, he withdrew. The IRP then endorsed Hassan Habibi, a lacklustre member of the IRC and minister of higher education. His chances of success were slim.

That left the field to three serious candidates: Ahmed Madani, Abol Hassan Bani-Sadr and Masoud Rajavi. A former defence minister and governor-general of Khuzistan, Madani had the backing of the National Front as well as Bazargan and his followers. But Bani-Sadr enjoyed much wider support. He started with the endorsement of two eminent members of Khomeini's household: Ahmed Khomeini and Hojatalislam Eshraqi. He also enjoyed the support of those ulema who did not like Beheshti. Among lay voters he was the favourite of all those who had regarded Bazargan as too moderate. Later he was to receive the backing of Masoud Rajavi, the thirty-two-year-old leader of the Mujahedin-e Khalq.

Rajavi backed Bani-Sadr after he had been barred as a candidate by Khomeini. On 17 January Khomeini ruled that only those who had voted for the constitution would be allowed to run for presidency. Since his party, the Mujahedin-e Khalq, had abstained from voting, Rajavi was disqualified. Some of the Mujahedin's objections against the constitution were on the same line as that of Shariatmadari. That is, the provisions for popularly elected president and parliament were at odds with Chapter Eight, containing Principles 107 to 110 about the powers of the Leader or the Leadership Council. Their other objections pertained to certain 'sectarian, anti-people and class based Principles'.[15]

Unlike the Fedai, the Mujahedin had participated in the Islamic Republic referendum. On the whole they did not feel as alienated from the Islamic regime as did the Fedai. They had come into existence as an Islamic party, and had a history of active resistance against the Shah and bloody repression by Savak.

Mujahedin-e Khalq

The Sazman-e Mujahedin-e Khalq-e Iran was formed in 1965 by young, former members of the Liberation Movement. In the aftermath of the Shah's crushing of the June 1963 uprising, they felt that their erstwhile leaders had been too moderate. The party's founders were all university students or graduates. They set up cells in Tehran, Tabriz, Isfahan and Shiraz. Some of them went to Jordan to receive military training at the PLO camps there.

From its inception the party stressed the importance of Islam. 'We have reached the firm conclusion that Islam, especially Shia Islam, will play a major role in inspiring the masses to join the revolution,' stated the party publication, *Sharh-e Tasis* (Description of the Foundation). 'It will do so because Shiaism, particularly Hussein's historic act of martyrdom and resistance, has both a revolutionary message and a special place in our popular culture.'[16]

Nahzat-e Husseini, Hussein's Movement, written by Ahmed Rezai, one of the founder-members, summed up the party ideology. In it the author described the Order of Divine Unity (Nizam-e Tauhid) sought by Prophet Muhammad as a united commonwealth: it worships one

God, and as a classless society works for the good of all. He argued that the rebellion led by Shia Imams, espcially Hussein, was as much against the usurping caliphs, who had abandoned the objective of the Order of Divine Unity, as it was against feudal lords and merchant capitalists. In present times, the author concluded, true Muslims must work to create a classless society by struggling against imperialism, capitalism, dictatorship and conservative clericalism. The other text adopted by the Mujahedin-e Khalq was Ayatollah Taleqani's *Labour and Property in Islam*, which took a similar, egalitarian view of Islam.

The Mujahedin carried out individual acts of violence against the state on the ground that by showing that the regime was vulnerable they were dispelling the despair and defeatism that had permeated the opposition. They started their guerrilla actions in August 1971 with a view to disrupting the celebrations of the 2,500 years of monarchy. Repression followed. As a result virtually all of the founder-members were either killed in armed clashes or by execution.

But repression proved to be a two-edged sword. While it destroyed Mujahedin leadership, it brought in a steady stream of young recruits, who were attracted by the party's action-oriented programme. Unlike the Fedai, the Mujahedin drew their members from the university students coming from bazaar merchant or trader families. The actual experience of confronting the Pahlavi regime and an inflow of recruits sympathetic to Marxism led the party to move leftwards, and embark on a process of synthesising Islam with Marxism. While party theorists drew their inspiration from Islam as an ideology and a culture, and rejected materialism, they used Marxism as an analytical tool. They argued that a decade of the White Revolution had destroyed feudalism and transformed Iran into a bourgeois society, which was tied to, and was dependent on, Western capitalism. Because of this relationship, Iran was facing the prospect of political, economic, cultural and military colonisation by the West, particularly America. As the Pahlavi king lacked support outside the small class of comprador bourgeoisie, agents of Western multinationals, he had to rely on despotic means and propaganda to maintain his rule. Only by carrying out dare devil acts against the autocratic regime could the party destroy the environment of terror that existed. Once the masses had got rid of their fear, and joined an armed struggle against the Pahlavi regime and overthrown it, the party would implement radical reforms. It would put Iranian economy on an independent footing and end its dependence on the West. It would try to establish the classless Order of the Divine Unity by redistributing wealth and guaranteeing basic freedoms to the struggling masses.

The leftwing drift of the party alienated many anti-Marxists. Finding themselves in the minority they dropped out steadily, thus inadvertently strengthening the position of the Marxists vis-à-vis the centrists. In mid-1974 the party began setting up cells in factories. A year later, the central committee, dominated by the Tehran-based leftists, accepted Marxism-Leninism as the party creed. The manifesto, adopted by the central committee, described Islam as 'the ideology of the middle class', and Marxism as 'the salvation of the working class', and concluded that Marxism was the truly revolutionary creed, not Islam.[17]

A majority of the members outside the capital rejected the central committee's decision, and refused to give up the party name. The party split between the centrists and the Marxists. Generally speaking, the centrists accepted and valued Marxism as a powerful means of analysis, but insisted that they were inspired primarily by Islam, and were against materialism.

Thus in 1975 there were two Mujahedin organisations: one leftist Islamic and the other Marxist-Leninist. They both carried out guerrilla actions, with the Marxist-Leninist being more daring, and in the process losing thirty activists in shoot-outs and through executions. The loss of cadres made both organisations reappraise their tactics. The next year they decided to downgrade armed actions in favour of propaganda. The Islamic organisation concentrated on students, and the Marxist-Leninist on workers.

When the revolutionary movement gathered steam, the Shah released all the Mujahedin except those serving life sentences. With this, both the Mujahedin organisations became active. They participated in demonstrations, particularly after the Black Friday massacre in early September. The release three months later of Masoud Rajavi, the only surviving member of the original central committee, boosted the morale of the Islamic Mujahedin. Born in 1947, Rajavi studied political science at Tehran University, and then went to a PLO camp in Jordan to receive guerrilla training. In 1971 he and Mahdi Abrishamchi were arrested for trying to abduct the American ambassador. He was tortured but did not recant. Twice he came close to being executed, but was saved by international pressure on the regime. Both Mujahedin organisations were active during the events of 10-13 February 1979: they armed their members with weapons captured from government armouries.

When the Bazargan government and Khomeini called for the surrender of these arms, Rajavi wrote to Khomeini that the (Islamic) Mujahedin were prepared to give up their weapons 'provided the people's rights are guaranteed'.[18] This was the beginning of the conflict between the Mujahedin and the regime which was to mature into open warfare in the summer of 1981.

Khomeini's call for the surrender of arms was rejected by the

Marxist-Leninist Mujahedin. Soon after the revolution it acquired a new name: Sazman-e Paykar dar Rah-e Azadi-e Tabaqah-e Kargar (The Combat Organisation on the Road to the Liberation of the Working Class), commonly known as the Paykar, Combat. The party saw the Shah's overthrow as a step towards a socialist revolution. While accepting the anti-imperialist credentials of Khomeini, it refused to regard him as the national leader. This put the Paykar in the same column as the Fedai Khalq. There was no common ground between the Paykar and the Islamic regime.

This was not the case with the Islamic Mujahedin led by Rajavi. Both the regime and the Mujahedin believed in Islam and the Quran. Where they differed was in their interpretations. For instance, Rajavi disagreed with Khomeini's view that democracy was alien to Islam. He cited the Quran and early Shia tradition to show that people had the right to hear all viewpoints and choose the best. According to Rajavi, Khomeini had 'a traditional, petty bourgeois and rightwing approach to Islam'. In contrast the Mujahedin by and large agreed with the interpretations offered by Ali Shariati, a radical Islamic thinker. 'We reject a class bound and traditional Islam, and our quarrel with Khomeini is about two kinds of Islam,' explained Rajavi. 'We do not believe that in true Islam there is room for oppression. . . . There is a problem of leadership, but this must not involve dictatorship. We therefore distinguish between reactionary dictatorship and democratic centralism. Khomeini's interpretation of the Quran is mechanical and deterministic.'[19]

On practical matters too Rajavi found himself at odds with Khomeini. He criticised the establishment of secret revolutionary courts. Later he endorsed the legitimate aspirations of minorities, particularly Kurds. He opposed the expansion of the Islamic Revolutionary Guards; and his party participated in the protest demonstrations against the closure of the *Ayandegan* in August 1979. Not surprisingly, the Mujahedin headquarters in Tehran was stormed by the IRG. It was the intervention of Ayatollah Taleqani – with whom the Mujahedin then had cordial relations – that prevented an irreparable breach between the Mujahedin and the regime. But after Taleqani's death in September, relations between the two sides deteriorated rapidly. As stated earlier, opposed to certain crucial articles in the Islamic constitution, the Mujahedin abstained in the referendum on the document. On the other hand, the Mujahedin supported the Militant Students' occupation of the US embassy. Rajavi decided to participate in the presidential elections mainly to demonstrate the size of the support his party had in the country. He was backed among others by Kurdish autonomists. Despite Rajavi's subsequent disqualification, the party decided to participate in the poll.

Rajavi asked the party supporters to vote for Bani-Sadr.

This was welcomed by Bani-Sadr, who had by now emerged as a strong favourite. Unlike his serious rivals, Bani-Sadr owned and edited a daily newspaper, *Inqilab-e Islami*. He used it as an effective campaigning tool. But, above all, he was helped by Khomeini's failure to contradict the rumour rife in the country that the Ayatollah favoured Bani-Sadr. In the final days of the campaign, the question was not who will win, but how large will Bani-Sadr's plurality be.

Bani-Sadr as president

On the election day 14.3 million voters turned up to vote. Of these, 10.7 million favoured Abol Hassan Bani-Sadr, a little over two million Ahmed Madani, and less than three-quarters of a million Hassan Habibi. With this, Bani-Sadr realised a life-long dream. He had resolved to become president of the (non-existent) republic of Iran in 1950, when he was barely seventeen, and an ardent admirer of Mussadiq.

Son of an ayatollah, Bani-Sadr was born in Hamadan. He pursued his university education in Tehran, specialising in economics, sociology and the Sharia. He had been in the capital for about a decade when the June 1963 uprising occurred. He was jailed for four months for his participation in a demonstration. After his release, a scholarship took him to the Sorbonne University in Paris. He gained a doctorate there, and stayed in Paris until the revolution in Iran. Among the books he authored was *The Economics of Divine Unity*. In it he expounded his theories of Islamic economics, and rejected both capitalism and Soviet socialism. He held that Islamic teachings were a means to a just and equitable society. Among those who noticed his work was Ayatollah Khomeini then living in Najaf.

Bani-Sadr had known Khomeini as a friend of his father, Ayatollah Nasurollah Bani-Sadr, and had been in touch with him from Paris. But it was only when Bani-Sadr visited Najaf in 1972 for his father's funeral that he actually met Khomeini. After this visit, Bani-Sadr became more active with the Islamic Student Society in Paris. When Khomeini arrived in the French capital in early October 1978, Bani-Sadr was among those who came to receive him at the airport. Soon Bani-Sadr became a member of Khomeini's inner circle of advisers. He emerged as a hardliner who advised rejecting any compromise with the Shah or Shahpour Bakhtiar. Khomeini came to like him.

Bani-Sadr returned to Tehran with Khomeini in February 1979. He soon became the country's chief architect of economic policies. In his paper *Inqilab-e Islami*, he attacked compromise and reformism. Since the Bazargan government manifested these characteristics, he was glad to see it fall in early November. As a member of the Experts' Assembly, he lobbied for the incorporation of a bill of rights into the constitution, and succeeded. But he failed to get the principle of 'divine unity' (tauhid) included in the constitution's fourteen general principles. He was opposed in this by Ayatollah Beheshti who argued, successfully, that the idea smacked too much of communism.

By winning 75 per cent of the votes cast in the presidential election, Bani-Sadr enhanced his stature. He was sworn in as president on 4 February by Khomeini. He was elected chairman of the Islamic Revolutionary Council, a position then held by Beheshti. Bani-Sadr thus became acting prime minister. A fortnight later Khomeini appointed him the commander-in-chief of the armed forces. In theory, Bani-Sadr was the second most powerful man in Iran. However, in practice, his authority was limited.

He asked for a twelve-month mandate from Khomeini to accomplish the following tasks: solving the American hostage crisis; stabilising the economy; resolving the minorities' problems, particularly the Kurdish rebellion; and reconstructing the armed forces. But Khomeini did or said nothing specific in return.

Bani-Sadr's achievement in each case was patchy. His own political standing was not such that he could impose his will on the different centres of power then existing. And Khomeini, holding different views from his own, either withheld his backing, or did something quite contrary.

The American hostage crisis was a good example. Khomeini undercut Bani-Sadr's position by announcing on 23 February that the fate of the American diplomats would be settled by 'the representatives of the people' who would meet in an Islamic Majlis. A few days later Beheshti said that the Majlis would not convene until April, and that it would take about a month before it could discuss the hostage issue. On 6 March the Militant Students refused to hand over the diplomats to the Islamic Revolutionary Council, as demanded by Bani-Sadr. Also contrary to the president's wish, they refused to allow the special five-member United Nations Commission, visiting Tehran, to meet the hostages. As a result, those students who agreed with Bani-Sadr's stance left the embassy, bringing down the number of Iranian occupiers from the original 450 to about 300.

On 14 March elections were held to the Majlis. The turnout of 6.1 million compared poorly with that for the presidential poll. Only ninety-eight candidates managed to win the requisite majority vote. The second round to settle the remaining 172 seats was then fixed for 9 May. This drove the US administration to despair. By now American diplomats had been held hostage for over five months. Realising this the IRC, led by Bani-Sadr, referred the matter of the diplomats' custody to Khomeini on 6 April. Khomeini decided in favour of the Militant Students. This ended Bani-Sadr's attempt to gain the upper hand in the American hostage issue and resolve it speedily.

Bani-Sadr did better in the economic field. As a trained economist who specialised in Islamic economics, he was on secure ground here. He had been handling economic affairs from the start of the revolution, and had been helped by a quick upturn in oil production.

Oil income was crucial to the economy. In 1977, oil revenue of $19.5 billion provided three-quarters of the government's annual income.[20] The expulsion of 1,600 foreign experts in the course of the revolutionary movement had no adverse effect on the industry.[21] After a break of ten weeks oil exports resumed on 5 March. Since the NIOC had terminated its supply contracts with the Western consortium, it now claimed that for the first time in the history of Iranian oil an Iranian company was handling all aspects of the industry – from prospecting to refining to sales. By early April oil output was running at over four million barrels/day versus 5.3 million barrels/day just before the revolution. During that period the loss of Iranian production to the international market had pushed the price for Iranian light crude from $13 a barrel to $20. Therefore by exporting 3.2 million b/d now Iran earned more than it did by shipping 4.5 million b/d before the revolution.

Given a firm demand for oil in the international market it was comparatively easy for the NIOC to remove the last vestige of dependence on Western companies. There was no opposition to this from any domestic quarter. But this did not apply to other Iranian industries. Such traditionalist economic thinkers as Bazargan and Nazih advocated maintaining economic ties with the West, and allowing multinational corporations to operate and expand in revolutionary Iran. Bani-Sadr opposed this. 'We must cut all organic [economic] ties that exist to make us dependent,' said Bani-Sadr. 'Our present economic links with foreign countries must be dissolved . . . by reorganising and redistributing our activities in various sectors of our economy.'[22] The traditionalists advocated encouraging private enterprise at home, and limiting the government's role to a regulatory agency. Bani-Sadr stood for direct government intervention as a means of creating an egalitarian society. He was the main force behind the official decision to nationalise banking, insurance and some key industries. His economic radicalism was inspired by a statement in the Quran which says that labour is the sole justification for the ownership of material wealth. That is, only those who labour to transform God-given resources into objects of value are entitled to the enjoyment of things they create.

The economic problem that the Islamic regime faced was twofold: falling output and rising unemployment. The revolutionary upheaval, followed by political and economic uncertainty, had caused a virtual halt in construction (which employed 650,000 in 1977) and a decline of 20 per cent in industry (which employed 1.8 million in 1977). The exodus of some 300,000 rich and upper middle class Iranians and foreigners had a catastrophic effect on hotels, holiday resorts, air travel, advertising, theatre and cinema. About 450,000 people lost their jobs.[23] At the same time 300,000 new job seekers were entering the market annually. The problem was made worse by the government's decision to cut the conscription period from two years to one. Little wonder the figure of estimated unemployed rose from 1.3 million in late 1978 to 2.2 million in early 1980 in a total workforce of 10.5 million.

Guided by the president, the authorities tried to counter economic ill-health in a variety of ways. The government cajoled factory managers not to dismiss workers even when the output had declined. In this it was helped by the presence of workers' councils in most of the large scale factories. The government tried to revive construction by allocating $4,000 million for this purpose out of the $12,600 million earmarked for development projects. The ministry of labour and social welfare offered unemployment loans to all those who had lost their jobs due to the revolution. During the first four months of the scheme, over 167,000 persons took advantage of it.[24] The government tried to balance its books by confirming the previous cancellations of orders for American weapons, and adding more items to the list. All told, the cancelled orders amounted to $9,000 million, and included fighter aircraft, Awacs, and fighter submarines.[25]

The regime won popularity among the poor by raising the minimum daily wage by 167 per cent: from Rials 210 to Rials 560. At the same time it encouraged rural emigrants to return to their villages and revive agriculture. With 480,000 people dependent on it in 1977, agriculture was an important part of the economy. But since the late 1960s, it had been afflicted by labour shortages. The Islamic government wanted to remedy the situation and make Iran self-sufficient in agricultural produce.

But a minor success in this proved problematical. With the return to rural Iran of recently politicised men, the traditional conflict between landlords and peasants sharpened – the major points of contention being the ownership of land and the share of crops paid as rent by tenants to their landlords.

This conflict was sharpest in Kurdistan. As upholders of law and order, the central security forces there often sided with landlords in their disputes with peasants. The election of Bani-Sadr as president made no difference to this state of affairs.

Bani-Sadr's efforts to resolve the Kurdish conflict during the period of truce between Kurdish guerrillas and central forces had been frustrated by Khomeini. The Ayatollah had rejected Bani-Sadr's proposal to hold a referendum in Kurdistan on self-rule. He had also overruled the agreement made in mid-December 1979 by a government delegation with Kurdish leaders on regional autonomy. On top of that he had disqualified Masoud Rajavi, the favourite of the Kurds, in the presidential contest.

Khomeini did not see Kurdish self-rule as an end in itself, but as a step towards secession and independence. He remembered the founding of an independent Kurdish republic in 1945. However, given the friendliness of the USSR to his regime, Khomeini did not expect the Soviets to aid the Kurds in their irredentist aim. He now saw the hand of America in a conspiracy to create an independent Kurdistan to be used as a pro-American base to destabilise neighbouring regimes, including the one in Tehran.[26]

Although the nationalist Kurdish coalition accepted the overall leadership of Shaikh Husseini, its constituents differed in their attitude to the Khomeini regime. The leftist Komala was bitterly hostile to it whereas the pro-Tudeh faction within the Kurdish Democratic Party was only mildly critical of it, and advocated a compromise with Tehran. This coalition controlled most of rural Kurdistan, with the Komala having its stronghold in the south and the KDP in the north.

At its fourth congress in mid-April 1980 in Mahabad, the KDP reiterated its demands: constitutional right of autonomy for all ethnic minorities; redrawing of provincial borders to include all Kurds into a single province; the election of an Executive Committee to administer the Kurdish region in all spheres except foreign affairs, defence and long-term planning; and the use of the Kurdish language in schools, offices and courts.[27]

As the central forces tried to extend their control, they were resisted by Kurdish partisans. The fighting lasted ten days. A temporary ceasefire was agreed on 29 April. The next day a government delegation flew to Mahabad to arrange a permanent ceasefire to a conflict which had so far claimed about 1,000 lives.[28] Bani-Sadr said that he was prepared to accept the KDP's demands 'with amendments'. But he was opposed by the hardliners in the Islamic Revolutionary Council and the commander of the IRG. They wanted nothing less than total destruction of the separatist forces. Some time later, when the Kurdish governor-general and seven Kurdish mayors arrived in the capital for talks, the IRG arrested them. It was only after Bani-Sadr had protested vehemently that the IRG released them.

Kurdish partisans were confident that they could sustain a guerrilla war against central forces for a long time. They had taken to a classical guerrilla tactic of withdrawing to mountain villages and returning to towns at night to harass the government forces. 'At night Kurdistan comes to life,' reported a correspondent of the London-based *Guardian*. 'Apparently sleepy mountain villages become hives of activity. At night guerrillas move men, arms, and supplies by Land Rover jeeps without lights – no easy task on mountain tracks.'[29]

Nonetheless, in early June the KDP and the Fedai Khalq said that once President Bani-Sadr had lifted the economic blockade of Kurdistan, and spelled out the amendments to the KDP demands he had in mind, they would negotiate. But nothing came of this. Kurdish guerrillas then cut off Iran's rail link with Turkey that passed through Kurdistan. This reduced the flow of much needed foreign imports into Iran.

The need to repair the rail link with Turkey, and the determination to strengthen Iran's security along its border with Iraq (of which Kurdistan was an important part), led the Tehran government to attack local guerrillas. Bloody clashes broke out between the two sides. The severity of the hostilities could be judged by the fact that in early August government forces killed 155 Kurdish partisans in Baneh. It had been a year since serious fighting had first erupted in Kurdistan. During that period various attempts at a peaceful solution to the Kurdish problem had failed primarily because Khomeini was unwilling to concede autonomy to Kurds, or any other minority.

Iraq's invasion of Iran in the third week of September helped Khomeini. It created a surge of nationalism in which ethnic differences were forgotten, for the time being. The war also provided Bani-Sadr with a proper opportunity to reorganise and rebuild the military. He had realised the need for this on his appointment as the commander-in-chief in February. But his attempts so far had been piecemeal.

The military

Before the revolution the Iranian military was the most powerful in the region: the army was 285,000 strong; the air force 100,000; and the navy 30,000. In addition the 75,000 strong gendarmerie was used partly for border security. The revolutionary upheaval affected all of these forces, except the navy. The gendarmerie lost 75 per cent of its ranks through desertions, the air force 20 per cent, and the army 60 per cent.[30] The depletion in the infantry was staggering, with some units losing all the ranks. 'I inherited an army that didn't have a single soldier in Tehran,' said General Qarani, the chief of staff, in early March 1979.[31]

A purge of the officers followed. But, as stated earlier, it stopped at the brigadier general level, leaving all the colonels in place. Encouraged by the Shah's overthrow, junior officers began to speak up – an unprecedented phenomenon in Iranian military history. When, for instance, Premier Bazargan appointed Major General Sayyed Mahdiyun commander of the air force, junior officers protested so vehemently that he had to go after three days in office. Bazargan's second appointee, Major General Shahpour Azarbarzin, lasted ten days.

As a result of the repression it carried out during the revolutionary movement, the military suffered a steep decline in public esteem. The stigma lingered on after the Shah's fall. Unsurprisingly, when the Islamic regime called on the deserters to report for duty, the response was lukewarm. In fact, the call-ups to conscripts had such poor response that the authorities had to give a two-month extension.

The chief of staff's decision in late March 1979 to use the army's elite units to crush the Kurdish rebellion proved contentious. Many junior officers and soldiers felt that it contravened the regime's promise of using the military only for external defence. There were reports of soldiers refusing to fight and being executed by Islamic military courts. Also, the fighting in Kurdistan made the officers of the military, equipped with American weapons, freshly aware of Iran's dependence on the US. Therefore they were critical of the Bazargan government's unilateral termination of the 1959 military cooperation agreement with the US in early November. Such a reaction made them suspect in the eyes of the Islamic camp. 'The Iranian army . . . [still] has a royalist organisation that has no connection at all with the current revolutionary Islamic regime,' said Abbas Zamani of the Islamic Revolutionary Guards on 1 December. 'There are a large number of army personnel who believe in the Islamic revolution but the army's organisational set-up is not Islamic, neither is its command. . . . The real [command] role is in the hands of senior officers of the previous regime.'[32]

There was thus much scope for a purge of the military. And once the Bazargan government had fallen, the Islamic Revolutionary Council undertook it with zeal. On the first anniversary of the revolution in February 1980, defence minister Mustapha Ali Chamran announced that 7,500 military personnel, mostly of high rank, had been purged during the previous two months.[33] But that was not enough. For every officer who had undergone training in the US was suspect. There were 11,000 officers who had received long-term training in America. In addition, there were many more thousands who had undergone short-term courses in the US.[34]

Not surprisingly, in March the government discovered a secret network of pro-American royalist officers inside the military. This in turn was to lead to further discoveries during the next four months, a process accelerated by the Carter administration's unsuccessful attempt to rescue the hostages by mounting a military campaign inside Iran on the night of 24-25 April. (The details of the operation are described in Chapter 10.) The failure of the Iranian radar system to detect the US helicopters and aircraft used in the operation; the wholesale transfer of the anti-aircraft batteries around Tehran to Kurdistan a few days before the American action; and the deliberate destruction of the abandoned US helicopters at Tabas airport: all these led the top political officials to conclude that some military leaders were colluding with the US. Among those suspected of collaboration with America was Major General Amir Bahman Bagheri, commander of the air force. Yet he was vehement in his call for 'full search of Iranian agents of the US'.[35] Official investigations led to the arrest in mid-May inter alia of Rear Admiral Muhammad Alayar, commander of the navy, for alleged links with America. He was a protégé of Ahmed Madani, who had once been a rear admiral in the Shah's navy, and who was later to be accused by some Majlis deputies of being in touch with the CIA. But before then he had fled Iran.

The Carter administration's claim that its military mission had been staged merely to rescue the hostages was widely disbelieved in Iran and elsewhere. Many Iranians and foreigners believed that the American operation was designed to overthrow the Khomeini regime, and that royalist military officers and politicians in Iran and abroad were involved. In any case, once the American venture had failed, the monarchists got to work on their plans. The most prominent among them were General Oveissi and Shahpour Bakhtiar, both of them resident in Paris. Oveissi headed the Iran Liberation Front, which was particularly active among royalist officers inside Iran.

An attempt at a coup planned for the early hours of 25 May was thwarted by the Khomeinists the night before. The government intensified its investigations into the loyalties of senior military officers. These led to the discovery of a tighter, more secret network than the one found before. It included among others Major General Bagheri of the air force. He was arrested in early June. This made Oveissi strike soon. The officers loyal to his Iran Liberation Front tried on 12 June to capture the army garrison in Piranshahr, Kurdistan. But they were thwarted. These developments worried the Ayatollah. 'I have appointed several people to check on the armed forces,' he said on 16 June. 'I shall appoint various people to act as inspectors so that they can inform me of all the things going on in the armed forces, and that everything [there] is in line with Islamic principles.'[36]

A few days later, with Khomeini's consent, President Bani-Sadr carried out a thorough reshuffle of military leadership. He promoted General Valiollah Fallahi, commander of the army, as the joint chief of staff, and gave his job to Brigadier General Qassem Ali Zahir-Nejad, commander of the gendarmerie. He appointed Colonel Javad Fakouri commander of the air force. Earlier he had posted Captain Bahram Afzali as commander of the navy. So now all the wings of the military had new commanders. On 29 June the president appointed Kazem Bojnurdi as commander of the Islamic Revolutionary Guards. These changes were in time. For the most serious challenge to the regime from senior military officers, conspiring with the pro-royalist forces abroad, was yet to come.

It was masterminded by Bakhtiar who worked with Oveissi and two other former Iranian generals. The plan was to take over Nouzheh garrison in Hamadan, and use it as a base to overpower the surrounding garrisons with a view to setting up a liberated territory and starting a civil war. The conspiring air force pilots had been instructed to take off from Hor (formerly Shahroki) air base near Hamadan and bomb Tehran's Mehrabad airport and such other targets as Khomeini's residence in north Tehran, the president's office and the IRG's headquarters. The coup was planned for the night of 9/10 July. But it was foiled before it could be mounted. According to Bakhtiar, some of his close associates sold the coup plans to President Bani-Sadr through the Iranian embassy in Paris.[37] Also, by early July, government investigations had led to the discovery of the innermost royalist network inside the military, codenamed Niqab (Mask). Bakhtiar admitted his involvement by issuing a statement which praised 'the courage and determination' of the plotters.[38]

Among the 300 suspected plotters who were arrested were Major General Mahdiyun, a former commander of the air force, and Lieutenant General Ahmed Mohagheghi, a former commander of the gendarmerie, and twenty air force pilots. On 16 July the government sealed the country's borders for forty-eight hours to stop the conspirators from fleeing. Khomeini called for a thorough purge, and warned that the mistakes of past leniency must not be repeated. 'As soon as victory had been achieved, all doors should have been closed, all comings and goings stopped, as other revolutions elsewhere in the world had done,' he said.[39]

Executions of the conspirators started on 14 July, and during the next two months claimed 108 lives. The revolutionary prosecutor general set up his court at Hor air base. The purges, which between the Revolution Day in February and mid-July had affected 4,500 military personnel,[40] were intensified. Both the executions and purges continued until the Iraqi invasion of Iran.

The Islamic regime found these military plots more menacing than the conflicts with its political or religious opponents. Khomeini was well-versed in orchestrating popular support to silence and overpower his political adversaries. But such a tactic was irrelevant when it came to dealing with conspiracies by military officers. The frequency with which military attempts were planned or mounted – on 24-25 April, 24 May, 12 June and 9-10 July – was another factor which worried the Ayatollah. At the very least royalist military officers wanted to carve out a territory of their own inside Iran and start a civil war. Such a development would have widened the cracks that had begun appearing within the Islamic regime, and which Khomeini seemed unable to repair.

Conflict between Bani-Sadr and the IRP

The American military operation on 24-25 April did not dissuade the Iranian authorities from calling off the second round of elections to the Majlis. It was conducted on 9 May as planned. Since the polling was not to be held in thirty-six seats in the Kurdish region, and parts of Khuzistan and Fars, a total of 136 seats was at stake. The Islamic Republican Party, which had won forty-one places in the first round, was the leading contender. In order to decisively beat off the challenge from its rivals, it combined with the Organisation of Militant Clergy and a breakaway faction of the Liberation Movement.

About five million people voted. The final breakdown of the Majlis seats was: the IRP, eighty-five; the IRP's allies, forty-five; the Liberation Movement, twenty; and independents, eighty-four. Among independent deputies, two had won the election with the support of the Mujahedin-e Khalq. Twenty-eight other independents, who had been backed by the Mujahedin, had lost.[41] None of the deputies belonged to, or was sympathetic to, the Tudeh or the Fedai. Taking the two election rounds together, the IRP won a total of four million votes out of 11.1 million.

The Majlis met on 28 May to check the credentials of the members. This went on for some weeks. Twenty deputies, including Ahmed Madani, were placed under investigation. Of these only six were cleared. Thus the final strength of the house was reduced from 234 to 220. Of these 130 members belonged to the IRP or were allied to it. On 17 July, in the wake of a failed military coup, the deputies elected six lawyers from a list submitted by the Supreme Judicial Council to complete the Guardians Council of twelve. With this the Majlis became operational, and the Islamic Revolutionary Council, a transitional body, came to an ena.

During its seventeen-month existence as a governing body, the IRC passed over one thousand bills. These included nationalising banks, insurance companies and major industries, introducing land reform, nationalising vacant plots within city limits, reducing conscription period, introducing narcotic control, establishing the Islamic Revolutionary Guards, cancelling some agreements with the US and the USSR and joining the Non-Aligned Movement.[42]

At the first business session of the Majlis, the deputies elected Hojatalislam Hashemi-Rafsanjani as speaker. He won 146 votes out of 206. This confirmed the IRP's control of the legislature. Earlier, in February, the party general secretary, Ayatollah Beheshti, had been appointed the supreme court chief by Khomeini. So now the IRP controlled two of the three governmental organs: legislature and judiciary. Since Beheshti's relations with President Bani-Sadr were at best strained, IRP dominance boded ill for the chief executive.

By all accounts Ayatollah Muhammad Husseini Beheshti was close to Khomeini. He had by now proved to be the most politically astute cleric, after Khomeini. While not shunning politics during the Shah's rule he had managed to stay out of jail, except for a brief period in 1975. Born in a religious family of Isfahan in 1928, Beheshti went to Qom for his theological studies when he was eighteen. Two years later he joined the theology faculty of Tehran University. There he participated in the oil nationalisation movement led by Mussadiq. After graduating in 1951, he taught in a Qom high school while pursuing his theological studies in the evenings. In 1959 he gained a doctorate of philosophy at Tehran University. During the 1962-3 turmoil he helped to form the Qom Students' Association.

His involvement with young Islamic militants led Savak to suspect him of association with those who assassinated Premier Mansur in January 1965. His peers therefore arranged for him to leave for Hamburg, West Germany, to supervise the mosque built there earlier with the blessing of Ayatollah Borujerdi.[43] During his five years in West Germany he was involved in the founding of the Muslim Student Union in Europe: the Persian-Speaking Group. In 1969 he travelled to Najaf to meet Khomeini.

On his return to Iran, Beheshti undertook a project of publishing religious texts. In 1971 he started a weeky Quranic commentary session in Tehran. This earned him a brief imprisonment in 1975. The following year he was involved in setting up a nucleus for the Organisation of Militant Clergy. The founders' intention was to form a secret or semi-secret Islamic political party. As the revolutionary movement built up in 1977-8, the OMC became active. Beheshti was a key figure in arranging the smuggling of Khomeini's speeches on cassettes.

He flew to Paris to see Khomeini when the latter was a fugitive there. Beheshti was one of the original members of the Islamic Revolutionary Council, and played a crucial role in the clandestine talks with Iranian military leaders before the revolution. He was the chairman of the IRC from September 1979 to February 1980.

If Khomeini had not ruled against a cleric as president, Beheshti would have certainly contested the office. He would have most probably won. Now, as the supreme court chief, and the leader of the party which controlled the Majlis, Beheshti was a serious rival to Bani-Sadr as the second most powerful man in the Republic.

Months before the IRP had established its supremacy in the Majlis, there were clear signs of conflict between it and the president. On the eve of the Iranian New Year, 21 March, Khomeini called for fundamental revolution in higher education. 'Our universities have changed into propaganda battlefield,' he said. 'Many university teachers are at the service of the West. What frightens us is cultural dependence. We fear . . . universities which train our youth to serve the West or serve communism.'[44]

Khomeini's call was taken up enthusiastically by IRP members and their associates, the Hezbollahis. They began harassing all the 'unIslamic' groups that had established offices on university campuses after having lost their other premises to the IRG and their allies. Since Khomeini had specifically denounced the Mujahedin-e Khalq in his New Year message, the Islamic militants made the Mujahedin their primary target. The campaign against opposition parties built up steadily, gaining impetus from the increasingly tough actions against Iran by the US administration. American pressure on the Islamic Republic concerning the hostage issue enabled Khomeini to mobilise the nation and turn its attention in any direction he wanted to, even if it happened to be against the Mujahedin and the Fedai who had always been hostile to US imperialism.

On 7 April President Carter broke off diplomatic relations with Iran. Khomeini called this a good omen worth celebrating, and declared the next Friday, 11 April, as the Unity Day. On 17 April, Thursday, Carter imposed an economic blockade against Iran. Predictably, Friday prayer sermons were used by the clergy to arouse the faithful to carry the Islamic revolution forward. Hojatalislam Khamanei, the Friday prayer leader of Tehran, warned that pictures of Lenin and the sign of the hammer and sickle would not be tolerated on university campuses. That day the Islamic Revolutionary Council announced that, accepting the Islamic students' demand, it wanted the eighteen political parties with their offices on university campuses to leave them within three days. Immediately clashes broke out between Islamic militants and leftist groups on university campuses in Shiraz, Isfahan and Mashhad.

IRP leaders reckoned that the ultimatum to the leftists on the campuses would damage Bani-Sadr. Given his background of many years of study and teaching at the Sorbonne University, they expected Bani-Sadr to stand up for freedom of expression and association in Iranian universities, and oppose Islamic militants' actions. They also hoped that the episode would expose Bani-Sadr's clandestine links with the Mujahedin. They were to be disappointed on both counts. The Mujahedin agreed to leave peacefully before 21 April, the IRC's deadline. On 22 April, instead of trying to stop attacks on 'unIslamic' groups on the campuses, Bani-Sadr led a column of Islamic students into the Tehran University campus, and described the day as the start of the cultural revolution. However, since the leftist groups (except the Mujahedin) refused to quit the campuses, pitched battles broke out between them on one side, and revolutionary guards and Hezbollahis on the other. These clashes went on for a few days in Tehran, Tabriz, Isfahan, Shiraz and Mashhad. The official toll was thirty-eight dead and 200 injured.[45]

Bani-Sadr's backing for the cultural revolution had much to do with the imminence of the second round of the Majlis elections. He hoped that his move would benefit the candidates endorsed by him. But nothing of the sort happened. Lacking the organisation and resources of their rival, the IRP, the supporters of Bani-Sadr did badly. Only about a score of them were elected.

The subsequent statements and actions by Bani-Sadr damaged his public standing and credibility. In early June he said, 'The whole of Kurdistan will be within our control in a week'.[46] This turned out to be a wildly optimistic estimate. At about the same time he promised to use security forces to stop the attacks on Mujahedin by 'stick-wielding persons'. But he failed to do so. The Mujahedin held a protest rally in Tehran, which drew a crowd of 200,000. Yet there was no end to the harassment being meted out to them. Unable to sustain repeated assaults on their remaining offices, Mujahedin leaders decided to close them. They held another protest rally on 29 June. It was broken up by the Hezbollahis. One man was killed and 300 injured.[47] Following this, public rallies were banned by the interior ministry. Instead, all political parties were invited to participate in a series of debates on television.

Bani-Sadr failed to translate his promises into reality because he lacked direct control over the Revolutionary Komitehs and the Islamic Revolution Guards, the two most effective arms of authority. He could not make up this deficiency by actuating a power base of his own: he lacked a political party of his own. To provide himself with some political ballast he turned to two diverse forces: Mujahedin leaders, and National Front personalities and Bazargan. The former had a party organisation of their own, and the latter had certain popular goodwill behind their names. But by so doing Bani-Sadr began to drift away from the mainstream of Khomeinist politics – a path which was to lead to his dramatic fall a year later.

Despite his basic political weakness Bani-Sadr played tough. But IRP leaders were in no mood to give in. They privately rejected his first three choices for prime minister: Ahmed Madani, Hassan Habibi and Mousa Kalantari, head of the civil service. On 23 July, the day after he had been sworn in as president by the Majlis, Bani-Sadr named Mustapha Mir-Salim, deputy interior minister, as his nominee for prime minister.

Mir-Salim had to be judged in the light of Khomeini's guidelines to the Majlis for approving ministerial appointments. Ministers, he said, had to be '100 per cent Muslim . . . dedicated and 100 per cent revolutionary'.[48] Although thirty-three-year-old Mir-Salim was an IRP member, the party leaders did not think that he met the Ayatollah's prerequisites for a minister. Also, most of the non-IRP deputies considered Mir-Salim to be inexperienced and incompetent. Faced with such opposition, Bani-Sadr agreed to a proposal made in the closed Majlis session on 27 July to let a three-man committee of the house examine the qualifications of all the ministerial candidates according to Khomeini's directive, and make recommendations.

On 8 August the Majlis committee recommended Muhammad Ali Rajai as prime minister. Bani-Sadr disapproved, arguing that Rajai lacked administrative experience. But Rajai had been education minister for about a year and had performed well. So when Rajai's name was offered to the Majlis, 153 of the 196 deputies voted for him.[49] This was a measure of the distance that existed between the president and the Majlis. The gap was to widen even further as months passed.

Muhammad Ali Rajai was a contrast to Bani-Sadr. He was born in a poor family of Qazvin in 1933. When he was four his father, a petty shopkeeper, died. Rajai drifted to Tehran when he was sixteen, and became a peddler. Two years later he joined the air force as an orderly and then as a maintenance trainee. He left the air force in 1956. After a brief stint at teaching in a primary shcool, he enrolled at a teachers' training college. He graduated in 1959. He then taught in a provincial town. From 1963 until his arrest in late 1974, he made his living as a high school teacher in Tehran.

His political career began at eighteen when he came into contact with the Fedaiyan-e Islam in Tehran. He was imprisoned briefly during the June 1963 uprising. Later he joined the Liberation Movement. In 1967, in association with Jalal al-Din Farsi and others, he set up the Islamic Welfare and Mutual Assistance Foundation, a front organisation for political activity. He was a member of the Mujahedin-e Kalq. But, unhappy at the leftward drift of the organisation, he left it in

1973. Soon he became one of the fifteen select students of Ayatollah Beheshti in Tehran. In November 1974 Rajai was arrested as a suspect in the planting of a bomb outside the Tehran office of El Al, the Israeli air line. He was tortured, and this left scars on his feet. During his imprisonment he came into contact with Ayatollah Taleqani and Hojatalislam Khamanei. He was released in November 1978.

A year later he was appointed education minister. He intensified the purge of unIslamic elements from schools, and set up a scheme to retrain teachers in imparting Islamic education to pupils. Even though he did not formally join the IRP, he was close to such IRP stalwarts as Beheshti and Khamanei. They regarded him as a devout Muslim, a maktabi (one who follows Islam in its totality), with a long history of opposition against the Shah, and his roots firmly planted into local politics and the mosque. He won a Majlis seat from Tehran as an associate of the IRP. The party leaders knew that the rise of someone of humble origins, like Rajai, to premiership would inspire tens of thousands of young Iranians from poor and lower middle class families, and enhance the regime's popularity. These young people would readily identify with Rajai, not Bani-Sadr. Rajai lived up to his image. In the speech outlining his government's programme, he said that 'redistribution of wealth' would be its main objective.[50]

The installation of Rajai as premier was a clear signal to Bani-Sadr by IRP leaders that he should expect no cooperation from them. As an IRP official put it, 'Anyone who has spent ten years in France is suspect'.[51] But Bani-Sadr had no intention of giving up his plans to establish his authority over everybody else. He based his claim on the fact that eleven million people had voted for him. The least he could do was to exercise his constitutional rights without inhibition. The constitution required that the president should approve the ministers before their names were submitted to the Majlis for a vote. On 31 August Rajai presented the president with a list of twenty ministers. Bani-Sadr rejected six, pertaining to such important ministries as foreign affairs, oil, economy and finance, and labour.

But he did not stop there. Addressing a rally to commemorate the first anniversary of the Black Friday on 8 September, Bani-Sadr accused the IRP of trying to 'monopolise Islam' and 'control the government by despotism'. However, he made a distinction between the IRP and Khomeini. Bani-Sadr said that he might have differences with Khomeini but he would never execute any decision against the Ayatollah.[52] That night, in a television programme, three IRP leaders attacked Bani-Sadr for dragging Khomeini, by name, into the controversy.

Two days later the Majlis approved all the ministers presented to it. Rajai's cabinet included only one cleric, Hojatalislam Mahdavi-Kani.

Of the fifteen members, nine belonged to the IRP; and they all had a record of active opposition to the Shah. Unsurprisingly, Rajai excluded Bani-Sadr's supporters from his cabinet.

Khomeini was unhappy about the conflict that had broken out. Administering the oath of office to the ministers, he appealed to 'all the authorities from the president downwards' to end their differences, and 'serve the interests of the nation'.[53] But it did nothing to heal the rift.

Oddly enough, the eruption of conflict within the Islamic regime was a symptom of the success that Khomeini and other leaders had in fulfilling the promise of giving Iran a republican constitutional system based on Islam. Within nineteen months of the revolution, a constitution had been adopted and implemented. An elected president was in office, and a representative parliament had approved the prime minister and his cabinet. The Islamic Republic had weathered quite a few storms, major and minor.

The chance of royalist military officers overthrowing the republic declined sharply when the Shah died of cancer on 27 July 1980 in Cairo. His death made redundant one of the main Iranian demands for releasing the American hostages. After the unsuccessful American attempt to secure the hostages' release in late April, the Iranian authorities had scattered the fifty-three diplomats to many unspecified cities. This ruled out any chance of the US mounting another military campaign to rescue the hostages. Once the Majlis had settled the main task of approving the prime minister and his cabinet, it applied itself to the hostage issue. On 16 September it decided to refer the matter to a special committee. The committee was formed on 2 October.

Having derived the maximum political dividend out of the hostage issue during a crucial period in the republic's life, Khomeini wanted it to be put on a back-burner. In any case, the Iraqi invasion of Iran in the third week of September engaged the urgent attention of the Majlis and other official bodies. During the next few years the Iraq-Iran war was to emerge as the most important event of the Islamic Republic's history.

THE GULF WAR

Competition and conflict between Iran and Iraq go far back in history, to the days of the Ottoman empire, when Iraq was the empire's easternmost province. In 1847 Britain and Czarist Russia imposed the Treaty of Erzerum on Iran and Ottoman Turkey. Reflecting the balance of forces between Iran and Ottoman Turkey, the treaty awarded both banks of the Shatt al Arab (The Arab River) to the Ottomans. When the British succeeded the Ottomans in Iraq after the 1914-18 War, they formally laid a claim to both sides of the waterway, but did not press it for fear of alienating the Qajar ruler then being wooed by the Bolsheviks in Russia.

However, when Iraq became independent (under British tutelage) in 1932, it pressed its claims on the Shatt al Arab as well as some disputed parts of the land border. This led to armed clashes between the two neighbours. In 1935 the matter was taken to the League of Nations, which referred it back to the disputants. With Turkey acting as a mediator, Iran and Iraq signed a treaty in July 1937 which – in line with the earlier agreements of 1847, 1913 and 1914 – allocated both sides of the Shatt al Arab to Iraq, except for small areas near Abadan and Khorramshahr.

A generation of fairly peaceful co-existence ended in July 1958, when Iraqi monarchy was overthrown by republican military officers. In November 1959 Muhammad Reza Shah of Iran demanded that the fluvial border be moved to the thalweg (median line of the deepest channel) of the Shatt al Arab. Iranian ships stopped using Iraqi pilots and paying toll fees to the Iraqis. Baghdad lacked the military strength to challenge Tehran.

The Shah became more hostile to Iraq when leaders of the radical Arab Baath Socialist Party seized power in Baghdad in July 1968. Border clashes between Iran and Iraq erupted in March 1969. On 15 April the Baathist government insisted that Iranian ships must pay entry tolls to it. The Shah refused. Iranian vessels entered the Shatt al Arab with a naval escort. Finding itself unequal to the Shah's military power the Iraqi government made no effort to stop the Iranian ships. On 19 April the Shah unilaterally abrogated the 1937 Frontier Treaty with Iraq.

By now the border issue had become a dramatic symptom of deeper conflicts between the two states on domestic social systems and international alignments. To counter-balance the Shah's fast expanding arsenal of Western weapons, Baghdad signed a fifteen-year Friendship and Cooperation Treaty with Moscow in April 1972. The Shah intensified his efforts to destabilise the Baathist regime by aiding Kurdish secessionists in Iraq. In turn Iraq encouraged secessionist elements among Arab, Kurdish and Baluch minorities in Iran.

The Shah soon realised that the activities of Iraqi Kurds were creating secessionist aspirations among Iranian Kurds. This made him amenable to compromise with Baghdad. First Turkey, and then Algeria mediated between the two sides. On 6 March 1975 the Shah signed an agreement with Saddam Hussein, then vice-president of Iraq, in Algiers during an OPEC summit conference. They agreed to delimit 'fluvial frontiers according to the thalweg line' and to 'end all acts of infiltration of a subversive character'.[1] Following this, a Treaty of International Boundaries and Good Neighbourliness between Iran and Iraq was signed in Baghdad on 13 June 1975. It was ratified by the two sides on 17 September.

But while this treaty eased the conflict between Kurds and the Baathist regime, it did nothing to alleviate the grievances of Shias in Iraq. Tension had been rising steadily between Shias, forming 55 per cent of the population and the ruling Baathist party dominated by secular-minded Sunnis.[2] In the late 1960s an ulema-dominated secret organisation Al Daawa al Islamiya (The Islamic Call) was formed in Najaf to articulate Shia grievances and counter secular trends among Shias. Hojatalislam Sayyed Mahdi Hakim, son of Ayatollah Muhsin Hakim, the marja-e taqlid, was one of the founders of the party. In 1974 the Ashura processions of Shias turned into political protest. As a result five Al Daawa leaders were executed. Three years later when police interfered with the Ashura procession midway between Najaf and Karbala (which has the shrine of Imam Hussein), the faithful attacked a police station at nearby Haidariya. To disperse the angry protestors, troops were pressed into action. Later eight Al Daawa protestors, including five clerics, were executed.[3]

When the Iranian revolutionary movement gathered momentum, the Iraqi government cooperated with the Shah – as required by the 1975 treaty – first to silence Khomeini and then expel him in October 1978. Some weeks later Saddam Hussein escorted the Shah's wife, Farah Diba, around Shia holy places in Iraq.

Later, while Baathist leaders viewed the victory of the revolution in

Iran with mounting anxiety, Ayatollah Muhammad Baqir Sadr, an eminent Shia leader based in Najaf, sent a congratulatory message to Khomeini, his long-term friend. 'Other tyrants have yet to see their day of reckoning,' said Sadr.[4] This was an undisguised reference to Baathist leaders.

As Khomeini took to appealing to Iraqis to overthrow the 'non-Muslim' Baathist regime, Baghdad encouraged the Iranian Arabs of Khuzistan to demand autonomy and sabotage oil installations. In Iraq the members of Al Daawa and the recently formed Al Mujahedin resorted to attacks on police stations, Baath Party offices and the People's Militia recruiting centres. Tehran Radio began increasingly to refer to Ayatollah Sadr as the 'Khomeini of Iraq', thus encouraging Iraqi Shias to seek his guidance.

In early June three Iraqi planes pursuing Kurdish rebels into Iran bombed several Iranian villages. This inflamed relations between Baghdad and Tehran. Soon the Iraqi authorities put Ayatollah Sadr under house arrest. This led to protest demonstrations in the Shia districts of Baghdad and in southern cities. The government used army firings to disperse the demonstrators. Scores were killed and some 3,000 arrested. Tehran Radio stepped up its anti-Baathist propaganda, calling on the faithful to replace 'the gangsters and tyrants of Baghdad' with 'the rule of divine justice'. The Iraqi government responded by smuggling among other things 170,000 AK-47 sub-machine guns to the Arab dissidents of Khuzistan.[5]

Intent on crushing Shia opposition, Saddam Hussein insisted on the execution of many Shia leaders and military officers found to have been Al Daawa members. President Ahmed Hassan Bakr reportedly refused to sign the execution orders, and offered to resign. Saddam Hussein became president on 17 July. Within a fortnight he discovered a major 'anti-state conspiracy'. It involved twenty-two top Baathist leaders, all of whom were executed.[6]

Relations between Iraq and Iran deteriorated rapidly, with their armies periodically clashing along the border. President Hussein followed the twin-headed policy of suppressing Shia religious leaders and portraying the Khomeini regime as representing Iranian imperialism, intent on expanding westward in the name of protecting Iraqi Shias. In December he called for the annulment of the 1975 Algiers Accord.

Saddam Hussein's persecution of Shia militants led to the execution in March 1980 of ninety-seven civilians and military personnel, half of them members of Al Daawa, an organisation whose membership was now punishable by death. On 1 April there was an unsuccessful hand grenade attack on Iraq's deputy premier, Tariq Aziz, in Baghdad. Al Daawa members were involved. The government intensified its repression of the organisation. On 8 April Khomeini called on the Iraqi army to overthrow Saddam Hussein. Iraq bombed Qasr-e Shirin, an Iranian border town, and deported over 15,000 Iraqi citizens of Iranian origin to Iran.[7] President Hussein pressured Ayatollah Sadr to reverse his religious judgement that the Baathist regime was 'unIslamic' and that relations with it were haram, religiously forbidden. Sadr refused. He was executed secretly, most probably on 8 April. Some days later the news leaked out. Khomeini declared three days of mourning in Iran.[8] While Tehran initiated a policy of imparting guerrilla training to Iraqi Shias and then sending them back to Iraq, the Baathist government continued its expulsions of Iraqi Shias.

The two countries severed diplomatic relations in June. Tensions rose sharply. Tehran Radio's Arabic service turned virulently anti-Saddam Hussein. On his part the Iraqi president allowed Shahpour Bakhtiar and General Oveissi a broadcasting station each on Iraqi territory. Besides conducting anti-Khomeini propaganda, these stations broadcast specific advice to the partisans of Bakhtiar and Oveissi among Iraqi tribals and armed forces. It was the hope of Hussein as well as Bakhtiar and Oveissi that their plans to establish an anti-Khomeini base inside Iran would succeed.

As stated earlier, all these plans, including the most serious one on 9/10 July, failed. The Iraqi government then seems to have decided to invade Iran with a view to changing the regime there. It was encouraged by persistent reports of conflict between President Bani-Sadr and IRP leaders, low morale among military officers, and rapid deterioration in the effectiveness of Iranian weaponry. The Baathist plan, apparently drawn up in consultations with Bakhtiar and Oveissi, visualised Iraqi forces capturing Khuzistan within a week, and then linking up with the Kurdish insurgents already fighting the Iranian troops. These liberated areas were then to be declared the 'Free Republic of Iran' under Bakhtiar, operating from the temporary capital of Ahvaz. This was seen as a catalyst to set off widespread uprisings against the Khomeini regime by the military as well as discontented civilians.[9]

Events moved fast during the first half of September. On 2 September clashes erupted between Iraqi and Iranian troops near Qasr-e Shirin. Fighting continued there and at other points along the border for the next ten days. On 6 September Iraq threatened to seize the 200 sq. kms in the Musian region (awarded to it by the Algiers Accord) if Iran did not cede them within a week. Five days later Baghdad claimed to have captured most of the territory. President Hussein informed the Iraqi parliament on 17 September that Iraq was abrogating the 1975 Treaty forthwith, and that Iranian ships entering or leaving the Shatt al Arab must take Iraqi pilots. Iran refused to do so. Heavy fighting broke out between the two sides along the waterway.

On 22 September Iraq invaded Iran, with its warplanes striking ten Iranian airfields. Artillery duels broke out on both sides of the Shatt al Arab. The next day, while Iraqi aircraft bombed Abadan refinery, nearly a third of the 200,000-strong Iraqi army marched into Khuzistan at various points.

The Iranian army was ill-prepared to repel the invaders. It was only on 20 September that the authorities finally got around to calling up military reserves. Most of the army troops were engaged in fighting Kurdish insurgents, and a big proportion of their 1,125 heavy tanks were stationed along the Soviet border.[10] On the other hand the 75,000 strong air force, with its over 400 combat aircraft, did well. Soon after the Iraqi invasion, 140 Iranian warplanes bombed the Iraqi oil centres of Mosul and Kirkuk, and the Basra petro-chemical complex. Fighting spread rapidly to the oil centres of both sides so that they had to suspend oil shipments on 26 September. Since all the Iraqi airbases were within the striking range of Iranian jets, the Baghdad government soon despatched most of its 332 combat aircraft to Jordan, Kuwait, Saudi Arabia, North Yemen and Oman.[11]

On 28 September the UN Security Council called for an end to the use of force by both countries. The resolution was supported by the superpowers, with the US stating that it was against 'any dismemberment of Iran'.[12] (The US statement was meant to smooth the way for the release of the American hostages in Iran.) President Bani-Sadr rejected the UN call, arguing that as long as Iraq was 'in violation of our territorial sovereignty', Iran saw 'no use in any discussion concerning the conflict'.[13]

As it happened, Bani-Sadr had learnt of Saddam Hussein's secret plans two months earlier. 'At the beginning of August we already had in our hands outlines of Saddam Hussein's [war] plans as well as a detailed account of the conversations which had taken place in France among the Iranian counter-revolutionaries, the Iraqi representatives, Americans, and Israeli military experts,' Bani-Sadr told Eric Rouleau of Le Monde in early October. 'We had to pay dearly for these documents which were bought in Paris. They have proved to be surprisingly accurate.'[14]

Now that the Iraqi invasion had occurred, Iran experienced a surge of patriotism. It engulfed the military, the IRG, and civilians – including Khuzistani Arabs and Kurdish autonomists. The vehicles that were used to evacuate women, children and old men from the threatened oil cities of Khorramshahr, Abadan and Ahvaz returned with volunteers from all over the country. They included clerics and theological students, young men in T-shirts and jeans, and tribals in their traditional costumes. Instead of being welcomed as liberators by Khuzistani Arabs, as they had been made to believe, the Iraqi troops found themselves facing spirited resistance.

Listening to Bani-Sadr's pleas, the revolutionary authorities virtually halted the purges and executions that had been set in motion by the failed military coup in July. This improved military morale. Speedy arrival of urgently needed weapons and ammunition from Syria and North Korea helped. Finally, the Soviet warning to the West on 8 October to stay out of the conflict worked in favour of Iran.[15]

Khomeini invested Bani-Sadr with 'exclusive powers' to conduct the war. As the head of the Supreme Defence Council, the Iranian president warned that Iran would strike against any Arab nation that gave military aid to Iraq. On his part Khomeini called on Iraqi Shias to rebel against Saddam Hussein.[16] Of the Arab countries, only Jordan sided with Iraq publicly. While sympathetic toward Iraq, the Gulf states restrained themselves from aiding it overtly. Syria and Libya did the same on the Iranian side.

President Hussein had hoped to end the war with victory for his country by Eid al Adha (the Festival of Sacrifice) due on 20 October. Instead, on the eve of the Eid, he blamed the slowness of Iraqi advance on the enemy cannons being 'greater in number', the enemy tanks being 'more advanced', and Iranian officers having had the benefit of the best of the American and other Western training.[17]

The ultimate responsibility for conducting the war lay with Saddam Hussein. In order to keep the casualties low, he had instructed the generals to rely heavily on artillery and mortar fire, and avoid hand to hand combat. While this restrained the generals, it kept the people united behind the president. On the ideological front Saddam Hussein tried to outdo Khomeini in Islamic fervour. He routinely described the present conflict as the 'Second Qadisiya', referring to the battle of Qadisiya in 637, when Arab Muslims defeated the Persian army of the Sassanians. Pictures of the President holding the Quran or at prayer filled the walls of city streets everywhere. He was quick to declare the birthday of Imam Ali, the most revered figure of Shias, as a national holiday.

Reflecting a mood of confidence, the Iraqi first deputy premier, Taha Yassin Ramadan, said on 21 October that Iraq would 'continue to clean up the region and take cities of Arabistan [i.e., Khuzistan]' as long as 'Tehran will not negotiate'.[18] The next day Bakhtiar declared his willingness to cooperate with Baghdad to overthrow the Khomeini regime. These statements put an official stamp on something that had been widely known and believed.

Just then the US was in the final stage of its presidential election campaign. Knowing the electoral value of the freed American diplomats returning home, President Carter offered concessions to Iran. On 2 November, after many procedural and other delays, the Iranian parliament endorsed its special committee's recommendation that the hostages be released after the US administration had accepted the conditions specified earlier by Khomeini: America must return the properties of the 'defunct Shah', cancel all financial claims against Iran, release Iran's frozen assets, and promise 'political and military non-intervention' in Iranian affairs.[19] While conceding the Iranian demands Carter pointed out that the issue of the Shah's assets was beyond his constitutional powers, and could only be settled by American courts. He had earlier promised to release the $300 worth of American weapons that had been paid for by Iran but had been withheld.[20]

Despite the keenness of both sides to clinch a deal before the polling day, 4 November, all that happened was that the Militant Students passed on the custody of the hostages to the Iranian government. Carter was thus robbed of a last minute coup on the hostage issue – something which, by all accounts, would have won him a second term of office. Carter's defeat pleased the Iranian regime, particularly Khomeini. After all the Ayatollah had once described Carter as one of three satanic figures confronting Iran, the other two being the Shah and Saddam Hussein. The Shah was dead, and Carter was out of office. That left Saddam Hussein.

On the eve of the Islamic New Year, 10 November, Khomeini called on Muslim countries throughout the world to rise up against Iraq for invading another Muslim state. The same day Saddam Hussein appealed for Muslim support everywhere for Iraq's 'holy war' against the descendants of the Persian empire, which was destroyed by Islam fourteen centuries ago.[21] He was in good form. Iraqi troops occupied a third of Khuzistan. They controlled a chain of cities and towns, extending from Khorramshahr in the south to Qasr-e Shiri on the central front. They had besieged Abadan.

Such losses hurt Bani-Sadr's standing with Khomeini. The shock of the Iraqi invasion had compelled Bani-Sadr and his rivals to sink their differences to fight the enemy. But once the immediate danger of the Islamic Republic's disintegration had passed, old frictions came to the surface. The Iranian president concentrated on building up the army whereas Premier Rajai and the IRP leaders focussed on bolstering the Islamic Revolutionary Guards. Bani-Sadr blamed the poor performance at the front on the incompetence of the Rajai government. In an unpublicised letter to Khomeini on 31 October he urged the Ayatollah to dismiss the Rajai government. In short, instead of the war creating a lasting national consensus and transforming the landscape of Iranian politics, it was being integrated into the existing political divisions.

Internalisation of the war

As Iran approached Muharram, the national mood was sombre. It was a contrast from the previous Muharram when, in the wake of the US embassy seizure, the mood was boisterous, with Iranians engaged in a drive to rid society of all American influences. Now the needs of the hour were unity and a capable fighting force led by professionals. In his pre-Muharram message, therefore, Khomeini criticised those ulema who 'interfere with the armies while being ignorant of military affairs just like myself'. He stressed that 'Experts should be allowed to perform tasks unencumbered by meddling from those who have no knowledge of the subject'.[22] He appealed for unity.

He privately advised that speech-making before the mourners in Tehran on the Ashura, 19 November, should be limited to strictly religious topics. A million people gathered for the traditional Ashura speeches. IRP speakers kept to Khomeini's guideline. But Bani-Sadr did not. He attacked the 'party' (meaning the IRP) for being repressive, dictatorial and practising torture on political prisoners.[23]

This fully revived the old conflicts. Bani-Sadr was unhappy at the way radio and television, run by IRP supporters, concentrated on the fighting prowess of the IRG, and neglected the achievements of the military and its commander-in-chief. He also opposed IRP leaders' insistence on holding by-elections to the forty vacant Majlis seats. He saw this as an IRP ploy to increase its majority to two-thirds of the house. He suggested that these elections be held after the war had ended. Disgusted at the vilification campaign against him by the IRP, Bani-Sadr took to spending most of his time at the front. This improved his relations with the officer corps but weakened his political base in the capital.

One of Bani-Sadr's regular forums was his newspaper, *Inqilab-e Islami*. In the 30 November issue he followed up his general charges against the IRP with specific accusations of torture and corruption by the anti-narcotic squad at Tehran's Qasr prison. This incensed his rivals. On 4 December Hussein Khomeini, a grandson of the Ayatollah, charged in a newspaper interview that Bani-Sadr partisans were plotting against Khomeini. Over the next two days, despite appeals for unity by Khomeini and Montazeri, fighting broke out between the opposing factions in a dozen cities. Five people were killed. Khomeini threatened to dissolve the Majlis and the presidency if internecine violence continued. He then appointed a three-man commission to investigate 'the rumours of torture'.[24]

But this changed little. At an Isfahan rally on 12 December Bani-

Sadr supporters tore up Khomeini's pictures. The IRG replied by attacking what it described as 'leftists, liberals and people intoxicated by the West'. Khomeini counselled restraint. 'To preserve unity, people should not react if I or my pictures are insulted', he said. The IRP cancelled its scheduled demonstrations.

On 17 December, in his column in the *Inqilab-e Islami*, Bani-Sadr tried to show how IRP leaders were hindering his war plans in order to advance the interests of the IRG. He argued that the army needed time to prepare an effective counter-offensive. Since he quoted from a closed session of the Majlis, held to discuss the war strategy, IRP leaders accused him of giving away 'war secrets'.[25] More importantly, his plea for time was weakened when the Iraqis invaded Kurdistan on 26 December. Bani-Sadr now had no choice but to mount a counter-offensive. As he made preparations, Khomeini ruled that any such action without the Islamic Revoutionary Guards would be haram, religiously forbidden.[26]

The Iranians launched an offensive in the Susangard, Dezful and Gilan-e Gharb areas on 5 January. This silenced the clerical critics of Bani-Sadr. The president urged the people to show patience. On 15 January Khomeini appealed to Iranians 'not to say things that upset the leaders of the army, the president or the government'.[27] So for a while there was comparative peace on the home front. But that made little difference to the battle front. The inadequately prepared Iranian offensive petered out after about a fortnight, achieving very little on the ground.

In any case this episode was overshadowed by rapid developments on the American hostage issue: an issue which Tehran and Washington wanted to resolve before Carter handed over the presidency to Ronald Reagan on 21 January. The deal struck by the Iranian government with the US administration had to be approved by the Majlis and necessary legislation passed. Between 12 and 14 January the Majlis passed two laws, one allowing international arbitration in the disputes with the US, and the other nationalising the assets of the former Shah and his fifty-eight Iranian and five American associates. This allowed Carter to declare, on 19 January, that a detailed agreement with Iran had been worked out. America agreed to unfreeze the Iranian assets of $12 billion. Of these $4 billion were to be retained by America against claims by 330 US companies and individuals. Of the remaining, $1.4 billion were to be held against international claims on Iran. The Iranian government agreed to repay $3.7 billion to various consortiums of foreign banks. That left a net sum of $2.3 billion for Iran. This was returned to Iran by 03:16 hours (Washington time) on 21 January. Nine hours later a plane carrying fifty-two American hostages left Tehran's Mehrabad airport for Algiers. Thus ended a 444-day-long saga. The final result was described by the Majlis speaker, Hojatalislam Hashemi-Rafsanjani, as 'a great victory over the Great Satan'.[28]

But President Bani-Sadr thought otherwise. He felt that Iran had done badly. He complained that Bahzad Nabavi, the minister in charge of the affair, had kept him informed of the developments only up to 12 January. After that he, the republic's president, had been ignored. It was obvious that Bani-Sadr would not let the matter rest.

The failure of Iran's January offensive did not affect the pace of the military build-up which had preceded it. At the outset of the war Iran could only muster one soldier to fight four Iraqis. But by late January Tehran was able to match the five divisions that Baghdad had deployed on the war fronts. The Iranians had by then killed 5,000 to 6,000 Iraqi troops, and lost 7,000 to 8,000 men of their own. Both sides had suffered economically. Iranian oil exports declined from 1.5 million b/d to 600,000 b/d. The fall was more steep in the case of Iraq: from 2.5 million b/d to 500,000 b/d.

The improved military strength seemed to encourage Bani-Sadr to pursue his dispute with the Rajai government and the Majlis on the resolution of the American hostage crisis. On 1 February he was reported as saying that a national debate should have been held on whether the release of the American diplomats was 'a great service or high treason'.[29] Three days later in his column in the *Inqilab-e Islami* he criticised the US hostages deal, and held the incompetence and inexperience of the Rajai government responsible for an agreement 'which fell much shorter than what could have been achieved early in the crisis'.

Khomeini tried to stay neutral in the rising conflict. On 2 February he instructed radio and television to 'take no side in the conflict' and not to serve 'any special group'.[30] He widened this call on the second anniversary of the revolution on 11 February. 'This is a strict reminder to the clergy in the judiciary, the Revolutionary Komitehs, the development foundations, and other organisations that they should not interfere at all in the affairs of the state for which they are not qualified,' he warned. 'Such meddling could cause the public to become distrustful of them, and the nation to break away from them.'[31]

Encouraged by this, thirty-eight writers, academics, lawyers and journalists addressed an open letter to Khomeini. In it they accused the IRP of monopolising power, looking down on the masses, abolishing judicial security, ending freedoms of expression and assembly, suppressing minorities, and being openly hostile to knowledge and the arts. Khomeini was quick to reply. The regime had its shortcomings, he conceded, but it was unfair to say that there had been no change except the replacement of the label 'Monarchy' with the term 'Islamic Republic'. To put it briefly, he added, 'The country's previous leaders had plundered Iran's wealth, lived in luxury, become corrupt, wrecked the economy, and made Iran dependent on foreigners'.[32]

By now a direct correlation could be discerned between the developments on the war front and those in domestic politics. An improvement on the battle front encouraged dissent at home. By mid-February the Iranians were strong enough in the battlefield to block further Iraqi advance. The result was a stalemate. This was conducive to the success of peacemaking efforts which had been initiated by the UN Security Council, the Non-Aligned Movement, and the Islamic Conference Organisation.

On 1 March Khomeini met the nine-member ICO delegation visiting Tehran. He urged them to 'sit in judgement on Iraq' and fight whosoever had 'launched the aggression'.[33] After consulting Baghdad, the ICO team offered a peace plan on 5 March. It specified a ceasefire in a week to be followed by Iraqi withdrawal from Iran. Ayatollah Montazeri said that Iran would accept nothing less than 'Saddam Hussein's overthrow and trial'. The Supreme Defence Council rejected the ICO plan unanimously. Two days later Iraq said that it would not withdraw from 'a single inch of Iranian territory before Tehran recognises Iraqi rights'.[34]

Khomeini had shrewdly allowed the ICO delegation a chance to define the terms of truce and thus test Iraqi morale. When Baghdad showed itself eager for peace, Khomeini was encouraged to fight on until victory – and Saddam Hussein's downfall. Realising the trap that he had fallen into, the Iraqi president tried to reverse the process. His forces made a determined attempt to capture Susangard on 19-20 March. They failed. This was a turning point in the war. It meant that having captured and retained 14,000 sq. kms of Iranian territory in the first six months of the conflict, Iraq had now reached the limit of its advance.[35] This marked the end of the first phase of the Gulf War.

The internal scene in Iran looked fractious. Street violence was a rising problem. Those who disagreed with the dominant faction in the regime were getting short shrift. In early February, Fedai and Paykar members tried to celebrate the tenth anniversary of the Fedai attack on the Siakal gendarmerie post. Some 5,000 leftists gathered for a demonstration in the capital. They were teargassed by revolutionary guards, and attacked by Hezbollahis armed with bricks and assault rifles. Fifty people were injured.[36] Disturbed by the episode and an open protest letter addressed to him by a group of writers, academics, lawyers and journalists, Khomeini sent a letter to the Majlis on 17 February urging it to act to end political violence. His call was taken up by forty opposition deputies. In an open letter of their own, they stated that failure to halt street violence, manifesting itself in counter-demonstrations by Islamic militants, would strengthen the suspicion that extremists had 'infiltrated the Republic's organs'.[37] A week later while 133 intellectuals charged government officials with practising torture, Bazargan stated that the IRP was trying to silence the Liberation Movement in the Majlis.

An event scheduled for 5 March, the anniversary of the death of Mussadiq, seemed well-suited to show whether or not opposition protests had been effective. A rally was to be held at the Tehran University campus. President Bani-Sadr – an ardent admirer of Mussadiq who kept a large portrait of the nationalist hero in his office – was invited to speak. He agreed. According to Ali-Reza Nobari, a confidant of the president, Khomeini (who disliked Mussadiq) sent messages to Bani-Sadr not to address the rally.[38] Bani-Sadr ignored the advice.

At this rally, attended by about 100,000 people, the Hezbollahis cut loudspeaker cables and shouted slogans. After the unarmed policemen present at the rally had failed to eject the disrupters, Bani-Sadr urged the audience and his presidential guards to arrest the trouble-makers. In the mêlée that followed forty-five people were injured. Bani-Sadr partisans seized sixty-seven disrupters, and frog-marched them, complete with their weapons and identity cards, to the platform. Bani-Sadr read out their identity cards to the audience. These showed that far from being irresponsible riff-raff, as the IRP-dominated media had portrayed them, the Hezbollahis were linked to the IRG, the Revolutionary Komitchs, and the IRP.[39] This was a coup of a sort for Bani-Sadr. Through this dramatic gesture, he damaged the credibility of the leaders of three important revolutionary organisations. It was a serious matter. That night the Ayatollah's office announced that Khomeini would not receive visitors for the next ten days. He went into retreat in order to focus his mind, something he did when faced with a major crisis.

During Khomeini's silence the conflict between Bani-Sadr and his opponents sharpened. In the Majlis, Hojatalislam Khalkhali argued that since the president had exceeded his authority by ordering arrests he had committed 'high treason against the constitutional law and must therefore be tried'. Ayatollah Beheshti, the supreme court chief, said that he could not rule out such a possibility. Bani-Sadr hit back. 'The question is whether the Pahlavis are to be replaced in the Islamic Republic by those wielding clubs,' he wrote in the *Inqilab-e Islami* on 9 March. The next day 130 Islamic judges called Bani-Sadr a traitor and condemned him for creating 'disunity, chaos and clashes'.[40]

On 11 March the Majlis passed a bill which authorised the prime minister to appoint acting cabinet ministers. It then approved such ministers for finance and economic affairs, and commerce. Opposing the move, Bazargan, the leader of the twelve Liberation Movement deputies, described it as a ploy to force Bani-Sadr to resign. That day the *Inqilab-e Islami* accused the IRP of appointing its members to 'almost all the judicial posts', and complained of summary trials and executions, torture and forced entry into private homes. On 12 March when Bani-Sadr supporters held a rally at the Tehran University campus, it was disrupted by IRP members and sympathisers. In the fighting that broke out gunfire was used.

As soon as Khomeini ended his public silence, he called a meeting of top level officials and politicians: Bani-Sadr, Rajai, Beheshti, Hashemi-Rafsanjani, Mousavi-Ardebili, Bazargan and Ahmed Khomeini. After a four-hour-long discussion Khomeini appointed a three-man concilia-tion committee to 'study complaints and problems relating to the war and other disputed issues'. This body was also to act as the watchdog of the media to see that they remained neutral in the conflict. The members of the conciliation committee were: Ayatollah Mousavi-Ardebili (Khomeini's nominee), Hojatalislam Eshraqi (Bani-Sadr's nominee), and Hojatalislam Muhammad Ali Yazdi, a Majlis deputy (the IRP's nominee). Khomeini replaced his appointees on the Supreme Defence Council, and ordered military officers to obey the commander-in-chief, Bani-Sadr. He also said that it would be 'better' if politicians 'gave no more speeches until the end of the war'. In his own speech to 218 Majlis deputies on the eve of the Iranian New Year he rebuked politicians for their 'lust for power', and decreed national unity for the customary ten days of the New Year celebrations.[41]

This time Khomeini's appeal worked. And the consequent political truce helped improve military morale. Khomeini mentioned this in his message on the second anniversary of the founding of the Islamic Republic on 1 April. Responding to the opposition criticism, the Ayatollah instructed judicial authorities to set up 'delegations to study the country's courts and dismiss unsuitable judges'. He called for the prosecution of all those revolutionary guards who were 'interfering in matters that are up to courts or other institutions [to settle]'.[42]

Khomeini's ban on political speeches hurt Bani-Sadr more than the other side. Bani-Sadr had no political party of his own. All he had was a Tehran-based newspaper. So the only way he could expand his following in the country was by addressing public rallies. According to Nobari's statements (made about a year later), ever since Rajai had been foisted as premier on Bani-Sadr, the Iranian president had known that he would have to part company with Khomeini. Bani-Sadr therefore wanted to use the intervening time to educate the public so that when the split came, a majority of the Iranian people would take his side.[43] But here he was, unable to deliver public speeches.

As for Bani-Sadr's opponents, they wished to retain the political initiative they had. On 8 April the interior minister informed all political parties that they needed official permits for their publications. The previous day the prosecutor general had charged the *Mizan* (Scales), the Liberation Movement's paper, with 'slander, libel, disturbing national security and false reporting', and ordered its closure.[44] Later he arrested the editor of the *Mizan* on a charge of divulging military secrets. In an interview with the *Inqilab-e Islami*, President Bani-Sadr described these acts as 'illegal' and 'a serious threat to freedom'. He revealed that he had written a protesting letter to Khomeini and that he had lodged complaints of criminal offence against Premier Rajai and his executive affairs minister, Bahzad Nabavi. These moves were effective: the *Mizan* reappeared on 26 April.

But Bani-Sadr's earlier charge of torture in Iranian prisons was not upheld by the commission appointed by Khomeini in December. One of its members told the Majlis on 12 April that after studying 3,620 files and visiting many civilian and military jails, the commission had concluded that torture did not exist.[45] A week later another member, Hojatalislam Muhammad Montazeri, said that instances of 'physical maltreatment' were few, and that these were committed by 'unauthorised people'. He added that warrants for the arrest and prosecution of these persons had been issued.[46]

Apart from these minor skirmishes between Bani-Sadr and his opponents, the period of mid-March to mid-May was one of comparative peace between the two sides. This had an uplifting effect on the armed forces. On 4 April the Iranian air force carried out its most daring raid on Iraq. Aided by the air cover provided by Syrian warplanes, Iranian jets struck deep into Iraq at Al Walid airbase, destroying up to forty-six Iraqi planes.[47] This was a severe blow to Baghdad. It came at a time when Tehran claimed that it had suffered war damages to the extent of $16,000 million: $12,000 million in lost oil revenue, and the rest in war expenditure and the cost of importing heating fuel and diesel. In contrast the annual defence budget for 1981-2 was $6,300 million.[48] The lack of strife at home was well-illustrated in mid-May, when General Fallahi, the joint chief of staff, gave an interview to the *Inqilab-e Islami*. In it he claimed that over the past three months Iranian soldiers and revolutionary guards had regained 40 per cent of the occupied territory of Iran.[49]

However, domestic political truce applied only to Bani-Sadr and his rivals. It did not include such opposition as the militant Fedai Khalq (Minority) – formed after a split in the party in June 1980 – or the Mujahedin-e Khalq. On 22 April, the first anniversary of the cultural revolution, Mujahedin supporters demonstrated in favour of the re-opening of universities. Clashes occurred between them and IRP partisans in the Caspian towns of Amol, Sari, and Qaemshahr. Four Mujahedin women were killed.[50] On 27 April some 100,000 Mujahedin supporters gathered for a rally in Tehran to honour the dead. They were attacked by Hezbollahis. One person was killed and many more were injured. On May Day the Mujahedin tried to join official celebrations by gathering outside the Tehran University campus. They were prevented, violently, from so doing. The resulting clashes led to three deaths and injuries to about 100.

Violence against the Mujahedin-e Khalq had become endemic. IRP leaders were hostile to the party for a variety of reasons. Some of them had been members of the organisation in the past: a fact which now embarrassed them. It was a party which had proved to be particularly attractive to young sons and daughters of traditional middle classes, the mainstay of the IRP. It had a history of armed resistance against the Shah in which its guerrillas had suffered many deaths, an element which appealed strongly to young Shias.

Khomeini was equally hostile to the Mujahedin. Initially he had attacked them without naming them. On their part Mujahedin leaders had criticised Khomeini obliquely. In April 1980 they had removed their offices from university campuses peacefully when they were ordered to do so. But the situation changed when the Mujahedin intervened directly in the power politics of Khomeini's regime. In mid-June 1980 Masoud Rajavi, the Mujahedin chief, passed on to President Bani-Sadr a tape-recording of a conversation that Hassan Ayat, an eminent IRP figure, had with some Islamic student leaders on a plan to undermine the president's authority. The *Inqilab-e Islami* published the conversation on 17 June. It caused a stir. IRP leaders were deeply embarrassed. They made their peace with Bani-Sadr in writing a week later. From then on Khomeini attacked the Mujahedin by name and routinely called them the munafiqin, hypocrites. There was a brief respite soon after the Iraqi invasion in September. The Mujahedin offered to fight for their country, and thousands of them rushed to the front to enlist. However, when the truce between Bani-Sadr and his rivals broke down in mid-November, and Bani-Sadr began courting the Mujahedin, the Ayatollah turned more overtly anti-Mujahedin.

The appointment of the conciliation committee in March 1981 lowered the political temperature but did not cure the underlying ailment of the Iranian body politic. Bani-Sadr found a way out of Khomeini's injunction against political speeches. He resorted to addressing military garrisons and giving interviews to foreign press. In these he alleged that the IRP was leading the country to 'new despotism' and that the Rajai government was failing to put the economy right.[51] In an interview with the Paris-based *Le Matin* (The Morning) published on 15 May, he claimed that he had more than 500 dossiers on the victims of torture. This was at sharp variance with what the official committee on torture had to say in its report released on 17 May.

That day two men from the presidential office were caught photocopying certain documents in the foreign ministry, and arrested. In the absence of a cabinet minister,[52] the foreign ministry was being run by an under-secretary, an appointee of Premier Rajai. He made a public issue of the thievish behaviour of the men from the presidential office. Bani-Sadr replied that the foreign ministry documents were needed for 'investigative purposes'. On 20 May the Majlis authorised the prime minister to appoint top officials to some forty national institutions – the Central Bank, the national police and so on. Since, constitutionally speaking, this power rested with the president, the Majlis decision was a clear move to curtail Bani-Sadr's authority.

Obviously the power struggle within the regime had now reached a crucial stage. The next move lay with Khomeini, the supreme arbiter. Would he side with Rajai or Bani-Sadr? At the time there was much speculation on the subject. However, going by the material published since then, it seems obvious that Khomeini had by then decided to move against Bani-Sadr. He had done so after he had been shown evidence of the CIA's contacts with Bani-Sadr in Paris and Tehran.

The ousting of Bani-Sadr

One of the main activities of the Militant Students occupying the US embassy in Tehran had been to collate and decode the massive collection of secret documents they had seized there, and to interrogate the diplomats who had been engaged in intelligence activities. They had even managed to reconstruct the shredded documents. By collating and decoding certain documents, and interrogating at length half a dozen CIA employees among their captives, the Militant Students reconstructed the following story about Bani-Sadr.

In the autumn of 1978, one William A. Foster of a consultancy firm in Philadelphia, USA, contacted Bani-Sadr in Paris with a view to hiring him as a consultant on the Iranian economy. Foster's real name was Vernon A. Cassin: he had been a CIA officer in the Middle East for nearly two decades. Nothing came of his overture to Bani-Sadr in Paris. Then in June 1979 a CIA source in Tehran, codenamed 'SDRotter' referred to the conversation that his cousin had had with Bani-Sadr over dinner, and urged the American intelligence agency to get in touch with Bani-Sadr, then a prominent member of the Islamic Revolutionary Council and in charge of Iran's economic and financial affairs. Two months later William A. Foster arrived in Tehran. Working closely with the local CIA station chief, Thomas Ahern (codename 'Paquin'), he contacted Bani-Sadr and offered him $1,000 a month as fees for consultation on the Iranian economy which was to take 'only half an hour from time to time'. Apparently meetings took place between Bani-Sadr and Foster/Ahern. For the captured documents showed that Ahern had seen Bani-Sadr three times when the latter had passed on to Ahern 'trivial information on the mechanism of the revolution'. What had helped the Militant Students to decode 'SDLure-1' as Bani-Sadr was the mention in the same cable of the phone number of Bani-Sadr's sister at whose place he was then staying.[53]

This information was passed on to Khomeini some time in April 1981. There was no evidence to show that Bani-Sadr had accepted any money from the CIA. But the mere fact that the CIA had considered him suitable to 'cultivate and recruit' as an informer, first in Paris and then in Tehran, was an important contributory factor to turn Khomeini decidedly against Bani-Sadr.

Khomeini backed the 20 May Majlis decision to strengthen Rajai's power at the expense of Bani-Sadr. He declared on 27 May that anyone attempting to overturn parliamentary laws would face charges leading to the death penalty. Bani-Sadr was unbowed by the warning. In a speech at Shiraz airbase he said that he was not afraid of threats to put him on trial. What is more, he revealed that before agreeing to let the Rajai government take over the American hostage issue he had insisted that any deal it made with the US administration must include the provision for the shipping of the US military parts for which Iran had already paid. He argued that by failing to do so, the Rajai government had 'simply made it impossible for our armed forces to perform their battle front duties effectively and conclusively'.[54] This was a highly contentious and sensitive issue, and Bani-Sadr's statements lost him whatever sympathy the three-man conciliation committee had for him.

On 30 May Rajai attacked Bani-Sadr without naming him. 'Those who studied abroad when the revolution occurred had little contact with the people,' Rajai said in the Majlis. 'But after they returned [to Iran] they demanded a role in the revolution.' That day at a press conference Bani-Sadr retorted, 'I shall not be outmanoeuvred by insults and abuse. I will not resign.'[55]

From then on events moved fast. On 1 June the conciliation committee rebuked Bani-Sadr for making inflammatory speeches, and countermanding Khomeini's advice to all politicians to maintain silence on controversial subjects. The next day, following the conciliation committee's recommendation, the supreme court chief, Ayatollah Beheshti, said that Bani-Sadr would be tried for violating the constitution by ordering arrests on 5 March rally and by refusing to endorse the ministerial appointments of Premier Rajai.[56] That day revolutionary guards arrested Manuchehr Masoudi, the president's legal adviser. The finance minister declared that Ali-Reza Nobari, the Central Bank's governor appointed by Bani-Sadr, was unfit for the job. These moves were part of a drive to dismiss Bani-Sadr's appointees, and reduce the presidency to the role of performing ceremonial functions.

On 6 June the prosecutor general closed down six newspapers, including the *Inqilab-e Islami*, licensed to Bani-Sadr. The following day, speaking in his home town of Hamadan, Bani-Sadr called on the youth to stand firm against 'all the violators of the law' and 'to resist tendencies towards dictatorship'. Addressing Bani-Sadr on state radio, Khomeini said, 'You call this dictatorship because you want to disobey the Islamic parliament and the Islamic prosecutor general.' Then he warned, 'You saw what I did to Muhammad Reza Pahlavi. I will do the same to you if you do not obey the Islamic parliament, the Islamic prosecutor general, and the Supreme Defence Council.'[57]

Khomeini banned all protest action on 9 June. The Hezbollahis, led by Hojatalislam Hadi Ghaffari, took over the presidential head-quarters. Revolutionary guards broke up pro-Bani-Sadr demonstrations mounted by the Mujahedin. Bani-Sadr, who was at the war front, said in Kermanshah that the efforts to strip him of his veto on ministerial appointments were illegal. On 10 June morning all military commanders, including the joint chief of staff, expressed their loyalty to Khomeini and the constitution. Later that day the Majlis passed a law which enjoined the president to sign legislation within five days or face its enforcement without his signature. In the evening Khomeini dismissed Bani-Sadr as the commander-in-chief. The next day he appointed General Fallahi, the joint chief of staff, as acting commander-in-chief.

On 12 June, Friday, in a statement issued by the presidential office, Bani-Sadr called for 'continued resistance to tyranny'. In a separate taped message he said that a coup was under way to overthrow him, and called on the people to 'rise against the move'.[58] Friday prayer meetings were held in Tehran. But to forestall such gatherings turning into pro-Bani-Sadr demonstrations, the authorities banned them in Isfahan, Shiraz, Sari and Yazd. There were reports of pro-Bani-Sadr demonstrations in Tabriz, Hamadan and Rasht.

Moves were now made to dismiss the president constitutionally. On Sunday the Majlis met to discuss Bani-Sadr's competence as president in the light of his 12 June statement. Tehran was gripped by tension as political gatherings were banned, and all important places guarded by tanks and armoured vehicles. The next day in a speech at his mosque in Jamran, a north Tehran suburb, Khomeini said that Bani-Sadr could continue in office if he apologised to the nation for urging the people to revolt. At the same time Khomeini condemned National Front leaders for planning a pro-Bani-Sadr rally. Bani-Sadr replied through his office. 'If I invite people for resistance against open violations of the law, have I invited them to revolt or [stand up] for the law?' he asked.[59] But his statement was ignored by the media. Some 50,000 IRP supporters gathered at Ferdousi Square in the evening to frustrate the National Front's plan to hold a pro-Bani-Sadr rally there. They succeeded. Thus Khomeini loyalists combined parliamentary moves with extra-parliamentary actions to achieve their objective.

On 17 June (Wednesday), at the end of a two-day debate, the Majlis passed a law which set out the procedure to judge the president's competence. The house then decided to settle the issue after the (Islamic) weekend, on Saturday, allotting five hours each on the pro- and anti-Bani-Sadr deputies, and inviting the president to defend himself in the chamber. As the authorities had lost track of Bani-Sadr's whereabouts since Tuesday afternoon, they sent out orders to the frontier guard posts and airports to stop him if he tried to leave.

The result of the Majlis vote on 20 June was a foregone conclusion. Given this, the pro-Bani-Sadr forces decided to muster popular support in the streets, and thus thwart the IRP plans. Twenty big and small parties combined to do so. Besides the Mujahedin-e Khalq, they included the Fedai Khalq (Minority), the Paykar, the pro-Peking Union of Communists, the KDP and the Komala.

As the Majlis assembled to debate the president's competence, these parties brought out an estimated 200,000 people into the streets of central Tehran. Revolutionary guards were pressed into action to disperse the protestors. Pitched battles broke out between the two sides. Thirty people, including fourteen guards, were killed, and over 200 injured. There were reports of rioting in Qom, Tabriz, Shiraz, Ahvaz, Bandar Abbas and Zahedan. The national total was put at 150 dead.[60]

The next day the Majlis declared Bani-Sadr to be incompetent by 177 votes to one, with twelve abstentions. A few hours later the prosecutor general ordered his arrest on sight on the charge of provoking 'groups' to resist the Republic's legal institutions. Once Khomeini had received the Majlis decision by letter from the speaker, Hashemi-Rafsanjani, he removed Bani-Sadr from office. Then, following Principle 103 of the constitution, he appointed Rajai, Hashemi-Rafsanjani and Beheshti as members of the temporary

Council of Presidency.

Thus ended the longest and the most acrimonious dispute between the Republic's elected leaders. It confirmed once more the pattern of Khomeini's political behaviour. He had allowed the differences between moderates and hardliners to mature into a full blown crisis, and had then come down on the side of radicals.

The IRP described the ouster of Bani-Sadr as 'the third revolution', the second revolution being the seizure of the US embassy. Bazargan's premiership until early November 1979 had reassured the modern middle class and ethnic minorities that they would not have to live under an uncompromisingly Shia regime. Likewise, Bani-Sadr's presidency had made the less committed citizens feel that the Islamic fundamentalists were willing to share power with others. In reality, however, the comparatively moderate leaders were of temporary value to Khomeinists. They were used by the fundamentalists to buy time to build up their organisations and consolidate their hold over the state apparatus and the religious network.

From the beginning there had been tension between two kinds of leaders within the Islamic camp: those who had been educated in the West and had spent many years in exile before returning home after the revolution; and those who had stayed home, actively resisted the Pahlavis and suffered imprisonment and torture. The difference between them was epitomised by Premier Rajai and President Bani-Sadr. Rajai's somewhat scruffy appearance, modest demeanour, and refusal to speak English, a foreign language, in public contrasted sharply with the haughty manner of a suave Bani-Sadr who revelled in his fluency in French.

Bani-Sadr carried his personal arrogance into the field of political strategy. Overlooking his basic weakness of lack of a political organisation of his own, he repeatedly refused offers of compromise with IRP leaders in the mistaken belief that he would win popular sympathy if he portrayed himself as an unflinching upholder of freedom and justice fighting a lone battle against the massive force of fundamentalist ulema bent on monopolising power and establishing dictatorship. He ignored the fact that since the ulema were in daily touch with Muslim masses, they enjoyed public respect and liking.

Beyond that there were deep differences between the two sides on the nature of the revolution and the direction it should take. Iranian revolutionaries faced a problem common to all revolutions: who should dominate the new order – the ideologue or the expert? Islamic militants put ideology first, Bani-Sadr professional skills.

With the outbreak of the war, this conflict was extended from running the civil service and the economy to fighting Iraq. The non-professional Islamic Revolutionary Guards and the Basij-e Mustazafin

(Mobilisation of the Deprived) volunteers, possessing more enthusiasm than expertise, swarmed to the front to fight. Military officers resented having to integrate non-professionals into their plans. In the dissension that developed, Bani-Sadr sided with the officer corps. This eroded his popularity among army troops who were being educated by the political-ideological department staffed by the ulema, and whose ranks were now swelled by fresh Islamic and leftist recruits.

The dramatic increase in the sizes of the IRG and the Basij worked against the interests of Bani-Sadr who had no control over these bodies. Since mosques were used as recruiting centres for these forces, their importance and standing rose. The ulema took to arms training at a special camp near Qom, and parading in city streets, thus dramatically demonstrating their patriotism. Moreover, mosques became integral parts of the civilian administration when the Revolutionary Komitehs decided to use them to implement the rationing system introduced in the aftermath of the war. In general, revolutionary organisations showed themselves to be flexible and energetic in meeting the exigencies of the war. All this worked in favour of IRP leaders, who controlled these bodies.

As a trained economist, Bani-Sadr was more aware of the poor shape of the Iranian economy, and an urgent need to repair it, than his rivals. He often urged ending the 'destructive phase' of the revolution and entering 'the period of reconstruction'.

But his opponents felt differently. To them the political-religious aspect of the revolution was far more significant than the economic. They knew instinctively that the masses regarded the Shah's overthrow as such a stupendous political and spiritual victory that they would not mind bearing economic hardship in its wake. Believing that the revolution was incomplete, Islamic radicals wanted to complete it by keeping up a permanent political ferment among the faithful. Since the exodus of the rich and super-rich had reduced the extent of socio-economic inequalities and corruption, the fundamentalists wanted to build on this, and accelerate the pace of Islamisation and redistribution of wealth.

Bani-Sadr's ideological concern lay elsewhere. 'The argument is over freedom, between those who want absolute rule and those who want freedom of choice,' he argued. 'If the people lose their freedom now, they'll never be able to live like a free nation again.'[61] But his warnings and speeches failed to unite the opposition to the IRP, which remained divided and incoherent. By the time opposition groups coalesced on 20 June 1981 to save Bani-Sadr's presidency, it was too late.

Going by Khomeini's public actions and statements, most Iranians felt that he had behaved impartially in the seven-month-long power struggle, from 19 November 1980 to 21 June 1981. During the first phase in November-December, Khomeini had called for restraint and won an immediate compliance by the IRP. During the second phase in March, he stuck to his promise of public silence for ten days. When he re-emerged, he appointed a well-balanced conciliation committee and took other steps which proved effective. It was Bani-Sadr's actions in mid-May which broke the truce and Khomeini's injunction on political speeches, and precipitated an acute crisis. Even then it was only after the Majlis, and then the conciliation committee, had moved against the president, that Khomeini acted against him. Finally, by offering to let Bani-Sadr stay as president if he apologised for disobeying the Majlis and the prosecutor general, and for calling on the people to 'rise against the move to oust him', Khomeini presented himself as a forgiving father figure. Such behaviour helped the Ayatollah to maintain popular support for the way he handled the thorniest internal problem yet faced by the Islamic Republic.

However, ousting Bani-Sadr from the presidency did not end the conflict. The event led the opposition groups, particularly the Mujahedin-e Khalq, to mount guerrilla warfare against the regime. How to counter this challenge to their authority became the prime concern of the Republic's leaders.

THE MUJAHEDIN CHALLENGE

Abol Hassan Bani-Sadr, president of Iran from 4 February 1980 to 21 June 1981, was now the most wanted man in the republic. The prosecutor general had charged him with inciting certain opposition groups to fight the Islamic government violently. The second most wanted man was Masoud Rajavi, leader of the Mujahedin-e Khalq. He had called on his party members to wage an armed struggle against Khomeini's regime. This set the scene for a bloody confrontation between the Mujahedin and the Islamic authorities. The official view of the Mujahedin was aptly summed up by Premier Rajai in an interview with the *The Middle East*, a London-based magazine. 'Differences of ideology are permissible [in Islam], but what is not permissible is to misguide others,' Rajai said. 'Since the Mujahedin were misguiding the people with their [Marxist] interpretations of Islam, they could not be tolerated in an Islamic republic.'[1]

To ensure that propaganda against the regime's newest enemies at home was conducted efficiently, the authorities sacked about 200 journalists suspected of lack of commitment to the Islamic revolution. They had been working in radio, television, the official newsagencies, and the publications owned by the Mustazafin Foundation.[2] Steps were also taken to purge the civil service, public sector undertakings and educational institutions of all those belonging to, or sympathetic with, the latest batch of opposition groups.

The recent events gave urgency to the passing of a law on political parties. The subject had been under discussion for some time, and an appropriate bill had been introduced by Rajai to the Majlis. Rajai declared himself to be in favour of 'freedom within the framework of Islamic ideology, not the criteria of Western democracy or Eastern dictatorship'.[3] He suggested four categories for political parties: Muslim, Sympathetic, Opposition and Enemy. The Muslim parties were those which followed, totally, Imam Khomeini's line. They were to run the government. The Sympathetic parties were those which were in sympathy with the Islamic revolution, but were not led or guided by the ulema. While they were to be allowed to have close links with the government they were to be excluded from certain key ministries and jobs. The Opposition parties were those which were at best lukewarm towards the Islamic revolution and which had so far refrained from plotting against the Islamic Republic. They were to be denied political power. The Enemy parties were the ones which had either taken up arms against the Islamic regime or were planning to do so. They were to be annihilated, both ideologically and militarily.

Obviously all monarchist groups at home or abroad were Enemy parties. Also the KDP, the Komala and the Fedai Khalq (Minority) had been Enemy parties for quite some time. They were joined by the Mujahedin and the Paykar when they raised arms against the government. Had the Mujahedin and the Paykar not done so, they would have been described as Opposition parties. The National Front was an Opposition group.

In contrast the Tudeh was a Sympathetic party. It had accepted Khomeini as the national leader, and was in sympathy with the Islamic revolution. It had backed most of the statements made by the radical Organisation of Militant Clergy. According to the Tudeh, Iran was being ruled by an anti-imperialist regime which faced threats from US imperialism and its counter-revolutionary allies. As such the party backed Khomeini's regime to help it withstand imperialist and counter-revolutionary pressures. In return, the Islamic Revolutionary Council had allowed it to exist legally and print daily, weekly and monthly publications. At the same time party members and sympathisers were excluded from certain areas of the administration. 'Of all the ministries there are three from which we are obliged to exclude the Marxists: the ministries of law and justice, defence and education,' said Rajai. 'Unless one firmly believes in the tenets of Islam and is quite conversant with it, one cannot dispense justice and decide cases according to the dictates of Islam. How can we entrust such a task to a Marxist? In the fight against Iraq, we cannot employ a Marxist, for he will fight only for his ideology. . . . We cannot have Marxists in the defence forces. Further, those who do not believe in Islam and Islamic Republic cannot be given the job of teaching. We cannot entrust education to Marxists.'[4]

Among the Muslim parties the Islamic Republican Party was of course pre-eminent. Then came such organisations as the Organisation of Militant Clergy (led by Montazeri), the Movement of Militant Muslims (led by Payman), and the Mujahedin of the Islamic Revolution (led by Bahzad Nabavi). They were followed by the Hezbollahis and the Fedaiyan-e Islam. They all believed completely in Imam Khomeini's Line.

To discuss the situation created by Bani-Sadr's dismissal and the

Mujahedin's revolt, IRP leadership called a secret, high-level meeting at the party headquarters in eastern Tehran. The party premises were adjacent to a school, with the conference hall sharing a wall with one of the school buildings. The IRP conclave was called to adopt a party candidate for the presidency, and to consider ways of broadening the government's popular base in order to meet successfully the Mujahedin challenge. The most favoured idea was to form an anti-imperialist ruling front of the Muslim and Sympathetic parties.

That evening over ninety party leaders assembled in the conference hall of the IRP headquarters. Beheshti was in the chair. Just before 9 pm, as he was addressing the assembly, an explosion rocked the hall. It was caused by a charge of thirty kilogrammes of dynamite stored in the adjoining room of the school. The ceiling came crashing down, and killed seventy-two people. Two more died later, bringing the total to seventy-four. The dead included Beheshti, four cabinet ministers, ten deputy ministers and twenty-seven Majlis deputies. Most of them were party moderates. Such hardliners as Hassan Ayat and Jalal al-Din Farsi had deliberately stayed away: they were against the idea of the IRP sharing power with Sympathetic parties. Hashemi-Rafsanjani and Rajai had attended the meeting, but had left a few minutes before the blast.

This was the most damaging blow the regime's enemies had inflicted on it since the revolution. The explosion killed not only the bulk of moderate IRP leadership but also the idea of a broad-based, anti-imperialist ruling front. Beheshti's death deprived the governing party of its most astute and pragmatic figure. He was the only top IRP leader who had lived abroad. He was as fluent in German and English as he was in Arabic. He was close to Khomeini, and enjoyed the respect of IRP ranks. While a fervent party man, he had established working relationships with the leaders of the Tudeh and the Fedai Khalq (Majority) – the parties which were candidates for inclusion in the anti-imperialist front.

Khomeini was shocked by the news. But he acted firmly and quickly. To foil any attempt at a military coup, he ordered the immediate encirclement of the army garrisons in and around Tehran by the Islamic Revolutionary Guards. However, the IRP headquarters explosion proved to be a solo act. Khomeini blamed 'the blind people who claim to be the Crusaders of the People [Mujahedin-e Khalq]' for the bomb blast, and called for a nationwide hunt to 'purge the American and Russian leftovers'.[5] This was at odds with the claim made by a Paris-based monarchist group, called the Military Organisation for National Equality, that it had carried out the explosion.

For the next few days while the regime was jittery and alert, its supporters were bewildered and grief-stricken. There was widespread sorrow for the loss of Beheshti, who was popularly regarded as being second only to Khomeini. On 30 June between 500,000 and 1,000,000 people joined the funeral procession of the dead IRP leaders to Behesht-e Zahra cemetery.[6] At Khomeini's urging the country's seniormost cleric, Ayatollah Golpaygani, joined the procession. The event did much to restore the confidence of the authorities. They were also helped by the imminence of Ramadan, due to begin on 2 July.

The IRP central committee met and appointed Hojatalislam Muhammad Javed Bahonar as the party general secretary. On 1 July he said that a Mujahedin plan to blow up the Majlis building had been foiled. This showed that intelligence and security organisations had become alert, and that the authorities held the Mujahedin responsible for the 28 June blast. About a fortnight later they announced the arrest of a twenty-three-year-old electrical engineer, employed as a maintenance engineer at the school adjoining the IRP headquarters, on the charge of causing the explosion. They said that he was a Mujahedin-e Khalq member.[7]

But the Mujahedin-e Khalq made no claim that it had carried out the blast. In a statement released in Tehran on 20 July the Mujahedin-e Khalq blamed Khomeini for 'all the disunity, crises, clashes, refugee problems, and the massacres of the revolution'. It pointedly refused to address him as Ayatollah or Imam. 'Mr Khomeini is so convinced of his divinity that he sees any opposition to himself as opposition to God, Islam and the Holy Quran,' said the Mujahedin communiqué. 'Although he thinks he is deputising for the Twelfth Imam, we have never accepted him in that role.'[8]

A communiqué such as this expressed the views of a party which claimed a membership of 10,000 in Greater Tehran, many of them armed. Its clandestine paper, The Mujahed, sold some 30,000 copies.[9] This showed that the nucleus of party members was surrounded by a ring of active sympathisers. Mujahedin-e Khalq members and sympathisers were predominantly young, male and female, and came from traditional middle class homes: merchants, shopkeepers, clerics, and artisans. They were drawn to the party because it offered modern, egalitarian interpretations of Islam – something quite apart from the medieval interpretations current among traditional ulema. They wanted to create an Islamic society which was forward-looking, democratic and egalitarian.

The 28 June explosion accelerated the process of retribution by the security and judicial authorities, which had been set off by the street fighting of 20 June in Tehran and elsewhere. A bomb blast at Qom railway station on 22 June killed eight and injured twenty-three. As a result eight leftists including Sayyed Sultanpuri, a playwright who had been imprisoned for illegally smuggling foreign currency, were executed. But this did not deter the regime's opponents. On 1 July a prison guard, shouting Mujahedin slogans, assassinated the governor of Tehran's Evin prison. By then the number of executions carried out since 20 June had reached eighty.[10] In the coming months the pattern of violence and counter-violence was to escalate in an ever-rising spiral.

Bani-Sadr's departure had a healthy effect on Iran's fighting forces, the military and the IRG. Since the early April Iranian attack on Iraq's Al Walid airbase, there had been little change on the battle front. The Iranians had stuck to their periodic attacks, aerial or ground, on the oil centres in northern Iraq and Basra in the south. They had failed to break the Iraqi siege of Abadan. As for the Iraqis, they had kept up sporadic air raids on Ahvaz and Kharg island, and made unsuccessful attempts to seize Susangard.

In the aftermath of Bani-Sadr's dismissal, the military high command made a determined attempt to regain Nowsud on 2 July. Success came on 8 July. This won General Fallahi a congratulatory message from Khomeini. In it the Ayatollah stressed the need for apprehending 'suspicious elements' within the military. 'At the same time as people are obliged to identify plotters and plotting groups and hand them over to the judicial authorities, it is incumbent on the armed forces all over the country to bring forward to their commanders those who are misguided or misled among them, so that they can be purged and punished', he said.[11] This was a clear reference to the Mujahedin members and sympathisers in the military.

Ramadan was an appropriate month to urge the faithful to be vigilant. The 28 June bombing had shown the state intelligence and security apparatus to be flawed. To make up the deficiency Khomeini called on the citizens to act as 'members of the intelligence organisation'. The *Jumhouri-ye Islami* took up the call. 'Inform the officials of every bit of information you may come across and they will investigate and identify the counter-revolutionaries,' it advised its readers on 10 July.

Yet Bani-Sadr and Rajavi, the two most wanted men, were still at large. They had by now agreed to work together and lead an armed opposition against the regime. In order to divert government attention they managed to plant stories abroad – including the one in the 12 July issue of the *Hurriyet* (Freedom), a Turkish daily – that the former president was hiding in the Kurdish region. He was in fact in Tehran; and so was Rajavi.

About a week later, in a well-publicised letter, Bani-Sadr suggested to Rajavi that they should unite all opposition forces under the umbrella of the National Resistance Council. For the immediate future they decided on frustrating the government plans to hold elections on

24 July to the presidency and forty-three Majlis seats.

The presidency was being contested by four candidates: Premier Rajai, the IRP nominee; Ali Akbar Parvarish, deputy speaker of the Majlis; and Habibollah Asghar-Owladi and Abbas Shaibani, both of them Majlis deputies. Mujahedin gunmen tried to assassinate Asghar-Owladi on 20 July, but failed. Bani-Sadr appealed to voters to abstain. But this had little impact. The regime was anxious to secure maximum voter participation. It also wanted to see the winner of the presidency obtain more votes than Bani-Sadr had done, both absolutely and relatively. Therefore the authorities lowered the voting age from sixteen to fifteen, thus adding 800,000 new voters to the rolls. Many ulema issued decrees stating that it was a religious duty to vote. In the presidential election, Rajai was a clear favourite from the start. A few days before the poll, two of his three rivals withdrew in his favour, thus ensuring a large majority for him. At 14.6 million, the voter turnout of 69 per cent compared favourably with the 70 per cent turnout in the January 1980 presidential poll. Eighty-eight per cent of them chose Rajai, a higher figure than that for Bani-Sadr.[12]

This was bad news for Bani-Sadr and Rajavi. It came along with the report that Muhammad Reza Sadati, an eminent Mujahedin figure, was executed on 26 July for masterminding the Evin prison governor's murder. Since Sadati had already been serving a sentence in Evin jail, when the assassination occurred, he was tried again. Bani-Sadr and Rajavi concluded that if they were caught they would be swiftly placed before a firing squad. They therefore decided to escape.

With the assistance of their partisans in the army and air force, Bani-Sadr and Rajavi boarded a Boeing 707 tanker plane on 28 July evening as it took off on a routine flight from Tehran's Doshan Tapeh military airbase. It was piloted by Colonel Bahzad Moezi. He had a colourful background. He had piloted the plane that carried the Shah out of Iran for the last time in January 1979, only to abandon his master in Morocco a few weeks later to fly back to Iran. He was one of the fifty-seven pilots arrested in July 1980 for plotting an unsuccessful military coup. Following the outbreak of the Gulf war, he was released by President Bani-Sadr to fight the Iraqis. This time he flew his tanker plane to Paris where it arrived in the early hours of 29 July. His two eminent passengers sought political asylum, and secured it. Iran called for Bani-Sadr's extradition on thirty charges, many of them carrying the death penalty, but to no avail.

The Iranian government was deeply embarrassed by the escape of Bani-Sadr and Rajavi. It tightened up security everywhere and intensified purges that had been started five weeks earlier. Immediately it arrested 100 air force personnel. Using the recently passed Law for the Reconstruction of the Government it set up purge committees to vet all civil servants.

Now that Bani-Sadr and Rajavi were safely abroad, their followers resorted to bolder actions to create insecurity and confusion in the country. On 2 August, the day Muhammad Ali Rajai was sworn in as president, two bomb explosions in Tehran and Kermanshah killed twenty people. President Rajai appealed to the Mujahedin to surrender their arms and 'return to Islam' to fight the Iraqi enemy. But the Mujahedin, now led by Mousa Khiyabani, were more interested in fighting Rajai than Saddam Hussein. 'With no more than a few hundred poorly armed members we made Savak and the imperial army desperate,' Khiyabani wrote in The Mujahed of 4 August. 'Now with several thousand well-armed Mujahedin and hundreds of thousands of genuine supporters throughout the country, we are a power to reckon with.' On 5 August gunmen assassinated Hassan Ayat, an IRP radical who had vehemently opposed Bani-Sadr. This was one of the thirty guerrilla actions staged during the week ending 8 August. All told these had caused fifty murders and fifty victims of bomb explosions.[13]

Ayat's murder led to an instant closure of the bazaar in Tehran. The Bazaari leaders protested against 'the lack of decisiveness by revolutionary courts'. This was hardly the case. Between 20 June and 4 August these courts had ordered the executions of some 300 members of the Mujahedin, Paykar, Fedai (Minority), Komala and the KDP.[14] Nonetheless the bazaar protest strengthened the hardliners' case in the government.

The Mujahedin launched their most daring raid yet when they attacked the IRG headquarters in Tehran with machine guns and rockets on 12 August. They failed to overrun it; but the boldness of their action illustrated their growing confidence. Following this, the army joined the IRG in patrolling government buildings in Tehran.[15] It was the first time since the revolution that the army had been co-opted into internal security operations in the capital. The IRG was clearly overstretched. It claimed to be discovering and destroying an average of ten hideouts of the Mujahedin and the Paykar daily.[16]

It was against this background that the Majlis approved Hojatalislam Muhammad Reza Bahonar, the IRP general secretary, as prime minister by 130 votes to twelve, on 5 August. This augured well for a smooth functioning of the government. Bahonar had much in common with Rajai. Born in 1933 of a poor family in Kerman, Bahonar went to study theology in Qom when he was twenty. There he became a student of Khomeini. Later, at Tehran University, be obtained a master's degree in education. During the tumultuous days of June 1963 he was imprisoned for his anti-Shah activities. His second period of imprisonment came in the early 1970s when he delivered a series of lectures against the Shah. During the revolutionary movement of 1977-

8, Khomeini (secretly) assigned him the task of organising strikes. He was among Khomeini's first appointees to the Islamic Revolutionary Council. Later he became one of the founders of the Islamic Republic Party. In July 1979 he was appointed deputy minister of education. He immediately set out to revise textbooks and abolish co-education in schools. He was an active member of the Assembly of Experts from August to November. Elected a Majlis deputy in the spring of 1980, he was appointed education minister by Premier Rajai. He worked closely with Beheshti, Rajai and Hashemi-Rafsanjani to remove Bani-Sadr from the presidency.

While introducing his cabinet of twenty-two ministers to the Majlis on 13 August, Bahonar outlined the priorities of his administration. 'The government is resolved to stand against the factionalists and not to allow society to become a haven for the factions attached to imperialism and international Zionism', he said. [17] Soon the Bahonar government set up ad hoc committees in many towns and cities to deal with the guerrilla problem, declared emergency in the worst affected towns and cities, and provided armed escorts for passenger and goods trains.

These actions were taken to thwart a political-economic plan of the Mujahedin and its allies to overthrow the regime. The plan involved debilitating the Majlis through assassinations of IRP leaders, weakening the IRG through repeated attacks, isolating the capital from the outside by striking at rail and bus traffic, and destroying food reserves by burning food storage silos.

The pace of executions quickened, and was defended by Khomeini. 'We don't fight anyone,' he said on 18 August. 'They are fighting us and anyone who does so will be smashed.' He then dismissed the perpetrators of violence as 'delirious flies in the last moment of their life'.[18] But this assessment proved to be premature. Three days later the Mujahedin attacked an IRG contingent in Tehran. Twelve people died in the skirmish. The Paris headquarters of the Mujahedin-e Khalq claimed that during the two months since 20 June party members had killed 500 revolutionary guards and forty Majlis deputies. Then came a claim that the Mujahedin had attacked the army garrisons outside Tehran and Tabriz on 24 and 27 August.[19] But the party's most sensational action was yet to come.

It occurred on 30 August. An incendiary bomb went off at the meeting of the National Security Council called to discuss ways of countering terrorist violence. Among those attending were President Rajai, Premier Bahonar, Colonel Hoshang Dastjerdi, head of the national police, and chiefs of military and IRG counter-intelligence as well as civilian intelligence. Rajai and Bajonar died immediately, and Dastjerdi later. Masoud Rajavi said in Paris that the action had been carried out by the National Resistance Council of which the Mujahedin-e Khalq was the leading constituent.[20] A week after the incident the government revealed that Masoud Kashmiri, a secretary of the prime minister in charge of national security, had taken a time-fused bomb in his attaché case into the room where the meeting was held, and that Kashmiri was a Mujahedin member.[21]

Khomeini declared four days of mourning. 'Grieved as we are upon the martyrdom of these people, and although they are precious to us and the Islamic Republic, we have others queueing up to fill their places,' he said on 31 August. 'The attackers are blind to the fact that every time we give a martyr, our people become more united.'[22] Hashemi-Rafsanjani called for tough action against the violent opposition. But Khomeini counselled restraint. He advised 'all the judges and all the people involved in this matter' to do 'no more than is God's order and Islam's law'.[23] This had no effect on the Mujahedin's actions. On 2 September they clashed with the IRG in southern Tehran: the battle lasted eight hours.

That day the Majlis approved of Hojatalislam Muhammad Reza Mahdavi-Kani as prime minister by 178 votes to ten. The fifty-year-old cleric was a confidant of Khomeini who had appointed him to the Islamic Revolutionary Council at its inception. Mahdavi-Kani was born in a rich religious family of Tehran. He obtained a degree in divinity, and was Khomeini's student in Qom in the mid-1950s. A politically active cleric, he had been imprisoned three times during the Shah's rule. His last incarceration began in 1975 and ended in November 1978. Soon after his release, his comfortable residence in Tehran became the venue of secret meetings between the IRC and the US ambassador Sullivan. When Khomeini returned to Tehran on 1 February he appointed Mahdavi-Kani head of the Central Revolutionary Komiteh. Later he became a cabinet minister holding the sensitive ministry of the interior. While governments changed, his control of this ministry did not. As interior minister he was a member of the National Security Council. On 30 August he was late for the fateful meeting, and thus escaped injury or death. Not surprisingly, when introducing his cabinet to the Majlis, Premier Mahdavi-Kani promised that his government would intensify the campaign against terrorism.

The sensational success of their 30 August operation made Masoud Rajavi ambitious. He announced a plan of selective assassinations of top Iranian leaders which – combined with a strategy of escalating small-scale confrontations with revolutionary guards into big demonstrations and strikes – would lead to the overthrow of Khomeini's regime. The Mujahedin 'hit list' included the Presidential Council of Premier Mahdavi-Kani, Majlis Speaker Hashemi-Rafsanjani, and Chief Justice Mousavi-Ardebili; Hojatalislam Khamanei, the new IRP general secretary; Hojatalislam Ali Qudusi, revolutionary prosecutor general; Muhsin Rezai, commander of the IRG; Assadollah Lajevardi, revolutionary prosecutor of Tehran; Hojatalislam Khoiniha, deputy speaker of the Majlis; Hojatalislam Muhammad Mahdi Rabani-Amlashi, chief high court judge; and Hojatalislam Ghaffari, leader of the Hezbollahis.[24]

What would follow the collapse of the present regime? The Mujahedin addressed this question by adopting a twelve-point programme. The Mujahedin blueprint offered a system of councils in all places of work and institutions as a basis for democracy in society. It guaranteed freedom of expression and political and religious beliefs. It recognised the right of all ethnic minorities, including Kurds, to manage their own internal affairs. In the economic field, it promised increased production. This was to be achieved by introducing workers' control of production and a new set of laws drawn up by workers through their councils. Likewise, peasants were to be organised in their councils. The state would abolish all peasant debts, and offer technical and financial aid to peasants. The Mujahedin programme committed itself to protecting the independence, territorial integrity and sovereignty of the Iranian nation. In foreign relations it promised to sever all links with imperialism by cancelling all unequal treaties and contracts and by nationalising all foreign assets.[25]

As planned, the Mujahedin graduated from staging clandestine attacks on revolutionary guards at night to baiting them in daylight. Small groups of young Mujahedin women shouted anti-Khomeini slogans in the streets as young armed Mujahedin men followed them. By the time revolutionary guards arrived on the scene, the women had melted into the crowd of spectators, and the armed men had disappeared into nearby side streets. The idea was to mount such demonstrations simultaneously in many places and overstretch the IRG, thus showing to the public that revolutionary guards were ineffective. This tactic was designed to encourage ordinary citizens to overcome their fear of the regime and join the resistance movement. It had been tried during the Shah's last days and had proved effective.

But this time the tactic failed. Revolutionary guards quickly learned to block escape routes as they approached a trouble spot. And they shot to kill. Agile and highly motivated, the young guards were a contrast to the Shah's professional soldiers who had been baffled by the Mujahedin manoeuvres. However, it took the Mujahedin some time to realise that their tactic was ineffective.

While engaging revolutionary guards in armed skirmishes, the Mujahedin continued their programme of assassinations, scoring such major targets as the Friday prayer leader of Tabriz, Ayatollah Assadollah Madani. With the Mujahedin activity showing no sign of decline, Khomeini lost his patience. He now called for severe actions against those who raised arms against the Islamic regime. 'When Prophet Muhammad failed to improve the people with advice, he hit them on the head with a sword until he made them human beings,' Khomeini said on 9 September. He then retired for two weeks as security and judicial authorities implemented his instructions. On 18 and 19 September alone they executed 182 people. In the three months since Bani-Sadr's dismissal, over 1,000 people had been executed by firing or hanging.[26]

The regime had become extremely security conscious. All buildings of the government and revolutionary organisations were guarded by the IRG, and illuminated at night by searchlights. To avoid car bombs, the areas surrounding these premises were cordoned off, and parking of vehicles was banned. Sandbagged command posts were set up at the entrances. The roads leading to these buildings were equipped with a series of speed breakers. Visitors to such places as the Majlis were searched three times and required to surrender all their belongings, including chains, keys, rings, pens and notebooks, before entering the building. Senior officials, governmental and religious, were instructed to change their routines and travel routes daily. Every cabinet minister was provided with bodyguards and a bullet-proof car. Out-of-town Majlis deputies were shifted to secret, top-security apartment blocks. Tehran-based deputies were provided with round-the-clock guards at their residences.

As 23 September, the beginning of the new academic year, approached, the Mujahedin promised a fresh upheaval. They claimed a large following among school teachers and older students.[27] Aware of this, on 22 September, Khomeini called on teachers and pupils to do their best to identify the 'satanic' elements and purge them. School children responded by marching in the streets and chanting slogans against 'heretic hypocrites' – meaning Mujahedin – and offering themselves as informers against counter-revolutionaries. Teachers responded by refusing to accept students they suspected of being pro-Mujahedin.[28]

Having failed to disrupt the educational system, the Mujahedin concentrated on thwarting plans for a presidential poll on 2 October. They wanted to secure the postponement of the election by creating large-scale disorders. On 27 September hundreds of Mujahedin clashed with revolutionary guards near the Tehran University campus. The fighting went on for seven hours. Seventeen people were killed and forty wounded.[29] To have chosen central Tehran to engage government forces in the most concentrated battle in the capital since the revolution was a daredevil act. But was it enough to force Khomeini to postpone the poll? The answer was quick to come.

'Disorder does not mean that Islamic rule is weak,' Khomeini said on 29 September. 'Islam is revived through this kind of bloodshed.'[30] The authorities proved the point by executing 153 persons for fighting the revolutionary guards on 27 September.

The leading candidate for presidency was Hojatalislam Khamanei. He was opposed by Hojatalislam Mahdavi-Kani, prime minister; Ali Akbar Parvarish, education minister; Hassan Ghafouri-Fard, energy minister; and Reza Zarvarei, former deputy interior minister. Of these only Mahdavi-Kani was a serious rival to Khamanei. But, on the eve of the election, he withdrew.

That day, in Paris, Bani-Sadr announced the formation of a government-in-exile, with himself as 'provisional president' and Rajavi as head of the National Resistance Council, consisting of the Mujahedin and the KDP. The NRC's programme was derivative of the Mujahedin's. It wanted to establish a Democratic Islamic Republic in which a system of councils at every level would ensure democracy. It guaranteed the rights of women, religious minorities and non-Persian nationalities. Among the democratic freedoms it promised were the rights to form trade unions and professional bodies. It wanted to nationalise foreign trade and implement a more equitable land reform. It wanted to boost the economy by reviving national industries.[31]

Elections to the presidency and vacant Majlis seats were held on schedule. These were peaceful except in Shiraz. There gunbattles between revolutionary guards and the Mujahedin caused six deaths. The turnout of about 80 per cent was the highest yet. Of the nearly 16,847,000 votes cast, Khamanei won over sixteen million.[32] In earlier presidential elections Rajai had secured 14.6 million votes, and Bani-Sadr 14.2 million. Khamanei was helped by the fact that he was not only the general secretary of the IRP but was also Khomeini's representative on the Supreme Defence Council.

Born in 1939, Ali Hussein Khamanei came from a religious family of Mashhad. At eighteen he went to Najaf to pursue his theological studies. Two years later he moved to Qom where he became a student of Khomeini. He participated in the June 1963 protest. After Khomeini had been deported in late 1964, Khamanei returned to Mashhad. He taught at the local theological college. During the next decade he was arrested six times for his anti-Shah activities. His release from jail in 1975 was followed by an internal exile to Iranshahr in Baluchistan-Sistan. An active leader of the revolutionary movement of 1977-8, he was one of the first appointees to the Islamic Revolutionary Council. He was one of the founders of the Islamic Republican Party. Later he became the IRC's representative at the defence ministry. He headed the political-ideological bureau of the military, which was charged with inculcating military personnel with

Islamic ideology and keeping a watchful eye on the officer corps. Following the death of Ayatollah Taleqani, Khomeini appointed Khamanei as the Friday prayer leader of Tehran, a position of considerable power and prestige. He was elected to the Majlis and was active in IRP politics. But he was not present at the fateful 28 June 1981 IRP meeting. This happened because only a day earlier he had been the target of an assassination attempt. As he was delivering a sermon at a south Tehran mosque a bomb, hidden in a tape recorder, exploded. The blast injured his arm and lung, and ruptured his vocal cords.

Having set up their government-in-exile, Bani-Sadr and Rajavi were determined to undermine the one at home. So the Mujahedin's guerrilla actions, directed in Iran by Khiyabani, continued. In late October a Mujahedin spokesman in Paris claimed that his party had assassinated 1,000 governmental and religious officials since Bani-Sadr's dismissal four months earlier.[33] But once Mujahedin partisans had failed to disrupt the presidential poll, their campaign lost impetus and direction. This was not the case with Khomeini. By sticking to the election schedule on 2 October he strengthened his position. He impressed Iranians anew with his firmness and refusal to be intimidated. And he underlined his commitment to securing legitimacy for his regime through popular vote. The high voter turnout boosted the morale of his supporters and demoralised his opponents. Those who had been neutral in the conflict now turned against the Mujahedin. In that sense the October 1981 presidential election was an important milestone in the Republic's brief life. Within three weeks of it, Hashemi-Rafsanjani could claim that the government had destroyed 90 per cent of the 'main opposition forces'.[34]

Once Khamanei was sworn in as president on 13 October, the question of the next government became uppermost. He disagreed with Premier Mahdavi-Kani on such important matters as land reform, foreign trade and the policy towards the armed opposition. Khamanei was for radical agrarian reform, nationalisation of foreign trade, and harsh treatment for the Mujahedin. Mahdavi-Kani was for a moderate approach all around. So he resigned on 15 October.

But Khamanei was reminded of the limitations of his constitutional powers when the Majlis rejected his nominee for prime minister, Ali Akbar Velayati, by eighty votes to seventy-four. Khamanei then offered Mir Hussein Mousavi, the foreign minister, as his choice for premier. On 28 October the Majlis approved Mousavi by 115 votes to thirty-nine. Mousavi became Iran's seventh prime minister since the Shah's departure in January 1979, his predecessors being Bakhtiar, Bazargan, Bani-Sadr, Rajai, Bahonar and Mahdavi-Kani. Born in 1942, Mousavi was the youngest prime minister yet.

During his days at the National University of Tehran, Mir Hussein Mousavi was active with local Islamic Associations. He was jailed briefly in 1973 for his anti-Shah actions. On his release he went to London to study interior design. After the revolution he became one of the founders of the IRP. He was appointed chief editor of the party paper, *Jumhouri-ye Islami*. In its editorials he demanded an immediate trial of the American hostages. He participated in the interrogation of the diplomats who worked for the CIA. An economic radical, he favoured redistribution of wealth, and nationalisation of both foreign and domestic trades. After Bani-Sadr's dismissal he was appointed foreign minister by the Presidential Council.

Since Mousavi and Khamanei had belonged to the IRP from the beginning, they were well-suited to work in accord. The IRP-dominated Majlis approved the twenty-one-member cabinet presented by Mousavi on 3 November. With both the Majlis speaker Hashemi-Rafsanjani and the supreme court chief Mousavi-Ardebili belonging to the IRP, the party controlled the legislative, judicial and executive organs of the state. And the daily administration was in the hands of second rank ulema, who were either IRP members or sympathisers. Thus, in less than three years, Khomeini had brought the Republic to the point where a fundamentalist Islamic party was firmly in power.

The Mousavi government intensified the policy of purging all governmental and revolutionary institutions of those with 'insufficient Islamic convictions' (as the prime minister put it), and accelerated the pace of Islamisation. The decision to dismiss all the Revolutionary Komiteh and the IRG officials whose sons or daughters had been found to be Mujahedin members was applied rigorously. The purge of the judiciary, which had so far affected thirty Islamic judges who had accepted bribes to commute capital punishment to life imprisonment,[35] was extended. The recently passed law on Islamic dress for women in public was implemented strictly. Special judges were appointed under the overall direction of Hojatalislam Murtaza Hussein to combat 'impious acts'. These included 'adultery, homosexuality, gambling, hypocrisy, sympathy for athiests and hypocrites, and treason'.[36]

A hardliner, Premier Mousavi decided to go beyond the lines drawn by Premier Rajai when it came to purging civil administration.[37] He wanted to remove Tudeh and Fedai (Majority) members and sympathisers from all civil service departments. Tudeh leaders protested. They argued that their party had consistently supported the Islamic revolution and its leader, Ayatollah Khomeini. This did not convince the government. In an interview with the *Ittilaat*, published on 22 November, Mousavi accused the Tudeh (as well as the Mujahedin) of infiltrating the Islamic Revolutionary Guards. On 1 December came the ban on the *Payam-e Mardom* (Message of the

People), a Tudeh publication, for violations of the press laws.

Government persecution was nothing new for the Tudeh. Its long history had been a tale of repression, punctuated with brief periods of activity and popularity.

The Tudeh Party

With its roots going back to June 1920 – when the Communist Party of Iran was formed – the Tudeh Party was Iran's oldest political organisation. The Communist Party helped to found the Soviet Republic of Gilan in the north. When the central forces of Iran crushed the republic in November 1921, the communist movement declined. Its remnants managed to survive under the cover of local Cultural and Sports Clubs. When Reza Shah's regime discovered this in 1931, it passed a law which forbade 'a group or association which aims to oppose the Iranian constitutional monarchy or advocates communist ideology or conduct'.[38] This law was used in April 1937 to arrest and convict fifty-eight members of the Marxist Circle in Tehran led by Taqi Arani.

Following the occupation of Iran by Soviet and British troops in August 1941 and the deposition of Reza Shah, all political prisoners were released. With this the communist movement revived. But in order to respect the 1931 law and make the new organisation attractive to workers, peasants and artisans, former Marxist Circle members decided to form a democratic front, and called it the Tudeh (Masses) Party. This happened in January 1942.

The party grew dramatically. It flexed its muscles in the autumn of 1944. Demonstrations sponsored by it brought down the conservative government of Premier Muhammad Saed. The party was strong among the industrial proletariat, particularly oil workers. By staging a series of strikes in Khuzistan, oil workers, led by the pro-Tudeh trade union, won impressive concessions from the Anglo-Iranian Oil Company. By 1946 the party had 25,000 members and 75,000 sympathisers. Its United Central Council of Unified Trade Unions of Iranian Workers had a total membership of 400,000.[39] The party's May Day rally in Tehran drew 500,000 people. The Tudeh drew its strength from modern middle classes and industrial workers. Its stress on modernism and progress in the socio-cultural field had a particular appeal for women and young people.

By the middle of 1946 the Tudeh was too strong to be smashed by force. A subtle approach was needed to stop its growth and then neutralise it. And it came from Premier Ahmed Qavam al Saltane. On 1 August he offered three cabinet posts to the Tudeh in a coalition government. The Tudeh leaders accepted. This caused a split in the party, with the radical ranks opposing the moderate leadership's decision. Soon the Qashqai tribals were in revolt demanding among other things the expulsion of the Tudeh from the government. This action had been instigated by the British and the Americans – as well as Premier Qavam al Saltane himself. To resolve the crisis the prime minister resigned, thus causing the coalition government to fall. When he reconstituted the cabinet, he excluded the Tudeh. This disrupted the Tudeh leaders' plans to contest the forthcoming Majlis elections in alliance with leftist and centrist parties, including the one headed by Qavam al Saltane.

In mid-November, intent on aborting a threatened strike in Tehran, Qavam al Saltane arrested hundreds of Tudeh members. Three weeks later, under the pretext of restoring normal conditions for Majlis elections in Azerbaijan, he sent troops to the province to overpower the year-old leftist, autonomous regime in Tabriz. The subsequent collapse of the leftist administration there, and in Kurdistan, was a setback for the Iranian communist movement as a whole.

Tudeh leaders tried to meet the crisis by boycotting the 1947 Majlis election and carrying out internal party reform. They held the second party congress in April 1948 in an optimistic mood. The Tudeh rally on 4 February 1949 to commemorate the anniversary of the death of Taqi Arani drew 25,000 people. As stated earlier, on that day an unsuccessful attempt was made to assassinate the Shah.[40] Since the attacker, a journalist, was carrying a membership card of a union affliated to the pro-Tudeh labour federation, the Shah used this to suppress the Tudeh. His government arrested a large number of party and trade union leaders, and confiscated party offices throughout Iran.

With the rise of the oil nationalisation movement, conditions for the revival of the Tudeh improved. The party's 1951 May Day demonstration attracted 30,000. However, Tudeh leaders considered Muahmmad Mussadiq an ally of America, who wanted to replace Britain with the US. Only in mid-1952 did they change their view of Mussadiq, and opt for an alliance with the National Front. Tudeh partisans were active in the pro-Mussadiq demonstrations on 21 July. This helped the party to expand its popular base rapidly. Its demonstration a year later to commemorate the events of 21 July 1952 drew 100,000 people. From then on the party was active until and soon after the Shah's flight from Iran on 16 August 1953. Oddly enough, the party leaders did not galvanise their supporters to resist the army when it struck on 19 August.

Once the Shah was back he repressed the Tudeh with vengeance. His government arrested 3,000 party activists. Of these forty were executed, fourteen tortured to death and 200 given life sentences.

Twenty-eight of those executed, and 144 of those jailed for life, were military personnel.[41] Khusro Ruzbeh, leader of the party's military organisation, was arrested in 1957 and executed the following year.

Unable to function inside Iran, the party leaders moved the headquarters to eastern Europe, alternating between East Berlin and Prague. As a result of a series of conferences between 1956 and 1964, the party opted for peaceful means to bring about the Shah's downfall and establish a democratic republic. It favoured the formation of an anti-imperialist, democratic front of all patriotic forces opposed to the US and the Shah. After its merger with the Democratic Party of Azerbaijan in 1960 the party acquired a new name, the Tudeh Party of Iran: the Party of Iranian Working Class. That year it helped form the Confederation of Iranian Students in Europe, a broadly based anti-Shah organisation. Four years later it applauded the 'progressive clergy', led by Khomeini, for their opposition to the 'Capitulations' offered to the American military personnel in Iran.

Such moderation brought charges of reformism against party leadership by radicals who left in 1965 to form a Maoist communist organisation of their own. Tudeh membership fell to about 3,000. However, assistance by the Communist Parties of the Soviet Union, East Germany, France and Italy enabled the Tudeh to engage fifty full-time cadres to run a radio station, called Peik-e Iran (The Courier of Iran), based in Bulgaria, and bring out two publications.[42]

Savak treated the Tudeh as its number one enemy: a party inimical not only to monarchy and private enterprise but also to Islam and Iran. But the Tudeh was no longer the favourite of leftist militants. While the guerrilla actions of the Fedai and the Mujahedin in the early 1970s captured the imagination of young Iranians, the Tudeh's continued stress on peaceful means made it increasingly irrelevant to the rising generation.

To make amends the party began underground activity in Iran in 1972 with secret cells in Tehran University, oil fields and major industrial centres. Two years later the party issued a call for the overthrow of the Shah and the founding of a republic. Its strength rose as the cadres of the Maoist organisation became disenchanted with Peking's policies after the death of Mao Tse-tung in 1976, and as the Fedai Khalq split into moderate and radical wings. The party membership in Iran and Europe rose to over 5,000.

In the autumn of 1977 Tudeh leadership revived secret party cells in Tehran, Abadan and Rasht, and put the production of the party publication on a regular basis. In September the Tudeh politbureau met in Prague to overhaul the party machine. It decided to establish contact with Islamic revolutionaries.[43] The following month the party instructed its followers in the oil fields – an important area of its traditional strength – to support Khomeini's call for a strike. This decision, more than any other single step, determined the Shah's fall.

At its meeting in December the Tudeh politbureau agreed that conditions were ripe for revolution, and instructed party members to prepare for an armed uprising. It also decided to replace Iraj Eskandri as the first secretary with Nur al-Din Kianouri. The latter had favoured a more active support for Khomeini than Eskandri. These decisions were endorsed by the party central committee when it met in mid-January.

Tudeh members participated actively in the final battles with the Shah's forces during the period of 9-13 February in Tehran and elsewhere. After the revolution, Kianouri and thirty cadres returned from abroad to revive the party openly. In March the central committee assembled in Tehran, its first meeting inside Iran for a quarter of a century.

Reviewing the current situation in August 1979, a Tudeh spokesman in Tehran described 'the political balance sheet' of the Khomeini regime as 'positive'. Expelling the Shah, declaring a republic, leaving Cento, removing American bases and foreign military advisers, breaking ties with Israel, stopping oil sales to South Africa, establishing links with the PLO, nationalising banks and insurance companies, and announcing a draft republican constitution: all these were seen as positive achievements of the Islamic revolution.[44]

In an interview with the Athens-based *Elevtherotipia* (Free Press), published on 28 November, Kianouri described 'the content of the revolution' as 'anti-imperialist, popular and democratic'. He stated that the revolution had occurred under 'Islam's umbrella'. 'After all, the role Islam played in the pre-revolutionary period, not only politically and organisationally, through the mosque, was catalytic, and principally indicative of its profound content,' he added. 'Shiaism is a revolutionary ideology which we shall never encounter blocking our road to socialism which . . . will be achieved through the cooperation of Muslim forces.'

All the same the Tudeh's endorsement of official policies was not unqualified. The party criticised the religious content of the constitution and the inferior position accorded to women. It openly disagreed with the Islamic government's foreign policy summed up by the slogan: 'Neither East Nor West'.

The Islamic government and the revolutionary organisations had been wary of the Tudeh from the beginning. Ignoring repeated Tudeh declarations of support for the Islamic revolution and Khomeini, they tended to lump the party with the Fedai and the Mujahedin. Not surprisingly, the IRG raided the Tudeh head office in Tehran in mid-August 1979 at the same time as it surrounded the Fedai and the

Mujahedin headquarters. But, unlike the Fedai and the Mujahedin occupants, the unarmed Tudeh members offered no resistance. The premises were later returned to the party.

Participation in the Experts' Assembly elections enabled Tudeh leaders to measure the party's popular appeal. Its candidates in Tehran won a total of 50,000, a poor achievement.[45] In view of this, and aware of the past pattern of dramatic growth and an equally dramatic decline, the party leaders opted for a low profile. They deliberately slowed down the processing of applications for new membership or even readmittance of the members of the pre-August 1953 period. In April 1980 they suspended issuing new membership cards altogether.

But this did nothing to dispel the deep mistrust of the Tudeh in the official circles. Among those who harboured strong anti-Tudeh views was Sadiq Qutbzadeh, then foreign minister. In late July, during Ramadan, the Islamic militants once again occupied the party headquarters in Tehran. However, the occupation was brief. About a month later Qutbzadeh publicly attacked the Tudeh. Freed from the constraints of office, he accused the Tudeh for much of the turmoil in Iran, and added that 'at the bidding of Moscow' the party was driving the young generation to 'political sabotage'.[46]

If the party had any Moscow connections it was using them for the benefit of Iran and the Islamic revolution. Kianouri had at least two secret meetings with President Bani-Sadr; and these had to do with Iraq's war preparations. Having acquired a blueprint of Iraqi plans in early August, Bani-Sadr listened carefully to the warnings coming from Kianouri about Iraq's aggressive designs.[47] Following the Iraqi attack on Qasr-e Shirin on 2 September, Kianouri called for mobilisation of the Iranian people to fight an invasion plotted by Iranian counter-revolutionaries and America. The plan, he warned, was to occupy Khuzistan, encourage Kurdish rebellion, deprive Iran of oil, and slowly strangle the Iranian economy.[48]

Later, after the Iraqi invasion had occurred, the anti-Tudeh elements within the Islamic regime treated Kianouri's advance warnings of the Iraqi plans as evidence of his contacts with the Soviet embassy in Tehran. Who else but the Soviet secret service, the KGB (Komitet Gosudarstvennoy Bezopasnosti, Committeee for State Security), would have access to the documents of the Iraqi defence ministry, they argued. Little wonder, the party's Tehran head office was once again raided in early November and its paper suspended.[49]

The party policy of supporting 'the anti-imperialist, anti-capitalist, anti-feudalist, anti-royalist, popular and freedom-seeking aims of the Imam's Line'[50] remained unchanged. Kianouri now advocated the formation of an anti-imperialist front to meet the threat faced by the Islamic Republic.' Unity of all revolutionary and anti-imperialist forces, particularly and including the religious revolutionaries who have a popular base, and the followers of theoretical socialism, is possible and necessary,' he said in March 1981.[51]

Unimpressed by this, the Islamic authorities arrested several Tudeh central committee members. It was only after the conflict between the IRP and Bani-Sadr had heightened in mid-May that they eased the pressure on the Tudeh. In the internecine struggle within the regime, the Tudeh sided firmly with the IRP. Eager to confront Bani-Sadr and his supporters with all the force they could muster in the country, IRP leaders welcomed the Tudeh's stance. They were helped in this by the Tudeh's fulfilment of the rules prescribed by the prosecutor general for a political party to function legally, including submitting the names and addressses of the organisation's executive authority, such as the central committee. The Tudeh was therefore able to operate more freely than before. For the first time since the revolution, the Islamic regime indirectly recognised the legal existence of the Tudeh by allowing its general secretary, Kianouri, to participate in a television discussion on 20 June 1981.[52]

When confronted with the guerrilla campaign by the Mujahedin, IRP leaders became receptive to Kianouri's idea of an anti-imperialist ruling front. As stated earlier, this was a main topic of discussion at the 28 June IRP meeting. The deaths of Beheshti and others sympathetic to Kianouri's proposal was a major setback to Tudeh hopes. Following the bomb explosion, Kianouri counselled the government to seek the aid of anti-imperialist states abroad and inflict 'exemplary revenge' on the terrorists at home.[53]

As before the party instructed its members and sympathisers to participate actively in elections. In fact Kianouri offered himself as a candidate for a vacant Majlis seat from Tehran. But he was disqualified, apparently because he was not considered 'one hundred per cent Muslim', a prerequisite for any official candidate.

The Tudeh advocated a tough line against the Mujahedin. In an interview cited in *The Times* of London, Kianouri attacked Bani-Sadr and Rajavi. 'Bani-Sadr is a traitor, with a mental illness that is politically very dangerous,' he said. 'He is incredibly egocentric and believes he is the greatest thinker of the century.' In Kianouri's view, the leaders of the 'counter-revolutionary groups' deserved the death penalty, but the young Iranians 'disturbed by the Mujahedin's propaganda' ought to be allowed to correct themselves through re-education in work camps. He acknowledged that one faction of the IRP wanted to ban the Tudeh while the other argued that non-violent leftist parties should be allowed to participate actively in politics 'according to the line defined by Imam Khomeini'.[54]

Once the governing party had weathered the storm created by the

Mujahedin and successfully held a presidential election in early October, it had no need for the backing of non-violent leftist parties. Therefore the anti-Tudeh faction prevailed in the internal IRP debate. Yet there was no outright ban on the Tudeh. Instead, the earlier policy of steady pressure on the party was resumed. Premier Mousavi indicated this when he said that Tudeh members and sympathisers would be weeded out of all state and revolutionary institutions. In December civil servants were ordered to fill in questionnaires stating among other things their political allegiance. Soon a thousand Tudeh members and sympathisers were dismissed from the foreign, oil and finance ministries.[55]

Further worsening of relations between the Tudeh and the government came six months later. It occurred in the context of developments in the Gulf War.

The war and the economy

The Islamic regime was anxious to show that Bani-Sadr's dismissal had improved the efficiency of its fighting forces. The best way to do so was to score gains on the battle fronts, preferably during the run up to the presidential election. On 27 September (the day the Mujahedin guerrillas attacked the IRG in central Tehran) Iranian forces launched an offensive which cleared the area between Abadan and Ahvaz of Iraqi troops. Then on the election day, 2 October, the Iranians mounted offensives in Ahvaz, Susangard, Dezful and Malak Shahi fronts. These were marginally successful, yielding 250 sq. kms of Iranian territory.

While the government was concentrating on countering the Mujahedin threat and expelling the Iraqis, the economy suffered a sharp downturn. This was caused by a steep decline in oil exports which provided 95 per cent of Iran's foreign currency earnings. During the third quarter of 1981, at 1.1 million b/d, Iran was producing only 5.2 per cent of the total OPEC output, down from 17.5 per cent in 1978 and 10.1 per cent in 1979.[56] Oil shipments running at a miserly 500,000 b/d were cut further by 200,000 b/d in late October 1981, when Iran's main oil terminal at Kharg island was hit by the Iraqis. Tehran's foreign reserves declined so steeply that soon it was unable to maintain its Bank of England account at $1,000 million, as required by the January 1981 agreement with the US to meet the claims by its American creditor companies. At the end of 1981, Iranian reserves were down to $500 million, just enough for a fortnight's imports.[57]

This was the most severe economic crisis that the Islamic regime has had to face. The only way it could balance its foreign trade was by reducing imports and increasing its oil exports. In order to achieve this it was compelled to act pragmatically. But pragmatism did not mean total abandonment of revolutionary ideology. It turned out to be a mixed bag. The decision to nationalise foreign trade to save foreign exchange on imports was radical, whereas oil exports could be raised only by compromising with a major objective of the revolution.

In the aftermath of the revolution, determined to loosen its economic links with the West, the Iranian oil ministry signed a series of barter deals with socialist and Third World countries. But such agreements proved disadvantageous to Tehran. Often what Iran got in return for its oil were overpriced, low quality goods it did not really need. On top of that came pressures generated by the Gulf War. Iran needed to import vital military goods to be paid for in foreign currencies. So Iran's salvation lay in selling oil for hard currencies to the countries which had them: the West and Japan.

But when the Iranians finally realised this, they found the international oil market depressed by oversupply, and Western and Japanese oil companies reluctant to do business with them. They had therefore to devise special means to interest these companies in Iranian oil. As a loyal member of OPEC, Iran did not want officially to undercut the OPEC price of $30 a barrel. Therefore the National Iranian Oil Company let it be known through intermediaries that its crude oil was available for less than the official price. It took some weeks for the news to spread, but it did. By early 1982 fresh orders for Iranian oil began arriving in Tehran.

So, within three years of the revolution, Iranian leaders had reversed two major points of their blueprint for the future: to conserve Iranian oil by severely curtailing production, and to sharply reduce Iranian trade with the West.

However, the impact of such decisions on the ordinary citizen was insignificant compared to the one on foreign trade. The commerce ministry devised a plan for nationalising foreign trade which was approved by Khomeini in late October 1981. It eliminated the middleman: his functions were taken over by the ministry. The new system was to operate through the ministry's Centres of Procurement and Distribution, each one specialising in a certain category of goods. A Centre was to buy quantities of a particular item abroad at the most competitive price, then sell it to traders at a certain profit margin, and specify a retail price. The plan was implemented along with severe restrictions on imports.

The new system served many useful purposes. It made the best possible use of scarce foreign reserves, ensured an efficient functioning of the rationing system introduced in the aftermath of the war, and increased government revenue by assigning it the role of the commercial middlemen. The only losers were large merchants and wholesalers, a small minority. Alienating them actually helped the Islamic regime to improve its popularity. Resorting to alternative ways of raising government revenue (to fight the war) by increasing direct or indirect taxes, or reducing official subsidies on basic necessities, would have certainly made the regime unpopular. Finally there was no ideological or constitutional hurdle to cross. According to Principle Forty-four of the constitution, foreign trade was to be part of the government sector.

Nationalisation of foreign trade, and selling oil for cash to the West and Japan at discount prices, proved to be the most important, and beneficial, economic decisions of the Islamic government. They gave it much leeway in the management of the economy, and contributed strongly to an economic recovery. They also helped it to pursue the war with greater vigour than before.

Iran followed up its offensive on 29 November 1981, codenamed Tariq al Quds (Road to Jerusalem) in the Susangard area with another a fortnight later, named Matla al Fajr (Rising of the Dawn), on the central front. The latter resulted in Iran regaining 160 sq. kms in the Qasr-e Shirin area.

On 15 December President Saddam Hussein expressed his readiness to end the war if Iran agreed to 'recognise Iraq's borders'. His willingness to compromise was seen in Tehran as an inadvertent admission that he was losing. This only led the Iranians to redouble their efforts in the field. After a three-day battle in mid-January 1982, they regained Bostan which, situated six miles from the international border, had been the heart of Iraqi logistics. By the time this offensive petered out, the Iranians had recovered 650 sq. kms in the southern region. The news that Egyptian and Jordanian volunteers were fighting on the side of Baghdad underlined a weakness of Iraq. With its military budget at $2.67 billion, Iraq was spending 8 per cent of its GNP on defence. The figure for Iran was $4.2 billion, or 5 per cent of its GNP.[58]

Iranian victories came at a time when the country was preparing to celebrate the third anniversary of the Islamic revolution on 12 February. The government was to score a major strike against its opponents at home before then. On 8 February an IRG raid on a Tehran house led to the deaths of ten central committee members of the Mujahedin-e Khalq, including Khiyabani. With this the authorities could claim to have struck a grievous blow to the declining guerrilla campaign of the Mujahedin.

This chapter of the Republic's domestic history was particularly bloody. By early February 1982 the Mujahedin claimed to have killed over 1,200 religious and political leaders of the regime. In return, the government had executed 4,000 guerrillas, most of them belonging to the Mujahedin. Masoud Rajavi, the Mujahedin leader, put the number of executions at twice the official figure. Whatever the actual number, there was little doubt that the government action had been effective. 'Though we were successful at first in shaking the regime to its very foundations, the brutality of its methods surprised us,' Rajavi said in an interview with *The Middle East*.[59]

In the face of relentless government repression the opposition groups severely curtailed their activities. 'The Mujahedin were confined mainly to assassinations of government personnel,' noted Fred Halliday, a British specialist on Iran. 'The Kurdish Democratic Party was somewhat on the defensive in the mountains of the west. Other opposition groups, such as the Fedai (Minority) and the Paykar, were restricted to sudden guerrilla actions, mainly in the north of the country.'[60]

Why did the Islamic regime hit back as fiercely as it did? An explanation came from Hashemi-Rafsanjani in an interview with *Arabia*, a London-based magazine. 'It was imperative to take action immediately otherwise . . . Iran would have become Lebanon,' he said. 'Islam commands determination.'[61] The reference was to the Lebanese civil war which broke out in April 1975 and was still in progress nine years later. During its most active phase, from April 1975 to October 1976, it had caused some 80,000 deaths in a country with a population of 3.5 million. The consequences of a civil war in Iran – with a population of nearly forty million and a long border with the Soviet Union – would have been much worse.

The pace of new orders for Iranian crude built up so rapidly in early 1982 that oil production was raised to 2 million b/d during the second quarter of the year, with 1.4 million b/d to be shipped abroad. Iran's foreign earnings were now more than adequate to cover its imports, civilian and military. This strengthened the hands of those officials who wanted to dislodge the Iraqis from the occupied Iranian territory in a massive, multi-pronged offensive.

This came on 22 March, the Iranian New Year, and was named Fatah al Mobin (The Clear Victory). It involved 200,000 soldiers, revolutionary guards and Basij volunteers, and was mounted in the Susangard-Dezful area. By staging a series of 'human waves' in the Dezful-Sush area, the Iranians succeeded in encircling the Iraqis and destroying two armoured and one mechanised Iraqi divisions.[62] The Iranian tactic involved pressing forward waves of about 1,000 combatants, carrying shoulder-held rockets, at intervals of 200 to 500 yards with a view to exhausting the ammunition supplies of the enemy troops, and then overpowering them. By the time the offensive ended, the Iranians claimed to have regained 2,400 sq. kms and captured

15,450 prisoners of war. Both sides suffered heavy casualties. The success of the Iranian tactics led Colonel Bahruz Suleimaz, deputy commander of the 21st Division, to declare: 'We are going to write our own [military] manuals, with absolutely new tactics that the American, British and French can study at their staff colleges.'[63]

On 8 April Iraq suffered another major setback. Protesting against Saddam Hussein's aid to the dissident Muslim Brotherhood in Syria, President Hafiz Assad closed the Syrian border with Iraq. Two days later he shut off the pipeline carrying Iraqi crude to the Syrian port of Banias, thus halving Iraqi oil income. This was bad news for Iraq as well as its Gulf Arab backers, from whom it had by now received $25 billion in grants and loans. Saddam Hussein promised Iraqi withdrawal from all Iranian territory if Iran agreed to respect 'Iraq's rights to its territory and waters'. The oil-rich Gulf states let it be known that they would set up a Gulf Reconstruction Fund to compensate Iran for its war damages.[64]

Iran ignored the Iraqi gestures. On 30 April it launched an offensive in Khuzistan with 65,000 men. A week later it regained a twenty-two-mile section of the border between Husseiniya and Khorramshahr.

This was a prelude to the Iranian move to recover Khorramshahr, and caused a nervous flurry of activity in the Gulf capitals. On 15 May the foreign ministers of the Gulf Cooperation Council – consisting of Saudi Arabia, Kuwait, Bahrain, Qatar, the United Arab Emirates and Oman – met in Kuwait to discuss the war. Khomeini warned them that by helping Iraq they would fall 'in the same trap as Iraq had fallen'.[65] Heeding the warning, the ministers adjourned their meeting. They said that they wanted to give time for the Islamic Conference Organisation's peace mission to succeed.

On 21 May, 70,000 Iranian combatants attacked Khorramshahr, defended by 35,000 Iraqi troops behind three well-fortified lines. Two days later Saddam Hussein invoked the Arab League's defence charter to secure military aid from the League's remaining twenty members.[66] But nothing came of it. The following day Khorramshahr fell to the Iranians. Over 12,000 Iraqi soldiers surrendered while the rest fled. The news was greeted with widespread jubilation in the streets of Iran. By recapturing Khorramshahr, the Iranians had reversed their biggest and most humiliating loss in the war. On 28 May the Iranian commanders moved some of their forces from the southern front to the central front to expel the Iraqis from the Iranian soil there. All told this offensive, codenamed Bait al Muqaddas (The Sacred House, that is, Jerusalem), secured Iran 5,380 sq. kms and 17,500 Iraqi prisoners of war.

The Iranian victory set off a chain of riots in Karbala, Basra, Hilleh and Nassariyeh – southern Iraqi cities with a predominantly Shia population – and Shia quarters of Baghdad on 30 May. The Iranian leaders let it be known that they would talk to their Iraqi counterparts only if they would replace Saddam Hussein as president. This led President Assad and King Fahd of Saudi Arabia to hold consultations on the successor to Saddam Hussein. The Syrian leader favoured Ahmed Hassan Bakr, former Iraqi president, while Fahd favoured Shafiq Daraji, the Iraqi ambassador to Riyadh.[67] They agreed on the formation of the Gulf Reconstruction Fund to be financed by the members of the Gulf Cooperation Council. On 2 June the GCC ministers, meeting in Riyadh, offered a peace plan: a ceasefire, withdrawal of the parties to the 1975 treaty borders, and negotiations to resolve the outstanding issue. But these concerted efforts were blown off course by the Israeli invasion of Lebanon on 5/6 June.

Israel's attack was triggered off by an attempt to assassinate Shlomo Argov, the Israeli ambassador to Britain, on the night of 3 June. The London operation was masterminded by Nawal al Rosan, an Iraqi 'carpet dealer', who was later found to be a colonel in the Iraqi intelligence.[68] The subsequent Iraqi behaviour lends credence to the theory that the Iraqi authorities ordered the killing of the Israeli envoy in order to provoke an Israeli invasion of south Lebanon – then a base for PLO operations against Israel – and create conditions suitable for an immediate ceasefire in the Gulf War to enable the combatants to fight their common foe: Israel.

On 10 June, when the Israelis reached the outskirts of Beirut, the ruling Revolutionary Command Council issued a statement saying that Iraq was ready for an immediate ceasefire, and would accept the verdict on war guilt by the ICO or the Non-Aligned Movement or the UN Security Council. The RCC said that it was responding to the ICO's appeal to Iraq and Iran to stop fighting and to 'direct their arms against the common enemy [Israel]'.

Khomeini spurned the offer, arguing that Iraq was using the same tactic as Israel: first occupying cities and then seeking a ceasefire. Going by the reports then current that Saddam Hussein was to be replaced by the triumvirate of Tariq Aziz, deputy president, Taha Yassin Ramadan, deputy premier, and Saddoun Hamadi, foreign minister, Khomeini probably concluded that Saddam Hussein's fall was imminent. But he was mistaken.

Saddam Hussein showed his prowess for survival. He announced on 20 June that the unilateral Iraqi withdrawal, begun that day, would end by 30 June. Two days before the deadline, he dismissed all the members of the ruling RCC, and reappointed a smaller RCC of nine members, with himself as chairman. He extended the purge to the cabinet and senior leadership of the military, thus aborting any chance of a coup against him. This left Khomeini with only one way to oust

Saddam Hussein: a military assault on his regime to be carried, if necessary, into Iraq.

When Baghdad reported on 29 June that its troops had vacated all Iranian territory, Tehran called it 'a lie'. For the next several days the Iranian Supreme Defence Council weighed the pros and cons of attacking Iraq. The doves argued that such an action would destroy much of the popular sympathy Iran had aroused in Muslim countries as a victim of Iraqi aggression, and undermine the Islamic Republic's moral standing. The hawks argued that at the very least there were two practical reasons for advancing into Iraq: to silence the Iraqi artillery that had been pounding Iranian civilian areas since the beginning of the war, and to capture Iraqi oilfields near the border for use as bargaining counters for securing compensation for Iran's war damages. The hawks won.

On 9 July Hashemi-Rafsanjani listed the Iranian conditions for a ceasefire: retaining the 1975 Iran-Iraq treaty, repatriation of over 100,000 Iraqi citizens expelled by the government, placing of war guilt on Iraq, payment of $100 billion to Iran for war damages, and punishment of Saddam Hussein. He added that if these demands were not met, then Iran would carry the war into Iraq.

It was significant that this statement was issued not by President Khamanei, chairman of the Supreme Defence Council, but by Hashemi-Rafsanjani, a representative of Khomeini on the Council. Apparently the ideas behind the statement had originated with Hashemi-Rafsanjani who had succeeded in winning the endorsement of the majority of the Council members. The argument to move into Iraq to knock out the Iraqi artillery was much too emotion-laden to be set aside easily.

By now Hojatalislam Ali Akbar Hashemi-Rafsanjani had emerged as the leader of hardliners not only on the Gulf War but also on economic reform and the policy towards the armed opposition. Born in 1933 he came from a religious family of Rafsanjan in south-east Iran. He went to Qom for his theological studies: there he became a student of Khomeini. Later he taught at the Faiziya seminary. As an active opponent of the Shah he suffered imprisonment. He was involved in the revolutionary movement of 1977-8, particularly the formation of the Revolutionary Komitehs. He was one of the original members of the Islamic Revolutionary Council, and one of the founders of the IRP. Furqan members made an unsuccessful attempt to assassinate him on 25 May 1979. He was later appointed deputy minister of the interior. He was an active member of the Assembly of Experts. After his election as a Majlis deputy from Tehran he was voted the speaker of the house in July 1980, a post to which he was re-elected a year later.

The prospect of Iran attacking Iraq disturbed both superpowers. They had been neutral in the Gulf War and had wanted an end to it. This sentiment was shared by others in the international community. Reflecting this, the UN Security Council passed a resolution on 12 July calling for a ceasefire and the withdrawal of the warring forces to the international border.

Tehran rejected the resolution, and launched an offensive, named Ramadan al Mubarak (The Blessed Ramadan), the next day on the southern front. With this the nature of the conflict changed. Iran was no longer fighting to expel the Iraqi aggressor. Instead it had staged an invasion of Iraq. This marked the fourth phase of the Gulf War, the earlier phases being the Iraqi advance into Iran (until late March 1981), the stalemate (until mid-March 1982), and the Iraqi retreat from Iran (until the end of June 1982).

Iran made a determined effort to capture Basra, a city with a Shia majority. The Iraqi defences consisted of earthworks and trenches, followed by minefields, barbed wire fences and well-placed machine gun and artillery positions. But by deploying five divisions of combatants, the Iranian commanders were able to break through Iraqi defence lines, and advance ten miles into Iraq. This brought the Iranians within seven miles of the city. Iraq launched an immediate counter-offensive with four divisions. Thus some 150,000 troops were locked in the largest infantry fighting since the Second World War. Fierce battles raged for a week.

Since the Iraqis were fighting a defensive war on their home ground their morale was high. They performed well. They first blunted the Iranian thrust, and then pushed the invading forces back. Determined to win, the Iranian commanders mounted another major offensive on 22 July. But this too was blocked by the Iraqis. A fortnight's intense fighting ended in a stalemate. Having at one point occupied 300 sq. kms of Iraqi territory, Iran had to give up all but eighty sq. kms. Iran suffered more casualties than Iraq. Independent observers put the number of Iranians killed, wounded or captured during the three weeks of fighting at 1,000 a day. Official Iranian sources said that 7,000 Iraqis had been killed or wounded and 1,400 taken captive.[69]

Like Iraqi leaders in the summer of 1980, Iranian officials had expected popular uprisings against the Baghdad government by Shias when the Iranian forces advanced towards Basra. To encourage such a development, Hojatalislam Muhammad Baqir Hakim – the prestigious leader of Iraqi Shias, living in exile in Tehran – had crossed the international border with the Iranians and appealed to fellow Iraqi Shias to rebel against Saddam Hussein. But neither this nor Khomeini's calls for rebellion against Saddam Hussein had worked. Facing a foreign invader, Iraqi Shias behaved in the same way as

Iranian Arabs and Kurds had done in September 1980; they rallied round their government. They shared the fears of Iraqi Sunnis that the Iranian occupation of their country could cause a violent disruption to their lives.

Nonetheless, Tehran gained something out of this offensive. The preparatory committee of the Non-Aligned Movement decided to move the venue of the seventh summit conference from Baghdad to Delhi. If the conference had been held in Baghdad in September, and chaired by Saddam Hussein, he would have become the leader of the ninety-seven-member Non-Aligned Movement for the next three years. This would have boosted Iraq's diplomatic standing in the Third World at the expense of Iran.

But this was not enough to satisfy the hawks in the Supreme Defence Council. When the doves said that securing the cancellation of the NAM conference in Baghdad and silencing the artillery guns across the border were enough to claim victory, the hawks argued that Iran must continue to fight for the objective summed up by the slogan: 'To Karbala and Najaf without Passports'.

Iran's invasion of Iraq had the effect of strengthening Saddam Hussein's position at home. It also led to the end of Soviet neutrality in the war in favour of Iraq. Moscow decided, secretly, to deliver the weapons it had contracted to sell to Baghdad in December 1978. These included MiG-25 aircraft, T-72 tanks, SAM-8 missiles, and Frog-7 ground-to-ground missiles.

Iraq strengthened its diplomatic position by subscribing to the Arab League peace plan adopted by the summit conference in Fez, Morocco, on 11 September: a ceasefire during the (imminent) hajj season, complete evacuation of the Iranian territory by Iraq, and compensation of £40 billion to Iran through the Islamic Reconstruction Fund.[70]

Iran rejected the Arab League proposals. It considered itself strong enough to evict Iraq from its soil in the central and northern sectors of the war front. On 1 October it mounted an offensive – named Muslim ibn Aqil, after Imam Hussein's younger brother – the central front near the Sumar hills overlooking the Iraqi town of Mandali. It deployed 50,000 troops. On 5 October the UN Security Council called for an end to hostilities and mutual withdrawals from occupied territories. Iraq accepted the ceasefire proviso of the resolution; Iran rejected it outright.

The Iranians captured the strategic Sumar hills but failed to make headway into Iraq towards Mandali, sixty-five miles north-east of Baghdad. Their commanders activated the southern front near Basra with a view to overstretching the Iraqis. But Baghdad had enough forces in place in the south to blunt the Iranian drive there. The total gain made by Iran in this offensive was 150 sq. kms of its own territory.

But there was to be no respite for Iraq. On 31 October Tehran launched another offensive, codenamed Muharram al Harram (The Holy Muharram), in the oil-bearing areas of Naft-e Shah in the central sector and Musian area near Dehloran, west of Dezful. Khomeini personally backed this move. In a speech on 31 October he said, 'War can be as holy as prayer when it is fought for the sake of defending Islam.' As such, he added, fighting at the front was a duty above all others.[71] In the central sector Iran gained 250 sq. kms including Bayat oilfield, but failed to achieve its overriding objective of seizing Mandali. Further south, the Iranians broke the Iraqi lines, and penetrated six miles into Iraq, capturing fifty oilwells on the way to Tabe. But they were unable to retain Tabe in the face of an Iraqi counter-offensive. At the end of this bout of fighting Iran had secured a total of 850 sq. kms, including 300 sq. kms of Iraqi territory.

Having found themselves on the defensive on the land front, the Iraqis chose to go on the offensive against Iranian targets in the Gulf. In mid-August Saddam Hussein declared the northern end of the Gulf as 'a naval exclusion zone' and threatened to bomb Iranian targets, including the oil terminal on Kharg island, situated about 100 miles south-east of Bandar Khomeini. Tehran warned that if the Kharg terminal were made inoperative, it would block the Hormuz Strait, and thus disrupt the daily flow of ten million barrels of oil bound for West European and Japanese ports.[72] Between 4 and 13 December Iraq claimed to have sunk six merchant and naval vessels in the Bandar Khomeini-Kharg region, most probably by using French-made F39 Exocet missiles fired from helicopter gunships. Of these only the loss of one vessel, a Turkish cargo ship, was confirmed. On 21 November, whereas Baghdad claimed to have sunk five oil tankers in the Kharg area, Lloyd's of London (Insurance) confirmed damage to two Iranian ships by the Iraqi action.[73]

Since 90 per cent of Iranian oil was shipped from Kharg, Tehran was anxious to protect the terminal, using all the military equipment it had. This was all the more so because Iranian exports of crude in the second quarter of 1982 were running at 1.8 million b/d and earning the country $1.3 billion a month, enough to pay for the civilian imports of $700 million and military imports of $400 million. In fact by the end of September Iran was believed to have built up foreign reserves of $4 billion.[74] 'What we lack now is not money but good planning,' said Bahzad Nabavi, minister for heavy industry.[75] In mid-October the Majlis voted an additional $1.9 billion to the defence budget of $5 billion.

The government had overcome the foreign exchange crisis by

banning all non-essential imports and severely limiting foreign travel, and by increasing its oil exports. It had managed to keep inflation around the 20 per cent level by sustaining the efficiency of the rationing system through imports, and by curbing public expenditure through such means as cutting civil servants' salaries and banning recruitment. Due mainly to an abrupt rise in oil output from early 1982 onwards, the GNP had risen modestly by 2.2 per cent in 1981-2. This reversed the trend of the past three years. During that period the GNP had declined by an average of 10.5 per cent each year.[76]

In tackling economic problems the government remained conscious of its political priorities. For instance, it did not tinker with subsidies on basic necessities or the Islamic system of social security. These cost the public exchequer $4 billion, or 10 per cent of the national budget. Subsidies amounted to $1.9 billion, with the one on flour and wheat alone costing over $500,000.[77] The government was keen to make a success of the rationing system, particularly for the poor. Whenever it received urgently needed imports of food, it first distributed them in the working class areas of cities and towns.[78] At the same time the authorities allowed a black market to function freely to allow the middle and upper classes to obtain whatever they could not get through the rationing system.

The government tried to increase agricultural production. It continued the policy of giving free chemical fertilisers to small farmers initiated by the Shah's regime. During the period of March-December 1981, its cheap loans to small peasants amounted to $1.8 billion. In 1981-2, 25,000 tractors were assembled in Iran, compared to 19,000 before the revolution.[79]

But no progress was made towards creating equitable ownership of arable land. The Mousavi government's effort to implement radical land reform was thwarted by the Guardians Council. In late 1981 the Majlis passed a bill which, among other things, imposed ceilings on land ownership – from five hectares to thirty hectares – depending on the quality of land and other factors. But the ulema section of the Guardians Council declared the legislation to be unIslamic. It objected to the bill's provision which authorised the state to buy excess land above the ceiling. It argued that blanket takeover of excess land meant that the state would buy up even the land acquired legitimately by an individual. This would undermine an individual's right to hold private property – a right which, according to the Quran, is inviolable. The Guardians' verdict was final. It disappointed those who were committed to the concept of redistribution of wealth under the aegis of Islam. Expectedly it was welcomed by landlords, who owned and managed large holdings, as well as by those bazaar merchants who had bought agricultural land to improve their social standing, and who were absentee landlords.

However, the Guardians Council decision did not affect the government's policy of reclaiming virgin land belonging to the state and allotting it to landless peasants. So this programme continued.

Industry was in a poor state. Premier Mousavi conceded this publicly. In a speech on 7 November 1982 he said: 'Only a small number of our factories are operational'.[80] This was the outcome of poor management and shortages of skilled personnel, industrial raw materials and spare parts. On the other hand the government was pressing ahead with its plans of rural electrification and extension of the telephone service to villages, as well as building a vast network of natural gas pipelines for heating and cooking.[81]

Shortage of skilled personnel co-existed with high unemployment. There were no official figures on the unemployed, but unofficial estimates put it around 15 to 20 per cent of the labour force.[82] The problem of lack of skilled personnel was being made worse by keeping universities and colleges shut. As elsewhere, this decision was dictated by political considerations. Universities and colleges were the main breeding grounds of the Mujahedin and other opposition parties. By keeping them closed the government was inhibiting the growth of its opponents. It is certain that if universities and colleges had been open at the time of Bani-Sadr's ouster, the regime would have faced a much bigger challenge than it actually did.

Since then the authorities had followed a policy of repression combined with rehabilitation of those who recanted in jail. This had gone on for about eighteen months. Yet the opposition, although weak, persisted.

The opposition

Following the killings of the Mujahedin central committee members in February 1982, the government eased up a bit on the opposition. In early March it announced an amnesty for 10,000 political prisoners on the eve of the Iranian New Year. But that still left an estimated 25,000 political dissidents behind bars.

Once Mujahedin leadership had overcome the shock of losing ten central committee members, it reorganised the party structure and replaced the lost comrades. Ali Zarkesh was appointed the new military commander. At the same time activity inside the military was stepped up. A sign of this came when an unconfirmed Mujahedin-inspired mutiny at Tehran's Lavizan garrison on 27 March led to fifteen deaths, including two colonels.[83]

The arrest on 8 April of Sadiq Qutbzadch on charges of plotting against the state, and reports of fighting between Qashqai tribals and revolutionary guards, revealed other sources of opposition. Qutbzadeh and his accomplices had allegedly devised a plan for a takeover of power along the following lines. Their supporters in the military would kill Khomeini by hitting his Jamran residence and offices with rockets, and assassinate the members of the Supreme Defence Council. Qutbzadeh and his associates would blame the outrage on the Tudeh, and seize power in order to avenge the killings.[84]

Sadiq Qutbzadeh had a chequered career. He was born in 1936 in a family of a minor lumber merchant of Tehran. Before he left Iran in 1959 he had been arrested twice for his anti-Shah activities. During the next two decades he lived in Egypt, Syria, Italy, Canada, America and France as a 'student'. When his Iranian passport was withdrawn by Savak he was given a Syrian passport by the government in Damascus. At one time he was known to have acted as a courier for Khomeini during his exile in Najaf. Finally, he settled down in Paris. Here he was actively involved with the Islamic Student Society. When Khomeini arrived in France in the autumn of 1978, Qutbzadeh became one of his close aides. He was one of the first appointees to the Islamic Revolutionary Council. On his return to Iran he was appointed head of radio and television. He dismissed women announcers and introduced religious programmes. In late November 1979 he became foreign minister and held the post until the Rajai government took office in August 1980. He retained his seat as a Majlis deputy. His application for starting a paper was rejected. In early November he was arrested after he had criticised the IRP in a television interview. He was released a few days later on Khomeini's orders. He soon fell into obscurity. Following Bani-Sadr's dismissal he was kept under surveillance.

His accomplices in the present plot included Ahmed Abbasi, a son-in-law of Ayatollah Shariatmadari. Abbasi's arrest on 17 April was accompanied by a revolutionary guards' raid on the house and the theological school of Shariatmadari. Simultaneously, the military officers, implicated in the plot, were being secretly arrested too. It was significant that, in his message for the Armed Forces Day on 18 April, Khomeini appealed for an end to 'discord among military personnel'.[85]

Just then the Militant Students, who had occupied the US embassy in late November for over a year, reprinted the first of a series of books, entitled *The Documents of the Nest of Spies: Volumes I to VI* (in Persian). These papers contained many references to Shariatmadari which were politically damaging to him, and showed that he had accepted funds for promoting non-alcoholic American drinks in Iran.[86] Earlier the Iranian media had published material from old Savak files showing Shariatmadari as being on the Shah's side – and evidence to prove that he had been in indirect touch with the US embassy after the revolution. On 20 April the elders of the Faiziya seminary in Qom stripped Shariatmadari of his religious title. The next day bazaars throughout Iran closed in solidarity with the Faiziya's action. About a week later Hojatalislam Khoiniha appeared on television to exhibit documents which showed that Shariatmadari had had contacts with the CIA. 'The main objective of the CIA, according to the existing documents, was to bring to power a government in Iran which would guarantee US interests in this country,' Khoiniha concluded.[87] On 3 May Shariatmadari confessed on television that he had been told of the plans by Qutbzadeh and his associates, but denied that he had given them his sanction.[88]

None of this had any impact on the Mujahedin. Having tightened up the organisation internally, Ali Zarkesh ordered a series of daring acts in early May. The Mujahedin blew up the Tehran office of the Reconstruction Crusade, a revolutionary organisation for rural development, and attacked an education centre and an interest-free loan centre. The government's retaliatory action led to the deaths or arrests of fifty Mujahedin.[89] Period attacks by the Mujahedin on revolutionary guards continued as before.

While public attention was focussed on the outcome of the Iranian offensives of late May and mid-July, the security and intelligence agencies concentrated on ferreting out those involved in the plot masterminded by Qutbzadeh. They arrested a total of 170 persons, including seventy military officers. The officers were tried secretly. But Qutbzadeh's trial by a military tribunal was televised on 14 August. In it he admitted participating in a conspiracy to oust some leading ulema from the government, but denied any plans for killing Khomeini. Had the plot succeeded, he said, Khomeini would have been sent to Qom and consigned to a strictly religious role. On 16 August the government announced that the seventy officers involved in the plot had been executed. A week later the trial of Qutbzadeh and his leading associates was postponed.

Early in September, after holding a brief hearing in secret, the military tribunal found Qutbzadeh guilty of conspiring to overthrow the Islamic government and sentenced him to death. The ultimate decision, however, lay with Khomeini. Appeals were made to him by Bazargan and others to spare Qutbzadeh's life. These were in vain. On the night of 15 September Qutbzadeh was executed by a firing squad in Tehran's Evin prison.

Qutbzadeh's execution marked a dramatic end to the co-option by the Islamic regime of lay Iranian intellectuals who had been active in the Islamic anti-Shah movement abroad. The process had begun with the removal from office of Ibrahim Yazdi in November 1979, and included Amir Abbas Entezam, Ahmed Madani and Bani-Sadr. Their many years in the West had cast them in a Western mould; and this did not fit the Islamic state that was being forged in Iran. Interestingly, most of them had been accused of contacts with the CIA. As for Qutbzadeh, once he had lost his official position, he combined with those elements who at the very least wanted to crush radical forces within the Islamic regime.

It was significant that during the period when Qutbzadeh's fate hung in the balance, the Mujahedin set off a series of bombs in central Tehran, causing dozens of deaths. After Qutbzadeh's execution, this activity ceased. In fact, when a bomb explosion in Tehran on 1 October killed sixty people and injured 700, the Mujahedin disclaimed responsibility and blamed the government for it.[90] But there was no end to the Mujahedin assaults on revolutionary guards. In mid-November the Mujahedin headquarters in Paris claimed that since 20 June 1981 the party had killed 2,000 political and religious leaders of the regime.[91] In return, according to its Paris head office, it had suffered executions of 3,000 Mujahedin.[92]

While being alert to plots at home, and sustaining its repression of violent opposition, the government kept up its programme of Islamisation. On 30 May the cabinet approved comprehensive plans to introduce Islamic legislation into current penal and legal codes, civil law, trade law, and registration of documents and land. Adherence to Islamic dress for women was enforced strictly. In August the government declared all secular law null and void. The Majlis passed a law on moral offences on 21 September.

The execution of Qutbzadeh about a week earlier signalled the end of the fourth, and the longest, phase of the revolution, which began with the dismissal of Bani-Sadr. The earlier phases had been shorter: from February to November 1979; from November 1979 to September 1980; and from September 1980 to June 1981.

As the opposition campaign during the last phase was launched in the Persian-speaking heartland of Iran, it caused the most severe turmoil since the revolution. The regime surmounted the challenge by using unrestrained force and propaganda. With war raging along 300 miles of its border with Iraq, the government convincingly labelled those creating disorder at home as unpatriotic agents of Iraq. It transformed patriotic feelings into a sustained drive for self-sufficiency, and was particularly successful in increasing oil exports. By painting the war in Islamic colours, Iranian leaders were able to galvanise the nation as well as raise Islamic consciousness in the country. Given this, they turned the tide on the battle front, and put Iraq on the defensive. In turn this increased the regime's popularity. On the other hand numerous instances of indiscriminate violence used by the Tehran government against its opponents tarnished its image in the West and the region.

Having surmounted the internal and external crises, Khomeini could afford to relax a little. And he did. Signs of this came soon after Ramadan, which ended in mid-August. These set the scene for consolidation of the revolution, which included electing an Assembly of Experts to settle the question of the successor(s) to Khomeini.

CONSOLIDATION OF THE REVOLUTION

The first sign of relaxation by the regime came in mid-August when Khomeini called on the purging committees of government ministries to exercise restraint.[1] Soon the campaign against music, involving confiscation of records, tapes and video-cassettes, was quietly abandoned. Then non-Muslim minorities were exempted from the ban on alcohol. This meant that half a million Christians, 50,000 Jews and 30,000 Zoroastrians could now legally consume alcohol at home. In October, Mahdi Bazargan was allowed to circulate a critical letter among Majlis deputies. In it he attacked the radicals in the IRP, and criticised the government for its violations of human rights, and for being inefficient and corrupt.[2]

After protracted internal discussion the government finally decided to face the problem of Khomeini's succession. On 20 November it announced an election on 10 December for an eighty-two-member Assembly of Experts to deal with the question of the next Leader or Leadership Council. Only clerics were allowed to run.

This was the eighth election or referendum since the revolution nearly four years ago. According to official sources, nearly 17,683,000 voters participated. The Assembly of Experts was to be a permanent body. Among the thirteen members elected from Tehran, Khamanei, Hashemi-Rafsanjani and Mousavi-Ardebili were at the top of the list. This was a measure of their popularity and the regime they led.

Thus reassured, Khomeini launched, what he described, 'a judicial revolution to protect the dignity and honour of individuals'. He issued an eight-point decree, entitled 'Islamisation of Judiciary', on 15 December. 'The legislation based on Sharia, and its approval and communication, must be carried out with necessary accuracy and speed,' stated Point One. 'The laws regarding judicial matters . . . must be given priority over other measures.' Point Two referred to the settlement of 'matters relating to the competence of judges and prosecutors and courts' so that 'the people's rights are protected'. The criterion lay in 'the present deeds of individuals, overlooking certain mistakes which they might have made during the former regime's rule'. Point Three called on Islamic judges 'both in the justice ministry and in revolutionary courts' to act 'independently, firmly and without consideration for any official'. Nobody was allowed to 'treat people in an unIslamic way', it concluded. Point Four warned that 'Nobody is allowed to arrest or summon anybody without a judge's order', and that 'Arrest or summons by force is an offence'. Point Five referred to the unlawfulness of usurping 'anybody's property or right . . . except on a Sharia judge's orders'. The same applied to impounding or confiscating somebody's property.

'Nobody is allowed to enter anyone's home, shop or private place of business without the owner's permission – or to arrest, pursue or detain anybody on the pretext of uncovering an offence or sin, or to insult anybody or to carry out unIslamic and inhumane actions, or eavesdrop on anybody's telephone conversations or listen to anybody's tapes in the name of uncovering an offence, centre of sin, or place of crime . . . or to investigate people's secrets or spy on other people's sins or discuss other people's secrets,' stated Point Six. 'All these are sins or offences . . . and anybody committing the aforesaid offences will be considered an offender.' However, Point Seven made an exception to the above. It stated that these restrictions did not apply to 'the cases relating to conspiracies and the mini-groups opposed to Islam and the regime of the Islamic Republic'. Such cases had to be dealt with 'firmly and severely . . . but in accordance with the prosecutors' and courts' orders'.

Point Eight called on the supreme court chief and the prime minister to implement the above instructions by setting up 'trustworthy and reliable councils' to which the aggrieved persons could refer their complaints about 'violations and transgressions by enforcement officers against their rights and properties'. These councils must report their findings to the supreme court chief and the prime minister; and the latter must punish the transgressors according to Sharia laws. 'From now on, which is the time for stability and construction,' concluded the decree, 'the nation must feel secure and at peace, and . . . should realise that judicial power is at its service in the enforcement of Islamic laws and regulations.'[3]

The issue of such a decree of Khomeini was an admission that there had been transgressions of the law in the past and that these had caused much resentment. Undoubtedly this was a most important document in the revolution's history. For several days it engaged the attention of Iranians at home and abroad. The opposition parties based in Europe dismissed it as a hoax meant to give the people a false sense of security. They saw it as an act of an unpopular government trying to win some popular backing. At the other end, hardliners in the

Islamic camp at home considered it as a step back from the radical position so far taken by the Islamic revolution.

Expressing an official view, Premier Mousavi called the decree 'a historic turning point' and 'a new phase in the revolution'. The leading papers in Tehran saw it as a confirmation of the strength and stability of the Islamic state. 'The regime could rely on the sword only to a certain degree,' explained Mousavi-Ardebili, the supreme court chief. 'In other cases reliance should be on justice, logic, faith and knowledge. . . . Encouragement should be given to an individual's fear of justice rather than the sword.'[4]

One of the main purposes of the eight-point decree was to reassure the modern middle classes at home, and to encourage the affluent and skilled Iranian expatriates to return. The wording of Point Two was significant. It instructed the judicial and other authorities to judge a person on 'the present deeds' and overlook his 'mistakes' of the past.

Khomeini made this move at a time when modern middle classes were feeling impotent and dejected. They had seen their hopes of the Mujahedin overthrowing the Islamic regime dashed, and were becoming resigned to the idea of a long spell under Khomeini's Islamic rule. The Ayatollah wanted to transform their disgruntled acceptance of his regime into something positive. He appealed to the self-exiled Iranians on economic grounds. 'Nobody should be afraid to come back and engage in business,' he said. 'We promise that as long as there is Islam there will be free enterprise also.'[5]

To further reassure these classes he transferred the trials for economic offences and breach of Islamic morals from harsh revolutionary courts to the justice ministry's public courts. But this had an undesirable impact in an unexpected quarter: the rate of price rises.

In order to control inflation the government had fixed official prices for most goods. In the absence of an effective price enforcement agency, the task of keeping traders in line had fallen on the local Revolutionary Komitehs and revolutionary guards, who had powers to arrest at will. But once Khomeini's eight-point decree and order to transfer economic offences to public courts had removed the threat of arbitrary arrest, traders felt free to overcharge. And they did. The price of a packet of cigarettes shot up from Rials 250 to Rials 750, and that of a car tyre from Rials 2,500 to Rials 12,500.[6]

This caused resentment among consumers. Voicing their grievances, newspapers and radio and television took to branding profiteers as 'economic terrorists'. The government appealed to merchants to stop overcharging. But this did nothing to alleviate the situation. Khomeini decided to step in. In late January he summoned the bazaar leaders of Tehran and other cities to his mosque at Jamran. After praising his audience for their support of the mosque and the revolution, Khomeini quoted from the Quran against excessive profiteering. Reminding them of the Islamic war that the country was waging against the infidel Iraqi leadership, he said that he expected every Muslim to make sacrifices for war, not enrich himself from it. He also appealed to them to ease the government's burden of waging a war, and assisting 1.5 million war refugees from western Iran as well as over one million Afghan political refugees in the country. Bazaar leaders donated about $130 million to the war effort.[7] Their concerted efforts brought down the prices, although not to the original levels. A packet of cigarettes now cost Rials 350, and a car tyre Rials 6,000.

Following his eight-point decree, Khomeini appointed a six-member committee, including the supreme court chief and the prime minister, to run the Headquarters for the Implementation of the Imam's Decree. By the end of December the HIID had dismissed the revolutionary prosecutors of Tehran municipality, Qom, Tabriz, Bushahr and Birjand on charges of violations of human rights and abuse of authority. To try these and other judicial officials, Khomeini established the Judicial Disciplinary Supreme Court. The HIID appointed twenty-three local committees to tour their areas and collect complaints about the malfunctioning of judicial and administrative systems.

Khomeini then turned his attention to methods being used by the vetting committees to determine the Islamic credentials of those employed by public agencies or applying for jobs with them. These committees had taken to giving tests to determine this. The tests contained many obscure theological questions which few laypersons, if any, could be expected to know. On the other hand they included questions which were unrelated to Islam. Also parents of many job applicants had been subjected to extensive interrogation by security organisations about matters unconnected with the job. Khomeini found all this unsatisfactory. On 5 January 1983 he instructed the HIID to dismiss the vetting committees, whether they be in the armed forces, ministries, departments or educational institutions. He reiterated that present behaviour was the only criterion to be considered in choosing a candidate for a job with the government or a revolutionary organisation. Furthermore, he instructed the HIID to find means to 'identify and re-employ those who had been wrongfully dismissed in the past'.[8] The HIID appointed a three-man Supreme Selection Committee to draft regulations, codes of conduct and duties of selection committees at lower levels.

Another sign of normalisation was the government's decision on 18 December to re-open universities and colleges. But this was to be done in stages – with medical, agricultural, engineering and technical faculties opening first, and humanities and the arts last. On the eve of the fourth anniversary of the revolution in February, the authorities announced the resumption of issuing exit visas: these had been suspended in the aftermath of the Gulf War. The decision was particularly welcomed by the middle and upper classes. Tens of thousands of them applied for new passports and exit visas.

During the next six months the passport office received 310,000 applications, including 190,000 originating in Tehran.[9] By early August the prime minister had set up a Special Office for the Attraction of Committed Iranian Experts, and planned to send representatives to European cities to persuade professionally qualified Iranians to return home. In some cases shortages were quite acute. The country needed 40,000 doctors, whereas it had only 15,000, with some 8,000 having migrated before and soon after the revolution.

The government's move to placate the middle classes seemed to complement its increasingly tough stance towards the Tudeh Party, which culminated in a ban on it. In a sense taking such a measure against a party which had been friendly towards the revolution was a sign of the growing self-confidence of the Islamic regime.

Banning the Tudeh

While Tudeh leaders felt irked by a series of purges of their members and sympathisers from the civil service, educational institutions and revolutionary organisations, the ruling IRP was not content with this. In mid-April 1982 the *Jumhouri-ye Islami* accused the 'treacherous Tudeh' of rushing to help 'liberals' and 'nationalists' against 'true Muslims' in the early 1950s, and of helping to reinstall the Shah in August 1953.[10] By this the newspaper meant that the Tudeh had not sided with Ayatollah Kashani when he split with Mussadiq. This was true. But to state that the Tudeh had assisted in the reinstallation of the Shah flew in the face of history – of such facts as the repression that the Shah unleashed against the Tudeh on his return. Tudeh leaders were unhappy about such accusations as well as at the ascendancy of conservative elements within the Islamic regime. Evidence of the latter came in early June when the Guardians Council rejected the foreign trade nationalisation bill passed by the Majlis on the ground that it was unIslamic.[11]

A month later, as government leaders weighed the merits and demerits of marching into Iraq, the Tudeh weekly, *Ittihad-e Mardom* (People's Unity), warned that Iranian invasion of Iraq would be detrimental to the future of the Islamic Republic. On 18 July the prosecutor general banned the publication for its 'clear opposition to Islam'. Soon Khomeini ordered that the purge of Tudeh members and sympathisers from the government and revolutionary bodies be accelerated. In protest the party's central committee published an open letter in an East Berlin paper. It accused the authorities of intimidating the party, and arresting its members, and preventing others from doing normal political work.[12]

The two sides were clearly on a collision course. In late October there was a strike at a car plant in Greater Tehran. The authorities broke the strike swiftly, and arrested scores of trade unionists at the factory and elsewhere. They made it a point to arrest all those suspected of membership of, or sympathies with, the Tudeh. This meant that the purge of Tudeh elements was now being extended to industry, which had been a traditional base of the party. Relations between the Tudeh and the government were now at their lowest ebb since the revolution.

Despite this the party leadership did not consider reversing its policy of functioning openly. It continued to hope that the balance of forces within the regime would change in favour of those who advocated radical socio-economic reform. It also continued to press for the restoration of democratic freedoms. Following Khomeini's promulgation of the eight-point decree, Kianouri, the Tudeh leader, wrote to Premier Mousavi complaining that 240 trade unionists were in jail without charges.[13] The government response was swift. Within days it put Tudeh trade unionists on trial.

This was a prelude to a more dramatic step. On 7 February 1983 – the day Iran launched a major offensive against Iraq – the authorities arrested seventy leaders and members of the Tudeh, including at least fourteen central committee members.[14] The principal charge against them, including Kianouri, was that they had been spying for the 'countries of the Eastern bloc'.

With all the Tudeh publications closed down, the National Voice of Iran Radio, operating from Baku, Soviet Azerbaijan, took up the party's cause. It did so more in sorrow than anger. Its 9 February broadcast referred to Khomeini's 11 May 1979 statement: 'All parties and groups can operate freely and express themselves freely as long as they are not at war with this Islamic country and do not engage in an armed rebellion against Islam'. On 23 and 24 March, the NVOI Radio broadcast a communiqué by the Tudeh central committee. It stated that the party had operated openly since the revolution, participated in all elections and referendums, and accepted the ten-point statement by the revolutionary prosecutor general concerning political parties' legal activities. 'During the four years [of the Islamic revolution] we have supported every positive step by the Islamic Republic of Iran and have sympathetically and frankly criticised any wrong and deficient measure,' it said.

Among the measures the Tudeh considered 'wrong and deficient' was the Labour Code drafted by Ahmed Tavakoli, the labour minister. This bill inter alia made no provision for legal strikes, and allowed an employer to dismiss a worker before the end of his contract without redundancy pay or any other compensation. A broadcast by the NVOI Radio on 5 April attacked the draft bill. After quoting leading government officials' description of the bill as 'a disgrace to the revolution', the NVOI broadcast categorised 'Tavakoli and his partners' as 'supporters of capitalism and feudalism'.

This went down badly with that faction in the regime which wanted to ban the Tudeh. Its case was strengthened by the Iraqi missile attacks on the civilian areas of Dezful on 20 and 22 April, which killed seventy-six people and wounded 405. Iraq used the recently acquired Soviet-made Frog-7 ground-to-ground missiles with a range of seventy-five miles. One way to avenge these deaths and injuries was to ban a party which was, at the very least, pro-Moscow. On 27 April the government arrested more leaders and members of the Tudeh. In Tehran's diplomatic circles these and earlier arrests were increasingly associated with the defection to the British in June 1982 of Vladimir Andreyvich Kuzichkin, a Soviet diplomat who monitored the Tudeh Party. He was reported to have given the names of some 400 Tudeh and Soviet agents in Iran to the British government, which had in turn passed them on to the Iranian authorities in October 1982.[15]

Certainly the main thrust of the Iranian government's charges against Tudeh leaders and members was that they had spied for the Soviet Union. On 30 April Iranian television showed Kianouri being questioned by an unseen interrogator. Kianouri said that the party had committed six major 'misdeeds'. It had trampled upon the country's major foreign policy slogan: 'Neither East nor West'. Blaming this on 'the adherence created over decades between our party and the Communist Party of the Soviet Union', he said: 'Our activities on the political scene changed on occasions to espionage'. Secondly, the party did not surrender all the weapons it had obtained during the period of the Islamic revolutionary movement. Thirdly, in violation of the revolutionary prosecutor general's ten-point guidance to political parties, the Tudeh did not dissolve its secret bodies. Fourthly, the party formed a secret organisation among military officers, who were 'very limited in number'. Nonetheless, these officers helped to collect information which was then transferred to the Soviet Union. Fifthly, the party frustrated the government's efforts to purge all its institutions and revolutionary bodies of people 'attached to outside organisations' by asking its members to deny association with the Tudeh. Finally, the party made arrangements for illegal trips abroad for its members. 'In my opinion, the mistakes we made are . . . espionage, deceit, treachery,' he concluded. 'They deserve the most severe punitive actions that the Islamic Republic may decide to mete out.'[16]

On 4 May the revolutionary prosecutor general dissolved the Tudeh Party, and ordered its members and supporters in Tehran to report to his office by 14 May, and those living outside the capital to do so within a month. According to a Tudeh spokesman in London, the government had arrested nearly 1,500 party members by early June. The party had some 2,500 to 3,000 members and three times as many active sympathisers. Many of those who escaped arrest did not surrender, and instead crossed into the leftist-ruled Afghanistan. There they were used by the Kabul government to fill in administrative jobs vacated by hostile Afghan nationals, and to help the ruling party to organise industrial workers and improve its propaganda apparatus.

Iranian officials had no reason to feel anxious about the Tudeh's current strength. It was the party's potential that worried them. After all the Tudeh had a long history, a party infrastructure, a disciplined cadre, and a body of politicians and ideologues of high calibre. It had shown itself to be resilient in the past. If in the future the IRP were to lose popularity, there was a chance that the Tudeh would expand rapidly. The Islamic regime was not prepared to allow this. It wanted to give a clear message to workers, and a certain section of the middle classes, that the Tudeh was finished for ever. So it combined a ban on the party with a political campaign based on its leaders' confessions.

The party faithful abroad found the government tactics damaging. In mid-May the West Berlin cell of the Tudeh published an article attacking the Iranian government. This was reproduced in *Pravda* (Truth), the newspaper of the Communist Party of the Soviet Union, on 24 May. 'The torturers from the Iranian security service, by resorting to the most barbarous medieval torture, have broken some of our comrades in the struggle and wrenched from them "admissions" which have no foundation and nothing in common with reality,' the article said.

In October the Iranian government showed another series of confessions by the arrested Tudeh leaders on television. In the first programme six party leaders admitted promoting Soviet interests in Iran, and instigating rebellion in Kurdish areas.[17] Ayatollah Reyshahri, the revolutionary prosecutor general, said in early December that 200 Tudeh members arrested in the military, gendarmerie and police would be tried soon. Among those arrested was Captain Bahram Afzali, former commander of the navy.

Later in December eighty-seven members of the military organisation of the Tudeh were found guilty of attempting to overthrow the government, espionage, possessing and concealing arms, and failing to observe the ban on political parties in the military. They were given sentences of a year in jail to life imprisonment. In late February 1984 there were further convictions. Ten Tudeh leaders, including Afzali, were executed.[18]

As in the past, the Tudeh continued to function abroad. In January 1984 the party's central committee held its eighteenth plenum in East Germany. It expelled all the arrested members, and elected Ali Khavari as the first secretary of the party. It adopted a new programme. 'Contrary to the belief of the counter-revolution, the revolution in Iran has not been banished,' it said. 'Progressive revolutionary and anti-imperialist forces, political and religious, possess extensive material and moral bases in society, and through unity and joint action, they can draw into their ranks all toiling classes and strata who are turning away from the reactionary ruling circle.'[19]

Among other things the plenum decided to establish 'healthy and constructive relations' with the Mujahedin-e Khalq. The one point on which both parties were agreed was the need to end the Iran-Iraq war. In his opposition to Khomeini, Masoud Rajavi had taken to cooperating with Iraqi leadership. In January 1983 Rajavi had a publicly acknowledged meeting with Tariq Aziz, deputy premier of Iraq, in Paris.

As the Soviet Union had been moving steadily towards a pro-Iraqi position since July 1982, and as the Tudeh was a pro-Moscow party, it now seemed logical for the Tudeh to establish working relationship with the Mujahedin-e Khalq. But none of this had any impact on the war policies of the Khomeini regime. It seemed as determined as ever to prosecute hostilities with Iraq until Saddam Hussein had fallen.

The war: pros and cons

One of the salient features of the war was that while Iran had by and large limited air raids to military and economic targets, Iraq had not been so discriminating. In late December 1982, for instance, Baghdad claimed to have mounted seventy-four air raids on targets in Khuzistan. Following this, fighting flared up on the southern front. On 18 January Iraq reported sixty-six bombing missions in the region. It renewed air attacks on 26 January and continued them for five days. Such tactics were costly. By then Iraq had lost 117 warplanes.[20] But because it had been taking delivery of military aircraft from France, and had been receiving Chinese-made MiG-19s and MiG-21s from Egypt, it had maintained its total of combat aircraft around the pre-war strength of 332.

In contrast Iran had failed to procure warplanes abroad. No member of the North Atlantic Treaty Organisation or the Warsaw Pact was prepared to sell military aircraft to Iran. This was also true of the neutral European nations: in most cases their planes were equipped with engines manufactured in a Nato country. Losses in the war, and lack of spares for its American combat planes, had reduced Iran's airworthy military aircraft from 440-plus before the war to about 120. Iran was therefore compelled to use its aircraft mainly for defensive purposes: protection of airfields, oilfields and installations, refineries and important cities. Because of lack of adequate air cover, Iranian offensives often resulted in heavy casualties.

This was particularly true of the Iranian offensive of 7 February in the Fakkeh region of Khuzistan, codenamed Wa al Fajr (By the Dawn). The Iranians crossed the border at Fakkeh and penetrated many miles into Iraq. Baghdad countered the Iranian move with a massive force. At its peak the fighting involved 100,000 troops. After a week's hostilities, Hashemi-Rafsanjani conceded that Iran's progress on the front had been slow. When pressed a few days later to explain what had happened, he replied: 'I don't consider the time ripe to tell the nation what had taken place. . . . Our forces crossed the enemy lines and then returned to positions more easily defensible.'[21] The Iranians suffered heavily at the hands of the Iraqis who made extensive use of aircraft and helicopter gunships. All told Iran regained 250 sq. kms of its territory. That still left Iraq in control of 850 sq. kms of Iranian soil in different regions.

The heavy losses of the Fakkeh offensive made Iranian leaders rethink the overall strategy. They decided to discard large, concentrated attacks in favour of building up pressure all along the 730-mile border with a view to overstretching Iraqi resources, and thus causing the collapse of the Baathist regime. By waging a long war of attrition, they wanted to reduce Iranian losses in men and materials.

In late March Iran had no difficulty in blunting an Iraqi offensive near Sharhan in the central sector – the first such Iraqi move since the early months of the war. On 10 April Iran mounted an offensive, codenamed Wa al Fajr-One, west of Ein Khosh in Khuzistan. It recovered 150 sq. kms of its territory.

What was unusual about the Wa al Fajr-Two offensive, launched on 22 July in the Piranshahr area of the northern sector, was that dissident Iraqi Kurds and Shias fought alongside the invading Iranians. Thus aided, the Iranian forces marched nine miles into Iraq, and captured Hajj Omran garrison as well as Mount Karmand. By so doing the Iranians cut off Iraqi supplies to the Iranian Kurdish insurgents. Iraq launched a counter-offensive, but failed to dislodge the Iranians. Altogether the Iranians secured 400 sq. kms of territory, half of it inside Iraq.

Having occupied Iraqi soil, Iranian officials allowed the Tehran-based Supreme Assembly of Islamic Revolution in Iraq to open offices in Hajj Omran. Formed in November 1982, the SAIRI was led by Hojatalislam Muhammad Baqir Hakim. By letting the SAIRI establish itself on Iraqi soil, Tehran wished to give succour to Iraqi opposition, which was then in a shambles.

Through a stick and carrot policy, Saddam Hussein had destroyed the opposition, consisting of Kurdish secessionists, communists, militant Shias and dissident Baathists. Divided into three parties, Kurds were at odds with one another. The repression unleashed on the communists since 1978 was intensified once they opposed the Iraqi invasion of Iran. Such militant Shia bodies as Al Daawa al Islamiya and the Iraqi Mujahedin were repressed with an iron hand, especially after the membership of these organisations was made a capital offence.

As for mainstream Shia religious leaders, Saddam Hussein found a modus vivendi with them by being generous in the renovation and beautification schemes of Shia shrines and holy cities. Since he had the power to vet prayer leaders in mosques he used it to his advantage, buying off the waverers and silencing the uncompromising opponents. By consistently presenting himself and the war in Islamic guise, he softened some of the Shia criticism of him. By harping on traditional ethnic animosity between Arabs and Persians, he helped Iraqi Shias to downgrade their sectarian differences with Iraqi Sunnis, and think of themselves as Arab first and Shia second. Finally, the Iranian invasion of Iraq aided Saddam Hussein at home: he could convincingly brand his opponents as traitors.

Just as Khomeini's regime aided and abetted Shia and Kurdish opposition to Saddam Hussein, the Baathist regime sided actively with Khomeini's opponents. It assisted the Iranian Kurdish insurgents, and established close ties with the leader of the Iranian Mujahedin, Masoud Rajavi.

Having gained the initiative in the war, Iran kept it up. On 30 July the Iranians staged Wa al Fajr-Three offensive west of Mehran in the central sector. They advanced six miles into Iraq. Fierce fighting ensued, with the Iraqis mounting 150 air sorties in a day. Yet Iran managed to retain 100 sq. kms of territory, half of it inside Iraq.

As the war approached its third anniversary there was growing anxiety among Iraq's friends and allies. The war had bankrupted Iraq. Besides having spent some $30 billion in foreign reserves of its own, Iraq had borrowed at least $38 billion abroad, mainly from the Gulf states.[22] Since Iraqi leaders maintained that they were fighting the war in order to preserve inter alia the future of the Gulf monarchies against the threat of Islamic republicanism propagated by Tehran, they regarded the aid from these countries as their rightful due.

Outside the Gulf, Paris was Baghdad's chief creditor. Leaving aside the $5 billion in military debts underwritten by the French government, Iraq owed private French companies $5 billion.[23] Thus Paris had a considerable stake in Saddam Hussein's survival, and an end to the war. It therefore joined Baghdad in exaggerating the threat that five Super Etendard planes and Exocet missiles (about to be delivered to Iraq by France) posed to Iran's Kharg island oil terminal. This was done to deter Iran from launching another offensive.

Tehran ignored the psychological warfare of Baghdad and Paris. Its forces crossed into Iraq in the northern sector's Marivan area in mid-September. Khomeini responded to threats with counter-threats. 'It should be announced to the world and emphasised that if they [the superpowers] continue to help Saddam [Hussein], their hands will be cut off from oil resources,' Khomeini said in a speech on 19 September. 'If they help Saddam to attack our economic resources, they will not see any more oil.'[24]

Iran moved its elite troops to Larak, Henqin and Sirri islands in the Hormuz Strait, and increased its artillery and anti-aircraft guns on Qeshm and Greater Tunb islands. At the Friday prayer congregation on 14 October, Hashemi-Rafsanjani explained three different methods of blocking the Hormuz – something Iran would do if its oil terminal at Kharg were destroyed. One way would be to create a 'wall of fire' with 130 mm. guns placed on Qeshm or Larak island, guns for which Iran manufactured ammunition at home. The second way would be to fire on passing ships with air-to-sea missiles from planes. 'Our underground depots are full of such missiles,' he said. 'The Americans know this.' The third method would be to sink a large oil tanker in the Strait, thus creating a vast oil slick which would make it 'very difficult to ply through the Strait'.[25]

The closure of the Hormuz was bound to damage the economies of West Europe and Japan. On an average fifty departing ships passed through the Hormuz daily, including twenty tankers carrying eight million barrels of oil, amounting to one-fifth of the non-communist world's consumption. Sixty-five per cent of Japanese oil imports, and 25 per cent of West European imports passed through the Hormuz.[26] According to a US Congressional study published in late 1982, the closure of the Hormuz Strait would cause oil prices to rise from $34 a barrel to $65 to $130.[27]

Little wonder that the Reagan administration reiterated former President Carter's policy statement that the Gulf was 'vital to US national security'. It moved another naval battle group to the Arabian Sea, where already many American, British and French naval vessels were gathered. France rushed emergency military supplies to Iraq worth $500 million, including Exocet missles, fragmentation bombs and anti-tank missiles.[28] Bahrain put its security forces on alert. Qatar closed its borders to all foreigners. And Oman moved its troops to Ras Masandam facing the Hormuz Strait.

It was against this background that the Iranians mounted the Wa al Fajr-Four offensive in the northern sector on 20 October. They removed the Iraqis from the territory between Baneh and Marivan, and then marched twenty-five miles into Iraq, capturing 650 sq. kms north and east of Penjwin. Due to the mountainous terrain the Iraqi helicopter gunships were not as effective as in the southern and central sectors. During the bout of fighting the Iraqis were alleged to have used bombs of nitrogen mustard gas against the Iranians.[29]

On 1 November, by twelve votes to nil, the UN Security Council called on the combatants to cease fire. Iraq accepted the resolution conditionally; Iran rejected it. A week later the GCC foreign ministers' conference in Doha, Qatar, considered the idea of 'step by step' ceasefire, starting with north Gulf ports, and then moving up in stages. But nothing came of it.

To avenge the loss of its territory, the Iraqi government mined Bandar Khomeini, and on 27 October fired missiles at Marivan, Dezful, Andimeshk, Nahavand, Masjid-e Suleiman and Bahbahan (130 miles from the border), killing 250 civilians. It was the first time the Iraqis had used Soviet-made Scud-B missiles with a range of 185 miles. The death of twenty-eight primary school children in Behbahan particularly outraged the Iranians. In general, far from demoralising the Iranians, such attacks steeled their resolve to continue the war.[30]

On 10 December Kuwait experienced five bomb explosions set off by resident Iraqi and Lebanese nationals thought to be pro-Khomeini. Six people were killed and eighty wounded. In retaliation Iraq fired Scud-B missiles at five Iranian towns – Dezful, Andimeshk, Behbahan, Ramhormuz and Nahavand – on 15 December, killing twenty-one people and injuring 222. In early February 1984 Tehran said that Iraqi air and missile attacks on civilian areas during the course of the war had left 4,700 Iranians dead, and 22,000 injured.[31] Iraq's response was to hit Dezful with missiles on 11 February, adding thirty-six to the total of the dead, and 140 to the score of the wounded. The Iranian government lost its temper. It retaliated by hitting Basra, Khanaquin and Mandali, an action which killed twenty and wounded eighty-nine. It then extended the attacks to three more towns.

Repeating the past year's pattern, the Iranians launched a major offensive around the time of the Islamic revolution's anniversary. Codenamed the Wa al Fajr-Five, it was mounted on 16 February in the Mehran-Dehloran area with the intention of reaching the strategic Basra-Baghdad highway between Amarah and Al Kut. The Iraqis had been expecting an invasion by the Iranians, and were well-prepared.

Nonetheless, Saddam Hussein wrote letters to the ICO peace mission's head, President Sekou Toure of Guinea, and the chairperson of the Non-Aligned Movement, Premier Indira Gandhi of India, saying that he was ready to 'end all military operations and start negotiations for a peaceful settlement of the conflict based on just and honest teachings of Islam'.[32] This was a futile exercise as far as the Iranians were concerned. On 21 February they mounted the Wa al Fajr-Six offensive at Chilat near Dehloran. The next day came still another offensive, named Kheibar. It was staged fifty miles south of Amarah with the intention of reaching the Basra-Baghdad highway at Qurna, and cutting off Basra before encircling it. Altogether Iran committed 300,000 combatants to these offensives.

Fearing the collapse of Iraq in the face of such a massive force, the American government ordered its naval force in the Arabian Sea, led by the aircraft carrier Midway, to sail up the Gulf. On 22 February President Reagan said that there was 'no way' the US would stand by and see the West's shipping lanes blocked. In the end, much to the relief of both the US and the USSR, Saddam Hussein's forces were able to absorb the Iranian offensive without much loss of territory or morale.

This time most of the fighting occurred in the marshlands of Hur al Howzeh, a difficult terrain. The tactics used by the Iranians were sufficiently innovative to be compared, by an Iraqi commander, to those of the North Vietnamese in fighting the Americans in South Vietnam. At the end of the three-week-long hostilities, Iran had seized the Majnoon islands, with proven oil reserves of seven billion barrels, amounting to a quarter of total Iraqi reserves. Not surprisingly, the Iraqis tried hard to regain these islands. But they failed. At their peak these offensives and counter-offensives involved 500,000 men. An estimated 27,000 of them died: 20,000 Iranians and 7,000 Iraqis.[33]

In order to beat back the invaders the Iraqis used bombs of nitrogen mustard gas and nerve gas. According to Tehran, the Iraqis had used chemical bombs forty-nine times between May 1981 and March 1984, and killed 1,200 Iranians and injured 5,000.[34] The Iranian government sent some of the recent victims to Austria, Sweden, Britain and France for treatment. The tests carried out there confirmed that the patients were suffering from chemical poisoning.

Iran complained to the UN general secretary, Javier Perez de Cuellar, about this. He sent an investigating team to Iran. According to the team's report, published on 26 March, nitrogen mustard gas and nerve gas had been used in the war. The UN Security Council unanimously adopted a resolution which called on both parties to abstain from using chemical weapons in accordance with the Geneva protocol of 1925 (to which Iraq and Iran were signatories). Since the UN resolution refrained from naming Iraq as the party which had used chemical weapons, Iran criticised the Security Council's action as 'unprincipled'.

There were reports, confirmed by US intelligence, that Iraq was producing and storing nerve gas at five sites, including the chemical plants complex at Akashat near Rutbah in western Iraq. Chemicals normally used for manufacturing pesticides were being used to produce poison gases. Apparently the Iraqis made an experimental use of chemical bombs during the Iranian offensives of February 1984 with a view to employing them on a large scale should the Iranians succeed in breaking Iraqi defences and march towards Basra or Baghdad.

By mid-April Iran had consolidated its hold on the Majnoon islands, and assembled a force of 300,000 to 500,000 men for major offensives against Iraq. To forestall the Iranians, the Iraqis flooded the marshes along the southern front. This, and the need to study a peace plan conceived by Egypt, forwarded to Tehran by Indira Gandhi, led to the postponement of Iranian offensives. The elements of the peace plan were: an immediate ceasefire, return to international borders by the combatants, stationing of an international force on the Iraqi side to supervise the ceasefire, an NAM commission to determine who started the war and who prolonged it, and the setting up of the Islamic Reconstruction Fund to finance reconstruction of the war-damaged zones of both countries.

Since this peace plan was forwarded by the chairperson of the Non-Aligned Movement, it was studied seriously in Tehran. It was some weeks before Iran responded. But the answer was the same as in the past: No. This meant that the hawks on the Supreme Defence Council had won the argument. In tune with Khomeini's thinking, they were for mounting a gigantic offensive to break through Iraqi defences and capture either Basra or Baghdad, and thus bring about the downfall of Saddam Hussein.

Three factors favoured the hawks: psychological, religious and demographic. Although Iran had not scored dramatic victories, such as the recovery of Khorramshahr, for a long time, it had had a series of minor successes. It had kept the initiative in the war that it had seized in the spring of 1982. In its attacks on Iraq it took two steps forward and got pushed back one step: that still left it one step ahead. Such a pattern kept alive a mood summed up by the Supreme Defence Council in June 1983: 'Now that we have come thus far we must persevere, resist and make sacrifices to rid the region of this [Baathist] cancer or [at least] weaken it to teach others a lesson.'[35]

However, sacrifices had been mounting. By the spring of 1984 it was estimated that over 170,000 Iranian combatants had died and twice as many had been injured – versus 80,000 Iraqis dead and 150,000 wounded.[36] Yet there was no dearth of conscripts or volunteeers to fight. The demographic composition of Iran is such that each year 422,000 males, amounting to about 1 per cent of the total population, reach the conscription age of eighteen. (The figure for Iraq is 161,000.) In addition there was the Basij volunteer force, operating from over 9,000 mosques, open to those below eighteen and above forty-five, and all women. By the spring of 1983 the Basij had trained 2.4 million Iranians in the use of arms, and sent 450,000 to the front.[37]

Underlying all this was the deep religiosity of Iranian Shias with strong overtones of 'martyr complex'. They considered it their religious duty to fight evil and oppression, which in this case they associated with Saddam Hussein. This struggle was part of another: to liberate Jerusalem from its Zionist occupiers and oppressors. They saw the march to Najaf and Karbala in the south or Baghdad in the centre as part of the advance to Jerusalem, the third holiest city of Islam, which in Arabic is called Al Quds (The Holy) or Bait al Muqqadas (The Holy Place). Since Syria was an ally of Iran and a staunch anti-Zionist state, all that stood between the Islamic Republic and Jerusalem was the infidel regime of Saddam Hussein. To die in removing this hurdle was to ensure passage to heaven in afterlife. The concept of afterlife is deeply embedded among Muslims; and this life is useful only in so far as it helps the believer to show his commitment to Islam and his yearning to close the distance between him and Allah, the Creator. On Iranian radio and television the audiences were constantly reminded of Prophet Muhammad's saying to the believers: 'Wish death and welcome afterlife'. One measure of the martyr complex of Iranian Shias was the disproportion between the number of war captives on each side. In early 1984 Iraq held only 7,300 Iranian prisoners of war, whereas Iran had over 50,000 Iraqi captives.[38]

The war had proved to be harmful in certain respects and helpful in others. It caused colossal losses in human lives and limbs, property and production. It distorted the economy, and channelled large sums into the military and weapons. It led to the postponement of rapid economic development of the country. It increasingly isolated Iran in the world arena. On the other hand the war provided an opportunity for the IRG to acquire battle experience and become proficient in handling heavy weapons and aircraft. This was an important factor in the balance of force between the military and the IRG. The war kept the military officers engaged at the front: this drastically reduced the chance of a coup against the civilian government. With the counter-revolutionaries and the Mujahedin siding with Baghdad, the Iranian regime was able to convincingly label them as unpatriotic, and curtail their influence inside the country. The war unified the nation, and bolstered popular support for the government. Finally, it created an environment conducive to governmental control of the economy which, in general, worked in favour of the dispossessed classes.

Under the pressure of war the drive for self-sufficiency gathered pace. The defence minister announced in March 1983 that the production of 'various military items' at home had tripled since the war. This referred to small arms as well as light and heavy ammunition, including mortars.[39] Repair facilities improved dramatically. In December 1982 the defence minister claimed that Iran was repairing American-made F-14 jet fighters on its own, and that 80 per cent of the spare parts for the planes were being procured domestically.[40] At the same time Iran diversified its sources of weapons purchases. It bought Soviet arms and ammunition from Syria and Libya. This enabled Tehran to use 1,460 Soviet-made tanks and armoured vehicles captured from the enemy.[41] Iran set up strong military links with North Korea, which supplied it with weapons modelled on Soviet and Chinese originals.

'War tempers our nation like steel,' said Hashemi-Rafsanjani on 22 April 1983. 'Many of our industries have become self-sufficient during this period.' A prime example of this was the oil industry. Its employees surprised the world five months later. Unaided by foreign expertise, they capped one of the three offshore oil wells which, having been hit in the previous March by the Iraqis, had been leaking.[42] A visit to the Tehran bazaar in the spring of 1983 showed many shops stocked with electrical appliances, stainless steel pots and pans, and jeans produced in factories established after the war.[43]

Despite the loss of crops in the war zones, the campaign for self-sufficiency in food and other agricultural products registered modest success. In 1981-2 agriculture accounted for 15 per cent of the GNP versus 13.9 per cent in the previous year.[44]

War conditions goaded the government to limit imports, introduce rationing and nationalise foreign trade. As these measures hurt the interests of rich merchants, and interfered with the consumption patterns of the middle and upper classes, they proved unpopular with the well-off. But this was not the case with the lower classes. Rationing assured them of basic necessities at fixed (and often subsidised) prices. Since rationing imposed equality of consumption, it helped the government to project itself as egalitarian. Except for the heavily subsidised and freely available bread, foodstuffs, washing powder and heating fuel were rationed. During the spring of 1983 the per capita weekly ration for rice was one pound, and for meat three-quarters of a pound. For those who needed more of these, or better quality, there was the free market. Rice sold there at twice the official rate of $1 a pound and meat at three times the official rate of $2 a pound.[45] The average weekly wage of a factory worker was $90.

Without impairing the efficiency of the war machine, the government tried to economise. It used captured weapons to equip the newly formed units of the military or the IRG. It paid a paltry stipend of $1 a day to conscripts. It encouraged the public to contribute to the war in cash and materials. At $7 billion, the military budget was just above 15 per cent of the total for 1983-4. But when war-related expenses – the running of the Basij and a large section of the IRG, the compensations and pensions to the war disabled and the families of the dead, the funding of the Foundation for the War Victims, and the war reconstruction fund – were added to the military expenditure, the total amounted to 30 per cent of the $45 billion budget. Of this, $1.7 billion was allocated to the war reconstruction fund.[46]

With about half a million people killed or maimed by the war, the cost of financing compensations and pensions was mounting. The government was generous to the survivors of the dead military personnel. It gave a man's family compensation of $24,000 and full salary as pension, and deposited $60 monthly in the bank account of each of his minor children until they came of age at eighteen. It assisted the family in renting, buying or building a house.[47] Less generous amounts were paid to the families of the dead IRG or Basij members, and those who were disabled on the front.

Iran managed to shoulder these burdens without borrowing anything abroad by keeping up its oil exports and sticking to good housekeeping. In 1982-3 oil exports earned Iran a record sum of $23 billion.[48] This was more than enough to pay for the imports worth $18 billion. Prudent housekeeping allowed the Islamic Republic to reduce its foreign debts to $1.1 billion from $15 billion before the revolution.

Such sums looked modest when juxtaposed with the Iranian government's calculations of the losses suffered by the economy due to the war. According to the official publication, *A Summary of the Economic Damages of the Iraqi-imposed War on Iran*, published in May 1983, the damages caused to Iranian production and wealth until March 1983 amounted to $135.8 billion. These included loss of oil revenue at $33 billion and agricultural output at $21.83 billion.[49] Six cities and 1,200 villages had been destroyed and another nineteen cities partially damaged. The war had created 1.5 million refugees.

Securing compensation for these losses was one of Iran's salient preconditions for a ceasefire. It also provided a strong incentive to continue fighting. It was one of the main motives behind Iran's successful offensives of February-March 1984 to capture the oil-rich Majnoon islands.

However, once these islands had passed into Iranian hands, the doves used their acquisition as an argument to stop fighting. They reasoned that by expelling Iraq from practically all of the occupied Iranian territory, and by seizing the Majnoon islands, Iran had won compliance of two of its three major demands. Punishment of Saddam Hussein, the remaining demand, was more likely to occur after the ceasefire rather than before, they argued. Iraqi military and political leaders would be more inclined to overthrow Saddam Hussein for his misdeeds, repression and disastrous judgement after the patriotic pressure on them to defend Iraq had ceased rather than when it continued.

The strength of the doves' argument, the need to consider the peace proposals sent by the NAM, and the flooding of the marshy border in the south, caused a stalemate in the Supreme Defence Council. It was not until early May that the peace proposals were rejected. This happened at a time when the country was in the process of electing the Second Islamic Majlis. The first round of the elections occurred on 15 April and the second on 17 May. One-third more voters participated in these polls than in 1980. Most of those elected belonged to the IRP.

But the IRP was far from being a cohesive political party. It was more an umbrella organisation under which Islamic individuals and groups with diverse political tendencies had assembled. At the same time there were fundamentalist organisations which existed outside the IRP umbrella and had friendly to intimate relations with it.

The Islamic camp

Within two years of Bani-Sadr's dismissal the political arena in Iran was occupied by what Muhammad Ali Rajai had described as 'the Muslim Parties', the only exception being the Liberation Movement of Iran. But these parties were of two kinds: those with a formal structure and known membership, and others with an informal organisation and unpublicised membership. The IRP, the Organisation of Militant Clergy, the Movement of Militant Muslims and the Mujahedin of the Islamic Revolution belonged to the first category; and the Hezbollah, the Fedaiyan-e Islam, and the Hotjatiyeh (Demanders of Proof) to the second.

Of the small, cohesive groups the Movement of Militant Muslims, led by Habibollah Payman, was the most radical. Payman entered politics as a member of the Tudeh. Although he left the party later he remained an economic radical. He set out his views in *Principles of Iranian People's Socialism* and *Labour, Ownership and Capital in Islam*. He believed in popular participation in the government, and suggested formation of the people's councils to run local affairs. The idea was not taken seriously by Iranian officials. A militant anti-imperialist, he visualised the Iranian revolution in pan-Islamic terms. When the Islamic constitution was being finalised he backed the idea of encouraging revolutionary movements in other Islamic countries. 'Otherwise like the Russian and Chinese revolutions, ours will be obliged to compromise with American imperialism,' he warned in an interview with the *Jumhouri-ye Islami*.[50] This concept was incorporated into the constitution. 'According to the [Quranic] verse "This your nation is a single nation, and I am your Lord, so worship me", all Muslims form a single nation, and the government of the Islamic Republic of Iran has the duty of formulating its general policies with a view to the merging and union of all Muslim peoples; and it must constantly strive to bring about political, economic and cultural unity of the Islamic world,' states Principle Ten of the constitution.

As stated earlier, the MMM played an important part in organising the occupation of the US embassy in Tehran. After the release of American diplomats in January 1981, the MMM became quiescent. This changed when the conflict between Bani-Sadr and the IRP heightened. The group became active and sided with the IRP. However, once the government had embarked on a policy of repressing the Mujahedin-e Khalq, its officials felt that given the radicalism of the MMM, it could unwittingly become a refuge for Mujahedin infiltrators. The group thus fell into disfavour with the authorities. In early 1982 Payman was appointed to the Cultural Revolution Committee, a body charged with Islamising the educational system. Following this the MMM, although not banned, became increasingly inactive.

Unlike the Movement of Militant Muslims, the Mujahedin of the Islamic Revolution was given a share of the power. This happened because the MIR was firmly allied to the IRP. As stated earlier, the organisation was formed by the merger of a few Islamic guerrilla groups, which had been active during the revolutionary movement of 1977-8.[51] The MIR saw itself as the hard core of the revolution, which would offer armed resistance should attempts to overthrow the revolutionary regime succeed. Later the idea of having an armed institution to protect the Islamic revolution was given shape in the form of the Islamic Revolutionary Guards. But the Mujahedin of the Islamic revolution continued to exist as a political group. It played a crucial role in the takeover of the US embassy in late 1979. Bahzad Nabavi, one of its leaders, was later appointed minister of executive affairs, and deputed to negotiate a deal with the US administration on the hostage issue along the lines spelled out by the Majlis.

The MIR worked in close alliance with the IRP. Its leaders were close to Mir Hussein Mousavi, then chief editor of the ruling party's *Jumhouri-ye Islami*. When Mousavi became premier in late 1981 he appointed three of them as ministers: Bahzad Nabavi (executive affairs), Muhammad Salamati (agriculture), and Muhammad Shahab

Gonabadi (housing and urban development). Some months later Nabavi was given the ministry of heavy industries. The performance of the Mousavi government left many MIR members dissatisfied. They felt that the administration lacked radical thrust. This led to a threeway split in the organisation in mid-1983.

The Organisation of Militant Clergy was different from the above bodies. With its membership open only to the ulema, it was a weightier body. As stated earlier,[52] the nucleus of this organisation was established among others by Ayatollah Beheshti in 1976. It came to surface gradually during the 1977-8 movement. After the revolution it played a key role in transforming the traditional religious infrastructure into a religio-political apparatus of the Islamic regime. It became the active political arm of the ulema, and helped the IRP in elections and referendums.

Since engaging in everyday politics had hitherto been seen as an extremist activity in clerical circles, the OMC straightaway acquired an aura of radicalism. In the early years of its open existence, it was led by Ayatollah Montazeri. He took a radical stance on many issues. In late 1982, when pressure of work compelled Montazeri to step down, the OMC's general secretaryship went to Hojatalislam Mahdavi-Kani. He was far from being radical. As a leading member of the Guardians Council, he declared the land reform and foreign trade nationalisation bills unIslamic.

Of the semi-public organisations, the Hezbollah was the most prominent. As described earlier the Hezbollahis took to the streets, or attacked the regime's critics, at crucial moments. By the spring of 1981 it had been established that they worked in league with the IRP, and that they were led by Hojatalislam Hadi Ghaffari. Most of the Hezbollahis were young men from the poorer districts of cities. They were zealous supporters of the Islamic revolution and Khomeini. Their strength was unofficially put at 20,000 in June 1981.

The term Party of Allah, Hezbollah, is generic, rather than specific. It was apt for an organisation which was loosely structured. Both these basic elements were seen as virtues. A definition of the Hezbollahi, given in a pamphlet published by the ministry of Islamic guidance, was instructive. 'The Hezbollahi is a wild torrent surpassing the imagination,' it said. 'He is a maktabi [one who follows Islam comprehensively], disgusted with any leaning to the East or West. He has a pocketful of documents exposing the treason of those who pose as intellectuals. He is simple, sincere and angry. Stay away from his anger, which destroys all in its path. Khomeini is his heart and soul. . . . . The Hezbollahi does not use eau de cologne, wear a tie or smoke American cigarettes. . . . You might wonder where he gets his information. He is everywhere, serving your food, selling you ice-cream.'[53]

Once political challenges to the regime had died down, Hezbollahis concentrated on social matters such as the observance of women's Islamic dress and the ban on alcohol. Not surprisingly, they were unhappy at the promulgation of Khomeini's eight-point decree on civil liberties and the transfer of trials for moral offences from revolutionary courts to public courts. In February 1983 they demonstrated in south Tehran to demand strict adherence to Islamic morals and warn those who might be tempted to transgress them due to the liberalisation measures taken.[54]

The Fedaiyan-e Islam, one of the oldest militant organisations, has been affected minimally by the onset of the Islamic revolution. It continues to exist as a shadowy organisation. Oddly, with the passage of time, Hojatalislam Khalkhali, its leader, grew distant from IRP officials. He failed to win a seat in the December 1982 election to the Assembly of Experts. On the other hand, even though he lacked the IRP endorsement, he retained his seat from Qom in the April-May 1984 Majlis elections.

Despite the revolution, one Islamic organisation still remains secret: the Hojatiyeh. Formed in the early 1930s, it was inspired by the writings of Mirza Mahdi Isfahani, who argued that the Twelfth Imam was infallible and that his authority could not be encroached upon by any Muslim, who could at most be considered his deputy. As Islamic purists, Hojatiyeh members advocated complete purification of Iranian Muslim society, starting with the elimination of (heretic) Bahais and (Godless) communists. They considered Bahais heretic, because their leader claimed to be a prophet of Allah, something contrary to a basic Muslim belief that Muhammad was the last prophet.[55] They secretly collected the names of Bahais in their neighbourhoods, and actively participated in the 1955-6 anti-Bahai riots.

Since the revolution, the Hojatiyeh has been directed by Shaikh Mahmoud Halabi from his home in Tehran. It stood for private enterprise and free market economy. Given this, and its staunch anti-communism, it was popular with rich merchants and landlords. It had members and sympathisers in the Majlis, government and the Guardians Council. In late 1981, of the twenty-one ministers in the Mousavi government, four were pro-Hojatiyeh: Muhammad Gharzai (oil), Ahmed Tavakoli (labour), Habibollah Asghar-Owladi (commerce) and Ali Akbar Parvarish (education). In the Guardians Council, Hojatalislam Abol Qassem Khazali was close to the Hojatiyeh.[56] More than once he openly criticised Hashemi-Rafsanjani as being too radical.

Thus the Hojatiyeh stood at the conservative end of the Islamic political spectrum, occupied by prosperous merchants, big landholders, affluent urban property owners, and rich ulema, who were either related to one of the above groups or administering vast religious endowments. At the other end of the political spectrum stood the ulema with poor or petty bourgeois backgrounds, theological students, small shopkeepers and semi-skilled employees of the bazaar, and Islamic laypersons from poor or lower middle class families. The radicals could roundly be called the Followers of Imam's Line, a generic term. In Hashemi-Rafsanjani, they had their best known and most powerful leader. The ground between radicals and conservatives was occupied by centrists.

Differences between conservatives and radicals were sharpest on economic policies, particularly those directed towards redistributing wealth and bolstering public and cooperatives sectors of the economy. Foreign trade nationalisation was a case in point. A draft bill was presented to the Majlis in May 1981. Six months later it was ratified by Khomeini. On 11 May 1982 the Majlis unanimously passed the legislation, and then submitted it to the Guardians Council.[57] The theologians on the Council declared the bill to be unIslamic and struck it down. They argued that by specifying total nationalisation, the bill excluded privately financed imports altogether – something contrary to Islamic tenets which hold private trading sacrosanct. The Council recommended that the foreign currencies earned by the private sector should be allocated to finance direct imports by traders' guilds. Since oil, produced in the public sector, secured 98 per cent of Iran's foreign earnings, this meant allotting only 2 per cent of foreign earnings to private importers. So the immediate impact of the Council's ruling on the financing and distributing of imports by the commerce ministry was minimal.

Nonetheless, the Council's ruling encouraged the commerce minister, Asghar-Owladi, himself a bazaar merchant, to transfer a greater share of imports from the ministry to the traders' guilds. In less than a year he raised the share of the traders' guilds in direct imports from less than 5 per cent to about 20 per cent.[58]

But this was not enough to overcome the growing unease of bazaar merchants and other affluent members of society at the trend of official policies and statements. For instance, at a Friday prayer congregation in Tehran in January 1983, Ayatollah Mousavi-Ardebili addressed himself to the housing shortage. He estimated that about 200,000 families in the capital were homeless, that is about one-seventh of the population. He described 'the landlords of empty houses [who are] not prepared to let their houses at any price' as 'economic terrorists'.[59] Some weeks later he suggested that the housing shortage could be solved by limiting an individual's ownership to one 'residential unit'.[60]

The most consistent and frequent critic of 'amassing of wealth by a small minority' at Tehran's Friday prayer congregations was Hashemi-Rafsanjani. And he made no distinction between secular and religious organisations. In his first sermon of the Iranian Year 1362 he pointed out that a major part of the nation's wealth belonged to the old religious endowments, and recommended that the endowments affairs be 'put right'.[61]

Such statements were attacked by conservative ulema and business-men. Hojatalislam Khazali, a pro-Hojatiyeh member of the Guardians Council, said that Hashemi-Rafsanjani's views on 'adjustment of wealth and filling the gap between the rich and the oppressed' were 'incorrect'. Tehran's merchants went further. They submitted a petition to Khomeini in which they requested him to instruct Hashemi-Rafsanjani to 'refrain from making provocative statements against the business community and wealthy persons'. Stating that Hashemi-Rafsanjani's words were 'in violation of the principles of Islam', they alleged that he was influenced 'mostly by Marxist thoughts'.[62]

Hashemi-Rafsanjani ignored these moves, and so did Khomeini. But thousands of theological students in Qom responded by signing a statement which described Hashemi-Rafsanjani as 'the worthiest personality analysing Islam in the path of the Islamic revolution and the Imam's Line'. Fakhr al-Din Hejazi, a radical Majlis deputy, said: 'Whenever the Majlis seeks to take a step for the welfare of the oppressed masses, it is accused of being "socialist".' He pointed out that the government had yet to enshrine into law Principle Forty-nine of the constitution, concerning illegitimately obtained wealth.[63]

Actions and statements such as the above worried bazaar merchants, who were unhappy about the growth of government-aided consumer cooperatives. They saw the cooperatives as a direct threat to their economic interests. The government action was in line with Principle Forty-four of the constitution. It described the Islamic Republic's economic system as consisting of three sectors: governmental, cooperative and private. The government sector comprised 'all major industries, foreign trade, major mines, banking, insurance, power generation, dams and major water-carrying networks, radio and television, postal, telegraph and telephone system, air, sea, land and railroad transportation and others . . . similar to the above'. The cooperative sector 'establishes and assigns the cooperative companies and organisations which have been created in cities and villages'. Finally, the private sector comprised 'those parts of agriculture, animal husbandry, industry, trade and services which supplement the activities of the governmental and cooperative sectors'.

The government had taken to promoting consumer cooperatives in its drive to curb profiteering by traders, encouraged by the shortages caused by the Gulf War and import controls. It combined this tactic with periodic threats and appeals to traders against hoarding and profiteering. But these measures failed to alter the basic laws of the market economy – of the relationship of price to supply and demand. Relations between the government and the bazaar reached a low point in the summer of 1983. In his interview with Tehran Radio on 10 July Premier Mousavi felt it necessary to devote much time to the subject. 'It is reasoned that the use of consumer cooperatives leads to the abolition of traditional distributive methods,' he said. 'Despite all the obstructions raised against consumer cooperatives, have they resulted in eliminating traders' guilds? We have hundreds of thousands of shops in Tehran. . . . Can one imagine that some 300 to 400 local consumer cooperatives can take over all these services?' He pointed out that the Guardians Council had not ruled the cooperatives to be against Islamic laws. 'The cooperatives are one of the revolutionary foundations in our country,' he said. 'Consequently, they are being strongly supported by the deprived people.'[64]

Mousavi also refuted the argument that the distribution of rice and wheat and other basic items through the government – undertaken 'due to exceptional circumstances' – was aimed at abolishing the private sector. 'When the issue of supporting the deprived people is raised, then these people claim that leftist measures are being taken, that the private sector is being challenged, and that the bazaar is being challenged,' he said.[65]

While the prime minister was making these statements his cabinet was seriously considering lifting price control on rice and derationing it. The idea was being pressed by Asghar-Owladi, the commerce minister. He won the approval of his colleagues, and in mid-July transferred rice distribution to the private sector. He had assured his fellow ministers that there were enough stocks of rice in the country to withstand upward pressures on price following price decontrol. But this was not to be. Within a few days of rice being taken out of the rationing system, its price trebled. Popular discontent rose sharply. As people formed long lines for subsidised bread, the distributive system for bread and flour came under strain. In the capital the rice crisis coincided with cuts in water supplies and electricity. This led to two noisy protest demonstrations in the Afsariyeh district of south Tehran, a power base of the regime. Revolutionary guards were used to disperse the demonstrators. These events shook the government. The prosecutor general of the guilds courts, dealing with economic offences, threatened 'Islamic justice' to the hoarders and profiteers, and warned that the guilty would be executed.[66]

Four days later the government reintroduced rice rationing. Asghar-Owladi resigned on 31 July; and so did Ahmed Tavakoli, another pro-Hojatiyeh minister who advocated free market economy. Their resignations were welcomed by the radicals who had earlier accepted foreign trade nationalisation as a compromise on their original demand for state monopoly in both foreign and domestic sectors of trade. In contrast, bazaar merchants were unhappy at the departure of Asghar-Owladi, who had headed the commerce ministry for two years. The absence of a strong spokesman of their interests in the cabinet, combined with a state-sponsored campaign against 'economic terrorists', created a gap between the bazaar and the administration.

Given the long history of alliance between merchants and the ulema, the alienation between the bazaar and the Islamic government was unprecedented. It worried Khomeini. He made this plain in his address to bazaar leaders, including Asghar-Owladi, in January 1984. 'If bazaars are not in step with the Islamic Republic, the public will suffer defeat,' Khomeini said. 'All the [foreign] powers have felt that Islam is doing them harm. Some of them say that they oppose the kind of Islam we have presented to the world; they would prefer the kind of Islam the Saudis have [in their country]. . . . We should ignore our grievances for the sake of Islam.'[67]

Whatever impact Khomeini might have had on dispelling bazaar leaders' alienation from the government, the basic conflict between the interests of the better-off and those of the worse-off remained unresolved in Iran. This was as true in urban areas as in rural.

The radicals saw land reform legislation as a means to redistribute wealth in rural Iran. But, as stated earlier, the provision for the purchase of land above a ceiling by the state for distribution to the landless was declared to be unIslamic.[68] However, this did not interfere with the government plans to allocate virgin land to the landless. In the spring of 1983 the agricultural ministry claimed to have distributed 350,000 hectares of state land to 50,000 peasant families over the past two years.[69] As the total cultivated area in Iran before then was only 4.5 million hectares, this was substantial progress.

There was one more important instance where the administration's egalitarian intentions were foiled by the Guardians Council. This had to do with confiscating the properties of the exiles. One of the reasons behind this move was the need to relieve the housing shortage. Most of the construction projects, abandoned during the revolutionary turmoil, had been in limbo due to financial and legal problems. The government lacked funds to complete the half-finished housing estates. It was also handicapped by the absence of legal owners of these properties: they had left Iran. To remove these hurdles the Majlis passed a bill on 11 January 1983, which authorised the government to confiscate the properties of those exiles who failed to return within two months of the law being enforced.[70] But the theologians on the Guardians Council struck this bill down on the ground that the state's confiscation of property acquired legitimately by an individual violated the right to hold private property, and was therefore unIslamic.

If the bills on foreign trade, land reform, and the exiles' properties showed the Mousavi government to be radically orientated, the draft bill on labour relations showed it to be otherwise. In early 1983 Ahmed Tavakoli, the labour minister, published a draft code for public discussion. It denied workers job security and the right to strike.[71] It deprived trade unions of such rights as bargaining the terms of insurance, retirement, minimum wages and working hours: rights which they enjoyed under the current law in force since the Shah's days. In short, the new bill favoured the employer at the expense of the worker. The radicals deplored the bias of the bill, as did the workers in their discussions of the legislation. Among those who publicly criticised it was Mustapha Hashemi, the industry minister.[72] In the face of such opposition, the government formed an eight-member committee to revise the bill. The resignation of Tavakoli in July boosted the critics' morale. This committee offered a new draft in January 1984. A conference of the Islamic Labour Council of Tehran, meeting in the following month, raised thirty-two objections to the draft. The revised bill was not ready for the First Islamic Majlis to consider before its dissolution in May.

While conservative elements, exercising authority in the strategically placed Guardians Council, had frustrated radical plans for redistribution of wealth, the radicals had succeeded, through popular pressure, to transform a reactionary labour relations bill into something different.

What divided the two sides on foreign issues were the general thrust of external relations with Muslim countries, and the Gulf War. The radicals wanted the government to actively implement Principle Ten of the constitution: it called for continuous effort 'to bring about political, economic and cultural unity of the Islamic world'. In practice, this meant exporting revolution to other Muslim countries. The arguments for following this line were not merely ideological. They were also pragmatic. Most Iranian leaders had concluded that an effective way to defend the revolution was by going on the offensive, by extending the influence of the revolution abroad. As President Khamanei put it, 'If the revolution is kept within the Iranian borders, it would become vulnerable'.[73]

There were obvious disadvantages in following this path. Efforts to export revolution to a foreign country vitiated relations between that country's government and Tehran, and further increased Iran's isolation in the international community. That was why this course of action was unpopular with officials of the foreign ministry, headed by Ali Akbar Velayati, a conservative.

Attempts were made to resolve the conflict. A separate department was set up in the foreign ministry to deal with national liberation movements. Its main task was to aid such movements, whether they were in Muslim countries or not. Also the secretariat of the Friday prayer leaders in Qom was used to maintain contacts with ulema throughout the world. Every year this body sponsored the World Congress of Friday Prayer Leaders. It drew delegates from more than forty countries. This was an effective way of creating and sustaining goodwill towards Iran's Islamic revolution in the Islamic circles of these states.

On the Gulf War radicals and conservatives were united until July 1982. Divisions arose on the question of attacking Iraq, with radicals being hawkish, and conservatives dovish. While the radical line has been consistently advocated by Hashemi-Rafsanjani, the dovish position has been taken at different times by President Khamanei, Premier Mousavi and Ayatollah Montazeri. But the ultimate director of the war was Khomeini, and by and large he has been a radical in his foreign and domestic policies.

To summarise, the Islamic camp has three major tendencies within it: conservative, radical and centrist; and differences between radicals and conservatives have surfaced on such issues as exporting the Islamic revolution, the conduct of the Gulf War, foreign trade nationalisation, the role of the cooperatives in the economy, agrarian reform, labour law, implementation of Principle Forty-nine of the constitution, confiscation of the exiles' properties, the administration of large religious endowments and civil liberties.

The two sides were also divided on the issue of Khomeini's succession. The radicals wanted Ayatollah Montazeri to succeed Khomeini as the marja-e taqlid and leader. The conservatives favoured Ayatollah Golpaygani. But, aware that he was unlikely to be accepted as the sole leader, they wanted the Leadership Council of three, consisting of Golpaygani, Montazeri and Mahdavi-Kani.

This seemed to be a fair compromise to the conservatives. But it was not likely to be accepted by the radicals, who dominated the Assembly of Experts. When the Assembly met on 14 July 1983, it elected Ayatollah Ali Meshkini as its chairman and Hashemi-Rafsanjani as its deputy chairman. The Friday prayer leader of Qom, Meshkini is a well-known radical. On his election as the Assembly's chairman, he was presented with Khomeini's sealed political will, to be opened after his death. It may be that Khomeini has issued specific instructions on succession in his will. Most likely he has not.

Besides the overtly political elements described so far, the Islamic camp included all the appointees of Khomeini to religious or secular positions. Responsible directly to Khomeini, they formed a substantial body of men. For this network included not only Khomeini's personal (religious) representatives to different regions of Iran and the Friday prayer leaders in cities and towns, but also his personal representatives on all important governmental and revolutionary institutions. Their primary tasks were to implement Khomeini's general directives and to keep him informed.

The first year of the revolution witnessed the establishment of many revolutionary organisations. Some were created later. By early 1984 all of them had taken root, and provided a firm base to the Islamic Republic.

Revolutionary organisations and Islamisation

The revolutionary organisations which sprung in the wake of the Shah's downfall covered all spheres of life: political, military, security, judicial, economic, social, cultural and religious. Some of these bodies functioned independently, others in tandem with government ministries. Later one of them was absorbed into an existing ministry, while a few of them were transformed into new ministries. These organisations were so preponderant that within three years of the revolution, one out of six Iranians above the age of fifteen belonged to one or more such bodies.[74]

With the Tudeh banned in May 1983, all pre-revolutionary political parties, excepting the Liberation Movement, were eliminated. Political life thus became the near monopoly of the Islamic Republican Party and its smaller allies. In the military, a series of purges resulted in the dismissal of all but a thousand officers of the pre-revolutionary period. Moreover, the regime took steps to inculcate Islamic ideas and values among military personnel. A political-ideological department was instituted in the military. It was often manned by young ulema, who were enthusiastically dedicated to the Islamic Republic. They educated officers and ranks in Islamic history and ideology. The information and guidance department performed the general task of creating and sustaining support for the actions and policies of the government, and the particular job of keeping an eye on dissidents or deviants. In addition, there were the Islamic Associations among military personnel – voluntary bodies which concerned themselves with raising the Islamic consciousness of their members and guarding the security of their units.

One of the important motives behind the establishment of the Islamic Revolutionary Guards was to create a counterforce to the army, then commanded by officers of dubious loyalty to the Islamic regime. As such, after the IRG nucleus was formed out of small

Islamic militias, recruitment to the force was strictly controlled. Each recruit had to pass tests in the Quran, *Nahaj al Balagheh* (Path of Eloquence) by Imam Ali, and *Hukumat-e Islami* by Khomeini.[75]

At first recruits underwent training for six months. But following the war the period was reduced to three months. Yet the standards of training – military, ideological and political – improved steadily, with the ulema playing a leading role in the ideological-political training. The IRG was involved in the fighting at the front from the day the war erupted. As it expanded it acquired an air unit of its own. It became the force on which IRP leaders lavished their attention and resources. Following Bani-Sadr's dismissal, cooperation between the IRG and the military improved dramatically. Revolutionary guards used unconventional tactics effectively on the front, and impressed military officers with their daring and flexibility. However, warfare was only one of the IRG's four functions, the others being internal security, anti-subversion and ethnic rebellions.

In November 1982 the Islamic Revolutionary Guards Corps ministry was created, with Muhsin Rafiqdust as its head. Soon an elite division was formed within the IRG with the specific purpose of protecting the capital against a possible military coup. In early 1983 the IRG was 170,000 strong, and included both ground and air forces. It remains the Islamic regime's most reliable and most effective fighting force.

Following the US embassy takeover in November 1979 – which made an American invasion of Iran a serious possibility – Khomeini gave a call for the creation of 'an army of twenty million'. This led to arms training for students at local mosques after school or college hours. In early 1980 the IRG formally set up the Vahid-e Basij-e Mustazafin (Unit of the Mobilisation of the Deprived). It drew volunteers from youths below the conscription age of eighteen, young women and middle aged men often from poor districts. Local mosques were used as recruiting and training centres. In March 1982 Basij volunteers were allowed for the first time to fight at the war front. During the next year about a fifth of the total force of 2.4 million participated in warfare. Often young Basij members volunteered to act as vanguards in the human wave attacks that the Iranians mounted against the enemy, performing such highly dangerous tasks as removing mines. These teenagers have grown up in an environment of revolutionary turmoil, and are more dedicated to the cause of Islam than most adults. This, combined with adolescent daring and a romantic view of war, explains their urge to go the battlefield and be in the front line. 'For them the war is like a movie, with bullets whizzing past them but not through them,' said one who had been to the front. 'They're so macho that they don't even wear helmets, and get blown up. But [they feel] they are on their way to heaven.'[76] Not surprisingly, the fatality rate among them is high. Those who stay home perform such routine tasks as night watch in neighbourhoods.

The government has ensured that the families of all those who die for Islam are properly looked after. This job has been assigned to the Martyrs Foundation, the country's most liberally endowed organisation. Khomeini decreed its formation in February 1980. Its initial task was to provide welfare to the families of those who had died in the revolutionary movement of 1977-9. Following the war, its budget rose manyfold.

Unlike the institutions described so far, the Islamic Revolutionary Komitehs were not formally established by Khomeini's decree. They emerged in the heat of the revolutionary struggle. After the revolution, they became the guardians of internal security. Later they were given the additional task of enforcing Islamic morality. They had their own armed militia. Following the war the Komitehs were authorised to administer the rationing system. With this, the Komitehs impinged on the life of every family. In late 1982 there were 6,137 Komitehs in the country. It was decided then to reduce their numbers and make them more accountable to the Central Komiteh. As a result the number of Komitehs in Tehran decreased from over 100 to thirty. A local Komiteh works in collaboration with the IRG unit, the mosques in its area, and the Islamic Associations, which existed in all workplaces, schools, universities, hospitals, neighbourhoods and large villages.

At the time of the bomb explosion at the IRP headquarters in June 1981, security and intelligence were being handled by fifteen different organisations. This was a contrast to the highly centralised system run by Savak during the Pahlavi period. After the revolution the government was intent on not reincarnating Savak under a different guise. But as the Mujahedin campaign mounted, the government was forced to streamline and centralise its security and intelligence arrangements. In March 1982 the Majlis passed a bill to set up the ministry of state security and intelligence. Since then the Central Komiteh and the IRG have been working in conjunction with this ministry in security and intelligence matters.

Following the revolution, the judicial system and the law were changed radically. Islamic revolutionary courts were introduced in civilian and military sectors. At first these courts dealt with counter-revolutionary activity and such serious offences as espionage and treason. Later, as the Islamisation campaign got going, they were ordered to deal with moral offences as well as Islamic deviation, described as 'hypocrisy'.

However, once the regime had met the political challenge by the Mujahedin, Khomeini reversed the trend. Following his decree on civil liberties in December 1982, he transferred trials for moral offences from revolutionary courts to public courts, run by the justice ministry. A year later the Supreme Judicial Council decided to abolish the posts of the revolutionary chief justice and prosecutor general, and to place revolutionary courts under the control of the state chief justice and prosecutor general of the justice ministry. The next step may well be to abolish revolutionary courts altogether. The normalisation process is likely to be aided by the fact that by the end of 1982 all secular laws had been abrogated, and civil and trade laws as well as the penal code had been Islamised.

The Islamic revolution created a vast economic conglomerate in the form of the Mustazafin Foundation. As described earlier, the Foundation came into being in early March 1979, when Khomeini ordered the consolidation of the properties of the Pahlavis and others. The fortunes of the Pahlavis amounted to one-fifth of the total private assets in Iran.[77] To this were added the multi-million dollar business empires of Habib Elqanian, Muhammad Wahabzadeh, Habib Sabet and Hozabr Yazdani. In the process the Foundation became the sole or part owner of over 100 companies.

Thereafter the Foundation's assets grew steadily as the authorities confiscated the properties of those who were executed and those who had been found to have acquired their assets through 'illegitimate means'. Among the latter were the Ayandegan, Ittilaat and Kayhan publishing companies. By the end of 1980 the Foundation owned, partially or wholly, 259 companies. During the next two-and-a-half years it took over 236 more companies. Of the total, 200 were manufacturing firms, 250 trading companies, and forty-five agro-industrial companies. With over 85,000 people working for it, the Mustazafin Foundation had far more employees than the National Iranian Oil Company.[78] The Foundation, headed by Sayyed Mahdi Tabatabai, was supervised by the Prime Minister. This will change when a bill to place it under the supervision of Khomeini is passed.

Since most of the Foundation's constituent companies were struggling to become profitable, the overall profits of the conglomerate were low. Property-owning companies were the exception. The Foundation had rented the villas of the rich to government ministries and other public bodies, and apartment blocks to those who could afford them. Mindful of Khomeini's directive to use its profits to meet the needs of the mustazafin, the deprived, the Foundation decided in the spring of 1983 to build 50,000 housing units in 1984-5, and rent them cheaply to the needy.[79] It had dovetailed its plans with those of the housing ministry and the Housing Foundation, formed after the revolution.

While the Housing Foundation had been given the specific job of building houses, the task assigned to the Reconstruction Crusade, formed in June 1979 was to bridge the gap between town and village. Since half of all Iranians lived in 65,000 villages, this was a very important assignment.[80] In practice it meant helping economic development in the countryside, increasing literacy, propagating Islamic culture and revolution among rural Iranians, improving communication between villagers and educated urban dwellers, and providing a constructive channel for the energies of the unemployed high school and university graduates. Not surprisingly, the Crusade set up branches in high schools, colleges and universities. Its annual budget of $690 million was divided almost evenly between operating costs and providing rural credit.[81]

After a brief period under the Bazargan government the Crusade was placed under the authority of the Islamic Revolutionary Council. Like the IRG, the Crusade soon became a professional body with a salaried cadre. But, unlike the IRG, the cadre were assisted by such professional volunteers as doctors, engineers and mechanics. In 1981 some 14,700 cadres were aided by 4,700 volunteers, giving a total strength of 19,400 to the Crusade. Two years later, at 35,000, the total had nearly doubled.[82] The Crusade members built civil works – roads, bridges, irrigation works, public baths, schools, health centres – distributed fertiliser, insecticide, water pumps and tractors, and gave loans to small farmers. In their construction projects, they were often aided by local volunteers as well as student volunteers from high schools during vacations. In the first two years of its existence, the Crusade claimed to have built 8,000 miles of roads, 1,700 schools, 1,600 public baths and 110 health centres.[83] A visit in April 1983 to five villages near Reyshahr, to the south of Tehran, showed that the Crusade had constructed two schools and two public baths, and introduced a scheme for loaning tractors to peasants. Also an irrigation scheme, consisting of underground water channels, was in progress in the area.

By purging upper and middle class cadres from the Crusade, IRP leaders consolidated their hold over the organisation by late 1981. Party members from urban lower middle class families ran the Crusade. Following Bani-Sadr's ouster, they campaigned for volunteers and materials to be sent to the war front. They also accelerated the programme of establishing Islamic Associations in rural areas. As a result, half of all villages had an Islamic Association by late 1983.[84]

In the internal struggle between conservatives and radicals within the Islamic camp, the Crusade members sided with the radicals. They pressed for land redistribution, and were disappointed when the Guardians Council rejected the land reform bill. In late 1983 the Guardians Council returned to the Majlis the bill to transform the Reconstruction Crusade into a ministry by declaring it to be in 'incomplete compliance with the constitution and Islamic law'.[85] The Majlis amended the legislation in the light of the Council's comments. Following the passage of the new bill, and its approval by the Guardians Council, the Ministry of Reconstruction Crusade was formed in February 1984.

To help the needy in rural areas the regime set up Imam Khomeini's Relief Committee in early 1979. During the next five years the Committee established 530 branches covering 40,000 villages, and provided medical, educational and welfare aid to 1.1 million families.[86] Simultaneously, efforts were made to reduce illiteracy in villages. For this purpose the Reconstruction Crusade worked in coordination with the Special Movement for Developing Education among the Deprived People, which was launched in 1980.

In the wake of the cultural revolution initiated by Khomeini in June 1980 came the University Crusade: it was meant to rid universities of unIslamic ideologies as well as staff and students. Though open to both students and teachers, the 'committed Muslim students' were the Crusade's main force. Long before the founding of this body, they had proved their Islamic zeal by engaging in pitched battles – in collusion with the Hezbollahis from outside the campuses – with their secular and leftist colleagues. At the same time, aided by the 'committed Muslim teachers', they had been vetting the teaching staff.[87] Once all the 200 universities and colleges had been closed down in June 1980, the authorities, acting on the information given by the University Crusade, dismissed all those teachers thought to be imbued with Eastern or Western ideologies: Marxism, capitalism, nationalism, liberalism, democracy. At the same time Iranian students were not allowed the facilities to join Western universities.

Composed of seven clerics and scholarly laymen, the Cultural Revolution Committee concentrated on countering cultural imperialism, whether of Eastern or Western variety, and imbuing universities with Islamic values. It redesigned curriculums; sponsored new textbooks, or modified the existing ones in the light of Islamic teachings; helped the teaching staff gain a better understanding of Islam; and replaced Western concepts in education with Islamic ones.

The ulema were active at different levels to help the CRC. They were intimately involved in the running of the Centre for Textbooks set up by the CRC. By the spring of 1983 this centre had produced 3,000 textbooks, either original or in translation. Most of these were on pure sciences, medicine and engineering: the disciplines where conflict between published knowledge and Islamic tenets was minimal. What proved daunting was the programme of producing textbooks in social sciences which were imbued with Islamic perspective and values.[88]

That is why the re-opening of universities and colleges, begun in mid-December 1982, was gradual. When all the higher education institutions re-opened fully in October 1983, they had far less students and teachers than before. At Tehran University the student body was down from 17,000 before the revolution to about 4,500. There was a similar drop in the size of the teaching staff. The ratio of women students dropped from 40 per cent of the total before the revolution to 10 per cent.[89] The Islamic regime is intent on forging stronger links between universities and theological colleges. Khomeini has specifically called for special ties between Tehran University and Faiziya seminary, the leading theological college of Qom. This is going ahead in stages.

Schools underwent Islamisation earlier and with far less upheaval. Within three years of the revolution, all co-educational schools had been transformed into single-sex schools, and about 40,000 teachers purged.[90] New Islamic teaching materials were made available to primary schools within six months of the revolution. Similar speed was shown in furnishing secondary schools with Islamic textbooks. Special stress was put on the teaching of Arabic, the language of the Quran. The resulting upsurge in Islamic devotion among teenage boys explained the enthusiasm with which they joined the Basij force and volunteered to fight at the front. In the aftermath of the revolution Islamic Associations sprung up in all schools. They identified unIslamic teachers and watched suspected dissidents among older students, particularly after the Mujahedin had taken up arms against the government.

Efforts to Islamise such popular institutions as schools, colleges and the military went hand in hand with tackling specific moral ills like prostitution and drugs. The Office for Propagation of Virtues and Prevention of Sins, formed in the wake of the revolution, was in the forefront of stamping out moral degeneracy. In May 1980, at its behest, the red light district of Tehran was pulled down, and about a thousand prostitutes rehabilitated.[91]

A concerted campaign was conducted to eradicate the consumption of soft and hard drugs. Addiction to heroin was widespread during the Shah's days, with the number of addicts put at 500,000 to 800,000. Hojatalislam Khalkhali, who was assigned the task of solving the drugs problem, resorted to awarding capital punishment to drugs dealers. Between 21 May and 18 July 1980, he ordered the execution of some 200 drug traffickers.[92] This was effective. Consumption of drugs dropped dramatically. But the problem did not disappear altogether. A visit in May 1983 to the Centre for the Rehabilitation of Drug Addicts at Shourabad near Tehran showed that the Centre had 1,100 patients. Although most of them were mature men in their early thirties to late fifties, who had acquired the habit during the Shah's rule, there were some young men in their early twenties as well. However, interviews at the Centre revealed that over the past few years it had become increasingly difficult to buy drugs outside the major cities – a sign of the overall success of the anti-drugs campaign. Of the 29,145 persons arrested on drugs charges during 1983-4, only 7,618 were addicts, the rest being smugglers.[93]

On the eve of Ramadan (in late June) in 1980, the revolutionary prosecutor general banned music in public places. At about the same time Islamic militants began protesting against certain unIslamic films. Vexed at this, the owners of 420 cinemas in the country closed their theatres, hoping that their action would cause a public outcry and compel the militants to end their agitation. But the public took the closures in their stride, and the zealots continued their protest. So the cinemas remained shut. Following the eruption of war in September, martial music was introduced on radio and television. In fact the authorities made frequent use of snatches of Beethoven's Fifth Symphony to inspire and energise the viewers and listeners. In the summer of 1982 the ban on playing of music in private was quietly relaxed. By then about fifty cinemas had re-opened in Greater Tehran, with changed names. The old Empire was now called Istiqlal (Independence), Universal as Pars, and Pacific as Aram (Comfort). The cinema owners had taken their cue from the municipal authorities: they had earlier changed Eisenhower Avenue to Azadi (Freedom), and Shah Reza Avenue to Inqilab (Revolution), and so on.

One of the victims of the Islamic revolution was the film industry with an annual output of some seventy feature films. There was a modest revival in 1981, when the industry produced seven movies. These films had been approved in advance by the ministry of Islamic guidance. The ministry also set up its own film production department. Financed by the Mustazafin Foundation, this department produced films with Islamic themes. The first batch of such movies was released in early 1983. *Safeer* was typical of the genre. A historical film, it portrayed its hero as an upright Muslim who stood firm against the intrigue and chicanery around him, and won. The film is an apt summary of the state of mind of present Iranian leaders. Although largely isolated in the world arena, they feel confident that they are following the righteous path, and that it will lead eventually to victory. The moral is that if a believer is steadfast in his faith he will overcome all hurdles.

These actions of the regime were part of a two-pronged process of the Islamisation of society: purification and enlightenment. Purification was defined as cleansing the soul of all vice, and enlightenment as removing the ill-effects of all the sins committed so far by an individual. An overall objective of the Islamic government was to make the social environment such that it would offer less and less temptation to the believer to stray from pious living.

In a society where some women are veiled and others not (as was the case during the Pahlavi rule), unveiled women are seen as temptresses, agents of corruption of wholesome family life. So, runs the Islamic argument, all women must wear at least a hejab, loose fitting clothing which hides the outlines of the figure, and a head scarf. If some women go further and use a chador, a shroud, of dark colour, so much the better. As described earlier, an order to impose chador on women employees of government ministries in March 1979 was withdrawn.[94] But that was not the end of the matter.

Aware of the religious atmosphere prevailing during Ramadan, the government ordered, on 5 July 1980, that all women in government and public offices must wear a hejab. The half a million urban women above the age of twelve who had jobs constituted 9 per cent of the female population.[95] A large majority of them worked in small, all-female workshops or sections of factories. So the government order affected about 3 per cent of the urban female population above the age of twelve. Due to this, and the frequent reiteration by the mass media that prescribing a proper dress for women had the sanction of the Quran, resistance to the government fiat was minimal. The appropriate verse in the Quran reads: 'And say to the believing women, that they cast down their eyes and guard their private parts . . . and let them cast their veils over their bosoms, and not reveal their adornment save to their husbands, or their fathers, or their husbands' fathers, or their sons, or their husbands' sons, or their brothers, or their brothers' sons, or their sisters' sons, or their women . . . or children who have not yet attained knowledge of women's private parts.'[96] Addressing the Friday prayer congregation in Tehran, Hojatalislam Khamanei, the Friday prayer leader, said, 'Hejab is an Islamic duty. Wearing of ornamental trinkets, elaborate hair styles and make-up is unIslamic.'[97] A year later the Majlis passed the Islamic Dress Law: it applied to all women in Iran, whether Muslim or not. Violation of the law was punishable by a maximum jail sentence of a year.

Following the revolution, the Family Protection Law of 1967/75, which restricted polygamy and gave women the right to initiate divorce proceedings, was first suspended and then abolished. However, in late 1983, a woman's right to divorce her husband was partly restored. There were hundreds of instances of public whippings or executions for adultery. There were also capital and other punishments for homosexuality. These were in accordance with the Quranic verses which describe allowable sexual relations, and punishments for transgressing them.

Relationships between men and women must conform to what the Quran has stated. 'Men are the managers of the affairs of women: for that God has preferred in bounty one of them over another, and for that they have expended of their property,' reads verse 38 of Chapter IV, 'Women' of the Quran. 'Righteous women are therefore obedient. . . . And those you fear may be rebellious, admonish, banish them to their couches, and beat them.'

Women's legal and financial positions are clearly defined by the Quran. 'God charges you, concerning your children: to the male the like of the portion of two females,' reads verse 11 of Chapter IV, 'Women'. 'And call in to witness two witnesses, men; or if the two be not men, then one man and two women, such witnesses as you approve of, that if one of the two women errs the other will remind her,' reads verse 282 of Chapter II, 'The Cow'. Following another Quranic verse, the Islamic regime dismissed all women judges and barred women lawyers from practising.

Great stress is laid on women as mothers. This fits into the long-term plan of the regime to foster a new generation of pure Muslims by providing children with an Islamic education at school and an Islamic environment at home, centred around the mother, who is modest in behaviour, faithful to her husband, and is always demurely dressed in public.

Islamic principles are also being applied increasingly to the economic aspect of life. The Majlis passed the interest-free banking bill in June 1983. It provided a transition period of eighteen months during which depositors were required to divide up their sums into the bank's two sections: 'interest-free' and 'term deposit'. The former would lend funds to needy customers without interest, and the latter to commercial companies, according to 'Islamic contracts'. The profits earned by lending funds to commercial firms would be shared by the depositors. In short, the idea of fixed interest rate is being replaced by variable profit margins by treating depositors as partners in a business.

Moreover, ideologues have been pondering the larger question of 'Islamic consumption'. Their ideas were accepted by the Mousavi administration and formalised into the Islamic Consumer Bill. In January 1984 the government described the purpose of the bill as 'changing the pattern of consumption in society and establishing a culture of Islamic consumption, divorced from waste and self-gratification'.[98]

While these fundamental changes were going apace, efforts were being made continually to create an Islamic ambience in the street, the media and the war front. One way to do this was by painting slogans on street walls. This was done on a vast scale in all Iranian cities and towns by the local Revolutionary Komitehs from a long, official list.

Slogans were of three kinds: political, religious and the war effort. The political slogans denounced the regime's external and internal enemies: the USA, the USSR, Israel and the Hypocrites (meaning Mujahedin). The religious ones either paid homage to a divine figure or quoted the Quran or Khomeini to denounce or prescribe a certain behaviour. 'Imam Hussein, our third martyr, is the headlight of our rescue vessel', was an example of the former. Those pertaining to the Gulf War were full of confidence. 'War, war, until victory', or simply, 'Islam is victorious'.

The mass media are helped in creating Islamic ambience by the proliferation of Islamic events throughout the year, not to mention the daily prayers which are strictly observed on radio and television. Besides the whole month of Ramadan, there are ten days of Muharram, the hajj season, the birthdays of Prophet Muhammad and twelve Imams, and two Eid festivals. To this must be added the events of Iran's revolutionary Islam: ten days of celebration of the revolution, a week of commemoration of the 'Iraqi-imposed war', and the founding days of the Islamic Republic, the IRG, the Basij, the Reconstruction Crusade, and so on.

A believer had the opportunity to involve himself in the revolutionary Islamic process by joining the Islamic Association at work or in the neighbourhood. These Associations performed many functions, such as identifying unIslamic elements, aiding the war effort, strengthening Islamic culture, and encouraging voter participation in elections and referendums.

It was as much a measure of the effectiveness of the Islamic Associations as it was of the degree of consolidation of the revolution that the voter turnout in the April-May 1984 Majlis election was one third up on the previous Majlis poll. About sixteen million out of a total of 24.5 million voters participated in this election.[99]

In all these activities, the ulema were in the forefront. They were now more numerous than ever before. Estimates of qualified clerics varied from 90,000 to 120,000.[100] In addition there was an unknown number of unqualified village preachers, prayer leaders, theological school teachers and procession organisers. To the important theological colleges in Qom, Mashhad, Tabriz, Isfahan, Shiraz and Yazd was added, in October 1983, the Imam Sadiq University in Tehran. The size of theology students trebled from the pre-revolution figure of 10,000.[101]

The number of mosques reached 22,000 in 1981, with urban mosques nearly doubling their pre-revolution total of 5,600. Some of these were newly built while others were created out of old property. Masjid al Nabi (Mosque of the Prophet) in Normak, a north-eastern district of Tehran, was an example of the latter. During the Shah's reign it was Monte Carlo cinema. The theatre gallery was altered into a library and a reading hall. A freshly-built dome over the hall, and Quranic verses inlaid around the frame of a large window facing the road, gave the place an Islamic look. Downstairs, the rectangular hall was partitioned to segregate the faithful by sex as they prayed. The mosque's office in the large room by the entrance was manned by volunteers. Their main task was to administer the rationing system for food and fuel for the 10,000 families living in the area. At the back the mosque had its own consumer cooperative store. The walled compound adjacent to the main building was used as a training ground for Basij volunteers. The periodic contributions made by the mosque's congregation to the war included two ambulances. The mosque offered classes in the Quran and Arabic as well as interest-free loans to those in dire need. At the time of elections and referendums the mosque was used as a polling station. This practice tended to favour the IRP or IRP-backed candidates.

Following the example of Prophet Muhammad, Khomeini set up his residence and administrative offices around a mosque in Jamran, a north Tehran suburb. As a marja-e taqlid, he stood at the apex of a religious network, in which the local Friday prayer leader was a key figure. Every week the Friday prayer leader delivers the main sermon which covers not only religious subjects but also contemporary political and social issues. In the main he supports official decisions, and galvanises public opinion behind the Islamic government. Under Khomeini's overall guidance Friday sermons have become highly political. While Khomeini wields the final authority to appoint or dismiss a Friday prayer leader, and is the head of the secretariat of Friday prayer leaders in Qom, Ayatollah Montazeri supervises the day-to-day administration of the secretariat.

As a marja-e taqlid Khomeini delivers periodic religious judgements on matters of import. He also looks after the religious welfare of the faithful. He instructed the Hajj Pilgrimage Committee in 1983 to provide funds to those poor Muslims who could not afford the journey to Mecca and Medina on their own. Since the revolution the number of hajj pilgrims has risen remarkably. In 1983 the figure was nearly 100,000, compared to 39,296 seven years earlier.[102] It was expected to go up to 150,000 in 1984.

It is obvious that the Islamisation process and the rise of revolutionary organisations have affected the lives of all Iranians. Most of them have either backed the change actively or gone along with it passively. A minority, consisting largely of upper middle and upper classes, has grumbled about the onset of Islamic values and behaviour. Its strength is estimated to be about a million families. (The figure excludes the supporters of the Mujahedin-e Khalq, which is committed to creating an Islamic society of a different kind.) They are almost invariably related to the Iranian exiles settled in the West. They stayed behind not because they sympathised with the Islamic revolution but because they wanted to safeguard their valuable properties. As long as there was a brother or sister, or a son or daughter, from a family present in Iran, the properties of the whole family were safe from the threat of confiscation. Had the bill to confiscate the exiles' properties become law in January 1983, a severe crisis would have arisen. But it did not.

The government decided not to pressure the secular rich for a variety of reasons. They lacked political power and had accepted their changed fortunes. Any pressure on them would negate the official efforts to attract skilled Iranians living abroad. Finally, the authorities felt confident that by Islamising education they had sown the seeds of a process which would mature into conflict between children and their unIslamic parents. So the future was decidedly loaded against those unwilling to Islamise themselves.

For the present the upper middle and upper classes found much to feel alienated from the regime: restrictions on women's dress in the street; a continued ban on music and dancing in public; the propagandistic output of radio, television and the press; the absence of good restaurants and places of entertainment; and a constant fear of reprisals if they expressed their disenchantment too loudly or too often.

At the same time they seemed to overlook a crucial fact: the Islamic regime upheld the right to private property as inviolable. This meant that the wealthy were free to rent houses and flats, buy and sell properties, and receive dividends on investments and bank deposits. Since Tehran had received about half of the 1.5 million war refugees as well as an influx of rural migrants (hopeful of receiving the fruits of the revolution in the capital) the demand for housing had risen sharply, pushing up property values and rents. So urban landlords were wealthier than before. In addition, their actions of the past ensured them continued high standards of living. During the Shah's days they had transferred huge sums abroad. Those accounts remained active, thanks largely to the presence of nearly a million Iranians living in the West. Since there was no restriction on receiving funds from abroad, the wealthy were free to draw on this source if all else failed. Finally, they were supported by the remnants of the cash savings they had literally hidden under the mattress during the Shah's last days. Under the circumstances, the rich continued to live a good life, albeit within the walls of their villas.

The centre piece of their existence was party-going. Here they met practically every evening of the week to console one another with the anti-regime news they had received by phone from their exiled relatives in Paris, Munich, London or Los Angeles, or by listening to the radio stations run by the opposition parties from abroad.

As expected, the opposition abroad exaggerates the differences within the regime, the problems of distribution of food and consumer goods, and the debate aroused by the stalemate in the war among Iranian leaders. But, above all, the regime's enemies are obsessed with Khomeini's health. For whatever their political hue might be – monarchist, Tudeh or Mujahedin – they are all putting their hopes and aspirations on the death of Khomeini.

On the other side the Islamic regime's number one priority is to keep Khomeini alive and in good health. Every month that he lives further consolidates the Islamic revolution, and ensures a smooth transfer of power to his successor(s) after his death.

Khomeini and the succession

Both the admirers and critics of the Islamic revolution are agreed on one point: Khomeini is popular with the Iranian masses. It is therefore vital for the regime to maintain him in robust health and protect him from assassination attempts. When Khomeini went to live in Qom in March 1979 he made himself available to ordinary Iranians who daily thronged to his unpretentious house, situated in a side street, in their hundreds. He received them in groups, listening to their problems and addressing them in return. This went on until January 1980 when he had a minor heart attack. He was taken to Tehran for proper medical treatment. After he had recovered he set up his headquarters in a complex of buildings around the mosque of Jamran in Shaheed Husseinkiya Street off Yasser Road. A series of coup attempts – in which Khomeini's headquarters figured prominently as a target – led the authorities to secure the premises by placing a ring of anti-aircraft guns around it and introducing an elaborate security system on the ground. Now computerised, semi-automatic Soviet-made SU-23 anti-aircraft guns are programmed to shoot any helicopter or aeroplane sighted in the area by the early warning radar screens. All vehicles using Yasser Road are stopped and searched and the identity papers of the travellers checked, by revolutionary guards.

Visits to Khomeini's headquarters are strictly controlled. Every visitor, no matter how high his rank, has to undergo an elaborate system of security checks before reaching it. Within these constraints, Khomeini is kept in public view through radio and television by reports of his weekly addresses to select groups of Iranians and foreigners. A wide cross-section of Muslim society at home and abroad is presented to the Ayatollah: the employees of the NIOC, the wives and children of the military officers who have died in the war, the cadres of the Reconstruction Crusade, leaders of bazaar merchants, Majlis deputies, the delegates to the World Congress of Friday Prayer Leaders, and so on.

Security checks begin at the junction of Shaheed Husseinkiya Street and Yasser Road. Here a visitor is frisked and made to surrender all his possessions – rings, cameras, watches, keys, pens and even notebooks. He undergoes two more body searches as he walks along the cobbled alleyway. Then he must give up his shoes before he can enter the mosque, a bare, closed, concrete building with a balcony that leads into Khomeini's offices. The moment Khomeini emerges from behind the balcony door he electrifies the audience who break into slogans. One has to witness the occasion in person to realise the magnetic pull that Khomeini has on Iranians.[103] The essence of the Islamic polity of Iran was expressed by Murtaza Sarmadi, a foreign ministry official, thus: 'The two main forces of the Islamic Republic are the Imam [Khomeini] and the unma [community]. We officials are merely following these forces'.[104]

Khomeini is a man of regular habits. He leads an orderly life, and is known for his serenity. He never leaves his premises and seldom, if ever, uses the phone. He keeps himself informed by receiving reports from a multitude of sources. He listens regularly to foreign radio stations, particularly the BBC's Persian service. He has no known ailment. Ayatollah Pasandida, his brother who is seven years his senior, is still alive. At this rate Khomeini can be counted on being the effective ruler of Iran for the next five to ten years.

Nonetheless the regime has already taken steps to ensure a smooth transition of power after Khomeini's death. As mentioned earlier, the Assembly of Experts charged with appointing his successor(s) met in July 1983. However, a year earlier the authorities had initiated a policy of projecting Ayatollah Hussein Ali Montazeri as the successor. The idea was first aired publicly by Ahmed Khomeini who said that he favoured Montazeri succeeding his father.[105]

Hussein Ali Montazeri was born in a peasant family of Najafabad in 1921. He had his early theological education in Isfahan, and then went to Qom. Here he became a student of Khomeini. In the early 1960s he taught at the Faiziya seminary. He participated in the events of June 1963. An active member of the anti-Shah clerical circles, he was close to Ayatollah Taleqani. In 1974 he was arrested, along with other prominent clerical opponents of the Shah. He was tortured in jail by Savak and released in November 1978.

On his return to Iran, Khomeini appointed Montazeri as the Friday prayer leader of Qom, a highly prestigious position. Then he was given a seat on the Islamic Revolutionary Council. In 1980 he was appointed the supreme guide of Iran's theological colleges. That entitled him to appoint personal representatives to the councils that ran these colleges. During that year a move was set afoot to declare him a Grand Ayatollah. Khomeini began to transfer to him some of his own religious-legal powers. For instance, he put him in charge of the secretariat of the Friday prayer leaders. He also authorised him to appoint members to the Supreme Judicial Council. Khomeini's closeness to Montazeri is well illustrated by the fact that Montazeri lived for many months in the house owned and occupied by Khomeini before his expulsion in late 1964, and which then became the exclusive residence of Khomeini's elder brother.

Like Khomeini, Montazeri daily receives various representatives, committees and delegates. They give him reports of their actions, and he sets out the guidelines for their future activity. He tends to exhort his audiences to improve their performance, and to stick to Islamic values and behaviour. In this address to clerical leaders he called on them to avoid luxurious living and abide by Islam's spartan values. During his meeting with top civil servants in mid-1983 he pointed out that there were still some laws and regulations which were not in line with Islam. Addressing the regional commanders of the IRG in January 1984, he called on them 'not to get involved in crippling protocol and red tape which is rife in many organisations and offices'. He warned that if revolutionary guards treated the public harshly the people would attribute their misbehaviour to 'Islam and the revolution'. He reminded them that they had no arbitrary right to arrest and needed court orders to do so, and that mere suspicion of 'a plot against the government' was not enough to enter private homes and arrest individuals.[106]

The official campaign to bolster Montazeri's image had reached a point where, by the spring of 1983, his bespectacled face appeared as frequently on television screen as did Khomeini's, although less prominently. In all government offices Khomeini's portraits were now accompanied by smaller pictures of Montazeri. In some instances, particularly in schools, Montazeri's portraits were given as much prominence as those of Khomeini.

Within the Islamic camp Montazeri was firmly on the side of the radicals. His son, Hojatalislam Muhammad Montazeri, led a contingent of 300 Iranian militiamen in mid-1979 to fight the Israelis alongside the Palestinians. After his death in the June 1981 bomb explosion, his followers joined the entourage of his father, thus strengthening the radical stance of Ayatollah Montazeri.

Since the Assembly of Experts is dominated by radicals the chances of Montazeri being selected as the successor to Khomeini are high. But if, by any chance, this does not happen, then the appointment of the Leadership Council of three – consisting of Montazeri, Hashemi-Rafsanjani, and Khamanei – is the most likely outcome.

While the regime has been steadily implementing its overall policies of strengthening the revolution and smoothing its future path, the opposition at home and abroad has been striving to maintain its existence through actions and words. Though much subdued, Kurdish insurgency persisted. Official pressure on the Mujahedin-e Khalq drove several hundreds of its members to Kurdistan where they operated under the guidance of the KDP. Between mid-March and mid-April 1983, Kurdish guerrillas claimed to have killed 500 government combatants.[107] In late October the Iranian forces combined the Wa al Fajr-Four offensive against the Iraqis in the northern sector with attacks on the KDP and Komala insurgents in the Shiler river area.[108]

Both the KDP and the Komala had joined the National Resistance Council in November 1981. They were followed by the National Democratic Front led by Hedayatollah Matine-Daftari. Thus the NRC had emerged as a middle of the road, democratic opposition to the Islamic regime, lying between the monarchists and the Tudeh.

Of the NRC's constituents, the Mujahedin-e Khalq was the most active in the Persian-speaking heartland of Iran. In early August 1983, it claimed that during the three years since the ouster of Bani-Sadr its members had killed 2,800 'agents of repression' – Islamic officials and revolutionary guards – in hundreds of assaults and defensive operations.[109] The government continued its actions against the Mujahedin, claiming in November 1983 to have destroyed their hideouts in Gilan and Mazandaran.[110]

Within the NRC strains developed between Rajavi and Bani-Sadr on the issue of Rajavi's relations with Iraq. Following his Paris meeting with Tariq Aziz in January 1983, Rajavi signed an agreement with Iraq whereby Baghdad promised not to attack Iran's civilian areas. However, this promise was not kept. All the same the Mujahedin-e Khalq concentrated its propaganda on the subject of war, calling for an immediate ceasefire and an end to the bombing of civilian areas by both sides. It argued that Khomeini continued to fight because he was afraid that if the war ended public attention would turn to internal problems, where his regime had fared badly. Efforts to patch up differences between Rajavi and Bani-Sadr, who opposed contacts with Iraq, failed. In early April 1984 Bani-Sadr broke with Rajavi, and quit the NRC.

The NRC had nothing to do with the monarchist groups which were also based mainly in Paris. In January 1982 Ali Amini, a former premier, formed the Front for the Liberation of Iran in the French capital. It brought together many anti-Khomeini groups around the programme of constitutional monarchy in Iran under the 1906 constitution with the objective of establishing political institutions 'as chosen by the people'. Among those who joined the Front were General Bahram Aryana and Rear-Admiral Ahmed Madani. Earlier Amini, Aryana and Madani were reported to be operating training camps of Iranian exiles in the Van region of south-east Turkey with a view to mounting a 'spring offensive' against the Khomeini regime. Although the plans were well advanced, and reportedly had the tacit support of the CIA, nothing more was heard of the venture.

About then twenty-two-year-old Reza Cyrus Pahlavi, residing in Cairo, declared his preference for a constitutional monarchy in Iran along the lines existing in Spain. Shahpour Bakhtiar, head of the National Resistance Movement of Iran, led a delegation of his supporters from Paris to Cairo to present the young pretender with a plan to overthrow the Islamic regime with the help of counter-revolutionary groups and pro-Western Arab states.[111] The plan was considered too unrealistic to be pursued. Nonetheless periodic attempts by the royalist contingent in the military to overthrow the Khomeini regime continued. For instance, in July 1982 five members of Nima, a monarchist group, were tried in Iran for attempting to overthrow the government.[112] On the other side, Islamic militants succeeded in assassinating General Oveissi, 'the Butcher of the Black Friday', in Paris on 7 February 1984.

Efforts to unite the major monarchist organisations reached fruition on 19 July 1983 when Ali Amini and Shahpour Bakhtiar adopted a joint programme: the acceptance of the 1906 constitution, confirmation of constitutional monarchy and 'the faithful implementation of the will of the general public', segregation of religion from politics, 'respect for the national traits of the people' within the context of national integrity, and the acceptance of rights and freedom specified in 'the universal charter of human rights'.[113]

As described earlier, the Tudeh re-established itself abroad, with the central committee holding its plenum in East Germany in January 1984. Such meetings in the future are likely to take place in Afghanistan, where many Tudeh members and sympathisers have taken refuge. There have been historic contacts between the Marxists of the two countries. President Babrak Karmal of Afghanistan was once a student of Ehsan Tabari, a leading Tudeh theoretician, who had spent twenty-two years in East Germany and eight years in the USSR. For the time being the Afghanistan connection is being played down, because Moscow does not wish to make Tehran even more intransigent than it has been on the issue of unconditional withdrawal of Soviet troops from Afghanistan.

On the other hand Moscow knows that whatever else might change during or after Khomeini's rule in Iran, one geopolitical fact will not: Iran has a 1,250-mile-long border with the Soviet Union.

PART III

IRAN AND THE WORLD

IRAN AND THE SOVIET BLOC

The current strain in relations between Iran and the Soviet Union is rooted in a long history of mutual hostility between the contiguous states: a history which has seen the northern neighbour emerge as one of the world's two superpowers, and the southern state often having to struggle to maintain its independence. In the eighteenth century the Iranian empire vied with the Ottoman and Czarist empires for hegemony in central Asia, whereas in the twentieth century Iran was twice partially occupied by Russia.

The idea of marching through Iran was first actively considered by Czar Paul I (1796-1801) when it was proposed to him by Napoleon I as part of the French drive to invade India, then under British tutelage. In the end Napoleon I opted for a naval route. His attack on Egypt in 1798 as part of his campaign for India failed. However, this had no effect on the long simmering Russo-Iranian dispute over Georgia. When Heraclius II, king of Georgia, was harassed by Aqa Muhammad Khan Qajar in 1795, he appealed to the Russian Czar for help. This appeal was repeated in 1798 by his successor George III. The following year the Georgian king renounced his crown in favour of the Czar. In 1801 the Czar incorporated Georgia into his empire.

This only steeled the resolve of the Iranian ruler, Fath Ali Shah, to recover Georgia from the Russians. He signed a treaty with Britain which promised him British weapons if the French marched towards Iran or India. Thus reassured, the Shah opened hostilities against the Czar in 1804. The First Russo-Iranian war lasted nine years. During the war the Czar forged an alliance with Napoleon I in 1807, which in turn led to the Anglo-Iranian alliance of 1809 and the presence of British officers in Iran. But that did not save Iran from defeat. According to the 1813 treaty of Gulistan, Iran surrendered to Russia most of its territory in the Caucasus to the north of its present border, and gave Russia the exclusive right to maintain warships on the Caspian Sea.

The ill-defined territorial clauses of the Gulistan treaty became a source of bitter disputes between Russia and Iran. Efforts at reconciliation failed. Demands were made in Iran for recapturing some of the disputed territory in Russian hands. Given this, and reports of maltreatment of Muslims in Czarist Russia, the ulema pressed the Shah to proclaim jihad against Russia. He did so in 1826. Despite its 1814 treaty with Britain, Iran got no aid from London. As it happened, Britain was then allied to Russia against the Ottoman empire. The Second Russo-Iranian war thus ended in Iranian defeat. According to the 1828 Turkomanchai treaty, Iran surrendered all the territory west of the Caspian Sea and north of its present border with the Soviet Union. It granted extra-territorial privileges to Russian nationals in Iran, and limited duties on Russian goods to 5 per cent. In return it received indemnities of $3 million.

In 1834 Russia conspired with Britain to ensure the coronation of Muhammad Mirza as the new Shah. In return the Shah gave further trade concessions to the Russians as well as the British.[1] Eight years later, responding to the Iranian appeal for help against Turkoman raiders from the north, the Russians set up a naval station on an Iranian island in the Caspian. They were able to help Iran further in this respect as their drive to conquer the independent regions east of the Caspian continued unabated. Once this process was completed in 1873, Russia shared common borders with Iran and Afghanistan. In 1881 Nasser al-Din Shah signed the treaty of Akhal-Khurasan to delineate Iran's north-eastern frontier with Russia. Three years earlier he had visited Russia, and on his return had formed the Cossack Brigade under Russian officers.

The Russians supported the tobacco boycott of 1891, and were glad to see the tobacco monopoly to a British company annulled. About the same time the Russian government obtained the rights to extend and operate the telegraph system from Tehran to its border town of Julfa, and build a paved road between the two destinations. A private Russian company received a fishing monopoly in the Caspian.

Russia shared its hegemony over Iran with Britain. Significantly, on Nasser al-Din Shah's death his son, Muzzafar al-Din, travelled from Tabriz to Tehran in the company of Russian and British envoys, and the Cossack Brigade kept the peace while the new Shah was being crowned. The sickly Shah wished at once to go to Europe for a cure. He raised a loan of $3 million from the Russian Banque d'Escompte by mortgaging customs receipts (except from south Tehran and the Gulf ports) to the bank, and by promising not to raise foreign loans or lower tariffs on foreign imports without prior Russian consent. He pledged to pay off the debt he had incurred earlier from the British-owned Imperial Bank of Persia. He excluded the five northern provinces along the Russian border from the oil concession he gave to D'Arcy in

1901. Two years later he borrowed again from Banque d'Escompte by ordering the customs chief to lower tariffs on Russian goods and raise them dramatically on British imports.

As described earlier, the constitutionalist movement in Russia had a direct impact on Iranian politics. Later the Russian Czar encouraged Muhammad Ali Shah to crush the Iranian constitutionalist movement. In this he was helped by the existence of the Anglo-Russian Entente of 1907. During the Iranian civil war of 1908-9 Russian troops entered the northern and eastern Iranian provinces of Azerbaijan, Gilan, Mazandaran and Khurasan. It was only after the Second Majlis had met in late 1909 and demanded Russian withdrawal, that the Czar agreed to remove his forces.[2]

Anxious to recover its independence, the Iranian government devised the concept of using a third power to beat off pressures by Russia and Britain. Out of this arose the appointment of an American economist, William Morgan Shuster, as the treasurer general. The Czar understood the wider implications of this appointment, and resolved to end it. He succeeded by threatening force. In the process he aroused widespread anti-Russian feeling in Iran. Confiscation of food by Russian troops in Enzeli and Rasht in early 1912 led to bloody rioting which left forty-three people dead. Later when a Russian officer was killed in Mashhad, the Russians bombed the Ali Reza shrine, where a large crowd had taken refuge, and ransacked the mosque. The Russian sacrilege of one of Iran's holiest shrines left a bitter feeling against Russia among Iranians.

However, dramatic events in Czarist Russia radically changed Russo-Iranian ties. Following the March 1917 Russian revolution the Czarist imperial army disintegrated. This encouraged the rise of nationalist and socialist groups in Iran's northern provinces. The Bolshevik revolution in November had a similar impact on all of Iran. Bolshevik officials wanted to open a new chapter in Russo-Iranian relations. In their notes of 14 January 1918 and 26 June 1919 to the Iranian government, they renounced all Czarist privileges and concessions. When the Anglo-Iranian agreement – which turned Iran into a virtual British protectorate – was made public in August 1919 the Bolsheviks opposed it. This was the background against which a twenty-five-article Russo-Iranian treaty of friendship was drafted. It was signed on 26 February 1921.

Articles One and Two confirmed the Russian notes of January 1918 and June 1919 renouncing all Czarist treaties and imperialist policies concerning Iran. Article Three recognised the borders of 1881. Article Four specified non-intervention by the signatories in each other's internal affairs. Article Five required the two parties to prohibit the formation or presence of 'any organisations or groups of persons whose object is to engage in acts of hostility against Persia or Russia'. This applied equally to troops. Both signatories were required to prevent the presence of forces of a third party in cases where the presence of such forces would be regarded as 'a menace to the frontiers, interests or safety' of the other party. 'If a third party should attempt to carry out a policy of usurpation by means of armed intervention in Persia, or if such power should desire to use Persian territory as a base of operations against Russia, or if a foreign power should threaten the frontiers of Federal Russia or those of its allies, and if the Persian government should not be able to put a stop to such menace after having been once called upon to do so by Russia, Russia shall have the right to advance her troops into the Persian interior for the purpose of carrying out the military operations necessary for its defence,' stated Article Six. 'Russia undertakes, however, to withdraw her troops from Persian territory as soon as the danger has been removed.' Article Seven applied the preceding one to the Caspian Sea. Articles Eight to Twelve invalidated all the economic privileges accorded in the past to Czarist Russia, and cancelled all Russian loans to Iran. Article Thirteen stipulated that the economic concessions returned by Russia to Iran would not be reallocated to a third party. The remaining Articles abrogated the extra-territorial rights that the Russians in Iran had enjoyed, and provided for the most favoured nation treatment on travel and transit facilities by the two parties, and resumption of commercial relations after the signing of the treaty.[3]

Articles Five and Six had been conceived against the background of civil war in Russia, whereby counter-revolutionary groups had set up bases in the adjoining countries and attacked the Bolshevik regime. Nonetheless, they were much criticised in the Majlis: they were seen as curtailing Iranian sovereignty. On 12 December the Russian envoy wrote a letter to the Majlis stating that these Articles applied only to 'cases in which preparations have been made for a considerable attack upon Russia or the Soviet Republics allied to her, by the partisans of the [Czarist] regime which has been overthrown or by its supporters among those foreign powers which are in a position to assist the enemies of the Workers' and Peasants' Republics, and at the same time to possess themselves – by force or by underhand methods – of part of Persian territory, thereby establishing a base for operations for any attacks . . . which they might mediate against Russia or the Soviet Republics.'[4] After this the treaty was ratified by the Iranian Majlis.

Until the commercial commissions provided by the February 1921 treaty had met to determine new trading terms, the low tariffs on Russian imports, as agreed in 1902, prevailed. This was detrimental to Iranian interests. In 1926 Reza Shah sent his aide, Abdul Hussein Teimurtash, to Moscow to get the process started. It reached fruition in 1927, the year when Reza Shah unilaterally abrogated the Capitulations to European countries.[5] By then economic cooperation between the two neighbours had been formalised through joint trading companies in cotton, wool and fisheries. Also a Russian trading bank in Iran had been authorised. In 1925 the Soviet government had managed to acquire 65 per cent of the shares of Kavir-e Khorian Company which held oil concessions in the Semnan-Damghan-Gorgan region of the vast, ill-defined province of Khurasan.

In the mid-1920s the Soviet Union initiated a series of non-aggression treaties with its neighbours in order to secure its borders. On 1 October 1927 it signed a Treaty of Guarantee and Neutrality with Iran. The signatories agreed to refrain from aggression against each other and remain neutral in the event of aggression by a third country. 'Each of the contracting parties agrees to take no part . . . in political alliances or agreements directed against the safety of the territory or territorial waters of the contracting party or against its integrity, independence or sovereignty,' stated Article Three. The same applied to economic boycotts or blockades organised by third parties. One of the two protocols accompanying the treaty reiterated that Article Six of the 1921 treaty remained in force.[6]

As Reza Shah consolidated his rule at home and began to assert Iranian independence in foreign affairs, he tried to end the remnants of Soviet domination of Iran. In December 1935 the Iranian government submitted to the USSR a protocol which repealed Article Six of the 1921 treaty and Protocol Two of the 1927 treaty. Moscow ignored the move. In the absence of the ratification of the Iranian proposal by the two parliaments, the treaties of 1921 and 1927 remained valid in their entirety.

With the German invasion of the USSR on 22 June 1941, these treaties became significant. On 26 June the Soviet Union sent a note to Iran (which was neutral in the war) drawing its attention to Articles Five and Six of the 1921 treaty, and referring to the presence of German agents in Iran. On 19 July Moscow joined London in delivering another protest note to Tehran on German spies. Finally, on 25 August Soviet and British envoys in Tehran informed the Iranian prime minister that their troops had entered Iran. They also demanded the abdication of Reza Shah. Soviet troops entered Iran at two points – in Azerbaijan and Khurasan.

On 30 August the Soviet Union requested Iran for help in developing the Kavir-e Khorian Company's oil concessions in the north. The Iranian government replied that this concession had expired with the 1921 treaty, and that it was prepared to discuss a new one. Nonetheless, the Soviets began drilling in the Semnan-Damghan-Gorgan region. But this was in vain.

The issue of exploitation of oil in northern Iran remained on the Soviet-Iranian agenda. In April 1944 it was reported that the Anglo-American oil conference then in session in Washington was considering the exploitation of Iranian oil. With pressure building up from the West and the USSR, the Iranian government decided on 2 September to postpone the issue of oil concessions until after the war. But that did not stop Soviet deputy foreign minister, Sergei Ivanovich Kavtaradze, visiting Tehran in late September, from pressing Soviet application for oil exploration rights in the north for five years. On 16 October the government of Muhammad Saed informed all applicants that no oil concession would be granted until after the war. Subsequent Soviet pressure, accompanied by Tudeh-led demonstrations, brought down the Saed administration on 9 November. But the Majlis was adamant. On 2 December it passed a resolution, introduced by Muhammad Mussadiq, which barred (on pain of three to eight years' imprisonment) any government official from discussing oil concessions with 'official or unofficial representatives of any country, or with the representatives of oil companies, or any other person', or signing any agreement connected with oil. A week later a disappointed Kavtaradze returned to Moscow. On the other hand, the overall Soviet objective may well have been to exclude British and American oil companies from northern Iran, and even to turn Iranian attention to the idea of annulling the existing concessions to Western companies in the south. If so, the Soviet purpose was well served by the events of the autumn of 1944.

According to a provision in the January 1942 Tripartite Agreement between Iran, the USSR and Britain, the Allied troops were to withdraw from Iran by 2 March 1946. But before then, there were rebellions in two northern provinces. The Democratic Party of Azerbaijan, consisting of local Tudeh members and other leftist and nationalist forces, proclaimed the Autonomous Government of Azerbaijan in Tabriz under Jaafar Pishevari on 12 December 1945. It declared Azeri-Turkish as the official language, nationalised banks, and began to distribute state-owned land to peasants. When Tehran sent its troops to Azerbaijan to quell the rebellion, Soviet forces barred their entry into the province. The Azerbaijani example was emulated by the Kurds in adjoining Kurdistan. On 15 December the Kurdish Democratic Party founded the Kurdish People's Republic of Mahabad. The two governments formed a military alliance against Tehran. These developments dovetailed with the primary Soviet objective in Iran: to prevent the formation of an anti-leftist administration in Tehran which, backed by the US, would expel all Soviet influence from Iran.

On 19 January 1946, at the behest of America, Premier Hakimi complained to the UN Security Council about Soviet interference in Iran's domestic affairs. But before the Security Council came up with its advice to the two parties to negotiate directly, the Hakimi government fell.

The new premier, Qavam al Saltane, negotiated not only with the Soviets but also with Pishevari. Intent on securing the withdrawal of Soviet troops, Qavam al Saltane compromised on Azerbaijani autonomy and oil concessions to Moscow. A draft agreement was reached on 4 April, and signed by the Shah four days later. Qavam al Saltane agreed to form a joint Soviet-Iranian oil company with 51 per cent Soviet interest, and promised to solve the Azerbaijani crisis peacefully. In return Moscow pledged to pull out its troops by 9 May. The draft agreement was to be ratified by 24 October by the new Majlis to be elected. Through this tactic Qavam al Saltane gave the Soviets a stake in normalising the political situation in Iran to enable the Majlis elections to take place.

Soviet troops withdrew on time. In mid-June, with Soviet mediation, Qavam al Saltane obtained a thirteen-point agreement with Tabriz. It promised major economic, cultural and autonomous reforms in Azerbaijan. On 6 October the Shah announced fresh elections to the Majlis. And on 21 November the Prime Minister said that security forces would be sent to different parts of the country during elections to maintain law and order. He ordered the troops to march into Azerbaijan on 9 December. Three days later they entered Tabriz. Fearing that resistance on its part would lead to Tehran calling on America and Britain for military aid and fighting along the Soviet border, the Autonomous Government of Azerbaijan decided to surrender. Tehran's forces entered Mahabad, the capital of the Kurdish People's Republic, on 17 December, and encountered no resistance.

Having got the electoral process started in the once troubled Azerbaijan and Kurdistan, Qavam al Saltane dragged it out in other provinces. Elections were not completed until June 1947. When finally he placed the agreement with Moscow before the Fifteenth Majlis on 22 October 1947 – a year later than promised – the deputies rejected it by 102 votes to two. They argued that it violated the 2 December 1944 oil law.[7]

But turning down the Soviet agreement was only part of the five-clause law. Its last clause instructed the government to undertake necessary measures to secure 'the national rights . . . in respect of the natural wealth of the country, including the southern oil'.[8] This pleased the Soviets. Having been deprived of a share in Iran's oil, they looked forward to the expulsion of Western interests from it.

As it was, the last clause of the 22 October 1947 oil law proved to be the seed which matured into a full blown oil nationalisation movement and which brought Mussadiq to power. On assuming office, he applied the principle of 'negative equilibrium' to Iran's foreign affairs. The concept was open to varied interpretations. The leftists interpreted it as breaking the British oil monopoly in the south by giving concessions to the Soviets in the north. The centrists saw it as being strictly neutral between the USSR and Britain with a view to ending their interference in Iranian affairs. The pro-Western nationalists considered it as a new variant of the old 'three power game' – the third power this time being the US – using America as a counterpoint to Britain and the USSR. Mussadiq's actions showed that he agreed with the last interpretation.

Once Mussadiq had broken with Britain and expelled the last British employee of the Anglo-Iranian Oil Company, the Soviet Union contracted to buy petroleum from the nationalised oil industry. It also signed a commercial agreement with Iran. Its lead was followed by Czechoslovakia and Hungary. But Mussadiq, a staunch anti-communist, shied away from strengthening economic ties with the Soviet bloc. He feared that such a move would destroy any chance of economic and military aid from Washington, something he badly needed. He remained hopeful to the last of separating the US from Britain, and achieving the objective of destroying British economic domination of Iran with American help. On its part, the Soviet Union could do nothing more than make offers of trade and economic aid.

After the Shah had regained his throne on 19 August 1953 with American complicity, he set out to do what Moscow had feared since the end of the Second World War: eradicate all Soviet influence from Iran, and further strengthen ties with the US. The Shah stressed that his foreign policy rested on the concept of 'positive nationalism'. Soviet leaders were not taken in. But, having just assumed power after Joseph Stalin's death in March 1953, they lacked the assurance to take vigorous counter-measures and push Iran back to a neutral path. It was only after the Shah had signed an agreement with a Western consortium on Iranian oil in August 1954, that they publicly criticised Iran for straying away from its avowed policy of neutrality.

Moscow was alarmed when Iran announced its intention to join the Baghdad Pact in October 1954. It pointed out that this would be contrary to the 1921 treaty. Tehran ignored the protest, and joined the alliance, later to be called the Central Treaty Organisation, Cento. Soviet leaders feared that following the lead of Turkey, a Baghdad Pact member, Iran would allow American bases on its soil. They wanted to prevent this. In a conciliatory move they invited the Shah to Moscow. He went in June 1956. According to the Shah, Soviet Premier Nikita Khrushchev suggested to him that 'some big power' might compel Iran 'against its will' to make its territory available for attack on the Soviet Union. The Shah replied, 'We would never allow either the [Baghdad] Pact or our territory to be used in furtherance of aggressive designs upon the Soviet Union'.[9]

Later when the US began deploying medium-range Jupiter and Thor missiles with nuclear warheads in Turkey, Soviet deputy foreign minister, I. Kuznestov, demanded and secured a repetition of the Iranian pledge on missile bases during his visit to Tehran in April 1957.

A new situation arose when, shaken by the July 1958 republican coup in Iraq, the Shah approached the US for a mutual defence treaty. Moscow protested that this was contrary to Article Three of the 1927 Soviet-Iranian Treaty. When the Shah ignored the Soviet protest, an authoritative article in *Pravda* of 6 December raised the prospect of Soviet troops marching into Iran under Article Six of the 1921 Treaty if Iran signed a military pact with the US. Then came an inducement. During his visit to Tehran in early 1959, Soviet deputy foreign minister, V. Semenov, offered a large amount of Soviet aid to Iranian heavy industry, a fifty-year non-aggression pact, changes in Articles Five and Six of the 1921 Treaty and Article Three of the 1927 Treaty, if Iran would abandon its plan to sign a military agreement with the US. Iran showed interest. Protracted talks ensued. But nothing came of it, because the Shah negotiated in bad faith. He used the negotiations with the Soviets to extract better terms from the US. As he revealed to C.L. Sulzberger of the *New York Times*, 'In its initial form the [American] draft was meaningless. We were so fed up that we turned a listening ear to Russian proposals for a non-aggression pact. . . . President Eisenhower [then] wrote begging me not to accept the Russian proposal'.[10] The Iranian-American pact was signed on 5 March 1959.

Soviet fears of Cento involvement with US military plans were confirmed when an American U-2 spy plane, shot down by the Soviets on 5 May 1960, was found to have flown from Pakistan, a Cento member. The Cento air exercises scheduled for 14 to 18 May now seemed particularly menacing to Moscow. The appointment of Ali Amini, a friend of President Kennedy, as Iranian premier in June 1961 indicated to the Soviets the extent of American influence in Iran. On 19 August *Pravda* published a secret Cento document which showed that nuclear arms bases existed in Turkey, Iran and Pakistan. Ali Amini's denial did not reassure Moscow.

In the early 1960s there was growing tension between Moscow and Peking. In order to face the Chinese threat in the east, Soviet leaders decided to secure the southern borders by improving relations with the bordering states. Aware of this, and resentful of the Kennedy administration's pressures to implement reform at home, the Shah resolved to dispel Soviet fears about missile bases and improve economic relations with Moscow. In September 1962 the two governments exchanged notes, with the Iranian administration pledging 'not to permit rocket bases of any sort on its soil' and not to allow Iran to become a base for aggression against the USSR.[11] This was a new chapter in Iran-Soviet relations under the Shah. It was a reflection of the Shah's growing confidence, and was meant to give him freedom to extend Iranian influence in the Gulf.

Within three months of the Iranian guarantees on foreign military bases the two states ratified transit and border accords signed earlier. In July 1963 the Soviets undertook joint projects with Iran concerning a hydro-electric project on the Aras river along the common border, and developing Caspian fisheries. They gave Iran low interest loans of $36 million. During his visit to Tehran in November 1963, Soviet leader Leonid Brezhnev signed the most favoured nation agreement on the transit of goods. This facilitated the growth of Iran's economic relations with East Europe. All told, these moves fitted Iran's ambitious Third Five Year Plan of 1963-7 well. Not surprisingly, in 1964 the Shah announced the launching of 'a new national independent foreign policy'.

In the summer of 1965 the Shah visited Moscow for the second time. The Soviets agreed to provide machinery and technical assistance for a steel mill in Isfahan with an annual capacity of 600,000 tons, and a machine tool and heavy engineering complex in Arak. They contracted to supply pipes for a pipeline project for natural gas from Khuzistan oil fields to Astara on the Soviet border in exchange for natural gas at the rate of seven billion cubic metres in 1970 and rising to ten billion cubic metres in 1976. The Soviets gave Iran $300 million in soft loans.

Having strengthened economic ties with Iran, Soviet officials offered weapons to Tehran at reasonable prices. At first the Shah declined the offer. But in 1966 he showed interest mainly in order to pressure the US to sell him the ground-to-air missiles he wanted. However, having started the negotiations, he could not back out completely. So in 1967 he ordered $110 million worth of military transport items from Moscow. Though he criticised Soviet armed intervention in Czechoslovakia in August 1968, he did not cancel his scheduled visit to Moscow in September. There he signed $280 million worth of economic agreements with the USSR. It was estimated that between 1965 and 1968 Iran had received more than one-fifth of all Soviet aid to Asia and Africa.[12] By the late 1960s over 1,500 Soviet experts were working in Iran on various projects.

Once the National Iranian Oil Company had acquired five million tons of oil annually from the Western consortium in 1967 for marketing on its own, it explored the East European market, and found it receptive. This improved economic relations between Tehran and East European capitals, particularly Bucharest.

During his visit to Tehran in March 1970, Soviet Premier Alexei Kosygin said, 'Iran is now strong enough to pick her own friends'.[13] This was a compliment to the Shah's efforts to balance Iran's close ties with the West by expanding links with the Soviet bloc. In October the Shah and Soviet President Nikolai Podgorny met in Astara to inaugurate the gas pipeline. By now the USSR had become the leading importer of Iran's non-oil exports. Soviet exports to Iran had grown tenfold in as many years. And the two countries had balanced trade.

However, expanded economic ties could not mask the very real political and diplomatic conflict that existed between the two states. In late 1971 Moscow deployed troops along the Iranian border to deter the Shah from aiding Pakistan in its war with India in its eastern wing on the issue of Bengali nationalism.[14] More importantly, when the Shah resorted to harassing the Baathist regime of Iraq from April 1969 onwards, the Soviets began arming Baghdad. Moscow formalised its warm relations with Baghdad in the form of a friendship and cooperation treaty in April 1972. This angered the Shah. To mollify him Soviet officials offered him a treaty of cooperation. He signed it during his visit to Moscow in October.[15] But this was more a symbolic gesture than a real one.

Starting in late 1972 the Shah embarked on a massive arms build-up financed by petro-dollars. During the next four years he spent $10 billion on American weapons. The secret $850 million electronic surveillance 'Ibex' project – designed to increase the CIA surveillance stations along the Iran-Soviet border from two to eleven – was directed specifically against the USSR.[16] At the same time the Shah kept up his periodic purchases of military transport from the Soviets. During his October 1976 visit to Moscow, the Iranian deputy war minister, General Hassan Toufanian, placed $150 million worth of orders for tank transporters, armoured personnel carriers and SAM-7s.[17]

An event concerning a Soviet defector in the autumn of 1976 showed that Moscow and Tehran were prepared occasionally to undertake political bargaining. In September 1976 a Soviet pilot defected to Iran with a view to seeking asylum in the US. Moscow pressured Tehran to return the defector. Following secret negotiations Iran handed over the pilot to Moscow in early 1977. In return the Soviet Union secured the closure of the pro-Tudeh Peik-e Iran radio station which had been operating from Sofia, Bulgaria, since 1959.[18]

Strengthening of economic links between the two neighbours continued. The five-year economic agreement between Tehran and Moscow signed in 1976 visualised transactions worth $3 billion, with Iran exporting natural gas and textiles and other consumer goods.

Since the trade in 1975-6 had amounted to $279 million, it meant more than doubling the current rate of transactions. The rail traffic agreement signed in June 1977 required the Soviet Union to transport 2.7 million tons of goods between Iran and Europe and Japan, an increase of 700,000 tons over the past year.[19] All this happened against the background of continued suspicion and hatred of the Soviet Union and Soviet officials in Iran. As Ayut Ajabee, a clearance agent in the border town of Julfa, put it, 'In the Shah's days you had to inform the local Savak before and after you went to see the Russian customs officer. You had to tell Savak the name of the Iranian company you represented, and the time you spent with the Russians.'[20]

There was growing unease in Moscow at the Iranian military build-up. Premier Kosygin said as much to Premier Hoveida during the latter's visit to Moscow in July 1977. Hoveida replied that Iran was only trying to stay even with the arms purchases going on elsewhere in the region.[21] But this was contrary to what the Shah had said in an interview with *Newsweek*. The Iranian build-up, he explained, was aimed as a deterrent against the Soviet Union, as a trip wire against a conventional attack, to resist 'long enough to wake up everybody'.[22]

In the final analysis, therefore, the Shah's Iran was a member of the Western camp which was poised against the Eastern bloc led by the USSR. As long as the Pahlavis were in power, Iran was going to stay firmly inside the Western orbit. Soviet leaders had reached this conclusion many years ago. They had also concluded that the Pahlavi dynasty was secure for the foreseeable future. These conclusions had led them to make the best of a bad bargain by developing strong economic ties with Tehran.

But as the events in Iran took a revolutionary turn in the summer of 1978 Soviet officials changed their assessment. As a result, they allowed the Tudeh Party to operate the National Voice of Iran Radio station from Baku in September 1978. Soviet media gave extensive coverage to the Iranian events. At the same time the government scrupulously avoided criticising the Shah. What Moscow was most anxious about was the prospect of American military intervention to beat off the revolutionary challenge to the Shah. That is why on 18 November Brezhnev publicly warned America against interference in Iran's internal affairs. The response of the US government that it had no such intention inadvertently worked for the revolutionaries and against the Shah.

After the revolution

The Soviet Union was one of the two countries to recognise the provisional government of Premier Bazargan on 12 February, the day he appointed three deputy premiers.[23] Soviet analysts hailed the acumen of the revolutionary leaders, particularly Khomeini, in giving a call to their followers for an armed confrontation with the army on 9-10 February when plans for a military coup were being hatched.

During the subsequent days and weeks, while Western media gave an impression of chaos prevailing in Iran, Soviet media stressed the positive side, stating that the provisional government was gaining control and that the situation was improving steadily. 'A process of stabilisation of the revolutionary regime in Iran . . . has become apparent in both its domestic and international aspects,' said *Pravda* on 1 March 1979. 'However, there are repeated calls for use of force in the Persian Gulf region to defend American interests. . . . Everything possible is being done to incite protests and plots by Iranian reaction within the country.'

Afraid that any rift among the revolutionaries would provide an opening to the monarchists among military officers and politicians to restore the former regime in some form, the Soviets advised leftist groups to support Khomeini unequivocally.

Moscow hoped that Khomeini would steer Iran away from the Western camp and into the non-aligned community of nations. Its hopes were realised. On 13 March Iran decided to quit Cento; and a fortnight later it applied for membership of the Non-Aligned Movement.

Relations between Tehran and Moscow became warm. Ayatollah Taleqani stressed in late February that Iran's ties with the Soviet Union must be 'good neighbourly'. On 3 March, while welcoming the victory of Iranian revolution, Brezhnev hoped that 'good neighbourly relations will develop fruitfully'.[24] Now that the revolutionary movement had won, the Soviet Union stressed the help it had given to it at crucial moments. As a Soviet radio commentary put it: 'During the Iranian people's struggle against the monarchy the USSR . . . did everything to prevent outside interference in Iran's affairs and to block plans for armed intervention against the revolution'.[25]

Tehran was quick to reassure Moscow that it would compensate the Soviets for its failure to supply natural gas due to the strikes in the oil fields. (It resumed supplies in April.) Moscow in turn reassured Tehran that it would continue its cooperation in economic and other matters. The importance of this lay in the fact that the Soviets had been involved in 140 industrial and other projects in Iran: together these accounted for 90 per cent of Iran's coal production, 87 per cent of its iron ore output, and 70 per cent of its steel production.[26] In October Moscow contracted to build an electric power station in Isfahan.

On the question of the American hostages, the Soviet Union made a distinction between the Iranian action and the American reaction. It considered hostage-taking as contravening international law and diplomatic immunity, and voted for the UN Security Council resolution of 4 December 1979 which called on Iran to release the diplomats. 'The seizure of the American embassy is undoubtedly not in keeping with the international convention on respect for diplomatic privileges and immunity,' said an editorial in *Pravda* of 5 December. 'This act, however, cannot be taken out of the overall context of American-Iranian relations. . . . The present attempts by the United States to blackmail Iran by massing armed forces on her frontiers and dictate a line of conduct to her by force are a gross violation of the standards of international law.'

Based on the information collected by their intelligence agencies, Soviet leaders concluded that under the guise of releasing its diplomats the US was planning an attack on Iran. Such a show of force by America would have encouraged President Hafizollah Amin of Afghanistan to loosen his ties with Moscow. Forestalling such a move was one of the main considerations which led Soviet officials to order their troops into Afghanistan on 27 December 1979.

Whatever purpose military intervention in Afghanistan served for Moscow, it alienated the Islamic regime of Iran. Tehran condemned the Soviet action. 'Because Afghanistan is a Muslim country and a neighbour of Iran,' said Qutbzadeh, Iran's foreign minister, 'the military intervention by the government of the Soviet Union . . . is considered a hostile measure not only against the people of that country but against all Muslims of the world.'[27]

But the Iranian condemnation did not stop the USSR from vetoing on 14 January 1980 the US-sponsored resolution at the UN Security Council (passed by ten votes to two) for economic sanctions against Iran. Moscow argued that an international economic boycott of Iran would be a severe blow to the fledgling republic.

It was obvious that Khomeini wanted to use the increased tension with the US to eliminate American influence from Iran – an objective in which the Soviets were only too willing to cooperate. On the eve of the first anniversary of the revolution, Khomeini declared that Iran would continue to struggle against America until 'all economic, military, political and cultural dependence on the US' had ended.[28]

However, such a statement was to be seen as part of the overall foreign policy of the Republic, encapsulated by the slogan: 'Neither East nor West'. On the eve of the Iranian New Year, Khomeini stated, 'We are the enemies of international communism in the same way as we are against the world predators of the West, headed by the United States'. He condemned the 'brutal intervention' in Afghanistan by 'looters and occupiers'.[29] Three weeks later Iran decided to boycott the Olympic Games to be held in Moscow in protest against the Soviet action in Afghanistan.

As for the Soviet policy towards Iran, it was dictated largely by the American behaviour towards Iran. In the US military build-up in the Gulf, and the economic boycott of Iran imposed on 7 April, Moscow saw clear signs of an impending American attack on Iran. To meet the eventuality, it moved half of its 100,000 troops in Afghanistan to the Iranian border.[30] Moscow's fears were vindicated when the US launched a military raid on 24-25 April on Iran with the purported objective of rescuing its hostages. Tass, the Soviet newsagency, condemned the American raid as 'a reckless gamble which might have started a war'. The Soviets believed that the American mission was a cover for a coup against Khomeini's regime.[31]

To help Iran overcome the consequences of the Western economic boycott, the USSR offered transit facilities to Iran across its territory. In early June the two governments signed a protocol whereby Moscow pledged to aid Tehran 'in extreme conditions' such as a naval blockade. In practice, active economic cooperation between the two neighbours had begun as early as December 1979. This was indicated by a dramatic jump in railway traffic at Julfa, where 300 freight cars were arriving daily from the USSR.[32] On 20 June the Iranian delegation in Moscow signed the Islamic Republic's first protocol on economic, technical and commercial links with the USSR. It provided for continued Soviet assistance in 142 projects, including coal and steel industries, and hydro-electric dams on the Aras, Atrak and Hari-Rud rivers. In September the USSR agreed to transport four million tons of goods annually over its territory to Iranian destinations, a record.[33]

Increasing economic links between Tehran and Moscow contrasted with a cooling of diplomatic relations. Qutbzadeh kept up his pressure against the USSR. He extended his attacks on Moscow for its intervention in Afghanistan to the Soviet embassy in Tehran. This drove *Pravda* on 19 June 1980 to accuse him of trying to 'discover Soviet plots against the Iranian revolution'. Undeterred, Qutbzadeh expelled Vladimir Golovanov, Soviet first secretary for spying, and demanded the reduction of the Soviet diplomatic contingent of forty by half, and the closure of the Soviet consulate in Rasht. In return he agreed to shut down the Iranian consulate in Leningrad.

Tehran-Moscow relations cooled further when, during summer, tension rose between Iran and Iraq, an ally of the USSR. In early August, protesting against Soviet arms supplies to Baghdad, Qutbzadeh threatened to recall the Iranian ambassador to Moscow. A few days later he addressed a long letter to Andrei Gromyko, Soviet foreign minister. In it he surveyed relations between their countries since 1941. 'You have proved in practice that you are no less satanic than the US,' he wrote. He accused the USSR of sending arms to the Kurdish insurgents, and attacked it for refusing to acknowledge Iran's abrogation (on 5 November 1979) of Articles Five and Six of the 1921 Treaty, thus adding to Iran's fears that the Treaty would be used 'as a pretext to launch aggression and attacks against our country'.[34] In his reply on 22 August, Gromyko offered to sell arms to Iran. But the latter rejected the offer. Regarding Articles Five and Six of the 1921 Treaty, the Soviet position was that their one-sided abrogation by Iran was meaningless. These articles were part of a multi-purpose treaty which included an article on the cancellation of Soviet loans to Iran. Abrogating the whole treaty would mean that Iranian debts would have to be repaid. At current prices they would amount to over $16,000 million. The abrogation would need to be ratified by the two parliaments to become effective.

It is quite possible that Soviet leaders had foreknowledge of Iraqi plans to invade Iran and tried in vain to persuade Baathist leadership to drop them.[35] Once Iraq had invaded Iran, the Soviet authorities immediately assured Iran that they would remain neutral in the conflict;[36] and this allowed the Iranians to move troops and equipment from the north to the south. They believed that Iraq had been encouraged to take this course by America and its Arab allies. 'Certain people in the West do not conceal their hopes that the present Iranian-Iraqi conflict will reduce the ability of the Republic of Iran to resist the imperialist pressure which is being exerted on it [in the context of the American hostage crisis],' reported *Izvestiya* (News) on 23 September. 'They also hope that the involvement of Iraq in military operations against Iran will enable the West to achieve the changes in Iraqi policy in the West's favour.' The same day *Pravda* accused the US of 'setting Iraq and Iran against each other'.

The Soviet appeal to both sides on 25 September to show 'restraint and common sense' was followed a few days later by an authorised article by Tass. It reminded Iraq and Iran that their war was 'undermining the national liberation movement in the Middle East in its struggle against imperialism and Zionism'.[37] In order to help end the war quickly, the Soviets stopped supplying weapons, or even spare parts, to Iraq. Since 85 per cent of Iraqi arms were Soviet-made, this move hurt Iraq.

While refraining from branding Iraq as the aggressor, the Soviet government made statements which showed its displeasure with Baghdad. On 30 September Brezhnev warned that the war might provide the US with an excuse to move into Iran militarily and control Gulf oil under the pretext of freeing American hostages.[38] Aware of the ill-effects of the Western economic and arms embargo on Iran – equipped almost exclusively with American, British and French weapons – and anxious to help Iran maintain its anti-imperialist stance, Moscow offered to sell weapons to Tehran. According to Premier Rajai, Soviet ambassador Vladimir Vinogradov made the offer on 4 October, and he rejected it.[39] Before the revolution the Soviets had sold small arms, Katyusha rocket artillery and surface-to-air missiles to Iran, not to mention military transport equipment.

Iran rejected Moscow's offer in the knowledge that it could buy Soviet weapons and ammunition from Syria, a Soviet ally, which had already airlifted such equipment to Iran. It was significant that the Syrian president, Hafiz Assad, discussed Iran with Brezhnev during his visit to Moscow in October to sign a Friendship and Cooperation Treaty with the USSR. In a joint statement the two leaders supported 'Iran's inalienable right to determine its destiny independently and without any foreign interference'.[40]

An article published in the Soviet army's paper, *Krasnaya Zvezda* (Red Star), on 26 October gave a strong hint of where Soviet sympathies lay. 'The declared aims of the [Iraqi] military actions are being changed,' said the article. 'At first Iraq claimed the comparatively small area of 508 kilometers . . . but now the Iraqi press is publishing maps in which the whole province of Khuzistan, called Arabistan in the Iraqi capital, is marked as Iraqi territory.' In the Soviet view, Iraq had compounded its culpability by combining its expansionist intention with cooperation with Washington. 'The Soviets . . . accept that Saddam Hussein wanted to emerge as a powerful leader of the Gulf and to protect himself from the instigated resentment of the Shia majority in Iraq,' reported the Moscow correspondent of *The Middle East* in December. 'But they maintain that he acted in concert with the Americans and with their help and guidance.'[41]

Moscow would have liked to see the impasse between Tehran and Washington on the American hostage issue continue. When negotiations between Tehran and Washington on the subject reached a point of resolution in mid-January 1981, Soviet media reported that the US was planning an attack on Iran while keeping up a facade of talks. On 17 January *Pravda* said that the US was preparing 'intimidating military operations' against Iran under the cover of a 'dishonourable game' about the American hostages.

Following the hostages' release on 21 January, Moscow expected the US to reduce its naval force in the region. But it did not. By now the Iran-Iraq war had become the main reason for America's large scale military presence in the area. Regarding their own role in the Gulf War, Soviet officials were prompt in denying periodic Iranian accusations of Soviet arms deliveries to Iraq. In early February 1981 Baghdad publicly confirmed that the USSR stopped implementing 'its pre-war arms contracts with Iraq' when the war erupted.[42]

However, since Soviet military embargo applied only to direct supplies, the Iraqis were able to bypass it by purchasing some Soviet arms and ammunition from other Warsaw Pact countries or such Arab states as North Yemen and Egypt whose armed forces were equipped with Soviet weaponry. 'If we had failed [to get Soviet arms altogether] we might have become irritated, very hostile, very hysterical against the Soviet Union which would have been a mistake,' said Tariq Aziz, Iraq's foreign minister. 'Now we can behave serenely with the Soviet Union without being hostile to it.'[43] Such statements, combined with an exchange of warm greetings by Brezhnev and Saddam Hussein on 9 April 1981 to commemorate the Soviet-Iraqi friendship treaty, neutralised Soviet warmth towards the Iranian revolution expressed recently by Brezhnev. Addressing the twenty-sixth congress of the Communist Party of the Soviet Union on 23 February, Brezhnev decribed the Iranian revolution as 'a major event on the international scene in recent years'. He added, 'However complex and contradictory, it is essentially an anti-imperialist revolution, though reaction at home and abroad is seeking to change this feature.'[44]

Iranian leaders considered Soviet intervention in Afghanistan as imperialistic, an action which among other things had created a major problem for their country. 'There are over one million Afghan refugees in Iran, and that acts as permanent counter-propaganda against the Soviets,' said President Bani-Sadr. 'I told the Soviet ambassador that . . . we will not allow any advantage to be given either to the Americans or the Russians. The ambassador asked if this ruled out collaboration between the two countries. I said, "No, collaboration is possible".'[45]

As before, this meant economic collaboration, with the USSR helping Iran to build up its heavy industry, mining and power generation. In May 1981 the Soviet Union contracted to expand the Isfahan steel mill's annual capacity to 1.9 million tons. The new mining projects in which the Soviets were involved were scheduled to produce two million tons of coal and three million tons of iron ore annually.[46] Trade between the two countries reached $1.1 billion, a record.[47] This happened despite the absence of Iranian gas exports to the USSR for most of the year. The supply of Iranian gas to the southern states of the Soviet Union, which had been resumed in April 1979, suffered when Iranian oil output slumped during the 1979-80 winter, and Iran insisted on raising its price. In early February the gas flow was down to about 15 per cent of the normal. An explosion in the pipeline later that month shut off supplies. In March the USSR offered to pay $2.66 per thousand cubic feet of gas versus $3.80 demanded by Iran, a dramatic jump from the original price of 65 cents.[48] Iran rejected the offer, and shut off supplies in April. Such a move had an ideological basis.

By the spring of 1980 Iran had developed a fairly coherent foreign policy around Principles 152 to 154 of its constitution. Among other things they prescribed 'non-alignment with respect to the hegemonist superpowers' and protection of 'the just struggles of the oppressed and the deprived in every corner of the globe'. Iranian leaders divided the world into oppressor nations and the oppressed. The two superpowers were the chief oppressors. Since Iran was one of the oppressed nations, it identified with others like itself. It was not enough to be merely non-aligned with power blocs, Iranian leaders argued. It was necessary to destroy their present economic, political, military and cultural domination of the Third World. By so doing revolutionary Third World states would inspire the oppressed peoples to intensify their national liberation movements. Out of this thinking arose Iran's decisions to aid certain national liberation movements, forge strong links with leading Third World countries, and to cultivate good relations with small nations within the power blocs and outside.

The last decision benefited East European states, particularly when it enabled them to buy Iranian oil on a barter basis. The chief beneficiary was Rumania. In April 1980 it contracted to buy 100,000 b/d, the largest amount for any Soviet bloc country. Good economic relations between Tehran and Bucharest dated back to the late 1960s when Rumania became Iran's main oil customer in East Europe. It was then assisting Iran to build a tractor assembly plant in Tabriz. With an output of 30,000 tractors a year in the early 1980s, this factory was able to meet most of the national demand.[49] The two-way trade between Iran and Rumania rose to $928 million in 1981-2, a record.

Bulgaria was the next most important trading partner of Iran in the Soviet bloc. Economic links between Tehran and Sofia grew in the mid-1970s during the oil boom: Bulgaria's nationalised truck company played a significant role in transporting goods from Europe to Iran via Turkey. At one stage, this activity engaged a third of Bulgaria's 7,500 trucks.[50] After the revolution, as the Islamic Republic prepared to face the Western embargo in the spring of 1980, it called on Bulgaria to transport goods overland to Iran. It did. That caused a spurt in trade which continued even after the embargo had been lifted. In 1982-3 the two-way trade between Iran and Bulgaria amounted to $400 million.[51]

While Poland has been assisting Iran in developing its coal industry, Czechoslovakia and East Germany have taken particular interest in Iran's power generation plans, and Hungary in its agricultural projects. In 1982 East Germany signed contracts for two power plants worth $22.5 million. Trade between Tehran and East Berlin rose fourfold in as many years since the revolution, and was in the neighbourhood of $200 million.

Iran has had no political or diplomatic problems with these (small) nations of the Eastern bloc. Its economic and diplomatic links with them have remained unaffected by the developments in the Gulf War. Contrary is the case with Tehran's political relations with Moscow.

When Iran considered attacking Iraq in early July 1982, the Soviet Union cautioned against the move. At the UN Security Council it voted for the resolution which called for a ceasefire and withdrawal to the international border. When Iran rejected the Security Council resolution and invaded Iraq, Moscow contrasted Tehran's action to the earlier Iraqi move to withdraw unilaterally from Iran. On 21 July the *Literaturnaya Gazeta* (Literary Gazette) commented that the Iranian invasion of Iraq benefited the US and Israel by distracting Arab states from Lebanon (then being invaded by Israel) and by giving a pretext to the US for increased military activity in the Gulf region. To Tehran such statements echoed sentiments expressed earlier by Baghdad.

Once Iraq was attacked, Moscow reassessed its position in the war in the context of its Friendship and Cooperation Treaty with Baghdad. According to this treaty, the two parties were required to contact each other in case of 'danger to the peace of either party or . . . danger to peace,' and to refrain from joining an alliance aimed against the other. The treaty called on the signatories to 'develop cooperation in the strengthening of their defence capacity'.[52] In view of this, Moscow decided to honour its pre-war arms contracts with Iraq, including those for advanced combat aircraft and tanks, but did so secretly. However, in late September, Saddam Hussein revealed the Soviet decision in order to deter Iran from launching an offensive against Iraq.

Ignoring the ploy, Iran carried out its attacks in October. It made some gains; but these were unequal to the effort it put into the offensives.[53] The Iraqis performed better than in the past. The Iranians attributed this to their newly received Soviet weapons. Tehran felt bitter towards Moscow. On 19 December the Iraqis fired two of their newly acquired Soviet-made ground-to-ground missiles, Frog-7, on Dezful, killing sixty-two and injuring 250. This made Iran more bitter towards the USSR. Reflecting the mood, the Afghan refugees' demonstration in Tehran on 27 December, to commemorate the Soviet intervention in Afghanistan, was particularly provocative. The Soviet ambassador protested. In reply the Iranian foreign ministry blamed 'abundant Soviet political and military aid to Iraq' as responsible for 'bringing many [Iranian] towns under Iraqi artillery fire'.[54] Expressing the view prevalent in the Soviet media, the National Voice of Iran Radio said in its broadcast of 11 January 1983 that Iranian backing for Afghan rebels would further strain relations between Tehran and Moscow, and isolate the Iranian revolution in the international arena. On 19 January a Tehran Radio commentary attacked the Soviet stand on the war. 'The Soviet Union took sides after seeing Saddam Hussein suffer one defeat after another, gradually making public its pro-Saddam attitude,' it said. A week later Iran expelled the Tass correspondent, Oleg Zuinko, by refusing to renew his visa.

The Iranian authorities took a series of actions against the Tudeh Party. These were as much specific moves against certain leaders and members of the party as they were efforts to destroy the political and cultural influence of one of the two superpowers in Iran – a major objective of Iranian foreign policy. As described earlier, the Tudeh was banned in early May 1983. The government coupled this action with the expulsion of eighteen Soviet diplomats, including four military attachés and four first secretaries. (In return the Soviet government expelled three Iranian diplomats.) It was significant that Iran's final moves against the Tudeh Party and Soviet diplomats came in the aftermath of the Iraqi attack on Dezful with three Soviet-made missiles on 22 April.

Soviet military assistance to Iraq was one major barrier to good relations between Moscow and Tehran, the other being the Soviet presence in Afghanistan. 'As long as the Soviets are in Afghanistan we cannot be your friend,' said Hashemi-Rafsanjani to V.K. Boldyrev, the Soviet ambassador in Tehran, in late May.[55]

But Iran was not content with merely reacting to other states' actions. It wanted to act in 'the defence of the rights of all Muslims', as stated in Principle 152 of the constitution. 'All Muslims' included those in the Soviet Union. In late May 1983 Iran launched a campaign on behalf of 'the oppressed Muslims in the USSR'. Propaganda posters showed the Kremlin as the capital of the Devil. 'Yesterday the Satan looked like Carter; today he wears the face of Yuri Andropov [the Soviet leader],' said Ayatollah Hojati Kermani. 'But we know the Satan behind the mask.'[56]

The Iranian campaign was directed at rekindling interest in Islam among the Muslims of the Soviet Union's southern republics of Azerbaijan, Kazhakistan, Kirghizia, Tajikistan, Turkmenia and Uzbekistan. Four-fifths of the USSR's forty-five million Muslims lived there. Secularisation of Soviet Muslims was obvious from the fact that there were only about 500 mosques in the USSR compared to an estimated 25,000 before the Bolshevik revolution, and that there were only two schools for training Muslim clerics.[57]

A mild revival in Islam had begun in these republics before the Iranian authorities took to beaming radio broadcasts at their inhabitants. One of the manifestations was the rise in the number of unofficial clerics. In late 1983 Turkmenia, with a population of 2.8 million, was reported to have 300 such clerics. Following his visit to the Soviet Union, Fakhr al-Din Hejazi, a Majlis deputy, said that he had been told by Muslims in Soviet Azerbaijan that during Ramadan they listened to Ardebil Radio to find out the correct times for breaking the fast.[58] Such statements tallied with Soviet assessments of the situation. Soviet officials agreed that Azerbaijan and Tajikistan had proved susceptible to Iranian propaganda. Like their counterparts in Iranian Azerbaijan, Muslims in Soviet Azerbaijan were Shia. (There was also an Iranian consulate in Baku.) With their language akin to Persian, Tajiks had always been culturally close to Iranians. In these republics there was a growing demand for mosques and religious schools, and more and more women were adopting Islamic dress.[59] These developments were viewed with disapproval by Soviet authorities, and created ill-will against the Islamic Republic of Iran.

Along with this came Tehran's ban on the Tudeh and intensification of the persecution of Tudeh members and sympathisers. The Soviet media turned decidedly anti-Tehran. A study by the Iranians of the Soviet broadcasts in Persian on Iran showed that of the 370 commentaries by Soviet radio stations between 23 August 1983 and 5 January 1984, two-thirds were concerned with the Tudeh and were critical of the Iranian government.[60] Others apparently referred to Iran's behaviour in the Gulf War.

Moscow blamed Tehran for its refusal to end the Gulf conflict. On 8 June *Krasnaya Zvezda* accused America of secretly supplying weapons and spare parts to Iran to keep the war going, and thus extending destabilisation in the region and giving itself an excuse to build up its military presence in the Gulf and the Arabian Sea. Six months later the paper accused Iran of deliberately blocking a settlement of the war.[61]

The strength of American as well as French and British navies in the region rose sharply in September 1983, when Iran threatened to close the Hormuz Strait. On 1 November the USSR backed the UN Security Council's call for a ceasefire, which was ignored by Iran. It was against this background that Tariq Aziz, Iran's foreign minister, held a series of meetings with his Soviet counterpart, Andrei Gromyko, in Moscow. Their joint statement expressed 'the shared desire of the two countries . . . to develop bilateral relations on the basis of the Soviet-Iraqi Treaty of Friendship and Cooperation'.[62] What the statement did not say was that the Soviet Union had agreed to sell fresh quantities of weapons to Iraq.[63]

This was as well, because otherwise the USSR Supreme Soviet's message in mid-January 1984 to the Iranian Majlis for cooperation between their countries 'in the struggle against world imperialism and US acts of aggression' would have been greeted in Tehran with contempt. As it was, Hashemi-Rafsanjani received the Soviet ambassador, bearing the message of the Supreme Soviet, with attentive courtesy. He pointed out that Saddam Hussein had attacked Iran as 'an agent of America' and that he was now being aided by 'Jordan, Sudan, Egypt, Morocco and reaction in the region'. He advised the Soviet Union to notice 'Iranian aid and presence, together with the Lebanese people, being active in Lebanon against the Western occupiers and Israel, and actively engaged in the anti-imperialist struggle'.[64]

Tehran was pursuing policies which damaged the interests of the West and pro-Western governments in the Gulf and elsewhere while being at odds with the Soviet Union which stood to gain by the diminution of Western influence. In a way Iran was following the old concept of 'negative balance', the only difference being that the revolutionary regime was now acting on its own rather than merely reacting to the moves of its northern neighbour or the West. That was one of the main differences between revolutionary Iran and Pahlavi Iran.

IRAN AND THE WEST

By the late eighteenth century Britain had emerged as the leading imperialist power in south Asia. In order to secure its empire in the Indian subcontinent from Russian encroachment, it tried to control Afghanistan and match Russian influence in Iran. The result was a series of British treaties with Fath Ali Shah in 1801, 1807 and 1814. During the next two decades British influence in Tehran had become so established that the Czar colluded with Britain to ensure the coronation of Muhammad Mirza as the new Shah in 1834. The 1841 Anglo-Iranian Treaty stipulated low tariffs on British imports and gave British subjects the same extra-territorial rights as had been given earlier to Russians.

Nasser al-Din Shah's attempt in 1856-7 to conquer Herat, Afghanistan, soured relations between Tehran and London. His forces were repulsed by the British. According to the Paris Treaty of 1857, Iran renounced its rights over Herat.

Following the Indian Mutiny in 1857, London pressed Tehran for rights to telegraphic lines through Iran. The Shah agreed. The work, begun in 1859, was completed in 1872. That year the Shah granted a multitude of rights to Baron de Reuter for a paltry sum.[1] 'The agreement contained the most complete surrender of the entire resources of a kingdom into foreign hands that had ever been dreamed of, much less accomplished, in history,' wrote Lord Curzon, British viceroy of India.[2] Although popular outcry against the concession led to its withdrawal, the Shah compensated Baron de Reuter by giving him banking and mineral rights in 1889. Baron de Reuter's company found no oil in the ten years it held the concession. In 1901 the Shah granted oil concessions over 500,000 sq. miles to William Knox D'Arcy for £20,000 advance, £20,000 in paid-up shares, and 16 per cent of net profits. D'Arcy was a British speculator who had earlier mined gold in Australia. It was not until 1908 that he found oil in commercial quantities at Masjid-e Suleiman. His firm expanded to become the Anglo-Persian Oil Company in 1909 (later called Anglo-Iranian Oil

Company and then British Petroleum). Commercial production began in 1912. With the British admiralty's decision to switch from coal to oil, the importance of petroleum increased. To ensure supplies, the British government acquired 40 per cent of APOC shares.

Following the Czar's success in securing the dismissal of Shuster as the treasurer general, Britain joined Russia in pressuring Tehran to formally accept the 1907 Anglo-Russian Entente. The regent agreed. But the Majlis had still to ratify the agreement when the First World War broke out in 1914. Britain and Russia controlled Iran to the extent of guarding the main roads and garrisoning cities in their respective sectors of influence.

By the end of the war the Iranian government was in such financial straits that only British subsidies of £225,000 a month kept it afloat. This encouraged Lord Curzon, British foreign minister, to realise his dream of absorbing Iran into the British empire. He secured the Iranian government's signature on the Anglo-Iranian Agreement of 1919, which reduced Iran to a British protectorate. When the terms were disclosed in August, there was a furore not only in Moscow but also in Washington. The American Petroleum Institute warned the US state department that the treaty would strengthen APOC's exclusive rights on Iranian oil.

As described earlier, the British aided Colonel Reza Khan of the Cossack Brigade to mount a successful coup against the government of Gilani.[3] General Edmund Ironside, commander of the British forces in Iran, was the key figure. When the newly appointed government of Zia al-Din Tabatabai presented the Anglo-Iranian Agreement to the Majlis, the latter rejected it. Yet this government requested London to allow British advisers to stay on to help reorganise military and civilian administrations. Tabatabai told the British envoy privately that the 1919 Agreement had to be abrogated 'to throw dust in the eyes of Bolsheviks and native malcontents', and allow the formation of a credible, reformist government.[4]

Having got himself installed on the Peacock Throne, Reza Shah tried to balance British influence with German. He appointed German financial experts to the Bank Melli (National Bank) established in 1928. Between then and 1932, Junkers, the German airline company, secured all rights for internal Iranian flights. Germany also developed shipping with Iran. Following a most favoured nation trade agreement with Germany, Tehran signed a friendship and cooperation treaty with Berlin.

All this made only a small dent in the British domination of Iran. Leaving aside APOC's imports and exports, Iranian foreign trade was dominated by Britain in the 1920s. APOC was the single largest employer in the country, engaging more people than all the Iranian industries together.[5] While APOC's output quadrupled during the 1920s, Iran's oil income only doubled. In 1930 APOC refused to pay 4 per cent tax on all income. This angered the Shah. On 7 November 1932 he cancelled the D'Arcy concession. His decision was greeted with national rejoicing in the streets.

The matter was taken to the Council of the League of Nations. Under its aegis a new agreement was signed in April 1933. This provided for reduction of the concession area from 500,000 sq. miles to 100,000 sq. miles in two stages, and the royalty to be paid at the rate of four shillings per tonne of oil sold or exported, rather than as a percentage of final profits. APOC guaranteed Iran a minimum annual sum of £750,000. In return Iran extended the agreement from 1961 to 1993, by which time all oil was expected to have been extracted.

When the Shah awarded the contract for building the Trans-Iranian Railway to a Scandinavian consortium in 1933, German companies were the main beneficiaries. The next year, at the suggestion of the Iranian legation in Germany – then under Nazi rule – the Shah changed the name of his country from Persia (a derivative of Fars) to Iran, the homeland of the Aryan race. This meshed well with Adolf Hitler's declaration of Iran as an Aryan country. Helped by Iran's Monopoly of Foreign Trade Law of 1931, and the presence of German experts at the Bank Melli, Iranian-German trade increased rapidly.

Hitler saw the military and political potential of Iran as an anti-Soviet bastion. With this, Germany's economic penetration of northern Iran deepened considerably. On the eve of the Second World War, Germany was Iran's leading trading partner, followed by the USSR, Britain and the US.

The January 1942 Tripartite Agreement of Britain, the USSR and Iran limited the Iranian army's role to one of internal security, and described the US as an adjunct to Britain in the task of delivering supplies to the Soviet Union through Iran. In March Iran was declared eligible for aid under the US Lend Lease Act of 1941. In October the US Persian Gulf Command Service was set up in Ahvaz under General Donald Connolly; and two months later non-combatant American troops began arriving. At their peak, 28,000 US troops were engaged in manning the Trans-Iranian Railway from the Gulf to the Soviet border, signals, road making and intelligence.

Muhammad Reza Shah saw in this development a chance to balance British and Soviet influence with American. In February 1943 Arthur Millspaugh was appointed the administrator general of finance of Iran, and was authorised to collect, transport and distribute foodgrains, and to control prices, rents, wages, distribution of goods and foreign trade. For all practical purposes he became Iran's economic overlord. The Shah declared war against Germany on 9 September 1943. He tried to win an independent status for American military in Iran, but failed.

Nonetheless, American penetration of Iran's military and civilian administrations had begun, and continued for the next thirty-five years. Colonel Norman Schwarzkopf, former New Jersey state police chief, was appointed an adviser to the interior minister in charge of gendarmerie affairs, and given 'attributes of command'. As chief of the US army mission, Major-General Clarence Ridley was authorised access to 'any and all records, correspondence, and plans relating to the administration of the [Iranian] army needed by him', and empowered to investigate, summon and question any member of the Iranian army in 'matters which in his opinion will assist him' in his duties.[6] Ridley helped the Shah to augment his army from 60,000 to 90,000, and assisted him in securing military equipment from Washington.

American missions to the Iranian army and gendarmerie were active in bolstering the efficiency of these forces. Soon after they had occupied Azerbaijan and Kurdistan in late 1946, members of the missions undertook inspection tours in the two provinces.

In the spring of 1947 America extended to Iran the Truman Doctrine of March 1947 which committed the US to aiding Greece and Turkey to maintain their integrity and independence. On 6 October Washington and Tehran signed an agreement which allowed the US to sell military equipment to Iran. It specified that Iranian army affairs may not be entrusted to a third party without American consent. Moscow protested at this, but in vain. In 1948 Washington provided Tehran with $60 million worth of weapons.

While Iran forged military links with the US, its grievances against the British-owned AIOC multiplied. Between 1941 and 1948 oil production rose from 50.8 million barrels to 190.4 million barrels; but Iran's oil revenue grew only from £4 million to £9.2 million. In contrast the AIOC paid £31.7 million in taxes to the British government in 1948.[7] Relations between management and workers at the AIOC were appallingly bad. There was a widespread strike in July 1946. It was broken only after troops had been used to fire on strikers, causing forty-seven deaths.

In September 1948 the Iranian government submitted a twenty-five-point memorandum to the AIOC outling the company's infringements of the 1933 agreement. It accused the AIOC of paying low royalties, evading local taxes, interfering in Iranian politics, and of having used the threat of force to secure the 1933 agreement. Iran pressed for a 50:50 sharing of net profits instead of the current 20 per cent. The AIOC refused.

Nonetheless, negotiations between the two sides ensued. These led to a Supplemental Agreement which was initialled on 17 July 1949. But because the current Majlis ended on 28 July, the ratification of the deal had to wait. The new Majlis appointed a committee in June 1950 to study the agreement. In November the committee rejected it. Against the background of popular demonstrations for cancelling the original 1933 deal with the AIOC, the government withdrew the Supplemental Agreement.

In February 1951, taking its cue from the Arabian American Oil Company's agreement of a 50:50 sharing of profits with Saudi Arabia, the AIOC promised to consider a similar deal with Iran. But it was too late. By now the Majlis oil committee was considering oil nationalisation. Following Premier Razmara's assassination on 7 March, the Majlis adopted the oil committee's recommendation for nationalisation. On 26 March, following a walkout by AIOC employees, the government declared martial law in Khuzistan. But disturbances continued. It took AIOC management a month to settle the strike. Between 28 April and 1 May the Iranian parliament's two houses passed the nationalisation bill and the Shah signed it. On 1 May Mussadiq became premier and immediately formed the National Iranian Oil Company. Sir Francis Shepherd, the British ambassador in Tehran, appealed to Henry Grady, the US ambassador, to intervene. Grady replied that he had no such instructions from Washington.

The US tried to mediate in the dispute. It pressed Britain to accept the principle of nationalisation, and condemned Iran for its unilateral abrogation of the 1933 agreement. It balanced its reassurance to Britain that US oil companies would not undertake operations in Iran with one to Mussadiq that US economic aid to Iran, including an Export-Import Bank loan of $25 million, would continue.[8] American pressure brought the two sides to the negotiating table, but the talks proved futile. The last batch of AIOC employees left Iran on 4 October 1951.

Britain took the dispute to the UN Security Council. The Council decided on 19 October to postpone discussion until after the ruling by the International Court of Justice at the Hague. A week later a Conservative government was elected to office in Britain. It took a harder line than the preceding Labour administration. Premier Winston Churchill and foreign minister Anthony Eden demanded compensation for Iranian actions. At the behest of the US, the World Bank tried to resolve the dispute. It failed.

Now the US gave up the pretence of neutrality, and sided with Britain. In January 1952 it cut off military aid to Iran. Two months later it rejected Iran's request for a loan of $100 million badly needed to cover the foreign trade deficit caused by the virtual stoppage of oil exports. Only the modest Point Four (economic) aid programme worth

$16 million was approved on 1 April.

On 22 July the ICJ ruled that the Iran-AIOC dispute was not within its jurisdiction. The verdict came a day after the reinstatement of Mussadiq as premier. The rising power of Mussadiq at the Shah's expense alarmed Britain and America. At the same time they knew that the economic crisis was deepening in Iran, and that time was on their side. Not surprisingly, Mussadiq suggested resumption of talks to Britain on the basis of nationalisation. In reply Churchill and American president Harry Truman demanded that compensation for the AIOC be decided by the ICJ. Mussadiq agreed, but Britain let the matter drop. This did not surprise Mussadiq. He knew that Britain had decided to destroy his government. The arrest on 13 October 1952 of an Iranian general and three businessmen for plotting with 'a foreign embassy' in Tehran showed Mussadiq that the danger was real.[9] To thwart a pro-British coup against him, Mussadiq severed diplomatic relations with Britain on 22 October.

In November Mussadiq appealed to the US for a loan of $100 million. Since these were the last days of the Truman administration, he received no reply. At the same time the fear of total stoppage of US economic aid made Mussadiq wary of implementing the oil and trade agreements he had signed in 1951 with the Soviet Union and its allies. Also strengthening ties with the USSR would have run counter to his interpretation of the 'negative equilibrium' in foreign policy: it amounted to a rehash of the old 'three power game', with the US being the third power to counter British and Soviet influence.

But he was mistaken. America was backing Britain. With the installing of General Dwight Eisenhower as American president and the appointment of John Foster Dulles as US secretary of state, Anglo-American cooperation in Iran grew stronger. As described earlier, the CIA took over the secret British plan to overthrow the Mussadiq government, codenamed it Operation Ajax, and assigned it to Kermit Roosevelt.[10]

In May 1953 Mussadiq combined his efforts to wrest control of the Iranian military from the Shah with securing more aid from the US. On 28 May he wrote to Eisenhower stating that if he failed to receive further American aid he would try 'elsewhere'. Iran was in dire straits. In 1952 it had produced only 10.1 million barrels of oil, 96 per cent down on the 1950 figure. The US aid of $21.3 million was being used to pay military and civilian bureaucracies.[11] After deliberate evasion of the issue for some weeks Eisenhower replied on 24 June saying that the US was not in a position either to give Iran more aid or buy its oil. The next day the US state department decided to activate its Operation Ajax.

Kermit Roosevelt arrived incognito in Iran on 19 July. Some days

later Brigadier-General Norman Schwarzkopf arrived in Tehran on a
diplomatic passport as part of his 'worldwide tour'. He had a meeting
with the Shah and then with Roosevelt. American military aid to Iran
since 1942 had enabled the US government to build up contacts with
Iranian military officers. These were being used extensively to plot the
downfall of Mussadiq.

But, as described earlier, the Roosevelt-Shah plan went awry when
the chief of staff, General Riahi, arrested Colonel Nasseri of the
Imperial Guards on 15/16 August.[12] As the Shah fled on 16 August,
Roosevelt and his co-plotters did some quick thinking. They decided to
mount a military coup on 19 August. They were inadvertently aided in
this by Mussadiq's decision to use troops and police on 19 August to
curb anti-Shah demonstrators in Tehran – a decision precipitated by
the US ambassador's promise of American aid if law and order were
restored.

Mussadiq fell on 19 August. 'The news of Mussadiq's fall from
power reached me during my convalescence, when my wife and I, with
my son, were cruising the Mediterranean between Greek islands,'
wrote Sir Anthony Eden, the British premier, in his memoirs. 'I slept
happily that night.'[13] As a bitter adversary of Mussadiq, the British
government had good reasons to celebrate his downfall. But it did not
yield the results Eden had anticipated.

The departure of Mussadiq did not lead to the restitution of the
AIOC. The three-year-long oil nationalisation movement had created
too much bitterness against the British among Iranians for them to
return in their old imperial glory. The final outcome of the oil episode
was that Britain ceased to be a superpower as it had been in Iran since
1841. The closing of the British embassy in Tehran in October 1952
ended an era, for ever. The new superpower in Iran now was America,
which had emerged as the undisputed leader of the West after the
Second World War.

The American era

It was a measure of American ascendancy in Iran that, following the
overthrow of Mussadiq, the US state department seriously considered
taking over the management of Iranian oil. The British protested
vehemently, and so did American oil companies. Finally the state
department, working closely with Torklid Reiber, a former oil
executive, decided to keep intact the oil nationalisation law and the
National Iranian Oil Company, with the latter awarding the rights to,
and management of, Iranian oil for the next forty years to a consortium
of Western oil companies. Its shares were divided thus: the AIOC, 40

per cent; Royal Dutch Shell, 14 per cent; five US oil companies (Exxon, Gulf, Mobil, Socal and Texaco), 8 per cent each; and Compagnie Française des Pétroles, 6 per cent.[14] The consortium's exploitation area of 100,000 sq. miles was limited to Khuzistan.

The new oil agreement between the NIOC and the consortium was signed in August 1954 and approved by the parliament two months later. The first oil shipment to a foreign country occurred in November. During the remaining two months of the year, 22.4 million barrels of oil were produced.

Washington was generous in its aid to Tehran. It provided Iran with emergency aid on 5 September 1953 of $45 million, twice the current level of annual assistance. Military aid quadrupled. Once Iran had signed an agreement with the Western oil consortium, American aid came pouring in. Between September 1953 and December 1956, US economic aid to Iran amounted to $280 million, and military assistance to $134 million. Comparative figures for 1949-52 were $16.4 million and $16.4 million.[15]

In October-November 1956, a military expedition by the British, French and Israeli governments to capture the recently nationalised Suez Canal in Egypt was frustrated. This marked the final expulsion of British and French imperialism from the region: a development seen by Eisenhower as creating a vacuum. 'The vacuum must be filled by the United States before it is filled by Russia,' he said in a speech on 1 January 1956.[16] From this arose his doctrine to protect any Middle East nation, or group of nations, from 'overt armed aggression' from any 'nation controlled by international communism'. This was endorsed by Congress in March.

President Camille Chamoun of Lebanon became the first leader in the region to endorse the Eisenhower Doctrine. Lebanon was in the midst of a civil war between pro-West, right wing forces and nationalist-leftist forces when a republican coup in July overthrew the Iraqi monarchy. Most Western capitals attributed this event to the machinations of Gamal Abdul Nasser, then president of the United Arab Republic, consisting of Egypt and Syria. Arguing that the UAR was 'a nation controlled by international communism', Chamoun asked for American troops in Lebanon, and secured them. Using the same argument about republican Iraq, the Shah tried to obtain military commitments from the US. But he found the terms offered by Washington unattractive. So, as described earlier, he used the threat of signing a non-aggression treaty with Moscow to gain better terms. This was a Machiavellian move which the Shah was fond of describing as part of his foreign policy of 'positive nationalism'. In March 1959 Iran signed an executive agreement on 'military cooperation' with the US. It fell within the purview of the Eisenhower Doctrine. Since it was not a treaty, it did not need US Senate approval. Among other things it provided for consultations between the parties in case of an aggression by a communist or communist-inspired country.

By the spring of 1959 America was involved in every aspect of Iranian life except religion. The US embassy in Tehran was as important a power centre as the Shah's palace. The extent of American influence over the Pahlavi regime could be judged by an unsigned memorandum (in English) found in the archives of the Shah's Marmar Palace after the revolution.

Written apparently by a group of experts, based either in Tehran or Washington, the memorandum provided guidelines to the Shah on his rule. First, an orchestrated campaign should be mounted to project the Shah as the Father of the People, Farmandeh. Second, all effort must be made to bolster the prestige of the Shah and the throne. Special attention must be paid to win the active support of women. Third, the middle class should be expanded and strengthened. Being secular, and averse to extremism, it could become a solid foundation for the Pahlavi regime. Fourth, old politicians should be phased out while new and young faces are introduced to public life. Fifth, the monarch should be active in international affairs, and seen to be so. Sixth, the monarch should take a keen interest in religious affairs, appear at mosques frequently, and try to displace Qom's ayatollahs from religious leadership. Seventh, intelligence should be organised and controlled with great care. There should be a special focus on the air force. It can speedily crush a mutiny in the army, and, being small and compact, it is much easier to control than the army.[17] It is worth noting that most of the Shah's actions during the first decade after the August 1953 coup stemmed from these recommendations.

The undated memorandum must have been written in late 1953 or in the following year. For a national intelligence body suggested by it (which was to become the forerunner of Savak) was formed in 1955. The law which formalised Savak was passed in March 1957. 'The Central Intelligence Agency provided the initial inspiration, training and guidance for Savak,' state Michael Leeden and William Lewis, American researchers. 'Later Israeli and Turkish intelligence agencies joined the American intelligence community in bolstering Savak's capabilities.'[18] The March 1959 agreement on military cooperation between Tehran and Washington provided formal channels for close cooperation in military intelligence.

With the arrival of John Kennedy at the White House in January 1961, American interference in Iran's domestic affairs grew. Kennedy addressed a letter to the Shah urging him to tackle corruption in the royal family and his personal entourage, and initiate socio-economic reform. He advised the Pahlavi ruler to appoint Ali Amini as prime minister. The Shah resented the pressure, but complied. Overcoming his personal dislike for Amini, the Shah appointed him premier in May 1961; and the compliant Majlis provided the necessary approval.

Though the Shah compelled Amini to resign in July 1962, the implementation of US-inspired reform – votes for women, agrarian reform etc. – continued. For the Shah wanted American arms, and these were forthcoming only if he persevered with reforming the social system. An ongoing military assistance programme from 1953 to 1962 had brought the total to $478.4 million – on a par with the total economic aid.[19]

The referendum in support of the White Revolution in January 1963 pleased the US administration. Kennedy congratulated the Shah on the result. In a secret memo to Kennedy on 28 April 1963, Dean Rusk, secretary of state, said, 'The US is strongly identified with the [Shah's] regime and the reform programme'. He then warned the president that 'the Shah's greatest liability may well be his vulnerability to charges of both reactionary and radical opposition that he is a foreign puppet'. More interestingly, in an appendix to the memorandum, Rusk outlined a five-point strategy on Iran's domestic affairs: 'Encouraging the Shah in his "White Revolution" on a course fast enough to maintain lower class support for the regime but slow enough to avoid social and/or economic collapse – i.e., revolution; maintaining the armed forces' morale and loyalty to the regime; improving the counter-insurgency capacity of the military and of rural and urban police forces; discouraging governmental impulses towards unduly harsh and repressive measures against non-communist opposition elements; and encouraging the detaching of moderate conservative and liberal opposition elements, and the enlistment of their loyalties and energies in the Shah's programme of social reform and emancipation'.[20]

Knowing the methods the Shah used to tackle the religious opposition in June 1963, it was obvious that the US administration failed to curb the Shah's 'unduly harsh and repressive measures against non-communist opposition'. From 1965 onwards Savak routinely employed torture on prisoners.

Iran's relations with America became a subject of public debate in the summer of 1964 when a bill granting diplomatic immunity to all US citizens working on military projects in Iran was presented to the Majlis. That this bill had to be passed before Washington would grant Tehran a $200 million loan to purchase American weapons was one more instance of Iran's dependence on the US.[21] Oddly enough, the Shah needed American arms to pursue, what he described, 'national independent foreign policy'.

The Shah saw the British withdrawal from Kuwait in June 1961 presaging total British withdrawal from the Gulf. This led him to improve relations with the Soviets in late 1962 so that he could shift the focus of Iranian defence from the north to the south. He did so in March 1965. He placed the newly formed Third Corps in Shiraz. This set him on an arms race with the Gulf Arab states, particularly Iraq and Egypt. To pay for the higher military budget he pressured the Western oil consortium in 1966 to raise production.

He was helped in this by the Arab-Israeli war of early June 1967, when Arab states imposed an oil embargo against the Western countries backing Israel. The embargo lasted until the end of August. Western oil companies in Iran raised output and filled the gap left by the Arabs. In 1967 Iranian oil production rose to 950 million barrels from 778 million in the previous year, and contributed $751 million to the government treasury.

With this, the Shah's ambition grew. He requested advanced weapons from Washington. The US defence department's International Security Agency recommended rejecting the Shah's request, arguing that Iran no longer faced an immediate threat from the USSR along its common border. But the state department argued otherwise, and won.

In June 1969 President Richard Nixon enunciated a doctrine which clearly favoured the Shah's arms build-up. Conceived against the background of the failure of direct US military involvement in South Vietnam, the Nixon Doctrine encouraged select American allies in the Third World to use US military and economic aid to bolster their fighting forces. In short, America was to be more of an arms supplier, and less of a gendarmerie, for its allies outside the North Atlantic Treaty Organisation. In this scheme of things, Iran was to continue occupying the pre-eminent position it had had since the August 1953 coup. Between 1953 and 1969 it had received as much US military assistance in grants as all other countries combined.[22]

By the end of 1971 Iran was in a position to ask the US to stop its grants. The reason was the rise in oil prices, caused in the first instance by a republican coup in Libya on 1 September 1969. Conscious of the rising demand for oil in the West, and the relaxing of the petroleum import quota for America by Nixon in 1970, Libya imposed production cuts on oil companies as a pressure tactic to secure higher taxes and royalties. It worked. Western oil corporations dreaded the idea of the Gulf states emulating Libya. They therefore agreed to negotiate with Iran, Iraq and Saudi Arabia as the representatives of all the Gulf states, and reached an accord with them in Tehran on 14 February 1971. The Shah played a prominent role in this. The agreement, valid for five years, required oil corporations to pay 55 per cent of their profits as tax, and raise the oil price immediately by 21 per cent, from $1.79 a barrel to $2.17. Following the American dollar's devaluation in

August 1971, oil price was raised by another 8.5 per cent. With its oil output at 1,657 million barrels in 1971, Iran earned $2,060 million.

The Shah was now preoccupied with military and foreign affairs: a preoccupation accentuated by his plan to fill the vacuum to be caused by the British withdrawal from the Gulf by late 1971. In this he had the backing of the US. As soon as the British announced their intention in January 1968 to leave the Gulf by December 1971, the Shah renewed the 150-year-old Iranian claim of sovereignty over Bahrain, an archipelago of islands. He protested when London included Bahrain in the Federal Council of seven trucial states and Qatar in July 1968. Early next year, however, he foreswore the use of force, and promised to abide by the wishes of the Bahraini people. In March 1970, at the Shah's suggestion, Iran and Britain referred the dispute to the UN secretary general, and agreed to accept his decision. Following consultations with the islanders, the secretary general's representative reported that an overwhelming majority wished Bahrain to become a sovereign state on its own. The Iranian Majlis accepted this in May 1970, thus preparing the way for Bahrain's independence in August 1971.

Just before the federation of trucial principalities – the United Arab Emirates – was to be declared independent in December 1971, the Shah pressed his claim to three islands at the mouth of the Gulf: Abu Musa, Little Tunb and Great Tunk. Abu Musa was administered by the principality of Sharjah, and the two Tunbs by Ras al Khaima. Britain aided the Shah to secure part possession of Abu Musa, with the Shah paying the Sharjah ruler £1.5 million annually. But the Ras al Khaima ruler proved intransigent, refusing even to join the United Arab Emirates. In November Iranian forces occupied the uninhabited Little Tunb, and captured Big Tunb after some fighting. British complicity in securing these islands to Iran was widely known. Protesting against this, Iraq severed diplomatic relations with both Tehran and London. The next year Sultan Qaboos ibn Saed of Oman handed over the tiny island of Umm al Ghanem to Iran when the Shah began aiding the Sultan in his campaign against the leftist insurgents in the western province of Dhofar. Thus the Iranian navy acquired a string of islands across the Gulf's mouth in the aftermath of British withdrawal. London had greater faith in the military capability of Iran than that of the fledgling UAE.

With British and American backing, the Shah was now becoming the gendarmerie of the Gulf, openly declaring that he would not tolerate any revolution on the Arab side of the Gulf. In the words of James Noyes, US assistant secretary of defence, Iran was 'the most determined and best equipped state in the Gulf to assert leadership'.[23] Iran was a shining example of the Nixon Doctrine at work, a matter of great pride to the American president.

Little wonder that, during his visit to Tehran in May 1972, Nixon promised the Shah that he could buy any non-nuclear weapons he wanted. Nixon also agreed that the US would train Iranians in the use and maintenance of these weapons, and that it would cooperate in instigating Kurdish insurgency in neighbouring Iraq, which had just concluded a friendship treaty with Moscow. American arms sales to Iran increased eightfold in two years: from $519 million in (fiscal) 1972 to $4,373 million in 1974. This happened at a time when the US arms manufacturing boom, caused by the Vietnam war, was tapering off, and weapons salesmen were looking desperately for fresh outlets.

Personal relations between Muhammad Reza Pahlavi and Richard Nixon were excellent. They had been friends since the first Eisenhower administration, when Nixon was vice-president. The Shah contributed generously to Nixon's presidential campaign fund in 1968.[24] Very early in his own administration President Nixon made a secret deal with the Iranian monarch: if the Shah would let the CIA set up two electronic surveillance stations in north Iran to eavesdrop on the communications traffic of Iran's neighbour – including the southern republics of the USSR containing Soviet testing sites for missiles and other weapons – he would let Savak operate inside the US to monitor the activities of tens of thousands of Iranian students and exiles. Direct links between the CIA and Savak developed to the point that in 1972 the CIA was annually training 400 Savak operatives at its headquarters in Langley, Virginia.[25]

Soon after being re-elected president in November 1972, Nixon appointed Richard Helms – a career intelligence officer and CIA director for over six years – as the ambassador to Tehran. Also the CIA's Middle East headquarters was moved from Cyprus to Tehran. With this, intelligence links between Tehran and Washington became even closer than before. 'The intelligence and covert operations portion of the American connection . . . permitted the Shah to play a complex game in which his personal ambitions could be accommodated, while ensuring a congruence of American and other interests with the goals and objectives of his government,' state Michael Leeden and William Lewis. 'These ventures included the establishment of escape routes for Soviet defectors wishing to flee to the West, reverse penetration for intelligence collection, reconnaissance missions into Soviet territory, the establishment of border listening posts to intercept Soviet communications, the launching of joint exercises to counter the efforts of Arab terrorists to destabilise sensitive geographic areas, and the sharing of intelligence estimates on particular countries of mutual interests to Tehran and Washington.'[26]

The multiplicity of America's joint projects with Iran underlined the vital significance of Tehran to Washington. In the American strategy of 'Three Pillars' in the Middle East – Israel, Iran and Saudi Arabia – Iran was the central pillar. This stemmed from the geographical position of Iran; a country with land or sea frontiers with ten states, including Iraq, Turkey, the Soviet Union, Afghanistan and Pakistan. Only by having both Iran and Saudi Arabia in its camp could the US ensure Western access to Gulf oil, which was crucial to the economies of the West and Japan. Thus Iran had a unique place in the global strategy of America.

Among those who had a full understanding of Iran's value to the West was Henry Kissinger, national security adviser to President Nixon from January 1969 to September 1973, and then US secretary of state. Nixon's resignation in the wake of the Watergate scandal[27] made no difference to US-Iran ties. Continuation of Kissinger as secretary of state under President Gerald Ford kept Washington-Tehran relations on the same keel as before.

Intelligence links were so close that every Saturday morning the Shah had a two-hour meeting with the CIA station chief in Tehran.[28] As for the military connection, it grew even stronger due to the October 1973 Arab-Israeli war and the subsequent events. Despite pressures on him, the Shah refused to join the Arab oil boycott of the West. Yet he gained handsomely by the fourfold oil price rise which stemmed from it. Between January 1973 and January 1974 the price of one barrel of Gulf oil rose from $2.37 to $11.65, with the host government's income rising from $1.37 a barrel to $7. With its petroleum output at 2,211 million barrels in 1974, Iran's oil income jumped to $19,300 from $4,400 million in the previous year. In 1974 Iran became the largest buyer of American arms.

Despite lower petroleum production of 1,965 million barrels in 1975, Iran earned a record $20,500 million, thanks to a higher oil price than before. Once again Iran was at the top of the list of US weapons purchasers. It had the largest US Military Assistance Advisory Group in the world. The Shah agreed to let the CIA listening posts along the Soviet border be increased to eleven. In March 1975, Alfred Atherton, under-secretary of state, described the bilateral US-Iran tie as 'a very special one'. By then US military presence in Iran had become a regular feature of life. For instance, every air flight arrival in Iranian cities was greeted by an American voice on a public address system saying. 'This way all United States military personnel'.[29] A local US Armed Forces radio network was established in Iran.

In his letter to the Shah on 21 February 1976, President Ford wrote: 'I have let it be known to the senior officials of my administration who deal with these issues that they should keep constantly in mind the very great importance which I attach to the special relationship that we enjoy with Iran'.[30]

By now Iran was taking military and political initiatives in the region that were complementary to American moves. During his visit to Tehran in mid-August 1976, Kissinger remarked that this 'convergence of interest' had resulted in 'parallelism of views on many key problems that has made our cooperation a matter that is in the most profound interest of both countries'.[31]

Links between the two states were set to grow even stronger. Between 1976 and 1980 the number of American military and civilian personnel was expected to double from the current level of 24,000. During that period the American arms deliveries to Iran were estimated to total $12 billion to $15 billion. (The corresponding figure for 1950-70 was $1.8 billion.)[32] The trade between the countries during 1976-80 was expected to rise to $40 billion – with American exports at $24 billion, and Iranian non-oil exports at $2 billion, and oil shipments at $14 billion.

In 1974 America imported 469,000 b/d of Iranian oil, a record. Following the relaxing of the petroleum import quota in 1970, shipments of foreign oil into the US doubled every three years: from 11.3 per cent of the total home consumption in 1970 to 23 per cent in 1973 to 45 per cent in 1976. About two-fifths of this petroleum came from the Gulf, with Iran supplying nearly half of it. This gave Iran a certain leverage over the US, particularly after the Shah acquired direct control over production levels in the aftermath of the nationalisation in March 1973 of the Western oil consortium.

The Shah's decision to nationalise the Western oil companies in Iran went down badly in Washington. Nixon urged him to reconsider, but to no avail. Similarly when President Ford pressed the Shah in early 1974 to reduce oil prices, the latter suggested that the industrialised countries should first slash the prices of their exports. Despite American pressure, OPEC (of which Iran was a prominent member) raised the oil price by 10 per cent.

In return America and other Western countries overcharged Iran for their services and goods. Iranians felt that they were being charged excessively for US weapons and personnel. In 1975 they paid over $100,000 for the services of a typical American military technician.[33] In a dramatic gesture General Toufanian, Iran's deputy war minister, picked up a helicopter door handle priced $11.62, and said, 'This costs us one barrel of oil'.[34] Earlier he had complained to General Howard Fish of the US Defence Security Assistance Agency that the price of one weapons system had been raised by 50 per cent in three years. 'The price of oil has tripled,' replied General Fish.[35]

Many American politicians questioned the wisdom of selling sophisticated aircraft to Iran even before they had been put into production. They also condemned the corruption that the handling of such arms orders as 160 F-16 aircraft worth $3,400 million had spawned in the US as well as the Iranian ruling circle. The report of US Senate Foreign Relations Committee, released in early 1976, was generally critical of the arms sales to Iran. It concluded that since Iran would be unable to engage in major military operations without 'sustained US support', the current policy had raised the possibility of America getting drawn into a local conflict at a time and place chosen by the Shah. Moreover, said the report, by overriding normal Congressional review procedures, Nixon's July 1972 executive order on arms sales to Iran had created 'a bonanza for US weapons manufacturers, the procurement branches of the three US [armed] services, and the Defence Security Assistance Agency.'[36] The report upset the Shah.

Speaking on behalf of the White House, Kissinger disagreed with the report. During his visit to Tehran shortly thereafter he said at a press conference that the current pace of US arms sales to Iran would continue until 1980.

But the Shah was not to be reassured. The memory of the American retreat from Vietnam in April 1975 was too fresh in his mind. 'I am afraid that today America's credibility is not too high,' he said. 'We have ten other markets to provide us with what we need. These people are just waiting for that moment.'[37] In fact, when the US Congress had refused to approve the sale of nuclear power stations to Iran, the Shah had placed the orders with France.

By then Iran had been loaning funds to France as well as Britain. In 1974-5 Iran's trade balance was so large that it disbursed $2.38 billion in foreign loans, grants and investments – including $887 million to the International Monetary Fund and the World Bank, and $728 million to Britain, France and Denmark. In mid-1974 it agreed to loan $1.2 billion to the National Water Council of Britain and deposit $1 billion with Banque de France over the next few years. Although it was unable to keep its promises in full, its moves had the effect of drawing Britain and France closer to itself.

Once the oil nationalisation dispute was solved in August 1954, Tehran's relations with London became normal, particularly when the AIOC (later British Petroleum) was given the largest single share in the oil consortium. With Iran joining the Baghdad Pact the following year, these relations warmed, since Britain was a fellow-member. As a supplier of army and naval weapons, Britain maintained training missions in Iran. As a Cento member, Iran allowed the British air force to use its northern air bases for spying over the Caspian Sea region of the Soviet Union.[38] By the time a dispute broke out between Britain and Iran about the future of Bahrain in mid-1968, London had supplied Tehran with 800 Chieftain tanks. This discord was resolved by the middle of 1970.

It was as well, because some time later, with the Shah embarking on a military build-up, British arms manufacturers gained handsomely by Iranian contracts. Chieftain tanks were especially popular with the Iranian army. It had more Chieftain tanks than the British army when the revolution came.[39] By 1978 Iran had become Britain's largest military exports market, and its second most important trading partner in the Middle East, with the two-way trade running at £1,585 million.[40]

Yet British investments in Iran at $170 million were modest, slightly more than those of France at $150 million.[41] French ties with Iran were mainly economic and cultural, with French arms supplies playing a very minor role. The biggest single order that French companies received was for a series of nuclear power stations, which was to be cancelled after the revolution.

In commercial links West Germany was well ahead of other West European countries – and even the US – until 1974. In 1972, following the visit to Tehran of the West German chancellor, Willy Brandt, Iran and West Germany signed an economic agreement which provided for Iranian exports of oil and natural gas (through the Soviet pipeline), and West German exports to and investments in Iran. However, given its huge surplus in foreign trade in 1974-5, the Iranian government bought 25 per cent of the shares of Krupp Huttenwerke, the steel subsidiary of the German conglomerate Krupp, in September 1974. While this provided the much needed cash injection to Krupp, it gave Iran access to German expertise to expand its steel industry. In 1975 West Germany became the second most important supplier of non-military goods to Iran. Valued at $404 million, West German imports amounted to nearly one-fifth of total Iranian imports.

As the European country with the largest Iranian expatriate community, the Shah's visits to West Germany became the focus of much protest. As repression in Iran became more intense, these demonstrations became more militant.

The same phenomenon began to occur during the Shah's visits to the US, his favourite country, which he visited a dozen times between October 1949 and November 1977. In the mid-1970s persistent reports of Savak's brutality towards the regime's real and suspected opponents – confirmed by Amnesty International, the International Commission of Jurists, and the International Commission of the Red Cross – began to tarnish the Shah's image in the US. The matter became entangled in US domestic politics when, in an interview with an American television network in October 1976, the Shah conceded that Savak functioned inside the United States. Fifteen to twenty Savak officials operated from Iranian consulates throughout the country, engaging fifty to 100 full-time informers, and many more part-timers.[42] Given the 60,000 Iranian students then in America, they had much to do. According to the Federal Bureau of Investigation, Savak activities violated American sovereignty. But being in league with the CIA, and protected at the very top, Savak could get away with a lot.

This was the time of the American presidential election, with the incumbent Ford being challenged by Jimmy Carter, the Democratic Party nominee. Untarnished by the chicanery of Washington politics, Carter tried to project himself as Mr Clean, concerned with moral issues, who was determined to cleanse American political life of lies and deceit and underhand methods characteristic of the Nixon administrations. He promised to cut down American arms exports – an activity which had made America 'the arms merchant of the whole world'[43] – and campaign for human rights abroad, including Iran. In the wake of the Watergate scandal, America's defeat in Vietnam, and the sensational exposures of the illegal deeds at home and abroad of the CIA and the FBI, his promises were well received. He won.

Once in office, President Carter set up the Bureau of Human Rights and Refugee Affairs. As stated earlier, this encouraged the Shah's middle class opponents to speak out.[44] The Shah loosened his grip somewhat in the spring of 1977. Faced with less than expected oil revenue for fiscal 1977, he curtailed the defence budget. Even then Iran bought a third of all the American weapons sold abroad. Carter's restriction on the future sales of arms had only a marginal effect on the Shah's plans. During the Pahlavi monarch's visit to Washington in mid-November, it was announced that Iranian arms sales already in the pipeline were worth $12 billion.[45]

While pro- and anti-Shah demonstrators battled with one another and police outside the White House in Washington, Carter praised the Shah for offering 'enlightened leadership' to Iran, to which America was bound with 'unbreakable ties' and an 'unshakeable' military pact.[46] A trade-off was agreed: the Shah promised to cooperate with Saudi Arabia at the next OPEC meeting to freeze oil prices; and Carter pledged to let all the arms supplies go through and play down the human rights issue. In any case by the end of 1977 the Iranian government claimed to have discontinued torture.

Carter's visit to Tehran on the New Year's Eve was an amiable affair, full of mutual praise. 'Iran is an island of stability in one of the most troubled areas of the world,' Carter said, offering a toast to the Shah. 'This is a great tribute to you, Your Majesty, and to your leadership and to the respect, admiration and love which your people give to you.'[47] These words must have haunted the American president as events unrolled in Iran during the next year.

Starting early 1978 most of the US government's Middle East

experts busied themselves with bringing about peace between Israel and Egypt: a process set in motion by the Egyptian president Anwar Sadat's visit in November 1977 to Jerusalem. Despite warnings from the French and Israeli intelligence services in the spring of 1978 to the US that the Shah would last only one to three years (the shorter estimation being that of the French intelligence representative in Tehran),[48] the Carter administration failed to realise the gravity of the situation.

In May, after having personally directed troops to quell demonstrators in Tehran, the Shah set up a direct line of communication with Zbigniew Brzezinski, Carter's national security adviser, through Ardeshir Zahedi, the Iranian ambassador in Washington. Son of General Zahedi, Ardeshir was married to Shahnaz, a daughter of the Shah. During the crisis that developed, Brzezinski maintained this contact, and backed the Shah consistently.

It was not until late August – after the fire in an Abadan cinema had raised popular hatred of the Shah to a high pitch – that the Carter administration finally grasped the situation. This was all the more ironic, because it had five intelligence agencies monitoring Iran: the Defence Intelligence Agency and the Military Assistance Advisory Group of the defence department, the Intelligence and Research Bureau of the state department, the CIA and the National Security Agency. 'Iran is not in a revolutionary or even a pre-revolutionary situation,' concluded a CIA study in early August. Apparently the CIA's links with Savak and the weekly meetings of Arthur Callaghan, the CIA station chief, with the Shah proved to be barriers to an objective assessment of the situation. By then the CIA had not acquired a single copy of the many works published by Khomeini. A Defence Intelligence Agency report of 28 September concluded that the Shah would remain 'actively in power' for the next ten years. This was three weeks after the Black Friday massacre of 7 September.

During that event Carter was engaged in intense negotiations with Sadat and Israeli Premier Menachem Begin at the mountain resort of Camp David in Maryland. On Sadat's suggestion he telephoned the Shah and reiterated American support for him. The immediate dissemination of this by the Iranian media strengthened the general feeling among Iranians that the US was in league with the Pahlavi monarch to crush the anti-Shah movement.

Other Western leaders too were in direct touch with Muhammad Reza Pahlavi. When, for instance, an approach was made in early October to the French government for political asylum for Khomeini in France, President Valéry Giscard d'Estaing first cleared this with the Shah.[49]

By then William Sullivan, the US ambassador in Tehran, had

concluded that the best course for the Shah to follow was to form a broad-based government including opposition leaders, and that the US should get involved in the process. This plan visualised the Shah stepping down at some point, and the military switching its allegiance to the civilian government led by National Front figures. The state department liked the plan, but not the White House. It felt that, like an American military intervention in Iran, implementing it would have meant flagrant interference in Iran's domestic affairs.

When in late October the Shah sought American approval for a military government, the state department drafted a cable advising a broad-based civilian, coalition government, and transfer of substantial powers to it by the Shah. But Brzezinski vetoed it. Instead he sent a message of support for a military administration. With Ardeshir Zahedi now in Tehran and telephoning him daily, Brzezinski had his own 'embassy' in the Iranian capital.

By early November Carter had set up a Special Coordinating Committee on Iran, consisting among others of Brzezinski, secretary of state Cyrus Vance, defence secretary Harold Brown, and the CIA director Stanfield Turner. Top officials in Washington were divided. Reflecting his department's views, Vance stated that he could not support massive repression by the Shah whereas Brzezinski argued that Iran was so vital to US interests that the nature of the Shah's regime was of secondary importance. Working through Zahedi, Brzezinski advised the Shah to crush the revolutionary movement. But the Shah was reluctant to do so. In the words of William Sullivan, 'The Shah told me that if he used force, he could suppress the spreading revolution only as long as he himself lived. Since he reckoned his mortality in a short-time frame, he felt the suppressed forces would blow up in the face of his son, and the dynasty would, in any event, be blasted away.'[50] Unknown to Sullivan and others, the Shah's cancer was well advanced, and he knew it.

Meanwhile the American embassy in Tehran was the scene of frequent visits by top Iranian military officers who urged tough action against the protestors but who, by virtue of many years of dependence on the Shah, showed little initiative of their own.

As General Azhari's government failed to reverse the process of the regime's disintegration, opinion in Washington swung in favour of the line proposed by Sullivan and backed by Vance. Sullivan's earlier suggestion that the White House contact Khomeini too was accepted in principle. Sullivan extended his secret contacts with the National Front figures to such clerical and military leaders as Shariatmadari, Beheshti and General Gharabaghi. On 27 November the *Washington Post* reported that the American government had opened secret talks with the Iranian opposition

About then Carter asked George Ball, a former under-secretary of state, to prepare an urgent report on Iran. While Ball was at work on this, Carter was briefed by Senator Robert Byrd, Democratic Party leader in the US Senate, after his visit to Tehran. He reportedly told the president that the Shah seemed unlikely either to crush the revolutionary movement or ride it out. Carter publicly aired his doubts about the Shah's future at a press conference on 7 December. Asked whether the Shah would survive, he replied, 'I don't know. I hope so. That is something in the hands of the Iranian people.'[51]

On 13 December Ball submitted his report to Carter and Brzezinski. Having concluded that the anti-Shah process was now irreversible, Ball recommended a broad-based transitional government (until fresh elections were held), which needed to be insulated from the Shah by the formation of a Council of Notables. The report was leaked to the press almost immediately, and made the Shah nervous. This, and the very disparate composition of the Council of Notables suggested by Ball, destroyed the report's value. Nothing came of it. Brzezinski kept up his position of strong US support for the Shah, and reiterated it in a speech on 20 December. But his position was weakened by the failure of the military government in Iran.

As the Shah seriously pursued Sullivan's earlier proposal of a broad-based government led by the National Front, and as army desertions mounted, Washington began to worry about the integrity of the Iranian armed forces. Following consultations with Vance during the Christmas-New Year holidays, Carter concluded that the transitional government to be appointed by the Shah before his departure would need US assistance, and that it was crucial to keep the Iranian military intact during the next delicate phase.

Once Shahpour Bakhtiar had been chosen premier by the Shah, Carter concentrated on securing for him the loyalty of military leaders. For this he sent to Tehran General Robert Huyser, commander of US forces in Europe, who also supervised the Military Assistance Advisory Groups in the Middle East. He arrived on 3 January 1979, the day Bakhtiar won the approval of the parliament's two houses. His tasks were to maintain the unity of Iranian military and ensure that there was no military coup against the Bakhtiar government. He worked closely with General Gharabaghi the newly appointed chief of staff, from the US MAAG office in the headquarters of Gharabaghi.

Carter tried to secure Bakhtiar's position politically. He sent a message to Khomeini through President Giscard d'Estaing. It said that the US was backing Bakhtiar, and since he had adopted the opposition's programme, Carter hoped Khomeini would call off agitation and support Bakhtiar. Otherwise, continued the message, the army would move to crush the protest and mount a coup. 'Azhari's government was a military coup,' retorted Khomeini in reply. 'Bakhtiar's government is no more than a facade for a military coup. . . . If the army does intervene it will be under the control of the Americans, in which case we would consider ourselves at war with America.' He advised Carter to remove the Shah, and withhold support from Bakhtiar.[52] Carter was unlikely to heed Khomeini's advice. As it was, Ambassador Sullivan tried hard to co-opt clerical and other leaders into the Bakhtiar government, but had little success.

It was some days after his arrival in Tehran that General Huyser sought to see the Shah. During the meeting he reportedly asked the monarch whether he had fixed his date of departure. The question was not impertinent; the Shah had announced on 1 January that he would like to take a vacation if the situation permitted.[53] But the Shah was not prepared to leave unless he had secured certain guarantees, the chief one being that he would retain command over the military while being on 'vacation'. He was the only coordinating link between different commanders, he argued. More importantly, as described earlier, he wanted to finalise plans for a military coup before leaving.[54]

Of the eight hardline generals and admirals only one, General Afshar Amini, director of the Shah's personal office, left with the monarch, on 16 January. The rest stayed behind. Between the Shah's departure and 12 February they tried twice to mount a coup, and failed.

Since his arrival in Tehran, Huyser kept up daily meetings with the generals and reporting the state of the Iranian military by telephone to Harold Brown, the defence secretary. Relying on what the generals told him, he informed Brown that troops were 85 per cent loyal, and would most probably obey Bakhtiar if he ordered them to crush the protest.[55] He promised US fuel to the Iranian armed forces, and impressed the generals by producing an oil tanker with 200,000 barrels a few days later. He conveyed the generals' request that America must guarantee that Khomeini would not be allowed to return to Iran. Of course no such assurance could be offered by Washington even if it wanted to.

In Khomeini's view America and the Shah were inextricably linked. 'America is an accessory [to the Shah] and has backed the massacre of our people by the Shah's ignoble regime,' he said in an interview in early January 1979.[56] Shortly after his return to Tehran on 1 February Khomeini warned his compatriots about the repetition of the events of August 1953, the memory of which was branded on the psyche of the Ayatollah as well as millions of Iranians. 'We will not let the United States bring back the Shah,' he said. 'This is what the Shah wants. Wake up. Watch out.'[57]

Given this, it was only a matter of days before Khomeini came into open conflict with the US. This happened on 6 February, a day after he appointed Mahdi Bazargan as the prime minister of the provisional government. Washington reiterated that it supported the government led by Bakhtiar.

Whatever influence the US now had in Iran was restricted to the armed forces. That made it all the more crucial for Washington that the military should hold together. In the first week of February it became clear that the army was disintegrating fast. Then came the rumblings in the air force at Doshan Tapeh air base in Tehran. There the fate of the trapped American air personnel became entangled in the internecine fighting within the Iranian military.[58] Given the deep involvement of the US in the Iranian armed forces, something like this was bound to happen sooner or later.

Khomeini was not being paranoid when he warned Iranians about the prospect of the Shah's restoration with American help. On the night of 10-11 February – as armed revolutionaries were delivering hammer blows to the army – Sullivan received a telephone call from Washington 'relaying a message from Brzezinski who asked whether I thought I could arrange a military coup against the revolution'.[59] Obviously the Carter administration was unwilling to accept the overthrow of the Shah. It would have been pleased if the Iranian generals' attempts at a coup had succeeded. When they did not, Carter's national security adviser made a desperate, but futile, attempt to instigate a coup on behalf of the US.

This was an ignominious end to American hegemony in Iran which began on 19 August 1953. On that occasion there was much jubilation in Washington. In the Cold War climate of the period the coup was seen as a triumph over the Soviet Union. In the process a representative government, which faithfully reflected the nationalist aspirations of Iranian people for economic and political independence, was destroyed, and a monarchist dictatorship imposed. For the next quarter of a century the Pahlavi regime served the interests of the Western camp led by the US. The nexus between Tehran and Washington became an important feature of international affairs. It gave impetus to the rapid capitalist development of Iran. But, by failing to match this with commensurate channels for political participation by the people, the system stored up pent-up frustrations of revolutionary proportions. For all the bravado he showed in the aftermath of the oil boom of the mid-1970s the Shah was dependent on the US for his military and political survival. His overthrow by Iranian revolutionaries was as much a defeat for the Pahlavis as it was for the US government. And it was a stunning event. Henry Kissinger described the 'loss of Iran' as 'the greatest single blow to the US foreign policy interests since the World War II'.[60] Khomeini echoed a similar sentiment differently: 'No other country was receiving the same benefits from Iran as much as was the United States'.[61]

After the revolution: troubled relations

Given the duration and strength of Iranian-American relations, the collapse of the Pahlavi dynasty was seen in Washington as a disaster. But the US administration tried to accept the loss with equanimity. Or at least the president did. Carter managed to put on a brave face at a press conference in Washington on 12 February, and said that the US would 'attempt to work closely with the existing government of Iran'.[62] It was a sign of the times that the US embassy in Tehran, which employed 1,000 staff during the heyday of the Shah, was now down to 100 personnel.

If the previous Iranian administrations had been pliant towards Washington, the one now headed by Mahdi Bazargan was going to be defiant. It had been catapulted to power by revolution in the streets, and that force had not yet played itself out. If anything, revolutionaries wanted to tackle the foreign power which had foisted Muhammad Reza Pahlavi on the Iranian people over twenty-five years ago: America. Unsurprisingly, 150 armed members of the Fedai Khalq attacked the US embassy in Tehran on 14 February. To them it was a continuation of the battles they had fought and won against the royalist forces since 9 February. The US marine guard at the embassy resisted the attackers for an hour before surrendering. The Fedai Khalq occupation ended a few hours later, when deputy premier Yazdi intervened. After that the task of securing the premises was assigned to a specially formed American Embassy Committee. This encouraged Washington to announce on 16 February that it would maintain diplomatic relations with the Bazargan government. At the same time the policy of further reducing the embassy staff continued.

The embassy's announcement on 1 March that 200 American personnel at the Kabkan electronic surveillance station had just left Iran embarrassed the Bazargan government. It did not know that the US had been continuing this activity after the revolution.[63]

In America the media turned steadily against the revolution, a process aided by the capital punishment meted out to many pro-American generals and politicians. The execution on 7 April of Amir Abbas Hoveida, a former premier, aroused widespread condemnation in the United States. On 17 May US Senate voiced its 'abhorrence' at 'the summary executions without due process' being carried out in Iran. The next day Tehran Radio retorted that the same Senate had said nothing against the massacre of Iranian revolutionaries in the

streets some months earlier.[64] Describing the US Senate action as a
clear interference in Iran's domestic affairs, the Bazargan government
asked Washington to delay the despatch of Walter Cutler to replace
Sullivan who had left the foreign service. On 25 May demonstrations
were held throughout Iran against the US Senate resolution. The main
theme was 'America is the number one enemy of the Islamic
revolution'. When Tehran objected to Cutler as America's envoy,
Washington refused to name a new ambassador.

In early June the Bazargan government accepted Bruce Laingen as
the US chargé d'affaires in Tehran. But it was unable to normalise
relations with America. It faced opposition from the Islamic Revolutionary Council at the policy-making level, and from the Islamic
Associations in the foreign ministry and the Iranian embassy in
Washington at the administrative level. The emphasis in Tehran was
on attenuating links with Washington. A clear indication of this came
on 10 August, when Iran cancelled three-quarters of its pending $12
billion worth of orders for US weapons.

Within this reduced framework, Yazdi in Tehran and his son-in-law,
Rouhani, in Washington tried to normalise links with America.
Bilateral relations improved somewhat. The US embassy staff in
Tehran rose from the record low of forty to seventy. The American
Embassy Committee was disbanded in September.

But the situation worsened dramatically when the Shah was allowed
into America on 22 October. Popular opinion turned hostile towards
the US government. On 1 November three million people marched in
Iran to demand the Shah's extradition from America. It was against
this background that the US embassy in Tehran was seized on 4
November.

When the Carter administration's diplomatic moves to free the
hostages failed, it began considering military options. According to
Brzezinski, it contemplated punishing Iran by attacking the Kharg
island oil installations, imposing a naval blockade and carrying out air
strikes against Iran. But after the Soviet intervention in Afghanistan in
late December 1979, the administration dropped the plan. It feared
that the ensuing military chaos in Iran would provide the Soviets with a
chance to advance through Iran to the Gulf.[65] On the other hand the
fear of American attack on Iran was one of the main reasons for the
Soviet march into Afghanistan.[66]

Later the US government narrowed its military options to two
rescue plans: one concerned itself exclusively with freeing the
hostages; and the other combined the rescue operation with military
strikes against Iran to mask the real mission. According to Brzezinski,
Carter overruled the second plan only a day before the operation was
launched from the US aircraft carrier Nimitz in the Arabian Sea on 24-

25 April.[67]

The basic idea was to sneak in six to eight helicopters to a disused air strip near Tabas, 380 miles south-east of Tehran, and fly in ninety specially trained American commandos by six C-130 transport planes from Quna air base in Egypt, carrying among other things fuel for helicopters. The commandos would then fly to Damavand, thirty miles east of Tehran, where many of the 400 Iranian agents of the US had already gathered. There the commandos and the Iranians would board trucks, and head for the US embassy in central Tehran, which would by then have been infiltrated by other Iranian agents. The commandos would use nerve gas to incapacitate the Iranian guards at the embassy. Once they had secured the embassy they would call the helicopters at Damavand. These helicopters would then take the American hostages and commandos to Manzariyeh airport, seventy miles south of Tehran. There they would all transfer to the waiting C-130 planes and fly out of Iran as other US aircraft, equipped with sophisticated devices, jammed Iran's radar systems.

But things went wrong. One of the six helicopters that had landed safely at Tabas air strip broke down, and could not be repaired. Then one of the arriving transport planes collided with a stationary helicopter, causing an explosion and the deaths of eight military personnel. Moreover, the secrecy of the mission was compromised by the totally unexpected passage of a bus with fifty passengers aboard, and its stoppage by the American officers on site. Therefore the leader of the mission was ordered to abort the mission. The order came directly from President Carter. In their hurry to evacuate the air strip, the Americans left a lot of incriminating material behind, including $1 million in Iranian currency. The sum was meant as payment to the American agents in Iran who were getting restive at not having been paid since the seizure of the US embassy in November 1979.[68]

A detailed report on the episode published two years later in the *Washington Post* stated that the raid was facilitated by a big gap in the Iranian radar and defences due to the CIA having recruited 'a high ranking Iranian defence official'. This official put 'on manoeuvres', or sent to Kurdistan, mobile ground-to-air missiles, anti-aircraft batteries, and some radar facilities around the areas of the planned American mission. He was probably Major General Bagheri, commander of the Iranian air force. It was not until early June 1980 that he was arrested.[69]

Contrary to the official American leaks, the back-up force waiting in Egypt was as large as 'up to 2,500'. Moreover, Carter was ready, if necessary, to authorise air cover or air strikes on military targets around Tehran to ensure the mission's success. In the case of crowds gathering outside the US embassy, the plan was for C-130 aircraft to fire their machine guns and cannons at them. The whole exercise was so complicated that it required the active cooperation of Egypt, Oman, Bahrain, Turkey and Israel. Even then it was estimated by outside experts that at best only about half of the fifty hostages at the embassy could or would have been rescued.[70]

Khomeini condemned the American mission. 'Landing military forces in an independent country is an unforgivable crime,' he said.[71] It confirmed his fears regarding American intentions about Iran. To forestall a repetition of the American action, the Iranian authorities dispersed the hostages to different cities. The precaution was not excessive. It was revealed later that Carter considered a second raid on Iran shortly after the April 1980 fiasco and that the Pentagon ordered another plan.[72]

By the time of the American mission, the student captors of the hostages had finished interrogating the eleven diplomats they had classified as spies. This enabled them to make better sense of the thousands of secret documents they had captured at the embassy. They had secured incontrovertible evidence of American interference in, and dominance over, Iran over the past many years. What was more, interference had continued after the revolution.

In early June 1980 the Iranian government held an International Conference on US Intervention in Iran. It was attended by 300 delegates from fifty-seven countries and organisations. The ten-member American delegation was led by Ramsay Clark, a former attorney general. Among the documents released at the conference was Brzezinski's secret memorandum to Vance which recommended 'destabilisation' of Khomeini's regime through Iran's neighbours. The immediate objective of the Carter administration after the revolution was to impose a 'moderate' government on Iran.[73] Typical of the lower level documents was a report sent by the US embassy in Tehran to the state department on 24 July 1979. It referred to one bazaar merchant Ali Eslami who was close to Ayatollah Shariatmadari, and who claimed to have his 'units' working against Khomeini. Of the two instances of Eslami's effectiveness, one pertained to an attack on Khomeini's residence in Qom in early July 'involving the use of a hand grenade'.[74]

By the spring of 1980 Carter had managed to integrate the hostage issue into American domestic politics. He used it effectively to beat off a serious challenge by Senator Edward Kennedy to his renomination as the Democratic Party's presidential nominee. But after the Tabas fiasco, which led to Vance resigning his post in protest, Carter's popular standing on this score fell steeply. Whereas in December 1979 66 per cent of voters supported Carter's handling of the hostage issue, in July 1980 the figure was down to 12 per cent.[75] From then on this subject remained as important to the voters as the state of the economy.

Soon after the Shah's death in late July, 187 members of the US House of Representatives addressed a letter to the Iranian Majlis urging consideration of the hostages issue. A month later the Majlis replied that the US should accept responsibility for the Shah's actions and compensate Iran for the financial and spiritual losses inflicted on the Iranian people. On 11 September Khomeini formulated these sentiments into specific demands: return of the Shah's assets to Iran, cancellation of US financial claims against Iran, unfreezing of Iranian assets, and an American promise of non-intervention in Iranian affairs. Ronald Reagan, the Republican candidate for president, said that he would accept three of these conditions, and leave the question of the Shah's assets for the US courts to decide.[76] Then came the appointment of a special Majlis commission to study the hostage issue.

On 22 September Iraq attacked Iran. According to President Bani-Sadr, the Americans had an inkling of Iraq's plans. The Carter administration may even have, through Saudi Arabia, encouraged Iraq to attack – seeing in the move the making of a solution to the hostages crisis.[77] Given that US intelligence had predicted Iran running out of its military spare parts for its predominantly American arsenal in three weeks, presidential aides visualised Tehran growing desperate to secure them from the Pentagon: a situation tailor-made for a swap, American spare parts for hostages.

In practice, however, Iran did not turn to the US. It approached Vietnam, which had huge stocks of leftover American spare parts and weapons. Vietnam helped Iran. As Iran offered spirited resistance to Iraq, and as the possibility of the war spreading to other Gulf states became real, Washington found its Arab allies in the region getting nervous. On 30 September the US sent four Awacs to Saudi Arabia. A week later it said that it would respond positively to requests for assistance from 'non-belligerent friends' in the Gulf.

Having thus reassured American allies, Carter concentrated on getting the hostages released before 4 November, the presidential election day. Behind the scene talks ensued between American and Iranian officials at the UN in New York. On 18 October Carter said that Iraqi forces had gone beyond 'the ultimate goal' stated by President Saddam Hussein, and that the US would like to see 'any invading forces withdrawn'. Two days later the US secretary of state said that Iraqi 'invasion' of Iran was threatening the Gulf's stability, adding that territory must not be seized by force, and that neither side should interfere in the internal affairs of the other. On 23 October the US ambassador to the UN said that 'the national integrity of Iran' was threatened by Iraqi 'invasion'.[78] These statements were enough to make the Iraqi foreign minister express doubts about US neutrality in the war.

It was against this background that the Majlis decided on 26 October to consider its committee's recommendations on the hostages. It held two closed sessions the following day without reaching any decision. On 28 October Carter promised that if the hostages were released the US would airlift the arms and spare parts that Iran had already paid for. He was anxious to parade the freed American hostages on television to boost his chance of re-election. The Majlis knew this. And the radical deputies were determined to inflict a damaging blow to Carter's electoral prospects. Twenty of them stayed away the next day, thus causing the Majlis session to be postponed for lack of quorum. When the Majlis reassembled on 2 November, Sunday, 185 of the 228 deputies were present. But two crucial days had been lost; and Carter's camp was in despair. By an overwhelming vote the deputies concurred with their committee's recommendation to release the hostages subject to the US accepting the demands made earlier by Khomeini. The next day Carter called the decision 'a positive basis' on which to resolve the crisis. The student captors handed over the hostages to the government. But all this was too close to the election day, 4 November, to help Carter. He lost.

Most Iranians regarded Carter's defeat as a case of poetic justice. America had imposed Muhammad Reza Pahlavi on them in 1953, and made them suffer his autocratic rule. Now they had been able to determine the outcome of an American presidential election. They had got even with Carter, a president who had been fulsome in his praise of the Shah, had backed the Pahlavi ruler throughout the revolutionary movement, and finally let him into America. Despite the placating promises about non-interference in the affairs of the Islamic regime, Carter had tried to destabilise it, and impose a government congenial to American interests.

At the same time Iranians knew that president-elect Ronald Reagan would be tough in his negotiations with them. He was determined to restore the image of America as a powerful nation, an image which had been tarnished by American impotence in the case of the hostage crisis. Tehran therefore concluded that it was best to settle the matter while Carter was still in the White House. On his part Carter dearly wanted to receive the freed hostages while he was still president. Although he managed to implement the deal with Iran before he formally handed over power to Reagan on 21 January 1981, the Iranians denied him the pleasure of receiving the freed hostages as American president.

After assuming office President Reagan said that there was nothing the US could do to take revenge on Iran for seizing American diplomats and keeping them captive for 444 days. He confirmed that he would honour the terms agreed by his predecessor. Accordingly, he lifted US economic sanctions against Iran.

In practice, the American economic boycott had been quite ineffective. Within a week of the boycott, some 300 US and West European companies offered to sell Tehran arms and other banned goods.[79] Many of them supplied the banned items to Iran by merely changing labels or re-routing the goods through third countries. Also Iran had no problem circumventing the restrictions of the European Economic Community. Since Austria, Switzerland and Sweden did not join the EEC move, the companies of these countries acted as intermediaries in supplying whatever Iran wanted. Such an activity by Austrian firms soon made Iran the second most important trading partner of Austria, a situation which continued even after the Western economic boycott was lifted in January 1981.

The net result of the Western sanctions was to force Iran to pay premiums on certain imports and use Dubai (in the UAE) as a transit port for many of its imported goods. Western action also encouraged the Islamic Republic to become self-sufficient and diversify its trade. Before the revolution 87.2 per cent of Iran's imports originated in the West; in 1980 the figure was down to 67 per cent.[80]

In 1978, the last year under the Shah, 45 per cent of Iranian imports came from the EEC, with West Germany accounting for nearly half of the total. The revolution made little difference to commercial links between Tehran and Bonn. West German imports into Iran fell by only a quarter, from Rials 151 billion in 1978 to Rials 123 billion in the following year. The April 1980 EEC restrictions reduced West German imports to Rials 117 billion.[81]

Since 10 per cent of West Germany's oil needs came from Iran, Bonn was more anxious than other European capitals to see the American hostage crisis resolved. Gerhard Ritzel, the West German ambassador in Tehran, played a crucial part in getting serious negotiations between the two sides started. He arranged a secret meeting between Warren Christopher, US under-secretary of state, and Sadiq Tabatabai, the Iranian government representative in Europe, in West Germany on 17 September 1980.[82]

In the EEC, Britain was Iran's second most important partner. Despite the EEC restrictions, British exports to Iran went up from Rials 47 billion to Rials 56.6 billion in 1980.[83] Like most other members of the EEC, Britain was neutral in the Gulf War, refusing to sell arms or spares to either party. This hurt Iran more than Iraq: before the revolution Britain was Iran's second most important supplier of weapons.

Falling slightly behind Britain in its commercial relations with Iran was Italy. Its exports to Iran in 1980 amounted to Rials 43 billion. In that year it secured a contract to build a steel plant in Isfahan. Once the EEC economic boycott was lifted in 1981, Italy became the second most important buyer of Iranian oil, after Japan. In October 1982 the state-owned oil company, Azeinda Generale Italiana Petroli won contracts for the construction of a natural gas pipeline in Iran. Snamprogetti, part of the state-run group Ente Nazionale Idro Carburi, secured contracts for service work in the Iranian oil industry.[84]

At the other end was France. Its relations with Iran deteriorated steadily. Since it gave refuge to Khomeini before the revolution, it had had good standing with the Islamic regime in the beginning. However, as most of the anti-Khomeini generals and politicians made Paris their base of operations against the Islamic Republic – and were allowed to do so by the French administration – relations between Tehran and Paris cooled. The outbreak of the Gulf War accelerated the process, with France emerging as Iraq's most important source of arms in the West. Tehran protested vehemently when the François Mitterrand administration gave political asylum to Bani-Sadr in France in late July 1981. It expelled the French ambassador in Iran. Soon 116 French citizens left the Islamic Republic. By then France had over 40,000 Iranian exiles, and its authorities allowed them to function politically.

Given the close ties that France had developed with Iraq – and its close ally, Saudi Arabia – it was not surprising to hear Paris state in December 1982 that it would not allow Iraq to lose the war. Such an outcome, it argued, would threaten Western interests in the Middle East. French officials repeated this argument in September 1983 to justify selling five Super-Etendard planes to Iraq. When the French delivered these aircraft to Iraq in October, Iran ended the special status that it had accorded to French banks nearly a century ago. It also placed French products on its black list, something it had done earlier with American products. Although the much reduced French embassy in Tehran was not closed down, France was now put in the same category as the US.

When conservative Reagan took office exiled Iranian monarchists hoped they would receive help from Washington in their plans to overthrow the Khomeini regime. But given a record of embarrassing failures by the CIA in Iran before and after the revolution, the Reagan administration was unwilling to undertake destabilisation activities in the Islamic Republic for the time being. On the other hand no US government could afford to be disinterested in the fate of Iran. Whether ruled by Khomeini or not, Iran's strategic importance remained unimpaired. Also, concentration of oil reserves in the Gulf made the region extremely important in the international balance of economic and military forces. According to an OPEC study in 1981, the eight Gulf states possessed 54 per cent of the world's known oil reserves of 671 billion barrels. At fifty-seven billion barrels, Iran's oil reserves were the third largest in the region.[85]

The subject of securing oil supplies from the Gulf was studied by the Congressional Research Service of the US Library of Congress in 1978. Anticipating the recommendations of this report by John M. Collins and Clyde R. Mark,[86] in February 1979 President Carter ordered the establishment of a joint task force of 50,000 to safeguard Gulf oil shipments, and the bolstering of the American Fifth Fleet in the Indian Ocean, operating from Diego Garcia near Mauritius. Following the Soviet intervention in Afghanistan in December, Carter declared that the Gulf was vital to the national security of America. This added urgency to the activation of the joint task force of infantry, marine, navy and air force personnel, to be called the Rapid Development Force. The function of the RDF was to aid any friendly nation in the region which sought US assistance. For this, the force had to be stationed in or near the Gulf, or had to be highly mobile.

With Iran's defection from the American camp, the oil fields of the pro-West Arab states in the Gulf became vulnerable. The vacuum left by Iran's departure was impossible to fill. The best that America could do was to strengthen its military and economic ties with Saudi Arabia, Bahrain, Kuwait and Oman – and induct Pakistan into the military plans of these states. And it did. The US established military bases on the Masirah island of Oman and at Gwadar on the Baluchistan coast of Pakistan. Every year the RDF held joint military exercises in the region in conjunction with Oman, Somalia and Egypt.

According to American military planners, the USSR is intent on marching to the warm waters of the Gulf, to realise the centuries old dream of Russian Czars. They, in turn, are determined to frustrate Soviet designs. The installing of Reagan in the White House encouraged military strategists to take a tougher line against the Soviets than before. In March 1982 the Pentagon issued a secret directive which said that the US could land troops in the area if the Persian Gulf were threatened by events short of an outright invasion because, it argued, the Soviets could exploit local unrest or internal subversion to enter the region by means 'other than outright invasion'.[87] Such a directive went beyond the Pentagon's publicly stated policy of countering specific Soviet military moves in the region.

By early 1983 the RDF had reached its full strength of 300,000, and was functioning under the US Central Command with its headquarters in Tampa, Florida. But military leaders did not think it enough to have a joint force designed mainly to assist American allies in trouble. So they decided to create a combat force to engage the Soviets inside Iran. The US government set out to form five light infantry divisions for use inside Iran against a Soviet attack.[88] Thus US military planners considered Iran as a potential theatre of war where the Americans and the Soviets would, or could, confront one another directly, without the presence of their respective European allies: a chilling prospect. But military planning did not stop there. According to Jack Anderson, an American columnist, the Pentagon had devised emergency plans for the use of nuclear weapons if it was faced with a Soviet takeover of Iran.[89] In short, when it came to keeping the Soviets out of Iran the Reagan administration was prepared to go to the farthest limit, including nuclear warfare.

Yet in its attitude to Iran in the Gulf War, the US steadily turned against Iran and in favour of Iraq. This happened after a fairly long period of 'balance' in its policies towards the combatants. It closed its eyes to the exports of weapons and spare parts to Iran by private companies either directly or through third parties. Simultaneously it passed on satellite and high altitude reconnaissance pictures of Iranian troop movements to Saudi Arabia, knowing that Saudi Arabia was transmitting these to Iraq.[90] The same applied to the information collected by four Awacs sent by the US to Saudi Arabia for round the clock surveillance of the Gulf. As Saddam Hussein was to reveal later, 'We in Iraq have benefited from Awacs'.[91]

Being equipped with mainly American weapons, the Iranian authorities had to keep on procuring American-made weapons and parts. Through Sadiq Tabatabai in West Germany they set up a network in West Europe and the Far East to obtain the necessary weapons and parts. Customs inspection in such places as Amsterdam, Singapore and Hong Kong was so lax that it was easy to redirect consignments arriving from the US or Canada straight to Iran without any inspection. Even during the period of American economic boycott there was no ban on the exports of food, medicines and agricultural machinery from the US to Iran. One American company regularly sent goods marked 'tractor engines' from Boston to Tehran. These were allowed for two years until a customs inspector with a military background noticed that the engines were equipped with super-chargers. The machines were replacements for engines used in American-made M-60 tanks.[92]

Once the American hostage crisis was resolved, commercial relations between Iran and America improved. In 1981 the two-way trade amounted to $363 million, heavily in favour of the US. The situation changed the next year when Iran offered price cuts on its oil. Among the parties to take advantage of this, through a Swiss trading company, was the US Defence Fuel Supply Centre. It ordered 1.8 million barrels for its strategic reserves at $29.41 a barrel, $4.59 below the OPEC price.[93] The two-way trade in 1982 rose to $706 million, and favoured Tehran. The Iranian authorities set up their companies in Dubai, Singapore and Hong Kong to procure the American goods they needed.

When Iran attacked Iraq in July 1982 the Reagan administration felt anxious. But Iraq managed to blunt the Iranian thrusts into its territory; and this brought relief in Washington. The subsequent stalemate suited the US: two unlikeable regimes were battering each other, and in the process dividing the Arab world and diverting Arab attention away from the Palestinian problem. Not surprisingly, the Office of Munitions Control of the state department continued to be lax about enforcing the ban on exports of weapons and spare parts to Iran. 'We don't give a damn as long as Iran-Iraq carnage does not affect our allies or alter the balance of power,' said a state department official in July 1983. 'Why save Iranians from themselves with US customs resources needed to protect Americans from the drug traffic [in the US]?'[94]

When the interests of American allies in the region were at stake with the Iranian threat to close the Hormuz Strait if the Kharg oil terminal were destroyed, President Reagan reiterated the earlier position that the US would keep the Strait open to shipping. He increased the American naval presence in the area to thirty warships. The French and British governments followed suit. The Soviets had twenty-six warships in the Arabian Sea.

As Iran began to gain an upper hand in the conflict, the US turned increasingly pro-Iraqi. Despite the continued inclusion of Iraq in the list of 'terrorist nations' – along with Libya, South Yemen, Syria and Cuba – the Reagan administration authorised the sale of sixty helicopters to Iraq for 'agricultural use' in June 1983. Later it provided credit of $460 million for the sale of 147,000 tons of rice to Baghdad.[95] During his visit to the United Nations in New York in September-October, Iraqi foreign minister, Tariq Aziz, had a meeting with US secretary of state, George Shultz.

Relations between Washington and Baghdad warmed, as Washington became progressively more hostile to Tehran. On 23 October a suicide bomb attack by a Lebanese Shia on US marines stationed in Beirut caused the death of 259 marines. Caspar Weinberger, US defence secretary, said that Iran was implicated in the outrage. Iran denied the charge. The US government seriously considered hitting the terrorists, but, lacking solid evidence, it took no action. However, it decided to get tough with Iran. The CIA support to the Iranian exiles in Turkey and France was increased.[96] The administration improved its monitoring of exports to Iran. It pressured its allies, particularly Britain and Israel, to help stop the flow of weapons and parts to Iran for its US-made military equipment.

American policy-makers concluded that Iraqi victory in the war was out of the question, and that there were two possibilities to the present conflict: Iranian victory or continued stalemate. In the case of Iranian victory, they visualised the collapse of the pro-Western monarchies in the Gulf states. Although the subsequent Islamic republics in Iraq and elsewhere were not expected to side with the Soviet Union, the overthrow of a group of pro-Western rulers in a region that contained more than half of the world's known oil reserves was seen as an unprecedented catastrophe. It was therefore decided to shore up Iraq morally and materially. In November the US national security adviser issued a secret directive to this effect, outlining the diplomatic and military steps that the US government should take. The Pentagon prepared contingency plans to assist Iraq militarily if it, or one of its allies, asked to 'stabilise the border'. In that case the US would use A-10 planes to attack Iranian tanks inside Iraq, fragmentation bombs to disperse Iranian troop concentrations, and 'air defence weapons' to enable Iraq to retain control of its air space.[97]

In mid-December Donald Rumsfeld, US special envoy to the Middle East, arrived in Baghdad with a letter from President Reagan to President Saddam Hussein. It was announced later that the two countries were 'ready' to restore diplomatic relations, broken off in June 1967.[98] Reagan then despatched a delegation of officials headed by deputy assistant secretary of state, James Placke, and deputy assistant secretary of defence, Major General Edward Tixier, to the capitals of the Gulf states. They informed Arab rulers that Washington would regard Iraq's defeat 'contrary to US interests'.[99] This was meant to reassure Iraq and dissuade Iran from launching its anticipated offensive against Iraq.

To prepare the ground for further aid to Iraq, the Reagan administration removed it from the list of 'terrorist nations' in mid-January 1984. However, the drive towards cordial relations between Washington and Baghdad was interrupted briefly when the issue of Iraq's use of chemical weapons came to the fore in March. To be consistent on this subject of international importance, the US administration first confirmed that Iraq had used chemical weapons, and then condemned it for so doing.

The US was aware of the financial crisis that Iraq faced due to its inability to export its full OPEC quota for oil of 1.2 million b/d. One way to overcome the problem was to build a pipeline from Kirkuk to the Jordanian post of Aqba. But Iraq feared that, given the proximity of Aqba to Israel, the pipeline would be vulnerable to Israeli attacks. It approached the US to obtain guarantees from Israel before undertaking the project. In mid-May 1984 the Israeli minister of energy, Yitzhak Modai, gave such a guarantee publicly. Soon Iraq awarded the $1,000 million contract to an American company, Leftbelt.[100] In short, as Soviet analysts had predicted, the Iraqi attack on Iran which got the Gulf War going, had brought Iraq closer to the West.[101]

On the other hand, deep hostility between Iran and the US, which existed at the start of the war, persisted. On 23 January 1984 Washington added Iran to its list of 'terrorist nations'. This meant that Iran was now subject to 'rigid US export controls'. Four months later at a press conference in Lahore, Pakistan, George Bush, US vice-president, stated that the 'wound' caused by the American hostage crisis was 'still open', and that 'Iran's fingerprints were all over the terror and murder of American marines in Lebanon'. He warned the Islamic Republic against attempts to overthrow other governments.[102] A few days later a US administration statement made it abundantly clear where its sympathies lay in the Gulf War. 'We do not want to see the government in Baghdad destabilised,' said an official spokesman in Washington. 'We want to see a stable and internally secure Iraq. We see it as the first line of defence against Iranian expansionism.'[103]

These statements were part of a drive to dissuade Iran from launching its spring offensive against Iraq. With the same aim in mind, Saddam Hussein intensified attacks on the ships inside the 'war exclusion zone' of fifty nautical miles around Kharg island and the Iranian ports north of it. He decided to escalate the conflict in the northern Gulf in order to induct US intervention and thus secure a halt to the hostilities. The 'air siege' of Kharg led to a reduction of Iranian oil exports by about half in a month: a considerable blow to Tehran's finances.

Since there were no ships selling to the narrow shoreline of Iraq, Iran retaliated by attacking the oil tankers of Saudi Arabia and Kuwait. It argued that by providing aid to Iraq these two countries had become 'virtual' participants in the conflict. Saudi and Kuwaiti aid consisted of providing Iraq with port facilities, information obtained by Awacs, and grants and loans – and producing and selling their own oil on behalf of Iraq. By doing what it did, Iran wanted to pressure Iraq, through Saudi Arabia and Kuwait, to lift the air siege of Kharg. Moreover, it wanted to prove to the US and its allies that Iran was capable of implementing its earlier threat: 'If we cannot export our oil we'll see that nobody else in the Gulf can'.

Attacks on eight ships in three weeks or so in May pushed up insurance rates from 2 per cent of the value of the vessel and its cargo to 7.5 per cent. This in itself became a strong disincentive for shipowners to use the Gulf, and alarmed the local regimes. Despite this, the Saudi and Kuwaiti governments refrained from calling on the US to help. Instead, they complained to the UN about Iranian attacks on their vessels.

Determined to keep Washington out of the conflict, President Khamanei warned the US that it would suffer 'more heavily than it did in Lebanon' if it intervened. With the memory of the deaths of hundreds of American Marines in Beirut still fresh, the Reagan administration took this warning seriously. At the same time it could not afford to stand idly by and see Gulf oil supplies disrupted. Although it imported only 5 per cent of its petroleum needs from the Gulf, West Europe imported a quarter of its needs, and Japan two-thirds. The stoppage of Gulf oil to West Europe and Japan was bound to damage their economies – and with it, finally, the American economy. The Reagan administration therefore devised a three-stage plan. At first it would help bolster the defence capabilities of its Arab allies, particularly Saudi Arabia and Kuwait. If that proved insufficient, it would then offer, along with Britain and France, naval escorts for the ships sailing into or out of friendly ports. If that failed it would finally, if invited, provide air cover for the ships and territories of its Arab allies.

Being members of the Gulf Cooperation Council, the Gulf states were expected to consult one another before seeking military assistance from a foreign power. Since Saudi Arabia was the dominant member of the GCC, the final decision lay with it. And leaders of Saudi Arabia, an Islamic monarchy, would ponder long and hard before seeking US aid against another Islamic regime, however truculent.

Before the Iranian revolution, all the Arab Gulf states (except Iraq) and Iran were in the same Western camp. If any dispute arose between them it was a matter within the family. With the Shah's downfall the situation changed. Even then, if Iranian revolutionaries had stopped at merely overthrowing the Shah, Washington would have found a modus vivendi with Tehran. But they went beyond that. They combined the campaign to expel all American influence from their society with calls for Islamic self-reliance and self-sufficiency in the region. Since the US was the dominant power in the area, it saw these appeals directed against it. Soon it became obvious that there was an inherent conflict of interests between Washington and Tehran, and that one could gain only at the expense of the other. Thus a superpower and a rising regional power were locked in a conflict that is unlikely to be settled in the near future.

For Washington, revolutionary Islam has proved to be more dangerous than it had visualised. It sees a strategic nation pursuing expansionist policies under the guise of Islam. How to tackle this threat to its military and economic interests in the region is Washington's major dilemma. In the past the US had been on the side of religion and religious movements, as these were seen to be powerful tools against Marxist forces. But here was a religious movement which had in its armoury ammunition directed at the US. Since the Iranian Islamic movement also vehemently opposed Marxists at home and the Soviet Union abroad, the US government could not accuse it of being leftist in disguise and discredit it, before destroying it. America's Arab allies in the region were equally baffled by this unprecedented phenonemon.

On top of that came geopolitical factors: Iran's contiguity with the Soviet Union, and its 1,000-mile-long coastline along the Gulf. Iran's 1921 treaty with the USSR made it virtually immune from a fully fledged attack by the US. Its coastline along the full length of the Gulf gave Iran unrivalled power to disrupt shipping in the Gulf. All these factors combined to inhibit the US from using its military might to cut Iran down to size. And America's inability to do so damaged its standing among its Arab allies in the region.

IRAN AND THE REGION

Historically, Saudi Arabia has been antithetical to Iran. Its Wahhabi rulers, belonging to the puritanical Sunni school of Hanbal, hold Shia Islam in low esteem. And as Arabs, they regard Iranians as outsiders. But these historical animosities did not stop the House of Saud and the Pahlavis from agreeing on the legitimacy of monarchy in Islam. Together they opposed the tide of radical republicanism that arose in the Middle East in the aftermath of the overthrow of King Farouq of Egypt in July 1952.

Among those who were pleased by the restoration of Muhammad Reza Pahlavi in August 1953 was King Saud ibn Abdul Aziz of Saudi Arabia. He visited the Shah in 1955, who returned the visit two years later. They were united in their opposition to President Nasser of Egypt. In 1960 they cooperated to form the Organisation of Petroleum Exporting Countries. Two years later both monarchs aided the royalists in North Yemen after the September 1962 republican coup there.

To stem the Nasserist tide, the Shah and King Faisal of Saudi Arabia combined to launch the Islamic Alliance in 1965 during the latter's visit to Tehran. This visit had been preceded by Iranian-Saudi agreement on territorial waters and the continental shelf. Both kings subscribed to the idea that OPEC should fix production quotas for its members. It did. Despite the Shah's recognition of Israel, and Iran's commercial, military and intelligence links with Israel, the Shah declared in March 1967 that the Palestinian problem was the concern of all Muslims. Yet when Arabs imposed an oil embargo on the West during the June 1967 war he did not join it.

In early 1968, after oil had been found near the median line of the Gulf, tension arose between Tehran and Riyadh. But it did not last long. By early October the dispute was settled. During the Shah's visit to Saudi Arabia in November, the two rulers agreed not to do anything detrimental to each other's interests and work together to counter the region's revolutionary forces.[1]

In the wake of the Nixon Doctrine enunciated in June 1969, the Shah offered a defensive alliance to all the Gulf states after the British withdrawal in late 1971. Washington visualised Iran and Saudi Arabia, both armed primarily with US weapons, as the Twin Sentinels of the Gulf. This was in line with the thinking of all the Gulf monarchs. Republican Iraq was the only dissenter.

By the middle of 1970 the Shah had settled the dispute with Britain on the future of Bahrain, signed an agreement with Qatar on offshore islands, exchanged visits with the Kuwaiti ruler, and signed an agreement with him on the continental shelf.

When Bahrain became independent on 14 August 1971 and Qatar on 1 September, Iran recognised them immediately. But relations with the UAE, which came into being on 1 December, started on a wrong note, with Iran taking over two Tunb islands and partially occupying Abu Musa island.

As the self-appointed gendarme of the Gulf, the Shah was keenly interested in the campaign by Sultan Qaboos of Oman to crush leftist insurgents in Dhofar province. When Qaboos asked for Iranian assistance in 1972, the Shah posted naval attachments on the Omani island of Umm al Ghanem at the entrance to the Gulf. He also offered joint defence of the navigable channels of the Hormuz Strait. The next year he lent combat troops to the Sultan, a step viewed with suspicion and disapproval in Riyadh. Saudi fears were aroused by the Shah's declaration in November 1972 that he was extending the 'security perimeter' of Iran beyond the Gulf to cover the north-west quadrant of the Indian Ocean, and combining this with a plan to increase the Iranian navy fivefold.

The Shah's refusal during the October 1973 Arab-Israeli war to join the Arab oil boycott of the West for its aid to Israel once again highlighted the chasm that lay between him and the Arab rulers of the Gulf. The growing commercial and military ties between Iran and Israel were a source of rising unease among Arabs. Besides being the main supplier of oil to Israel, Iran used the Eilat-Ashkelon pipeline (built with Iranian finance, to overcome the Suez Canal closure after the June 1967 war) to ship oil to such destinations as Italy and Rumania.

When the Omani ruler failed to quell the leftist rebellion in Dhofar, the Shah increased the Iranian task force from a brigade to a division in mid-1975. Aided by the Iranians and the British, the Sultan's forces defeated the insurgents in early 1976, and secured a formal ceasefire in April. But the Iranian troops did not leave Oman, nor did they stop patrolling the air space and coastline of Dhofar. This, and Iran's dramatic military build-up, fuelled fears of the Shah's expansionist aims among the other Gulf rulers. The Pahlavi had taken to acting haughtily. For instance, when the Arab states decided to form the Arab Gulf News Agency in January 1976, the Shah protested at the name and recalled his ambassadors from the capitals of the seven Gulf countries. It was only after the name was changed to the Gulf News Agency in June that he sent the ambassadors back to their posts. But such highhandedness proved counter-productive. It destroyed the support that the Shah had built up over the years for the Gulf Security Pact for the states in the region. At a meeting in Muscat in December, the Gulf foreign ministers shelved the proposal that Iran should join the Pact. That virtually killed the Shah's pet project.

Arab Gulf monarchies said little about Iran's rapprochement with Iraq in March 1975, mainly because of the fear and dislike of the radical Baathist regime in Baghdad. The general feeling among Gulf rulers was that by agreeing to share the ownership of Shatt al Arab with Iran, Iraq had compromised historic Arab rights.

As the anti-Shah movement gathered momentum from 1977 onwards, Gulf rulers watched it with growing consternation. The Shah's overthrow, they feared, would encourage republican forces in their own countries. They were ill-equipped to tackle such a threat, since they had all along sought legitimacy of their rule within Islamic precepts. Khomeini's view, based on an interpretation of the Quran, that hereditary power was unIslamic, was the most serious ideological challenge they had faced so far.

Khomeini's interpretation was readily accepted by most Shia ulema in the Gulf. This made Bahrain the most vulnerable to revolutionary upheaval. While 60 per cent of its 400,000 inhabitants were Shia, it had been ruled since 1783 by the Sunni Khalifa family. The current ruler, Shaikh Issa ibn Salman, had been at odds with the elected representatives, and had dissolved the national assembly and suspended the constitution in August 1975, and driven all opposition underground.

The Iranian revolution in early 1979 buoyed the opposition. Aware of the popularity of Khomeini and the Islamic revolution among the Shia majority – consisting of workers, civil servants and merchants – the ruler banned all news on the subject. The security forces broke up a demonstration on Jerusalem Day (15 May) with 900 arrests. Undaunted, forty leading ulema issued a twelve-point charter, demanding inter alia that Bahrain be declared an Islamic republic. The ruler's response was to suppress the subsequent demonstrations by students and others in support of the charter, and to expel Sayyed Hadi al Modaresi, an eminent Shia leader.[2]

Kuwait was the other state to feel the winds of the Iranian revolution. Thirty per cent of its 600,000 nationals were Shia.[3] Consisting mainly of poor urban dwellers, bedouins (nomadic tribes) and small merchants, Kuwaiti Shias were receptive to Khomeini's attacks on the Gulf rulers, whom he often described as 'mini-Shahs'. In July 1979 a delegation of local Shia notables flew to Tehran to congratulate Khomeini. Later thirty former parliamentary deputies out of a total of fifty petitioned the ruler, Shaikh Jabar al Sabah, to revive the national assembly dissolved in August 1976. The ruler responded by further restricting press freedom and banning discussion of public affairs even at private meetings of less than twenty persons. He resorted to ordering wholesale expulsions of 'undesirable' aliens, chiefly Shia Iranians.

With the seizure of American hostages in Tehran in late 1979, political tensions in the region sharpened. It was in this context that information ministers of the Gulf states met in Riyadh and decided on guidelines for the state-controlled and state-guided media regarding the Iranian revolution. These guidelines stressed 'playing down the news from Tehran' and demoting 'the Iranian revolution from the status of an all-Muslim one to a purely Shia one, and then to downgrade it to a purely Iranian Shia one'.[4] It was significant that Saudi Arabia was the main force behind calling the conference and shaping its outcome.

The House of Saud was shaken by the seizure of Islam's holiest shrine, the Grand Mosque of Mecca, by some 400 well-armed guerrillas at dawn on 20 November 1979, which marked the start of the Islamic fifteenth century. It took the authorities a fortnight to clear the vast mosque of the rebels. In the process, according to official sources, 127 troops, twenty-five pilgrims and 117 rebels were killed. Of the 170 guerrillas captured, 103 received long prison sentences, and the rest were beheaded by sword in public places.[5] Encouraged by the air of defiance engendered by the events in Mecca, the 400,000 strong Shia minority[6], concentrated in the oil-rich province of Al Hasa, broke the long-established ban in the kingdom on Ashura on 27 November. To the alarm of the authorities, the Ashura processions turned into pro-Khomeini demonstrations in eight important towns in the oil region. They pressed into action 20,000 security forces to break them up.[7] But sporadic demonstrations by Shia militants continued for the next two months.

Khomeini regarded the Gulf rulers as corrupt men who fostered what he called 'American Islam' or 'golden Islam'. He was scathing about their policy of depleting the valuable oil resources of their countries to satisfy the ever-growing demands of America, which he described as the Great Satan, the number one source of corruption on earth. He denounced them for denying their subjects any role in the decision-making processes of the state. The creation of a representative system in Iran, with a popularly elected president and parliament, made his argument for republicanism attractive to many in the Gulf countries.

In the wake of the Mecca episode, King Khalid ibn Abdul Aziz reshuffled seventeen top civilian and military positions. He appointed a committee to produce a draft constitution. This was followed by an announcement by Crown Prince Fahd ibn Abdul Aziz that a consultative assembly of sixty to seventy nominated members would be established 'in the near future'. The promise was not kept.

By making the US appear helpless in securing the release of its diplomats, the Khomeini regime hurt American prestige in the Gulf. This was detrimental to the interests of the Gulf rulers, since they were tied closely, commercially and militarily, to the US. Following the British withdrawal in 1971, Bahrain's ruler signed a secret agreement with America to lease naval facilities at Al Jufair. Bahrain thus became the headquarters of the US Middle East Force. On the expiry of this agreement in June 1977, it was renewed clandestinely. It offered naval and air facilities to American armed forces. In the wake of the American hostage crisis there was an upsurge in US naval and air activity in Bahrain. This reached a peak during the American military mission on 24/25 April 1980. Following the failure of this mission, US military planes refuelled in Bahrain before taking off for Turkey.

The news of this activity triggered off protest demonstrations in Bahrain and Kuwait. Interestingly, Riyadh criticised the US adminis- tration for its raid on Iran. It described the American action as 'an affront to the sovereignty of the countries of the area' which jeopardised 'the sea's security and stability'.[8]

Local security had been uppermost in the minds of Saudi leaders in the aftermath of the Mecca episode. They began canvassing support for an internal security pact covering Saudi Arabia, Kuwait, Bahrain, Qatar, the UAE and Oman. The outbreak of the Gulf War in September 1980 gave urgency to the proposition. They were now advised by Britain and France to create a supra-national body of the Gulf states which could call on the West for military assistance in the event of serious internal or external threat to one or more of its members.

The third summit of the Islamic Conference Organisation in late January 1981 in Taif, Saudi Arabia, provided a chance for the Gulf rulers to meet without undue publicity. They decided to form the Gulf Cooperation Council. At the Gulf summit in Abu Dhabi, the GCC was formally established on 26 May. Its objectives went beyond what Saudi leaders had proposed at first. The GCC's objectives were to coordinate internal security, procurement of arms and the national economies of the member states, and settle border disputes.

In the early days of the Gulf war, Iraq wanted to bomb the islands of Abu Musa and two Tunbs from the UAE or Oman. Since this would have caused the conflict to spread, Saudi Arabia pressured Iraq to drop the idea. It did. After all Iraq was close to Saudi Arabia. In fact, according to Tehran, Iraq had signed secret agreements with Saudi Arabia and Kuwait ten days before invading Iran. Saudi Arabia and Kuwait agreed to raise their respective oil outputs by 1,000,000 b/d and 800,000 b/d, and contribute the sales revenue to Iraq's war effort.[9] While keeping to their secret agreements, Saudi Arabia and Kuwait refrained from joining Iraq in the war. Once they had succeeded in containing the conflict and keeping intact their oil exporting facilities, they felt confident to face the Iranian threat ideologically and politically.

Saudi Arabia had to deal with Iran every year on the subject of hajj pilgrims. As the season approached in September 1981, tension between Tehran and Riyadh rose. Over 70,000 Iranian pilgrims were determined to use the occasion to spread Khomeini's message of politically active Islam. On 25 September fighting broke out between Iranian pilgrims and Saudi security forces in Medina when the Iranians raised slogans against the US and Israel. Twenty-two pilgrims and six Saudi soldiers were injured. Intent on curbing the use of hajj for political purposes, Saudi leaders were in an intransigent mood. As it was they had to deal with more than two million pilgrims, three-quarters of them alien, an exercise which was a great strain on their security system.[10]

Violence during the hajj made Riyadh even more security conscious and anti-Khomeini. Saudi leaders were aware of the publicly stated policy of Khomeini's regime since the early days that it considered it its 'Islamic duty' to support the national liberation movements of 'the deprived peoples' of the world. Explaining the policy, Iranian foreign minister Yazdi said, 'These liberation movements had stemmed from internal and natural conditions. They only wanted to benefit from Iran's experience [of national liberation] and gain strength from Iran's support'.[11] Among the movements being backed by Tehran were the Organisation of the Islamic Revolution in the Arabian Peninsula in Saudi Arabia and the Islamic League of Bahraini Students.[12]

Addressing GCC interior ministers in Bahrain in December 1981, Prince Nayif ibn Abdul Aziz, Saudi Arabian interior minister, stated, 'The Iranians, who said after their revolution that they did not want to be the policeman of the Gulf, have become the terrorists of the Gulf'.[13]

In early January the Bahraini government arrested sixty people – forty-five of them Bahraini and most of the rest Saudi – on charges of plotting a coup. It alleged that they had been trained in sabotage by Sayyed Hadi al Moderasi, who after his expulsion from Bahrain had been living in Iran. Prince Nayif arrived in Manama to meet his Bahraini counterpart, Shaikh Muhammad ibn Khalifa, and offered to send Saudi troops. 'The sabotage plot was engineered by the Iranian government and was directed against Saudi Arabia,' said Prince Nayif.[14] The two ministers signed a security cooperation agreement and hoped that a unified agreement would be adopted by all GCC members. 'The external danger [to the Gulf states] is Iran and the present regime in Tehran,' said Bahraini premier Shaikh Khalifa ibn Salman al Khalifa. 'The Iranian regime is instigating the Shias in Bahrain and the Gulf under the slogans of the Islamic revolution . . . training them in the use of weapons and acts of sabotage and sending them to their countries [of origin] to foment chaos and destroy security'.[15] Following the trials of the accused a few months later, three were given life sentences, and the rest shorter prison terms.

During his visit to Riyadh on 8 February 1982, Caspar Weinberger, US defence secretary, got the Saudi government's agreement to form a joint Saudi-American Military Committee – something the Saudi government had been unwilling to do in the past. What brought about the change in Riyadh was its fear of the Iranian threat. This was the background against which the Pentagon issued a secret directive in March which widened the scope of US military involvement in the Gulf. Significantly, the directive stated, 'Whatever the circumstances, we should be prepared to introduce American forces into the region should it appear [that our] security of access to Persian Gulf oil is threatened'.[16] Clearly this was meant to include the 'circumstances' created by Iranian activities in the region.

Debates inside the GCC on external security were being conducted within the limits set by Kuwait on the one hand and Oman on the other. Kuwait advocated the formation of a joint military command which was self-reliant, whereas Oman proposed a joint Arab Gulf force for the purpose of defending the Hormuz Strait under a Western umbrella. Consensus had grown around the idea of coordinating the defence plans of the members, and letting Oman and Bahrain strengthen their individual ties with the US. However, the overall thinking of the GCC members on external security could not be insulated from the developments in the Gulf War.

As Iran began scoring victories in the battlefield from the spring of 1982 onwards, GCC members paid close attention to what Tehran said or did. Khomeini called on the Gulf states to abandon their 'obedience to the US and [other] international predators'. Addressing the people of the Gulf he stated: 'The people and government of Iran want to free you of the disgraceful load of being under the control of the superpowers. These powers want to force your black gold [of oil] out of your throats'.[17]

Afraid of further Iranian gains in the war and their adverse impact on the stability of their regimes, Gulf leaders adopted a peace plan which favoured Tehran. But, as stated earlier, their efforts were swept aside by the Israeli invasion of Lebanon in early June.[18]

Iran's advance into Iraq in July and its threat to block the Hormuz Strait the following month distressed Saudi Arabia. This was the prelude to the hajj season in September. Khomeini instructed Hojatalislam Khoiniha, the leader of the Iranian Hajj Committee, to 'Acquaint Muslims with what is taking place in dear Lebanon, in crusading Iran, and in oppressed Afghanistan. Inform them of their great duties in confronting aggressors and international plunderers.'[19] During the pilgrimage Khoiniha called for mass prayers by fellow-pilgrims to smash the conspiracies of 'the deviated people' – a clear reference to Saudi rulers. In Mecca security forces arrested 100 Iranian pilgrims for attempting to address gatherings. It seemed that while the Iranians had become bolder in their actions the Saudis had become more skilled in frustrating Iranian attempts.

Having failed to get Iran interested in a ceasefire through conciliatory moves, Saudi Arabia adopted a tough stance. In early October Riyadh warned Tehran that it would face 'no holds barred' war with all Arab states if it continued to refuse mediation.[20] The reference to 'all Arab states' stemmed from the fact that the recently held Arab League summit in Fez had adopted a peace plan to end the Gulf War. The Saudi threat was meant to abort Iran's impending offensive against Iraq. It was in vain. Iran launched its offensives as planned, although they failed to achieve their full objectives. That encouraged Saudi Arabia to seek endorsement of its stand by fellow members of the GCC. It succeeded. 'Iran's tresspassing over its borders with Iraq endangered the safety of the Arab nation and also threatened its security and sovereignty,' said the GCC communiqué in November.[21]

Tehran knew that the Gulf states lacked the political will and military wherewithal to go beyond what they had been doing so far to help Iran provide funds, and transit facilities for military and other goods. As it was, the financial ability of the Gulf states to aid Iraq was waning. International demand for oil was slack, and Iranian discounts on oil prices hurt the interests of other Gulf states. Saudi Arabia has had to curtail its oil production from the peak of 9.5 million b/d in the late 1970s to 4.5 million b/d in early 1983.[22] The same was the case with other major oil producers in the region: Kuwait, Qatar and the UAE.

In early 1983 the UAE's financial aid to Iraq was running at the annual rate of $500 million. Alone among the Gulf states the UAE had maintained correct relations with Iran since the revolution. While limiting its aid to Iraq to modest grants and loans, the UAE kept up its trade with Iran. Dubai, where most of the UAE's 20,000 Iranian merchants were based, did thriving business with Iran. In April 1983 Iran Air resumed flights from Bandar Abbas to Dubai and Sharjah. Six months later ferry services between Sharjah and Bandar Abbas were restarted. Not surprisingly, the UAE was one of the two Gulf states to maintain diplomatic relations with Tehran at the ambassadorial level, the other being Kuwait.

Continuation of the Gulf War helped the GCC to become a cohesive body, particularly in military matters. Taken together, GCC states had 190,000 military personnel and 300 aircraft, a substantial force. Iran was loath to see this force placed under a unified command. Its government and media combined their criticism of the GCC with political-ideological appeals, aimed at both the ruler and the ruled, to overthrow the foreign domination of the Gulf. On the eve of the GCC foreign ministers conference in Riyadh on 20 February 1983, the Iranian daily, *Azadegan* (The Free), advised GCC rulers to 'return to the lap of Islam, abandon the Saddam Hussein regime in Baghdad, and stop squandering the wealth of their peoples'.[23] A few months later, in an interview with the Tehran-based Voice of the Gulf Radio, Khomeini said, 'Islamic Iran is ready to help the countries of the region in their liberation and salvation from the arrogant forces. . . . We believe that the superpowers led by the US are trying to prevent the unit of Islamic countries, especially in this sensitive region of the world.'[24]

But the reasons for the split in Islamic ranks in the Gulf, and elsewhere, lay in Tehran's actions: so argued the Saudi government and media. 'Ever since the Iranian and Islamic peoples were afflicted by the Khomeini regime, this regime has failed to render any noteworthy service to Islam, and the Muslims,' said *Al Medina* (The City), a Saudi daily, in July. 'This regime has tried to create schism among Muslims, not only in their politics but also in their mosques. The Khomeini regime sends its agents everywhere to foment discord.'[25]

As the hajj season approached, Riyadh and Tehran exchanged diatribes. Prince Nayif, Saudi interior minister, stated that by staging noisy demonstrations in Mecca and Medina in praise of Khomeini the Iranian pilgrims had, in the past, behaved in a manner incompatible with Prophet Muhammad's injunctions about the hajj. Undesirable though this behaviour was, what worried the Saudi authorities even more was the fact that the pilgrims from among the Shia tribes of the Arabian Peninsula had taken to contacting the Iranian ulema during the hajj.[26] Such links posed a threat to the Saudi kingdom's internal security.

In September nearly 100,000 Iranian pilgrims arrived in Saudi Arabia for hajj. Although they defied official regulations by shouting slogans against the US, USSR and Israel in Mecca and Medina, there were no violent incidents. It seemed that after repeated trials the Saudi security forces had found a way of containing militant Iranians in their midst.

Significantly, as the Gulf War entered its fourth year, Riyadh Radio announced that a three-week-long joint military exercise by GCC forces would be conducted in the UAE desert in early October. The commander of the UAE armed forces explained that the exercise, codenamed Jazira Shield, had been necessitated by 'the worrying and complex events as a result of the Iraq-Iran war and the situation in Lebanon'. It was reported that the forces participating in the exercise would form the nucleus of the Rapid Deployment Force of the GCC. 'Who will the Rapid Deployment Force of the GCC confront?' asked Tehran Radio's Arabic service on 26 September. 'Just as the formation of the GCC [in May 1981] was intended to confront the Islamic tide, it is equally true that these exercises have the same purpose'.

One way Iran could retaliate against this was by intensifying its support of the national liberation movements in GCC countries. In any case, there were periodic reports of Iranian agents landing secretly on the beaches of Bahrain and Kuwait. According to the Kuwaiti interior ministry, quoted by Qatar News Agency on 24 October 1983, forty Iranian infiltrators were arrested as they tried to enter Kuwait by sea.[27] But in the prevailing atmosphere of tension and fear in Kuwait, the figure of forty was exaggerated to 'several hundred' with everyone of them armed with lethal weapons. In the mind of the Sunni majority, Iran and Shias had become synonymous: both were considered dangerous and destabilising. As a Kuwaiti minister put it, 'The Iranian revolution does not seem to accept the legitimacy of our system of government. It exports Shiaism in the guise of pan-Islam.' Earlier that month militant Sunnis had attacked workers building a Shia mosque in a suburb of the capital. It was the first incident of its kind, and heightened Sunni-Shia tension.[28]

As a small country contiguous with Iraq and aiding it, Kuwait had great difficulty insulating itself from the consequences of the Gulf War. A reminder of this came on 12 December. That day five bomb explosions killed six people and injured eighty. The targets included US and French embassies, the compound of an American residential complex accommodating US missile experts, and Kuwait airport. Eighteen Kuwaiti residents of Iraqi and Lebanese nationality were arrested. They were reported to be members of Al Daawa al Islamiya of Iraq.[29] Alleging that these explosions were directed by the Iranian government, Iraq attacked five Iranian towns with ground to ground missiles.

With Iran showing no sign of stopping the war, the mood in the Gulf capitals became increasingly despondent. Iran's seizure of the Majnoon Islands in its offensives of February 1984 made GCC members realise that time was running against Iraq. GCC foreign ministers meeting in Riyadh in mid-March made an attempt to mediate in the war. As before, it was in vain. Following this, Kuwait announced a 'public mobilisation plan'. After three-and-a-half years of aiding Iraq in the conflict, Kuwait prepared to bear the full consequences of its policy.

As reports of the impending spring offensive by Iran gained currency, Iraq used its Super-Etendard planes and Exocet missiles in late March to escalate the conflict in the one theatre of war where it could use its initiative: the northern Gulf ports of Iran. However, the victims of Iraqi attacks were a Kuwaiti oil tanker and a Saudi cargo vessel. This embarrassed Baghdad as much as it did Riyadh and Kuwait.

There was respite for some weeks before Iraq intensified its naval attacks again. During the first week of May, Iraqi planes damaged two vessels, an Iranian tanker and a Saudi vessel. But on 13 May Iran changed the rules of the game. Its planes hit a Kuwaiti ship carrying fuel oil between Kuwait and Bahrain – that is, outside the Iraqi-declared war zone. The next day they damaged a Kuwaiti oil tanker. On 16 May they hit a 212,000 ton Saudi tanker near Ras Tanura in Saudi territorial waters. Since Tehran did not claim responsibility for these attacks, it was a few days before the facts were established. But when they were, alarm bells rang out in Western capitals. Iran had carried out its threat of damaging the oil exports of the Gulf states if its own exports were reduced.

During the week of 13-19 May Iraq hit three ships, and Iran three. This was equal to the total for the past several months. Insurance rates jumped. Diplomatic activity increased. America reiterated its determination to keep the Gulf open for shipping. This suited Saddam Hussein. He wanted to internationalise the conflict in the hope that it would mean an immediate ceasefire, and a respite for his beleaguered regime. He expected that Saudi Arabia and Kuwait would join the war and/or America would move its warships into the Gulf to protect sealanes. But he was to be disappointed.

Saudi Arabia and Kuwait acted through the GCC. The latter lodged a complaint against Iran with the UN Security Council for its attacks on ships bound for Saudi Arabia and Kuwaiti ports outside the war zone. At the same time King Fahd ibn Abdul Aziz of Saudi Arabia approached President Assad of Syria to ascertain Iran's intentions. Assad sent Vice-President Abdul Halim Khaddam to Tehran. Iranian leaders told Khaddam that they had no intention of extending the war to Kuwait or Saudi Arabia, and that what they had done was merely to show that any threat to Iranian shipping would equally threaten all other shipping in the Gulf.[30] On 28 May President Khamanei publicly urged the Gulf states to stay neutral in the war or be 'forced to put up with the consequences'.

What these consequences might be for Saudi Arabia and Kuwait had been hinted at earlier by the semi-official *Kayhan International*. 'Military speaking they [Saudi Arabia and Kuwait] are weaker and more penetrable than they think,' stated the paper in its editorial of 20 May. 'It would take our forces less than a few days to manifest this deficiency.' Outside of the military, too, Saudi Arabia and Kuwait were vulnerable. For its water and electricity, Kuwait was dependent on a few desalination and electricity plants. Their destruction by aerial bombing or internal sabotage would cause an exodus from the country. Saudi Arabia faced a similar situation in its oil rich province of A1 Hasa. Most of its oil facilities were clustered around Ras Tanura. By inviting the US to protect their sealanes Saudi Arabia and Kuwait would have solved that problem. But in the process they would have aroused Tehran's anger and invited acts of sabotage by Khomeinist elements within their borders. No foreign government or agency could offer them protection against internal terrorism or sabotage.

Saudi Arabia and Kuwait therefore decided to use their own forces to defend the sealanes against future Iranian attacks. Riyadh approached Washington for equipment to bolster its defence capabilities. Washington agreed to sell Riyadh 400 shoulder-held Stinger ground-to-air missiles to be carried by ships approaching or leaving Saudi ports.

Iraq had the satisfaction of having scared off many buyers of Iranian oil and reducing Tehran's oil exports by 1.8 million b/d to less than one million b/d. On the other hand a nearly fourfold increase in insurance rates for ships bound for northern Gulf had adversely affected the interests not only of Iran but also of Kuwait, Bahrain and Saudi Arabia. The number of oil tankers anchored off the UAE coast in southern Gulf rose from the past average of nine to twenty-five. Above all, the events of mid-May did not alter the Iranian plans to stage major land offensives against Iraq.

Faced with the stark options of declaring war against Iran and/or inviting the US to protect the Gulf sealanes – or continuing the status quo – Saudi Arabia and Kuwait chose the latter. By so doing they inadvertently edged towards Tehran's position that Gulf security was the business of the Gulf states, and that the superpowers had to be kept out.

It was significant that at a crucial moment in the crisis, Saudi Arabia selected Syria to sound out Iran. The very choice of Syria did a lot to reduce tension. Damascus was friendly with Riyadh. At the same time it had been close to Tehran since the revolution and had not deviated.

Other Arab states and immediate neighbours

Syria was the first Arab country to recognise the Khomeini regime. President Assad, an ally of the Soviet Union, was in sympathy with the Iranian revolution's militant anti-Americanism. What further attracted him to the new regime was its Shia character. As a member of the Alawi sect, Assad held Imam Ali ibn Abi Talib in greater esteem than any other successor to Prophet Muhammad. So do Shias. Soon after Assad seized power in November 1970, Imam Mousa Sadr, an eminent Shia leader in Beirut, ruled that Alawis were part of the Shia school of Islam.

The Iranian revolution occurred at a time when Syria and Iraq were committed to achieving political unity. However, after Saddam Hussein became president in July 1979, chances of such a union dwindled fast. Soon the Iraqi and Syrian governments reverted to their earlier querulous relationship. Since the Assad regime shared its hostility towards Baghdad with Khomeini, Damascus felt all the more cordial towards Tehran.

Not surprisingly, when Iraq attacked Iran in September 1980, Syria supplied weapons and ammunition to Iran by staging flights over Greece, Bulgaria and the USSR. Syria also provided Iran with intelligence on Iraq. And at least on one occasion, in April 1981, Syrian planes gave air cover to the Iranian aircraft as they bombed the Iraqi air base of Al Walid.

Tehran's strong anti-Zionist line was popular in Damascus. Syria was then the leader of the Front of Steadfastness and Confrontation (with Israel), consisting of Libya, Algeria, South Yemen and the PLO. The Front invited Iran to its foreign ministers conference in Tripoli, Libya, in mid-September 1981 as an observer. Mir Hussein Mousavi, then Iran's foreign minister, attended. A month later Iran signed an arms deal with Syria.[31]

This was a prelude to the forging of long-term commercial links between the two states. In March 1982 they signed a ten-year trade pact. Iran agreed to sell, over the next year, five million tons of oil to Syria for cash, and exchange another 700,000 tons for Syrian phosphates and manufactured goods. Having thus secured its oil needs, Syria closed the Iraqi pipeline passing through its territory in early April. It thus deprived Iraq of 40 per cent of its oil revenue.[32] Assad then severed all ties with Iraq, and came out publicly in favour of overthrowing the Saddam Hussein regime.

Soon after Syria came to Iran's aid again. In the wake of the loss of Khorramshahr to the Iranians in May, Saddam Hussein sent out urgent appeals to Arab leaders to join him in the war. President Hosni Mubarak of Egypt showed his willingness to do so. Assad warned that if Egypt fought on Iraq's side, Syria would line up with Iran. This dissuaded Mubarak from joining the fray.

When Israel attacked Lebanon in June, Iran expressed its solidarity with Lebanon. The government offered to send volunteers to fight Israel in Lebanon. For this it needed Syria's cooperation. Assad allowed about one thousand members of Iran's Islamic Revolutionary Guards safe passage through Syria to Baalbek in the Shia enclave of eastern Lebanon. After the ceasefire, Baalbek became a centre of militant anti-Israeli activity.

In January 1983 the foreign ministers of Iran, Syria and Libya met in Damascus for consultations. In a joint communiqué issued by Syria and Libya, they condemned Iraq for its invasion of Iran and pledged to stand by Iran against 'hostile forces'.[33] Iran showed its appreciation of the Syrian stand. When drawing up trade terms for the next financial year Iran agreed to sell Syria not only five million tons of oil for cash and barter but also offered Syria one million tons of oil – worth nearly $200 million – as a grant, to assist it in its fight against Israel.[34]

The Syrian government derived political and diplomatic advantages from its alliance with Iran. By having Iraq engaged in war with Iran, it had a quiet eastern front for itself. Saddam Hussein was unable to instigate destabilising activities against the Assad regime. This allowed Assad to concentrate on resolving the Lebanese crisis caused by the Israeli invasion and occupation.

In the autumn of 1982 Lebanon was in a sorry state. It was occupied by Israeli forces in the south and Syrian troops in the north and east, leaving only an enclave around Beirut under the Lebanese government of President Amin Gemayel, a Maronite Christian.[35] His administration was to be assisted by the peace-keeping forces of America, France, Italy and Britain to extend its area of control. The presence of Western troops was opposed by most Lebanese Muslims. This was particularly true of Shias. On 23 October 1983 two suicide bomb attacks on US marines and French paratroopers in Beirut caused nearly 300 deaths. These assaults were widely attributed to militant Shias, who believe in religious martyrdom.

Being about 30 per cent of the Lebanese population of 3.6 million, Shias were the largest community, more numerous than the 900,000 Maronite Christians. Yet the 1943 National Pact, based on the 1932 census, gave Shias only nineteen parliamentary seats to the Maronites' thirty in a house of ninety-nine deputies.[36] In the 1930s Shias were concentrated in southern Lebanon where they had arrived from adjoining areas in the eleventh century to escape persecution. Political convulsions of the 1950s caused them to move north, to Sidon and Beirut, in search of work and shelter.

Lebanese Shias had close contacts with their holy cities in Iraq, and thus with Qom. In 1957 Imam Mousa Sadr, born in Qom of a leading theological family, was sent to Lebanon to offer religious guidance to local Shias. As a result of his condemnation of the Shah's suppression of the June 1963 uprising, Sadr was deprived of his Iranian nationality. He then became a Lebanese citizen. Four years later he formed the Higher Shia Communal Council under his leadership. He founded the Movement of the Deprived which attracted many Shias, dissatisfied as they were with their traditional, pro-establishment leaders. Through strikes and demonstrations Sadr made Shias aware of their political strength. To protect Shias during the 1975-6 civil war, Sadr established a militia, called Al Amal (The Hope). It was armed and trained by Al Fatah (The Victory), a Palestinian organisation.

Throughout his stay in Lebanon, Sadr was in touch with Khomeini, who was his close friend. Not surprisingly, Lebanese Shias watched with growing interest the rise of the revolutionary movement in Iran under Khomeini. But Sadr did not live to see it succeed. During a trip to Libya and Italy in late August 1978 he 'disappeared'.

Following Sadr's death, leadership of the Higher Shia Communal Council passed to Shaikh Muhammad Mahdi Shams al-Din. The Amal congress of April 1980 elected a new Leadership Council, with Nabih Berri, a lawyer, as the general secretary. Under him the Amal expanded and became one of the most important fighting forces. In October 1981 a delegation from the Amal visited Tehran and had a meeting with President Khamanei.

However, Berri's policies were considered too constitutionalist by some of his colleagues, particularly Hussein Mousavi, a young teacher. Mousavi left the Amal to form the Islamic Amal with its headquarters in Baalbek in the Syrian-controlled Bekka valley. Baalbek was also the centre of the Hezbollahis of Lebanon, led by Shaikh Muhammad Hassan Fadlollah and Shaikh Ragheb Harb. Later it was in Baalbek that Iranian revolutionary guards set up their offices.

Baalbek was reported to be the centre of the Islamic Jihad, a shadowy organisation which claimed responsibility for the bombing of American and French barracks in Beirut in late October – and a similar attack on the Israeli headquarters in Tyre on 4 November, which killed twenty-nine Israelis and thirty-two non-Israelis. In retribution Israeli and French warplanes (the latter operating from offshore warships) raided Baalbek on 20 November. Of the forty-four people killed, fourteen were Iranian revolutionary guards.[37] The deaths of Iranians by Israeli bombs further inflamed the anti-Israeli feelings of the Tehran regime.

This set off a fresh cycle of violence and counter-violence, leading to an intensification of hit and run attacks on Israeli forces in south Lebanon, where 60 per cent of the one million inhabitants were Shia. On 3 and 4 January 1984 sixteen Israeli planes bombed Baalbek and two adjoining villages, killing nearly 100 people and injuring 400, most of them civilian. Two days later the Iranian deputy foreign minister, Hussein Shaikholislam, visited Baalbek. In his statements he was reported to have praised suicide bomb attacks on American, French and Israeli troops.[38] This was taken to be an affirmation of the earlier allegations by US, French, Israeli and Lebanese intelligence officials that Iran was masterminding suicide assaults in conjunction with Syria. President Gemayel had already reached this conclusion, and ordered the closure of the Iranian embassy in Beirut in December.

Tehran denied these charges, and replied that the Western powers and Israel were looking for scapegoats for the failure of their policies in Lebanon: a Muslim majority country ruled by a Maronite minority allied to the West and Israel. Ayatollah Hadi Khosrowshahi, the Iranian ambassador to the Vatican, explained the religio-political context of suicide attacks. Arguing that the Muslim peoples of Iran, Afghanistan, Palestine and Lebanon had the right to defend their 'freedom, faith, honour and independence from the aggressor' by 'whatever means they see fit', he said: 'This honourable defence is a right for every free human being, and dying in this noble cause is in our view martyrdom in the way of God'.[39]

Soon Lebanese Shias showed themselves to be well-versed in conventional means of fighting. When President Gemayel's order to the Lebanese army to flatten the Shia suburbs of south Beirut was carried out on 3 February, Berri ordered Amal militia to attack the army. Aided by the militia of the Druze Progressive Socialist Party, operating mainly from the adjoining Shouf mountains, the Amal captured West Beirut, and dealt Gemayel's army and administration a body blow. The Lebanese army disintegrated and the government, led by Premier Shafiq al Wazzan, collapsed. The success of the Muslim forces, supported by Syria, over the Gemayel administration, backed by the US and Israel, pleased Tehran as much as it did Damascus.

Tehran saw the victory of Lebanese Muslims in the Beirut area as the first step – to be followed by the expulsion of the Israelis from south Lebanon[40] – towards the final goal of liberating Jerusalem. It was not accidental that the Islamic Republic portrayed its struggle to free Najaf and Karbala from the 'non-Muslim' regime of Saddam Hussein as part of the march to liberate Jerusalem. Known in Arabic as Al Quds (The Holy) or Bait al Muqaddas (The Holy Place),

Jerusalem is the third holiest place of Muslims. It is the city of the Holy Rock, the site to which Prophet Muhammad flew miraculously by night and was escorted up a staircase of light by the archangel Gabriel to receive divine instructions for his followers. This was the beginning of his prophethood.

Khomeini had maintained all along that the Zionists had usurped the Muslim land of Palestine, and that the process must be reversed. During his exile in Najaf he issued a religious decree saying that part of the donations made to the Twelfth Imam must be given to the Palestinian cause.[41]

Within a week of the revolution in early February 1979 Yasser Arafat, chairman of the PLO, accompanied by thirty-one aides, arrived in Tehran and had a meeting with Khomeini. The building, which until then had housed the Israeli mission in Tehran, was turned over to the PLO. Arafat appointed Hassan al Hani, his foremost political adviser, as the PLO ambassador to Iran. It showed the importance he attached to revolutionary Iran. He and other PLO leaders saw the change in Tehran as compensating the loss that the Palestinian cause had suffered due to the defection of Egypt from Arab ranks, ready to sign a separate peace treaty with Israel. The Iranian government pledged financial aid to the PLO, linked to the country's oil exports.

When American diplomats were taken hostage Arafat tried to mediate, but was persuaded by Tehran not to. After the Gulf War erupted, he mediated between the Iranians and the Iraqis, but to no avail. The ouster of Bani-Sadr as president by Islamic militants caused a cooling of relations between the PLO and the Khomeini regime. In August 1981 Hassan al Hani left Tehran. Early next month Masoud Rajavi announced that Hani had had a meeting with him in Paris. The PLO headquarters in Beirut stated that Hani was not authorised to carry out any official duties.[42] All the same Tehran-PLO relations grew cooler.

Iran lost further goodwill among PLO leaders when it rejected the Iraqi offer of a ceasefire in June 1982, which would have enabled the erstwhile combatants in the Gulf War to combine and fight Israel and thus help the PLO, then under an Israeli siege in Beirut. After this Arafat began siding with Iraq in its war with Iran. Among other things Baghdad provided facilities to run a broadcasting station inside Iraq, called the Voice of Palestine Radio.

In May 1983 there was a split in the leading constituent of the PLO, Al Fatah: the power base of Arafat. This showed Tehran that Arafat's popularity among Palestinians was waning. Iran's sympathies lay with the pro-Syrian faction within Al Fatah which opposed Arafat, and which wanted to abide strictly by the PLO covenant that all of

Palestine, not just the West Bank and the Gaza Strip, must be liberated.

Some months later President Khamanei articulated the Iranian government's misgivings about the PLO and Palestinians. 'The Palestinians are weak because their movement's criteria are not in accordance with genuine Islamic principles,' he said. 'The people who speak in the name of Palestinians never speak in the name of Islam.'[43] In short, secularism was the root cause of the weakness of the Palestinian liberation movement.

It was obvious that the Islamic Republic was quite selective in choosing its friends and allies in the Arab world. The case of the PLO was illustrative. Yet the same strict criteria did not always apply when it came to the Republic's ties with its immediate neighbours. Turkey was a good example. It was a secular state as well as a member of Nato; yet it enjoyed excellent relations with Iran.

Following the EEC trade sanctions against Iran in April 1980, commercial links between the two neighbours grew dramatically. Between 1980 and 1982 Turkish exports of foodgrains, sugar, meat, farm machinery and electrical appliances rose from $87 million to $600 million. Iran exported 80,000 b/d of oil to Turkey. The two-way trade in 1982-3 amounted to $2,200 million.[44] In September 1982 Iran agreed to supply natural gas to Turkey and build a pipeline for the purpose. Tehran and Ankara initiated a feasibility study for an oil pipeline from Iran to the Turkish port of Mersin.

Long before the Islamic movement gathered pace in Iran, Turkey experienced a campaign for Islamic revival. This was led by the National Order Party formed in 1969 by Necmettin Erbakan. Since Turkey's secular constitution of 1923 forbade propaganda for a theocratic state, the party was outlawed by the constitution court. Erbakan then formed the National Salvation Party in October 1972. It emerged as the third largest party in parliamentary elections held a year later, winning nearly 12 per cent of popular vote, mainly in rural areas. Erbakan became deputy premier in the two coalition governments formed between 1974 and 1977. Defying the constitution, he propagated Islamic ideas, and called for the formation of the Islamic Common Market consisting of Turkey and the Arab Middle East. Although the NSP's vote declined to 8.6 per cent in the June 1977 election, Islamisation of politics did not. 'Politics has even entered the mosques and lower forms of secondary schools,' said Turkey's interior minister in April 1978.[45]

Intensification of the revolutionary movement in Iran in the latter half of 1978 engaged the attention of the Shias in Turkey (known as Alewis) who, forming one-sixth of the national population of forty-two million, were concentrated in the south-east. Turkey itself was being rocked by violence between extreme right and extreme left, which claimed seventy lives a month. As strife in urban areas spilled into villages, it rekindled old racial and sectarian hatreds, between Turks and Kurds, and Shia and Sunni. The underprivileged Shias, who by and large favoured the left, became targets of attack by neofascists, who worked in league with militant Sunnis. A three-day sectarian-political riot in Kahranmaras in December left 117 people dead and over 1,000 injured, most of them Shia. This embarrassed and alarmed the Turkish government. Premier Bulent Ecevit put twelve eastern provinces under martial law to reassure the Shia minority.

Aware of the historic ties that have existed between Turkish Shias and their Iranian counterparts, Ecevit was keen to see that this did not become a destabilising factor after the Shah's overthrow in early 1979. He was therefore quick to recognise the Khomeini regime and establish normal relations with it. On his part Khomeini – who had spent a year of his exile in Turkey in the mid-1960s – was aware of the importance of Turkey in the history of Islam, and wanted good relations with Ankara. The first foreign diplomat he received after his return to Tehran was the Turkish ambassador to Iran.

Although the regime in Turkey changed twice during the next five years, Turkish-Iranian relations did not. Improvement in commercial links between the two states, in the wake of the Western embargo of Iran in the spring of 1980, aided Turkey's ailing economy. But it had only a marginal impact on the deteriorating law and order situation in Turkey. While conflict between right and left intensified, the movement for Islamic revival gained ground. In early September the World Assembly of Islamic Youth for the Liberation of Palestine, sponsored by the National Salvation Party and held in Konya, drew large crowds. Among other things the rally called for the establishment of an Islamic state in Turkey. This triggered off a military coup on 12 September. The communiqué issued by the military leaders described their action as being against 'the followers of fascist and communist ideologies as well as religious fanatics'.[46]

In normal circumstances Iranian leaders would have probably acted on their view which holds military dictatorship as unIslamic, and disapproved of the military takeover of Turkey. But with tension on the Iran-Iraq border building up to open warfare, they took a pragmatic stance on the subject. When the Gulf War erupted Turkey declared itself neutral. This meant an upturn in its trade with Iraq (whose southern ports were soon blocked) and a continued flow of oil through the 900-mile-long pipeline from Kirkuk to the Turkish port of Yumurtalik. In early August 1982 Turkey's military premier, Bulent Ulusu, visited Tehran. He offered to mediate in the war, but nothing came of it.[47] A year later Hashemi-Rafsanjani summed up Tehran-

Ankara ties thus: 'We have extensive relations with Turkey. We do not think we are a threat to Turkey's interests in the region'.[48]

Turkey continued to give top priority to its links with Iran. This was as true of the military government as of the elected civilian administration, headed by Turgut Ozal, which followed in December 1983. The Ozal government reiterated Turkish neutrality in the Gulf War. In late April 1984 Ozal visited Tehran, thereby highlighting the significance that Turkey attached to its ties with the Islamic Republic. Turkey remained Iran's third most important trading partner, after Japan and West Germany. Iran tried to balance its trade with Turkey by increasing its sale of oil to Ankara. Exports of 100,000 b/d to Turkey in early 1984 for nearly $1 billion showed that its efforts were successful.

The other neighbour with whom Iran tried to balance its trade by using the same tactic was Pakistan. In 1980 Pakistan benefited commercially by two diverse events: the Western embargo of Iran and Tehran's severance of all links with Kabul. Pakistan's exports to Iran shot up from $45 million in 1978-9 to $250 million four years later. The Islamic Republic tried to balance the trade by exporting 10,000 b/d of oil, worth about $100 million a year, to Pakistan.[49]

Like Turkey, Pakistan was once a member of the Baghdad Pact, to which Iran belonged. In 1964 the three countries formed an organisation, called the Regional Cooperation for Development: it concentrated on improving communications in the region. During the Indo-Pakistan war of 1965, the Shah provided Pakistan with some military aid. But when the next Indo-Pakistan war broke out in December 1971 in Pakistan's eastern wing, the Shah was unable to do much to help the military regime of Pakistan.[50] The Shah deplored the dismemberment of Pakistan as a result of the war.

He established cordial relations with Zulfikar Ali Bhutto, who became the civilian head of Pakistan. Following his November 1972 statement extending the Iranian security perimeter to include the north-west quadrant of the Indian Ocean, the Shah virtually regarded the Baluchistan province of Pakistan (adjacent to Iranian Baluchistan) as part of Iran's security perimeter. He opposed the autonomist demands of the popularly elected provincial government of Pakistani Baluchistan, arguing that conceding these would give Iranian Baluchs 'dangerous ideas'.[51] In February 1973, yielding to the Shah's pressures, Bhutto dismissed the Baluchistan government on the ground that, working in league with Iraq and the Soviet Union, Baluch autonomists were plotting to dismember Pakistan and Iran.

During his visit to Tehran, Bhutto was offered emergency financial and military aid. 'We strongly reaffirm that we will not close our eyes to any secessionist movement in Pakistan,' said the Shah.[52] Urging Bhutto to use the air force as well as the army to crush Baluchi insurgency, he lent Pakistan scores of Iranian helicopter gunships. The insurgency continued for three years. Buoyed by booming oil revenue, the Shah gave increased financial and military aid to Pakistan.

The Shah became obsessed with the idea of Pakistan falling apart. 'What would happen if what remains of Pakistan were to disintegrate?' he asked in an interview with *Newsweek* in November 1977. 'If we don't assume the responsibility for the security of the region, who will do it?'[53]

By then Pakistan was being ruled by General Muhammad Zia al-Haq. He had seized power in a military coup in early July 1977, and had the support of local Islamic parties. 'Pakistan, which was created in the name of Islam, will continue to survive only if it sticks to Islam,' Zia al-Haq said on assuming power. 'That is why I consider the introduction of an Islamic system an essential prerequisite for the country.'[54]

Not surprisingly, Pakistan recognised the Bazargan government the day it was formed. There was a pragmatic reason behind this as well. Pakistan was indebted to Iran to the tune of several hundred million dollars. In July 1979 Khomeini received Agha Shahi, Pakistan's foreign minister, a sign of the importance he attached to relations with the Islamic Republic of Pakistan.

In the charged political atmosphere engendered by the American hostage crisis, radical Islamic elements in Iran placed Zia al-Haq in the same category as President Sadat of Egypt, a lackey of American imperialism. Addressing a group of Pakistani naval officers in late November, Khomeini called on them to initiate Islamic revolution at home.[55]

What arrested the progression of this policy line was the Soviet military intervention in Afghanistan in late December. In fact, Moscow's action brought Tehran and Islamabad together to follow a common objective: to secure Soviet withdrawal from Afghanistan. Relations between the two capitals remained cordial even though Pakistan was to draw closer to the US and Saudi Arabia militarily and financially.

The histories of Iranians and Afghans have been intertwined for many centuries. It was the rebellion by Afghan tribes in 1722 which ended the Safavid rule in Iran. The fate of Herat in western Afghanistan was a source of recurring conflict between Iran and British India. In more recent times relations between Tehran and Kabul were soured by the dispute over the Helmund river and its marshes.

In the wake of Iraq's friendship treaty with Moscow in April 1972, the Shah decided to improve relations with Afghanistan by resolving the border issue in the marshy area of Helmund. Negotiations between the two sides on this issue were in progress when King Muhammad

Zahir Shah was overthrown in a bloodless coup by his brother-in-law and former premier, Muhammad Daud Khan, on 17 July 1973. Daud Khan declared Afghanistan a republic. The Shah of Iran recognised the new regime; and the Iranian parliament approved the Helmund river treaty between the two states.

The Shah tried to influence the republican regime in Kabul by offering aid for such massive projects as a steel mill in Afghanistan and a rail link between the republic and Bandar Abbas in Iran. He attempted to veer Daud Khan away from reformist policies at home and a pro-Soviet stance abroad. In 1976 he pledged to underwrite half of Afghanistan's $2,500 million seven-year plan. In response Daud Khan began orienting Afghan policy towards the West, particularly America. Afghan intelligence services worked in cooperation with Savak and the CIA. Leftist elements in Afghanistan bore the brunt of these agencies' actions. Under this pressure two leftist groups, Parcham (Flag) and Khalq (People), merged to form the People's Democratic Party. This was a serious challenge to Daud Khan's rule. He tried to counter it by repressing the leftists further.

The assassination of Mir Akbar Kheibar, a respected PDP leader, in Kabul on 17 April 1978 was typical of the tactics being used by Afghan intelligence services against the leftists. The funeral procession for Kheibar turned into a massive demonstration against the Daud Khan government. It set off a chain of events which culminated in the overthrow of Daud Khan on 27 April by leftist military officers allied to the PDP. The new regime was headed by Noor Muhammad Taraki (of the PDP's Khalq faction), with Hafizollah Amin (of the Khalq faction) and Babrak Karmal (of the Parcham faction) as deputy premiers. Along with social and economic reforms, the PDP government promised to promote 'genuine Islamic tradition'.

These events alarmed the Shah. Despite his preoccupation with stemming the rising discontent in Iran, he supplied arms to traditionalist Afghan elements to fight the leftist authorities. Among Iranian ulema Shariatmadari was prominent in his support for Islamic forces ranged against the Afghan government, then riven by internal wrangling which saw Karmal being posted as Afghan ambassador to Czechoslovakia in December 1978.

The PDP regime welcomed the Shah's downfall, which held a promise of improved ties with Tehran. But the revolutionary government in Iran soon began deporting Afghan workers, alleging that they were criminals. This soured relations between Kabul and Tehran. On 18 March 1979 Iran closed its borders with Afghanistan. When fighting broke out in Herat between security forces and Islamic rebels, the PDP government expelled the Iranian consul in Herat, alleging an Iranian hand in fomenting the trouble.[56]

As guerrilla activity in Afghanistan increased, Taraki blamed Pakistan, Iran and the CIA for it. Internal rivalries in the PDP government reached a point where there was a shoot-out in September between the rival followers of Taraki and Amin. Taraki was killed. As the new head of state, Amin pursued counter-insurgency measures with greater vigour than Taraki. He also accelerated the pace of secularisation. These policies alienated large sections of Afghan society. Kabul's relations with Tehran cooled further.

On 27 December Soviet troops marched into Afghanistan, with the Kremlin claiming that they had been invited by the Afghan government to help foil foreign conspiracies against it. In the fighting that erupted at the presidential palace, Amin and many of his aides were killed. Babrak Karmal, who had been living in exile in Moscow for many months, returned to become the president of Afghanistan. Tehran condemned the Soviet action.

The Karmal administration immediately freed thousands of political prisoners and returned to the country's original green-black-red flag, which had been replaced in August 1978 by an all-red flag. It also restored the customary invocation to Allah which is used as the preamble to all public statements. But these gestures had no impact on the Islamic Conference Organisation foreign ministers meeting in Islamabad, Pakistan in January. Working with Pakistan, Iran rallied Islamic sentiment against the leftist regime in Afghanistan. The ICO suspended Afghanistan's membership.

Karmal addressed a letter to Khomeini suggesting 'consolidation of fraternal and friendly Islamic relations between the Afghan and Iranian peoples' with the objective of delivering 'an ultimate rebuke to the world-craving imperialism and Zionism'.[57] Khomeini was unmoved.

At the next ICO foreign ministers conference in May, the Iranian delegation included two Afghan rebel leaders. A few weeks later the Iranian foreign minister, Qutbzadeh, said that Iran was ready to supply arms to Afghan insurgents. 'Independence of Afghanistan is as sacred as the liberation of Palestine,' he said. 'If Iran accepts the Soviet presence in Afghanistan it will fall from the hand of one superpower into the hand of another superpower.'[58]

Qutbzadeh was a member of the three-member ICO commission appointed to unite various rebel Afghan parties. But the differences among them proved to be irreconcilable. In the summer of 1981 the Karmal administration tried to implement its conscription law. This led to an exodus of young men to Pakistan and Iran. As a result the number of Afghan refugees in Iran – which stood at 900,000 in early 1981 – rose further. About a third of these were in the Tayabad district near Herat, and most of the rest in and around Mashhad and Tehran.

Anti-government activities in Afghanistan were high in the areas contiguous to Pakistan or Iran. The effectiveness of the guerrillas inside Afghanistan depended on how well they had coordinated their activities with those outside the country.

In due course the CIA became the coordinator of foreign aid, in cash and weapons, that flowed to Afghan rebels from the US, China, Saudi Arabia, Egypt and Pakistan. This applied to the activities of the rebels on the Pakistani side. Being on the opposite side of the Pakistani border, the Iranians kept well clear of the CIA and its activities among Afghan rebels.

At the same time Iran cooperated with Pakistan in strengthening Afghan resistance against the Karmal government. In late July 1982 it helped to create the United Front for the Liberation of Afghanistan, headed by Gulb al-Din Hikmatyar. The Front committed itself to getting the Soviets out of Afghanistan and establishing an Islamic regime there.

Iran was one of the four parties invited to participate in the talks to be held under the aegis of the UN General Secretary's office to find a solution to the problem and secure the withdrawal of Soviet troops, as recommended by the UN General Assembly. (The other three parties were Afghanistan, Pakistan and the USSR.) But Iran refused to conduct face-to-face negotiations with the Karmal government, a government it did not recognise. Pakistan too had withdrawn recognition from the Karmal administration. Yet in the spring of 1983 it agreed to hold talks with the Afghan government under the UN aegis in order to create conditions conducive to Soviet withdrawal. However, Iran said that it would not take part until 'the real representatives of the Afghan people' participated in these negotiations.[59] So the stalemate continued.

Tehran's intransigence on this issue was characteristic of its behaviour in other instances. Even in the Islamic Conference Organisation it had taken positions which had made it stand out as a radical loner. However, that was not the case in the beginning. In fact the eleventh ICO foreign ministers conference in Islamabad in January 1980 supported the Islamic revolution in Iran and opposed 'the external pressures' being applied on it.[60] The situation changed with the Iraqi attack on Iran. Khomeini expected that the ICO would condemn Iraq for its aggression against another Muslim country. But nothing of the sort happened. On the contrary, the ruler of Saudi Arabia (which housed the headquarters of the ICO in Jeddah) phoned Saddam Hussein to congratulate him on his action.

At the December 1980 ICO foreign ministers conference in Rabat, Morocco Iran argued that the item on the agenda for the third Islamic summit should read 'The Iraqi invasion and occupation of Iran' and not 'The Iraq-Iran war'. It was outvoted. Therefore it boycotted the summit held in Taif, Saudi Arabia.[61]

Khomeini saw the ICO peace mission when it visited Tehran in March 1981. But, as described earlier, he used it as a ploy to test Iraqi morale.[62] The subsequent ICO attempts to mediate in the war were equally futile. Khomeini insisted that the aggressor must be punished to set an example for ICO members not to attack a fellow Muslim state in the future. But his was a minority voice.

The fourteenth ICO foreign ministers conference in Dhaka, Bangladesh, in December 1983 failed to adopt a resolution on the Gulf War. Iran boycotted the fourth Islamic summit in Casablanca, Morocco, the following month because the ICO did not send a delegation to Iran to inspect the results of Iraqi bombing of Iran's civilian areas.

Behind these specific objections lay something more profound which informed Iranian policies towards other Muslim countries. Iranian leaders believed that it was only in their country that the will of Allah, as expressed through the Quran, was being implemented. A country such as Saudi Arabia was ruled under a monarchical system which was in itself unIslamic. Moreover, those who ruled the state were deviants. In their personal lives they broke the Quranic injunctions on drink, extra-marital sex, gambling etc. In so far as its nationals were Muslim, Saudi Arabia was a Muslim state; but it was not an Islamic state. As for an Islamic state like Libya, it was deficient in another sense. The present system there had been instituted by army officers after they had mounted a coup against the monarchy. There had been no involvement of ordinary Muslims in changing the regime, something which Iranian Muslims had done. In Iran the faithful had struggled in their millions to overthrow a corrupt regime and institute a government of God. Iran was therefore unique. It provided a model for people in other Muslim countries to follow.

Such an assessment of their revolution and country made Iranian leaders feel self-righteous. If this had isolated Iran in the community of Muslim countries, Iranians should not feel dejected by it, they argued. The faithful must look at the life of Imam Ali. He was a perfect Muslim. Yet he was ignored and made to suffer. But ultimately the Muslim community realised his worth and elected him the successor to Prophet Muhammad. Like a true Muslim the Islamic Republic must stay firmly on a correctly interpreted Islamic path. Ultimately others will see the correctness of its policies and come around to its views and interpretations. It was a matter of faith, correct interpretation of the Quran, perseverance and time.

CONCLUSION

The Iranian revolution stands apart from similar upheavals in the Middle East. During the period of 1952-62, the monarchs of Egypt, Iraq and North Yemen were overthrown by groups of military officers, and republics established. These coups were welcomed by the people; and they set the scene for widespread political and economic reform. In Iran, however, the involvement of millions of people in the process of toppling the Pahlavi regime made a qualitative difference.

Since Iranians had suffered decades of oppressive dictatorship, they genuinely desired freedoms of expression and association. They enjoyed these after the revolution, but only briefly. Some of Ayatollah Khomeini's confidants during his exile in Paris maintained that the Ayatollah had promised basic freedoms as an integral part of the post-Pahlavi state, and that it was only after he had returned to Iran that he reneged. They held Ayatollah Bcheshti mainly responsible for this change. If Beheshti played any role in this, it was most probably to express his preference for Khomeini's blueprint for an Islamic government and society as elaborated in his written works. It is obvious from Khomeini's writings that he draws his inspiration exclusively from Islam – with not the slightest reference to such Western concepts as democracy, nationalism or socialism – that he takes a literalist view of Sharia, and that he believes firmly in direct rule by the ulema. Khomeini has been consistent in his views, and he has had the reputation of being uncompromising. It is true that he did not issue a clear-cut political programme of his own during the revolutionary movement. But his writings provided a fair indication of what to expect if the movement being led by him succeeded in overthrowing the Shah.

Islamic leaders like Beheshti decided to work with Bazargan, or even Bani-Sadr, out of expediency and lack of political party of their own. In his address to the IRP leaders on the last day of his life, 28 June 1981, Beheshti said: 'At the time [in February 1979] we cast a vote of confidence for the Bazargan government we were not so well organised as we are today. . . . We had not fully discovered our potential resources'.[1]

While the IRP discovered its 'potential resources', counter-revolutionary forces at home and abroad attempted to derail and destroy the revolution. The greater the pressure of its opponents on the regime, the more intolerant it became towards dissent, whether malevolent or not. In the process, basic freedoms suffered. The more ruthless the Islamic government became, the more its opponents vilified it; and so the cycle went on, upwards.

These developments occurred in the context of the assassinations and deaths of top leaders. The assassination of Ayatollah Motahhari, the moderate chairman of the Islamic Revolutionary Council, by the Furqan in May 1979 removed an important figure capable of conciliating different trends within the Islamic camp, which then included the Mujahedin-e Khalq. The death of Ayatollah Taleqani in September 1979 deprived the top layer of clerical leadership of the balance that had existed so far: Shariatmadari, inclined towards liberal, pro-Western forces; Taleqani, sympathetic towards the domestic left; and Khomeini somewhere in between. Taleqani was also a bridge between the radical IRC and the moderate Bazargan government. While being close to Khomeini, Taleqani had cordial relations with Mujahedin leaders. He enjoyed the respect of the Persian-speaking majority as well as the non-Persian-speaking minorities. His national stature was such that he was a credible bridge between the left, whether Islamic or secular, on one hand, and the conservative Islamic right on the other. Following his death, a violent confrontation first between the secular left and the Islamic right, and then between the Islamic left and the Islamic right, became inevitable.

With Taleqani's balancing presence gone, the Islamic establishment became bipolar. Shariatmadari represented the liberal school which advocated non-intervention by the ulema in the day-to-day administration of society; and Khomeini represented the interventionist school. Differences between the two became irreconcilable, and were settled by their respective followers in the streets of Tabriz and Qom. In such a contest Shariatmadari had no chance of winning. Khomeini was a seasoned fighter; and this time he had the weight of the Iranian state behind him.

Once Shariatmadari was eliminated as a potential rival to Khomeini, anti-Khomeini forces switched their loyalties to President Bani-Sadr. With their favourite occupying the presidency, they had a fair chance of destabilising the regime. But the Khomeinists, now organised as the Islamic Republican Party, were well entrenched in seats of power. They controlled the Majlis, the judiciary, all revolutionary organisations and, most importantly, the media. When their long-expected confrontation with Bani-Sadr finally came in June 1981, they employed all their resources to defeat him.

But removing Bani-Sadr from the presidency was one thing, eliminating all opposition forces quite another. Finding themselves pushed against the wall, the Mujahedin-e Khalq, the principal backers of Bani-Sadr, hit back hard. It took the ruling party and the government a long time to counter the Mujahedin challenge. The previous threat to them had come from the Marxist-Leninist Fedai Khalq, with its base chiefly among the secular professional classes, and from ethnic minorities in the outlying regions of the Republic. But the Mujahedin drew their main support from the same sections of society as the IRP did: traders and merchants, artisans, and the ulema in the Persian-speaking heartland of Iran. Many young men and women from traditional middle class families found the Mujahedin interpretations of Islam, often based on Ali Shariati's dialectical approach to Islam, more attractive than Khomeini's literalist interpretations of Sharia and the Quran. They believed more in the 'spirit of Islam', as articulated by Mujahedin ideologues, than in the corpus of Islam, which was the sole source of inspiration for the Khomeinists. Being young and angry, they were critical, even contemptuous, of the traditional ulema, whom they saw as the epitome of conservatism.

The regime was aware of the appeal that the Mujahedin had among the young. By giving its backing to the Khomeinist students' seizure of the US embassy in Tehran, it tried to impress on the young that it was as militantly anti-imperialist as the Mujahedin or the Fedai. Access to the secret documents captured at the US embassy enabled it to weed out almost all the pro-American elements in the country. Time and again it was made aware of the strength of American influence even in post-Pahlavi Iran. To find the Iranian air force commander implicated in cooperating with the CIA to facilitate Washington's military mission against Iran in April 1980 shocked and alarmed the Islamic leadership. Such discoveries increased its paranoia and vigilance.

It was significant that while pursuing an anti-imperialist line abroad, and making repeated statements in favour of the poor at home, Khomeini did not use phraseology which could conceivably be termed Marxist. He avoided such terms as capitalists, landlords, bourgeoisie, toilers, and feudal. Instead of talking of exploiters and exploited, he referred to oppressors and oppressed.[2] In general he championed the cause of the lower classes. Yet he also said, 'The foundation of an Islamic state is based on no one class being dominant over other classes'.[3]

Had the Iranian government and media used terms which smacked even vaguely of Marxism, they would have provided the US and the anti-Khomeinist forces at home with an alibi to label the regime as

Marxist, and conduct virulent propaganda against it with a view to destroying it. The same thing would have happened if the Tudeh Party had been taken into the government as a junior partner. This would also have subverted the Republic's main foreign policy platform, 'Neither East nor West'.

The propensity with which propertied classes at home and abroad painted all those who advocated egalitarian policies with Marxism was well illustrated in March 1983 when Tehran's bazaar merchants accused Hojatalislam Hashemi-Rafsanjani of being inspired by Marxism. Later the government's modest efforts to promote consumers' cooperatives were attacked by merchants as being 'socialistic'.[4]

Like revolutions elsewhere, the Iranian revolution has destroyed the old power structure, consisting of the Shah, the aristocracy, and the Westernised upper and upper middle classes. In the new power structure, the lower middle class has a pre-eminent place. It is a feature which the Iranian revolution shares with the republican revolutions of Egypt, Iraq and North Yemen. There the old ruling elite, consisting of the monarch, aristocrats, feudal lords and urban rich, was replaced by military officers from lower middle class families. Once in power, these officers pursued policies which hurt the old propertied classes and benefited, primarily, the petty bourgeoisie. In other words, the interests of the petty bourgeoisie were advanced by the members of this class wearing military uniforms. A similar process is at work in Iran, with one difference. Here the interests of the petty bourgeoisie are being served by the members of this class in clerical robes.

A large majority of the Iranian ulema come from urban or rural petty bourgeois families. They are often related to traders or shopkeepers. Those who come from better-off homes are linked with rich merchants and landlords. So, although the petty bourgeoisie is the dominant class in the Islamic camp, it has to contend with the interests of the mercantile bourgeoisie and rich landlords. Therein lies the root of conflict between conservatives and radicals within the IRP and the Guardians Council: a conflict which has manifested itself on such issues as land redistribution, foreign trade nationalisation, and confiscation of the exiles' properties. Though the overall bias of the regime is towards the working and lower middle classes, it is unwilling to alienate bazaar merchants. In Iran, as elsewhere in the Islamic world, merchants have been close to the ulema and the mosque, and have supported them.

In short, the Islamic regime rests on a foundation which has working and lower middle classes at its core and bazaar merchants on the periphery. In the Pahlavi era, the working class and petty bourgeoisie were powerless. The post-Pahlavi regime has inducted them into powerful revolutionary organisations, and armed them. They feel that they have a stake in the system. They are loyal to Khomeini, whom they consider to be a divine figure, an aide to the Twelfth Imam. His success in overthrowing the Shah is regarded by them as a superhuman feat. Carter's defeat in the American presidential election is seen by them as another manifestation of Khomeini's divine powers. So too is the failure of the April 1980 American military mission to free the hostages. That Saddam Hussein has not fallen yet does not alter the view of Khomeini's admirers: they point out that the Shah did not go down when he first confronted Khomeini in 1963.

It is hardly surprising that the secular upper and upper middle classes in Iran are by and large alienated from the present system, and oppose it. The Islamic regime knows this. It knows too that imparting Islamic education to their children, and Islamising society at large, will further weaken these social strata. It therefore pays scant attention to their grievances.

This is not the case with the criticism or protest by working or lower middle class. That draws the immediate attention of Iranian officials. This was well illustrated by the reaction to the protest demonstration in the Afsariyeh district of Tehran in July 1983 due to the shortages of water and electricity. The government tried to improve the situation. The prime minister went to considerable length to explain why these shortages had occurred and what his administration was doing to alleviate them.[5]

When it comes to allocating supplies of rationed goods, the government gives priority to the poor and lower middle class districts of cities. Despite the demands of war on the budget, it has maintained subsidies on basic goods at the old rates. By curbing the luxurious lifestyle of the rich (in public), through the process of Islamisation, the authorities have removed an important source of envy and anger among the lower classes, which reached revolutionary proportions during the Pahlavi period.

The political upheaval caused by a revolution plays havoc with the economy. In the wake of the Bolshevik Revolution, the Russian GNP fell by 70 per cent. Iran has suffered far less. Its GNP declined by 21 per cent. The main reason is that oil, the primary product which Iran has to offer in the international market, is in demand.

On the other hand, the revolutionary regime has failed to keep its promise of ending the economy's dependence on oil. Like its predecessor, it treats oil as the number one industry. However, the oil industry has become self-sufficient in technical expertise to an extent not thought possible before. This is part of the drive for self-reliance which has been one of the major objectives of the revolution.

Iran is today an independent nation, a status it had not enjoyed for the past few centuries. It is independent politically, militarily and culturally. It is able to choose its trading partners with greater freedom than before. Above all Iran now has its own political ideology which is rooted in its own history. Since this ideology is derived from Islam, it does not have to relate overtly to capitalism or socialism. In a world accustomed to thinking in bipolar terms of capitalism and socialism, the emergence of the Islamic political ideology, as expounded by Iran, has caused much confusion. Private enterprise is sacrosanct in Iran. At the same time, in the mixed economy of Iran, the state plays a leading role, except in agriculture (which accounts for only one-sixth of the GDP) and distribution.

Another confusing feature of the Iranian revolution is that it is trying to recreate an idyll which existed in the seventh-century Arabia of the days of Prophet Muhammad and Imam Ali. So far, the revolutions in Europe and elsewhere have been future-orientated. The revolutionaries were fired by a vision of society which was to be quite different from the past or the present, and which was to be fashioned by forward-looking concepts. In Iran, the clergy who were in the forefront of the revolutionary movement, and who now run the revolutionary state, believe that the Quran and Sharia are self-contained, and provide the model for an ideal society. This has led some analysts to conclude that the regime in Tehran is reactionary, not revolutionary.

While some of the features of the Iranian revolution are unique, others are not. The regime in Tehran has had to face problems which other revolutionary states have done in the past: how to repel the attacks by counter-revolutionaries, how to keep the promise of granting basic freedoms without endangering the revolution, how to resolve the conflict between ideologues and technocrats, how to revive an ailing economy, and what line to take on the issue of exporting revolution.

The Iranian revolution was a result of specific national conditions; and so was the Bolshevik revolution in Russia. Just as the Bolsheviks tried to present their revolution as something of global importance and applicability, so too have Iranian revolutionaries. Arguing that their revolution has stemmed from the universalist ideology of Islam, they see the change in Iran as the first step towards the recreation of the Domain of Islam of the seventh century. If nothing else, such an appraisal provides them with a rationale for spreading the revolution in the adjoining Muslim states. They considered the neighbouring Iraqis as being most receptive to the ideas of Islamic revolution. Their attempts to stoke revolutionary fervour among Iraqi Muslims aroused the anger and alarm of the Baathist regime in Baghdad. The result was war.

Its progress has become bound up with the future of the regimes in

Tehran and Baghdad. On balance, the war has helped, rather than hindered, the Iranian revolution. It created conditions which enabled Islamic leaders to consolidate the revolution. The holding of the Majlis elections on schedule in April-May 1984, with greater voter participation than before, illustrated the degree to which the consolidation has occurred.

Long-term factors favour Iran on the battlefield. It is five times as large as Iraq, and three times more populous. While important Iranian urban and economic centres are distant from the war fronts, the strategic north-south highway of Iraq is dangerously close to the international border. Being infused with a potent ideology, the Iranian combatants are better motivated to fight than the Iraqis. On the other hand, in the early summer of 1984, Iraq had two to one superiority in tanks over Iran, and nearly four to one superiority in combat aircraft. The Iraqis had established a solid first line of defence, with a supportive force which was highly mobile. Its financial backers were so committed to saving it from defeat that Baghdad had no difficulty in replenishing its military stocks speedily. This was not the case with Iran.

Yet Iraq was on the defensive, anxious to end the fighting and start talking. Iranian officials were unwilling to do so unless Saddam Hussein had been replaced, even if by another Baathist leader. They feel that the departure of Saddam Hussein, whether voluntary or forced, will trigger off widespread political turmoil in Iraq, which will not subside until there is a Shia-dominated government in Baghdad. Such an administration, they are confident, will work in harmony with the Islamic Republic of Iran.

However, there is no evidence to suggest that Saddam Hussein will step down voluntarily. There is of course always the possibility of assassination. President Sadat's assasination in October 1981, despite the strictest security precautions, showed how real such a prospect is in the Middle East. If Saddam Hussein were to meet the same fate as Sadat, the Iranian government would soon agree to a ceasefire.

Short of that eventuality, the progress of the war will be decided by the outcome of the offensives Iran was preparing to launch in the early summer of 1984. Iran may be able to break through the Iraqi defences and surround or capture Basra in the south, or Baghdad in the centre, thus causing the downfall of the Saddam Hussein regime and/or direct intervention by one or both superpowers. It is equally possible that the Iranian offensives will fail to break Iraqi defences. In that case Iran may show its willingness to negotiate a settlement. Of the three mediators in the field – the United Nations, the Islamic Conference Organisation and the Non-Aligned Movement – the last one is most likely to be acceptable to Iran. But the negotiations will be long and thorny. There is no guarantee that the hostilities will not erupt again. Neither side is likely to disband the war machine it has assembled over the past years. Khomeini is unlikely to abandon his ambition to overthrow Saddam Hussein.

If the tanker war in the Gulf escalates, and if, in the process of protecting Gulf sealanes, the US hits Iranian targets, that will make Tehran seriously consider seeking Soviet aid under the 1921 treaty. Even if Tehran does not do so, Moscow may feel obliged to invoke Articles Five and Six of the treaty to provide defensive measures to Iran against America. That will open up the prospect of direct confrontation between the superpowers, without the involvement of their allies. In short, the present understanding between the superpowers is based on the premise that the US will refrain from attacking Iran. If Washington breaks the promise, then Moscow will side with Tehran.

However displeased the Soviet Union may be with the Islamic Republic's current policies at home and abroad, it considers the present regime preferable to the one it replaced. The Kremlin does not want Iran to return to the Western military camp. As long as Tehran stays out of the American bloc, it will have the overt or covert goodwill of Moscow. Since there is no evidence to suggest that Iran intends to abandon, or even modify, its policy of strict non-alignment and refusal to join any military bloc, relations between Tehran and Moscow will remain correct to cordial.

As far as the West, especially America, is concerned, it seems to have no short-term or long-term plan to work for restoring monarchy in Iran. That means the Pahlavi dynasty is finished for ever. What the West will try doing – particularly after Khomeini's departure – is to shape the regime in Tehran along the lines of what exists in Saudi Arabia today, and reintegrate it commercially and politically, if not militarily, into the Western camp.

If that were to happen, the image of Islamic Iran in the Western media will change. Iran will then by and large receive the blandly positive treatment that has customarily been accorded to Saudi Arabia, a conservative Islamic monarchy tied to the West. What turned Western capitals and media against Iran after the revolution was not just that the Westernised Shah had been replaced by an Islamic regime, but that the new entity set out systematically to eliminate all Western commercial, political, military and cultural influences from Iran.

The present hostility of Western governments and commentators towards Iran does not surprise or upset Iranian officials. They expect it. In fact they see it as a confirmation that they are really expelling all Western influence from their midst, and re-establishing their true

Islamic identity. They would be concerned if they found themselves consistently praised, or even liked, in Western media or capitals.

Given the continued Iranian intransigence on the war front, and the composition of the newly elected Majlis, pro-Iranian sentiment is unlikely to develop in the West. The new Majlis has a greater proportion of radicals than the old one. It is most likely to concentrate on redistributing wealth and implementing Principle Forty-nine of the constitution concerning illegitimately acquired wealth. It is also likely to accelerate the process of Islamisation, and ensure strict enforcement of the laws pertaining to it.

The actual course of the present and future parliaments will be set by the outcome of the war, the longevity of Khomeini, and the contents of his political will. It will also be determined by the temper of the Iranian people and the impact that the Iranian revolution is able to have on the Muslim world at large.

Iranian leaders see their country as a pace-setter in recreating a model Islamic society, and feel that their progress along this path is of general interest to Muslims everywhere, and of particular interest to the inhabitants of the forty-three member-countries of the Islamic Conference Organisation. They have shown that by carrying out an Islamic revolution in Iran they have ousted a corrupt ruling elite, freed the country from the domination of a superpower, and reclaimed its national independence. These achievements are highly valued in many Third World capitals, which find the choice of linking up with the Soviet or the American bloc incompatible with their newly acquired political independence. What Iran has shown to the Muslim states of the Third World is the Third Way of Islam, quite apart from the Eastern or Western path. In a world riven with superpower rivalries and tensions, it is an attractive proposition. When it is combined with the moral intransigence and radical anti-imperialism of a Khomeini, the mixture becomes irresistible, particularly to the young and educated in many Muslim states. Following Khomeini's line means not only rejecting the rise of capitalism, with its concomitant corruption, but also atheistic Marxism. This explains why it has followers everywhere in the Muslim world.

In the Middle East proper, the failure of the radical Arab nationalism of Nasser, allied to Moscow, and the Arab conservatism of the House of Saud, allied to Washington, to secure the liberation of Palestine, has led many Palestinians to consider seriously the path of revolutionary Islam to liberate Palestine. The rise of a non-aligned Iran has inhibited the conservative states of the Gulf from forging closer links with the USA. The fall of the Shah discouraged the Saudi monarch from joining, in the summer of 1979, the Camp David peace process which had earlier led to a separate peace treaty between

Egypt and Israel.

While Iran's revolutionary regime has proved its durability and strength by defeating numerous attacks, it has in the process taken actions which have lost it much of the goodwill it enjoyed abroad during the early period of the revolution. In those days, while secular leftists everywhere saw in the revolution a promise of socialist democracy, Muslim opinion in the region and outside thought of the upheaval in Iran as constituting Islamic revolution. But within a year most of the secular leftists at home and abroad had turned hostile to the regime. And within the next few years, a strong opinion grew among non-Iranian Muslims that what was happening in Iran had more to do with Shias in particular than Muslims in general. Since Shias are only one-sixth of the global Muslim population of 850 million, this perception has worked against the interests of the Tehran regime. The success of the Islamic revolution in Iran gave a fillip to fundamentalism throughout the Muslim world. Yet Sunni fundamentalists, while pursuing the same objective of recreating the ideal society of the seventh century, have kept their distance from the Khomeinists in their countries.

The excesses of the Iranian revolution have provided effective ammunition to the critics of Tehran's regime. According to Amnesty International, more than 5,000 people have been executed in Iran during the first five years of the revolution. The Mujahedin-e Khalq put the total of executions at 30,000.[6] Whatever the true figure, such actions by the Islamic Republic have damaged its image not only in the West but also in the region. As Prince Nayif of Saudi Arabia put it in July 1983, 'It is odd that the Iranian government denies the Saudi government the right to preserve Saudi Arabia's security during this crucial period of the pilgrimage season, while Iranian departments commit oppressive actions and massacres every day against their citizens in Iran on the pretext of preserving security.'[7] Also the manner in which all dissenting voices in Iran's theological circles have been silenced has disturbed many sympathisers of the Iranian revolution. This may have been necessary to help unify and strengthen the Republic, but it has alienated much Islamic opinion abroad. In addition, many religious and lay Muslims outside Iran are uneasy about the centralisation of power into Khomeini's hands. Such a development is likely to work against the future welfare of the Islamic Republic, they argue. The more dependent the state becomes on Khomeini, the more difficult it would be to fill the vacuum when he goes.

What exactly will happen after Khomeini's death is hard to forecast in detail. However, given the existence of the Assembly of Experts and Khomeini's political will, the chances are that the succession will not be problematical. Whosoever succeeds Khomeini will have to be satisfied with far less popular respect, admiration and loyalty than was accorded to Khomeini. On the other hand, Khomeini's successor(s) will have lesser problems to tackle than he had to. During a most turbulent period following the revolution – when the Islamic regime came under repeated counter-revolutionary attacks, Iran's territorial integrity was threatened, and a civil war seemed imminent – Khomeini's strong, charismatic leadership saved the day.

There is little doubt that the opponents of the Islamic regime will come to active life on Khomeini's death. Knowing well the odds against their success in seizing power, they would aim at starting a civil war. But they are unlikely to succeed. They are divided among themselves. The constitutional monarchists hate the leftists, whether secular or religious; and the leftists reciprocate the feeling. Whether the two factions act singly or jointly, they would encounter severe resistance by those wielding power and arms in the Islamic Republic.

But supposing a civil war were to ensue, and bring to power a secular or an Islamic leftist regime, biased against the traditional ulema, what would be the chances of its survival? Minimal. In view of what has happened in Iran since 1977, it is difficult to see how a political system which specifically excludes the ulema from power can survive for long. Iranian history shows that even the most repressive and ambitious of the Pahlavi or Qajar kings failed to keep the clergy out of politics or destroy their popular standing. If this was the case before the Islamic revolution – and the subsequent control of state power by the ulema – their hostility towards a regime which ignores them, or excludes them from seats of power, can be well imagined.

Whatever else might happen after Khomeini's death, Iran will not revert to monarchy, whether constitutional or absolute. And it will not acquire a political system which excludes the clergy.

POSTSCRIPT*

The tanker war in the Gulf, which reached a climax in mid-May 1984, subsided in June. Iraq hit only two ships during the month, and Iran one. By late June Iranian oil exports from Kharg were back to normal, around 1.8 million b/d, and insurance rates were down from 7.5 per cent of the value of the cargo to 5 per cent. The main reason for this was economic. There was such a surfeit of oil tankers in the international market that the owners gained a lot more in compensation for the loss of a vessel on the high seas than from scrapping it. Maritime insurers were more interested in improving their profits through higher charges than in removing the cover altogether. Finally, there were lots of 'cowboy sailors' ready to earn $5,000 for a single trip to Kharg island. Even at the height of the crisis, ships owned by Norwegian, Swedish, Danish and Greek companies kept up traffic to and from the Iranian ports in the upper Gulf.

Iran had less success at the United Nations. In early June, responding to the GCC members' complaint, the UN Security Council condemned (by thirteen votes to nil) attacks on the ships sailing to and from Saudi Arabian and Kuwaiti ports. It called on 'all states' to respect free navigation in the Gulf.

After lengthy consultations GCC members rejected the idea of restricting the movement of the ships trading with them to their territorial waters, and opted for providing them with air cover in the international waters of the Gulf. The arrival in Saudi Arabia from the US of 400 Stinger anti-aircraft missiles and a super-Awacs plane, capable of monitoring air and sea traffic, bolstered Saudi defences. Eight American naval ships began escorting Saudi and Kuwaiti tankers in the Gulf. On 5 June US Awacs helped the Saudi air force to shoot down an Iranian F-4 plane. Iran protested, saying that its aircraft was in international airspace. Riyadh stated that the plane was in Saudi territory, but added that it did not wish to escalate the conflict in the

---

* The notes are at the end of the Postscript.

Gulf. Saudi Arabia reiterated its non-belligerent intentions through Syria. But this was not enough to satisfy Tehran. Iranian planes hit a Kuwaiti supertanker on 10 June in the lower Gulf, about 100 miles off the coast of Qatar. On 5 July an unidentified aircraft (most probably belonging to Iran) attacked a Liberian tanker, loaded with Saudi oil, in the lower Gulf.[1]

The overall Iraqi purpose in initiating the tanker war was to draw in the superpowers by internationalising the conflict, and/or force Saudi Arabia and Kuwait to join the hostilities on its side. The latter development would have opened up a new front for Iran and severely strained its already depleted air force. This would have torpedoed the Iranian plans to mount land offensives against Iraq. In the event, Iraq failed to achieve either of its objectives.

While sympathetic to Iraq, both the US and the USSR desisted from active intervention in the conflict. The two superpowers held top level consultations and reached a limited understanding that the Gulf must remain a free waterway. Moscow was reported to have informed Washington in advance that it was sending long-range ground-to-ground missiles to Iraq. And the US was known to have told the USSR that it did not wish to go beyond supplying defence equipment to Saudi Arabia and Kuwait, and escorting their tankers. Aware of the temptations that the escalating conflict offered to America to increase its influence, Moscow reportedly warned Washington that it would 'resist' any American attempts to use the current crisis to impose a pro-West regime in Tehran.[2]

Saudi Arabia and Kuwait had good reasons to refrain from declaring war against Iran. They seemed to have heeded both friendly advice from Damascus and dire warnings from Tehran. 'The life style of the littoral states of the Persian Gulf . . . depends on ports, installations and their oil pipelines,' said Hashemi-Rafsanjani. 'All of them could be destroyed by shelling, let alone air attacks.'[3] In any case these countries needed time, equipment and practice to make their defences effective. The US came to their aid. Besides airlifting fresh weapons to Saudi Arabia, it sent military personnel to Kuwait to upgrade the Hawk anti-aircraft missiles there. It extended the Awacs' cover to Kuwait's refineries and desalination plants.[4]

In mid-July the Saudi government made a gesture to Iran which surprised most observers. Through its hajj pilgrimage office it invited Hashemi-Rafsanjani to hajj, due in September. Acknowledging the invitation publicly, the Iranian leader said, 'Such journeys could be useful'.

At the same time President Mubarak of Egypt went on canvassing support for his plan to end the Gulf War, despite its rejection by Iran in May, and secured Yugoslavia's backing for it. These states, as well as the seven members of the ICO commission on the Gulf War, were encouraged by two events. In mid-June, following attacks on civilian targets which resulted in over 900 casualties in a week, Iran and Iraq agreed to cease such operations and have UN observers stationed in their capitals to monitor breaches. Secondly, the much-awaited Iran land offensive was postponed in early July.

By now the Iraqis had set up a four-tier defensive system in the south: minefields, barbed wire, anti-tank trenches, and heavy artillery placed on high ground. Abundantly armed, the Iraqis were in high spirits. To block Iranian penetration, they had created an artificial lake fifteen miles long and half a mile to three miles wide south of the Hur al Howzeh marshes. On the south and west of the lake hundreds of bunkers were filled with soldiers and militia men.[5] The Iraqis were as numerous on the southern front as the Iranians: 200,000.

To be able to breach such defences, Tehran needed more men, and more and better military hardware. This was bound to take time. Therefore the Iranian officials decided to give diplomacy a chance. Yet diplomacy was narrowly defined in Tehran. Any talks with Saudi or Kuwaiti leaders were to be aimed at convincing them that only by ousting Saddam Hussein from power could Iran, Iraq and other Gulf states live in peace. These leaders were to be persuaded to cease aiding the Iraqi president.

Khomeini takes a moral-religious view of the Gulf conflict. 'Those who criticise us and say "why don't you compromise with these corrupt powers" analyse things from a materialistic viewpoint,' he told senior officials in his Eid al Fitr message. 'They do not know the views of God and the prophets, how they dealt with oppressors. . . . To compromise with oppressors is to oppress the oppressed.' He brushed aside the opinion that the nation was growing war weary. 'Our revolutionary guards who lead a less than normal life do not fear war,' he continued. 'Our military men who lead a normal life do not fear war. War would not do them any harm. It is those who have palaces and the like who should fear war, because they would lose out.'[6]

He had good reasons to believe that the nation was more united than before. The composition of the Second Islamic Majlis was an important indicator of this. Unlike its predecessor, it lacked any members of the Liberation Movement: the party had boycotted the elections. The Second Majlis confirmed Mousavi as Prime Minsiter on 5 August 1984 by 163 votes to twenty-one, an improvement on the 115 votes he had secured in the First Majlis. Hashemi-Rafsanjani was re-elected speaker by 181 votes to nil, an increase of thirty-five votes over his performance four years before.[7] Under his leadership the Majlis had emerged as the most important political institution. Its decision to allow its proceedings to be broadcast live on radio manifested the confidence that the Islamic regime felt.

At the time of hajj in late August there were signs of easing of tension between Iran and Saudi Arabia. 150,000 Iranian pilgrims were allowed to demonstrate peacefully one mile from the Grand Mosque in Mecca. In his message to the pilgrims Khomeini called on the faithful to 'mobilise against world arrogance and strive for the liberation of Jerusalem'. King Fahd echoed similar sentiments when, in his address to the heads of numerous hajj delegations, he said: 'The enemy is still spilling the blood of the innocent and spreading corruption while the Muslim world spent tens of years suffering, and biding in the labyrinths of conferences and international forums, without a solution to the painful tragedy.' The 'enemy' was apparently Israel, and the 'painful tragedy' pertained to the Palestinians. Fahd combined his statement with an appeal for an end to 'the shedding of Muslim blood', an obvious reference to the Iran-Iraq war.[8]

In his early August speech Khomeini publicly expressed disappointment at Iran's isolation. 'We have no more friends than can be counted on the fingers of one hand,' he said.[9] To strengthen existing friendships President Khamanei toured Syria, Libya and Algeria. In Damascus President Assad reportedly advised Khamanei against mounting a major land offensive against Iraq and further alienating the Gulf monarchies. At the same time Assad had been trying to convince the Gulf rulers that Syria's friendship with Tehran was a better guarantee for their security than the armed might of Iraq.[10]

However, Assad's argument did not seem to prevail. For the GCC summit in Kuwait in late November decided to set up a Rapid Deployment Force of two brigades under a senior Saudi officer.[11] Kuwait strengthened its defences of Bubiyan and Warba islands. But Iran showed the vulnerability of Saudi and Kuwaiti defences when its aircraft penetrated the Saudi air defence shield in northern Gulf and hit a Kuwait-bound freighter.[12]

Baghdad continued its attacks on ships in the Gulf area adjacent to Iran that it had declared as a war exclusion zone because Iran had denied Iraq its legitimate right to export oil from its southern ports of Fao and Umm Qasr. In October Iran mounted a minor offensive in the central sector near Dehloran, and made some gains. Yet Iraq still controlled pockets of Iranian territory in the central sector and the Abadan area, totalling 400 sq. miles.

An indication that the doctrine of 'military caution' was being adopted officially came in October when Khomeini appointed Brigadier General Zahir-Nejad as his second personal representative on the Supreme Defence Council. Zahir-Nejad had resigned as chief of staff in July in response to the Islamic Revolutionary Guards commanders' criticism that he had failed to exploit the early gains of the Majnoon islands offensive in February.

Since a major offensive could only be launched properly after procuring sufficient arms and ammunition, Iran went on purchasing trainer aircraft from Switzerland, Chieftain tank parts from Britain (for which orders had been placed before the revolution), Soviet-made tanks from Syria and Libya, and placing orders for arms with Brazil through Libya.[13]

Iraq expected an Iranian land offensive, and to pre-empt it the Iraqi forces tried to recapture Majnoon islands. But they failed. The Arab League committee on the Gulf conflict reiterated its backing for Iraq and called on Iran to heed the peace pleas.

As Iranians prepared to celebrate the sixth anniversary of the revolution in February 1985 there were some signs of relaxation at home. Assadollah Lajevardi, the revolutionary prosecutor of Tehran and governor of Evin jail (used for political prisoners), known for his harsh treatment of the imprisoned, was eased out of his posts. Ayatollah Montazeri stated that only those who endangered state security should be jailed. As part of the anniversary celebrations several hundred political prisoners were released.

On the eve of the anniversary Bazargan and twenty-five others of the Liberation Movement criticised the regime for 'lack of freedom' and creating 'a political and economic crisis', and called for an end to the war.[14] Similar statements were made by the Mujahedin and Tudeh leaders from abroad.

These dissenting voices were soon drowned by the 'war of the cities' that erupted after Iraq had bombed a steel factory in Ahvaz and an unfinished nuclear power plant in Bushahr on 5 March. By so doing, Iran argued, Iraq had breached the June 1984 agreement, reached through the UN, to refrain from attacking civilian targets. Iran shelled Basra. In return Iraq carried out air attacks on various Iranian cities and towns, including Isfahan, 250 miles from the border. Iran retaliated by raiding a Baghdad suburb on 11 March. The next day Iraq hit sixteen cities and town of Iran, and gave one week's notice before treating Iranian airspace as enemy zone.

On 11 March the Iranian commanders pressed 30,000 to 50,000 soldiers and revolutionary guards into a major offensive in the Hur al Howzeh marshland to breach the Iraqi lines and sever the Basra-Baghdad road, Highway 6, just north of Qurna. Swampy conditions helped the Iranians to offset the Iraqi advantage in tanks as they negotiated the marshes in boats and along the narrow strips of dry land in the area. Once they reached the dry plain they waited to build up their forces before pushing four miles through huge tracts of barbed wire, and across minefields, to the Tigris under heavy fire from the Iraqi machine guns. A brigade of some 5,000 Iranians set up pontoon bridges across the river, and captured Highway 6, as Tehran claimed on 18 March that its forces controlled all of the Hur al Howzeh marshes south of Amrah. 'The Iranians were so outgunned yet they were able to advance and cross the river,' said an analyst in Washington.' It's significant that they were able to make it that far.'[15] The news that the Iraqi defences painstakingly built over four years had been breached by an Iranian brigade set alarm bells ringing in Baghdad. Soon the Iraqis mounted a massive counter-offensive, with Uzayr in the north and Qurna in the south as the two points of a pincer. Lacking sufficient armour, logistical backing or air power to resist the Iraqi onslaught, the Iranians failed to maintain their position. By the time the battle was over, some 20,000 Iranians and 14,000 Iraqis were dead.[16]

Iran hit the Iraqi city of Kirkuk on 14 March with a ground-to-ground missile, probably a Soviet-made Scud-B, reported to have been obtained from Libya. The next day Iraq bombed Tehran. Thousands of foreigners left the capital as 19 March, the deadline for the termination of foreign airlines' flights to Iran, approached. Iran responded to Iraq's air raids on Tehran with missile attacks on Baghdad. On 31 March, when the UN general secretary undertook a tour of four Gulf states, including Iran and Iraq, Tehran reported that the Iraqi raids had killed 1,450 Iranians and injured more than 4,000.[17] 'We want to bring the Iranian people into the frontlines of the war,' said Major General Thabit Sultan, commander of the Iraqi Fourth Corps. 'We hope this will encourage the Iranian people to rebel against their government and bring the war to an end.'[18] This hope was unrealised since the Islamic regime in Tehran presented the Iraqi air raids on civilian areas as further evidence of Saddam Hussein's inhumanity. Nonetheless, on 6 April both sides agreed to stop attacking each other's cities.

On 18 April, the Iranian Army Day, Khomeini argued that Iran was fighting a 'defensive war'. 'Defence does not mean that we give up as soon as the other side offers peace,' he explained. 'Are you telling us to extend the hand of friendship to someone who has smashed Islam? We'll resist to the end.'[19] Pointing out that this was the fifteenth century of Islam, the *Guardian* commented: 'At a comparable period Christianity was capable of equally extreme, equally murderous, and equally uncompromising expressions of religious idealism.'[20]

Taking advantage of the comparative lull in the fighting, the Saudi foreign minister, Prince Saud al Faisal, visited Tehran to seek a ceasefire on the eve of Ramadan beginning on 20 May. Nothing came of it. On 25 May a suicide bomber driving a car packed with explosives made an unsuccessful attempt to assassinate Shaikh Sabah al Sabah, the Kuwaiti ruler. Claiming that the action had been directed by Iran,[21] Suddam Hussein resumed air raids on Tehran, and intensified attacks on vessels in the Gulf. On 4 June Kharg island and the petroleum complex in Bandar Khomeini were subjected to particularly severe air raids. Since the Iranians lacked long range anti-aircraft guns, they were unable to bring down the Iraqi planes which dropped bombs or fired rockets from an altitude of 10,000 feet. All Iran could do was to hit Baghdad with long range ground-to-ground missiles and use its F-4s based in Lavan island to hit ships trading with Saudi Arabia or Kuwait near the Qatari coast.

The Iranian government resolved to use the occasion of Jerusalem Day, celebrated since the revolution on the last Friday of Ramadan, to prove to the world that it had popular support to continue the war. On 14 June Tehran witnessed a congregation variously estimated to be one to five million strong. The next day Baghdad announced that it was suspending air raids on cities for a fortnight. As it did not resume them on 30 June, or later, the rationale offered by Tehran that the massive turnout of Iranians in Tehran on 14 June had convinced Iraq that the Islamic regime enjoyed popular backing and that its bombing of Tehran had failed to undermine the clerical rule, gained credence.[22]

Among those who were most vociferous to keep up the fight were the million-odd relative of the nearly 200,000 Iranians killed in the war: they were bent on taking revenge. On its part the Islamic regime was unwilling to cease hostilities until and unless it had something tangible, political or military, to show for the sacrifices its people had made.

Furthermore, none of those who offered to mediate met Tehran's criteria of 'honesty, sincerity and fairness'. This included the Japanese leaders whom Hashemi-Rafsanjani met in Tokyo in early July after his successful trip to Peking. Though earlier reports of a Sino-Iranian arms deal worth $1.6 billion – including fighter aircraft, tanks, and surface-to-air missiles – were denied in Peking and Tehran,[23] there was much substance to the news from Damascus that Iran was purchasing surface-to-air missiles from China, military helicopters from Italy, and light weapons from Spain.[24]

The close coordination between the military and the Islamic Revolutionary Guards, which had first been noted in the February 1984 Majnoon islands offensive – the guards advancing with the backing of the military, which transported commandos by helicopters, and provided anti-aircraft fire and logistical support – was further strengthened. Following this pattern of action, Iran launched a series of small offensives, codenamed Quds and Ashura, in the central sector and the Hur al Howzeh marshes, and made some gains. The Iranian strategy of nibbling small areas all along the 735-mile long border meant that Iraq had to swiftly match enemy troops concentrations. This strained the Iraqi army, which was increasingly manned by conscripts.

It was against this background that presidential elections were held in Iran on 16 August. Among the fifty who registered as candidates with the Guardians Council was Mahdi Bazargan. His party, the Liberation Movement, favoured opening talks with Iraq, and advocated combining diplomacy with military action. It argued that Iran had wrongly rejected such an opportunity thrice: in May 1982 at the time of the recapture of Khorramshahr; in March 1984 after the Majnoon islands offensive; and in May 1985 when the Iraqi offer of a ceasefire during Ramadan was conveyed through the Saudi foreign minister. War was in the interest of imperialism and Zionism, and lethal to Islam and the revolution, it stated.[25] The party also demanded that conditions of 'freedom, security and honesty' be created in the country to enable it to contest the presidential poll freely and fairly.

Forty-seven of the candidates, including Bazargan, were rejected by the Guardians Council. Ayatollah Khazali, one of its members, explained that the Council turned down Bazargan because of his 'lack of adherence' to the Vilayat-e faqih doctrine which underlined the Iranian constitution.[26] Unofficial reports stated that the Council was divided on the issue. Those who opposed Bazargan's candidature argued that besides his own doubts about the Vilayat-e faqih doctrine, his party, by being pro-Western, violated the Islamic Republic's leading tenet of 'Neither East nor West'. If Bazargan were allowed to contest, so the argument went, his views would get a lot of publicity. Those who favoured his candidature stated that by letting him run, the government would reassure the Western media and opinion-makers that the elections were free.[27] Apparently the latter argument did not prove strong enough to win majority support in the Guardians Council.

The three who were allowed to contest were: Ali Khamanei, the current president; Mahmoud Kashani, an eminent lawyer; and Habibollah Asghar-Owladi, a former minister. The government wanted maximum voter participation, and the media exhorted citizens to vote. On the eve of the poll the *Jumhouri-ye Islami* wrote: 'Boycotting elections or casting a discarded vote is a clear betrayal of the blood of martyrs who joined God to consolidate this (our) divine system.' Yet, at 14,244,630 out of a total of 25,138,000 voters, the turnout of 57 per cent was much lower than the 75 per cent for the October 1981 presidential election. Since the previous election was held in the wake of President Rajai's assassination the circumstances were exceptional. This time the situation was quite normal. Khamanei won. But he secured only 85 per cent of the votes versus the 95 per cent that he had done in the previous poll. His total vote fell from sixteen million to 12.6 million.[28] The regime's critics attributed the decline to the growing unpopularity of the official policies, particularly on the war and the running of the economy.

His re-election provided Khamanei a chance to change the Prime Minister. He was widely known to be unhappy with the performance of the government of Mousavi, his reluctant choice in October 1981. Mousavi's supporters mounted a grass roots campaign for his re-selection. The atmosphere became so charged that 135 Majlis members sought Ayatollah Khomeini's guidance on the formation of the next government. In his reply Khomeini stated: 'I consider Mr Mousavi to be a pious and dedicated Muslim, and his government to be a successful one under extremely complicated conditions prevailing in the country. I don't consider it advisable to replace the Mousavi government, but the President and the Islamic Majlis are the final powers to choose.'[29] By so doing the Ayatollah opted for maintaining continuity in the state administration, with Mousavi, Khamanei and Hashemi-Rafsanjani occupying the leading positions they had done for the previous several years.

Once Khomeini had issued his guideline on the subject, President Khamanei had virtually no choice but to present Mousavi to the Majlis as Prime Minister. He did so on 13 October. Of the 261 Majlis deputies present, 162 voted for Mousavi, and seventy-three against, with twenty-six abstaining. It was significant that despite Khomeini's public backing for Mousavi, ninety-nine deputies either voted against him or abstained. Obviously Majlis members were becoming increasingly conscious of their constitutional rights, and determined to exercise them.

The opposition criticised the Mousavi government for its continued reliance on oil for more than half of its revenue, growing dependence on food imports, faulty distribution of foodstuffs and other necessities, and falling living standards.

Instability in the oil market and distruption in the Gulf shipping reduced Iran's oil income. In fiscal 1984-5 Iran earned $14.7 billion in oil revenue versus the projected $21.2 billion, a drop of 30 per cent. The government responded by slashing its expenditure by 40 per cent, and severely restricting imports, including industrial materials and spares. This, and the periodic power cuts due to the excess of demand over supply, had a debilitating effect on the economy. Industrial output during March-June 1985 fell by 17 per cent over the same period in 1984.

The war and import restrictions have distorted the economy and fuelled inflation. The Mousavi government claimed that by curtailing its expenditure – mainly on development projects – and reducing money supply growth from 23 per cent in 1981 to 6 per cent in 1984, it halved the inflation rate from 21.2 per cent to 10.5 per cent. However, the official statement that inflation in late 1985 was running at 3.4 per cent was widely distrusted.[30] The Paris-based Organisation for Economic Cooperation and Development put the inflation rate around 30 per cent.

Those with fixed incomes felt the pinch. This included the country's 1.5 million civil servants. They found the salary increase, pegged to the official inflation rate, inadequate to counter the real inflation. To balance their domestic budgets, some resorted to doing second jobs, others to taking bribes – a practice that had disappeared in the wake of the revolution. A series of investigative articles in the *Jumhouri-ye Islami* in early September showed that bribery had crept back into the government offices most frequently visited by the public – including customs, the Centres for Procurement and Distribution of commerce ministry, town halls, the deeds and personal status registration office, and justice administration. Hojatalislam Ali Akbar Nateq-Nouri, the interior minister, said that the government was not as much worried about the war as 'the threat posed by corruption'.[31]

The government encouraged people to complain, and ran a daily Complaints Slot on its radio. Newspapers urged readers to send in complaints by letter or phone. And many did. These concerned erratic distribution of rationed goods, sharp increases in prices, power cuts, bribery and bureaucratic sloth. By so doing the officials and editors allowed the disgruntled to blow off steam, and not to let dissatisfaction build up to explosive proportions.

Mousavi had his own frustrations to cope with. 'It is now two years since we sent to the Majlis bills on taxation, land distribution, foreign trade, and the limits of private sector,' he said in December 1984.[32]

Principle Forty-four of the constitution describes the Republic's economy as consisting of public, cooperative and private sectors. It seemed logical for the government to flesh out the principle with specific laws, setting out clear-cut boundaries for each sector. But this had not happened yet. Lacking such laws, the government conducted the economy according to the decrees and orders issued by the Islamic Revolutionary Council that ruled before the constitution was promulgated and elections held.

In the case of foreign trade – listed in Principle Forty-four as being in the public sector – the bill to nationalise it had been returned to the Majlis three times in as many years by the conservative Guardians Council for being in conflict with Islamic precepts.[33] There was ill-concealed friction between bazaar leaders and the government led by Mousavi, who was publicly committed to 'review the distribution system to eliminate control by intermediaries'.[34] He had been encouraging the establishment of consumer cooperative stores in mosques, factories and other workplaces – a development which was seen by leading merchants as a threat to their very existence of the bazaar. This fear was exaggerated: the cooperative stores had a very small share of the market. In foreign trade they accounted for only 2 per cent of the imports versus the private sector's 17 per cent, which was about half of its share before the revolution.

However, the matter was not purely economic. Bazaar leaders had hoped that the onset of the Islamic revolution – in whose success they had played a crucial role – would transform them into power brokers. But their hopes remained unfulfilled. The young, radical leaders of the revolution had different ideas about the political and economic role of the bazaar. 'What we have opposed and still oppose is the investment on an unlimited scale by the private sector in distribution and non-essential middleman activities,' said Bahzad Nabavi, minister of heavy industry, and a confidante of Mousavi.[35]

Bazaar merchants realised to their chagrin that whenever they appealed directly to the public for support they fared badly. For instance, Asghar-Owladi, the best known among them, secured only 2 per cent of the popular vote in the August 1985 presidential election. Earlier he had lost his Majlis seat from Tehran. Under the circumstances bazaar leaders were obliged to exercise their influence behind the scenes on such bodies as the Guardians Council whose jurist members, being predominantly conservative, believed in giving the private sector maximum area for growth.

Whenever their differences with the Mousavi government became acute the bazaar leaders approached Khomeini. Keen to maintain a balance between his radical and conservative followers, and not to let one side prevail over the other and thus reduce his base of support, Khomeini would intervene to shift the balance in the private sector's favour. For example, in August 1984 he stated that in general private enterprise should be permitted to realise its 'full potential', and instructed the government to remove unnecessary restrictions on businessmen. Addressing the newly appointed cabinet led by Mousavi on 31 October 1985, Khomeini said, 'Give the committed businessmen – those who want to serve the country – a free hand, and do not nationalise everything.[36]

Earlier, in March 1985, the government had decided to implement Principle Forty-nine of the constitution – which empowers the authorities to confiscate properties acquired through 'illigitimate means'[37] by appointing a special Islamic Revolutionary Tribunal. The number of such properties and their value were substantial; and they fell into three categories. First, following the revolution, the cinemas showing pornographic movies were expropriated on the orders of Khomeini or Islamic revolutionary courts, and handed over to the Revolutionary Prosecutor-General's office. Second, the assets of those who were found guilty of spreading 'corruption on earth' and executed, or put to flight, were impounded, and passed on to various revolutionary bodies. Finally, 7,475 properties belonging to some 3,000 Iranians, living at home or abroad, were confiscated by courts without proper investigation, and handed over to either a revolutionary organisation (such as the Mustazafin Foundation, the Martyrs Foundation, the Reconstruction Crusade, or the Islamic Propagation Organisation), or the prosecutor-general's office, or a special office in the Prime Minister's secretariat.[38]

There was no dispute about the first two categories. Controversy arose about the last one after the promulgation of the Eight Point decree by Khomeini in December 1982. Since Point Five of the decree stated that it was unlawful to usurp 'anybody's property or right . . . except on a Sharia judge's orders', and since this principle also applied to 'impounding or confiscation of somebody's property', many confiscations came under review when the authorities were challenged by the former owners. Some 2,000 Iranian exiles returned home to file petitions. Vast sums were involved, the confiscations in Tehran alone amounting to Rials 120 billion, about $1.5 billion.[39] Many of the affluent Iranians succeeded in getting the previous orders reversed, often by pressuring or bribing the Sharia judges. This went down badly with the rank and file of the ruling party, who began to protest privately.

To correct this shift in favour of rich Iranians, Khomeini appointed in early July 1985 Hojatalislam Khoiniha, a radical cleric, prosecutor-general to replace Ayatollah Yusuf Sanei. Three months later Khoiniha instructed all revolutionary and public courts to forward to his office the names of the 'fugitive capitalists' and the details of their properties. Chief Justice Mousavi-Ardebili warned the 'influence peddlers' not to pressure or bribe judges to reverse the confiscation orders. As Khoiniha mounted a campaign against the machinations of the 'fugitive capitalists', the subject caught the popular imagination. In his Friday sermon on 8 November Mousavi-Ardebili cited the guidelines Khomeini had issued on 'the rights of the oppressed' to a recent assembly of jurisprudents, including those on the Guardians Council. While expressing his opposition to arbitrary action in expropriating private assets, Khomeini was reported to have stressed the need to 'support the deprived and deal strongly with the capitalists'. He criticised those who interpreted such an action against capitalists as being 'Communistic'.[40] This was enough to indicate that Khomeini endorsed Khoiniha's hard line on implementing Principle

Forty-nine, a stand welcomed no doubt by such radicals as Mousavi.

While Khomeini remained the supreme leader, efforts were being made continually by officials to make him less and less indispensable. Khomeini himself was keen to see this happen. In mid-September 1985 he instructed his followers to remove his portraits from all mosques, and directed the state-run media to stop the practice of frequently invoking his name on radio and showing his face on television.

The question of succession to Khomeini was high on the agenda of the Experts Assembly when it began its third session on 16 November. Three days later, in line with Principle 107 of the constitution,[41] it chose Ayatollah Montazeri as the future Leader. But, oddly, it did not make its decision public. On 22 November Hojatalislam Barikbin, the Friday prayer leader of Qazvin, leaked the Assembly's decision during his sermon. It was immediately picked up by two of Tehran's four dailies. But the radio and television ignored it.

Observers attributed this behaviour to the state media's unwillingness to highlight future leadership while Khomeini was actively discharging his duties. On the other hand official sources said that the Experts Assembly decided to act to prevent a leadership vacuum should something drastic happen suddenly to eighty-three-year-old Khomeini.

Iranian officials said that more than two-thirds of the Experts present resolved that 'As the sole manifestation of the first part of Principle 107 of the constitution, Ayatollah Montazeri is acceptable to an overwhelming majority of the people for future Leadership'.[42] But the actual number of the Experts present was not revealed.

In any event this resolution ended the debate on future leadership in favour of those who, like Hashemi-Rafsanjani, wanted to settle the issue while Khomeini was alive with a view to securing his endorsement, and thus aborting any damaging controversy that might arise after his death. It meant the defeat of the conservatives within the Experts Assembly who were opposed to Hashemi-Rafsanjani's stand on principle. They did not wish to extend the exceptional authority accorded to Khomeini, due to his extraordinary qualities and achievements, to any other personality. Instead they wanted to nominate a Leadership Council of three, comprising the different Islamic trends within the regime, with Montazeri playing a pre-eminent role.

Unlike Khomeini, who speaks in public only rarely, Montazeri delivers an hour-long lecture every morning at his headquarters in Qom. However, the subject is invariably theological, and his audience limited to a few hundred graduate students in theology. Just as at Khomeini's headquarters in Jamran, these robed students undergo strict security checks, surrendering all their possessions – except books, notebooks and pens – to the guards before being let into the lecture hall.

Underneath his genial appearance, sixty-three year old Montazeri is said to be a tough man. A Muslim diplomat, who has had a few meetings with Montazeri, was reported as saying, 'Every time I meet him I come away feeling more and more impressed with him. He is his own man, and has grown with the job.'[43] Daily the media carry reports of Montazeri's meetings with various delegations and officials, local or foreign. Almost every week he gives a televised lecture on *Nahaj al Balagheh*, the sayings of Imam Ali.

Montazeri's nomination to high office caused no surprise at home or abroad. It was widely seen as an important step towards further stabilisation of the Islamic regime which had been showing increasing signs of normalising relations with its Gulf neighbours.

It seemed Iranian leaders had concluded that in order to channel all their energies into achieving the overriding objective of ousting the Iraqi president they needed to end their less significant feuds with the Gulf states. They also appeared to have discovered merit in balancing their intransigence on the battlefield with flexibility in diplomatic and commercial links with their neighbours.

On the other side, the confidence of the Gulf rulers in the durability of their dynasties, badly shaken in the early days of the Iranian revolution, had revived. Having weathered the squalls of Islamic republicanism created by Tehran, the Gulf monarchs now felt secure enough to normalise relations with Iran. Also, much to their relief, the nighmarish scenario of Iran blocking the Hormuz Straits had not materialised, even though Iraq had once succeeded in damaging the Kharg oil terminal substantially. Moreover, they seemed to trust Tehran when it said that it wanted to keep the waterway open, if only for its own economic benefit.

Yet, given the intense animosity between revolutionary Iran and conservative Gulf states, these factors were not enough to bring about rapprochement. An honest broker was needed. He materialised in the person of President Assad of Syria. A trusted ally of Tehran, and an important member of the Arab League, he had been urging the Gulf states, particularly Saudi Arabia, to mend fences with Iran.[44]

The first sign of improvement in Tehran-Riyadh relations came in May 1985 when the Saudi foreign minister, Prince Saud al Faisal, visited Tehran and met President Khamanei. Though the ceasefire in the Gulf War that Prince Saud was seeking during Ramadan did not materialise, his visit established dialogue at the highest level. This came in handy when arrangements for 150,000 Iranian pilgrims to Mecca and Medina had to be finalised in early August. A compromise was reached. The Saudi authorities agreed to allow the Iranians to demonstrate in favour of Islamic unity and against the US, the Soviet Union and Israel provided they did so peacefully and without banners or pictures. The event passed off without incident.

In December the Iranian foreign minister, Velayati, returned the Saudi visit. In Riyadh he met his counterpart as well as King Fahd. According to the Islamic Republic News Agency, King Fahd said that his country respected the Iranian nation and its leaders, and that the former regime of Iran had been neglectful of Islam. Stressing the need for unity among Muslims, King Fahd stated that both Iran and Saudi Arabia could play an important role in strengthening Muslim unity. In reply Velayati declared that 'peaceful coexistence with its neighbours' was an important principle of Iran's foreign policy.[45] To show its goodwill towards Riyadh, Iran put on trial two South Yemenis who about a year before had hijacked a Saudi plane on a Jeddah-Riyadh flight to Tehran.

Iran improved its relations with all the Gulf states except Kuwait. Following the failed assassination attempt on its ruler in late May, Kuwait took to deporting 'undesirable elements'. By early September it had deported 6,270 people, most of them Iranians.[46] So relations between Kuwait and Tehran remained tense.

About a month before the GCC summit in Muscat, Oman, in early November, the Iranian government sent Ali Muhammad Besharati, vice-foreign minister, on a tour of Bahrain, Qatar and the UAE. In each of the three capitals Besharati repeated Khomeini's statement: 'We want Arab countries to be dignified and glorious. We want to improve relations with them'.[47]

The end result of Besharati's tour was a conciliatory communique issued by the GCC summit. For the first time since its formation in May 1981, the GCC refrained from mentioning Iraq's peace efforts and condemning Iran for continuing the Gulf War. Instead, it stated that Iran's views had to be considered in order to end the conflict. Iranian leaders saw this as a small, but significant, move towards neutrality by the GCC, something they were aiming at.

According to Iranian officials, relations with Bahrain were 'on the mend'. Those with Qatar were back to normal. Evidence of this came in early December 1985 when Shaikh Hamad al Thani, crown prince of Qatar, stated: 'We admire Iran as a country in the forefront of our struggle against Israel'.[48]

Iranian leaders put a partisan interpretation on these events. 'In the beginning the Gulf states made mistakes in evaluating our revolution and our policies,' said Hussein Shaikholislam, deputy foreign minister. 'Recently, however, they have shown that they want to rectify their mistakes.'[49]

Since the UAE came nearest to being neutral in the Gulf War, Tehran had close ties with it. Exchanges of ministerial visits were frequent. Dubai, an entrepot of the UAE, was an ideal place for Iran to procure food, industrial raw materials, machinery and spare parts it badly needed. In 1985-6 the two-way trade between Iran and the UAE reached the record level of $1,000 million a year.[50]

The other neighbour with whom Iran enjoyed flourishing commerce was Turkey. The annual transactions between the two countries in 1985-6 were running in the region of $2,500 million. In January 1986 the Turkish prime minister, Turgut Ozal, made his second visit to Tehran in as many years. The fact that Turkey was a member of Nato, and had a secular constitution which banned mixing religion with politics, was counterbalanced by such considerations that Turkey was Iran's neighbour, a Third World state, and a country whose nationals were 99 per cent Muslim.

Similar considerations applied to the Zia al-Haq regime in Pakistan, which was pro-American. The visit in January 1986 of President Khamanei to Islamabad underlined friendly relations between the two neighbours.

Iran continued to aid the Afghan guerrillas fighting the Karmal regime in Kabul, particularly in the Hazarajat mountain region of central Afghanistan, where most inhabitants are Shia. During the 1985-6 winter Iran despatched about 1,000 camel loads of light arms and ammunition to this region.[51]

The Soviet presence in Afghanistan continued to be the main hurdle for close ties between Tehran and Moscow. Their two-way trade at $439 million in 1984 was half the level of the previous year.[52] Relations turned sour when, in the wake of the Iraqi air raids on the Soviet-aided industrial projects in Ahvaz and Isfahan in March 1985, some 1,200 Soviet specialists working in Iran left the country on the grounds of lack of safety. Tehran protested, but to no avail. Still, an Iranian delegation, led by Kazem Ardebili, deputy foreign minister, visited Moscow in April to improve 'political and technical cooperation'. Three months later the Iranian foreign minister said, 'We intend to increase and expand our relations with the Soviet Union.'[53] As Iraqi aerial raids on Kharg became frequent and more intense during the summer – thus increasing the possibility of the Iranian blocking of the Hormuz Straits and the consequent American intervention – Iran felt a tactical need to improve ties with Moscow. In early October Hashemi-Rafsanjani reminded his Friday prayer audience that the Soviets had said that they would not stand by if the US were to intervene militarily in the Gulf.[54] The visit in early February 1986 to Tehran by a Soviet delegation led by Georgy Kornienko, first deputy foreign minister, showed the importance that the Kremlin attached to its links with Iran.

But any improvement in Soviet relations with Iran was not to be at the expense of Moscow's close ties with Baghdad. In late 1984 the Soviet Union was the source of 70 per cent of arms supplies to Iraq; and a year later Tariq Aziz, Iraq's foreign minister, confirmed that his country was getting most of its weapons from the Soviets on 'easy terms'. Some 6,000 Soviet military advisers were posted in Iraq.[55]

Iraq was also being courted by Washington. On 26 November the US restored diplomatic links with Baghdad after a lapse of seventeen years. President Reagan received Tariq Aziz at the White House. This was part of the American strategy to strengthen the forces opposed to Islamic radicalism which was seen as much of an enemy of Western interests in the Middle East as Marxism. Following the Reagan-Aziz meeting the US made its intelligence in the Gulf available to Iraq on a regular basis. According to European intelligence sources, warnings of attacks by Iranian planes on ships in the busy Gulf sea lanes were relayed to the Iraqis 'within minutes' of the Iranian pilots' take-off, monitored by the American-piloted Awacs in the Gulf. These were supplemented by a report every twelve hours on the Iranian military activity on the ground – culled from the information gathered from the many American satellites orbiting over the Gulf and from the American Awacs – which was passed on to Baghdad through Riyadh.[56] The Pentagon denied these reports. However, an official spokesman had stated in late July 1985 that being neutral in the Gulf War did not mean that 'We don't have sympathies'.[57] American sympathies were certainly not with Iran.

In Spetember 1984 the US imposed further restrictions on exports to Iran which had earlier been listed as 'a nation which helps international terrorism'. The hijacking in June 1985 of a Trans-World Airways plane flying out of Athens, and the murder of an American navy diver on board, seemed to increase American hostility towards Iran.

Washington tightened up on those trying to smuggle arms and spares from the US to Iran. According to the reports published in the *New York Times* and *Washington Post* in August 1985, during the previous year the Federal Bureau of Investigation had secured fourteen indictments against forty-four individuals and eight companies, twice the total of the past three years. Among those arrested was a deputy chief of staff of army materials command: he was reported to be working on an arms deal worth $140 million. The smugglers were aided by the fact that every year about 1 per cent of the total US arms and spares stockpile worth $80 billion 'disappeared', often due to misplacement.[58] American authorities claimed to have broken up five weapons-exporting groups using London as their shipping and financing centre. They allegedly met orders emanating from the National Iranian Oil Company building in London, which was shared by the Iranian air force's logistical support centre in Europe. Washington pressured London to tighten up on the activities of such arms dealers. British officials protested, complaining that 'The

Americans are paranoid about Iran and are becoming heavy-handed in their dealings with us.'[59]

Britain maintained good commercial links with Iran, and continued to have about 6 per cent of the Iranian market. In July 1985 Britain delivered to Iran the last of the three military transport vessels it had agreed to supply according to a pre-revolution contract. On the same basis it delivered to Iran Chieftain tank parts in September.[60] With this relations between London and Tehran improved markedly.

However, the most significant pro-Iranian move by any Western nation had been made by West Germany in July 1984, when its foreign minister, Hans Dietrich Genscher, became the first senior West European politician to visit the Islamic Republic. During his stay in Tehran he stated that the Western attempt to isolate an important country like Iran was 'one of the biggest mistakes made by the Western powers'.[61] In 1983-4 West Germany was the largest exporter of goods to Iran, a position it surrendered to Japan the following year. This happened mainly because Iran resolved to balance its trade by pressuring the leading exporters to Iran to buy more of Iranian oil, something that West Germany was not as willing to do as Japan.

As an OPEC member Iran was expected to stay within the exports quota of 1.2 million b/d alloted to it. But its ability to reach even this modest figure was compromised when Iraq intensified its air raids on the Kharg oil terminal in mid-August 1985. So far Baghdad had reckoned that if it destroyed the Kharg terminal then Tehran would retaliate by mounting a punishing land offensive against it. But once Iraq had succeeded in blunting repeated Iranian offensives, it lost its fear of Iranian reprisals on land, and decided to attack Kharg in a big way. It was inadvertently helped by the fact that the defence capacity of Kharg had been whittled down by the transfer of computers and other automatic equipment to Tehran in spring 1985 to protect the city from the Iraqi bombing. On 16 August, the day of the Iranian presidential poll, Iraqi planes flew low over Kharg and succeeded in hitting the oil terminal. In the next three weeks Iraq launched three more raids on Kharg to impede repairs; but as these were carried out from high altitudes they were ineffective. These attacks coincided with Iran's limited land offensives, codenamed Ashura and Zafar, in the Hur al Howzeh marshland and the central Dehloran sector.

In response to the Iraqi damage to Kharg, Iran raided Iraqi oilfields in the north and began searching ships in the Gulf suspected of carrying arms to Iraq. Also it carried out a limited offensive in the north near the Iraqi-Turkish border. In this it was aided by the guerrillas of the Kurdish Democratic Party of Iraq. Opposed to Saddam Hussein, these Kursish guerrillas claimed to control the Iraqi territory in the region up to the Syrian border except around the oil pipeline going to Turkey, and to have tied down two of Iraq's seven army corps.[63] Following this venture, Tehran claimed that its forces were twenty-five miles deep into northern Iraq.

All along the Iranians continued to operate a shuttle service between Kharg island and the temporary oil terminal on Sirri island, 350 miles to the south, out of the range of the Iraqi jets, thus obviating the need for Iran's oil buyers to expose their tankers to Iraqi attacks. Also, the fixed oil terminal on Lavan island in southern Gulf, with 400,000 b/d capacity, remained fully operational. Thus by mid-October Iran had established that Iraq was incapable of destroying the Kharg oil facilities, and that any disruption in Iranian oil exports could only be temporary. This improved the morale of the Iranian Supreme Defence Council as well as ordinary citizens.

Around this time Tehran initiated a programme of constructing twelve floating jetties near and outside the Gulf, and a string of a well-protected fixed oil terminals south of Kharg. The jetties in Jask, Bandar Lengeh and on Qeshm island were expected to be finished by the Iranian New Year, 20 March 1986. Fixed oil terminals at Taheri, 170 miles south of Kharg, and Bandar Asaluyeh, thirty miles further south, were scheduled to be ready by December. The new facilities would bring the total export capacity of Iran to 13 million b/d, including 6.5 million b/d from Kharg.

In a general sense the Gulf War, now in its sixth year, was stalemated. During the previous year Iraq had devised two new tactics – air raids on Iranian cities and intense bombing of Kharg – to weaken the Iranian resolve, and failed. Having frustrated the Iraqi moves the Iranian leaders mounted the 'Caravan to Karbala' campaign to enlist further popular backing for the war. Coinciding with the partial mobilisation ordered by the government in early October 1985, numerous cities and towns of Iran began to send their respective 'Caravan to Karbala' to the war front in a blaze of publicity. Karbala was a particularly emotive war cry. It was in Karbala that Imam Hussein had been killed in 681, along with his seventy-two ill-equipped followers while fighting a well-armed enemy force of 4,000. The event is re-enacted as a passion play every year by Shias in a ten-day ceremony, which is accompanied by mass flagellation. The charter of the Basij-e Mustazafin, which had by the end of 1985 reportedly trained three million Iranians, is to 'liberate Karbala' from the control of the secular government of Iraq. Often the red headbands worn by the Basij volunteers carry the words: 'Lover of Karbala'. Now the local Basij units marching off to the battle fronts were being hailed as the 'Caravans to Karbala'.

A steady increase in Iran's fighting forces has brought the total to 1.25 million, nearly half of them revolutionary guards. Yet the proportion of the war and war-related expenditure in the virtually stagnant budget of $42 to $46 billion over the past few years has remained constant: about one third.

This has been achieved mainly by gradually shifting the war burden to the voluntary sector. Not only is the Basij-e Mustazafin, where a volunteer is paid nominally, now contributing a quarter of the total manpower at the front, but also more and more materials and cash are coming directly from the public. The list of the War Contributions published daily in the *Kayhan International* is illustrative. In December 1985 it included: 'Semirom: 8,394 kilos of wheat and wheat flour, 847 bars of soap and boxes of detergent. Roodehen: seventeen trucks, fifteen gas stoves, ten air conditioners, one truckload of apples.' There were of course cash contributions, ranging from Rials 90,000 to Rials 6,930,000.

Every large mosque and workplace has its Basij unit. Enquiries made at Saadi Tile Company's works in the Tehran suburb of Shahr Rey revealed that half of its 1,440 workers donated one day's wages every month to the War Fund. About a third of them were members of the Basij unit at the factory, and had been to the front for three months or more.[64]

Those who have spent six months or more at the front get preference in promotion at work. This applies as much to factories as to offices, private or public. The government thus combines monetary incentives with an appeal to the Islamic zeal of potential war volunteers. The fate of those who die for Islam is described in the Quran thus: 'Count not those who are slain in God's way as dead, but rather living with their lord, by Him provided, rejoicing in the bounty that God has given them.'[65]

The much publicised Iranian mobilisation was as much part of the Tehran's psychological warfare to signal Iran's will to fight on as it was to strengthen the Iranian military position on the ground. Mousavi summed up the official thinking in Tehran thus: 'This is a war in which the party which is more steadfast will win'.[66]

Iraq was not idle either. In January 1986 it claimed to have mounted an offensive and retaken part of the Majnoon islands it had lost to Iran nearly two years back. At about the same time, in the course of monitoring ships in the Gulf for the war materials destined for Iraq, Iranian marines boarded and searched an American vessel, thus demonstrating Tehran's resolve not to make an exception of a super-power. They found nothing objectionable, and let the ship proceed. Interestingly, Washington responded in a low key, with its official spokesman stating that 'The rules of naval warfare traditionally accord a belligerent certain rights to ascertain whether neutral shipping is being used to provide contraband to the opposing belligerent'.[67] Since mid-August 1985 Iran's navy had taken fourteen ships belonging to Italy, West Germany, Denmark, Kuwait, Poland and Japan to Iranian ports for a thorough search.

If nothing else, these actions showed that the Iranian navy was in a good shape. It played a leading role in the successful mounting of an offensive, codenamed Wa Al Fajr-Eight, at the mouth of the Gulf at Fao, on the night of 9-10 February, the eve of the seventh anniversary of the Islamic revolution. Iran combined this move with an assault on Iraq in the Hur al Howzeh marshes north of Basra, and on Umm al Rassas island inside Shatt al Arab near Khorramshahr twenty-five miles south-east of Basra. Iraq claimed to have beaten back the Iranian assaults on Umm al Rassas and in the Howzeh marshes, but not the one in the Fao peninsula.

Having gained a foothold on the western bank of Shatt al Arab, the Iranians pushed northwards from the disused oil port of Fao to Basra, sixty miles away, and to Umm Qasr, thirty-four miles to the west, near the Kuwaiti border. Within a week they claimed to have occupied 320 sq. miles of Fao peninsula. By then they had achieved their short-term objectives of virtually cutting off Iraq from the Gulf, destroying and capturing a large number of men and weapons, taking over the missile station in the area, and seizing a radar station which gave cover to the Iraqi planes on their raiding missions in the Gulf.

The Iranian success stemmed from the surprise they sprung on the Iraqis who had been expecting a major offensive in the Howzeh marshes (and only there), their three-to-one numerical superiority in manpower, and the soft, marshy terrain which neutralised Iraqi advantage in armour. As for the superior Iraqi air force, the Iranians surprised their enemy by transporting across the Shatt al Arab waterway one, or possibly two, air defence systems they had reportedly purchased from China, and making an effective use of the Chinese-made HQ2 surface-to-air missiles (equivalent of the Soviet SAM-2s). Also, following their success in clandestinely procuring spare parts from the US, the Iranians had made twenty-four F-14s airworthy, so doubling the previous total. Thus, within a fortnight of the offensive Tehran could claim to have shot down fifty-five Iraqi planes and helicopters.[68] 'This offensive disproves the lies that we are unable to continue the war,' said Hashemi-Rafsanjani to the Friday prayer assembly in Tehran on 21 February 1986. 'The American Awacs in Saudi Arabia are watching us, but we have devised a technique so that they cannot find out what our forces are doing.'[69]

Tehran's move was part of a bigger plan to cut off the Kuwait-Basra highway in the south and deprive Iraq of vital military and civilian supplies from Kuwait and Saudi Arabia, and sever Basra-Baghdad highway in the north, thus isolating Basra from the rest of the country.

Such a development, Iranian leaders reckoned, would be so devastating to Iraq's prestige that it would generate moves within the Iraqi establishment to overthrow Saddam Hussein, and this would pave the way for a ceasefire.

On 14 February Iraq mounted a counter-offensive with three armoured columns backed up by heavy artillery and air force – and periodic use of chemical weapons. But the Iranians offered stiff resistance. Saddam Hussein strengthened the local 7th Army Corps with units from the Presidential Guard, used exclusively in Baghdad for the security of his government, and the battle-experienced 3rd Army Corps in the Hur al Howzeh area, in order to expel the Iranians from the Fao peninsula. But due to the soft, marshy soil, the armoured columns could only use narrow roads. As they did so they encountered Iranian defensive positions every 300 yards. Also the Iranians were by now armed with the tanks and armoured personnel carriers they had earlier captured from the Iraqis. The Iraqi commanders were unwilling to commit infantry to overwhelm the 30,000 Iranians who had dug in. Yet by early March the Iraqi casualities had reportedly reached 10,000 versus 20,000 for the Iranians,[70] a ratio unacceptable to Baghdad.

To ensure that the Iraqi high command did not transfer too many units of its 3rd Army Corps to the Fao peninsula, Tehran maintained a high military profile in the Howzeh marshland. While the Iraqi attention was focussed on the southern front, on 24 February Iran mounted an offensive, codenamed Wa Al Fajr-Nine, in Iraqi Kurdistan near Sulaimaniya. By early March the Iranians claimed to have come within ten miles of Sulaimaniya, an important oil centre of Iraq, and captured 130 sq. miles of Iraqi soil. They either wanted to disrupt oil production in the area, or control the dam on Darbandikhan Lake, which is the main source of electricity to Baghdad.

While hailing the Fao offensive as a great success, Tehran insisted that it was of limited nature, more political than military. By moving close to the Kuwaiti border, said the *Kayhan* on 23 February, the Iranian armed forces were sending a message to the conservative Arab states along the Gulf. 'The time has come to believe that a close friend of our enemy could also be regarded as our enemy.'

The intimate ties of Kuwait and Saudi Arabia with Iraq were apparent from the fact that they continued to sell 300,000 b/d of the oil extracted from the neutral zone along the Saudi-Iraqi border – and touching the Kuwaiti frontier – to Iraq's customers. 'We cannot allow other countries to sell oil on behalf of our enemy and pass safely through the Persian Gulf waters,' said Mousavi on 26 February.[71] Iran was thus giving notice that it would extend its policy of confiscating the Iraq-bound arms passing through the Gulf to the oil being shipped to Iraq's customers.

In early March Iran hit four ships leaving or approaching the western side of the Gulf in as many days in retaliation for the Iraqi attacks on four tankers plying between Kharg and Sirri islands during the previous week, thus proving its potential for enforcing its threats against the countries aiding Iraq. The later reports that, in addition to its Lavan island-based F-4s, Iran was using military helicopters from Rostam island, the centre of an oilfield sixty-five miles from the mainland, and that the Iranian helicopters had struck fourteen ships during the first three months of 1986, signified an escalation in the naval conflict.[72]

But neither Kuwait nor Riyadh showed any sign of loosening its close links with Baghdad. Kuwait condemned the Iranian offensive in Fao and put its forces on alert. Kuwaiti and Saudi foreign ministers flew to Damascus to advise President Assad to warn Iran against invading Kuwait, and added that if he failed to restrain Tehran he would lose financial aid for Syria from the Gulf states.[73]

Of course the Gulf states may well reduce or cut off aid to Syria due to sharply falling oil prices. As it was, Saudi Arabia played the leading role in putting oil prices on skids by boosting its oil exports from an average of two million b/d in late 1985 to 4.5 million b/d in early 1986. It argued that sharply lower oil price would hurt such non-OPEC producers as Britain and Norway, and make their oil industry uneconomic, thus compelling them to cooperate with OPEC in fixing prices and making them stick worldwide. Privately, however, both Saudi Arabia and Kuwait hoped that by depressing oil price they would *inter alia* reduce Iran's oil income to the extent of seriously impairing its ability to prosecute the Gulf War.[74]

But the Saudi-inspired tactic failed to win British or Norwegian cooperation with OPEC. In early April oil price fell to below $10 a barrel from an average of $27 in December 1985. Even if prices were to rise a bit later, and average out at $13 to $14 a barrel for 1986, Iran's actual oil revenue for the fiscal year 1986-7 is likely to be half of the projected $16 billion, barely enough for the imports of war materials ($4 to $5 billion) and food and medicines ($3.75 billion). However, in early 1986 Iran was known to have total foreign reserves of about $5 billion.[75] Also Iran had already embarked on barter trading, exchanging oil for food and industrial raw materials, thus obviating the need for payments in hard currencies. Moreover the Majlis, which has so far specifically forbidden the government from borrowing money abroad, is likely to relax its policy and allow the government to resort to securing medium term credit to finance imports. All told, therefore, Iran is unlikely to slow down its war effort, particularly when it has recently made territorial and diplomatic gains.

For instance, in its unanimously passed resolution on 24 February 1986, the UN Security Council referred to the 'first aggression' that sparked off the Gulf War. It was a move in the right direction, but was not enough for Iran, which had boycotted the Security Council meeting.

A month later the UN Security Council adopted the report of a UN team of four experts which concluded, after examining over 700 casualties of chemical weapons in Tehran and Ahvaz, that Iraq had used mustard gas and nerve gas against the Iranian forces on many occasions. 'It is our impression that the use of chemical weapons in 1986 appears to be more extensive than in 1984,' the report said. While condemning Iraq by name (for the first time) for resorting to chemical weapons, the Security Council unanimously registered its condemnation of 'the prolongation of the conflict which continues to take a heavy toll of human lives'. Once again, for Iran the Security Council's condemnation of Iraq by name was a step in the right direction, but was not enough. 'The UN Security Council should not consider its task finished by merely issuing a statement, but should take steps to punish the aggressor,' said the Iranian foreign ministry.[76]

As Iranians prepared to celebrate the seventh anniversary of the founding of the Islamic Republic on 1 April 1986, Khomeini gave one of his strongest calls for the mobilisation of all able-minded men and the continuation of the war until the fall of Saddam Hussein. On 1 April ten divisions of the Iranian reserve forces joined the civilians in their march to the Tehran University campus for a rally. Describing the US as Iran's 'arch enemy', Prime Minister Mousavi said, 'We will continue to struggle against America in Iran, in the Gulf region and throughout the world.'[77]

It was not surprising therefore that, following the American air raids on the Libyan cities of Tripoli and Benghazi on the night of 14-15 April to hit 'the terrorist infrastructure', President Khamanei described the American action as 'an attack on Islam'. He added: 'We, in our turn, are prepared to take any action in retaliation for such a savage act.'[78] The fact that Iraq was the only Arab country not to condemn the American bombing of Libya helped Iran to argue that Saddam Hussein had proved himself to be a renegade even in Arab eyes.

War with Saddam Hussein's Iraq and confrontation with America abroad have by now become as much fixtures of Iranian life as Islamisation and revolution at home. Plans to impart weapons training to ever-increasing segments of Iranian society are going ahead. Starting the new academic year in 1986, military training will be extended to the upper forms of secondary schools, a step which will ultimately involve 4.5 million students.[79]

It is only a matter of time when, having consolidated their hold over the Fao peninsula, the Iranian military leaders will stage offensives to seal off the Iraqi-Kuwaiti borders and cut off Basra from Baghdad.

To the extent that mobilistion for war is easier and more dramatic than for revolution, the hostilities with Iraq are serving a valuable purpose for the Islamic regime. Khomeini's death is unlikely to change the situation.

30 April 1986

Notes

1 In mid-August Iranian planes attacked two more ships trading with the Gulf states. By so doing Tehran intended to prove to these countries that despite US protection their ships were vulnerable.
2 *Sunday Times*, 3 June 1984; and *The Times*, 14 June 1984.
3 Tehran Radio, 31 May 1984.
4 *Sunday Times*, 23 June 1984.
5 *Guardian*, 28 June 1984; and *Washington Post*, 21 July 1984.
6 *BBC Summary of World Broadcasts*, 14 August 1984.
7 See pp. 198 and 146.
8 *Daily Telegraph*, 3 September 1984.
9 *BBC Summary of World Broadcasts*, 11 August 1984.
10 *Observer*, 9 September 1984.
11 *The Times*, 1 December 1984.
12 *Guardian*, 19 December 1984.
13 Ibid., 20 August 1984; and *The Middle East*, December 1984, p. 26.
14 *Guardian*, 5 March 1985.
15 *Newsweek*, 1 April 1985, p. 15.
16 *Sunday Times*, 7 April 1985; and *The Times*, 31 July 1985.
17 *Newsweek*, 1 April 1985, p. 16. Since the beginning of the Gulf War some 7,000 Iranian civilians were killed and over 30,000 injured. *Guardian*, 9 April 1985.
18 *Sunday Times*, 7 April 1985.
19 *Guardian*, 19 April 1985.
20 10 April 1985.
21 The Beirut-based Islamic Jihad organisation claimed responsibility for the attack, and demanded the release of those arrested in connection with the December 1983 bombings in Kuwait. See p. 234.
22 During the seven-week period in March-April and May-June 1985, Iraqi planes hit Tehran forty-three times. Twelve Iranian ground-to-ground missiles landed in Baghdad.
23 The political reasons for Sino-Iranian friendship were articulated by Hashemi-Rafsanjani thus: 'We consider China to be really independent and without domineering intentions. It pursues a policy of support for the oppressed, and is opposed to the superpower domination'. *Ittilaat*, 28 June 1985.
24 *Observer*, 5 May 1985.
25 Cited in *Iran Press Digest*, 29 July 1985.
26 *Kayhan*, 13 August 1985.
27 *Iran Press Digest*, 6 August 1985.

28 Kashani secured 1,403,000 votes, and Asghar-Owladi 283,000. *Guardian*, 20 August 1985.
29 *Kayhan*, 29 September 1985.
30 Interviews in Tehran, December 1985.
31 *Observer*, 30 June 1985.
32 *The Middle East*, April 1985, p. 51.
33 See p. 244.
34 *Iran Press Digest*, 5 November 1985.
35 *The Middle East*, April 1985, p. 52.
36 *International Herald Tribune*, 1 November 1985.
37 See p. 123.
38 *Iran Press Digest*, 11 November 1985.
39 *Abrar*, 9 October 1985. In 1984-85 the Prime Minsiter's office sold properties worth Rials 50 billion and was still left with assets worth Rials 350 billion. *Iran Press Digest*, 11 November 1985.
40 Ibid.
41 See p. 121.
42 *Jumhouri-ye Islami*, 1 December 1985. One of the facts which recommended Montazeri to the high office was that he had actively opposed the Shah, and suffered imprisonment and torture. This could not be said of such senior clerics as Ayatollahs Marashi-Najafi and Golpaygani.
43 *Washington Post*, 13 February 1986.
44 Assad has an economic interest in easing tensions between Iran and the Gulf monarchies. His alliance with Iran had cost him cuts in subsidies from the oil-rich kingdoms. At the same time he had been unable to pay for the annual import of five million tonnes of Iranian oil and owed Tehran $900 million.
45 *Kayhan International*, 10 December 1985.
46 *Guardian*, 6 September 1985.
47 *Jumhouri-ye Islami*, 14 October 1985.
48 Tehran Radio, 5 December 1985.
49 Interview in Tehran, 18 December 1985.
50 *Jumhouri-ye Islami*, 14 October 1985.
51 *Guardian*, 31 January 1986. Shias form about a third of the population of Afghanistan.
52 *Iran Press Digest*, 15 July 1985.
53 *Ittilaat*, 20 July 1985.
54 *Iran Press Digest*, 7 October 1985.
55 *Economist*, 24 November 1985, p. 57; and Tehran Radio, 1 December 1985.
56 *Sunday Times*, 17 March 1985.
57 *The Times*, 31 July 1985. America sold fortyeight Bell troops carrier helicopters to Iraq. Ibid.
58 *Iran Press Digest*, 3 September 1985; and *New York Times*, 29 September 1985.
59 *Sunday Times*, 18 August 1985. Next April US and Bermudan authorities arrested ten of the seventeen Americans, Europeans and Israelis charged with conspiring to sell US-made warplanes, tanks and other arms worth $2.5 billion to Iran from the supplies held by other countries. *Observer*, 27 April 1986.
60 *Iran Press Digest*, 30 September 1985.
61 *BBC Summary of World Broadcasts*, 28 July 1984.

62 Of the thirteen Iraqi attacks on Kharg between mid-August and late September only two were effective. *Washington Post*, 27 September 1985. Even at the worst of times Kharg, with the maximum capacity of 6.5 million b/d, was capable of exporting 1.5 million b/d. *Guardian*, 5 October 1985.
63 Ibid., 25 February 1986.
64 Interviews on 23 December 1985.
65 Arthur J. Arberry, *The Koran Interpreted*, Chapter III, 'The House of Imran', verse 164, p. 66.
66 *Toronto Star*, 26 January 1986.
67 *Guardian*, 14 January 1986.
68 *Observer*, 23 February 1986; and *Guardian*, 24 February 1986.
69 Ibid., 22 February 1986.
70 BBC World Service Radio, 5 March 1986.
71 *Guardian*, 27 February 1986.
72 Ibid., 3 April 1986. On an average one ship was hit every week in 1984 and 1985. So far 200 vessels had been struck since the beginning of the Gulf War, with the aggregate tonnage equal to one-fifth the total during the Second World War. BBC World Service Radio, 17 April 1986.
73 *Economist*, 28 February 1986, p. 37
74 *Observer*, 20 April 1986.
75 *Washington Post*, 9 January 1986.
76 *Guardian*, 15 March 1986; and Associated Press, 24 March 1986. A single Iraqi raid with chemical bombs on 28 February alone wounded 8,500 Iranian soldiers and civilians. Of these 200 died soon after. *Guardian*, 25 March 1986.
77 Islamic Republic News Agency, 1 April 1986.
78 *Guardian*, 16 April 1986.
79 *Kayhan*, 7 October 1985.

NOTES

Introduction

1 *Iran Almanac, 1975*, Echo of Iran, Tehran, p. 395.

Chapter 1 The Islamic heritage

1 *Race & Class*, Vol. XXI, Summer 1979, p. 5.
2 Zaidi Shias are an exception to this.
3 In contrast, Ismailis and Twelvers believe in the following five Imams: Ali, Hassan, Hussein, Zain al Abidin and Muhammad al Baqir.
4 Nikki R. Keddie, *Roots of Revolution: An Interpretive History of Modern Iran*, Princeton University Press, Princeton, N.J. and Guildford, 1981, pp. 21-2.
5 See p. 272.
6 See pp. 272, 294.
7 Ervand Abrahamian, *Iran Between Two Revolutions*, Yale University Press, New Haven, Conn., and London, 1982, p. 55.
8 It is widely believed that Jamal al-Din was born in 1838 of Shia parents in the Iranian town of Assadabad near Hamadan. But, insisting that his birthplace was Assadabad near Konar in the district of Kabul in Afghanistan, he called himself Afghani. This implied that he was Sunni.
9 Abrahamian, op. cit., p. 73.
10 See pp. 68–9.
11 A man claiming to be a descendant of Prophet Muhammad.
12 Edward G. Browne, *The Persian Revolution of 1905-1909*, Cambridge University Press, Cambridge, 1910, p. 365.
13 A photograph of the Majlis members shows sixty of them wearing turbans (compulsory for the ulema) and forty fez caps. Browne, op. cit., photograph facing p. 124.
14 Shahrough Akhavi, *Religion and Politics in Contemporary Iran: Clergy-State Relations in the Pahlavi Period*, State University of New York Press, Albany, N.Y., 1980, p. 26.
15 Browne, op. cit., pp. 374-8; and Akhavi, op. cit., pp. 35-7.
16 See p. 295.
17 See p. 273.
18 Cited in Akhavi, op. cit., pp. 29-30.
19 Abdul-Hadi Hairi, *Shi'ism and Constitutionalism: A Study of the Life and*

Views of Mirza Muhammad Husayn Na'ini, E.J. Brill, Leiden, 1977, p. 270.
20 Cited in Abrahamian, op. cit., p. 135.

Chapter 2 The Pahlavis

1 Cited in Shahroukh Akhavi, *Religion and Politics in Contemporary Iran*, p. 58.
2 Donald Wilber, *Riza Shah Pahlavi: The Resurrection and Reconstruction of Iran*, Exposition Press, Hicksville, N.Y., 1975, p. 263.
3 See p. 296.
4 See p. 258.
5 Ervand Abrahamian, *Iran Between Two Revolutions*, p. 152.
6 Wilber, op. cit., p. 263.
7 Nikki R. Keddie, *Roots of Revolution*, p. 117.
8 D.N. Wilber, *Iran: Past and Present*, Princeton University Press, Princeton, N.J., 1948, p. 132.
9 Keddie, op. cit., p. 110. Also see p. 53.
10 T.H.V. Motter, *The Persian Corridor and Aid to Russia*, Office of the Chief of Military History, Department of the Army, Washington, D.C., 1952, p. 161.
11 See pp. 273-4.
12 From there Reza Pahlavi Shah went to Johannesburg, South Africa, then part of the British empire. He died there in July 1944.
13 Keddie, op. cit., p. 111.
14 See p. 201 and pp. 276-7.
15 Cited in Abrahamian, op. cit., pp. 265-6.
16 Cited in Akhavi, op. cit., p. 64.
17 Following the unsuccessful attempt on his life, the Shah convened a constituent assembly. It resolved to establish the Senate with half of its sixty members nominated by the Shah, as stated in the constitution. The first Senate was convened in 1950, and its tenure fixed at six years.
18 *Bakhtar-e Emruz* (Today's West), 6 March 1952, cited in Richard W. Cottam, *Nationalism in Iran: Updated through 1978*, University of Pittsburgh Press, Pittsburgh, Pa., 1979, p. 152.
19 *Shahed* (Witness), 19 July 1952, cited in Abrahamian, op. cit., p. 271.
20 *Ittilaat* (Information), 3 September 1952.
21 Ibid., 9 June 1952.
22 The actual figures were: 2,043,300 for the dissolution; and 1,300 against. *New York Times*, 14 August 1953.
23 L.P. Elwell-Sutton, *Persian Oil: A Study in Power Politics*, Lawrence and Wishart, London, 1955, p. 310.
24 Abrahamian, op. cit., pp. 278-9.
25 Kermit Roosevelt, *Countercoup: The Struggle for the Control of Iran*, McGraw-Hill, New York, 1979, pp. 163-7.
26 Following the dissolution of the Senate in late October 1952, General Zahedi lost his parliamentary immunity.
27 Abrahamian, op. cit., p. 280.
28 *Ittilaat*, 20 August 1979.
29 *Christian Science Monitor*, 28 May 1963. Seventy-two-year-old Mussadiq was sentenced to three years' solitary imprisonment. After his release he was placed under house arrest until his death in 1967.

30 Mohamed Heikal, *The Return of the Ayatollah: The Iranian Revolution from Mossadeq to Khomeini*, André Deutsch, London, 1981, p. 70.
31 *Ittilaat*, 10 October 1953.
32 Cited in Akhavi, op. cit., p. 75.
33 A stratified social organisation, an Iranian bazaar consists of: wholesalers, commission agents, brokers, middlemen, merchants, money-changers, workshop owners, artisans, craftsmen, apprentices, shopkeepers, shop assistants, hawkers, peddlers and porters.
34 See p. 32.
35 Abrahamian, op. cit., p. 275.
36 *Ittilaat*, 10 May 1955.
37 Richard W. Cottam cites three sources and as many estimates: 10,000; 200,000; and 1,000,000. Op. cit., p. 87. In the Majlis, Assadollah Alam, interior minister, referred to '700,000 Bahais in 500 communities'. *Kayhan* (The World), 9 August 1955.
38 *Ittilaat*, 20 October 1955.
39 See p. 301.
40 Cited in Ali-Reza Nobari (ed.), *Iran Erupts*, The Iran-America Documentation Group, Stanford, Calif., 1978, p. 70.
41 Peter Mansfield (ed.), *The Middle East: A Political and Economic Survey*, Oxford University Press, Oxford and New York, Fourth Edition, 1973, pp. 27-8.
42 Robert Graham, *Iran: The Illusion of Power*, Croom Helm, London, 1978, p. 40.
43 Eric Hooglund, *Reform and Revolution in Rural Iran*, University of Texas Press, Austin, Tex., 1982, p. 17 and p. 22.
44 Keddie, op. cit., pp. 289-90, notes 7 and 8. Though other clerics spoke and wrote against the compulsory purchase of excess land by the state, none of them issued a religious decree, fatwa, on the subject. In its campaign against the clergy, the Pahlavi regime never produced any such decree.
45 In 1957, of the 39,409 villages, 9,234 belonged to large landlords owning one or more villages; 1,444 to the state; 812 to the Shah; and 713 to the religious trusts. K. Khosravi, *The Sociology of Rural Iran* (in Persian), Tehran, 1972, pp. 28-9.
46 'No to the arbitrary rule of the Shah, his interference in the affairs of the state, the rule of terror and Savak activities, colonial domination of the country, police violations, and gendarmerie oppression,' said the National Front manifesto. Cited in Marvin Zonis, *The Political Elite of Iran*, Princeton University Press, Princeton, N.J., 1971, p. 74.
47 *Ittilaat*, 25 January 1963.
48 Ibid., 31 January 1963.
49 Ibid., 7, 8 and 9 March 1963.
50 Michael M.J. Fischer, *Iran: From Religious Dispute to Revolution*, Harvard University Press, Cambridge, Mass., and London, 1980, p. 188.
51 Ruh Allah Khumayni, *Islam and Revolution*, translated by Hamid Algar, Mizan Press, Berkeley, Calif., 1981, p. 176.
52 Anonymous, *Biography of the Leader, Vol. II* (in Persian), 15 Khurdad Publications, Tehran, 1979, p. 42.
53 Interview with Reza Nasseri, a shopkeeper, in Qom in December 1979.
54 Mansfield (ed.), op. cit., p. 281.
55 *New York Times*, 7 June 1963.
56 Zonis, op. cit., p 63, note 15.

57 *Payam-e Emruz* (Today's Message), 10 June 1963.

58 Fischer, op. cit., p. 188.

59 Anonymous, op. cit., p. 72.

60 Mansfield (ed.), op. cit., p. 283.

61 Khumayni, op. cit., p. 186.

62 Cited in Zonis, op. cit., p. 46.

63 Mousavi means a descendant of Imam Mousa al Kazem, the seventh Imam. Sayyed Ahmed Mousavi was called al Hindi (the Indian), because he was born in the Oudh principality in northern India, where his forefathers had moved from the Iranian province of Khurasan many decades earlier at the invitation of the Shia ruler of Oudh.

64 Cited in Khumayni, op. cit., p. 170.

65 Shia religious titles in the ascending order are: thiqatalislam (trusted one of Islam), hojatalislam (proof of Islam), ayatollah (sign or token of Allah), ayatollah al ozma (grand ayatollah). An ayatollah al ozma is automatically a marja-e taqlid, source of emulation, to the faithful.

66 Cited in *Time*, 7 January 1980, p. 14.

67 Interview with Ayatollah Murtaza Pasandida in Qom in December 1979.

68 Cited in Akhavi, op. cit., p. 101.

69 Mansfield (ed.), op. cit., pp. 301-2.

70 Keddie, op. cit., p. 162; and Abrahamian, op. cit., p. 429.

71 Abrahamian, op. cit., p. 430.

72 Ibid., pp. 430-1.

73 Julian Bharier, *Economic Development of Iran, 1900-1970*, Oxford University Press, Oxford and New York, 1971, p. 36.

74 Abrahamian, op. cit., p. 431.

75 See p. 304.

76 Hossein Amirsadeghi (ed.), *Twentieth Century Iran*, Holmes and Meier, New York, 1977, p. 280.

77 Shahram Chubin and Sepehr Zabih, *The Foreign Relations of Iran: A Developing State in a Zone of Great-Power Conflict*, University of California Press, Los Angeles, Calif., 1974, Appendix Table I.

78 Fred Halliday, *Iran: Dictatorship and Development*, Penguin Books, Harmondsworth, 1979, p. 30.

79 Graham, op. cit., p. 145.

80 Akhavi, op. cit., pp. 160-1.

81 David H. Albert (ed.), *Tell the American People: Perspectives on the Iranian Revolution*, Movement for a New Society, Philadelphia, Pa., 1980, p. 17. Also see p. 306.

82 Cited in Khumayni, op. cit., p. 190.

83 The Shah explained the long-postponed coronation thus: 'I long ago promised myself that I would never be king over a people who were beggars or oppressed. But now that everyone is happy I allow my coronation to take place'. Cited in Heikal, op. cit., p. 93.

84 Hamid Algar, 'The Oppositional Role of the Ulema in Twentieth Century Iran' in Nikki R. Keddie (ed.), *Scholars, Saints and Sufis*, University of California, Los Angeles and Berkeley, Calif., 1972, pp. 250-2.

85 Ibid., p. 253. Since there was no national dynastic rule in Iran from 641 to 1501, the Shah's claim of 2,500 years of continuous monarchy was false.

86 See p. 304.

87 Cottam, op. cit., p. 329.

88 Heikal, op. cit., p. 94. The *New York Times* correspondent put the expenses at $100 million. 12 October 1971.

89 Cited in Khumayni, op. cit., p. 202.
90 Akhavi, op. cit., pp. 164-6.
91 Ibid., p. 141.
92 This memorandum was discovered after the revolution in official files, and published in the *Kayhan* of 19 March 1979.
93 *Iran Almanac, 1975*, Echo of Iran, Tehran, p. 395. Part of the increase was no doubt due to the rising prosperity of Iranians during that period.
94 *New Republic*, 1 September 1973, p. 7.
95 The other founder-members were: Iraq, Kuwait, Saudi Arabia and Venezuela. In October 1973, besides the founders, the members of OPEC were: Algeria, Ecuador, Indonesia, Libya, Nigeria, Qatar, Trinidad and Tobago and the United Arab Emirates.
96 Dilip Hiro, *Inside the Middle East*, Routledge & Kegan Paul, London, and McGraw-Hill, New York, 1982, p. 334.
97 The members of OAPEC, formed in 1968, were: Algeria, Bahrain, Egypt, Iraq, Libya, Oman, Qatar, Saudi Arabia, Syria and the United Arab Emirates.
98 Amirsadeghi, op. cit., p. 280.
99 *The Economist*, 31 October 1970, p. 48; and *New York Times*, 4 February 1976.
100 Cited in Graham, op. cit., p. 136.
101 Chubin and Zabih, op. cit., Appendix Table I.
102 Graham, op. cit., p. 224.
103 This was exclusive of the 60,000 foreign managers and technicians working in Iran at that time.
104 Abrahamian, op. cit., p. 434.
105 Ibid., pp. 434-5.
106 Barry Rubin, *Paved with Good Intentions: The American Experience and Iran*, Penguin Books, Harmondsworth and New York, 1981, p. 156.
107 *Ittilaat*, 6 October 1979.
108 See p. 58. *Mujahed* (Combatant), March 1975, pp. 6-10.
109 Abrahamian, op. cit., p. 431.
110 *P.E.N. Country Reports*, March 1978, p. 12.
111 *Human Rights and the Legal System in Iran*, Geneva, 1976, pp. 21-2.
112 *Mujahed*, March 1975, pp. 1-11.
113 Ibid., May 1975, p. 7.
114 Cited in *Khabarnameh* (Newsletter), June 1975, p. 1.
115 Graham, op. cit., p. 243, note 43.

Chapter 3 The end of monarchy

1 See p. 306.
2 Robert Graham, *Iran: The Illusion of Power* pp. 260-1.
3 Hojatalislam Mustapha Khomeini was active in the training of Islamic guerrillas at the Palestinian camps in south Lebanon, a stronghold of the Shias. *The Dawn of the Islamic Revolution, Vol. I*, Ministry of Islamic Guidance, Tehran, No date, p. 342.
4 Interviews in Tehran bazaar, December 1979.
5 Parviz Radji, *In the Service of the Peacock Throne*, Hamish Hamilton, London, 1983, p. 171.
6 Cited in Nikki R. Keddie, *Roots of Revolution*, p. 243. The reference to India had to do with Khomeini's grandfather, Ahmed. See p. 49.

7 Throughout this chapter the low casualty figure is the one given by official sources, and the high figure is an unofficial estimate.
8 These figures were given by Nouri Albala, a French lawyer, who visited Tabriz after the riots, and interviewed many eye-witnesses. Ali-Reza Nobari (ed.), *Iran Erupts*, p. 102.
9 Ruh Allah Khumayni, *Islam and Revolution*, p. 212.
10 Ibid., p. 228.
11 These figures were complied by Ervand Abrahamian from the *Ittilaat*, a Tehran-based newspaper, of February to June 1978, and the *Mujahed*, the organ of the National Front in North America, of the same period. *Iran Between Two Revolutions*, p. 508.
12 *Iran Times*, 2 June 1978.
13 Cited in *Mardom* (People), 11 February 1979.
14 *The Middle East*, July 1978, p. 14.
15 Keddie, op. cit., p. 107.
16 *Washington Post*, 20 August 1978.
17 Savak ran 600 goverment-sponsored trade unions. Fred Halliday, *Iran*, p. 81.
18 Pp. 254-5.
19 Graham, op. cit., p. 228.
20 Khumayni, op. cit., p. 232.
21 *Iran Times*, 1 September 1978.
22 But unknown to Sharif-Emami, the Shah set up a watchdog committee within the cabinet headed by Hushang Nahavandi, minister of science and higher education, to see that the prime minister did not go too far in meeting the opposition's demands.
23 Khumayni, op. cit., pp. 234-6.
24 *The Dawn of the Islamic Revolution, Vol. I*, p. 263.
25 Nobari, op. cit., p. 196; and *The Dawn of the Islamic Revolution*, p. 257. Allowing for the natural deaths which occurred during those few days in that part of Tehran, the number of those killed by troops exceeded 4,000.
26 The Iran-Iraq treaty of 1975 required each signatory to stop all subversive activities directed from its territory against the other. Due to the restrictions imposed on him by the Iraqi authorities, Khomeini was unable to comment on the events of the Black Friday.
27 *Events*, 3 November 1978, p. 48.
28 Khumayni, op. cit., pp. 240-1.
29 Abrahamian, op. cit., p. 518.
30 Michael Leeden and William Lewis, *Debacle: The American Failure in Iran*, Knopf, New York, 1981, p. 153.
31 Ibid.
32 *Events*, 17 November 1978, p. 27.
33 Mohamed Heikal, *The Return of the Ayatollah*, pp. 155-6.
34 *BBC Summary of World Broadcasts*, 7 November 1978.
35 Abrahamian, op. cit., pp. 519-20.
36 *Khabarnameh*, 9 November 1978, p. 1.
37 *Washington Post*, 19 November 1978.
38 See pp. 273-4.
39 See p. 28.
40 Khumayni, op. cit., pp. 243-4.
41 Michael M.J. Fischer, *Iran*, p. 204.
42 *Washington Post*, 19 December 1978; and *New York Times*, 19 December 1978.

43 *New York Times*, 2 February 1979.
44 *Mardom*, 11 February 1979.
45 *Guardian*, 21 February 1979.
46 *New York Times*, 2 January 1979.
47 South Africa bought 60 per cent of its oil imports from Iran, and Israel 90 per cent.
48 *Foreign Broadcast Information Service*, 10 January 1979.
49 The other members of the Regency Council were: Abdullah Entezam, Muhammad Ali Varastah, Abdul Hussein Ali Abadi, Ali Qoli Ardalan, Muhammad Sajadi and Javad Sayyed. *New York Times*, 13 January 1979.
50 Khumayni, op. cit., pp. 246-7.
51 Ibid., pp. 247-8.
52 The Tehran-based members of the Islamic Revolutionary Council included Ayatollah Beheshti, Ayatollah Taleqani, Ayatollah Motahhari, Hojatalislam Ali Akbar Hashemi-Rafsanjani and Bazargan. Of those acting as aides to Khomeini in Paris, the following were appointed to the IRC: Abol Hassan Bani-Sadr, Qutbzadeh, and Ibrahim Yazdi.
53 *Wall Street Journal*, 10 December 1982.
54 Heikal, op. cit., p. 172.
55 Khomeini saw Tehrani later only to accept his resignation from the Regency Council.
56 *The Dawn of the Islamic Revolution, Vol. I*, p. 9.
57 See p. 315.
58 *The Dawn of the Islamic Revolution, Vol. I*, p. 11.
59 Named after homa, a mythical Iranian bird, a homafar stands midway between a sergeant and a warrant officer.
60 Heikal, op. cit., p. 177.
61 *New York Times*, 4 February 1979.
62 *Daily Telegraph*, 9 February 1981.
63 Interview with William Sullivan, the then US ambassador to Iran, broadcast on BBC Radio 4 on 23 January 1983.
64 *The Dawn of the Islamic Revolution, Vol. I*, p. 21.
65 Barry Rubin, *Paved with Good Intentions*, pp. 280-1.
66 *Events*, 23 February 1979, p. 11.
67 Gharabaghi made this statement after he had left Iran in early August 1980. *Guardian*, 7 August 1980.
68 *MERIP Reports*, March-April 1981, p. 13.
69 See p. 317.
70 The lower figure was given by *Newsweek*, 3 March 1980, p. 12, and the higher figure by Hojatalislam Hashemi-Rafsanjani in an interview with *Arabia: The Islamic World Review*, August 1982, p. 89.
71 Asked when exactly he expected the revolution to succeed, Ayatollah Pasandida, the elder brother of Khomeini, replied: 'I did not expect the revolution to succeed at all'. Interview in Qom, December 1979.
72 This would have meant amending the constitution to replace the regency of Princess Ashraf, a mere formality. See p. 69.
73 *The Middle East*, March 1979, p. 31; and *Iran Week*, 28 December 1979, p. 22.
74 *Financial Times*, 17 December 1977.
75 See p. 78.
76 *Events*, 30 June 1978, p. 26.
77 *Financial Times*, 29 July 1980.
78 Graham, op. cit., p. 146.

79 Cited in *Newsweek*, 3 March 1980, p. 12.
80 Abrahamian, op. cit., pp. 531-2.
81 Bazargan's interview with Oriana Fallaci, *Corriere Della Sera* (Evening Mail), 30 September 1979. Though Bazargan said that he gave in to Khomeini, he later returned to Paris to persuade Khomeini to accept the Regency Council. *Jumhouri-ye Islami* (The Islamic Republic), 5 April 1983.
82 Cited in *Sunday Times*, 13 April 1980.
83 Ibid.

Chapter 4 The founding of the Islamic Republic

1 Shahrough Akhavi, *Religion and Politics in Contemporary Iran*, p. 110.
2 *New York Times*, 14 and 18 February 1979.
3 *Guardian*, 24 February 1979.
4 Ibid.
5 Ibid., 7 March 1979.
6 Cited in Michael M.J. Fischer, *Iran*, pp. 218-19.
7 *New York Times*, 14 May 1979. Four-fifths of the first 200 persons sentenced to capital punishment belonged to the Shah's military-security apparatus. They included twenty-three military generals and thirty officers of the national police, mostly majors and captains.
8 Later General Jam was appointed defence minister by Bakhtiar, but refused to take up the job. *New York Times*, 9 January 1979.
9 *Guardian*, 2 March 1979.
10 Among those who witnessed this phenomenon at first hand was a Tehran businessman, who acted as the presiding officer at a polling station in a southern part of the city. Interview in Tehran in December 1979.
11 *The Islamic Republic Party: Plan, Basis and Ideology* (in Persian), Tehran, 1979, pp. 2, 4, 6, 12 and 13.
12 Interview in Tehran with Hamid Nazari, editor of *The Iranian*, in November 1979.
13 *The Middle East*, September 1979, pp. 49-50.
14 Ibid., p. 27.
15 *New York Times*, 26 April 1979; and *The Middle East*, August 1979, p. 16 and p. 42.
16 *Guardian*, 12 March 1979.
17 *New York Times*, 31 May 1979; and *The Middle East*, August 1979, p. 16.
18 *The Middle East*, August 1979, p. 16.
19 Head of military intelligence during the Shah's rule, Qarani was dismissed by the monarch for his alleged involvement in an anti-state plot. Fred Halliday, *Iran*, p. 68.
20 Michael Leeden and William Lewis, *Debacle*, p. 199.
21 Interview with Hamid Nazari, editor of *The Iranian*, November 1979.
22 Based on interviews with government officials in Tehran, May 1983.
23 Of the thirty-seven banks in pre-revolutionary Iran, the government owned nine wholly, and six partly. *The Middle East*, September 1979, p. 42.
24 *Islamic Government: Rule of the Faqih* (in Persian), Najaf, 1971, p. 48.
25 Khumayni, op. cit., p. 75.
26 'The Ideological Conditions for Khomeini's Doctrine of Government' in *Economy and Society*, May 1982, London and Boston, Mass., p. 149.
27 *Iran Times*, 25 May 1979; *New York Times*, 25 May 1979; and *Daily Telegraph*, 29 May 1979.

28 *Le Monde*, 12 and 13 November 1978.
29 *Iran Times*, 9 February 1979.
30 Ibid., 16 March 1979.
31 Fischer, op. cit., pp. 221-2.
32 See pp. 108-9.
33 The wording of the constitution is mainly from *Constitution of the Islamic Republic of Iran*, translated by Hamid Algar, Mizan Press, Berkeley, Calif., 1980, and *Constitution of the Islamic Republic of Iran*, published in the *Middle East Journal*, Washington, D.C., Spring 1980, pp. 184-204.
34 Parliament was later called the Islamic Consultative Assembly.
35 See p. 19.
36 See p. 109.
37 *New York Times*, 18 April 1979.
38 Ibid., 20 April 1979.
39 *The Iranian*, 19 September 1979, p. 4.
40 *New York Times*, 4 and 7 July 1979.
41 According to Sharia, he who commits an action is capable of explaining it. Therefore the accused is entitled to defend himself, but unaided by anybody else.
42 *The Middle East*, September 1979, p. 31.
43 *New York Times*, 10 July 1979.
44 Mohamed Heikal, *The Return of the Ayatollah*, p. 71.
45 Of the 172 Fedai guerrillas killed during the period of 1971-6, three-quarters were university students or teachers, and other professionals. Ervand Abrahamian, *Iran Between Two Revolutions*, p. 481.
46 *MERIP Reports*, March-April 1980, p. 18; and Robert Graham *Iran*, p. 237.
47 Later the Ayandegan publishing company was declared 'illegally acquired assets' and taken over by the Mustazafin Foundation. *The Iranian*, 17 October 1979, p. 6.
48 *Guardian*, 17 August 1979.
49 Interview with Ahmed Jaffrey in Tehran, December 1979.
50 *The Iranian*, 4 July 1979, p. 15.
51 'We won't purge the colonels,' said Bazargan. *Guardian*, 5 March 1979.
52 *The Iranian*, 17 October 1979, p. 5.
53 *New York Times*, 14 March 1979.
54 See p. 318.
55 Khomeini had set up similar networks in other ministries and government institutions. For instance, when the Bazargan administration authorised payment for American military spare parts, the managers of the Central Bank refused to issue cheques. Interviews in Tehran, December 1979; and Leeden and Lewis, op. cit., p. 224.
56 *The Iranian*, 18 July 1979, p. 3 and p. 15.
57 Leeden and Lewis, op. cit., p. 224.
58 *The Dawn of the Islamic Revolution, Vol. I*, p. 348.

Chapter 5 The American hostage crisis

1 Mohamed Heikal, *The Return of the Ayatollah*, pp. 16-19.
2 Michael Leeden and William Lewis, *Debacle*, p. 223.
3 *Foreign Broadcast Information Service*, 11 November 1979.
4 Michael M.J. Fischer, *Iran*, p. 233.

5 *The Dawn of the Islamic Revolution, Vol. I*, p. 378.
6 *New York Times*, 2 January 1980.
7 Interview in Qom on 12 December 1979.
8 *New York Times*, 10 December 1979.
9 Interviews by the author in Tabriz in late December 1979.
10 *Sunday Times*, 16 December 1979.
11 Fischer, op. cit., p. 238.
12 *The Iranian*, 19 January 1980, p. 3.
13 Ibid., p. 3 and p. 15.
14 With the banning of foreign journalists from Tabriz on 13 January, independent sources of news dried up.
15 Suroosh Irfani, *Revolutionary Islam in Iran*, Zed Press, London, 1983, p. 199.
16 Cited in Ervand Abrahamian, *Iran Between Two Revolutions*, p. 491.
17 Cited in ibid., p. 493.
18 Interview with Masoud Rajavi, *MERIP Reports*, March-April 1982, p. 9.
19 Ibid., p. 8 and p. 10.
20 Robert Graham, *Iran*, p. 264.
21 *Observer*, 25 February 1980.
22 *The Iranian*, 24 November 1979, p. 6.
23 *New Statesman*, 8 February 1980, p. 202; and *The Iranian*, 16 February 1980, p. 6.
24 *The Iranian*, 26 July 1979, p. 6.
25 Ibid., 19 September 1979, p. 4. Also see p. 82.
26 Interviews in Tehran in December 1979; and Sepehr Zabih, *Iran Since the Revolution*, Croom Helm, London, 1982, p. 86.
27 *Kayhan*, 18 April 1980.
28 *Guardian*, 1 May 1980.
29 Ibid., 9 June 1980.
30 *Daily Telegraph*, 21 April 1980.
31 *Guardian*, 5 March 1979.
32 *Al Safir* (The Blast of a Trumpet).
33 *Daily Telegraph*, 11 February 1980.
34 BBC Radio 4 documentary on Iran, 23 January 1983. Between 1953 and 1978, over 15,000 officers underwent long-term training, ranging from two to three years, in the US. Heikal, op. cit., p. 68.
35 *The Times*, 28 April 1980.
36 *Daily Telegraph*, 17 June 1980.
37 *8 Days*, 7 March 1981, p. 14.
38 *New York Times*, 12 July 1980.
39 *Guardian*, 22 July 1980.
40 *Daily Telegraph*, 15 July 1980. Altogether 12,000 military personnel had been purged during the past seven months.
41 *Daily Telegraph*, 12 May 1980.
42 *Guardian*, 19 July 1980.
43 *The Dawn of the Islamic Revolution, Vol. I*, pp. 180-1.
44 *Guardian*, 23 April 1980.
45 *Daily Telegraph*, 27 April 1980.
46 *New Statesman*, 13 June 1980, p. 884.
47 *Guardian*, 30 June 1980.
48 Ibid., 23 July 1980.
49 Twenty-four deputies voted against, and nineteen abstained. *Daily Telegraph*, 11 August 1980.

50 Zabih, op. cit., p. 73.
51 *Guardian*, 15 August 1980.
52 *MERIP Reports*, July-August 1981, p. 7, and March-April 1982, p. 16.
53 *New York Times*, 12 September 1980.

Chapter 6 The Gulf War

 1 Tareq Y. Ismael, *Iraq and Iran: Roots of Conflict*, Syracuse University Press, Syracuse, N.Y., 1982, p. 61.
 2 Leaving aside Kurds, who formed 15 per cent of the national population of thirteen million in the late 1970s, Arabs in Iraq were divided thus: Shia, 55 per cent; Sunni, 25 per cent; and Christian, 5 per cent.
 3 *The Middle East*, March 1977, p. 44; and *Guardian*, 6 April 1977.
 4 *Guardian*, 28 February 1979.
 5 *Observer*, 24 June 1979; and *Guardian*, 6 July 1979.
 6 *New York Times*, 8 August 1979.
 7 *Al Safir*, 15 April 1980.
 8 Since then Iran has been observing a week of mourning to commemorate Ayatollah Sadr's execution.
 9 *MERIP Reports*, July-August 1981, pp. 3-4.
10 The military high command had taken seriously the assessment put forward by Qutbzadeh, the foreign minister, that the USSR was planning to move into Iran.
11 *New York Times*, 3 October 1980.
12 Ibid., 29 September 1980.
13 Ibid., 2 October 1980.
14 *Le Monde*, 8 October 1980.
15 *Guardian*, 9 October 1980.
16 *Daily Telegraph*, 15 October 1980.
17 *Guardian*, 20 October 1980.
18 *New York Times*, 22 October 1980.
19 Ibid., 13 September and 2 November 1980. See p. 321.
20 *New York Times*, 29 October 1980.
21 *Guardian*, 10 November 1980.
22 *Sunday Times*, 9 November 1980.
23 *8 Days*, 6 December 1980, p. 17; and *The Middle East*, February 1981, p. 20.
24 *Daily Telegraph*, 6 and 10 December 1980; *Sunday Times*, 7 December 1980; and *Guardiun*, 8 December 1980.
25 *New York Times*, 18 December 1980.
26 *Guardian*, 5 January 1981.
27 Ibid., 16 January 1981.
28 Ibid., 22 January 1981.
29 *New York Times*, 2 February 1981.
30 *Guardian*, 3 February 1981.
31 *Daily Telegraph*, 12 February 1981.
32 Ibid., 17 February 1981.
33 *New York Times*, 2 March 1981.
34 Ibid., 8 March 1981.
35 At their peak in late 1980, the Iraqis had occupied 24,000 sq. kms of Iranian territory.
36 *Guardian*, 7 February 1981.

37 *New York Times*, 19 February 1981.
38 *MERIP Reports*, March-April 1982, pp. 16-17.
39 *The Times*, 6 March 1981; *Daily Telegraph*, 7 March 1981; *Guardian*, 9 March 1981; and *MERIP Reports*, March-April 1982, p. 16 and p. 29.
40 *New York Times*, 9 March 1981; and *Guardian*, 10 and 11 March 1981.
41 *New York Times*, 17 March 1981; and *Guardian*, 18 and 20 March 1981.
42 *New York Times*, 2 April 1981.
43 *MERIP Reports*, March-April 1982, p. 16 and p. 29.
44 *Guardian*, 8 April 1981.
45 Ibid., 13 April 1981.
46 *Daily Telegraph*, 20 April 1981.
47 *New York Times*, 5 April 1981; and *Foreign Broadcast Information Service*, 21 May 1981.
48 The military budget for 1981-2 was thus lower than the $8,000 million defence budget for 1975-6. *The Middle East*, March 1979, p. 32; and *Guardian*, 4 April 1981.
49 *Inqilab-e Islami*, 17 May 1981.
50 *Daily Telegraph*, 23 April 1981.
51 Sepehr Zabih, *Iran Since the Revolution*, p. 131.
52 See pp. 62 and 175-6.
53 Based on an account of the episode by Scott Armstrong, a Washington-based journalist, published in *Current*, a Bombay weekly. 13 February 1982, p. 20.
54 Zabih, op. cit., p. 131.
55 *The Times*, 1 June 1981.
56 *Washington Post*, 3 June 1981.
57 *The Times*, 9 June 1981.
58 Ibid., 13 June 1981.
59 Ibid., 16 June 1981.
60 *Sunday Times*, 21 June 1981; *8 Days*, 4 July 1981, p. 13; and *The Middle East*, September 1981, p. 18.
61 Cited in *The Middle East*, February 1981, p. 20.

Chapter 7 The Mujahedin challenge

1 *The Middle East*, July 1981, p. 37.
2 *Sunday Times*, 28 June 1981.
3 *MERIP Reports*, July-August 1981, p. 7.
4 *The Middle East*, July 1981, p. 37.
5 *New York Times*, 1 July 1981.
6 *Sunday Times*, 5 July 1981; and *The Dawn of the Islamic Revolution, Vol. I*, p. 164.
7 *8 Days*, 17 July 1981, p. 8. In late December the government announced the execution of three persons found guilty of causing the 28 June bomb explosion. *New York Times*, 29 December 1981.
8 *Guardian*, 21 July 1981.
9 *Sunday Times*, 14 June 1981; and *The Middle East*, September 1981, p. 20.
10 *The Times*, 30 June 1981.
11 *Guardian*, 10 July 1981.
12 *The Times*, 23 and 27 July 1981.
13 *Sunday Times*, 9 August 1981.
14 *The Times*, 5 and 6 August 1981.

15 *Foreign Broadcast Information Service*, 13 August 1981.
16 Ibid., 14 August 1981.
17 Sepehr Zabih, *Iran Since the Revolution*, pp. 148-9.
18 *The Times*, 19 August 1981.
19 *Sunday Times*, 23 and 30 August 1981.
20 *New York Times*, 1 September 1981.
21 *Jumhouri-ye Islami*, 6 September 1981; and Tehran Radio, 13 September 1981.
22 *The Times*, 1 September 1981; and *The Dawn of the Islamic Revolution, Vol. I*, p. 247.
23 *Washington Post*, 2 September 1981.
24 *Sunday Times*, 6 September 1981.
25 *The Middle East*, September 1981, p. 20.
26 *The Times*, 10 and 21 September 1981.
27 Colleges and universities were closed.
28 *New York Times*, 24 September 1981.
29 *Foreign Broadcast Information Service*, 27 September 1981.
30 *New York Times*, 30 September 1981.
31 *MERIP Reports*, March-April 1982, p. 4.
32 *Foreign Broadcast Information Service*, 5 October 1981.
33 *New York Times*, 27 October 1981.
34 Ibid., 24 October 1981.
35 *Sunday Times*, 1 November 1981.
36 Ibid., 26 September 1981.
37 See p. 186.
38 Sepehr Zabih, *The Communist Movement in Iran*, University of California Press, Los Angeles, Calif., 1966, p. 62.
39 Ibid., p. 114 and p. 153.
40 See p. 31.
41 Ervand Abrahamian, *Iran Between Two Revolutions*, p. 338 and p. 451.
42 Ibid., p. 454. This radio station operated from Bulgaria from 1959 to 1976. Fred Halliday, *Iran*, p. 229.
43 Mohamed Heikal, *The Return of the Ayatollah*, p. 156.
44 *MERIP Reports*, March-April 1980, p. 21.
45 *Le Matin* (The Morning), 27 November 1979.
46 *Time*, 30 August 1980, p. 15.
47 See p. 168.
48 *MERIP Reports*, July-August 1981, p. 3.
49 *Sunday Times*, 9 November 1980.
50 National Voice of Iran Radio, 15 March 1981.
51 Ibid., 24 March 1981.
52 Yet an official licence was not issued to the Tudeh Party by the prosecutor general's office then or later.
53 *Sunday Times*, 5 July 1981.
54 *The Times*, 29 July 1981.
55 *Sunday Times*, 3 January 1982.
56 *Middle East Economic Survey*, February 1983, p. 10.
57 *Financial Times*, 10 November 1981, and 28 January 1983.
58 *The Military Balance, 1981-82*, International Institute for Strategic Studies, London, 1982, p. 43 and p. 50.
59 *The Middle East*, March 1982, p. 26.
60 *MERIP Reports*, March-April 1982, p. 4.
61 *Arabia*, August 1982, p. 19.

62 *Washington Post*, 30 March 1982.
63 *New York Times*, 8 April 1982.
64 *Guardian*, 10 and 13 April 1982.
65 Ibid., 17 May 1982.
66 *Christian Science Monitor*, 25 May 1982.
67 *Guardian*, 2 June 1982.
68 Ibid., 7 March 1983.
69 *Financial Times*, 16 August 1982; and Islamic Republic News Agency, 16 February 1984.
70 *Daily Telegraph*, 11 September 1982.
71 *Tehran Times*, 2 November 1982.
72 *New York Times*, 19 August 1982.
73 *Washington Post*, 23 November 1982.
74 *Wall Street Journal*, 11 November 1982.
75 *Christian Science Monitor*, 13 October 1982.
76 Islamic Republic News Agency, 8 August 1983.
77 *BBC Summary of World Broadcasts*, 16 March and 14 July 1983.
78 Interview with a Third World diplomat in Tehran, May 1983.
79 *Arabia: The Islamic World Review*, April 1982, p. 42.
80 *BBC Summary of World Broadcasts*, 10 November 1982.
81 *Christian Science Monitor*, 13 October 1982.
82 *Wall Street Journal*, 9 November 1982.
83 *New York Times*, 19 April 1982; and *MERIP Reports*, March-April 1983, p. 5.
84 *Guardian*, 11 and 12 April 1982; and National Voice of Iran Radio, 28 March 1983.
85 *New York Times*, 19 April 1982.
86 BBC World Service Radio, 20 April 1982.
87 *Guardian*, 30 April 1982.
88 Ibid., 5 May 1982. Shariatmadari died of cancer in early April 1986.
89 Ibid., 5 and 8 May 1982; and *Foreign Broadcast Information Service*, 6 May 1982.
90 *New York Times*, 3 October 1982.
91 *New Statesman*, 19 November 1982, p. 20.
92 *Christian Science Monitor*, 8 October 1982. This figure was less than half of the one mentioned by the Mujahedin headquarters in early 1982. See p. 209.

Chapter 8 Consolidation of the revolution

1 *Guardian*, 17 August 1982.
2 *Economist*, 15 January 1983, p. 34.
3 Tehran Radio, 15 December 1982. Explaining the decree a week later, Khomeini said: 'To spy and search is contrary to Islam. . . . We should not engage in oppression. We should not investigate what is going on in people's homes.' *Foreign Broadcast Information Service*, 23 December 1982. Copies of Khomeini's eight-point decree were displayed at all government offices and police stations.
4 *BBC Summary of World Broadcasts*, 30 December 1982.
5 *Sunday Times*, 9 January 1983.
6 Interviews in Tehran bazaar, April 1983.
7 Islamic Republic News Agency, 30 January 1983.
8 Tehran Radio, 5 January 1983.

9 Islamic Republic News Agency, 16 August 1983.
10 *Jumhouri-ye Islami*, 16 April 1982.
11 See pp. 207-8.
12 *Strategic Survey, 1982-83*, International Institute of Strategic Studies, London, 1984, p. 84.
13 *Daily Telegraph*, 6 January 1983.
14 *Tehran Times*, 3 May 1983.
15 Interviews in Tehran, May 1983.
16 Significantly, the government chose 30 April, the eve of May Day, which is celebrated officially, to show Kianouri's confessions. These were transmitted immediately after a documentary on Iranian workers, laudatory in tone to labour, and sprinkled with such sayings of Khomeini as 'Workers' Day is People's Day', and 'Peasants and workers are the foundation of the country's independence'.
17 *Guardian*, 5 October 1983.
18 *Sunday Times*, 26 February 1984; and National Voice of Iran Radio, 27 February 1984.
19 *BBC Summary of World Broadcasts*, 28 January 1984.
20 *Washington Post*, 2 February 1983; and *Guardian*, 10 February 1983.
21 *The Middle East*, April 1983, p. 4.
22 *New Statesman*, 23 September 1983, p. 19. In 1980 and 1981 the Gulf states, chiefly Saudi Arabia and Kuwait, gave Iraq $18 to $20 billion in grants and loans. In the following two years the Gulf aid to Baghdad amounted to about half of the previous total. It was offered in cash and oil, with Saudi Arabia and Kuwait supplying some of Iraq's customers with their own oil.
23 *International Herald Tribune*, 30 September 1983.
24 Tehran Radio, 19 September 1983.
25 Ibid., 14 October 1983.
26 The corresponding figure for the US was 5 per cent. *Economist*, 29 October 1983, p. 9; *Sunday Times*, 20 May 1984; and BBC World Service Radio, 21 May 1984.
27 *Guardian*, 11 November 1983.
28 Ibid., 14 October 1983; and *Sunday Times*, 16 October 1983.
29 *BBC Summary of World Broadcasts*, 1 and 12 November 1983.
30 A visit by the author to Dezful after an Iraqi missile attack in April 1983 showed a quarter of the city's male population joining the funeral procession of the victims.
31 *Financial Times*, 7 February 1984.
32 *Guardian*, 18 February 1984.
33 *Sunday Times*, 11 March 1984.
34 Ibid., 18 March 1984.
35 *BBC Summary of World Broadcasts*, 11 June 1983.
36 *Wall Street Journal*, 9 December 1983; and *Sunday Times*, 29 April 1984.
37 *Tehran Times*, 21 April 1983.
38 *Guardian*, 16 February 1984.
39 Tehran Radio, 1 March 1983; and Islamic Republic News Agency, 28 September 1983.
40 Tehran Radio, 11 December 1982.
41 *Guardian*, 10 February 1983.
42 *Kayhan International*, 24 September 1983.
43 A pair of imported jeans cost $100 whereas a locally made pair cost only $20.

44 *BBC Summary of World Broadcasts*, 5 April 1983.
45 Petrol rationing, introduced in the wake of the war, was lifted on 3 January 1983.
46 *Kayhan International*, 28 November 1983.
47 Interview with an official of the Martyr's Foundation in Tehran, May 1983.
48 *Tehran Times*, 1 May 1983.
49 *BBC Summary of World Broadcasts*, 9 May 1983.
50 *Jumhouri-ye Islami*, 17 October 1979.
51 See p. 109.
52 See p. 158.
53 Cited in the *Guardian*, 16 July 1981.
54 Interviews in Tehran, April 1983.
55 See p. 39.
56 Interviews in Tehran, April-May 1983.
57 *Foreign Broadcast Information Service*, 12 May 1982. See p. 207.
58 Interviews in Tehran, April 1983.
59 Tehran Radio, 28 January 1983.
60 *Iran Press Digest*, 13 March 1983, p. 1.
61 *Ittilaat*, 26 March 1983.
62 *Iran Press Digest*, 27 March 1983, p. 3.
63 Ibid., pp. 3-4. See p. 123.
64 Tehran Radio, 10 July 1983.
65 Ibid.
66 *Guardian*, 30 July 1983. Two weeks later thirteen bazaar merchants had been convicted of hoarding and fined a total of $540,000. *Middle East Economic Digest*, 15 July 1983, p. 8.
67 Tehran Radio, 2 January 1984.
68 See p. 216.
69 Interview in Tehran, May 1983. Some of this land belonged to the state in its own right while the rest was the 'illegally acquired property' of individuals and companies confiscated by the government after the revolution.
70 *New York Times*, 12 January 1983.
71 See p. 228.
72 *Kayhan*, 13 March 1983.
73 Islamic Republic News Agency, 2 November 1983.
74 *Sunday Times*, 11 April 1982.
75 Sepehr Zabih, *Iran Since the Revolution*, p. 99.
76 *Toronto Star*, 12 March 1984.
77 See pp. 107, 132.
78 Interview with a Mustazafin Foundation official in Tehran, April 1983; and Islamic Republic News Agency, 24 July 1983. If the claims of unjust confiscation by some former owners of property are upheld by the Headquarters for the Implementation of the Imam's Decree, the Foundation will have to give up these properties.
79 Interview in Tehran, April 1983.
80 A village was defined as a place with less than 5,000 people. Of the 65,000 villages, only 18,000 had more than 250 inhabitants. *Iran Almanac, 1977*, Echo of Iran, Tehran, p. 415.
81 *MERIP Reports*, March-April 1983, p. 12.
82 Interview with a Reconstruction Crusade official in Reyshahr, April 1983.
83 *MERIP Reports*, March-April 1983, p. 12.

84 *Kayhan International*, 10 November 1983.
85 Ibid., 11 November 1983.
86 Ibid., 4 March 1984.
87 Interview with a University Crusade official in Tehran, April 1983.
88 Ibid.
89 *Times Higher Education Supplement*, 8 July 1983; and *Sunday Times*, 23 October 1983.
90 *The Middle East*, February 1982, p. 30.
91 *Daily Telegraph*, 21 May 1980.
92 Ibid., 11 June and 19 July 1980.
93 Tehran Radio, 2 May 1984.
94 See p. 132.
95 *MERIP Reports*, February 1982, p. 23.
96 Arthur J. Arberry, *The Koran Interpreted*, Oxford University Press, Oxford and New York, 1964, Chapter XXIV, 'Light', verse 31, pp. 355-6.
97 *Daily Telegraph*, 5 July 1980.
98 *BBC Summary of World Broadcasts*, 17 January 1984.
99 Islamic Republic News Agency, 15 May 1984.
100 Interviews in Tehran, April-May 1983.
101 Ervand Abrahamian, *Iran Between Two Revolutions*, p. 433; and *Sunday Times*, 4 April 1982.
102 Tehran Radio, 29 September 1983; and Robert Graham, *Iran*, p. 206. Making a pilgrimage to Mecca is one of the five edicts enjoined upon a true Muslim, the others being reciting the central precept 'There is no god but Allah, Muhammad is the messenger of Allah', praying five times a day, abstaining from food and sex between sunrise and sunset during Ramadan, and giving anonymously one-fortieth of his annual income as charity.
103 Based on a visit to the Jamran headquarters on 18 April 1983.
104 Interview on 16 April 1983.
105 *Washington Post*, 29 April 1982.
106 Tehran Radio, 30 January 1984. The issuing of such warnings in public showed that revolutionary guards were not always following Khomeini's eight-point decree on civil liberties.
107 *The Middle East*, August 1983, p. 25.
108 *Kayhan International*, 20 October 1983.
109 *Guardian*, 5 August 1983.
110 *Kayhan International*, 19 November 1983.
111 *Sunday Times*, 24 January 1982.
112 *Middle East Economic Digest*, 8 July 1982, p. 17.
113 *BBC Summary of World Broadcasts*, 21 July 1983.

Chapter 9 Iran and the Soviet bloc

1 See p. 16.
2 See pp. 18-21.
3 J.C. Hurewitz, *Diplomacy in the Near and Middle East: A Documentary Record, Vol. II*, Van Nostrand, Wokingham, 1956, pp. 90-4. The treaty was signed by Persia and the Russian Soviet Federated Socialist Republic. The reference to Federal Russia's allies pertained to other Soviet Republics. The Union of Soviet Socialist Republics was not formed until late 1922.
4 Peter Avery, *Modern Iran*, Ernst Benn, London, 1967, p. 249.

5 The trade agreement was renewed in 1931, 1935 and 1939.
6 Hurewitz, op. cit., pp. 154-6.
7 The Soviets argued that once the Shah had signed the agreement on 8 April 1946, the oil concession to them became operational. All that was needed was the formation of a joint Soviet-Iranian company.
8 L.P. Elwell-Sutton, *Persian Oil: A Study in Power Politics*, p. 119.
9 Mohammed Reza Shah Pahlavi, *Mission for my Country*, Hutchinson, London, 1960 and McGraw-Hill, New York, 1961, p. 129.
10 *New York Times*, 17 July 1961.
11 *Pravda*, 17 September 1962.
12 Shahram Chubin and Sepehr Zabih, *The Foreign Relations of Iran*, p. 79.
13 *Kayhan International*, 3 March 1970.
14 *New York Times*, 30 November 1971.
15 *Kayhan*, 29 October 1972.
16 Barry Rubin, *Paved with Good Intentions*, p. 168; and Robert Graham, *Iran*, p. 174. One of the two existing stations was at Kabkan.
17 Graham, op. cit., p. 189.
18 Ibid., p. 215; and Fred Halliday, *Iran*, p. 229.
19 *The Middle East*, January 1978, p. 51.
20 Interview in Julfa, December 1979.
21 *The Middle East*, January 1978, p. 50.
22 *Newsweek*, 1 March 1976, p. 25.
23 The other country was Pakistan.
24 *Pravda*, 4 March 1979.
25 *Foreign Broadcast Information Service*, 25 April 1979.
26 *Events*, 6 October 1978, p. 21.
27 *Kayhan International*, 29 December 1979.
28 *New York Times*, 12 February 1980.
29 *Daily Telegraph*, 22 March 1980.
30 *Sunday Times*, 13 April 1980.
31 *Daily Telegraph*, 2 November 1981.
32 Interviews in Julfa, December 1979.
33 *8 Days*, 27 September 1980, p. 60.
34 *Foreign Broadcast Information Service*, 15 August 1980; and *Guardian*, 15 August 1980.
35 See p. 204.
36 Tehran Radio, 23 September 1980.
37 Tass, 28 September 1980.
38 *New York Times*, 1 October 1980.
39 *The Times*, 6 October 1980.
40 *Pravda*, 11 October 1980.
41 *The Middle East*, December 1980, p. 12.
42 *New York Times*, 4 February 1981.
43 *Washington Post*, 19 April 1981.
44 *Report of the Central Committee of the CPSU to the XXVI Congress of the Communist Party of the Soviet Union, 23 February 1981*, Novosti Press Agency Publishing House, Moscow, 1981, p. 23.
45 *8 Days*, 23 May 1981, p. 5.
46 *BBC Summary of World Broadcasts*, 12 April 1983.
47 *Middle East Economic Survey*, 15 February 1982.
48 *International Affairs*, Autumn 1981, p. 613.
49 *Tehran Times*, 20 April 1983.
50 *8 Days*, 3 May 1980, p. 5.

51 *BBC Summary of World Broadcasts*, 2 September 1983.
52 Dilip Hiro, *Inside the Middle East*, p. 281.
53 See pp. 214-15.
54 *BBC Summary of World Broadcasts*, 3 January 1983.
55 Ibid., 14 May 1983.
56 *Sunday Times*, 5 June 1983.
57 *8 Days*, 16 February 1980, p. 6.
58 Tehran Radio, 8 December 1983.
59 *MERIP Reports*, January 1983, p. 22.
60 *BBC Summary of World Broadcasts*, 21 January 1984.
61 *Krasnaya Zvezda*, 7 December 1983. Four months later the Soviet Union put an official stamp on this when a joint statement by Premier Nikolai Tikhonov and Iraq's vice-premier, Taha Yassin Ramadan, blamed Iran for not ending the hostilities. *Guardian*, 26 April 1984.
62 *Guardian*, 28 November 1983.
63 Ibid., 20 March 1984.
64 Tehran Radio, 17 January 1984.

Chapter 10 Iran and the West

1 See p. 16.
2 George N. Curzon, *Persia and the Persian Question, Vol. I*, Longman, London, 1892, p. 480.
3 See p. 22.
4 *Documents on British Foreign Policy, 1919-39, Vol. XIII*, London, p. 731.
5 Nikki R. Keddie, *Roots of Revolution*, p. 109.
6 T.H.V. Motter, *The Persian Corridor and Aid to Russia*, p. 462.
7 *MERIP Reports*, May 1975, p. 14.
8 Rouhollah K. Ramazani, *Iran's Foreign Policy, 1941-1973: A Study of Foreign Policy in Modernising Nations*, University Press of Virginia, Charlottesville, Va., 1975, p. 206.
9 See p. 34.
10 See p. 35.
11 Barry Rubin, *Paved with Good Intentions*, p. 61.
12 See p. 35.
13 Anthony Eden, *The Memoirs of Sir Anthony Eden: Full Circle*, Cassell, London, 1960, p. 214.
14 The AIOC was awarded compensation of $510 million, paid mostly by the US oil companies.
15 Marvin Zonis, *The Political Elite of Iran*, pp. 108-9; and *Arms Trade with the Third World*, Stockholm International Peace Research Institute, Stockholm, 1971, p. 146.
16 Dilip Hiro, *Inside the Middle East*, p. 412, note 26.
17 Cited in Mohamed Heikal, *The Return of the Ayatollah*, p. 67.
18 Michael Leeden and William Lewis, *Debacle*, p. 39.
19 *Arms Trade with the Third World*, Stockholm International Peace Research Institute, Stockholm 1971, p. 146; and Ali-Reza Nobari (ed.), *Iran Erupts*, p. 70.
20 Cited in Nobari (ed.), op. cit., pp. 104-6.
21 See p. 49.
22 Robert Pranger and Dale Tahtinen, *United States Policy in the Persian Gulf*, American Enterprise Institute, Washington, D.C., 1979, p. 7.

23 Rubin, op. cit., p. 139.
24 Ibid., p. 153.
25 *New York Magazine*, 18 September 1978, p. 45.
26 Leeden and Lewis, op. cit., p. 55.
27 The political scandal was named after the apartment block in Washington D.C., where the offices of the Democratic Party were broken into by the agents of President Nixon's (Republican Party) campaign managers in the summer of 1972.
28 Heikal, op. cit., p. 16.
29 *Observer*, 22 November 1975.
30 Rubin, op. cit., p. 154.
31 *Department of State Bulletin*, 6 September 1976, p. 303.
32 Hossein Amirsadeghi (ed.),*Twentieth Century Iran*, p. 212; and Rubin, op. cit., p. 155.
33 Robert Graham, *Iran*, p. 91.
34 *Washington Post*, 9 December 1976.
35 *New York Times*, 4 February 1976.
36 Cited in Rubin, op. cit., pp. 173-4.
37 *Washington Post*, 9 February 1976.
38 Fred Halliday, *Iran*, p. 256.
39 Keddie, op. cit., p. 176.
40 *Guardian*, 5 March 1979; and *Sunday Times*, 29 May 1983.
41 *Events*, 15 December 1978, p. 13.
42 Rubin, op. cit., p. 180.
43 *New York Times*, 7 October 1976.
44 See p. 66.
45 *Washington Post*, 18 November 1977. In contrast, the annual dollar limit imposed by Carter on new US arms exports was $8.6 billion.
46 Rubin, op. cit., p. 201.
47 *New York Times*, 2 January 1978.
48 Leeden and Lewis, op. cit., p. 126.
49 Ibid., p. 150.
50 *Foreign Policy*, Fall 1980, p. 178. However, as the Shah's subsequent actions showed, he did his utmost to retain the throne, including plotting royalist military coups. See pp. 87, 90 and 94.
51 *Washington Post*, 8 December 1978.
52 Ibid., 19 January 1979; and Heikal, op. cit., pp. 170-1.
53 *New York Times*, 2 January 1979.
54 See p. 87.
55 Rubin, op. cit., p. 246.
56 *Monday Morning*, 8-14 January 1979.
57 Cited in Rubin, op. cit., p. 249.
58 See p. 92.
59 *Foreign Policy*, Fall 1980, p. 186.
60 David H. Albert, *Tell the American People*, p. 8.
61 Tehran Radio, 19 May 1979.
62 *New York Times*, 13 February 1979.
63 *Guardian*, 2 March 1979.
64 *Washington Post*, 18 May 1979; and *Foreign Broadcast Information Service*, 18 May 1979.
65 Zbigniew Brzezinski, *Power and Principle: Memoirs of the National Security Adviser, 1977-1981*, Weidenfeld and Nicolson, London, 1983, pp. 488-9.

66 See p. 284.
67 Brzezinski, op. cit., p. 496.
68 *Guardian*, 30 April 1980.
69 See p. 155.
70 *Washington Post*, 25 April 1980; *Daily Telegraph*, 26 April and 2 May 1980; *Guardian*, 2 May 1980; and *The Middle East*, December 1980, p. 30.
71 *Daily Telegraph*, 3 June 1980.
72 *Washington Post*, 25 January 1981.
73 *Daily Telegraph*, 29 January 1981.
74 *Tabas, A Confrontation of the Chapter of the Elephant: An Examination of the Adventure at Tabas* (in Persian), Muslim Students Following the Imam's Line, Tehran, 1982, pp. 54-5.
75 *Guardian*, 31 July 1980.
76 *Daily Telegraph*, 15 September 1980.
77 See p. 168. Iraq had no diplomatic ties with the US, having severed them during the Arab-Israeli war of June 1967.
78 *New York Times*, 19, 21 and 24 October 1980.
79 *Time*, 25 July 1983, p. 19.
80 *Middle East Economic Survey*, 19 February 1983, p. 11.
81 *Kayhan International*, 9 October 1983.
82 *Daily Telegraph*, 23 January 1981.
83 *Kayhan International*, 9 October 1983.
84 *Wall Street Journal*, 4 November 1982.
85 The oil reserves of other Gulf states were: Saudi Arabia, 168 billion barrels; Kuwait, sixty-eight billion barrels; Iraq, thirty-five billion barrels; the UAE, thirty-two billion barrels; Oman, 2.4 billion barrels; and Bahrain, twenty-four million barrels. *Kayhan International*, 6 November 1983. Iran has the world's second largest reserves of natural gas, after the Soviet Union.
86 The authors discussed two possibilities of American involvement in the region: the US seizing selected oilfields if embargoes or unbearable price rises created chaos in the US or elsewhere in the industrial world; or the US assisting a government in the Gulf which faced the risk of losing oil resources as a result of internal turmoil or attacks by a hostile power. The report was published in April 1979. Hiro, op. cit., p. 346.
87 *Daily Telegraph*, 19 January 1983.
88 *BBC Summary of World Broadcasts*, 20 August 1983.
89 *Times of India*, 31 March 1983.
90 *Guardian*, 22 July 1983.
91 *Financial Times*, 12 May 1984. These planes, leased to Saudi Arabia, were manned by American military personnel.
92 *Time*, 25 July 1983, p. 20.
93 *Guardian*, 27 April 1982.
94 *Time*, 25 July 1983, p. 20.
95 *Kayhan International*, 1 October 1983. Earlier the US had authorised the sale of six 'small' jets to Iraq for $25 million. *Washington Post*, 14 September 1982.
96 *Newsweek*, 10 October 1983, p. 33.
97 *Newsday*, 22 May 1984.
98 *Guardian*, 20 December 1984.
99 *Washington Post*, 4 January 1984.
100 *Guardian*, 25 May 1984.
101 See p. 286.
102 *Guardian*, 19 May 1984.
103 Ibid., 22 May 1984.

Chapter 11 Iran and the region

1 *New York Times*, 17 November 1968.
2 *The Middle East*, September 1979, p. 18.
3 Kuwaiti nationals are a minority in the total population of 1.3 million. *Guardian*, 5 December 1983.
4 *Sunday Times*, 30 December 1979.
5 *Guardian*, 10 January 1980.
6 Estimates of Shias in the kingdom varied from 7 per cent to 15 per cent of the population of four million. Mohamed Heikal, *The Return of the Ayatollah*, p. 203. The above population figure excluded the over two million expatriates living in Saudi Arabia.
7 *International Herald Tribune*, 4 December 1979.
8 *The Times*, 28 April 1980.
9 *Daily Telegraph*, 4 February 1981.
10 Of the 1.9 million hajj pilgrims in 1978, 1.5 million were foreigners: of the latter, 669,000 were resident in Saudi Arabia. *Arab Dawn*, January-February 1979, p. 9.
11 *Iranvoice*, 30 July 1979.
12 A.H.H. Abidi, 'Iran and Non-Alignment', in K.P. Misra (ed.), *Non-Alignment: Frontiers and Dynamics*, Vikas, New Delhi, 1982, p. 349, note 28.
13 *The Times*, 21 December 1981.
14 *The Middle East*, February 1982, p. 14.
15 *Foreign Broadcast Information Service*, 28 January 1982.
16 *Daily Telegraph*, 19 January 1983. Also see p. 325.
17 *Guardian*, 31 May 1982.
18 See p. 211.
19 *Guardian* 14 September 1982.
20 *International Herald Tribune*, 4 October 1982.
21 *New York Times*, 12 November 1982.
22 *Financial Times*, 28 January 1983.
23 Tehran Radio, 20 February 1983.
24 *BBC Summary of World Broadcasts*, 24 June 1983.
25 Riyadh Radio, 24 July 1983.
26 *Sunday Times*, 18 September 1983.
27 *BBC Summary of World Broadcasts*, 27 October 1983.
28 *Guardian*, 5 December 1983.
29 Six of the accused were executed, seven given life sentences, and the rest freed. BBC World Service Radio, 28 March 1984.
30 *Guardian*, 18 and 26 May 1984.
31 *Sunday Times*, 1 November 1981.
32 *Middle East International*, 23 April 1982, p. 3.
33 *BBC Summary of World Broadcasts*, 25 January 1983.
34 Ibid., 12 April 1983.
35 Maronites are followers of Saint Maron, a fourth-century Christian hermit, who lived in north-eastern Syria. They are affliated to the Holy See.
36 Dilip Hiro, *Inside the Middle East*, p. 390, note 29.
37 *Kayhan International*, 28 November 1983.
38 *Guardian*, 7 January 1984.
39 *Sunday Times*, 15 January 1984.

40 It was significant that Nabih Berri was appointed minister of south Lebanon affairs in the government of national reconciliation formed in April 1984.
41 Heikal, op. cit., p. 139.
42 *Foreign Broadcast Information Service*, 2 September 1981.
43 Islamic Republic News Agency, 17 October 1983.
44 *Washington Post*, 11 March 1982; *Wall Street Journal*, 15 November 1982; and *Kayhan International*, 24 April 1983.
45 *The Middle East*, May 1978, p. 10.
46 Ibid., November 1980, p. 25.
47 *Christian Science Monitor*, 4 August 1982; and *Foreign Broadcast Information Service*, 9 August 1982.
48 *BBC Summary of World Broadcasts*, 11 August 1983.
49 *Kayhan International*, 22 September 1983.
50 See p. 281.
51 Selig S. Harrison, *In Afghanistan's Shadow: Baluch Nationalism and Soviet Temptations*, Carnegie Endowment for International Peace, Washington, D.C., 1981, p. 97.
52 *Middle East Monitor*, 16 July 1973, p. 2.
53 *Newsweek*, 14 November 1977, p. 70.
54 *The Times*, 7 July 1977.
55 Edward Mortimer, *Faith and Power: The Politics of Islam*, Faber and Faber, London, 1982, p. 371.
56 The National Islamic Front of Aghanistan was one of the liberation movement groups that the Iranian government then supported. A.H.H. Abidi, 'Iran and Non-Alignment' in K.P. Misra (ed.), op. cit., p. 349, note 28.
57 Cited in Mortimer, op. cit., p. 375.
58 *Guardian*, 19 May 1980; and *Daily Telegraph*, 2 and 6 June 1980.
59 *Indian Express*, 9 April 1983.
60 *Guardian*, 29 January and 10 April 1980.
61 The first Islamic summit was held in 1969 in Rabat, Morocco, and the second in Lahore, Pakistan, in 1974. The ICO was established in July 1969 in the aftermath of an unsuccessful attempt to burn down Al Aqsa mosque in Jerusalem. In 1981 it had forty-three members.
62 See p. 174.

Conclusion

1 *Jumhouri-ye Islami*, 5 April 1983.
2 Before the revolution Khomeini sometimes used leftist terms. See his advice to theological students in the summer of 1978, p. 83.
3 *Kayhan*, 22 December 1979.
4 See pp. 245-6.
5 See pp. 246-7.
6 *Guardian*, 8 September 1984. About 5,000 people were executed by the Shah's regime after his return to Iran in August 1953. Iran's population then was about half of the present forty-one million. See p. 36.
7 *BBC Summary of World Broadcasts*, 29 July 1983.

SELECT BIBLIOGRAPHY

Abrahamian, Ervand, *Iran Between Two Revolutions*, Princeton University Press, Princeton, N.J. and Guildford, 1982.

Akhavi, Shahrough, *Religion and Politics in Contemporary Iran: Clergy-State Relations in the Pahlavi Period*, State University of New York Press, Albany, N.Y., 1980.

Albert, David H. (ed.), *Tell the American People: Perspectives on the Iranian Revolution*, Movement for a New Society, Philadelphia, Pa., 1980.

Amirsadeghi, Hossein (ed.), *Twentieth Century Iran*, Holmes and Meier, New York, 1977.

Arberry, Arthur J., *The Koran Interpreted*, Oxford University Press, Oxford and New York, 1964.

Avery, Peter, *Modern Iran*, Ernest Benn, London, 1967.

Bharier, Julian, *Economic Development of Iran, 1900-1970*, Oxford University Press, Oxford and New York, 1971.

Browne, Edward G., *The Persian Revolution of 1905-1909*, Cambridge University Press, Cambridge, 1910.

Chubin, Shahram and Zabih, Sepehr, *The Foreign Relations of Iran: A Developing State in a Zone of Great-Power Conflict*, University of California Press, Los Angeles, Calif., 1974.

Constitution of the Islamic Republic of Iran, translated by Hamid Algar, Mizan Press, Berkeley, Calif., 1980.

Cottam, Richard W., *Nationalism in Iran: Updated through 1978*, University of Pittsburgh Press, Pittsburgh, Pa., 1979.

The Dawn of the Islamic Revolution: Vol I, Ministry of Islamic Guidance, Tehran, No date.

Elwell-Sutton, L.P., *Persian Oil: A Study in Power Politics*, Lawrence and Wishart, London, 1955.

Fischer, Michael M.J., *Iran: From Religious Dispute to Revolution*, Harvard University Press, Cambridge, Mass., and London, 1980.

Graham, Robert, *Iran: The Illusion of Power*, Croom Helm, London, 1978.

Halliday, Fred, *Iran: Dictatorship and Development*, Penguin Books, Harmondsworth, 1979.

Heikal, Mohamed, *The Return of the Ayatollah: The Iranian Revolution from Mossadeq to Khomeini*, André Deutsch, London, 1981.

Hiro, Dilip, *Inside the Middle East*, Routledge & Kegan Paul, London, and McGraw-Hill, New York, 1982.

Hooglund, Eric, *Reform and Revolution in Rural Iran*, University of Texas Press, Austin, Tex., 1982.

Irfani, Suroosh, *Revolutionary Islam in Iran*, Zed Press, London, 1983.

Ismael, Tareq Y., *Iraq and Iran: Roots of Conflict*, Syracuse University Press, Syracuse, N.Y., 1982.

Keddie, Nikki R., *Roots of Revolution: An Interpretive History of Modern Iran*, Yale University Press, New Haven, Conn., and London, 1981.

Khumayni, Ruh Allah, *Islamic Government: Rule of the Faqih* (in Persian), Najaf, Iraq, 1971.

Khumayni, Ruh Allah, *Islam and Revolution*, translated by Hamid Algar, Mizan Press, Berkeley, Calif., 1981.

Leeden, Michael, and Lewis, William, *Debacle: The American Failure in Iran*, Knopf, New York, 1981.

Mansfield, Peter (ed.), *The Middle East: A Political and Economic Survey*, Oxford University Press, Oxford and New York, Fourth Edition, 1973.

Mortimer Edward, *Faith and Power: The Politics of Islam*, Faber & Faber, London, 1982.

Nobari, Ali-Reza (ed.), *Iran Erupts*, The Iran-America Documentation Group, Stanford, Calif., 1978.

Pahlavi, Mohammed Reza Shah, *Mission for my Country*, Hutchinson, London, 1960 and McGraw-Hill, New York, 1961.

Pranger, Robert and Tahtinen, Dale, *United States Policy in the Persian Gulf*, American Enterprise Institute, Washington, D.C., 1979.

Radji, Parviz, *In the Service of the Peacock Throne*, Hamish Hamilton, London, 1983.

Ramazani, Rouhollah K., *Iran's Foreign Policy, 1941-1973: A Study of Foreign Policy in Modernising Nations*, University Press of Virginia, Charlottesville, Va., 1975.

Roosevelt, Kermit, *Countercoup: The Struggle for the Control of Iran*, McGraw-Hill, New York, 1979.

Rubin, Barry, *Paved with Good Intentions: The American Experience and Iran*, Penguin Books, Harmondsworth and New York, 1981.

Wilber, D.N., *Iran: Past and Present*, Princeton University Press, Princeton, N.J., 1948.

Wilber, Donald, *Riza Shah Pahlavi: The Resurrection and Reconstruction of Iran*, Exposition Press, Hicksville, N.Y., 1975.

Zabih, Sepehr, *The Communist Movement in Iran*, University of California Press, Los Angeles, Calif., 1966.

Zabih, Sepehr, *Iran Since the Revolution*, Croom Helm, London, 1982.

Zonis, Marvin, *The Political Elite of Iran*, Princeton University Press, Princeton, N.J., 1971.

NEWSAGENCIES, NEWSPAPERS AND PERIODICALS

Abrar (Tehran)
Arabia: The Islamic World Review (Slough)
Azadegan (Tehran)
BBC Summary of World Broadcasts (Reading)
Christian Science Monitor (Boston)
Daily Telegraph (London)
Economist (London)
Economy and Society (London)
8 Days (London)
Events (London)
Financial Times (London)

Foreign Broadcast Information Service (Washington)
Guardian (London)
Inqilab-e Islami (Tehran)
International Affairs (London)
International Herald Tribune (Paris)
Iran Almanac (Tehran)
Iran Press Digest (Tehran)
Iran Times (Washington)
Iran Week (Tehran)
The Iranian (Tehran)
Islamic Republic News Agency (Tehran)
Ittilaat (Tehran)
Izvestia (Moscow)
Jumhouri-ye Islami (Tehran)
Kayhan (Tehran)
Kayhan International (Tehran)
Krasnaya Zvezda (Moscow)
Mardom (Tehran)
MERIP Reports (Washington)
The Middle East (London)
Middle East Economic Digest (London)
Middle East Economic Survey (Nicosia)
Middle East International (London)
Middle East Journal (Washington)
Le Monde (Paris)
New Republic (Washington)
New Statesman (London)
New York Times (New York)
Newsweek (New York)
Observer (London)
Pravda (Moscow)
Race & Class (London)
Al Safir (Beirut)
Tass (Moscow)
Tehran Times (Tehran)
The Times (London)
Time (New York)
The Times Higher Education Supplement (London)
Toronto Star (Toronto)
Wall Street Journal (New York)
Washington Post (Washington)

INDEX

For a name starting with Al, El, Ol or Ul, see its second part.
A person's religious or secular title has been exluded.
For a member of the Iranian royal family, see the dynastic name.